SECOND EDITION

The Quiddler®

Short Word

Dictionary

QUIDDLER *n pl* **-S** someone who spends a great
deal of time on very small details

Manufactured & distributed by:

ENTERPRISES, INC.
16537 E. Laser Drive, Suite 10
Fountain Hills, AZ 85268
under license from Cannei, LLC.

The Quiddler SHORT Word Dictionary - SECOND EDITION

ISBN 978-0-9824586-1-7

Distributed by Set Enterprises, Inc.

The typeface used is Calibri.

All correspondence and inquiries should be directed to
quiddler@setgame.com
or
Quiddler Dictionary Editor
Set Enterprises, Inc.
16537 E. Laser Drive, Suite 10
Fountain Hills, AZ 85268

Manufactured in China.

SPECIAL THANKS

Set Enterprises would like to extend special thanks

To our family, friends and friends of friends

Compilation
Barbara Zahno

Editor in Chief
Bree Popp

Quiddler Inventor & Special Consultant
Marsha Falco

Associate Editors
Ginger Keymer, Christina Wainwright

Assistant Editors
Julie Contadino, Patrice Rakers, Robert Falco, Tracy Howe, Carrie Kerr, Jason Levy, Julie Levy, Jen Patterson, Kristina Perkins, Pat Romano, Sarah Schmid, Kyra Troyan, Vernon Vehmeier, Patricia Will & Ron Will

The hard work, perseverance and willingness of all of these people to quibble for way too long over minute details made this dictionary possible.

PREFACE

Thanks to input from many of our devoted Quiddler fans, this second edition is a new and improved version of *The Quiddler SHORT Word Dictionary*. This dictionary was created to help Quiddler players increase their scores and take advantage of the short word bonus in each round. After many years of playing with different dictionaries and answering questions from Quiddler players around the world, and after being beat many times by Barbara, the compiler of this dictionary who carried her own pocket-size version, we decided to create a short word dictionary to level the playing field a little. We hope you enjoy using this dictionary to increase your Quiddler score while learning a few new words along the way.

The Quiddler SHORT Word Dictionary is not intended to be a comprehensive reference tool, but rather was designed to be used when playing the card game Quiddler as well as other word games. *The Quiddler SHORT Word Dictionary* only contains allowable words that are between two and five letters. Keep in mind, of course, that longer words are allowed (don't forget the long word bonus) while playing Quiddler. Quiddler is a family game to be enjoyed by children and adults alike. This dictionary has been edited for content with that in mind. Of course, any words you agree to allow, that are admissible under the rules, can be used, even if they are not contained in this dictionary.

This dictionary includes slang and obsolete terms as well as words that are used in English-speaking countries around the world. Words were only included if they could be verified with at least two sources. We have tried to compile an accurate and exhaustive list, but as with any large undertaking and especially one that requires some subjectivity, we are sure that there are mistakes and omissions. We have created an email address solely for the purpose of collecting comments related to this dictionary. Please send all comments to quiddler@setgame.com. If you are suggesting the addition of a word for the next edition, please include at least two sources where the word can be found.

INTRODUCTION

This dictionary is intended to be used as an aid while playing Quiddler, it is not intended for use as a general English dictionary. There are several special features of this dictionary you should be aware of. Many features included in general dictionaries, such as definitions of multiple senses, pronunciation guides, and etymologies, are omitted.

1. **Main Entries:** Instead of a straight alphabetical listing, *The Quiddler SHORT Word Dictionary* divides each letter by word length. This should help you locate words with the exact number of letters you are looking for. Thus you will find two letter words that begin with A in alphabetical order, then three letter words that begin with A, and so on for each letter.

The main entries in this dictionary are confined to words between two and five letters in length that are acceptable under the rules of Quiddler. No proper nouns, prefixes, suffixes, abbreviated or hyphenated words can be used. However, abbreviations that have become commonplace standalone words, such as **intro**, can be used and are included in this dictionary. In addition, slang and obsolete words, as well as words used in English-speaking countries around the world can be used and are included in this dictionary. All words must use at least two cards; there will never be an acceptable word with less than two letters.

2. **Parts of Speech:** Many words have more than one part of speech, i.e., a word can be both a noun and a verb, or both an adjective and an adverb. *The Quiddler SHORT Word Dictionary* only presents and defines one part of speech for each entry. Because the aim of this dictionary is to help you maximize your score (and maybe learn something along the way), it does not necessarily

include the most common definition of a word. Instead, the part of speech defined is the part with the most inflected forms.

Abbreviations used:

adj	adjective
adv	adverb
aux v	auxiliary verb
comp of	comparative of
conj	conjunction
indef art	indefinite article
interj	interjection
n	noun
n/pl	only used in plural form
[obs]	obsolete
pl	plural
p part	past participle
pr part	present participle
prep	preposition
pron	pronoun
pr t	present tense
p t	past tense
v	verb (includes transitive and intransitive verbs)
SCOT.	Scottish
BRIT.	British
AUS.	Australian
N.Z.	New Zealand

3. **Inflected Forms:** All inflected forms for the part of speech defined are included. The inflected forms are listed immediately after the part of speech and are in **BOLD** and **ALL CAPS**. If the inflected form is created by adding letters to the end of the root word, those letters are listed preceded by a dash. If any change is necessary to the root word, the entire inflected form is spelled out.

Principal Parts of Verbs

The principal parts of all verbs are entered in the following order: past tense, past participle, present participle, and third person singular present tense. When the past tense and past participle are identical, however, one form represents both.

Comparison of Adjectives and Adverbs

Comparative and superlative degrees of adjectives and adverbs are listed with the comparative first and the superlative last.

4. **Cross References:** Alternate spellings of words are indicated at the end of an entry in **BOLD** and **ALL CAPS**, preceded by the word *also*. Please note that because only one definition is provided for each word and because we tried to maximize the number of words per main entry, the word referred to by the *also* may not have the same definition in this dictionary.

AA *n pl* **-S** rough, cindery lava

AB *n pl* **-S** commonly used abbreviation for an abdominal muscle

AD *n pl* **-S** an advertisement

AE *adj* SCOT. one, singular

AG *n* commonly used abbreviation for agriculture

AH *v* **-ED, -ING, -S** to exclaim in amazement or surprise; *also* **AAH**

AI *n pl* **-S** a three-toed sloth

AL *n pl* **-S** an evergreen East Indian tree

AM *v p t* first person singular of to be

AN *indef art* used before words with a vowel sound

AR *n pl* **-S** the letter "R"

AS *adv* to the same degree

AT *prep* in the position of

AW *interj* expressing protest, disgust, or disbelief

AX *v* **-ED, -ING, -ES** to chop, to cut down; *also* **AXE**

AY *n pl* **-S** an affirmative vote; *also* **AYE**

THREE LETTERS

AAH *v* **-ED, -ING, -S** to exclaim in amazement or surprise; *also* **AH**

AAL *n pl* **-S** an East Indian shrub, mulberry

AAS *n pl of* **AA**; rough, cindery lavas

ABA *n pl* **-S** a gownlike, sleeveless outergarment worn by Arabs; *also* **ABBA**

ABB *n pl* **-S** among weavers, yarn for the warp

ABS *n pl of* **AB**; commonly used abbreviation for abdominal muscles

ABY *v* **ABOUGHT, ABYING, -S** [obs] to atone, make amends for; *also* **ABYE**

ACE *v* **-D, ACING, -S** to win a point in tennis with a serve that the opponent cannot reach

ACH *interj* used to express impatience

ACT *v* **-ED, -ING, -S** to do something; to perform; to execute

ADD *v* **-ED, -ING, -S** to increase or combine

ADO *n pl* **-S** a bustling excitement

ADS *n pl of* **AD**; commonly used abbreviation for advertisements

ADZ *v* **-ED, -ING, -S** to shape wood with a tool similar to an ax, with an arched blaze set at right angles to the handle; *also* **ADZE**

AFF *adv* SCOT. off

AFT *adv* toward the stern

AGA *n pl* **-S** a civil or military leader, especially in Turkey; *also* **AGHA**

AGE *v* **-D, AGING, -S** to grow old; *also* **EILD**

AGO *adv* in the past

AHA *interj* to express surprise or triumph

AHI *n pl* **-S** yellowfin tuna

AHS *v pr t of* **AH** exclaims in amazement or surprise; *also* **AAHS**

AHU *n pl* **-S** stone heap used by the Polynesians as a memorial

AID *v* **-ED, -ING, -S** to help

AIL *v* **-ED, -ING, -S** to be ill or indisposed

AIM *v* **-ED, -ING, -S** to direct toward a specific object or goal

AIN *n pl* **-S** the 16th letter of the Hebrew alphabet; *also* **AYIN**

AIR *v* **-ED, -ING, -S** to make opinions known publicly

AIS *n pl of* **AI** three-toed sloths

AIT *n pl* **-S** BRIT. a small island or islet; *also* **EY, AYT, EYET, EYGHT, EYOT**

AKE *v* **-D, AKING, -S** [obs] to suffer a dull, sustained pain; ache

ALA *n pl* **-E** a wing or wing-like structure

ALB *n pl* **-S** a long white linen robe with tapered sleeves worn by a priest at Mass; *also* **AUBE**

ALE *n pl* **-S** a type of beer; alcoholic beverage; *also* **EALE**

ALF *n pl* **-S** somebody, especially an Australian, regarded as unsophisticated

ALL *adj* the total number, amount or quantity

ALP *n pl* **-S** a high mountain

ALS *n pl of* **AL**; evergreen East Indian trees

ALT *n pl* **-S** the first octave above the treble staff

AMA *n pl* **-S** a housemaid, especially a wet nurse, in India; *also* **AMAH**

AMI *n pl* **-S** a male friend

AMP *v* **-ED, -ING, -S** to increase volume

AMU *n pl* **-S** a unit of atomic mass

ANA *n pl* **-S** a collection of anecdotes

AND *conj* also, plus, as a result

ANE *adj* SCOT. one

ANI *n pl* **-S** any of several tropical American birds

ANT *n pl* **-S** a social insect living in organized colonies

ANY *adj* some; whichever, no matter which

APE *v* **-D, APING, -S** to imitate, to mimic

APO *n pl* **-S** a protein made by the liver

APP *n pl* **-S** commonly used abbreviation for application

APT *adj* suitable; mentally quick and resourceful

ARB *abbr pl* **-S** a commonly used abbreviation for arbitrageur

ARC *v* **-ED** or **-KED, -ING** or **-KING, -S** to move in a curved course

ARD *n pl* **-S** a primitive plough

ARE *n pl* **-S** a metric surface measure

ARF *interj* used to imitate the bark of a dog

ARK *n pl* **-S** a large boat

ARM *v* **-ED, -ING, -S**, to provide with weapons

ARS *n pl of* **AR** more than one of the letter "R"

ART *n pl* **-S** a work of beauty or a significant thing

ASH *n pl* **-ES** matter left after something has burned

ASK *v* **-ED, -ING, -S** to put a question to

ASP *n pl* **-S** a venomous snake

ASS *n pl* **-ES** a long-haired, hoofed, horse-like animal

ATE *v p t of* **EAT** consumed food

AUA *n pl* **-S** yellow-eyed mullet fish native to New Zealand

AUF *n pl* **-S** [obs] a changeling or elf child

AUK *n pl* **-S** a diving sea-bird of northern seas

AUM *n* a mystic syllable used in meditation, affirmations or blessings; *also* **OM**

AVA *n* variety of shrub common to the Pacific Islands

AVE *n pl* **-S** expression of greeting or farewell

AVO *n pl* **-S** a monetary unit of Macao

AWA *adv* SCOT. away, in a different direction

AWE *v* **-D, AWING, -S** to inspire with a feeling of wonderment

AWL *n pl* **-S** a pointed tool for making small holes

AWN *n pl* **-S** a bristle-like tip of certain grasses

AXE *v* **-D, AXING, -S** to chop, to cut down; *also* **AX**

AYE *n pl* **-S** an affirmative vote; *also* **AY**

AYS *n pl of* **AY** affirmative votes; *also* **AYES**

AYT *n pl* **-S** BRIT. a small island or islet; *also* **EY, AIT, EYET, EYGHT, EYOT**

AYU *n pl* **AYU** a small edible fish; sweetfish

AZO *adj* compound containing nitrogen, as in azo dye

ALEC *n pl* **-S** [obs] a herring; a sauce or relish made from herring

ALEE *adv* on or toward the side away from the wind

ALEF *n pl* **-S** the first letter of the Hebrew alphabet; *also* **ALEPH**

ALES *n pl of* **ALE** types of beer; alcoholic beverages

ALEW *n pl* **-S** [obs] a loud exclamation; a call to invite attention; *also* **HALLO**

ALFA *n pl* **-S** a communication code for the letter "A"

ALFS *n pl of* **ALF** people, especially Australians, regarded as unsophisticated

ALGA *n pl* **-S** or **-E** a kind of seaweed; a primitive aquatic plant without true stems, roots or leaves

ALIF *n pl* **-S** the first letter of the Arabic alphabet

ALIT *v p t of* **ALIGHT**; descended and settled; rested

ALLY *v* **ALLIED, ALLYING, ALLIES** to unite or associate for a specific purpose

ALMA *n pl* **-S** a woman or girl who dances or sings professionally in Egypt; *also* **ALME, ALMAH, ALMEH**

ALME *n pl* **-S** a woman or girl who dances or sings professionally in Egypt; *also* **ALMA, ALMAH, ALMEH**

ALMS *n pl of* **ALM** gifts of charity; money for the poor

ALOE *n pl* **-S** a succulent plant mostly found in Africa

ALOW *adv* nautical term meaning below decks

ALPS *n pl of* **ALP** high mountains

ALSO *adv* in addition; in like manner; likewise

ALTO *n pl* **-S** the lowest female singing voice or the highest male singing voice

ALTS *n pl of* **ALT** notes in the first octave above the treble staff

ALUM *n pl* **-S** any of various double sulfates of a trivalent metal

AMAH *n pl* **-S** a housemaid, especially a wet nurse, in India; *also* **AMA**

AMAS *n pl of* **AMA**; housemaids, especially wet nurses, in India; *also* **AMAHS**

AMBO *n pl* **-S** or **-NES** a large pulpit in early Christian churches; *also* **AMBON**

AMEN *n pl* **-S** used at the end of prayers, meaning "so be it"

AMEL *v* **-S** [obs] to form a glossy surface on; *also* **ENAMEL**

AMID *prep* in the midst or middle of; surrounded by; among

AMIR *n pl* **-S** a ruler or nobleman of Asia or Africa; *also* **AMEER, EMEER, EMIR**

AMIS *n pl of* **AMI** male friends

AMIT *v* **-TED, -TING, -S** [obs] to lose

AMMA *n pl* **-S** an abbes or spiritual mother

AMMO *n* commonly used abbreviation for ammunition; projectiles fired from a gun

AMOK *adv* in a frenzied and reckless manner; *also* **AMUCK**

AMPS *v pr t of* **AMP** increases volume

AMUS *n pl of* **AMU** units of atomic mass

AMYL *n pl* **-S** a univalent hydrocarbon radical

ANAL *adj* pertaining to, or situated near, the anus

ANAN *interj* [obs] expression equivalent to "What did you say?," "Eh?"

ANAS *n pl of* **ANA** collections of anecdotes

ANES *adv* SCOT. once

ANET *n* [obs] the herb dill or dill seed

ANEW *adv* once more; over again; another time

ANGA *n pl* **-S** any of eight fundamental categories of the yogic path

ANIL *n pl* **-S** a West Indian shrub from which indigo dye is made

5

ANIS *n pl* **-ES** a French or Spanish liqueur flavored with aniseed; *also* **ANISE**

ANKH *n pl* **-S** a cross with a loop on the top, representing life, rebirth, reincarnation and love in ancient Egypt

ANNA *n pl* **-S** a former coin of Pakistan and India, equal to 1/16 of a rupee

ANOA *n pl* **-S** a small buffalo native to Indonesia

ANON *adv* at another time; straightway; at once

ANSA *n pl* **-E** the protruding part of planetary rings

ANTA *n pl* **-S** or **-E** a pier produced by thickening a wall at its termination

ANTE *v* **-D, -ING, -S** to put a fixed stake into the pool before cards are dealt in poker

ANTI *n pl* **-S** a person that is not in favor of an action or proposal

ANTS *n pl of* **ANT** social insects living in organized colonies

ANUS *n pl* **-ES** or **ANI** excretory opening at the end of the alimentary canal

APAR *n pl* **-S** a South American armadillo with three bands of bony plates

APED *v p t of* **APE** imitated or mimicked

APER *n pl* **-S** one who apes or mimics

APES *v pr t of* **APE**; imitates or mimics

APEX *n pl* **-ES** or **APICES** the top point or angular summit of anything

APOD *n pl* **-S** or **-ES** a footless animal; *also* **APODE**

APOS *n pl of* **APO** proteins made by the liver

APPS *n pl of* **APP** commonly used abbreviation for applications

APSE *n pl* **-S** a domed or vaulted recess or projection on a building, esp. the east end of a church; it usually contains the altar; *also* **ABSIS, APSIS**

AQUA *n pl* **-S** or **-E** a light bluish green color

ARAK *n pl* **-S** strong liquor distilled from fermented palm sap, rice or molasses; *also* **ARRACK**

ARBS *n pl of* **ARB** a commonly used abbreviation for arbitrageurs

ARCA *n pl* **-E** a chest used to store valuables in medieval Spain and Italy

ARCH *v* **-ED, -ING, -ES** to form a curve

ARCO *adj* bowed; often used as a musical direction to performers on stringed instruments

ARCS *v pr t of* **ARC** moves in a curved course

ARDS *n pl of* **ARD** primitive ploughs

AREA *n pl* **-S** fields of study, or branches of fields of study

ARES *n pl of* **ARE** metric surface measures

ARET *v* **-TED, -TING** [obs] to reckon; to ascribe; to impute

AREW *adv* [obs] in a row

ARIA *n pl* **-S** an elaborate song for a solo voice

ARID *adj* lacking sufficient water or rainfall

ARIL *n pl* **-S** a fleshy and usually brightly colored seed covering that forms on some plants after fertilization

ARKS *n pl of* **ARK** large boats

ARMS *v pr t of* **ARM** provides with weapons

ARMY *n pl* **ARMIES** a large body of persons trained and armed for war

AROW *adv* in a row, line or rank; successively; in order

ARTS *n pl of* **ART** works of beauty or significant things

ARTY *adj* **ARTIER, ARTIEST** characterized by a showy, pretentious display of artistic interest; *also* **ARTSY**

ARUI *n* a wild sheep of North Africa; *also* **AOUDAD, AUDAD, UDAD**

ARUM *n pl* **-S** any plant of the arum family, which is characterized by small flowers on a thick spike, within a hood-like leaf

ARVO *n pl* **-S** AUS., N.Z. afternoon

ARYL *n pl* **-S** a univalent radical

ASCI *n pl of* **ASCUS** small spore sacs in certain lichens and fungi

ASEA *adv* at sea; in the direction of the sea

ASHY *adj* **ASHIER, ASHIEST** ash-colored; whitish gray; deadly pale

ASKS *v pr t of* **ASK** puts a question to

ASPS *n pl of* **ASP** venomous snakes

ASSE *n pl* **-S** a small fox of S. Africa

ATAP *n pl* **-S** thatch for native huts in Malaya, made of nipa palm leaves; *also* **ATTAP**

ATAR *n* essential oil or perfume obtained from flowers; *also* **ATHAR, ATTAR, OTTAR, OTTO**

ATMA *n pl* **-S** the individual soul, the principle of life in Hinduism; *also* **ATMAN**

ATOM *n pl* **-S** an ultimate indivisible particle of matter

ATOP *adv* on or at the top

AUAS *n pl of* **AUA** yellow-eyed mullet fish native to New Zealand

AUBE *n pl* **-S** [obs] a long white linen robe with tapered sleeves worn by a priest at Mass; *also* **ALB**

AUFS *n pl of* **AUF** [obs] changelings or elf children

AUKS *n pl of* **AUK** diving sea-birds of northern seas

AULD *adj* **-ER, -EST** SCOT. old; as in auld lang syne, the good old days

AUNT *n pl* **-S** the sister of your father or mother; the wife of your uncle

AURA *n pl* **-S** or **-E** a characteristic or distinctive impression created by someone or something

AUTO *v* **-ED , -ING , -S** to go by or ride in a four-wheeled motor vehicle

AVER *v* **-RED, -RING, -S** to assert or prove the truth of something

AVES *n pl of* **AVE** expressions of greeting or farewell

AVID *adj* longing eagerly for; eager

AVIE *adv* [obs] emulously; rivaling; envious

AVIS *n* [obs] advice; opinion; deliberation

AVOS *n pl of* **AVO** monetary units of Macao

AVOW *v* **-ED, -ING, -S** to declare openly that something is true

AWAY *adv* absent; gone; at a distance; aside; off

AWED *v p t of* **AWE** inspired by a feeling of wonderment

AWES *v pr t of* **AWE** inspires by a feeling of wonderment

AWLS *n pl of* **AWL** pointed tools for making small holes

AWNS *n pl of* **AWN** bristle-like tips of certain grasses

AWNY *adj* bearded

AWOL *n pl* **-S** informal for one who is truant or absent, originally a military acronym

AWRY *adv* with a twist to the side; not straight; askew

AXAL *adj* of or pertaining to a straight line on which an object rotates; *also* **AXIAL, AXILE**

AXED *v p t of* **AXE** chopped, cut down

AXEL *n pl* **-S** a figure skating jump with a forward takeoff and a backward landing

AXES *v pr t of* **AXE** chops, cuts down

AXIL *n pl* **-S** the upper angle between a leaf or twig and the stem from which it grows

AXIS *n pl* **AXES** a straight line, real or imaginary, on which an object rotates or is regarded as rotating

AXLE *n pl* **-S** the pin or spindle on which a wheel revolves

AXON *n pl* **-S** a long nerve fiber that conducts impulses away from the body of the nerve cell; *also* **AXONE**

AYAH *n pl* **-S** a native nurse or maid in India

AYEN *adv* [obs] again; back against; *also* **AYEINS**

AYES *n pl of* **AYE** affirmative votes; *also* **AYS**

AYIN *n pl* **-S** the 16th letter of the Hebrew alphabet; *also* **AIN**

AYLE *n pl* **-S** [obs] a grandfather; *also* **AIEL**

AYRY *n pl* **AYRIES** the nest of a bird of prey; *also* **AERY, AERIE, AYRIE, EYRE, EYRIE, EYRY**

AZAN *n pl* **-S** a Muslim call to prayer which happens five times a day

AZON *n pl* **-S** a radio-controlled aerial bomb

AZYM *n pl* **-S** [obs] unleavened bread; matzoh; *also* **AZYME**

FIVE LETTERS

AAHED *v p t of* **AAH** exclaimed in amazement or surprise; *also* **AHED**

AALII *n pl* **-S** a small Hawaiian tree with hard dark wood

AARGH *interj* used to express disgust

ABACA *n pl* **-S** a banana-like plant native to the Philippines

ABACI *n pl of* **ABACUS** frames with bars and beads that are used to make mathematical calculations

ABACK *adv* by surprise

ABAFT *adv* toward the stern

ABAMP *n pl* **-S** a unit of electric current equal to 10 amperes; *also* **ABAMPERE**

ABAND *v* **-ED, -ING, -S** to banish; to expel

ABASE *v* **-D, ABASING, -S** to lower in rank, prestige or esteem

ABASH *v* **-ED, -ING, -ES** to make ashamed or embarrassed

ABATE *v* **-D ABATING, -S** to reduce in degree or intensity

ABAYA *n pl* **-S** a long loose robe worn by Muslim women

ABBAS *n pl of* **ABBA** gown-like, sleeveless outer garments worn by Arabs; *also* **ABAS**

ABBES *n pl of* **ABBE** members of the secular clergy, especially in France

ABBEY *n pl* **-S** a monastery or convent of nuns

ABBOT *n pl* **-S** the superior or head of a monastery

ABDAL *n pl* **-S** a religious devotee or dervish in Persia

ABEAM *adv* at right angles to the length of a ship or airplane

ABEAR *v* **-ED, -ING, -S** to put up with; to endure

ABELE *n pl* **-S** a white poplar

ABERR *v* **-ED, -ING, -S** to wander; to stray

ABETS *v pr t of* **ABET** encourages and supports

ABHAL *n pl* **-S** the berry of a cypress tree in the East Indies

ABHOR *v* **-RED, -RING, -S** to detest; loathe

ABIDE *v* **-D, ABIDING, -S** to put up with; tolerate

ABIME *n pl* **-S** [obs] a bottomless gulf or pit; *also* **ABYME, ABYSM, ABYSS**

ABLED *adj* capable of unimpaired function

ABLEN *n pl* **-S** a small freshwater fish; *also* **ABLET**

ABLER *adj* having more sufficient power, skills, or resources than another

ABLET *n pl* **-S** a small freshwater fish; *also* **ABLEN**

ABMHO *n pl* **-S** the centimeter-gram-second unit of conductance

ABNET *n pl* **-S** the girdle of a Jewish priest or officer

ABODE *n pl* **-S** a dwelling place; a home

ABOHM *n pl* **-S** the centimeter-gram-second electromagnetic unit of resistance, equal to one billionth of an ohm

ABOIL *adj* in an excited or tumultuous state

ABOMA *n pl* **-S** a large South American serpent

ABOON *adv* BRIT., SCOT. above

ABORD *v* **-ED, -ING, -S** [obs] to approach; to accost

ABORT *v* **-ED, -ING, -S** to bring to a premature end

ABOUT *adv* approximately

ABOVE *adv* in or to a higher place; overhead

ABRIS *n pl of* **ABRI** rock shelters formed by the overhang of a cliff

ABSIS *n pl* **-ES** a domed or vaulted recess or projection on a building, especially the east end of a church containing the altar; *also* **APSIS, APSE**

ABUSE *v* **-D, ABUSING, -S** to hurt by treating badly

ABUTS *v pr t of* **ABUT** touches along a border

ABUZZ *adj* noisy like the sound of a bee, buzzing

ABYES *v pr t of* **ABYE** [obs] atones, makes amends for; *also* **ABYS**

ABYME *n pl* **-S** a bottomless gulf or pit; *also* **ABIME, ABYSM, ABYSS**

ABYSM *n pl* **-S** a bottomless gulf or pit; *also* **ABIME, ABYME, ABYSS**

ABYSS *n pl* **-ES** a bottomless gulf or pit; *also* **ABIME, ABYME, ABYSM**

ACARI *n pl of* **ACARUS** small mites

ACCOY *v* **-ED, -ING, -S** to render quiet; to soothe

ACERB *adj* **-ER, -EST** sour or bitter in taste; *also* **ACERBIC**

ACERS *n pl of* **ACER** trees or shrubs with winged fruit

ACETA *n pl of* **ACETUM** preparations having vinegar or dilute acetic acid as the solvent

ACHED *v p t of* **ACHE** suffered a dull continuous pain

ACHES *v pr t of* **ACHE** suffers a dull continuous pain

ACHOO *interj* used to suggest or imitate the sound of a sneeze

ACIDS *n pl of* **ACID** chemical compounds that yield hydrogen ions when dissolved in water

ACIDY *adj* sharp or sour in taste

ACING *v pr part of* **ACE** winning a point in tennis with a serve that the opponent cannot reach

ACINI *n pl of* **ACINUS** berries, as grapes or currants

ACKEE *n pl* **-S** the fruit of an African tree of the soapberry family grown in the Caribbean; *also* **AKEE**

ACMES *n pl of* **ACME** the highest points of achievement or excellence

ACMIC *adj* from **ACME** at the highest point of achievement or excellence

ACNED *adj* having acne, a skin disorder

ACOCK *adj* in a tilted or turned up position; not straight

ACOLD *adj* [obs] being chilled; having a low or inadequate temperature

ACORN *n pl* **-S** the fruit of the oak tree

ACRED *adj* possessing acres or landed property

ACRES *n pl of* **ACRE** units of area equal to 43,560 square feet each

ACRID *adj* sharp and harsh; bitter to taste and smell

ACTED *v p t of* **ACT** did something; performed; executed

ACTIN *n pl* **-S** a protein that together with myosin functions to contract muscles

ACTON *n pl* **-S** a quilted jacket worn under armor

ACTOR *n pl* **-S** a theatrical performer; a stage player

ACUTE *adj* extremely sharp or intense

ACYLS *n pl of* **ACYL** radicals derived from organic acids

ADACT *v* **-ED, -ING, -S** [obs] to compel; to drive

ADAGE *n pl* **-S** a long-used old saying; a proverb

ADAPT *v* **-ED, -ING, -S** to make suitable; to adjust

ADAYS *adv* [obs] by day, or every day

ADDAX *n pl* **-ES** large African antelope with lightly spiraled horns

ADDED *v p t of* **ADD** increased or combined

ADDER *n pl* **-S** one who, or that which, increases or combines

ADDLE *v* **-ED, -ING, -S** mix up or confuse

ADEEM *v* **-ED, -ING, -S** to revoke, as a legacy; grant

ADEPS *n pl* **ADIPES** animal fat; lard

ADEPT *adj* well skilled; completely versed; thoroughly proficient

ADIEU *n pl* **-S** good-bye; farewell

ADIOS *interj* used to express farewell

ADITS *n pl of* **ADIT** entrances

ADMAN *n pl* **ADMEN** informal term for one whose profession is writing, designing, or selling advertisements

ADMEN *n pl of* **ADMAN** commonly used abbreviation for those whose profession is writing, designing, or selling advertisements

ADMIT *v* **-TED, -TING, -S** to give a right of entrance

ADMIX *v* **-ED, -ING, -ES** to mingle with something else

ADOBE *n pl* **-S** a sun-dried brick; used in hot dry climates

ADOBO *n pl* **-S** a dish of marinated vegetables and meat or fish

ADOPT *v* **-ED, -ING, -S** to take into one's family through legal means and raise as one's own child

ADORE *v* **-D, ADORING, -S** to love in the highest degree

ADORN *v* **-ED, -ING, -S** to deck or dress with ornaments; to embellish

ADOWN *adv* [obs] from a higher to a lower situation; downward

ADOZE *adj* napping; asleep

ADRAD *p part of* **ADREAD** [obs]; put in dread; made afraid

ADRIP *adv* [obs] in a state of falling in drops; as, leaves all adrip

ADULT *n pl* **-S** a person, animal or plant who has reached maturity

ADUNC *adj* curved inward; hooked, as in a parrot's bill; *also* **ADUNQUE**

ADURE *v* **-D, ADURING, -S** [obs] to burn up

ADUST *adj* dried out by heat or excessive exposure to sunlight

ADYTA *n pl of* **ADYTUM** innermost sanctuaries or shrines in ancient temples

ADZED *v p t of* **ADZE** shaped wood with a tool similar to an ax, with an arched blaze set at right angles to the handle

ADZES *v pr t of* **ADZE** shapes wood with a tool similar to an ax, with an arched blaze set at right angles to the handle; *also* **ADZS**

AECIA *n pl of* **AECIUM** the fruiting bodies of rust fungi

AEGIR *n pl* **-S** an often dangerous high wave caused by tidal flow

AEGIS *n pl* **-ES** kindly endorsement and guidance; *also* **EGIS**

AEONS *n pl of* **AEON** indefinitely long periods of time; *also* **EONS**

AERIE *n pl* **-S** the nest of a bird of prey; *also* **AERY**, **AYRY**, **AYRIE**, **EYRE**, **EYRIE**, **EYRY**

AFFIX *v* **-ED, -ING, -S** to fix or fasten in any way

AFIRE *adj* aflame, burning

AFLAT *adv* [obs] level with the ground; flat

AFLOW *adj* moving freely, flowing

AFOOT *adv* walking, on foot

AFORE *prep* [obs] earlier, before

AFOUL *adj* entangled; in collision

AFRIT *n pl* **-S** a powerful evil spirit in Arabian mythology; *also* **AFREET**

AFROS *n pl of* **AFRO** rounded, thick, tightly curled hair styles

AFTER *prep* behind in place or order

AGAIN *adv* once more

AGALS *n pl of* **AGAL** cords of goat's hair that Bedouins wind around their heads to hold down kaffiyehs

AGAMA *n pl* **-S** a small terrestrial lizard of warm regions

AGAMI *n pl* **-S** a South American crane-like bird

AGAPE *n pl* **AGAPAE** love that is wholly selfless and spiritual; brotherly love

AGARS *n pl of* **AGAR** gelatinous substances obtained from certain marine algae

AGASP *adj* in a state of choking or breathing with effort

AGATE *n pl* **-S** an impure form of quartz used as a gemstone

AGATY *adj* of or containing agate

AGAVE *n pl* **-S** a tropical American plant with tall flower stalks and thick leaves

AGAZE *adj* looking intently, fixed as if in fear or wonder

AGENE *n pl* **-S** a yellow pungent volatile oil

AGENT *n pl* **-S** a representative who acts on behalf of other persons or organizations

AGGER *n pl* **-S** an earthwork or mound in ancient Roman building

AGGIE *n pl* **-S** a playing marble

AGGRI *adj* of or related to aigris stone, used to refer to a type of ancient glass bead; *also* **AGGRY**

AGGRO *n pl* **-S** BRIT. aggressive or violent behavior

AGGRY *adj* of or related to aigris stone, used to refer to a type of ancient glass bead; *also* **AGGRI**

AGHAS *n pl of* **AGHA** civil or military leaders, especially in Turkey; *also* **AGAS**

AGILE *adj* moving quickly and lightly

AGING *v pr part of* **AGE** growing old; *also* **AGEING**

AGIOS *n pl of* **AGIO** fees charged for exchanging currencies

AGISM *n pl* **-S** discrimination against middle-aged and elderly people; *also* **AGEISM**

AGIST *v* **-ED, -ING, -S** to feed or pasture for a fee

AGITA *n pl* **-S** acid indigestion; heartburn

AGLET *n pl* **-S** the metal or plastic sheath at the end of a shoelace

AGLEY *adv* SCOT. awry; askew; *also* **AGLY**

AGLOW *adj* radiating light, warmth, excitement or happiness; glowing

AGMAS *n pl of* **AGMA** velar nasal consonant speech sounds

AGONE *adv* [obs] in the past; gone by

AGONY *n pl* **AGONIES** intense feelings of suffering

AGOOD *adv* [obs] in earnest; heartily

AGORA *n pl* **AGOROT** or **AGOROTH** a place of assembly for the people of ancient Greece

AGREE *v* **-D, -ING, -S** to correspond in gender, number, case or person

AGRIA *n pl* **-S** an extensive pustular eruption

AGRIN *adj* in the act of smiling broadly

AGUES *n pl of* **AGUE** acute fevers, usually associated with malaria

AGUSH *adj* in a state of flowing suddenly and plentifully

AHEAD *adv* in front of

AHEAP *adj* huddled together; in a pile, mass or mound

AHIGH *adv* [obs] at or to a height

AHOLD *n* informal for a grip or grasp, as in get ahold of

AHULL *adj* with the sails furled and the helm lashed to head into the wind

AIDED *v p t of* **AID** helped

AIDER *n pl* **-S** someone who helps

AIDES *n pl of* **AIDE** those who act as assistants

AIELS *n pl of* **AIEL** [obs] grandfathers; *also* **AYLES**

AIGRE *adj* [obs] sour

AILED *v p t of* **AIL** was ill or indisposed

AIMED *v p t of* **AIM** directed toward a specific object or goal

AIMER *n pl* **-S** one who aims, directs or points

AIOLI *n pl* **-S** a garlic mayonnaise

AIRED *v p t of* **AIR** made opinions known publicly

AIRER *n pl* **-S** BRIT. a frame on which clothes are dried

AIRNS *n pl of* **AIRN** SCOT. mineral elements, iron

AIRTH *v* **-ED, -ING, -S** SCOT. to point out the way; direct; guide; *also* **AIRT**

AIRTS *v pr t of* **AIRT** SCOT. points out the way; directs; guides; *also* **AIRTHS**

AISLE *n pl* **-S** a passageway between seating areas

AITCH *n pl* **-ES** the letter "H"

AIVER *n pl* **-S** a draft horse

AJIVA *n pl* **-S** inanimate matter

AJUGA *n pl* **-S** bugle

AKEES *n pl of* **AKEE** the fruit of an African tree of the soapberry family grown in the Caribbean; *also* **ACKEES**

AKELA *n pl* **-S** a pack leader, in the Cub Scouts

AKENE *n pl* **-S** a small, dry fruit that remains closed at maturity, as in the sunflower; *also* **ACHENE**

AKING *v pr part of* **AKE** [obs] suffering a dull continuous pain; aching

AKNEE *adv* on the knee

ALACK *interj* used to express sorrow or regret

ALAMO *n pl* **-S** a poplar tree, especially a cottonwood

ALAND *adv* on land; to the land; ashore

ALANS *n pl of* **ALAN** [obs] large hunting dogs; wolfhounds; *also* **ALANTS**

ALANT *n pl* **-S** [obs] a large hunting dog; a wolfhound; *also* **ALAN**

ALARM *v* **-ED, -ING, -S** to make somebody frightened or apprehensive

ALARY *adj* pertaining to, or having wings; *also* **ALAR**

ALATE *adj* having wing-like extensions

ALBAN *n pl* **-S** a white crystalline resinous substance extracted from gutta-percha

ALBAS *n pl of* **ALBA** troubadour love songs or poems

ALBEE *conj* [obs] although; albeit; *also* **ALBE**

ALBUM *n pl* **-S** a book with blank pages for photographs or stamps

ALCID *n pl* **-S** a web-footed diving bird

ALCOS *n pl* **-S** small South American dogs domesticated by the Aborigines

ALDAY *adv* [obs] continually

ALDER *n pl* **-S** a shrub or small tree having toothed leaves and cone-like fruit

ALDOL *n pl* **-S** a thick, colorless to pale yellow liquid used in perfumery and as a solvent

ALEAK *adj* in a condition of allowing liquid to pass in or out accidentally; leaky

ALECS *n pl of* **ALEC** [obs] herrings; sauces or relishes made from herring

ALEFS *n pl of* **ALEF** more than one of the first letter of the Hebrew alphabet; *also* **ALEPH**

ALEPH *n pl* **-S** more than one of the first letter of the Hebrew alphabet; *also* **ALEF**

ALERT *adj* **-ER, -EST** watchful; vigilant; ready for sudden action

ALEWS *n pl of* **ALEW** [obs] loud exclamations; calls to invite attention; *also* **HALLOOS**

ALFAS *n pl of* **ALFA** communication codes for more than one of the letter "A"

ALFET *n pl* **-S** a cauldron of boiling water into which an accused person in early English history plunged his forearm as a test of innocence

ALGAE *n pl of* **ALGA** seaweeds; primitive aquatic plants without true stems, roots and leaves; *also* **ALGAS**

ALGAL *adj* pertaining to, or like, algae

ALGAS *n pl of* **ALGA** seaweeds; primitive aquatic plants without true stems, roots and leaves; *also* **ALGAE**

ALGID *adj* cold; chilly

ALGIN *n pl* **-S** a gelatinous substance used as a thickener or emulsifier

ALGOR *n pl* **-S** coldness; chilliness

ALGUM *n pl* **-S** a tree mentioned in the Bible; *also* **ALMUG**

ALIAS *n pl* **-ES** an assumed name

ALIBI *v* **-ED, -ING, -S** or **-ES** to make an excuse or offer a justification for something

ALIEN *adj* owing political allegiance to another country or government; foreign

ALIFE *adv* [obs] on my life; dearly

ALIFS *n pl of* **ALIF** more than one of the first letter of the Arabic alphabet

ALIGN *v* **-ED, -ING, -S** to place something in an orderly position in relation to something else; *also* **ALINE**

ALIKE *adj* having resemblance; without difference

ALINE *v* **-ED, -ING, -S** to place something in an orderly position in relation to something else; *also* **ALIGN**

ALISH *adj* having a taste like a fermented drink made from malt, hops and yeast, similar to beer

ALIST *adj* leaning to one side

ALIVE *adj* having life; in a state of action

ALIYA *n pl* **-S** the act of proceeding to the reading table in a synagogue for the reading of a portion from the Torah; *also* **ALIYAH**

ALKYD *n pl* **-S** a synthetic resin

ALKYL *n pl* **-S** a univalent radical

ALLAY *v* **-ED, -ING, -S** to subdue or reduce in intensity

ALLEY *n pl* **-S** a narrow street with walls on both sides

ALLOD *n pl* **-S** a freehold estate; land which is the absolute property of the owner; *also* **ALLODIUM**

ALLOO *v* [obs] to incite dogs by a call; to halloo

ALLOT *v* **-TED, -TING, -S** to give out in small portions

ALLOW *v* **-ED, -ING, -S** to approve of; to grant

ALLOY *n pl* **-S** a mixture containing two or more metallic elements

ALLYL *n pl* **-S** an organic radical

ALMAH *n pl* **-S** a woman or girl who dances or sings professionally in Egypt; *also* **ALMA, ALME, ALMEH**

ALMAN *n pl* **-S** a kind of dance; *also* **ALLEMANDE**

ALMAS *n pl of* **ALMA** women or girls who dance or sing professionally in Egypt; *also* **ALMAHS, ALMEHS, ALMES**

ALMEH *n pl* **-S** a woman or girl who dances or sings professionally in Egypt; *also* **ALMA, ALME, ALMAH**

ALMES *n pl of* **ALME** women or girls who dance or sing professionally in Egypt; *also* **ALMAS, ALMAHS, ALMEHS**

ALMUG *n pl* **-S** a tree mentioned in the Bible; *also* **ALGUM**

ALOES *n pl of* **ALOE** succulent plants found in Africa

ALOFT *adv* in or into the air; high above the ground

ALOGY *n pl* **ALOGIES** [obs] unreasonableness; absurdity

ALOHA *n pl* **-S** a Hawaiian greeting or farewell

ALOIN *n pl* **-S** a bitter purgative obtained from aloes

ALONE *adj* of or by itself; by themselves

ALONG *adv* lengthwise

ALOOF *adj* away from; clear from

ALOUD *adv* with a loud voice, or great noise

ALPHA *n pl* **-S** the first letter in the Greek alphabet

ALPIA *n pl* **-S** the seed of canary grass

ALTAR *n pl* **-S** a table in Christian churches used as a focus of worship

ALTER *v* **-ED, -ING, -S** to make otherwise; to change

ALTHO *conj* variant of although; in spite of the fact that

ALTOS *n pl of* **ALTO** low female singing voices

ALULA *n pl* **-E** part of a bird's wing

ALUMS *n pl of* **ALUM** double sulfates of a trivalent metal

ALWAYS *adv* at all times; forever

AMAHS *n pl of* **AMAH** housemaids, especially wet nurses, in India; *also* **AMAS**

AMAIN *adv* with full strength; at or with great speed

AMASS *v* **-ING, -ES** to collect into a mass or heap

AMATE *v* **-D, -ING** [obs] to dismay; daunt

AMAZE *v* **-D, AMAZING, -S** to bewilder; stupefy

AMBER *n pl* **-S** a yellowish translucent resin resembling copal

AMBIT *n pl* **-S** the scope, extent or bounds of something

AMBLE *v* **-D, AMBLING, -S** to walk or move at a leisurely pace

AMBON *n pl* **-ES** a large pulpit in early Christian churches; *also* **AMBO**

AMBOS *n pl of* **AMBO** large pulpits or reading desks in early Christian churches; *also* **AMBONES**

AMBRY *n pl* **AMBRIES** a small recess near the altar in a church, where sacred vessels are kept

AMEBA *n pl* **-S** or **-E** one-celled organism with no definite form; *also* **AMOEBA**

AMEER *n pl* **-S** ruler, chieftain or commander in Islamic countries; *also* **AMIR, EMEER, EMIR**

AMEND *v* **-ED, -ING, -S** to change or modify for the better

AMENS *n pl of* **AMEN** used at the end of prayers, meaning "so be it"

AMENT *n pl* **-S** a cylindrical spike-like cluster of flowers found in willows, birches and oaks; *also* **CATKIN**

AMESS *n pl* **-ES** a hood or cape; *also* **AMICE, AMYSS**

AMICE *n pl* **-S** a hood or cape; *also* **AMESS, AMYSS**

AMICI *n pl of* **AMICUS** persons or organizations that are not a party to a lawsuit but who provide information to a court on issues involved in a case

AMIDE *n pl* **-S** an acidic derivative of ammonia; *also* **IMID, IMIDE**

AMIDO *adj* containing, or derived from, amidogen

AMIES *n pl of* **AMIE** female friends

AMIGA *n pl* **-S** a female friend

AMIGO *n pl* **-S** a male friend

AMINE *n pl* **-S** a nonacidic compound derived from ammonia; *also* **IMINE**

AMINO *adj* of or containing an amine in combination with certain non-acidic organic radicals

AMIRS *n pl of* **AMIR** rulers or noblemen of Asia or Africa; *also* **AMEERS, EMEERS, EMIRS**

AMISS *adj* wrong; faulty; out of order; improper

AMITS *v pr t of* **AMIT** [obs] loses

AMITY *n pl* **AMITIES** a cordial disposition; friendly relations

AMMAS *n pl of* **AMMA** abbesses or spiritual mothers

AMNIA *n pl of* **AMNION** thin membranes forming a closed sac about the embryos of reptiles, birds, and mammals; *also* **AMNIONS**

AMNIC *adj* characterized by developing an anionic membrane; *also* **AMNIONIC, AMNIOTIC**

AMNIO *n pl* **-S** informal for amniocentesis, a surgical procedure for obtaining a sample of amniotic fluid from the amniotic sac

AMOLE *n pl* **-S** the root, bulb, or other plant parts of several plants native to western North America, used as a substitute for soap

AMONG *prep* in the midst of

AMORT *adj* spiritless; lifeless

AMOUR *n pl* **-S** a love affair

AMOVE *v* **-D, AMOVING, -S** [obs] to remove a person or thing from a position

AMPED *v p t of* **AMP** increased volume

AMPLE *adj* large; great in size, extent, or capacity

AMPLY *adv* sufficiently or abundantly; in an ample manner

AMPUL *n pl* **-S** a small bottle that contains medication for injection; *also* **AMPULE, AMPOULE**

AMUCK *adv* in a frenzied and reckless manner; *also* **AMOK**

AMUSE *v* **-D, AMUSING, -S** to entertain or occupy in a pleasant manner

AMYLS *n pl of* **AMYL** univalent hydrocarbon radicals

AMYSS *n pl* **-S** a hood or cape; *also* **AMESS, AMISS**

ANCHO *n pl* **-S** a dried poblano pepper

ANCON *n pl* **-ES** a projecting bracket used in classical architecture to carry the upper elements of a cornice

ANEAR *adv* [obs] close; to a point or place not far away

ANELE *v* **-D, ANELING, -S** [obs] to anoint

ANENT *prep* about; concerning; in respect

ANGAS *n pl of* **ANGA** the eight fundamental categories of the yogic path

ANGEL *n pl* **-S** a good spiritual creature in stories or some religions, usually represented as a human with wings

ANGER *v* **-ED, -ING, -S** to provoke a strong feeling of annoyance in

ANGLE *v* **-D, -ING, -S** to incline or bend from a vertical position

ANGOR *n pl* **-S** extreme distress or mental anguish, usually of physical origin

ANGRY *adj* **ANGRIER, ANGRIEST** troublesome; rigorous

ANGST *n pl* **-S** a feeling of anxiety or apprehension often accompanied by depression

ANILE *adj* old-womanish; senile

ANILS *n pl of* **ANIL** West Indian shrubs from which indigo dye is made

ANIMA *n pl* **-S** the inner self of an individual; the soul

ANIME *n pl* **-S** any of various resins or oleoresins

ANIMI *n pl of* **ANIMUS** feelings of ill will arousing active hostility

ANION *n pl* **-S** a negatively charged ion

ANISE *n pl* **-S** a French or Spanish liqueur flavored with aniseed; also **ANIS**

ANJOU *n pl* **-S** a green-skinned pear with firm flesh

ANKER *n pl* **-S** a liquid measure in various countries of Europe

ANKHS *n pl of* **ANKH** crosses with a loop on the top, representing life, rebirth, reincarnation and love in ancient Egypt

ANKLE *n pl* **-S** the joint that connects the foot with the leg

ANKUS *n pl* **-ES** an elephant goad with a sharp spike and a hook

ANNAL *n pl* **-S** the record of a single year

ANNAS *n pl of* **ANNA** former coins of Pakistan and India, equal to 1/16 of a rupee

ANNEX *v* **-ED, -ING, -ES** to join or attach

ANNOY *v* **-ED, -ING, -S** to disturb or irritate

ANNUL *v* **-LED, -LING, -S** to reduce to nothing; to obliterate

ANOAS *n pl of* **ANOA** small buffalo native to Indonesia

ANODE *n pl* **-S** a positively charged electrode

ANOLE *n pl* **-S** a small tropical American insectivorous lizard with the ability to change skin color

ANOMY *n pl* **ANOMIES** social instability resulting from a breakdown of standards and values; also **ANOMIE**

ANSAE *n pl of* **ANSA** protruding parts of planetary rings

ANTAE *n pl of* **ANTA** piers produced by thickening walls at their termination; also **ANTAS**

ANTAS *n pl of* **ANTA** piers produced by thickening walls at their termination; also **ANTAE**

ANTED *v p t of* **ANTE** put a fixed stake into the pool before the cards are dealt in poker

ANTES *v pr t of* **ANTE** puts a fixed stake into the pool before the cards are dealt in poker

ANTIC *n pl* **-S** prank; trick; mischief

ANTIS *n pl of* **ANTI** people that are not in favor of an action or proposal

ANTRA *n pl of* **ANTRUM** cavities or chambers, especially those in bones

ANTRE *n pl* **-S** a cavern; a cave

ANTSY *adj* **ANTSIER, ANTSIEST** restless or impatient; fidgety

ANURY *n pl* **ANURIES** non-secretion or defective secretion of urine; ischury

ANVIL *n pl* **-S** an iron block, usually with a steel face, upon which metals are hammered and shaped

ANYON *n pl* **-S** a subatomic particle

AORTA *n pl* **-S** or **-E** the main trunk of the arterial system

APACE *adj* with a quick pace; speedily

APAID *adj* [obs] paid; pleased

APAIR *v* **-ED, -ING, -S** [obs] to impair or become impaired; to injure

APARS *n pl of* **APAR** South American armadillos with three bands of bony plates

APART *adv* aside; away; not together

APEAK *adv* in a vertical line or position; *also* **APEEK**

APEEK *adv* in a vertical line or position; *also* **APEAK**

APERS *n pl of* **APER** those who ape or mimic

APERT *adj* open; evident; undisguised

APERY *n pl* **APERIES** apish behavior; mimicry

APHID *n pl* **-S** various small plant-sucking insects; *also* **APHIS**

APHIS *n pl* **APHIDES** various small plant-sucking insects; *also* **APHID**

APIAN *adj* pertaining to bees

APING *pr part of* **APE** imitating or mimicking

APIOL *n pl* **-S** an oily liquid derived from parsley

APISH *adj* having the qualities of an ape; fantastically silly

APNEA *n pl* **-S** temporary absence or cessation of breathing; *also* **APNOEA**

APODA *n* an order of Amphibia without feet

APODE *n pl* **-S** a footless animal; *also* **APOD**

APODS *n pl of* **APOD** footless animals; *also* **APODES**

APORT *adv* on or towards the port or left side of a ship

APPAL *v* **-LED, -LING, -S** to strike with disgust or revulsion; *also* **APPALL**

APPAY *v* **-AID, -ING, -S** [obs] to pay; to satisfy or appease

APPEL *n pl* **-S** a tap or stamp of the foot in fencing to show intent to attack

APPLE *n pl* **-S** the fleshy, usually rounded, red, yellow or green edible pome fruit of a tree of the rose family

APPLY *v* **APPLIED, -ING, APPLIES** to lay or place; to put or adjust

APPUI *n pl* **-S** [obs] a support or supporter; a prop

APRES *prep* after; following

APRON *v* **-ED, -ING, -S** to cover or protect with an apron, a structure along a shoreline to prevent erosion

APSES *n pl of* **APSE** domed or vaulted recesses or projections on a building, especially the east ends of churches containing the altars; *also* **ABSISES, APSIDES**

APSIS *n pl* **APSIDES** a domed or vaulted recess or projection on a building, especially the east end of a church containing the altar; *also* **APSE, ABSIS**

APTLY *adv* in a suitable manner; properly

AQUAE *n pl of* **AQUA** light bluish green colors; *also* **AQUAS**

AQUAS *n pl of* **AQUA** light bluish green colors; *also* **AQUAE**

ARACE *v* **-D, ARACING** [obs] to tear up by the roots; to draw away

ARAKS *n pl of* **ARAK** strong liquors distilled from fermented palm sap, rice or molasses; *also* **ARRACKS**

ARAME *n pl* **-S** an edible, mild-flavored seaweed

ARARA *n pl* **-S** the palm cockatoo of Australia

ARBOR *n pl* **-ES** a structure covered with lattice-worked branches or vines

ARCAE *n pl of* **ARCA** chests used to store valuables in medieval Spain and Italy

ARCED *v p t of* **ARC** moved in a curved course; *also* **ARCKED**

ARCUS *n pl* **-ES** a dense, horizontal, roll-shaped cloud sometimes occurring at the lower front portion of a cumulonimbus

ARDEB *n pl* **-S** a unit of capacity used for dry measure in Egypt and surrounding countries, about 5.2 bushels

ARDOR *n pl* **-S** an intense feeling of love

AREAL *adj* of or pertaining to an area

AREAR *v* [obs] to raise; to set up; *also* **ARERE**

AREAS *n pl of* **AREA** fields of study, or branches of fields of study

ARECA *n pl* **-S** any of several tropical Asian palms; especially the betel palm

AREEK *adj* in a condition of having a strong, unpleasant smell

AREFY *v* **AREFIED, -ING, AREFIES** to dry, or make dry

AREIC *adj* land without surface drainage, that is without streams or rivers

ARENA *n pl* **-S** a playing field where sports events take place

ARENE *n pl* **-S** a hydrocarbon that contains at least one aromatic ring

AREPA *n pl* **-S** a South American baked or fried cornmeal cake

ARERE *v* [obs] to raise; to set up; *also* **AREAR**

AREST *n pl* **AREST** [obs] a support for a spear when couched for the attack

ARETE *n pl* **-S** a sharp mountain ridge

ARGAL *n pl* **-S** a crude tartar deposit from wine making; *also* **ARGOL**

ARGIL *n pl* **-S** a white clay used by potters

ARGLE *v* **-D, ARGLING, -S** SCOT. to argue

ARGOL *n pl* **-S** a crude tartar deposit from wine making; *also* **ARGAL**

ARGON *n pl* **-S** a colorless and odorless inert gas

ARGOT *n pl* **-S** a specialized vocabulary or set of slang used by a particular group

ARGUE *v* **-D, ARGUING, -S** to debate or discuss; to treat by reasoning

ARGUS *n pl* **-ES** one who is very vigilant; a guardian; always watchful

ARHAT *n pl* **-S** a Buddhist who has attained enlightenment

ARIAS *n pl of* **ARIA** elaborate songs for solo voices

ARIEL *n pl* **-S** an African gazelle

ARILS *n pl of* **ARIL** fleshy and usually brightly colored seed coverings that form on some plants after fertilization

ARISE *v* **AROSE, ARISEN, ARISING** to get up

ARISH *n* the stubble of wheat or grass; a stubble field; *also* **ARRISH, EARSH, ERSH**

ARLES *n pl of* **ARLE** earnest money; money paid to bind a bargain

ARMED *v p t of* **ARM** provided with weapons

ARMER *n pl* **-S** one who provides with weapons

ARMET *n pl* **-S** a medieval helmet with a visor and a neck guard

ARMIL *n pl* **-S** an ancient astronomical instrument

ARMOR *n pl* **-S** a protective covering made of metal and used in combat

ARNEE *n pl* **-S** a large wild buffalo of India

ARNOT *n pl* **-S** SCOT. [obs] burnium, pignut or earthnut; *also* **ARNUT**

ARNUT *n pl* **-S** SCOT. [obs] burnium, pignut or earthnut; *also* **ARNOT**

AROID *n* any plant of the arum family

AROMA *n pl* **-S** a distinctive odor that is pleasant

AROPH *n* [obs] a name by which saffron is sometimes called

AROSE *v p t of* **ARISE** got up

ARPEN *n pl* **-S** an old measure of land in France; *also* **ARPENT**

ARRAS *n pl* **-ES** a wall hanging or tapestry, especially of Flemish origin

ARRAY *v* **-ED, -ING, -S** display or arrange in a neat or impressive way

ARRET *n pl* **-S** a judgment, decision, or decree of a court or high tribunal

ARRIS *n pl* **-ES** the sharp edge or ridge formed by two surfaces meeting each other

ARROW *n pl* **-S** a slender, pointed, and usually feathered projectile weapon shot from a bow

ARSES *n pl of* **ARSIS** the unaccented parts of a musical measure

ARSIS *n pl* **ARSES** the unaccented part of a musical measure

ARSON *n pl* **-S** a malicious burning to destroy property

ARTAL *n pl of* **ROTL** a unit of weight used in Muslim regions, which varies from about one to five pounds

ARTEL *n pl* **-S** a collective farm in Russia

ARTSY *adj* **ARTSIER, ARTSIEST** characterized by a showy, pretentious display of artistic interest; *also* **ARTY**

ARUMS *n pl of* **ARUM** plants of the arum family, which is characterized by small flowers on a thick spike, within a hood-like leaf

ARVAL *n pl* **-S** a funeral feast

ARVOS *n pl of* **ARVO** AUS., N.Z. afternoons

ARYLS *n pl of* **ARYL** univalent radicals

ASANA *n pl* **-S** any of various bodily positions in yoga

ASCOT *n pl* **-S** a broad neck scarf knotted so that its ends lie flat

ASCUS *n pl* **ASCI** a spore sac in certain lichens and fungi

ASDIC *n pl* **-S** a form of sonar used for detecting submarines

ASHEN *adj* very pale

ASHES *n pl of* **ASH** matter left after something has burned

ASIDE *n pl* **-S** a remark made by a stage player which the other players are not supposed to hear

ASKED *v p t of* **ASK** put a question to

ASKER *n pl* **-S** one who poses a question

ASKEW *adj* not straight or level

ASKOI *n pl of* **ASKOS** ancient Grecian oil or wine jars

ASKOS *n pl* **ASKOI** an ancient Grecian oil or wine jar

ASLUG *adv* [obs] in a slow manner

ASPEN *n pl* **-S** a poplar tree with small rounded leaves

ASPER *n pl* **-S** a former silver coin of Turkey and Egypt

ASPIC *n pl* **-S** a savory jelly made from meat or fish stock

ASPIS *n pl* **ASPIDES** a type of shield carried by ancient Greek soldiers

ASSAI *n pl* **-S** any of several South American palm trees

ASSAY *v* **-ED, -ING, -S** to subject to chemical analysis

ASSES *n pl of* **ASS**; long-haired, hoofed, horse-like animals

ASSET *n pl* **-S** a useful or valuable quality or thing

ASSOT *v* **-ED, -ING, -S** to infatuate

ASTAY *adv* at an acute angle to the surface of the water, said of the cable when heaving an anchor

ASTER *n pl* **-S** annual plant of the daisy family

ASTIR *adj* moving about; being in motion

ASTUN *v* **-NED, -NING, -S** to stun

ASYLA *n pl of* **ASYLUM** sanctuaries or places of refuge and protection

ATAKE *v* [obs] to overtake

ATAPS *n pl of* **ATAP** thatches for native huts in Malaya, made of nipa palm leaves; *also* **ATTAPS**

ATAXY *n pl* **ATAXIES** inability to coordinate voluntary muscle movements; *also* **ATAXIA**

ATHAR *n* an essential oil or perfume obtained from flowers; *also* **ATAR, ATTAR, ATHAR, OTTAR, OTTO**

ATILT *adv* in a tilted position; inclined upward

ATIMY *n pl* **ATIMIES** a public disgrace or stigma; infamy

ATLAS *n pl* **-ES** a book of maps or charts

ATMAN *n pl* **-S** the individual soul, the principle of life in Hinduism; *also* **ATMA**

ATMAS *n pl of* **ATMA** more than one individual soul, the principle of life in Hinduism; *also* **ATMANS**

ATOLE *n pl* **-S** a porridge or gruel of maize meal and water or milk

ATOLL *n pl* **-S** a ring-like coral reef that nearly or entirely encloses a lagoon

ATOMS *n pl of* **ATOM** ultimate indivisible particles of matter

ATOMY *n pl* **-IES** [obs] a tiny particle or being; a mite

ATONE *v* **-D, ATONING, -S** to make amends

ATONY *n pl* **ATONIES** lack of normal muscular tension; *also* **ATONIA**

ATOPY *n pl* **ATOPIES** a type of allergy where a reaction may occur in a part of the body not in contact with the allergen; *also* **ATOPIC**

ATRIA *n pl of* **ATRIUM** usually skylighted central areas, often containing plants, in some modern buildings

ATRIP *adj* just clear of the bottom, as an anchor

ATTAL *n* rubbish or refuse consisting of broken rock containing little or no ore; *also* **ATTLE**

ATTAP *n pl* **-S** thatch for native huts in Malaya, made of nipa palm leaves; *also* **ATAP**

ATTAR *n* an essential oil or perfume obtained from flowers; *also* **ATAR, ATHAR, OTTAR, OTTO**

ATTER *n* [obs] a poison; venom

ATTIC *n pl* **-S** a room consisting of open space at the top of a house just below the roof

ATTLE *n* rubbish or refuse consisting of broken rock containing little or no ore; *also* **ATTAL**

ATTRY *adj* [obs] poisonous; malicious

AUBES *n pl of* **AUBE** [obs] long white linen robes with tapered sleeves worn by a priest at Mass; *also* **ALBS**

AUBIN *n* a broken gait of a horse, between an amble and a gallop; a Canterbury gallop

AUCHT *n pl* **-S** [obs] a property; a possession

AUDAD *n* a wild sheep of North Africa; *also* **AOUDAD, UDAD, ARUI**

AUDIO *adj* of or relating to audible sound

AUDIT *v* **-ED, -ING, -S** to examine records or accounts to check their accuracy

AUGER *n pl* **-S** a hand tool for boring holes

AUGET *n pl* **-S** in mining a priming tube connecting a charge chamber with the place where a slow match is applied

AUGHT *n pl* **-S** nothing; zero; quantity of no importance

AUGUR *v* **-ED, -ING, -S** to predict, especially from signs or omens; foretell

AULIC *adj* of or pertaining to a royal court

AUNTS *n pl of* **AUNT** the sisters of your father or mother; the wives of your uncles

AUNTY *n pl* **AUNTIES** informal for an aunt, a sister of your mother or father or the wife of your uncle; *also* **AUNTIE**

AURAE *n pl of* **AURA** characteristic or distinctive impressions created by someone or something; *also* **AURAS**

AURAL *adj* of, relating to or perceived by the ear

AURAR *n pl of* **EYRIR** monetary units of Icelandic currency, each equal to one hundredth of a krona

AURAS *n pl of* **AURA** characteristic or distinctive impressions created by someone or something; *also* **AURAE**

AUREI *n pl of* **AUREUS** gold coins that were a unit of currency in ancient Rome

AURES *n pl of* **AURIS** ears

AURIC *adj* of or pertaining to gold

AURIN *n pl* **-S** a red coloring matter derived from phenol

AURIS *n pl* **AURES** an ear

AURUM *n pl* **-S** gold

AUTOS *v pr t of* **AUTO** goes by or rides in a four-wheeled motor vehicle

AUXIN *n pl* **-S** a plant hormone that promotes root formation and bud growth

AVAIL *v* **-ED, -ING, -S** to assist or aid; to be of value or advantage

AVALE *v* **-D, AVALING, -S** [obs] to cause to descend; to lower

AVANT *adj* culturally and stylistically new or advanced

AVAST *interj* a nautical term used as a command to cease; stop

AVENS *n pl-***ES** a perennial herb of the rose family with pinnate basal leaves and colored flowers

AVERS *v p t of* **AVER** asserts or proves the truth of something

AVERT *v* **-ED, -ING, -S** to turn aside, or away

AVGAS *n* gasoline for use in piston-driven airplanes

AVIAN *adj* of or related to birds

AVILE *v* **-D, AVILING,** [obs] to abase or debase; to depreciate

AVION *n pl* **-S** an airplane

AVISE *v* **-D, AVISING, -S** [obs] to look at; to think of

AVISO *n pl* **-S** information; advice

AVOID *v* **-ED, -ING, -S** to keep away from

AVOKE *v* **-D, AVOKING, -S** to call from or back again

AVOWS *v pr t of* **AVOW** declares openly that something is true

AWAIT *v* **-ED, -ING, -S** to watch for; to look out for

AWAKE *v* **-D** or **AWOKE, AWOKEN, AWAKING, -S** to rouse from sleep

AWARD *v* **-ED, -ING, -S** to grant or bestow an honor upon

AWARE *adj* having perception or knowledge

AWARN *v* **-ED, -S** [obs] to warn

AWASH *adj* covered in water or another liquid

AWFUL *adj* **-LER, -LEST** extremely bad and unpleasant

AWING *v pr part of* **AWE** inspiring with a feeling of wonderment

AWKLY *adv* [obs] in an unlucky or clumsy manner

AWNED *adj* having the bristle-like tip of certain grasses

AWOKE *v p t of* **AWAKE** roused from sleep

AWOLS *n pl of* **AWOL** informal for those who are truant or absent, originally a military acronym

AWORK *adv* [obs] at work; in action

AXELS *n pl of* **AXEL** figure skating jumps with forward takeoffs and backward landings

AXIAL *adj* of or pertaining to a straight line on which an object rotates; *also* **AXAL, AXILE**

AXILE *adj* of or pertaining to a straight line on which an object rotates; *also* **AXAL**, **AXIAL**

AXILS *n pl of* **AXIL** the upper angles between leaves or twigs and the stems from which they grow

AXING *v pr part of* **AXE** chopping, cutting down

AXIOM *n pl* **-S** a self-evident or universally recognized truth

AXION *n pl* **-S** a hypothetical subatomic particle having no charge and zero spin

AXITE *n pl* **-S** a fiber of an axon

AXLED *adj* having pins or spindles upon which wheels revolve

AXLES *n pl of* **AXLE** pins or spindles upon which wheels revolve

AXMAN *n pl* **AXMEN** informal term for a person who is assigned to perform a task involving ruthless reduction, as of a work force or budget

AXMEN *n pl of* **AXMAN** informal term for people who are assigned to perform a task involving ruthless reduction, as of a work force or budget

AXONE *n pl* **-S** a long nerve fiber that conducts impulses away from the body of the nerve cell; *also* **AXON**

AXONS *n pl of* **AXON** long nerve fibers that conduct impulses away from the body of the nerve cell; *also* **AXONES**

AYAHS *n pl of* **AYAH** native nurses or maids in India

AYINS *n pl of* **AYIN** more than one of the 16th letter of the Hebrew alphabet; *also* **AINS**

AYLES *n pl of* **AYLE** [obs] grandfathers; *also* **AIELS**

AYOND *adv* SCOT. beyond; *also* **AYONT**

AYONT *adv* SCOT. beyond; *also* **AYOND**

AYRIE *n pl* **-S** the nest of a bird of prey; *also* **AERY, AERIE, AYRY, EYRE, EYRIE, EYRY**

AZANS *n pl of* **AZAN** Muslim calls to prayer which happen five times a day

AZIDE *n pl* **-S** any chemical compound containing the azido group, N_3

AZIDO *adj* containing the chemical compound N_3

AZINE *n pl* **-S** an organic compound that contains one or more nitrogen atoms

AZLON *n pl* **-S** a textile fiber derived from protein

AZOIC *adj* before the appearance of life

AZOLE *n pl* **-S** any of a group of five-membered heterocyclic compounds containing one or more nitrogen atoms in the ring

AZONS *n pl of* **AZON** radio-controlled aerial bombs

AZOTE *n pl* **-S** [obs] nitrogen

AZOTH *n pl* **-S** [obs] mercury

AZUKI *n pl* **-S** an Asian herb with edible sprouts and reddish beans used to make flour; *also* **ADZUKI**

AZURE *n pl* **-S** the clear blue color of the sky

AZURN *adj* [obs] sky-blue in color

AZYME *n pl* **-S** [obs] unleavened bread; matzoh; *also* **AZYM**

AZYMS *n pl of* **AZYM** [obs] unleavened breads; matzohs; *also* **AZYMES**

BA *n pl* **-S** the eternal soul in Egyptian mythology

BE *v* **WAS** or **WERE**, **-EN**, **-ING**, **AM** or **ARE** or **IS** to exist

BO *n pl* **-S** a friend; a pal

BY *n pl* **-S** the position of those who draw no opponent for a round in a tournament and so advance to the next round; *also* **BYE**

THREE LETTERS

BAA *v* **-ED, -ING, -S** to bleat like a sheep

BAC *n pl* **-S** a broad flat-bottomed ferryboat

BAD *adj* below average in quality or performance; evil

BAG *v* **-GED, -GING, -S** to put into a pouch or sack

BAH *interj* to express disgust or contempt; *also* **PAH, PAU**

BAL *n pl* **-S** commonly used abbreviation for balmoral, a heavy, laced walking shoe

BAM *v* **-MED, -MING, -S** to strike with a dull resounding noise

BAN *v* **-NED, -NING, -S** to prohibit

BAP *n pl* **-S** BRIT. a small bun or roll

BAR *v* **-RED, -RING, -S** to exclude

BAS *n pl of* **BA**, eternal souls in Egyptian mythology

BAT *v* **-TED, -TING, -S** to hit a baseball

BAY *v* **-ED, -ING, -S** to make a barking sound, as of hounds

BED *n pl* **-S** a piece of furniture to sleep on

BEE *n pl* **-S** a honey making insect

BEG *v* **-GED, -GING, -S** to ask for; to plead

BEL *n pl* **-S** a measure of noise equal to ten decibels

BEN *n pl* **-S** SCOT. the inner room or living room of a cottage

BES *n pl* **-ES** the second letter of the Hebrew alphabet; *also* **BETH**

BET *v* **-TED, -TING, -S** to wager

BEY *n pl* **-S** a provincial governor in the Ottoman Empire

BIB *n pl* **-S** a napkin tied under the chin of a child while eating

BID *v* **-DED** or **BADE, -DING, -S** to make an offer

BIG *adj* **-GER, -GEST** of great size; large

BIN *v* **-NED, -NING, -S** to place or store in a large receptacle

BIO *n pl* **-S** commonly used abbreviation for a biography, a written account of a person's life

BIS *adv* again; encore

BIT *v* **-TED, -TING, -S** to place the metal mouthpiece of a bridle in the mouth of a horse

BIZ *n pl* **-S** commonly used abbreviation for business

BOA *n pl* **-S** a snake that kills by constricting

BOB *v* **-BED, -BING, -S** to move quickly up and down

BOD *n pl* **-S** commonly used abbreviation for a body

BOG *v* **-GED, -GING -S** to sink; to impede

BOH *interj* exclamation used to startle

BON *adj* [obs] good; valid as security for something

BOO *v* **-ED, -ING, -S** to express contempt, scorn, or disapproval

BOP *v* **-PED, -PING, -S** to hit or strike

BOS *n pl of* **BO** friends; pals

BOT *n pl* **-S** the parasitic larva of a botfly; *also* **BOTT**

BOW *v* **-ED, -ING, -S** to bend the body in respect

BOX *v* **-ED, -ING, -ES** to fight with fists

BOY *n pl* **-S** a male child

BRA *n pl* **-S** commonly used abbreviation for a brassiere; a woman's undergarment

BRO *n pl* **-S** commonly used abbreviation for brother, a male having the same parents as another

BRR *interj* exclamation of feeling cold

BUB *n pl* **-S** used as a term of familiar address for a man or boy

BUD *v* **-DED, -DING, -S** to begin to develop or grow

BUG *v* **-GED, -GING, -S** to annoy

BUM *v* **-MED, -MING, -S** to borrow without expectation of returning

BUN *n pl* **-S** small rounded bread, either plain or sweet; *also* **BUNN**

BUR *v* **-RED, -RING, -S** to remove rough edges from metal; *also* **BURR**

BUS *v* **-ED** or **-SED, -ING** or **-SING, -ES** or **-SES** to ride a long motor vehicle that carries passengers

BUT *conj* on the contrary; with the exception that

BUY *v* **BOUGHT, -ING, -S** to purchase

BYE *n pl* **-S** the position of those who draw no opponent for a round in a tournament and so advance to the next round; *also* **BY**

BYS *n pl of* **BY** the positions of those who draw no opponent for a round in a tournament and so advance to the next round; *also* **BYES**

FOUR LETTERS

BAAL *n pl* **-S** or **BALIM** a false god or idol

BAAS *v pr t of* **BAA** bleats like a sheep

BABA *n pl* **-S** a leavened rum cake, usually made with raisins

BABE *n pl* **-S** an infant; a young child of either sex; a baby

BABU *n pl* **-S** a Hindi courtesy title for a gentleman, equivalent to sir; *also* **BABOO**

BABY *n pl* **BABIES** an infant or young child of either sex; a babe

BACE *n* [obs] a starting point or point of departure

BACH *v* **-ED, -ING, -ES** to live as a bachelor

BACK *v* **-ED, -ING, -S** to support

BACS *n pl of* **BAC** broad flat-bottomed ferryboats

BADE *v p t of* **BID** made an offer

BADS *n* in economics, any goods with a negative value to the consumer or a negative price in the marketplace

BAFF *v* **-ED, -ING, -S** to strike the ground with a club in making a stroke

BAFT *n pl* **-S** a coarse stuffing of cotton from India; *also* **BAFTA**

BAGS *v pr t of* **BAG** puts into a pouch or sack

BAHT *n pl* **BAHT, -S** the basic monetary unit of Thailand

BAIL *v* **-ED, -ING, -S** to remove water from a boat by repeatedly filling a bucket and emptying it over the side

BAIN *n pl* **-S** [obs] a bathhouse; a bagnio in Italy or Turkey

BAIT *v* **-ED, -ING, -S** to lure or entice, especially by trickery or strategy

BAKE *v* **-D, BAKING, -S** to prepare food by cooking in dry heat

BALD *v* **-ED, -ING, -S** to lose the hair on one's head

BALE *v* **-D, BALING, -S** to create a large package of raw or finished material tightly bound with twine or wire

BALK *v* **-ED, -ING, -S** to stop short and refuse to go on; *also* **BAULK, BAUK**

BALL *v* **-ED, -ING, -S** to form into a round body or mass

BALM *n pl* **-S** a fragrant ointment that mitigates pain

BALS *n pl of* **BAL** commonly used abbreviation for balmoral, heavy, laced walking shoes

BAMS *v pr t of* **BAM** strikes with a dull resounding noise

BANC *n pl* **-S** a bench; high seat of distinction or judgment

BAND *v* **-ED, -ING, -S** to tie, bind or encircle with a narrow strip of cloth or other material

BANE *v* **-D, BANING, -S** [obs] to kill especially with poison

BANG *v* **-ED, -ING, -S** to strike sharply

BANI *n pl of* **BAN** monetary units of Romania

BANK *v* **-ED, -ING, -S** to construct a slope rising on the outside edge

BANS *v pr t of* **BAN** prohibits

BAPS *n pl of* **BAP** BRIT. small buns or rolls

24

BARB *v* **-ED, -ING, -S** to provide or furnish with a hair or bristle ending in a double hook

BARD *v* **-ED, -ING, -S** to equip a horse with armor protection

BARE *v* **-D, -ING, -S** to strip of covering

BARF *v* **-ED, -ING, -S** to vomit

BARK *v* **-ED, -ING, -S** to make a loud sound like a dog

BARM *n pl* **-S** the yeasty foam that rises to the surface of fermenting malt liquors

BARN *n pl* **-S** a covered building used to store grain or hay

BARS *v pr t of* **BAR** excludes

BART *n pl* **-S** a baronet, a member of the British order of honor below a baron but above a knight

BASE *v* **-D, -BASING, -S** to establish as a fact or conclusion

BASH *v* **-ED, -ING, -ES** to strike with a heavy, crushing blow

BASK *v* **-ED, -ING, -S** to lie in warmth; to be exposed to genial heat

BASS *n pl* **-ES** an edible, spiny-finned fish

BAST *n pl* **-S** fibrous material from various plants used to make cordage and textiles

BATE *v* **-ED, BATING, -S** to moderate or restrain

BATH *n pl* **-S** a tub of water for washing or soaking the body

BATS *v pr t of* **BAT** hits a baseball

BATT *n pl* **-S** a sheet of cotton used for stuffing

BATZ *n pl* **-EN** a small copper coin with a silver mixture, formerly used in Germany and Switzerland

BAUD *n pl* **-S** a unit of data transmission speed

BAUK *v* **-ED, -ING, -S** to stop short and refuse to go on; *also* **BALK, BAULK**

BAWL *v* **-ED, -ING, -S** to cry out with a loud, full sound

BAYS *v pr t of* **BAY** makes a barking sound, as of hounds

BEAD *v* **-ED, -ING, -S** to furnish with small, ball-shaped pieces of material pierced for stringing or threading

BEAK *n pl* **-S** the bill or nib of a bird, consisting of a horny sheath

BEAL *v* **-ED, -ING, -S** to gather matter; to swell and come to a head, as a pimple

BEAM *v* **-ED, -ING, -S** to radiate light; shine

BEAN *n pl* **-S** the seed of certain leguminous herbs

BEAR *v* **BORE, BORNE** or **BORN, -ING, -S** to support or sustain; to hold up

BEAT *v* **-EN, -ING, -S** to strike repeatedly

BEAU *n pl* **-S** or **-X** a frequent and attentive male companion

BECK *n pl* **-S** a gesture of the head, hand, etc. meant to summon

BEDE *v* [obs] to offer; to proffer

BEDS *n pl of* **BED** pieces of furniture to sleep on

BEEF *v* **-ED, -ING, -S** to complain

BEEM *n* [obs] a trumpet

BEEN *v p part of* **BE** existed

BEEP *v* **-ED, -ING, -S** to honk a horn

BEER *n pl* **-S** a fermented liquor made from malted grain

BEES *n pl of* **BEE** honey making insects

BEET *n pl* **-S** a round red root vegetable

BEGA *n pl* **-S** a measure of land in India; *also* **BIGHA**

BEGS *v pr t of* **BEG** asks for, pleads

BEHN *n pl* **-S** an herb, whose leaves resemble ears of corn; saffron; *also* **BEHEN**

BELK *v* **-ED, -ING, -S** [obs] to vomit

BELL *n pl* **-S** a hollow device made of metal that makes a ringing sound when struck

BELS *n pl of* **BEL** measures of noise equal to ten decibels

BELT *v* **-ED, -ING, -S** to hit something or somebody hard; to encircle

BEMA *n pl* **-S** or **-TA** area around the altar in an Eastern Orthodox church; a platform in a synagogue; *also* **BIMA, BIMAH**

BEND *v* **BENT, -ING, -S** to turn toward some certain point; to direct; to incline

BENE *n pl* **-S** a sesame plant; *also* **BENNE, BENNI**

BENS *n pl of* **BEN** SCOT. inner rooms or living rooms of a cottage

BENT *v p part of* **BEND** turned toward some certain point; directed; inclined

BERE *v* **-D, BERING, -S** [obs] to pierce

BERG *n pl* **-S** commonly used abbreviation for iceberg, a mass of floating or stationary ice

BERK *n pl* **-S** BRIT. a foolish person; *also* **BURK**

BERM *n pl* **-S** a shoulder of a road, *also* **BERME**

BEST *v* **-ED, -ING, -S** to get the better of; surpass

BETA *n pl* **-S** the second letter of the Greek alphabet

BETE *v* **-D, BETING, -S** [obs] to mend; to repair; *also* **BEETE**

BETH *n pl* **-S** the second letter of the Hebrew alphabet; *also* **BES**

BETS *v pr t of* **BET** wagers

BEVY *n pl* **BEVIES** a group of animals or birds, especially larks or quail

BEYS *n pl of* **BEY** provincial governors in the Ottoman Empire

BHUT *n pl* **-S** a spirit or demon in Indian mythology; *also* **BHOOT**

BIAS *v* **-ED** or **-SED, -ING** or **-SING, -ES** or **-SES** to cause to have a prejudiced view

BIBB *n pl* **-S** a bracket on the mast of a ship to support the trestletrees

BIBS *n pl of* **BIB** napkins tied under the chin of a child while eating

BICE *n pl* **-S** a pale blue pigment, prepared from the native blue carbonate of copper; *also* **BISE**

BIDE *v* **-D** or **BODE, BIDING, -S** to remain in a condition or state; to wait

BIDI *n pl* **-S** a thin, often flavored Indian cigarette made of tobacco wrapped in a tendu leaf; *also* **BEEDI, BIRI**

BIDS *v pr t of* **BID** makes an offer

BIER *n pl* **-S** a movable platform on which a coffin or corpse is placed before burial

BIFF *v* **-ED, -ING, -S** to hit

BIGA *n pl* **-S** a two-wheeled chariot drawn by two horses harnessed abreast

BIGG *n pl* **-S** SCOT. barley, especially the hardy four-rowed kind

BIKE *v* **-D, BIKING, -S** to ride on a vehicle with two wheels and a seat that is moved by pushing pedals with the feet

BIKH *n pl* **-S** a virulent poison extracted from aconite plants; *also* **BISH**

BILE *n pl* **-S** a yellowish digestive juice secreted by the liver

BILK *v* **-ED, -ING, -S** to defraud, cheat or swindle

BILL *v* **-ED, -ING, -S** to present a statement of costs or charges

BIMA *n pl* **-S** area around the altar in an Eastern Orthodox church; a platform in a synagogue; *also* **BIMAH, BEMA**

BIND *v* **BOUND, -ING, -S** to tie or confine with a cord

BINE *n pl* **-S** the winding or twining stem of various climbing plants, such as the hop, woodbine or bindweed

BING *n pl* **-S** SCOT., BRIT. a heap or pile; as of wood

BINK *n pl* **-S** SCOT., BRIT. a bench

BINS *v pr t of* **BIN** stores in a large receptacle

BION *n* the physiological individual, characterized by independence of function

BIOS *n pl of* **BIO** commonly used abbreviation for biographies, written accounts of a person's life

BIRD *n pl* **-S** a warm-blooded, feathered, winged animal

BIRI *n pl* **-S** a thin, often flavored Indian cigarette made of tobacco wrapped in a tendu leaf; *also* **BEEDI, BIDI**

BIRK *n pl* **-S** BRIT. a birch tree; *also* **BIRKEN**

BIRL *v* **-ED, -ING, -S** to revolve a floating log by treading

BIRO *n pl* **-S** a pen that has a small metal ball as a point of transfer of ink to paper

BIRR *n pl* **-S** a whirring sound, as of a spinning wheel

BIRT *n pl* **-S** BRIT. a fish of the turbot kind; the brill; *also* **BURT, BRET, BRUT**

BISE *n pl* **-S** a pale blue pigment prepared from the native blue carbonate of copper; *also* **BICE**

BISH *n pl* **-ES** a virulent poison extracted from aconite plants; *also* **BIKH**

BISK *n pl* **-S** a thick cream soup, especially of pureed shellfish or vegetables; *also* **BISQUE**

BITE *v* **BIT, BITTEN, BITING, -S** to seize something forcibly with the teeth

BITS *v pr t of* **BIT** places the metal mouthpiece of a bridle in the mouth of a horse

BITT *v* **-ED, -ING, -S** to wind a cable around a vertical post on the deck of a ship

BIZE *n pl* **-S** a dry cold north wind in southeastern France

BIZS *n pl of* **BIZ** commonly used abbreviation for businesses

BLAB *v* **-BED, -BING, -S** to talk thoughtlessly or without discretion; to tattle

BLAE *adj* SCOT. dark blue or bluish gray; lead-colored

BLAH *n pl* **-S** a general feeling of physical or psychological discomfort or dissatisfaction

BLAM *interj* used to suggest the sound of a shot or explosion

BLAT *v* **-TED, -TING, -S** to cry, as a calf or sheep; to bleat

BLAW *v* **-ED, -N, -ING** SCOT. to blow

BLEA *n pl* **-S** the part of a tree which lies immediately under the bark; the alburnum or sapwood

BLEB *n pl* **-S** a small blister; a bubble

BLED *v p part of* **BLEED** lost blood

BLEE *n pl* **-S** [obs] complexion; color; hue; likeness; form

BLEK *v* **-KED, -KING, -S** [obs] to blacken; to defile

BLET *v* **-TED, -TING** to decay internally when overripe

BLEW *v p t of* **BLOW** expelled air from the mouth

BLIN *v* **-NED, -NING, -S** [obs] to stop; to cease; to desist

BLIP *v* **-PED, -PING, -S** to interrupt recorded sounds, as on a videotape

BLOB *n pl* **-S** an indistinct shapeless form

BLOC *n pl* **-S** a coalition; a group of allied countries

BLOG *n pl* **-S** a personal journal on a website

BLOT *v* **-TED, -TING, -S** to spot; to stain

BLOW *v* **BLEW, -N, -ING, -S** to expel air from the mouth

BLUB *v* **-BED, -BING, -S** to weep noisily in an uncontrolled way

BLUE *v* **-D, BLUING** or **-ING, -S** to make or become the color of a clear sky

BLUR *v* **-RED, -RING, -S** to cause imperfection of vision in; smudge; obscure

BOAR *n pl* **-S** an uncastrated male swine; a wild hog

BOAS *n pl of* **BOA** snakes that kill by constricting

BOAT *n pl* **-S** a small open vessel or water craft

27

BOBS *v pr t of* **BOB** moves quickly up and down

BOCE *n pl* **-S** a European fish having a compressed body and bright colors

BOCK *n pl* **-S** a dark beer

BODE *v* **-D, BODING, -S** to be an omen of

BODS *n pl of* **BOD** commonly used abbreviation for bodies

BODY *n pl* **BODIES** the main part; the physical form of a person, animal or plant.

BOES *v pr t of* **BEHOVE** is appropriate or necessary

BOFF *n pl* **-S** a big laugh; *also* **BOFFOLA**

BOGS *v pr t of* **BOG** sinks; impedes

BOGY *v* **-ED, -ING, -S** to shoot a hole in golf one stroke over par; *also* **BOGEY**

BOHO *n pl* **-S** a bohemian, a person, especially a poet or artist that lives in a nonconforming way

BOIL *v* **-ED, -ING, -S** to reach or cause to reach the temperature at which liquid turns to vapor

BOKE *v* **-D, BOKING, -S** [obs] to poke; to thrust

BOLA *n pl* **-S** a rope with weights attached, esp. in S. Am., used to catch cattle or game by entangling their legs

BOLD *adj* **-ER, -EST** clear and distinct to the eye; conspicuous

BOLE *n pl* **-S** the trunk or stem of a tree

BOLL *n pl* **-S** the pod or capsule of a plant, as of flax or cotton

BOLN *v* **-ED, -ING, -S** to swell; to puff

BOLO *n pl* **-S** a long, heavy, single-edged machete

BOLT *v* **-ED, -ING, -S** to secure or lock with a long metal pin that screws into a nut

BOMB *v* **-ED, -ING, -S** to attack with explosive devices

BOND *v* **-ED, -ING, -S** bring together in a common cause or emotion

BONE *n pl* **-S** the hard, calcified tissue of the skeleton of vertebrates

BONG *v* **-ED, -ING, -S** to make deep ringing sound, as of a bell or gong

BONK *v* **-ED, -ING, -S** to strike or cause to come into contact; to hit hard on the head

BONY *adj* **BONIER, BONIEST** of, relating to, or resembling the hard, calcified tissue of the skeleton of vertebrates; *also* **BONEY**

BOOB *v* **-ED, -ING, -S** to commit a faux pas or mistake

BOOK *n pl* **-S** a written, published work

BOOM *v* **-ED, -ING, -S** to make a deep, resonant sound

BOON *n pl* **-S** a timely blessing or benefit

BOOR *n pl* **-S** a peasant; a rustic; an unrefined countryman

BOOS *v pr t of* **BOO** expresses contempt, scorns, or disapproves

BOOT *v* **-ED, -ING, -S** to kick

BOPS *v pr t of* **BOP** hits or strikes

BORA *n pl* **-S** a violent, cold winter wind on the Adriatic Sea

BORD *n pl* **-S** [obs] a board; a table

BORE *v* **-D, BORING, -S** to make a hole in or through with a drill

BORK *v* **-ED, -ING, -S** to deny Senate confirmation of a nominee, especially for the US Supreme Court

BORN *v p part of* **BEAR** supported or sustained; held up

BORT *n pl* **-S** imperfectly crystallized or coarse diamond used for industrial cutting or abrasion; *also* **BOART, BORTZ, BOORT**

BOSA *n pl* **-S** an acidulated fermented drink of Middle Eastern countries; *also* **BOZA, BOZAH, BOUZA**

BOSC *n pl* **-S** a greenish-yellow variety of a pear

BOSH *n pl* **-ES** empty talk; nonsense; trash; humbug

BOSK *n pl* **-S** a thicket; a small wooded area

28

BOSS *v* **-ED, -ING, -ES** to give orders in a domineering manner

BOTA *n pl* **-S** a leather bag or sack for holding wine

BOTE *n pl* **-S** compensation, such as for injury to person or honor

BOTH *adj* the one and the other; the two; the pair

BOTS *n pl of* **BOT** parasitic larvae of botflies; *also* **BOTTS**

BOTT *n pl* **-S** the parasitic larva of a botfly; *also* **BOT**

BOUD *n pl* **-S** [obs] a weevil; a worm that breeds in malt or biscuits

BOUK *n pl* **-S** [obs] the body; bulk or volume

BOUL *n pl* **-S** a curved handle

BOUN *adj* [obs] ready; prepared; destined; tending

BOUR *n pl* **-S** [obs] a chamber; a cottage

BOUT *n pl* **-S** a temporary attack of illness

BOWL *v* **-ED, -ING, -S** to roll a round object, as a bowling or cricket ball, along the ground

BOWS *v pr t of* **BOW** bends the body in respect

BOXY *adj* **BOXIER, BOXIEST** squarish in shape

BOYO *n pl* **-S** IRISH a boy, chap, fellow, feller

BOYS *n pl of* **BOY** male children

BOZA *n pl* **-S** an acidulated fermented drink of Middle Eastern countries; *also* **BOSA; BOZAH, BOUZA**

BOZO *n pl* **-S** a dunce; fool

BRAD *n pl* **-S** a thin, small nail

BRAE *n pl* **-S** SCOT. a hillside; a slope; a bank

BRAG *v* **-GED, -GING, -S** to boast; to show off

BRAN *n pl* **-S** the outer coating of the seed of wheat, rye or other cereal grain

BRAS *n pl of* **BRA** commonly used abbreviation for brassieres; women's undergarments

BRAT *n pl* **-S** a spoiled child

BRAW *adj* SCOT. fine; splendid; dressed in a fine or showy manner

BRAY *v* **-ED, -ING, -S** to pound, beat, rub, or grind small or fine as if in a mortar

BRED *v p part of* **BREED** produced as offspring; brought forth; bore

BREE *n pl* **-S** a thin, watery soup; a broth

BREN *n pl* **-S** a submachine gun operated by gas pressure and used by the British army during WWII

BRET *n pl* **-S** BRIT. a fish of the turbot kind; the brill; *also* **BURT, BIRT, BRUT**

BREW *v* **-ED, -ING, -S** to boil; to cook; to make beer

BRID *n pl* **-S** [obs] a bird

BRIE *n pl* **-S** a French soft, creamy, white cheese

BRIG *n pl* **-S** a two-masted square-rigged vessel

BRIM *n pl* **-S** the rim, border or upper edge of a cup, dish or any hollow vessel

BRIN *n pl* **-S** one of the radiating sticks of a fan

BRIO *n pl* **-S** vigor; vivacity, liveliness

BRIS *n pl* **-ES**, the Jewish ceremony of male circumcision; *also* **BRISS, BRITH**

BRIT *n pl* **-S** the young of a herring, sprat or similar fish; *also* **BRITT**

BROB *n pl* **-S** a wedge-shaped spike for securing an end of a timber butting against the side of another

BROG *v* **-GED, -GING, -S** SCOT. to prod with a pointed instrument, as a lance; *also* **BROGGLE**

BROO *n pl* **-S** a bree; a broth

BROS *n pl of* **BRO** commonly used abbreviation for brothers, males having the same parents as another

BROW *n pl* **-S** the prominent ridge over the eye

29

BRRR *interj* used to signify that one feels cold

BRUH *n pl* **-S** the rhesus monkey

BRUN *n pl* **-S** a natural stream of water smaller than a river or creek; *also* **BROOK**

BRUT *n pl* **-S** BRIT. a fish of the turbot kind; the brill; *also* **BURT, BRET, BIRT**

BRUX *v* **-ED, -ING, -ES** to clench or grind one's teeth

BUBO *n pl* **-ES** a lymph node that is inflamed and swollen

BUBS *n pl of* **BUB** used as a term of familiar address for men or boys

BUBU *n pl* **-S** a loose, flowing, usually full-length garment worn in some African countries; *also* **BOUBOU**

BUCK *v* **-ED, -ING, -S** to leap forward and upward suddenly; rear up, as a horse

BUDS *v pr t of* **BUD** begins developing or growing

BUFF *v* **-ED, -ING, -S** to polish or shine with a soft, undyed leather

BUGS *v pr t of* **BUG** annoys

BUHL *n pl* **-S** an inlaid furniture decoration; *also* **BOULE, BOULLE**

BUHR *n pl* **-S** a hard, siliceous rock used to make millstones

BULB *n pl* **-S** an underground stem, such as that of the onion or tulip

BULK *v* **-ED, -ING, -S** to grow or increase in size or magnitude

BULL *v* **-ED, -ING, -S** to push ahead or through forcefully

BUMF *n pl* **-S** BRIT. paperwork; a pamphlet, form or memorandum; *also* **BUMPH**

BUMP *v* **-ED, -ING, -S** to come in violent contact with something; to thump

BUMS *v pr t of* **BUM** borrows without expectation of returning

BUND *n pl* **-S** a street running along a harbor or waterway, especially in the Far East

BUNG *v* **-ED, -ING, -S** to close with or as with a cork or stopper

BUNK *v* **-ED, -ING, -S** to sleep in a small compartment, shelf, box or recess used as a sleeping place

BUNN *n pl* **-S** [obs] a small rounded bread, either plain or sweet; *also* **BUN**

BUNS *n pl of* **BUN** small rounded breads, either plain or sweet; *also* **BUNNS**

BUNT *v* **-ED, -ING, -S** to push or strike with or as if with the horns or head

BUOY *v* **-ED, -ING, -S** to keep afloat

BURA *n* a Chadic language spoken south of Lake Chad

BURB *n pl* **-S** commonly used abbreviation for suburb, a usually residential area outlying a city

BURD *n pl* **-S** SCOT. a young lady; maiden

BURG *n pl* **-S** a fortified or walled town in medieval Europe; *also* **BURH**

BURH *n pl* **-S** [obs] a fortified or walled town in medieval Europe; *also* **BURG**

BURK *n pl* **-S** BRIT. a foolish person; *also* **BERK**

BURL *v* **-ED, -ING, -S** to dress or finish cloth by removing lumps, slubs or loose threads

BURN *v* **-ED, -T, -ING, -S** to destroy by fire

BURP *v* **-ED, -ING, -S** to belch

BURR *v* **-ED, -ING, -S** to remove rough edges from metal; *also* **BUR**

BURS *v pr t of* **BUR** removes rough edges from metal; *also* **BURRS**

BURT *n pl* **-S** BRIT. a fish of the turbot kind; the brill; *also* **BIRT, BRET, BRUT**

BURY *v* **BURIED, BURING, BURIES** place in a grave or tomb; cover from sight

BUSH *v* **-ED, -ING, -ES** to grow or branch out like a bush, a low, branching woody plant

BUSK _v_ **-ED, -ING, -S** BRIT. to entertain by singing and dancing, especially in streets and public places

BUSS _v_ **-ED, -ING, -ES** [obs] to kiss; smack

BUST _v_ **-ED, -ING, -S** to burst

BUSY _v_ **BUSIED, -ING, BUSIES** to make busy, constantly at work; diligent; active

BUTE _n pl_ **-S** commonly used abbreviation for phenylbutazone, a drug used to treat arthritis

BUTS _n/pl_ reservations or objections

BUTT _v_ **-ED, -ING, -S** to hit or push against with the head or horns; to ram

BUYS _v pr t of_ **BUY** purchases

BUZZ _v_ **-ED, -ING, -ES** to make a low, continuous, humming or sibilant sound

BYES _n pl of_ **BYE** positions of those who draw no opponent for a round in a tournament and so advance to the next round; _also_ **BYS**

BYRE _n pl_ **-S** BRIT. a cowshed or barn

BYTE _n pl_ **-S** a unit of data that is eight binary digits long

FIVE LETTERS

BAAED _v p t of_ **BAA** bleated like a sheep

BAALS _n pl of_ **BAAL** false gods or idols; _also_ **BALIM**

BABAS _n pl of_ **BABA** leavened rum cakes, usually made with raisins

BABEL _n pl_ **-S** a place or scene of noise and confusion

BABES _n pl of_ **BABE** infants; young children of either sex; babies

BABKA _n pl_ **-S** a coffee cake with orange rind, rum, almonds and raisins

BABOO _n pl_ **-S** a Hindi courtesy title for a gentleman, equivalent to sir; _also_ **BABU**

BABUL _n pl_ **-S** an African acacia tree; _also_ **BABOOL**

BABUS _n pl of_ **BABU** Hindi courtesy titles for gentlemen, equivalent to sirs; _also_ **BABOOS**

BACCA _n pl_ **-E** a berry

BACCY _n pl_ **BACCIES** leaves of the tobacco plant dried and prepared for smoking or ingestion

BACKS _v pr t of_ **BACK** supports

BACON _n pl_ **-S** hog back and sides salted and dried or smoked

BADDY _n pl_ **BADDIES** one that is bad; an opponent of the hero; _also_ **BADDIE**

BADGE _n pl_ **-S** a distinctive mark, token or sign worn on the person

BADLY _adv_ in a bad manner; poorly; not well

BAFFS _v pr t of_ **BAFF** strikes the ground with a club in making a stroke

BAFFY _n pl_ **BAFFIES** a short wooden club with a steep-sloped face, for lofting the ball; number four wood

BAFTA _n pl_ **-S** a coarse stuffing, usually of cotton from India; _also_ **BAFT**

BAFTS _n pl of_ **BAFT** coarse stuffings of cotton from India; _also_ **BAFTAS**

BAGEL _n pl_ **-S** a dense ring-shaped bread roll

BAGGY _adj_ **BAGGIER, BAGGIEST** bulging or hanging loosely

BAGUE _n pl_ **-S** small convex molding found at the top of the shaft of most columns in Classical architecture

BAHAR _n pl_ **-S** a measure of weight used in certain parts of the E. Indies

BAHTS _n pl of_ **BAHT** monetary units of Thailand

BAILS _v pr t of_ **BAIL** removes water from a boat by repeatedly filling a bucket and emptying it over the side

BAINS *n pl of* **BAIN** [obs] bathhouses; bagnios in Italy or Turkey

BAIRN *n pl* **-S** SCOT. a child; *also* **BEARN**

BAITH *adj* SCOT. both

BAITS *v pr t of* **BAIT** lures or entices, especially by trickery or strategy

BAIZA *n pl* **-S** a monetary unit of Oman

BAIZE *v* **-D, BAIZING, -S** to cover or line with

BAKED *v p t of* **BAKE** prepared food by cooking in dry heat

BAKEN *v p part of* **BAKE** [obs] prepared food by cooking in dry heat

BAKER *n pl* **-S** one whose business it is to bake bread

BAKES *v pr t of* **BAKE** prepares food by cooking in dry heat

BALAS *n pl* **-ES** a rose-red to orange semiprecious gem

BALDS *v pr t of* **BALD** loses the hair on one's head

BALDY *n pl* **BALDIES** an unkind name for someone who has lost or is losing the hair on their head; *also* **BALDIE**

BALED *v p t of* **BALE** created a large package of raw or finished material tightly bound with twine or wire

BALER *n pl* **-S** one who creates a large package of raw or finished material tightly bound with twine or wire

BALES *v pr t of* **BALE** creates a large package of raw or finished material tightly bound with twine or wire

BALIM *n pl of* **BAAL** false gods or idols; *also* **BAALS**

BALKS *v pr t of* **BALK** stops short and refuses to go on; *also* **BAULKS, BAUKS**

BALKY *adj* **BALKIER, BALKIEST** stubborn; hesitant to move

BALLS *v pr t of* **BALL** forms into a round body or mass

BALLY *n* a noisy uproar; *also* **BALLYHOO**

BALMS *n pl of* **BALM** fragrant ointments that mitigate pain

BALMY *adj* having the qualities of balm; aromatic; soothing

BALSA *n pl* **-S** a tropical tree used for making floats and rafts

BANAL *adj* obvious and dull; ordinary

BANAT *n pl* **-S** the territory governed by a ban

BANCH *n pl* **-ES** the seat for judges in a courtroom

BANCO *n pl* **-S** a bet in certain gambling games

BANCS *n pl of* **BANC** benches; high seats of distinction or judgment

BANDA *n pl* **-S** a style of Mexican dance music

BANDS *v pr t of* **BAND** ties, binds, or encircles with a narrow strip of cloth or other material

BANDY *v* **BANDIED, BANDING, BANDIES** to toss a ball back and forth

BANED *v p t of* **BANE** [obs] killed with poison

BANES *v pr t of* **BANE** [obs] kills with poison

BANGS *v pr t of* **BANG** strikes sharply

BANJO *n pl* **-S** a stringed instrument of the guitar family that has long neck and circular body

BANKS *v pr t of* **BANK** constructs a slope rising on the outside edge

BANNS *n/pl* a public announcement of a proposed marriage

BANTY *n pl* **BANTIES** a bantam; a small fowl

BARBE *n pl* **-S** a medieval cloth headdress

BARBS *v pr t of* **BARB** provides or furnishes with hairs or bristles ending in a double hook

BARCA *n pl* **-S** a double-ended boat, skiff or barge

BARDE *n pl* **-S** a defensive armor formerly worn by a horse

BARDS *v pr t of* **BARD** equips a horse with armor protection

BARED *v p t of* **BARE** stripped of covering

BARER *adj* more lacking in clothing

BARES *v pr t of* **BARE** strips of covering

BARFS *v pr t of* **BARF** vomits

BARGE *n pl* **-S** a pleasure boat elegantly furnished and decorated

BARIC *adj* of or pertaining to barium

BARKS *v pr t of* **BARK** makes a loud sound like a dog

BARKY *adj* covered with, or containing, bark

BARMS *n pl of* **BARM** yeasty foams that rise to the surface of fermenting malt liquors

BARNS *n pl of* **BARNS** covered buildings used for storing grain or hay

BARNY *adj* **BARNIER, BARNIEST** resembling a barn

BARON *n pl* **-S** a nobleman next in rank below a count

BARRE *n pl* **-S** a handrail fixed to a wall, as in a dance studio

BARRY *adj* divided into bars

BARSE *n* the common perch

BARTH *n* a place of shelter for cattle

BARTS *n pl of* **BART** baronets, members of the British order of honor below a baron but above a knight

BARYE *n pl* **-S** a unit of pressure

BASAL *adj* of or like the bottom of something

BASAN *n pl* **-S** a type of sheepskin

BASED *v p t of* **BASE** established as a fact or conclusion

BASER *adj* of lower birth or station

BASES *v pr t of* **BASE** establishes as a fact or conclusion

BASIC *n pl* **-S** the most important thing

BASIL *n pl* **-S** an aromatic herb of the mint family

BASIN *n pl* **-S** a bowl-shaped vessel which holds foods or liquids; *also* **BASON**

BASIS *n pl* **BASES** the foundation or necessary part of something

BASKS *v pr t of* **BASK** lies in warmth; exposes to genial heat

BASON *n pl* **-S** a bowl-shaped vessel which holds foods or liquids; *also* **BASIN**

BASSI *n pl of* **BASSO** the lowest adult male singing voices; *also* **BASSOS**

BASSO *n pl* **BASSI** or **-S** the lowest adult male singing voice

BASSY *interj* to express enough; stop

BASTA *interj* enough; stop

BASTE *v* **-D, BASTING, -S** to cover with liquid before or while cooking

BASTO *n* the ace of clubs in a game of quadrille

BASTS *n pl of* **BAST** fibrous materials from various plants used to make cordage and textiles

BATCH *v* **-ED, -ING, -ES** to process or assemble in groups or amounts

BATED *v p t of* **BATE** moderated or restrained

BATES *v pr t of* **BATE** moderates or restrains

BATHE *v* **-D, BATHING, -S** to take a bath

BATHS *n pl of* **BATH** tubs of water for washing or soaking the body

BATIK *v* **-ED, -ING, -S** to print fabric in which areas not to be dyed are covered by wax; *also* **BATTIK**

BATON *n pl* **-S** a slender wooden stick or rod

BATTA *n* an extra pay; also rate of exchange

BATTS *n pl of* **BATT** sheets of cotton used for stuffing

BATTU *n* a ballet movement performed by striking the legs together

BATTY *adj* **BATTIER, BATTISET** slightly eccentric

33

BAUDS *n pl of* **BAUD** units of data transmission speeds

BAUKS *v pr t of* **BAUK** stops short and refuses to go on; *also* **BALKS**, **BAULKS**

BAULK *v* **-ED, -ING, -S** to stop short and refuse to go on; *also* **BALK, BAUK**

BAVIN *n pl* **-S** BRIT. a bundle of brushwood; a piece of kindling

BAWDY *adj* **BAWDIER, BAWDIEST** humorously coarse

BAWLS *v pr t of* **BAWL** cries out with a loud, full sound

BAYAD *n pl* **-S** a large, edible, siluroid fish of the Nile; *also* **BAYATTE**

BAYAT *n pl* **-S** an oath of allegiance to an emir

BAYED *v p t of* **BAY** made a barking sound, as of hounds

BAYOU *n pl* **-S** a swampy arm or slow-moving outlet of a lake

BAYZE *n* [obs] an often bright-green cotton or woolen material napped to imitate felt and used chiefly as a cover for gaming tables

BAZAR *n pl* **-S** an exchange, a marketplace; *also* **BAZAAR**

BAZOO *n pl* **-S** the mouth

BEACH *v* **-ED, -ING, -ES** to run or drive a boat ashore

BEADS *v pr t of* **BEAD** furnishes with small, ball-shaped pieces of material pierced for stringing or threading

BEADY *adj* **BEADIER, BEADIEST** resembling beads; small, round and glistening

BEAKS *n pl of* **BEAK** bills or nibs of birds, consisting of a horny sheath

BEAKY *adj* **BEAKIER, BEAKIEST** having a large beak

BEALS *v pr t of* **BEAL** gathers matter; swells and come to a head, as a pimple

BEAMS *v pr t of* **BEAM** radiates light; shines

BEAMY *adj* **BEAMIER, BEAMIEST** emitting beams of light; radiant

BEANO *n pl* **-S** a form of bingo, esp. one using beans as markers

BEANS *n pl of* **BEAN** the seeds of certain leguminous herbs

BEANY *n pl* **BEANIES** a small skullcap worn by schoolboys; *also* **BEANIE**

BEARD *n pl* **-S** hair that grows on the chin, lips and adjacent parts of the human face

BEARN *n pl* **-S** SCOT.[obs] a child; *also* **BAIRN**

BEARS *v pr t of* **BEAR** supports or sustains; holds up

BEAST *n pl* **-S** an animal

BEATH *v* **-ED, -ING, -ES** [obs] to bathe

BEATS *v pr t of* **BEAT** strikes repeatedly

BEAUS *n pl of* **BEAU** frequent or attentive male companions; *also* **BEAUX**

BEAUT *n pl* **-S** something outstanding, beautiful of its kind

BEAUX *n pl of* **BEAU** frequent or attentive male companions; *also* **BEAUS**

BEBOP *n pl* **-S** a fast complex jazz style

BECAP *v* **-ED, -ING, -S** to put a cap on

BECKS *n pl of* **BECK** gestures of the head, hand, etc. meant to summon

BEDEL *n pl* **-S** [obs] an officer in a university; also a messenger or crier of a court; *also* **BEADLE**, **BEDELL**

BEDEN *n pl* **-S** an Arabian ibex; wild goat

BEDEW *v* **-ED, -ING, -S** to moisten with or as with dew

BEDIM *v* **-MED, -MING, -S** to make dim or indistinct

BEDYE *v* **-D, -ING, -S** to dye or stain

BEECH *n pl* **-ES** a large deciduous tree

BEEDI *n pl* **-S** or **-ES** a thin, often flavored Indian cigarette made of tobacco wrapped in a tendu leaf; *also* **BIDI, BIRI**

BEEFS *v pr t of* **BEEF** complaints

BEEFY *adj* **BEEFIER, BEEFIEST** having much or resembling beef; muscular in build

BEELD *n pl* **-S** SCOT. a place of shelter; refuge; *also* **BEILD, BIELD**

BEEPS *v pr t of* **BEEP** honks a horn

BEERS *n pl of* **BEER** fermented liquors made from malted grain

BEERY *adj* **BEERIER, BEERIEST** resembling or affected by beer

BEETE *v* **-D, BEETING, -S** [obs] to mend; to repair; *also* **BETE**

BEETS *n pl* **-S** round red root vegetables

BEEVE *n pl* **-S** cattle that are reared for their meat

BEFIT *v* **-TED, -TING, -S** to be suitable to; to suit; to become

BEFOG *v* **-GED, -GING, -S** to cover or obscure as with fog

BEGAN *v p t of* **BEGIN** started; commenced

BEGAS *n pl of* **BEGA** measures of land in India; *also* **BIGHAS**

BEGAT *v p t of* **BEGET** [obs] caused to exist

BEGET *v* **BEGOT** or **BEGOTTEN, BEGOT** or **-TING, -S**, to cause to exist

BEGIN *v* **BEGAN** or **BEGUN, -NING, -S** to start; to commence

BEGOT *v p t of* **BEGET** caused to exist

BEGUM *n pl* **-S** a Muslim woman of high rank

BEGUN *v p part of* **BEGIN** started; commenced

BEHEN *n pl* **-S** an herb, whose leaves resemble ears of corn, saffron; *also* **BEHN**

BEHNS *n pl of* **BEHN** herbs, whose leaves resemble ears of corn; saffron; *also* **BEHENS**

BEIGE *n pl* **-S** a light grayish-brown color

BEIGY *adj* a light grayish-brown color; beige

BEILD *n pl* **-S** SCOT. place of shelter; refuge; *also* **BEELD, BIELD**

BEING *n pl* **-S** the state or fact of existing; self

BEKAH *n pl* **-S** a monetary unit in Israel; half a shekel

BELAM *v* **-MED, -MING, -S** BRIT. to beat or bang

BELAY *v* **-ED, -ING, -S** to be made secure; to cause to stop

BELCH *v* **-ED, -ING, -S** to expel gas noisily from the stomach through the mouth

BELEE *v* **-D, -ING, -S** to place under the lee, or unfavorably to the wind

BELGA *n pl* **-S** a former Belgian monetary unit worth five francs

BELIE *v* **-D, BELYING, -S** to picture falsely; misrepresent

BELKS *v pr t of* **BELK** [obs] vomits

BELLE *n pl* **-S** a lady of superior beauty and attractions

BELLS *n pl of* **BELL** hollow devices made of metal that make a ringing sound when struck

BELLY *n pl* **BELLIES** the abdomen; the stomach

BELON *n pl* **-S** a flat oyster of coastal waters of France

BELOW *adv* under, or lower in place; beneath; not so high

BELTS *v p t of* **BELT** hits something or somebody hard; encircles

BEMAD *v* **-DED, -DING, -S** [obs] to make mad

BEMAS *n pl of* **BEMA** areas around the altars in Eastern Orthodox churches; platforms in a synagogue; *also* **BIMAS, BIMAHS**

BEMOL *n pl* **-S** [obs] the sign the same as B flat

BENCH *n pl* **-ES** a long seat for more than one person

BENDS *v pr t of* **BEND** turns toward some certain point; directs; inclines

BENDY *adj* **BENDIER, BENDIEST** flexible; with many curves or angles

BENES *n pl of* **BENE** sesame plants; *also* **BENNES, BENNIS**

35

BENET v -TED, -TING, -S to catch in a net; to ensnare

BENIM v -MED, -MING, -S [obs] to take away

BENNE n pl -S a sesame plant; also **BENE, BENNI**

BENNI n pl -S a sesame plant; also **BENE, BENNE**

BENTO n pl -S a Japanese meal packaged in a portioned lacquered box; also **OBENTO**

BENTS n pl of **BENT** the stiff stalks of various grasses

BENTY adj **BENTIER, BENTIEST** full of the stalks of coarse, stiff, withered grass; as, benty fields

BERAY v [obs] to make foul; to soil; to defile

BERED v p t of **BERE** [obs] pierced

BERES v pr t of **BERE** [obs] pierces

BERET n pl -S a round, soft, brimless cap

BERGH n [obs] a hill

BERGS n pl of **BERG** commonly used abbreviation for icebergs, masses of floating or stationary ice

BERKS n pl of **BERK** BRIT. foolish persons; also **BURKS**

BERME n pl -S a shoulder of a road; also **BERM**

BERMS n pl of **BERM** shoulders of roads; also **BERMES**

BEROB v -BED, -BING, -S [obs] to rob; to plunder

BEROE n/pl small, oval, transparent jellyfish

BERRY n pl **BERRIES** any small fleshy, edible fruit

BERTH v -ED, -ING, -S to bring a ship to a space to dock or anchor at a wharf

BERYL n pl -S a hard, crystalline mineral used as gems

BESEE v -D, -ING, -S [obs] to see; to look; to mind

BESES n pl of **BES** more than one of the 2nd letter of the Hebrew alphabet; also **BETHS**

BESET v -TING, -S to assail or attack on all sides

BESIT v -TED, -TING, -S [obs] to suit; to fit; to become

BESOM n pl -S a bundle of twigs for sweeping; a broom

BESOT v -TED, -TING, -S to muddle or stupefy, especially with liquor

BESTS v pr t of **BEST** gets the better of; surpasses

BETAS n pl of **BETA** more than one of the second letter of the Greek alphabet

BETED v p t of **BETE** [obs] mended, repaired; also **BEETED**

BETEL n pl -S a climbing Asiatic species of plant, whose leaves are chewed with the betel nut by people in Southeast Asia

BETES v pr t of **BETE** [obs] mends; repairs; also **BEETES**

BETHS n pl of **BETH** more than one of the 2nd letter of the Hebrew alphabet; also **BESES**

BETON n pl -S a type of concrete

BETSO n pl -S [obs] a small brass Venetian coin

BETTY n pl **BETTIES** a short bar used by thieves to wrench doors open; also **BETTEE**

BEVEL v -ED or -LED, -ING or -LING, -S to cut at that forms any angle other than a right angle

BEVER v -RED, -RING, -S [obs] to make a snack or light refreshment between meals

BEVOR n pl -S a piece of plate armor designed to protect the neck and lower face

BEWET v -TED, -TING, -S to wet or moisten.

BEWIG v -GED, -GING, -S to cover the head with a wig

BEZEL n pl -S the sloping edge of a cutting tool

BHOOT n pl -S a spirit or demon in Indian mythology; also **BHUT**

BHUTS *n pl of* **BHUT** spirits or demons in Indian mythology; *also* **BHOOTS**

BIALI *n pl* **-S** a flat bread roll made with gluten flour and topped with chopped onions; *also* **BIALY**

BIALY *n pl* **BIALIES** a flat bread roll made with gluten flour and topped with chopped onions; *also* **BIALI**

BIBBE *v* **-D, BIBBING, -S** [obs] to drink; to tipple

BIBBS *n pl of* **BIBB** brackets on the mast of a ship to support the trestletrees

BIBLE *n pl* **-S** a book with an authoritative exposition

BICEP *n pl* **-S** a muscle having two heads or points of origin

BICES *n pl of* **BICE** pale blue pigments, prepared from the native blue carbonates of copper; *also* **BISES**

BIDDY *n pl* **BIDDIES** a hen or chicken

BIDED *v p t of* **BIDE** remained in a condition or state; waited

BIDER *n pl* **-S** one who waits

BIDES *v pr t of* **BIDE** remains in a condition or state; waits

BIDET *n pl* **-S** a basin-like fixture for bathing the posterior parts of the body

BIDIS *n pl of* **BIDI** thin, often flavored Indian cigarettes made of tobacco wrapped in a tendu leaf; *also* **BEEDIS, BIRIS**

BIELD *n pl* **-S** SCOT. a place of shelter; refuge; *also* **BEILD, BEELD**

BIERS *n pl of* **BIER** movable platforms on which coffins or corpses are placed before burial

BIFFS *n pl of* **BIFF** hits

BIFFY *n pl* **BIFFIES** upper Midwest dialect for a toilet, especially an outhouse

BIFID *adj* forked or cleft into two parts

BIGAS *n pl of* **BIGA** two-wheeled chariots drawn by two horses harnessed abreast

BIGGS *n pl of* **BIGG** SCOT. barleys, especially the hardy four-rowed kinds

BIGGY *n pl* **BIGGIES** a bigwig; something, as a corporation, that is considered to be big or important

BIGHA *n pl* **-S** a measure of land in India; *also* **BEGA**

BIGHT *v* **-ED, -ING, -S** to fasten with a loop in a rope

BIGLY *adv* in a tumid, swelling, blustering manner; violently

BIGOS *n pl* **-ES** a Polish stew of cabbage and meat

BIGOT *n pl* **-S** a prejudiced person who is devoted to his own group, religion, race or politics and is intolerant of those who differ

BIJOU *n pl* **-S** or **-X** a small and delicately worked piece; a jewel

BIKED *v p t of* **BIKE** rode on a vehicle with two wheels and a seat that is moved by pushing pedals with the feet

BIKER *n pl* **-S** one that rides a vehicle with two wheels and a seat

BIKES *v pr t of* **BIKE** rides on a vehicle with two wheels and a seat that is moved by pushing pedals with the feet

BIKHS *n pl of* **BIKH** virulent poisons extracted from aconite plants; *also* **BISHES**

BIKIE *n pl* **-S** AUST. one who rides on a vehicle with two wheels and a seat that is moved by pushing pedals with the feet

BILBO *n pl* **-S** or **-ES** an iron bar with sliding fetters formerly used to shackle the feet of prisoners

BILBY *n pl* **BILBIES** a carnivorous marsupial that lives in Australia and looks like a rat with grey fur and long ears

BILES *n pl of* **BILE** yellowish digestive juices secreted by the liver

BILGE v **-D, BILGING, -S** to cause the lowest inner part of a ship's hull to leak

BILGY adj **BILGIER, BILGIEST** looking or smelling like bilge water

BILIN n/pl a mixture of the sodium salts of the bile acids

BILKS v pr t of **BILK** defrauds, cheats or swindles

BILLS v pr t of **BILL** presents a statement of costs or charges

BILLY n pl **BILLIES** a short stout club used primarily by policemen

BIMAH n pl **-S** area around the altar in an Eastern Orthodox church; a platform in a synagogue; also **BIMA, BEMA**

BIMAS n pl of **BIMA** areas around the altars in Eastern Orthodox churches; platforms in a synagogue; also **BIMAHS, BEMAS**

BIMBO n pl **-S** an offensive term for a person who is regarded as unintelligent and shallow

BINAL adj twofold; double

BINDI n pl **-S** a small dot worn on the forehead by women in India

BINDS v pr t of **BIND** ties or confines with a cord

BINER n pl **-S** a soldier armed with a carbine

BINES n pl of **BINE** winding or twining stems of various climbing plants, such as the hop, woodbine or bindweed

BINGE v **-D, -ING** or **BINGING, -S** to be uncontrolled and self-indulgent

BINGO n pl **-S** or **-ES** a game of chance

BINGS n pl of **BING** BRIT., SCOT. heaps or piles; as of wood

BINIT n pl **-S** [obs] a binary digit

BINKS n pl of **BINK** BRIT., SCOT. benches

BINNY n pl **BINNIES** a large edible species of yaburnu, found in the Nile

BIOME n pl **-S** a major regional or global biotic community

BIONT n pl **-S** a living organism

BIOTA n pl **-S** the combined flora and fauna of a region

BIPED n pl **-S** an animal with two feet

BIPOD n pl **-S** a supporting stand with two legs

BIRCH v **-ED, -ING, -ES** to whip with or as with a rod from a birch tree

BIRDS n pl of **BIRD** warm-blooded, feathered, winged animals

BIRIS n pl of **BIRI** thin, often flavored Indian cigarettes made of tobacco wrapped in a tendu leaf; also **BEEDIS, BIDIS**

BIRKS n pl of **BIRK** BRIT. birch trees; also **BIRKENS**

BIRLE v **-D, BIRLING, -S** SCOT. to ply with drink

BIRLS v pr t of **BIRL** revolves a floating log by treading

BIROS n pl of **BIRO** pens that have a small metal ball as the point of transfer of ink to paper

BIRRS n pl of **BIRR** whirring sounds, as of spinning wheels

BIRSE n pl **-S** SCOT. a bristle; or tuft of bristles

BIRTH v **-ED, -ING, -S** to deliver a baby

BIRTS n pl of **BIRT** BRIT. fishes of the turbot kind; brills; also **BURTS, BRETS, BRUTS**

BISES n pl of **BISE** pale blue pigments, prepared from the native blue carbonates of copper; also **BICES**

BISKS n pl of **BISK** thick cream soups, especially of pureed shellfish or vegetables; also **BISQUES**

BISON n/pl a bovine mammal with a massive head, shaggy forequarters and a humped back

BITCH n pl **-ES** a female dog or other canine animal

BITER n pl **-S** one who seizes something forcibly with the teeth

BITES v pr t of **BITE** seizes something forcibly with the teeth

BITOK *n pl* **-S** a Russian dish made with patties of ground meat

BITSY *adj* **BITSIER, BITSIEST** very small, tiny, bitty

BITTS *v pr t of* **BITT** winds a cable around a vertical post on the deck of a ship

BITTY *adj* BITTIER, **BITTIEST** tiny

BIZES *n pl of* BIZE dry cold north winds in southeastern France

BLABS *v pr t of* **BLAB** talks thoughtlessly or without discretion; tattles

BLACK *adj* **-ER, -EST** being of the darkest color

BLADE *n pl* **-S** the cutting part of an instrument, of a knife

BLAFF *n pl* **-S** a West Indian stew of fish or pork, seasonings such as lime and garlic and often fruits and vegetables

BLAHS *n pl of* **BLAH** feelings of physical or psychological discomfort or dissatisfaction

BLAIN *n pl* **-S** a blister; a sore

BLAME *v* **-D, BLAMING, -S** to hold someone or something at fault

BLAND *adj* mild; soft; gentle; smooth and soothing in manner

BLANK *adj* bearing no writing, print or marking of any kind; empty

BLARE *v* **-D, BLARING, -S** to sound loudly and somewhat harshly

BLASÉ *adj* nonchalant unconcerned; indifferent

BLAST *v* **-ED, -ING, -S** to use an explosive

BLATE *adj* SCOT. timid; bashful

BLATS *v pr t of* **BLAT** cries, as a calf or sheep; bleats

BLAWN *v p part of* **BLAW** SCOT. blown

BLAZE *v* **-D, BLAZING, -S** to burn brightly and intensely

BLEAK *adj* **-ER, -EST** depressing; dreary

BLEAR *v* **-ED, -ING, -S** to make dim or indistinct

BLEAS *n pl of* **BLEA** the parts of a tree which lie immediately under the bark; the alburnum or sapwood

BLEAT *v* **-ED, -ING, -S** to cry like a sheep or calf

BLEBS *n pl of* **BLEB** small blisters; bubbles

BLEED *v* **BLED, -ING, -S** to lose blood

BLEEP *n pl* **-S** a short high-pitched signal made by an electronic device

BLEES *n pl of* **BLEE** [obs] complexions; colors; hues; likenesses; forms

BLEKS *v pr t of* **BLEK** [obs] blackens; defiles

BLEND *v* **-ED** or **BLENT, -ING, -S** to mix or mingle together

BLENK *v* **-ED, -ING** [obs] to blink; to shine; to look

BLENT *v p t of* **BLEND** mixed or mingled together

BLESS *v* **-ED** or **BLEST, -ING, -S** to make or pronounce holy; to consecrate

BLEST *v p t of* **BLESS** made or pronounced holy; consecrated

BLIMP *n pl* **-S** a non-rigid, buoyant airship

BLIMY *interj* BRIT. used to express surprise or excitement; *also* **BLIMEY**

BLIND *adj* **-ER, -EST** sightless

BLING *n* showy or expensive jewelry

BLINI *n pl of* **BLIN** small buckwheat pancake served with sour cream or caviar; *also* **BLINY**

BLINK *v* **-ED, -ING, -S** to close and open the eyes rapidly

BLINS *v pr t of* **BLIN** [obs] stops; ceases; desists

BLINY *n pl of* **BLIN** small buckwheat pancake served with sour cream or caviar; *also* **BLINI**

BLIPS *v pr t of* **BLIP** interrupts recorded sounds, as on a videotape

BLIRT *n pl* **-S** a gust of wind and rain

BLISS *v* -ED, -ING, -ES to experience a state of extreme happiness

BLITE *n pl* -S an annual herb

BLITZ *v* -ED, -ING, -ES to attack suddenly and without warning

BLIVE *adv* [obs] quickly; forthwith

BLOAT *v* -ED, -ING, -S to inflate; to puff up

BLOBS *n pl of* **BLOB** indistinct shapeless forms

BLOCK *v* -ED, -ING, -S to obstruct

BLOCS *n pl of* **BLOC** coalitions; groups of countries in special alliance

BLOGS *n pl of* **BLOG** personal journals on a website

BLOKE *n pl* -S BRIT. a fellow; man

BLOND *adj* -ER, -EST having fair skin and hair; *also* **BLONDE**

BLOOD *n pl* -S the fluid circulated through the body by the heart

BLOOM *v* -ED, -ING, -S to blossom; to flower or be in flower

BLOOP *v* -ED, -ING, -S to ruin; botch

BLORE *n pl* -S [obs] the act of blowing; a roaring wind; a blast

BLOTE *v* -D, BLOTING, -S [obs] to cure, as herrings, by salting and smoking them; to bloat

BLOTS *v pr t of* **BLOT** spots, stains

BLOWN *v p part of* **BLOW** expelled air from the mouth

BLOWS *v pr t of* **BLOW** expels air from the mouth

BLOWY *adj* BLOWIER, BLOWIEST windy; breezy

BLUBS *v pr t of* **BLUB** weeps noisily in an uncontrolled way

BLUED *v p t of* **BLUE** made or became the color of a clear sky

BLUER *adj* of the color of a clear sky

BLUES *v pr t of* **BLUE** makes or becomes the color of a clear sky

BLUET *n pl* -S a small plant of the madder family, having little, pale-blue, four-lobed flowers

BLUEY *adj* almost or partly the color of a clear sky; *also* **BLUISH**

BLUFF *v* -ED, -ING, -S to mislead

BLUNT *v* -ED, -ING, -S to dull the edge of; to make less effective

BLURB *n pl* -S a brief publicity notice, as on a book jacket

BLURS *v pr t of* **BLUR** causes imperfection of vision in; smudges; obscures

BLURT *v* -ED, -ING, -S to utter suddenly and impulsively

BLUSH *v* -ED, -ING, -S to become red in the face, especially from modesty or embarrassment

BLYPE *n pl* -S SCOT. a small piece of skin; a shred

BOARD *v* -ED, -ING, -S to cover or close with planks

BOARS *n pl of* **BOAR** uncastrated male pigs; wild hogs

BOART *n pl* -S imperfectly crystallized or coarse diamond used for industrial cutting or abrasion; *also* **BORT, BORTZ, BOORT**

BOAST *v* -ED, -ING, -S to glorify oneself in speech; talk in a self-admiring way

BOATS *n pl of* **BOAT** small open vessels, or water crafts

BOBBY *n pl* BOBBIES BRIT. a police officer

BOCAL *n pl* -S a cylindrical glass vessel, with a large and short neck

BOCCA *n pl* -S the round hole in the furnace of a glass manufactory through which the glass is taken out

BOCCE *n* a game of Italian origin similar to lawn bowling; *also* **BOCCI, BOCCIE**

BOCCI *n* a game of Italian origin similar to lawn bowling; *also* **BOCCE, BOCCIE**

BOCES *n pl of* **BOCE** European fish having compressed bodies and bright colors

BOCKS *n pl of* **BOCK** dark beers

BODED *v p t of* **BODE** was an omen of

BODES *v pr t of* **BODE** is an omen of

BODGE *v* -D BRIT. to do a clumsy inelegant job; botch

BODLE *n pl* -S a small monetary unit of Scotland

BOEUF *n* meat from an adult domestic bovine

BOFFO *adj* extremely successful; great

BOFFS *n pl of* **BOFF** big laughs; **BOFFOLAS**

BOGAN *n pl* -S a backwater, usually narrow and tranquil

BOGEY *v* -ED, -ING, -S to shoot a hole in golf one stroke over par; *also* **BOGY**

BOGGY *adj* soft and watery soil

BOGIE *n pl* -S a framework mounted on a set of wheels on the undercarriage of a vehicle

BOGLE *n pl* -S a goblin; a specter; a frightful phantom

BOGUE *v* -D, BOGUING, -S to fall off from the wind; to edge away to leeward, of a sailing vessel

BOGUS *adj* fraudulent; having a misleading appearance

BOGYS *v pr t of* **BOGY** shoots a hole in golf one stroke over par

BOHEA *n pl* -S a black Chinese tea

BOHOS *n pl of* **BOHO** bohemian people, poets or artists that lives in a nonconforming way

BOILS *v pr t of* **BOIL** reaches or causes to reach the temperature at which liquid turns to vapor

BOING *n pl* -S a sound suggesting a reverberation or vibration, as of a rebounding metal spring

BOITE *n pl* -S a small restaurant or nightclub

BOIST *n pl* -S [obs] a box

BOKED *v p t of* **BOKE** [obs] poked; thrust

BOKES *v pr t of* **BOKE** [obs] pokes; thrusts

BOLAR *adj* of or pertaining to bole or clay

BOLAS *n pl of* **BOLA** ropes with weights attached used to catch cattle or game by entangling their legs

BOLDO *n pl* -S a fragrant evergreen shrub; *also* **BOLDU**

BOLDS *v pr t of* **BOLD** makes clear and distinct to the eye; makes conspicuous

BOLDU *n pl* -S a fragrant evergreen shrub; *also* **BOLDO**

BOLES *n pl of* **BOLE** trunks or stems of trees

BOLLS *n pl of* **BOLL** the pods or capsules of a plant, as of flax or cotton

BOLNS *v pr t of* **BOLN** swells; puffs

BOLOS *n pl of* **BOLO** long, heavy, single-edged machetes

BOLTS *v pr t of* **BOLT** secures or locks with a long metal pin that screws into a nut

BOLTY *n pl* BOLTIES an edible fish of the Nile; *also* **BULTI**

BOLUS *n pl* -ES a small rounded mass of something, especially of food being swallowed

BOMBE *n pl* -S a dessert consisting of two or more layers of ice cream frozen in a round mold

BOMBS *v pr t of* **BOMB** attacks with explosive devices

BONDS *v pr t of* **BOND** brings together in a common cause or emotion

BONED *adj* braced or supported with stays, as a dress or corset

BONES *n pl of* **BONE** hard, calcified tissues of the skeleton of vertebrates

BONEY *adj* BONIER, BONIEST of, relating to, resembling, or consisting of the hard, calcified tissue of the skeleton of vertebrates; *also* **BONY**

BONGO *n pl* -S or -ES one of a pair of connected tuned drums that are played by beating with the hands

BONGS v pr t of **BONG** makes deep ringing sound, as of a bell or gong

BONKS v pr t of **BONK** strikes or causes to come into contact; hits hard on the head

BONNE n pl **-S** a female servant; a housemaid

BONNY adj **BONNIER, BONNIEST** SCOT. handsome; beautiful; pretty

BONUS n pl **-ES** something given in addition to what is usual or expected

BONZE n pl **-S** a Buddhist monk, especially of China, Japan or nearby countries

BOOBS v pr t of **BOOB** commits a faux pas or mistake

BOOBY n pl **BOOBIES** dunce; a stupid person

BOODH n pl **-S** a buddah; one who has achieved a state of perfect spiritual enlightenment in accordance with the teachings of Buddah

BOOED v pt of **BOO** expressed contempt, scorned or disapproved

BOOFY adj AUS. (of the hair) voluminous

BOOGY v **BOOGIED, -ING, BOOGIES** to dance to rock music; also **BOOGIE, BOOGEY**

BOOKS n pl of **BOOK** written, published works

BOOKY adj given to reading; fond of study; bookish

BOOLY n pl **BOOLIES** [obs] Irish herdsman wandering from place to place

BOOMS v pr t of **BOOM** makes deep, resonant sounds

BOONS n pl of **BOON** timely blessings or benefits

BOORS n pl of **BOOR** peasants, rustics or unrefined countrymen

BOORT n imperfectly crystallized or coarse diamond used for industrial cutting or abrasion; also **BORT, BORTZ, BOART**

BOOSE n pl **-S** a stall or a crib for an ox, cow, or other animal

BOOST v **-ED, -ING, -S** to increase, support or raise

BOOTH n pl **-S** a small area set off by walls for special use

BOOTS v pr t of **BOOT** kicks

BOOTY n pl **BOOTIES** goods or money obtained illegally by force

BOOZE v **-D, BOOZING, -S** to drink liquor greedily or immoderately

BOOZY adj a little intoxicated; fuddled; stupid with liquor; also **BOUSY**

BORAL n pl **-S** a mixture of boron carbide and aluminum

BORAS n pl of **BORA** violent, cold winter winds on the Adriatic Sea

BORAX n pl **-ES** or **BORACES** a white or gray mineral consisting of hydrated sodium borate

BORDS n pl of **BORD** [obs] boards; tables

BORED v pt of **BORE** made a hole in or through, with a drill

BOREL n pl **-S** coarse woolen cloth; also **BORREL**

BORER n pl **-S** one that bores; also an instrument for boring

BORES v pr t of **BORE** makes a hole in or through with a drill

BORIC adj of, pertaining to, or containing boron

BORKS v pr t of **BORK** denies Senate confirmation of a nominee, especially for the US Supreme Court

BORNE v p part of **BEAR** supported or sustained; held up

BORON n pl **-S** a nonmetallic element extracted from kernite and borax

BORSH n pl **-S** a Russian soup with beet juice as a foundation; also **BORSCHT, BORSHT**

BORTS *n pl of* **BORT** imperfectly crystallized or coarse diamonds used for industrial cutting or abrasion; *also* **BOARTS, BORTZES**

BORTY *adj* poorly crystallized diamonds

BORTZ *n pl* **-ES** imperfectly crystallized or coarse diamond used for industrial cutting or abrasion; *also* **BOART, BOORT, BORT**

BOSAS *n pl of* **BOSA** acidulated fermented drinks of Middle Eastern countries; *also* **BOZAS**

BOSCS *n pl of* **BOSC** greenish-yellow variety of pears

BOSKS *n pl of* **BOSK** thickets; small wooded areas

BOSKY *adj* **BOSKIER, BOSKIEST** covered with bushes, shrubs or trees

BOSOM *v* **-ED, -ING, -S** to embrace; cherish

BOSON *n pl* **-S** a subatomic particle that has zero or integral spin; photons and alpha particles

BOSSY *adj* **BOSSIER, BOSSIEST** domineering

BOSUN *n pl* **-S** a ship's officer in charge of equipment and the crew

BOTAS *n pl of* **BOTA** leather bags or sacks for holding wine

BOTCH *v* **-ED, -ES, -ING** to ruin through carelessness or clumsiness

BOTEL *n pl* **-S** a ship that functions as a hotel; *also* **BOATEL**

BOTES *n pl of* **BOTE** compensations, such as for injuries to person or honor

BOTHY *n pl* **BOTHIES** SCOT. a hut or small cottage

BOTTS *n pl of* **BOTT** the parasitic larvae of botflies; *also* **BOTS**

BOUDS *n pl of* **BOUD** [obs] weevils; worms that breeds in malt or biscuits

BOUGE *v* **-D, BOUGING, -S** [obs] to swell out; to bilge

BOUGH *n pl* **-S** a large tree branch

BOUKS *n pl of* **BOUK** [obs] bodies; bulks or volumes

BOULE *n pl* **-S** an inlaid furniture decoration; *also* **BUHL, BOULLE**

BOULS *n pl of* **BOUL** curved handles

BOUND *v* **-ED, -ING, -S** to leap

BOURD *v* **-ED, -ING, -S** to jest

BOURG *n pl* **-S** a medieval village, especially one situated near a castle

BOURI *n* a fish found in rivers of Europe and Africa

BOURN *n pl* **-S** a stream or rivulet; *also* **BOURNE**

BOURS *n pl of* **BOUR** [obs] chambers; cottages

BOUSE *v* **-D, BOUSING, -S** to haul with a tackle; *also* **BOWSE**

BOUSY *adj* a little intoxicated; fuddled; stupid with liquor; *also* **BOOZY**

BOUTS *n pl of* **BOUT** temporary attacks of illness

BOUZA *n* an acidulated fermented drink of Middle Eastern countries; *also* **BOSA, BOZA, BOZAH**

BOVID *n pl* **-S** a hollow-horned ruminant; a bovine

BOWED *v p t of* **BOW** bent the body in respect

BOWEL *n pl* **-S** the intestine

BOWER *v* **-ED, -ING, -S** to enclose in or as if in a shaded, leafy recess or arbor

BOWLS *v pr t of* **BOWL** rolls a round object, as a bowling or cricket ball, along the ground

BOWNE *v* **-D, BOWNING, -S** [obs] to make ready; to prepare; to dress

BOWSE *v* **-D, BOWSING, -S** to haul with a tackle; *also* **BOUSE**

BOXED *v p t of* **BOX** fought with fists

BOXEN *adj* made of boxwood; pertaining to or resembling a box

BOXER *n pl* **-S** one that fights with the fists

BOXES *v pr t of* **BOX** fights with the fists

BOYAR *n pl* **-S** a member of a former Russian aristocratic order; *also* **BOYARD**

BOYAU *n pl* **-S** or **-X** a winding or zigzag trench

BOYER *n pl* **-S** a Flemish sloop with a castle at each end

BOYLA *n pl* **-S** AUS. a witch doctor; a sorcerer

BOYOS *n pl of* **BOYO** IRISH boys, chaps, fellows or fellers

BOZAH *n* an acidulated fermented drink of Middle Eastern countries; *also* **BOSA, BOZA, BOUZA**

BOZAS *n pl of* **BOZA** acidulated fermented drinks of Middle Eastern countries; *also* **BOSAS**

BOZOS *n pl of* **BOZO** dunces; fools

BRACE *v* **-D, BRACING, -S** to support; to tighten

BRACH *n pl* **-S** or **-ES** a female hound

BRACK *n pl* **-S** a crack or breach; a flaw

BRACT *n pl* **-S** leaf-like plant part located just below a flower

BRADS *n pl of* **BRAD** thin, small nails

BRAES *n pl of* **BRAE** SCOT. hillsides; slopes; banks

BRAGS *v pr t of* **BRAG** boasts; shows off

BRAID *v* **-ED, -ING, -S** to weave, interlace, or entwine together

BRAIL *v* **-ED, -ING, -S** take in a sail with a line used to furl loose-footed sails

BRAIN *n pl* **-S** the organ inside the head that controls thought, memory, feelings and activity

BRAIT *n pl* **-S** a rough diamond

BRAKE *n pl* **-S** a restraint used to slow or stop a vehicle

BRAKY *adj* **BRAKIER, BRAKIEST** covered with brambles, ferns and other undergrowth

BRAND *v* **-ED, -ING, -S** to mark by burning with a hot iron

BRANK *v* **-ED, -ING, -S** to hold up and toss the head, as a horse when spurning the bit or prancing

BRANS *n pl of* **BRAN** outer coatings of the seeds of wheat, rye or other cereal grain

BRANT *n pl* **-S** a small, dark wild goose of the genus *Branta* that breed in Arctic regions; *also* **BRENT**

BRASH *adj* **-ER, -EST** hasty in temper; impetuous

BRASS *n* an alloy of copper and zinc

BRAST *v* **-ED, -ING, -S** [obs] to burst

BRATS *n pl of* **BRAT** spoiled children

BRAVA *interj* used to express approval of a woman, especially for a performance

BRAVE *adj* **-R, -ST** bold; courageous; daring

BRAVO *interj* well done; excellent; used to praise a performer

BRAWL *v* **-ED, -ING, -S** to quarrel noisily and outrageously

BRAWN *n pl* **-S** solid and well-developed muscles

BRAXY *n pl* **BRAXIES** a fatal disease of sheep caused by a bacterium

BRAYS *v pr t of* **BRAY** pounds, beats, rubs or grinds small or fine as if in a mortar

BRAZA *n pl* **-S** a unit of length in some Spanish-speaking countries, representing the reach of outspread arms

BRAZE *v* **-D, BRAZING, -S** to solder two pieces of metal together using a hard solder with a high melting point

BREAD *n pl* **-S** a food made from dough of flour or meal mixed with liquid and a leavening agent and then baked in loaves

BREAK *v* **BROKE, BROKEN, -ING, -S** to cause to separate into pieces suddenly or violently; to smash

BREAM *v* **-ED, -ING, -S** to clean a ship's bottom with heat

BREDE *n pl* **-S** a braid, a narrow fabric for binding, trimming

BREED v **BRED, -ING, -S** to produce as offspring; to bring forth; to bear

BREES n pl of **BREE** thin, watery soups; broths

BREME adj [obs] fierce; sharp; severe; cruel

BRENS n pl of **BREN** submachine guns operated by gas pressure and used by the British army during WWII

BRENT n pl **-S** a small, dark wild goose of the genus *Branta* that breed in Arctic regions; *also* **BRANT**

BRETS n pl of **BRET** BRIT. fishes of the turbot kind; brills; *also* **BURTS, BIRTS, BRUTS**

BRETT n a long carriage with a calash top that has space for reclining at night when used on a journey; *also* **BRITZSKA**

BREVE n pl **-S** a symbol placed over a vowel to indicate a short sound

BREWS v pr t of **BREW** boils; cooks; makes beer

BRIAR n pl **-S** a shrub or small tree of southern Europe having a hard, woody root used to make tobacco pipes; *also* **BRIER**

BRIBE n pl **-S** something offered or serving to influence or persuade

BRICK n pl **-S** a block of clay baked by the sun or in a kiln until hard and used as a building material

BRIDE n pl **-S** a woman newly married, or who is about to be married

BRIDS n pl of **BRID** [obs] birds

BRIEF v **-ED, -ING, -S** to give concise preparatory instructions or advice to

BRIER n pl **-S** a shrub or small tree of southern Europe having a hard, woody root used to make tobacco pipes; *also* **BRIAR**

BRIES n pl of **BRIE** French soft, creamy, white cheeses

BRIGS n pl of **BRIG** two-masted, square-rigged vessels

BRIKE n pl **-S** [obs] a breach; ruin; downfall; peril

BRILL n pl **-S** an edible flatfish of European waters

BRIMS n pl of **BRIM** the rims, borders or upper edges of cups, dishes or hollow vessels

BRINE n pl **-S** water saturated or strongly impregnated with salt

BRING v **BROUGHT, -ING, -S** to convey or carry along; to move

BRINK n pl **-S** the edge of a steep slope

BRINS n pl of **BRIN** the radiating sticks of fans

BRINY adj **BRINIER, BRINIEST** of or pertaining to water saturated or strongly impregnated with salt; salty

BRIOS n pl of **BRIO** vigor; vivacity, liveliness

BRISK adj **-ER, -EST** full of liveliness and activity

BRISS n pl **-ES** the Jewish ceremony of male circumcision; *also* **BRIS, BRITH**

BRITH n pl **-S** the Jewish rite or ceremony of male circumcision; *also* **BRISS, BRIS**

BRITS n pl of **BRIT** the young of herrings, sprats or similar fish; *also* **BRITTS**

BRITT n pl **-S** the young of a herring or sprat or similar fish; *also* **BRIT**

BROAD adj **-ER, -EST** wide from side to side

BROBS n pl of **BROB** wedge-shaped spikes for securing an end of a timber butting against the side of another

BROCK n pl **-S** BRIT. a badger

BROGS v pr t of **BROG** SCOT. prods with a pointed instrument, as a lance; *also* **BROGGLES**

BROIL v **-ED, -ING, -S** to cook by direct radiant heat, as over a grill or under an electric coil

BROKE v p t of **BREAK** caused to separate into pieces suddenly or violently; to smash

45

BROMA *n* a light form of prepared cocoa or cacao

BROME *n pl* **-S** any of various grasses of the genus *Bromus*, having spikelets in loose, often drooping clusters; *also* **BROMEGRASS**

BRONC *n pl* **-S** a commonly used abbreviation for a wild horse; a bronco

BROOD *v* **-ED, -ING, -S** to sit on or hatch eggs

BROOK *n pl* **-S** a natural stream of water smaller than a river or creek; *also* **BRUN**

BROOM *v* **-ED, -ING, -S** to sweep with or as with a bundle of bristles bound together and attached to a handle

BROOS *n pl of* **BROO** brees; broths

BROSE *n pl* **-S** SCOT. a porridge made with oatmeal or dried peas

BROSY *adj* SCOT. pertaining to brose porridge

BROTH *n pl* **-S** a thin soup of meat, fish or vegetable stock

BROWN *v* **-ED, -ING, -S** to make or become similar to the color or wood or soil, as in cooking or sunbathing

BROWS *n pl of* **BROW** the prominent ridges over the eyes

BRUHS *n pl of* **BRUH** rhesus monkeys

BRUIN *n pl* **-S** a large ferocious bear

BRUIT *v* **-ED, -ING, -S** to spread news of; repeat

BRUME *n pl* **-S** heavy fog or mist

BRUNS *n pl of* **BRUN** natural streams of water smaller than a river or creek; *also* **BROOKS**

BRUNT *n pl* **-S** the main impact, force or burden

BRUSH *v* **-ED, -ING, -ES** to touch in passing; to pass lightly over

BRUSK *adj* **-ER, -EST** markedly short and abrupt; *also* **BRUSQUE**

BRUTA *n/pl* an order of mammals including the armadillos, sloths and anteaters

BRUTE *n pl* **-S** entirely physical or instinctive person; lacking reason

BRUTS *n pl of* **BRUT** BRIT. fishes of the turbot kind; brills; *also* **BURTS, BRETS, BIRTS**

BUBAL *n pl* **-IS** an antelope of N. Africa; *also* **BUBALE**

BUBBA *n pl* **-S** brother; used as a familiar term of address in the Southern United States

BUBBY *n* a term of familiar or affectionate address to a small boy

BUBUS *n pl of* **BUBU** loose, flowing, usually full-length garments worn in some African countries; *also* **BOUBOUS**

BUCHU *n pl* **-S** a S. African shrub with leaves that are used as a mild diuretic

BUCKO *n pl* **-S** or **-ES** a blustering or bossy person

BUCKS *v pr t of* **BUCK** leaps forward and upward suddenly; rears up, as a horse

BUDDY *n pl* **BUDDIES** a close friend

BUDGE *v* **-D, BUDGING, -S** to move or stir slightly; to alter position or attitude

BUDGY *adj* [obs] consisting of fur

BUFFA *n pl* **BUFFE** a female singer of comic roles in an opera

BUFFI *n pl of* **BUFFO** male singers of comic roles in opera

BUFFO *n pl* **-S** or **BUFFI** a male singer of comic roles in opera

BUFFS *v pr t of* **BUFF** polishes or shines with a soft, undyed leather

BUFFY *adj* **BUFFIER, BUFFIEST** resembling or characterized by buff, a pale, light yellowish-brown color

BUGGY *n pl* **BUGGIES** a small, light one-horse carriage

BUGLE *v* -D, BUGLING, -S to play a bugle, a brass wind instrument shorter than a trumpet and lacking keys or valves

BUHLS *n pl of* BUHL inlaid furniture decorations; *also* BOULES, BOULLES

BUHRS *n pl of* BUHR hard, siliceous rocks used to make millstones

BUILD *v* BUILT, -ING, -S to erect or construct

BUILT *v p t of* BUILD erected or constructed

BULAU *n pl* -S a rat-like insectivorous mammal of E. India

BULBS *n pl of* BULB underground stems, such as those of the onion or tulip

BULGE *v* -D, BULGING, -S to cause to curve outward

BULGY *adj* BULGIER, BULGIEST having an outward curve

BULKS *v pr t of* BULK grows or increases in size or magnitude

BULKY *adj* BULKIER, BULKIEST extremely large; massive

BULLA *n pl* -E a large blister or vesicle

BULLS *v pr t of* BULL pushes ahead or through forcefully

BULLY *v* BULLIED, -ING, BULLIES to intimidate with superior size or strength

BULTI *n* an edible fish of the Nile; *also* BOLTY

BUMFS *n pl of* BUMF BRIT. paperwork; pamphlets, forms, or memorandums; *also* BUMPHS

BUMPH *n pl* -S BRIT. paperwork; a pamphlet, form or memorandum; *also* BUMF

BUMPS *v pr t of* BUMP comes in violent contact with something; thumps

BUMPY *adj* BUMPIER, BUMPIEST having an uneven surface

BUNCE *n pl* -S a sudden happening that brings good fortune

BUNCH *v* -ED, -ING, -ES to collect or cluster things of the same kind

BUNCO *v* -ED, -ING, -S to swindle, as by a confidence game; *also* BUNKO

BUNDS *n pl of* BUND streets running along a harbor or waterways, especially in the Far East

BUNDT *n pl* -S a type of tube pan with fluted sides

BUNGS *v pr t of* BUNG closes with or as with corks or stoppers

BUNKO *v* -ED, -ING, -S to swindle, as by a confidence game; *also* BUNCO

BUNKS *v pr t of* BUNK sleeps in a small compartment, shelf, box or recess used as a sleeping place

BUNNS *n pl of* BUNN [obs] small rounded breads, either plain or sweet; *also* BUNS

BUNNY *n pl* BUNNIES a rabbit

BUNTS *v pr t of* BUNT pushes or strikes with or as if with the horns or head

BUNYA *n pl* -S an evergreen tree native to Australia

BUOYS *v pr t of* BUOY keeps afloat

BURAN *n pl* -S a strong wind of the Eurasian steppes, bringing blizzards in the winter and dust in the summer

BURBS *n pl of* BURB commonly used abbreviation for suburbs, usually residential areas outlying a city

BURDS *n pl of* BURD SCOT. young ladies; maidens

BUREL *n pl* -S [obs] a coarse woolen cloth; *also* BORREL

BURET *n pl* -S a measuring cylindrical glass tube used in laboratories; *also* BURETTE

BURGA *n pl* -S a loose garment worn by Muslim women; *also* BURKA, BOURKHA, BURKHA, BURQA

BURGH *n pl* -S SCOT. a chartered or incorporated town in Scotland

BURGS *n pl of* BURG fortified or walled towns in medieval Europe; *also* BURHS

BURHS *n pl of* **BURH** [obs] fortified or walled towns in medieval Europe; *also* **BURGS**

BURIN *n pl* **-S** a cutting tool used in engraving stone

BURKA *n pl* **-S** a loose garment worn by Muslim women; *also* **BURGA, BOURKHA, BURKHA, BURQA**

BURKE *v* **-D, BURKING, -S** to murder by suffocation or strangulation

BURKS *n pl of* **BURK** BRIT. foolish persons, *also* **BERKS**

BURLS *v pr t of* **BURL** dresses or finishes cloth by removing lumps, slubs or loose threads

BURLY *adj* **BURLIER, BURLIEST** having a large, strong, or gross body

BURNS *v pr t of* **BURN** destroys by fire

BURNT *v p t of* **BURN** destroyed by fire

BURPS *v pr t of* **BURP** belches

BURQA *n pl* **-S** a loose garment worn by Muslim women; *also* **BURKA, BURGA, BOURKHA, BURKHA**

BURRO *n pl* **-S** a small donkey, used as a pack animal

BURRS *v pr t of* **BURR** removes rough edges from metal; *also* **BURS**

BURRY *adj* **BURRIER, BURRIEST** prickly

BURSA *n pl* **-S** or **-E** a saclike body cavity, especially one located between joints

BURSE *n pl* **-S** a purse

BURST *v* **BURST, -ING, -S** to come open or fly apart suddenly

BURTS *n pl of* **BURT** BRIT. fishes of the turbot kind; brills; *also* **BIRTS, BRETS, BRUTS**

BUSBY *n pl* **BUSBIES** a military headdress or cap worn in some regiments of the British army

BUSED *v p t of* **BUS** rode a long motor vehicle that carries passengers

BUSES *v pr t of* **BUS** rides a long motor vehicle that carries passengers

BUSHY *adj* **BUSHIER, BUSHIEST** thick and shaggy; overgrown with bushes

BUSKS *v pr t of* **BUSK** BRIT. entertains by singing and dancing, especially in streets and public places

BUSTO *n pl* **-ES** a bust; a statue

BUSTS *v pr t of* **BUST** bursts

BUSTY *adj* **BUSTIER, BUSTIEST** full-bosomed

BUTCH *n pl* **-ES** a haircut in which the hair is cropped close to the head; a crew cut

BUTES *n pl of* **BUTE** commonly used abbreviation for phenylbutazones, drugs used to treat arthritis

BUTLE *v* **-D, BUTLING, -S** to serve as a butler

BUTTE *n pl* **-S** a detached low mountain with a flat top

BUTTS *v pr t of* **BUTT** hits or pushes against with the head or horns; rams

BUTTY *n pl* **BUTTIES** a sandwich; *also* **BUTTIE**

BUTUT *n pl* **BUTUT** or **-S** a unit of currency in Gambia

BUTYL *n pl* **-S** a hydrocarbon radical

BUXOM *adj* having a healthily plump and ample of figure

BUYER *n pl* **-S** one who buys; a purchaser

BWANA *n pl* **-S** a form of respectful address in parts of Africa; master; boss

BYARD *n pl* **-S** a piece of leather crossing the breast, used by coal miners

BYLAW *n pl* **-S** a law or rule governing the internal affairs of an organization

BYRES *n pl of* **BYRE** BRIT. cowsheds or barns

BYSSI *n pl of* **BYSSUS** a fine linen, used by the Egyptians for wrapping mummies

BYTES *n pl of* **BYTE** units of data that are eight binary digits long

BYWAY *n pl* **-S** a side road

CAB v **-BED, -BING, -S** to travel in a taxicab

CAD n pl **-S** an ungentlemanly man

CAG n [obs] BRIT. a small cask or barrel

CAM n pl **-S** a rotating or sliding piece of machinery that transfers motion

CAN v **-NED, -NING, -S** to seal in an airtight container

CAP v **-PED, -PING, -S** to put a limit on

CAR n pl **-S** an automobile

CAT n pl **-S** an animal of various species; a domesticated pet

CAW v **-ED, -ING, -S** to cry like a crow, rook or raven; also **KAW**

CAY n **-S** a small low island or reef in the ocean, made of coral or sand

CEE n pl **-S** the letter "C"

CEL n pl **-S** a transparent sheet of celluloid used in animation

CEP n pl **-S** an edible mushroom that grows wild under pine or other evergreen trees; also **CEPE**

CHA n the Chinese name for a kind of rolled tea used in Central Asia

CHI n pl **-S** the circulating life energy that in Chinese philosophy is thought to be inherent in all things; also **KI, QI**

CIG n pl **-S** informal term for cigarette

CIS adj having two atoms on the same side of a double bond in a molecule

CIT n informal term for a citizen; an inhabitant of a city

COB n pl **-S** a male swan

COD n pl **-S** an important fish for food in Northern Atlantic waters

COG v **-GED, -GING, -S** to load or manipulate dice fraudulently

COL n pl **-S** a pass between two mountain peaks

CON v **-NED, -NING, -S** deceive into doing or believe something by lying

COO v **-ED, -ING, -S** to cry softly, as a pigeon

COP n pl **-S** a cone-shaped or cylindrical roll of yarn or thread wound on a spindle

COR n an ancient Hebrew and Phoenician measure of capacity; also **KOR**

COS n pl **-ES** a variety of crisp, long-leaved lettuce

COT n pl **-S** a light, narrow bed

COW v **-ED, -ING, -S** to intimidate; to frighten with threats or show of force

COX v **-ED, -ING, -ES** to act as a coxswain; a person who steers a boat

COY adj **-ER, -EST** shy; reserved

COZ n pl **-ES** informal term for a cousin; also **CUZ**

CRU n pl **-S** a grade or class of wine

CRY v **CRIED, -ING, CRIES** to weep

CUB n pl **-S** the young of certain carnivorous mammals, such as the bear, wolf or lion

CUD n food regurgitated from the first stomach of a ruminant and chewed again

CUE v **-D, CUING** or **-ING, -S** to give a signal to an actor

CUM prep together with; also used as

CUP v **-PED, -PING, -S** to place in or as in a small, open container used for drinking

CUR n pl **-S** a mongrel dog

CUT v **CUT, -TING, -S** to divide with a sharp-edged instrument

CUZ n pl **CUZES** informal term for a cousin; also **COZ**

CWM n pl **-S** a valley; a cirque, especially in the Welsh mountains

FOUR LETTERS

CAAS *n* [obs] a box; a case

CABS *v pr t of* **CAB** takes or drives a taxicab

CACA *n* Spanish for excrement, commonly used by children in the United States

CACK *v* -ED, -ING, -S to ease the body by passing stool

CADE *n pl* -S a bushy Mediterranean juniper

CADI *n pl* -S Islamic magistrate; *also* **QADI, KADI**

CADS *n pl of* **CAD** ungentlemanly men

CADY *n pl* **CADIES** SCOT. one who does errands or other odd jobs; *also* **CADIE**

CAFE *n pl* -S a coffeehouse; a small restaurant

CAFF *n pl* -S BRIT. a cafe, especially one serving tea and fried breakfasts in unstylish surroundings

CAGE *v* -D, **CAGING,** -S to confine or lock up

CAGY *adj* **CAGIER, CAGIEST** crafty; shrewd; *also* **CAGEY**

CAID *n* a Muslim tribal chief, judge or senior official; *also* **QAID**

CAIN *n pl* -S SCOT. rent paid in livestock or produce; *also* **KAIN**

CAKE *v* -D, **CAKING,** -S to form into a hard mass or crust

CAKY *adj* **CAKIER, CAKIEST** tending to form lumps; cake-like; *also* **CAKEY**

CALF *n pl* -S or **CALVES** a young cow

CALK *v* -ED, -ING, -S to make watertight or airtight with a filler or sealant; *also* **CAULK**

CALL *v* -ED, -ING, -S to request to be present; to summon

CALM *v* -ED, -ING, -S to make or become quiet

CALX *n pl* -ES or **CALCES** the residue left after a mineral or metal has been calcined

CAME *v p t of* **COME** moved forward; drew near

CAMO *n pl* -S commonly used abbreviation for camouflage fabric or a garment made of it

CAMP *v* -ED, -ING, -S to stay in temporary accommodations, especially in a tent

CAMS *n pl of* **CAM** rotating or sliding pieces of machinery that transfers motion

CANE *v* -D, **CANING,** -S to make or furnish with a strong slender often flexible woody material

CANS *v pr t of* **CAN** to seal in an airtight container

CANT *v* -ED, -ING, -S to tilt or slant

CANY *adj* of or pertaining to cane

CAPE *n pl* -S land jutting into water

CAPH *n* the 11th letter of the Hebrew alphabet; *also* **KAF, KAPH, KHAF**

CAPO *n pl* -S a small movable bar placed across a guitar's fingerboard to raise the pitch of all the strings uniformly

CAPS *v pr t of* **CAP** puts a limit on something

CARB *n pl* -S commonly used abbreviation for a carbohydrate

CARD *n pl* -S thick stiff paper or thin cardboard

CARE *v* -D, -CARING, -S to be concerned or interested

CARF *v pr t of* **CARVE** [obs] cuts, as wood, stone or other material

CARK *v* -ED, -ING, -S [obs] to worry or be worried

CARL *n pl* -S SCOT. a strong, robust fellow, especially a manual laborer; *also* **CARLE, KERL**

CARN *n* a mound of stones erected as a memorial or marker; *also* **CAIRN**

CARP *v* -ED, -ING, -S to find fault in a disagreeable way; complain fretfully

CARR *n* BRIT. a marsh with trees

CARS *n pl of* **CAR** automobiles

CART *v* -ED, -ING, -S to carry in a small wheeled vehicle

CASA *n pl* -S a house; a dwelling

CASE *v* **-D, CASING, -S** to enclose in a box, sheath or covering

CASH *v* **-ED, -ING, -ES** to convert into ready money

CASK *n pl* **-S** a barrel for the storage of liquid, especially alcoholic drink

CASS *v* **-ED, -ES** [obs] to render useless or void; to annul

CAST *v* **CAST, -ING, -S** to send or drive by force; to throw

CATE *n pl* **-S** [obs] a choice or dainty food; a delicacy

CATS *n pl of* **CAT** animals of various species; domesticated pets

CAUF *n pl* **CAUVES** a chest with holes for keeping fish alive in water

CAUK *n* an opaque, compact variety of barite or heavy spar; *also* **CAWK**

CAUL *n pl* **-S** the inner fetal membrane of higher vertebrates that covers the head at birth; *also* **CALLE**

CAVA *n pl of* **CAVUM** natural hollows or sinuses within the body

CAVE *v* **-D, CAVING, -S** to cause to collapse or fall in

CAVY *n pl* **CAVIES** a guinea pig or related S. American rodent

CAWK *n pl* **-S** an opaque, compact variety of barite or heavy spar; *also* **CAUK**

CAWS *v pr t of* **CAW** cries like a crow, rook or raven; *also* **KAWS**

CAYS *n pl of* **CAY** small low islands or reefs in the ocean, made of coral or sand

CECA *n pl of* **CECUM** pouches that form the beginning of the large intestines; *also* **CAECA**

CEDE *v* **-D, CEDING, -S** to yield or surrender; to give up

CEDI *n pl* **CEDI** or **-S** the basic monetary unit of Ghana

CEES *n pl of* **CEE** the letter "C"

CEIL *v* **-ED, -ING, -S** to overlay, as a ceiling, with wood, plaster, etc.

CELL *n pl* **-S** a small room for a prisoner, monk or nun

CELS *n pl of* **CEL** transparent sheets of celluloid used in animation

CELT *n pl* **-S** a primitive weapon or implement of stone or metal, shaped like a chisel or ax head

CENT *n pl* **-S** a subunit of currency in the United States, worth one-hundredth of a dollar

CEPE *n pl* **-S** an edible mushroom that grows wild under pine or other evergreen trees, prized for its flavor; *also* **CEP**

CEPS *n pl of* **CEP** edible mushrooms that grow wild under pine or other evergreen trees; *also* **CEPES**

CERA *n* wax in prescriptions

CERE *v* **-D, CERING, -S** to wrap in or as if in a cerecloth, a cloth treated with wax formerly used to wrap a body for burial

CERO *n pl* **-S** or **CERO** a large mackerel with a long, pointed snout

CERT *n pl* **-S** BRIT. somebody who is certain to do something; a foregone conclusion or certain outcome

CESS *n pl* **-ES** local tax or levy in Ireland

CETE *n pl* **-S** a group or company of badgers

CHAB *n* the red-bellied woodpecker

CHAD *n pl* **-S** a tiny bit of paper left over from punching a data card

CHAI *n pl* **-S** shed or other aboveground building where a winemaker stores wine in casks

CHAK *v* to toss up the head frequently, as a horse to avoid the restraint of the bridle

CHAM *v* [obs] a title held by hereditary rulers or tribal chiefs; *also* **KHAN**

CHAP *v* **-PED, -PING, -S** to cause the skin to split or roughen due to exposure

CHAR *v* **-RED, -RING, -S** to scorch or become scorched

CHAT *v* **-TED, -TING, -S** to talk in a light and familiar manner

CHAW *v* **-ED, -ING, -S** to grind with the teeth; to masticate; *also* **CHEW**

CHAY n pl **-S** a light, open carriage; also **CHAISE, SHAY**

CHEF n pl **-S** a professional cook

CHES v pr t of **CHESE** [obs] chooses

CHEW v **-ED, -ING, -S** to grind with the teeth; to masticate; also **CHAW**

CHEZ prep at the home of

CHIA n an aromatic annual plant in the mint family, native to Mexico and the southwest United States

CHIC adj **-ER, -EST** elegant and stylish

CHID v p t of **CHIDE** rebuked; reproved; scolded

CHIN n pl **-S** the lower portion of the face below the mouth

CHIP v **-PED, -PING, -S** to break or crack

CHIS n pl of **CHI** the circulating life energy that in Chinese philosophy is thought to be inherent in all things; also **KIS, QIS**

CHIT n pl **-S** a statement of money owed, especially for food or drink

CHON n pl **CHON** a Korean monetary unit; also **JEON**

CHOP v **-PED, -PING, -S** to cut into pieces; to mince

CHOU n pl **-X** a puff filled with cream or custard

CHOW v **-ED, -ING, -S** to eat

CHUB n pl **-S** or **CHUB** a freshwater game fish with a thick spindle-shaped body

CHUD v **-DED, -DING** [obs] to champ; to bite

CHUG v **-GED, -GING, -S** to move with or give out a series of dull explosive sounds

CHUM v **-MED, -MING, -S** to display good-natured friendliness

CIAO interj used to express greeting or farewell

CIGS n pl of **CIG** informal term for cigarettes

CILL n pl **-S** a shelf or slab at the foot of a doorway or window; also **SILL**

CINE n pl **-S** a motion picture

CION n pl **-S** a detached shoot or twig containing buds from a woody plant, used in grafting; also **CYON**

CIRE n a highly glazed finish for fabrics, usually achieved by applying wax to the fabric

CIST n pl **-S** a burial chamber typically lined with stone; also **KIST**

CITE v **-D, CITING, -S** to quote a book or author as evidence for an argument

CITY n pl **CITIES** a town of significant size and importance

CIZE n pl **-S** [obs] bulk; largeness; also **SIZE**

CLAD v **CLAD, -DING, -S** to sheath or cover with a metal

CLAG v **-GED, -GING, -S** to clog or cover with mud

CLAM n pl **-S** a burrowing marine mollusk that lives on sand or in mud

CLAN n pl **-S** a tribe or collection of families; a clique

CLAP v **-PED** or **CLAPT, -PING, -S** to strike the hands together; to applaud

CLAW v **-ED, -ING, -S** to scratch, dig, tear or pull with or as if with claws

CLAY n pl **-S** a fine-grained, firm earthy material that is malleable when wet and hardens when heated

CLEE n pl **-S** a sharp, hooked nail, as of a beast or bird

CLEF n pl **-S** a musical notation showing the pitch of notes

CLEG n SCOT. a small breeze

CLEM v **-MED, -MING, -S** BRIT. to be or make hungry

CLEW v **-ED, -ING, -S** to roll or coil into a ball

CLIP v **-PED** or **CLIPT, -PING, -S** to cut off, as with shears or scissors

CLOD n pl **-S** a lump, especially of earth, turf or clay

CLOG *v* **-GED, -GING, -S** to obstruct; to burden

CLON *n pl* **-S** a group of genetically identical cells derived from a single cell by asexual reproduction; *also* **CLONE**

CLOP *v* **-PED, -PING, -S** to make a sound, as of a horse's hooves striking the ground

CLOT *v* **-TED, -TING, -S** to coagulate or thicken

CLOY *v* **-ED, -ING, -S** to cause distaste or disgust by supplying too much of something rich or sweet

CLUB *v* **-BED, -BING, -S** to strike or beat with or as if with a club, a stout heavy stick

CLUE *v* **-D, -ING, -S** to give guiding information

CLUM *interj* [obs] silence; hush

COAK *n pl* **-S** a dowel through overlapping timbers to prevent one from sliding across the other

COAL *n pl* **-S** a black or brownish black solid, combustible material used as a fuel

COAT *v* **-ED, -ING, -S** to provide with or form a layer or covering

COAX *v* **-ED, -ING, -ES** to persuade by gentle, insinuating courtesy; to wheedle

COBB *n pl* **-S** BRIT. a sea mew or gull

COBS *n pl of* **COB** male swans

COCA *n* a shrub grown for its leaves, which are the source of cocaine

COCK *n pl* **-S** an adult male chicken

COCO *n pl* **-S** a tall palm tree bearing coconut fruit

CODA *n pl* **-S** the closing section of a musical composition

CODE *v* **-D, CODING, -S** to convert ordinary language into symbols or letters for security purposes

CODS *n pl of* **COD** important food fish of Northern Atlantic waters

COED *n pl* **-S** woman at a two-gender college

COFF *v* **-ED or COFT, -ING, -S** SCOT. to buy

COFT *v p t of* **COFF** SCOT. bought

COGS *v pr t of* **COG** loads or manipulates dice fraudulently

COHO *n pl* **-S** or **COHO** a small salmon, originally of Pacific waters; *also* **COHOE**

COIF *v* **-ED, -ING, -S** to arrange or dress the hair

COIL *v* **-ED, -ING, -S** to wind in spirals

COIN *v* **-ED, -ING, -S** to invent a word or phrase

COIR *n pl* **-S** the fiber obtained from the husk of the coconut, used in making rope and matting; *also* **KYAR**

COKE *v* **-D, COKING, -S** to change into a carbon fuel

COKY *adj* coke-like; like a carbon fuel

COLA *n pl* **-S** a carbonated beverage

COLD *adj* **-ER, -EST** without heat; having a low temperature

COLE *n* a hardy cabbage with coarse curly leaves; *also* **BORECOLE, COLEWORT, COLLARD, KALE, KAIL**

COLL *v* [obs] to embrace

COLP *n* a small slice of meat, especially a small rasher of bacon; *also* **COLLOP**

COLS *n pl of* **COL** passes between mountain peaks

COLT *n pl* **-S** a young male horse, donkey, etc.

COLY *n pl* **COLIES** a small African bird with a long tail and a crested head

COMA *n pl* **-S** a state of deep, often prolonged unconsciousness caused by injury or disease

COMB *v* **-ED, -ING, -S** to straighten with an instrument that has teeth for arranging hair

COME *v* **CAME, COMING, -S** to move forward; to draw near

COMP *v* **-ED, -ING, -S** to play a jazz accompaniment, as on a piano or guitar

COND v **CONNED, CONNING, CONNS** to conduct or direct the steering of a vessel; *also* **CONN**

CONE v **-D, CONING, -S** to shape like a cone, a pointed object with a round base

CONI n pl of **CONUS** cone shaped structures, pointed objects with round bases

CONK v **-ED, -ING, -S** to hit on the head; *also* **KONK**

CONN v **-ED, -ING, -S** to conduct or direct the steering of a vessel; *also* **COND**

CONS v pr t of **CON** deceives into doing or believing something

CONY n pl **CONIES** BRIT. a rabbit; *also* **CONEY**

COOF n pl **-S** SCOT. a silly person; a dolt

COOK v **-ED, -ING, -S** to prepare food for eating by subjecting it to heat

COOL v **-ED, -ING, -S** to make less warm

COOM n pl **-S** SCOT. soot; coal dust

COON n pl **-S** informal term for a raccoon

COOP n pl **-S** an enclosure for confining small animals

COOS v pr t of **COO** cries softly, as a pigeon

COOT n pl **-S** or **COOT** a duck-like wading bird with lobed toes

COPE v **-D, COPING, -S** to deal with or come to terms with

COPS n pl of **COP** cone-shaped or cylindrical rolls of yarn or thread wound on a spindle

COPY n pl **COPIES** an imitation, transcript or reproduction of an original work

CORB n pl **CORVES** a basket used to carry coal; *also* **CORF, CORVE**

CORD n pl **-S** a small rope of several strands twisted together

CORE v **-D, CORING, -S** to remove the core or central part of

CORF n pl **CORVES** a basket used to carry coal; *also* **CORB, CORVE**

CORK v **-ED, -ING, -S** to seal container with a cork, a stopper for a bottle or cask

CORM n pl **-S** a short thick solid food-storing underground stem, sometimes bearing papery scale leaves

CORN v **-ED, -ING, -S** to preserve or pickle with salt or in brine

COSH v **-ED, -ING, -ES** BRIT. to hit on the head with a cosh, a thick heavy stick or bar

COSS n an Indian unit of length having different values in different localities; *also* **KOS, KOSS**

COST v **COST, -ING, -S** to require a specified payment

COSY adj **COSIER, COSIEST** BRIT. marked by or providing contentment or comfort

COTE n pl **-S** a small shed or shelter for sheep or birds

COTS n pl of **COT** light, narrow beds

COUP n pl **-S** a sudden appropriation of leadership or power; a takeover

COVE v **-D, COVING, -S** to have or give an inward curve

COWL n pl **-S** a draped neckline on a garment

COWS n pl of **COW** domesticated bovine animals as a group; *also* **KEE, KIE, KINE, KY**

COWY adj like a domesticated bovine animal; cow-like

COXA n pl **-E** the hip or hip joint

COYS v pr t of **COY** [obs] caresses, pets; coaxes, entices

COZY adj **COZIER, COZIEST** snug; comfortable; content

CRAB v **-BED, -BING, -S** to head an airplane into a crosswind to counteract drift

CRAG n pl **-S** a steep, rugged rock; a rough, broken cliff

CRAM v **-MED, -MING, -S** to stuff; to crowd or pack to capacity

CRAN n pl **-S** or **CRAN** a unit of capacity formerly used for measuring fresh herring

CRAW *n pl* **-S** the stomach of an animal

CRED *n* informal term for credibility, believability

CREW *v* **-ED, -ING, -S** to serve as a member of a group of people who work on and operate a ship, boat, aircraft or train

CRIB *n pl* **-S** a small enclosed bed for a child

CRIC *n* the ring which turns inward and condenses the flame of a lamp

CRIT *n pl* **-S** BRIT. the smallest or weakest pig in a litter

CROC *n pl* **-S** commonly used abbreviation for a crocodile

CROP *v* **-PED, -PING, -S** to cut very short or trim the edges off of

CROW *v* **-ED, -ING, -S** to shout in exultation or defiance; to brag

CRUD *n* a disgustingly foul or unpleasant substance

CRUP *adj* short; brittle; i.e., crup cake

CRUS *n pl* **CRURA** the part of the leg from the knee to the foot

CRUT *n* the rough, shaggy part of oak bark

CRUX *n pl* **CRUXES** or **CRUCES** the most important point; something difficult to explain

CUBE *v* **-ED, -ING, -S** to form into regular solid bodies with six equal square sides

CUBS *n pl of* **CUB** the young of certain carnivorous mammals, such as the bear, wolf or lion

CUED *v p t of* **CUE** gave a signal to an actor

CUES *v pr t of* **CUE** gives signals to actors

CUFF *v* **-ED, -ING, -S** to fight; to scuffle; to box

CUKE *n pl* **-S** a cylindrical green fruit with thin green rind and white flesh eaten as a vegetable; a cucumber

CULL *v* **-ED, -ING, -S** to reduce the number of animals by selective slaughter

CULM *n pl* **-S** the stalk or stem of grain and grasses, jointed and usually hollow

CULT *n pl* **-S** a group of people who share religious or spiritual beliefs, especially beliefs regarded by others as misguided, unorthodox, extremist or false

CUPS *v pr t of* **CUP** places in or as in a small, open container used for drinking

CURB *n pl* **–S** edge between the sidewalk and roadway; *also* **KERB**

CURD *n pl* **-S** a soft white substance formed when milk coagulates, used as the basis for cheese

CURE *v* **-D, CURING, -S** to restore to health; to heal

CURL *v* **-ED, -ING, -S** to twist or form into ringlets

CURN *n* SCOT. a grain; a small quantity or number

CURR *v* to coo; to make a murmuring sound, as of doves

CURS *n pl of* **CUR** mongrel dogs

CURT *adj* brief and to the point; effectively cut short; abrupt

CUSK *n pl* **-S** or **CUSK** a large, edible, marine fish; *also* **BURBOT**

CUSP *n pl* **-S** a sharp and rigid point

CUSS *v* **-ED, -ING, -ES** to curse

CUTE *adj* **-R, -ST** pleasing; attractive

CUTS *v pr t of* **CUT** divides with a sharp-edged instrument

CWMS *n pl of* **CWM** valleys; cirques, especially in the Welsh mountains

CYAN *n* a blue color

CYMA *n pl* **-S** or **-E** a flat topped or convex flower cluster; *also* **CYME**

CYME *n pl* **-S** a flat-topped or convex flower cluster; *also* **CYMA**

CYON *n pl* **-S** a detached shoot or twig containing buds from a woody plant, used in grafting; *also* **CION**

CYST *n pl* **-S** a small sac or bladder-like structure

CZAR *n pl* **-S** a male monarch or emperor, especially one of the former emperors of Russia

FIVE LETTERS

CABAL *v* **-LED, -LING, -S** to enter into a conspiracy

CABBY *n pl* **-IES** informal term for cabdriver; *also* **CABBIE**

CABER *n pl* **-S** a heavy wooden pole tossed as a trial of strength in Scottish Highland Games

CABIN *n pl* **-S** a cottage or small house; a hut

CABLE *v* **-D, -ING, -S** to send a telegram

CABOB *n pl* **-S** a small piece of mutton or other meat roasted on a skewer; *also* **KABOB, KEBAB, KEBOB, KABAB**

CACAO *n pl* **-S** the bean-like seeds from which chocolate, cocoa, and cocoa butter are made

CACHE *v* **-D, CACHING, -S** to hide or store provisions or valuables

CACKS *v pr t of* **CACK** eases the body by passing stool

CACTI *n pl of* **CACTUS** spiny succulent plants

CADDY *v* **CADDIED, -ING, CADDIES** to serve as a golfer's assistant who carries clubs and performs other duties during a round; *also* **CADDIE**

CADER *n pl* **-S** a nucleus of trained military personnel around which an organization can be built; *also* **CADRE**

CADES *n pl of* **CADE** bushy Mediterranean junipers

CADET *n pl* **-S** a student at a military academy training to be an officer

CADGE *v* **-D, CADGING, -S** to beg or get by begging

CADGY *adj* SCOT. cheerful; merry

CADIE *n pl* **CADIES** SCOT. one who does errands or other odd jobs; *also* **CADY**

CADIS *n pl of* **CADI** Islamic magistrates; *also* **QADIS, KADIS**

CADRE *n pl* **-S** a nucleus of trained military personnel around which an organization can be built; *also* **CADER**

CAECA *n pl of* **CAECUM** pouches that form the beginning of the large intestines; *also* **CECA**

CAFES *n pl of* **CAFE** coffeehouses; small restaurants

CAFFS *n pl of* **CAFF** BRIT. cafes, especially ones serving tea and fried breakfasts in unstylish surroundings

CAGED *v p t of* **CAGE** confined or locked up

CAGER *n pl* **-S** informal term for a basketball player

CAGES *v pr t of* **CAGE** confines or locks up

CAGEY *adj* **CAGIER, CAGIEST** crafty; shrewd; *also* **CAGY**

CAGIT *n* a green parrot found in the Philippine Islands

CAHOW *n pl* **-S** a nearly extinct, dark-colored petrel found in Bermuda

CAIDS *n pl of* **CAID** Muslim tribal chiefs

CAIRD *n* SCOT. a traveling tinker; a tramp or sturdy beggar

CAIRN *n pl* **-S** a mound of stones erected as a memorial or marker; *also* **CARN**

CAKED *v p t of* **CAKE** formed into a hard mass or crust

CAKES *v pr t of* **CAKE** forms into a hard mass or crust

CAKEY *adj* **CAKIER, CAKIEST** tending to form lumps; cake-like; *also* **CAKY**

CALFS *n pl of* **CALF** young cows or bulls

CALID *adj* [obs] hot; burning; ardent

CALIF *n pl* **-S** a Muslim leader; *also* **CALIPH, KALIF, KALIPH, KHALIF**

CALIN *n* an alloy of lead and tin used to make Chinese tea canisters

CALIX *n pl* **CALICES** a cup for the wine of a Eucharist; *also* **CHALICE**

CALKS *v pr t of* **CALK** makes watertight or airtight with fillers or sealants; *also* **CAULKS**

CALLA *n pl* **-S** an ornamental lily that has a white funnel-shaped cone around a long yellow flower spike

CALLE *n pl* **-S** the inner fetal membrane of higher vertebrates that covers the head at birth; *also* **CAUL**

CALLS *v pr t of* **CALL** requests to be present; summons

CALMS *v pr t of* **CALM** makes or becomes quiet

CALVE *v* **-D, CALVING, -S** to give birth to a calf

CALYX *n pl* **-ES** or **CALYCES** a cuplike part of a flower

CAMAS *n pl* **-SES** a blue-flowered perennial herb; *also* **CAMASS**

CAMEL *n pl* **-S** a humped, long-necked ruminant mammal

CAMEO *n pl* **-S** an engraving or carving in low relief on a stone

CAMES *n pl of* **CAME** grooved bars of lead for holding together the pieces of glass in stained glass windows

CAMIS *n pl* **-ES** a light, loose dress or robe

CAMOS *n pl of* **CAMO** commonly used abbreviation for camouflage fabrics or garments made of it

CAMPO *n pl* **-S** a level, grassy plain

CAMPS *v pr t of* **CAMP** stays in temporary accommodations, especially in a tent

CAMPY *adj* **CAMPIER, CAMPIEST** comically exaggerated

CANAL *n pl* **-S** an artificial channel filled with water

CANDY *v* **CANDIED, -ING, CANDIES** to coat with sugar

CANED *v p t of* **CANE** made or furnished with a strong slender often flexible woody material

CANER *n pl* **-S** one that makes or supplies with cane or rattan

CANES *v pr t of* **CANE** makes or furnishes with a strong slender often flexible woody material

CANID *n pl* **-S** an impromptu, informal photograph

CANNA *n pl* **-S** a tropical plant with showy flowers

CANNY *adj* **CANNIER, CANNIEST** artful; cunning; shrewd; *also* **CANNIE**

CANOE *n pl* **-S** a boat made of bark or skins

CANON *n pl* **-S** a law or rule

CANST *v pr t of* **CAN** [obs] to be able to do; can

CANTO *n pl* **-S** a major division of a long poem

CANTS *v pr t of* **CANT** tilts or slants

CANTY *adj* **CANTIER, CANTIEST** cheerful; sprightly; lively; merry

CAPED *v p t of* **CAPE** headed or pointed; kept a course

CAPEL *n* a horse; a nag; *also* **CAPLE**

CAPER *n pl* **-S** a frolicsome leap or spring; a skip; a jump

CAPES *n pl of* **CAPE** lands jutting into water

CAPIZ *n pl* **-ES** a small mollusk with hinged shell

CAPLE *n* a horse; a nag; *also* **CAPEL**

CAPOC *n pl* **-S** a fine and short cotton that cannot be spun

CAPON *n pl* **-S** a castrated rooster

CAPOS *n pl of* **CAPO** small movable bars placed across the fingerboards of guitars to raise the pitch of all the strings uniformly

CAPUT *n pl* **CAPITA** the top or superior part of a thing

CARAC *n* a galleon; a large ship; *also* **CARACK**

CARAT *n pl* **-S** the weight by which precious stones and pearls are weighed

CARBO *n pl* **-S** informal term for a carbohydrate

CARBS *n pl of* **CARB** commonly used abbreviation for carbohydrates

CARDO *n* the hinge of a bivalve shell

CARDS *n pl of* **CARD** thick stiff papers or thin cardboards

CARED *v p t of* **CARE** was concerned or interested

CARER *n pl* **-S** someone who is concerned or interested

CARES *v pr t of* **CARE** has concern or interest

CARET *n pl* **-S** a mark used by writers and proof readers

CAREX *n pl* **CARICES** a marsh plant

CARGO *n pl* **-S** the lading or freight of a ship

CARKS *v pr t of* **CARK** [obs] worries

CARLE *n pl* **-S** SCOT. a strong, robust fellow, especially a manual laborer; *also* **CARL, KERL**

CARLS *n pl* **CARL** SCOT. strong, robust fellows, especially manual laborers; *also* **CARLES, KERLS**

CARNY *n pl* **-IES** informal term for a person employed by a carnival

CAROB *n pl* **-S** the edible pod of an Arabian tree

CAROL *v* **-ED, -ING, -S** to sing joyously

CAROM *v* **-ED, -ING, -S** to rebound after hitting; *also* **CARROM**

CARPI *n pl of* **CARPUS** bone in wrist joint

CARPS *v pr t of* **CARP** finds fault in a disagreeable way; complains fretfully

CARRY *v* **CARRIED, -ING, CARRIES** to move; to convey by force; to impel

CARSE *n* SCOT. low, fertile land; a river valley

CARTE *n pl* **-S** a bill of fare

CARTS *v pr t of* **CART** carries in a small wheeled vehicle

CARUS *n* coma with complete insensibility; deep lethargy

CARVE *v* **-D, CARVING, -S** to cut

CASAL *adj* of or pertaining to case

CASAS *n pl of* **CASA** houses; dwellings

CASED *v p t of* **CASE** enclosed in a box, sheath or covering

CASES *v pr t of* **CASE** encloses in a box, sheath or covering

CASKS *n pl of* **CASK** barrels for the storage of liquid, especially alcoholic drink

CASKY *adj* resembling a cask, a barrel for the storage of liquid

CASTE *n pl* **-S** a separate and fixed order or class of persons in society

CASTS *v pr t of* **CAST** sends or drives by force; throws

CASUS *n pl* a legal case; an occurrence; an occasion

CATCH *v* **CAUGHT, -ING, -ES** to lay hold on; to seize

CATEL *n* [obs] property; *also* **CHATTEL**

CATER *v* **-ED, -ING, -S** to provide food and service for

CATES *n pl of* **CATE** [obs] choice or dainty foods; delicacies

CATSO *n pl* **-S** a base fellow; a rogue; a cheat

CATTY *adj* **CATTIER, CATTIEST** catlike; spiteful

CAUDA *n pl* **-E** any tail-like structure

CAULD *n* SCOT. cold

CAULK *v* **-ED, -ING, -S** to make watertight or airtight with a filler or sealant; *also* **CALK**

CAULS *n pl of* **CAUL** the inner fetal membranes of higher vertebrates that covers the head at birth; *also* **CALLES**

CAUMA *n pl* **-S** great heat, as of the body in fever

CAUSA *n* a comprehensive term for any proceeding in a court of law

CAUSE *v* **-D, CAUSING, -S** to bring about; make happen

CAVED v p t of **CAVE** caused to collapse or fall in

CAVER n pl **-S** one who explores or studies caves, large underground hollows

CAVES v pr t of **CAVE** causes to collapse or fall in

CAVIL v **-ED** or **-LED**, **-ING** or **-LING**, **-S** to raise trivial objections; to find fault unnecessarily

CAVIN n a hollow way, adapted to cover troops

CAVUM n pl **CAVA** a natural hollows or sinuses within the body

CAWED v p t of **CAW** cried like a crow, rook or raven; *also* **KAWED**

CAWKS n pl of **CAWK** opaque, compact varieties of barite or heavy spar

CAWKY adj **CAWKIER**, **CAWKIEST** of or pertaining to cawk; like cawk, opaque, compact varieties of barite or heavy spar

CAXON n [obs] a kind of wig

CEASE v **-D**, **CEASING**, **-S** to come to an end; to stop

CECAL adj pertaining to the pouch that forms the beginning of the large intestine

CECUM n pl **-S** the pouch that forms the beginning of the large intestine

CEDAR n pl **-S** an evergreen tree

CEDED v p t of **CEDE** yielded or surrendered; gave up

CEDER n pl **-S** one who yields, surrenders or gives up

CEDES v pr t of **CEDE** yields or surrenders; gives up

CEDIS n pl of **CEDI** the basic monetary units of Ghana

CEDRY adj of the nature of cedar

CEIBA n pl **-S** a tropical tree of the silk-cotton family

CEIBO n a small S. American spiny tree with dark crimson and scarlet flowers

CEILI n pl **-S** a social event with traditional Irish or Scottish music and dancing; *also* **CEILIDH**

CEILS v pr t of **CEIL** overlays, as a ceiling, with wood, plaster, etc.

CEINT n [obs] a girdle

CELEB n pl **-S** commonly used abbreviation for a celebrity; a famous person

CELLA n pl **-E** the inner room or sanctuary of an ancient Greek or Roman temple; *also* **NAOS**

CELLO n pl **-S** a large stringed instrument; the bass member of the violin family

CELLS n pl of **CELL** small rooms for prisoners, monks or nuns

CELOM n pl **-S** or **-ATA** the body cavity in some animals; *also* **COELOM, COELOME**

CELTS n pl of **CELT** primitive weapons or implements of stone or metal, shaped like chisels or ax heads

CENSE v **-D**, **CENSING**, **-S** to perfume a place or worshipers with incense

CENTO n pl **-S** a literary or a musical composition formed by selections from different authors

CENTS n pl of **CENT** subunits of currency in the United States, each worth one-hundredth of a dollar

CENTU n pl of **CENTAS** Lithuanian monetary units; *also* **CENTAI**

CEORL n [obs] a freeman of the lowest class in Anglo-Saxon England; *also* **CHURL**

CEPES n pl of **CEPE** edible mushrooms that grow wild under pine or other evergreen trees, prized for their flavor; *also* **CEPS**

CERAS n one of the hornlike structures on the back of mollusks, which serve as gills

CERCI n pl of **CERCUS** sensory appendages of certain insects

CERED *v p t of* **CERE** wrapped in or as if in a cerecloth, a cloth treated with wax formerly used to wrap a body for burial

CERES *v pr t of* **CERE** wraps in or as if in a cerecloth, a cloth treated with wax formerly used to wrap a body for burial

CERIA *n pl of* **CERIUM** white crystalline compounds used in the manufacture of ceramics

CERIC *adj* of or containing cerium; a metallic element

CERIN *n* a waxy substance extracted by alcohol or ether from cork

CEROS *n pl of* **CERO** large mackerels with long pointed snouts

CERTS *n pl of* **CERT** BRIT. somebody who is certain to do something; a foregone conclusion or certain outcome

CERYL *n pl* -S a radical obtained from beeswax

CESTA *n pl* -S a scoop-shaped wicker basket used for catching and throwing in the sport of jai alai

CESTI *n pl of* **CESTUS** women's belts or girdles, especially as worn in ancient Greece

CETES *n pl of* **CETE** groups or companies of badgers

CETIC *adj* of or pertaining to a whale

CETIN *n pl* -S a white, crystalline, water-insoluble fat used in making pharmaceuticals, cosmetics, soaps and candles

CHACE *v* -D, **CHACING**, -S to pursue; *also* **CHASE**

CHADS *n pl of* **CHAD** tiny bits of paper left over from punching data cards

CHAFE *v* -D, **CHAFING**, -S to warm by rubbing

CHAFF *v* -ED, -ING, -S to make fun of in a good-natured way; to tease; to banter

CHAIN *v* -ED, -ING, -S to fasten or secure with a chain or a series of objects linked together

CHAIR *v* -ED, -ING, -S to preside over something

CHAIS *n pl of* **CHAI** sheds or other above ground buildings where a winemaker stores wine in casks

CHAJA *n pl* -S the crested screamer of Brazil, often domesticated and used to guard other poultry; *also* **CHAUNA**

CHALK *v* -ED, -ING, -S to write with a soft, compact calcium carbonate

CHAMP *v* -ED, -ING, -S to bite into small pieces; to crunch

CHANK *v* -ED, -ING, -S informal term meaning to eat noisily or greedily; to chomp

CHANT *v* -ED, -ING, -S to utter with a melodious voice; to sing

CHAOS *n* a state of extreme confusion and disorder

CHAPE *n pl* -S a metal tip or mounting on a scabbard or sheath

CHAPS *v pr t of* **CHAP** causes the skin to split or roughen due to exposure

CHAPT *v p t of* **CHAP** to crack or open in slits; to split

CHARD *n pl* -S or **CHARD** a variety of beet whose large edible leaves and stems are similar to spinach

CHARE *v* -D, **CHARING**, -S to perform daily household work; to do chores; *also* **CHORE**

CHARK *v* -ED, -ING, -S BRIT. [obs] to char; to burn to a coal

CHARM *v* -ED, -ING, -S to attract or delight greatly

CHARR *n pl* -S BRIT. a brook trout

CHARS *v pr t of* **CHAR** scorches or becomes scorched

CHART *v* -ED, -ING, -S to make a map of; plot or record information in a table or graph

CHARY *adj* **CHARIER, CHARIEST** careful; wary; cautious

CHASE *v* **-D, CHASING, -S** to pursue; *also* **CHACE**

CHASM *n pl* **-S** a deep fissure in the earth's surface; gorge

CHAST *v* **-ED, -ING, -S** [obs] to correct by punishment; *also* **CHASTEN, CHASTISE**

CHATI *n* a small South African species of tiger

CHATS *v pr t of* **CHAT** talks in a light and familiar manner

CHAUN *v* **-ED, -ING, -S** [obs] to open; to yawn

CHAUS *n pl* **-ES** a lynx-like animal of Asia and Africa

CHAWS *v pr t of* **CHAW** grinds with the teeth; masticates

CHAYS *n pl of* **CHAY** roots native to India that produce a red dye

CHEAP *adj* **-ER, -EST** low in price or cost; a bargain

CHEAT *v* **-ED, -ING, -S** to deceive by trickery; swindle

CHECK *v* **-ED, -ING, -S** to verify or confirm by consulting a source

CHEEK *n pl* **-S** the side of the face below the eye

CHEEP *v* **-ED, -ING, -S** to chirp, as a young bird

CHEER *v* **-ED, -ING, -S** to cause to rejoice; to gladden; fill with joy

CHEFS *n pl of* **CHEF** professional cooks

CHELA *n pl* **-E** a pincer-like claw, especially of a crab or other crustacean; *also* **CHELY**

CHELY *n pl* **CHELIES** [obs] a pincer-like claw, especially of a crab or other crustacean; *also* **CHELA**

CHEMO *n* commonly used abbreviation for chemotherapy, a treatment of a disease with chemical agents

CHENG *n pl* **-S** a Chinese reed instrument, with tubes, blown by the mouth

CHERT *n pl* **-S** a variety of silica that contains microcrystalline quartz

CHESE *v* **-D, -ING, CHES** [obs] to choose

CHESS *n pl* **-ES** one of the plants forming the roadway of a floating bridge

CHEST *n pl* **-S** the part of the human body enclosed by the ribs

CHETH *n* the eighth letter of the Hebrew alphabet; *also* **HETH**

CHEVE *v* **-D, CHEVING, -S** [obs] to come to an issue; to turn out; to succeed; *also* **CHIEVE**

CHEVY *v* **CHEVIED, -ING, CHEVIES** to vex or harass with petty attacks; *also* **CHIVY, CHIVVY**

CHEWS *v pr t of* **CHEW** grinds with the teeth; masticates

CHEWY *adj* **CHEWIER, CHEWIEST** needing much chewing, grinding with the teeth

CHIAO *n pl* **CHIAO** a monetary unit of China; *also* **JIAO**

CHICA *n pl* **-S** a girl or young woman, often used as a term of affectionate address

CHICH *n pl* **-ES** the chick-pea

CHICK *n pl* **-S** a young bird

CHICO *n pl* **-S** a thorny plant having fleshy leaves; the greasewood plant

CHIDE *v* **-D** or **CHID** or **CHIDDEN, CHIDING, -S** to rebuke; to reprove; to scold

CHIEF *n pl* **-S** one who is highest in rank or authority

CHIEL *n pl* **-S** SCOT. a boy or young man; *also* **CHIELD**

CHILD *n pl* **-REN** a human offspring

CHILE *n pl* **-S** very hot and finely tapering pepper; *also* **CHILI**

CHILI *n pl* **-ES** very hot and finely tapering pepper; *also* **CHILE**

CHILL *v* **-ED, -ING, -S** to make somebody or something cold

CHIMB *n pl* **-S** the edge of a cask or a barrel

CHIME *v* **-D, CHIMING, -S** to sound harmoniously, as a set of bells or musical instruments

CHIMP *n pl* **-S** commonly used abbreviation for a chimpanzee; an intelligent arboreal ape of tropical Africa

CHINA *n* a high quality porcelain

CHINE *v* **-D, CHINING, -S** to cut meat along or across the backbone

CHINK *v* **-ED, -ING, -S** to make or cause glass or metallic objects to make a short sharp ringing sound

CHINO *n pl* **-S** a durable coarse cotton twill fabric

CHINS *n pl of* **CHIN** lower portions of faces below mouths

CHIPS *v pr t of* **CHIP** breaks or cracks

CHIRK *v* **-ED, -ING, -S** to cheer up; to enliven

CHIRM *v* **-ED, -ING, -S** [obs] to chirp or to make a mournful cry, as a bird

CHIRO *n pl* **-S** the ladyfish; *also* **CHEIRO**

CHIRP *v* **-ED, -ING, -S** to make a short high-pitched sound, such as that made by small birds or insects

CHIRR *v* **-ED, -ING, -S** to make a harsh trilled sound, such as that made by grasshoppers; *also* **CHURR, CHIRRE**

CHIRU *n pl* **-S** a Tibetan goat antelope

CHITS *n pl of* **CHIT** statements of money owed, especially for food or drink

CHIVE *n pl* **-S** a perennial herb used as a seasoning

CHIVY *v* **CHIVIED, -ING, CHIVIES** to vex or harass with petty attacks; *also* **CHEVY, CHIVVY**

CHOCK *v* **-ED, -ING, -S** to stop from turning, moving or falling by using a wedge or block

CHOIR *n pl* **-S** a band or organized company of singers

CHOKE *v* **-D, CHOKING, -S** to struggle for breath; have insufficient oxygen intake

CHOKY *adj* **CHOKIER, CHOKIEST** tending to cause choking

CHOMP *v* **-ED, -ING, -S** to chew loudly and greedily; to champ

CHOOK *n pl* **-S** AUS. a hen or chicken

CHOPS *v pr t of* **CHOP** cuts into pieces; minces

CHORD *n pl* **-S** to or more musical notes played or sung simultaneously

CHORE *n pl* **-S** a routine or minor duty or task; *also* **CHARE**

CHOSE *v p t of* **CHOOSE** selected from among a range of options

CHOUT *n pl* **-S** an assessment equal to a fourth of the revenue, exacted as a tribute by the Mahrattas in India

CHOUX *n pl of* **CHOU** puffs filled with cream or custard

CHOTT *n pl* **-S** the bed of a dried salt marsh

CHOWS *v pr t of* **CHOW** eats

CHUBS *n pl of* **CHUB** freshwater game fish with thick spindle-shaped bodies

CHUCK *v* **-ED, -ING, -S** to throw something carelessly

CHUET *n pl* **-S** [obs] minced meat

CHUFA *n pl* **-S** a European sedge with small edible nutlike tubers

CHUFF *v* **-ED, -ING, -S** to produce or move with noisy puffing or explosive sounds, such as those made by locomotives

CHUGS *v pr t of* **CHUG** moves with or gives out a series of dull explosive sounds

CHUMP *n pl* **-S** a foolish person; a dolt

CHUMS *v pr t of* **CHUM** displays good-natured friendliness

CHUNK *n pl* **-S** a thick, solid piece of something

CHURL *n pl* **-S** [obs] a freeman of the lowest class in Anglo-Saxon England; *also* **CEORL**

CHURN *v* **-ED, -ING, -S** to stir, beat or agitate milk or cream to make butter

CHURR *v* **-ED, -ING, -S** to make a harsh trilled sound, such as that made by grasshoppers; *also* **CHIERE, CHIRR**

CHUTE *v* **-D, CHUTING, -S** to convey something such as coal or dirty laundry down an inclined trough, passage or channel through which things may pass

CHYLE *n pl* **-S** a milky digestive fluid in the small intestine

CHYME *n pl* **-S** a partially digested food passed from the stomach to the small intestine

CIBOL *n pl* **-S** a perennial onion plant; its fistular leaves are used in cookery

CIDER *n pl* **-S** the expressed juice of apples used to make a beverage or other products such as vinegar; *also* **CYDER**

CIGAR *n pl* **-S** a small roll of tobacco leaves for smoking

CILIA *n pl of* **CILIUM** short hair-like projections that beat rhythmically to aid the movement of fluid past the cell

CILLS *n pl of* **CILL** shelves or slabs at the foot of doorways or windows; *also* **SILLS**

CINCH *v* **-ED, -ING, -ES** to tighten something by constricting it

CINES *n pl of* **CINE** motion pictures

CIONS *n pl of* **CION** detached shoots or twigs containing buds from a woody plant, used in grafting; *also* **CYONS, SCIONS**

CIPPI *n pl of* **CIPPUS** small square or round low pillars, used in ancient societies to indicate distances of places, for a landmark or sepulchral inscriptions

CIRCA *prep* approximately, about, used before a date to indicate that it is estimated

CIRRI *n pl of* **CIRRUS** thin wispy clouds that form at the highest and coldest point of the cloud region

CISCO *n pl* **-S** or **-ES** a silvery freshwater fish found in deep lakes

CISTS *n pl of* **CIST** burial chambers typically lined with stone; *also* **KISTS**

CITAL *n* summons to appear, as before a judge

CITED *v p t of* **CITE** quoted a book or author as evidence for an argument

CITER *n pl* **-S** one who quotes a book or author as evidence for an argument

CITES *v pr t of* **CITE** quotes a book or author as evidence for an argument

CIVET *n pl* **-S** a catlike mammal native to Africa and Asia

CIVIC *adj* relating to or connected with city administration

CIVIE *n pl* **-S** commonly used abbreviation for a civilian, a non-military person; *also* **CIVVY**

CIVIL *adj* polite, but in a way that is cold and formal

CIVVY *n pl* **CIVVIES** commonly used abbreviation for a civilian, a non-military person; *also* **CIVIE**

CIZAR *v* [obs] to clip with scissors

CIZES *n pl of* **CIZE** [obs] bulk; largeness; *also* **SIZES**

CLACK *v* **-ED, -ING, -S** to make a sudden, sharp noise

CLADE *n pl* **-S** a group of organisms derived from a common ancestor, such as a species

CLADS *v pr t of* **CLAD** sheaths or covers with a metal

CLAGS *v pr t of* **CLAG** clogs or covers with mud

CLAIM *v* **-ED, -ING, -S** to ask for, or seek to obtain, by virtue of authority

CLAMP *v* **-ED, -ING, -S** to fasten together with a mechanical device with movable jaws

63

CLAMS *n pl of* **CLAM** burrowing marine mollusks that live on sand or in mud

CLANG *v* **-ED, -ING, -S** to strike together so as to produce a ringing metallic sound

CLANK *v* **-ED, -ING, -S** to make the short loud sound of two heavy metal objects hitting each other

CLANS *n pl of* **CLAN** tribes or collections of families; cliques

CLAPS *v pr t of* **CLAP** strikes the hands together; applauds

CLAPT *v p t of* **CLAP** [obs] struck the hands together; applauded

CLARO *n pl* **-S** a mild cigar

CLART *v* **-ED, -ING, -S** to daub, smear or spread, as with mud

CLARY *n pl* **CLARIES** a perennial plant of the mint family native to southern Europe

CLASH *v* **-ED, -ING, -ES** to disagree violently

CLASP *v* **-ED** or **CLASPT, -ING, -S** to hold and embrace tightly

CLASS *n pl* **-ES** a group of individuals ranked together as possessing common characteristics

CLAST *n pl* **-S** a rock fragment from the breakdown of larger rocks

CLAVE *n pl* **-S** one of a pair of percussion sticks hit together to make a clicking sound

CLAVI *n pl of* **CLAVUS** intense headaches where the pains are likened to that which would be produced by a sharp object driven into the skull

CLAVY *n pl* **CLAVIES** a mantelpiece

CLAWS *v pr t of* **CLAW** scratches, digs, tears, or pulls with or as if with claws

CLAYS *n pl of* **CLAY** fine-grained, firm earthy materials that are malleable when wet and harden when heated

CLEAN *v* **-ED, -ING, -S** to remove dirt, soil, etc.

CLEAR *v* **-ED, -ING, -S** to remove people or objects from

CLEAT *v* **-ED, -ING, -S** to fasten to a cleat, a spur-like device used in gripping a tree or pole in climbing

CLEEK *v* **-ED, -ING, -S** SCOT. to grasp or seize something suddenly and eagerly

CLEFS *n pl of* **CLEF** musical notations showing the pitch of notes

CLEFT *v p t of* **CLEAVE** split or made something split, especially along a plane of natural weakness

CLEGG *n* large blood-sucking swift fly; a horsefly

CLEMS *v pr t of* **CLEM** BRIT. is or makes hungry

CLEPE *v* **-D** or **CLEPT** or **YCLEPED** or **YCLEPT, CLEPING, -S** [obs] to call or address by name

CLEPT *v p t of* **CLEPE** called or addressed by name

CLERK *v* **-ED, -ING, -S** to act or work as an official who is responsible for correspondence, records and accounts and who is vested with specified powers or authority

CLEWS *v pr t of* **CLEW** rolls or coils into a ball

CLICK *v* **-ED, -ING, -S** to make a slight, sharp noise

CLIFF *n pl* **-S** a high, steep rock; a precipice

CLIFT *n* [obs] a cliff

CLIMB *v* **-ED, -ING, -S** to ascend or mount by using the hands and feet

CLIME *n pl* **-S** a climate; a tract or region of the earth

CLINE *n pl* **-S** a series of differing characteristics within a species

CLING *v* **CLUNG, -ING, -S** to adhere closely; to stick; to hold fast

CLINK *v* **-ED, -ING, -S** to cause to give out a slight, sharp, tinkling sound

CLIPS *v pr t of* **CLIP** cuts off, as with shears or scissors

CLIPT *v p t of* **CLIP** cut off, as with shears or scissors

CLOAK *n pl* **-S** a loose outer garment; *also* **CLOKE**

CLOCK *v* **-ED, -ING, -S** to record the time or speed of, as with a stopwatch

CLODS *n pl of* **CLOD** lumps, especially of earth, turf or clay

CLOFF *n* small deductions from the original weight; *also* **CLOUGH**

CLOGS *v pr t of* **CLOG** obstructs; burdens

CLOKE *n pl* **-S** a loose outer garment; *also* **CLOAK**

CLOMB *v p t of* **CLIMB** [obs] ascended or mounted by using the hands and feet

CLOMP *v* **-ED, -ING, -S** to walk or move with a heavy thumping sound

CLONE *v* **-D, CLONING, -S** to make a group of genetically identical cells derived from a single cell by asexual reproduction; *also* **CLON**

CLONK *v* **-ED, -ING, -S** to make a loud dull thud; *also* **CLUNK**

CLONS *n pl of* **CLON** groups of genetically identical cells derived from a single cell by asexual reproduction; *also* **CLONES**

CLOOM *v* [obs] to close with glutinous matter

CLOOP *n* the sound made when a cork is forcibly drawn from a bottle

CLOOT *n pl* **-S** SCOT. a hoof, or either of the two halves of a cloven hoof

CLOPS *n pl of* **CLOP** makes sounds, as of a horse's hooves striking the ground

CLOSE *v* **-D, CLOSING, -S** to stop, or fill up; to shut

CLOSH *n* a disease in the feet of cattle; laminitis

CLOTE *n* [obs] the common burdock, biennial herbs; *also* **CLOTBUR**

CLOTH *n pl* **-S** fabric

CLOTS *v pr t of* **CLOT** coagulates or thickens

CLOUD *v* **-ED, -ING, -S** to make muddy or foggy

CLOUR *v* **-ED, -ING, -S** SCOT. to strike off the surface of something, as to level uneven stonework

CLOUT *v* **-ED, -ING, -S** to hit somebody or something hard with the hand

CLOVE *n pl* **-S** a dried aromatic flower used as a spice

CLOWN *v* **-ED, -ING, -S** to behave in a silly or funny way

CLOYS *n pl of* **CLOY** causes distaste or disgust by supplying too much of something rich or sweet

CLOZE *adj* based on or being a test of reading comprehension in which the test taker fills in words that have been deleted from a text

CLUBS *v pr t of* **CLUB** strikes or beats with or as if with a club, a stout heavy stick

CLUCK *v* **-ED, -ING, -S** to make the call of a hen to her chickens

CLUED *v p t of* **CLUE** gave guiding information

CLUES *v pr t of* **CLUE** gives guiding information

CLUMP *n pl* **-S** an unshaped piece or mass

CLUNG *v p t of* **CLING** to adhere closely; to stick; to hold fast

CLUNK *v* **-ED, -ING, -S** to make a loud dull thud; *also* **CLONK**

CNIDA *n pl* **-E** a peculiar stinging cell found in a jellyfish

COACH *v* **-ED, -ING, -ES** to train or tutor by special instruction

COACT *v* **-ED, -ING, -S** to work or act together

COAKS *n pl of* **COAK** dowels through overlapping timbers to prevent one from sliding across the other

COALA *n* a sluggish, tailless, gray, furry, arboreal marsupial; *also* **KOALA**

COALS *n pl of* **COAL** black or brownish black solid, combustible materials used as fuel

COALY *adj* **COALIER, COALIEST** pertaining to, or resembling coal, a combustible mineral substance used as fuel

COAPT *v* **-ED, -ING, -S** to join or bring displaced parts close together in their correct alignment

COAST *v* **-ED, -ING, -S** to move effortlessly; by force of gravity

COATI *n pl* **-S** or **COATI** a tropical mammal related to the raccoon

COATS *v pr t of* **COAT** provides with or forms a layer or covering

COBBS *n pl of* **COBB** BRIT. sea mews or gulls

COBBY *adj* **COBBIER, COBBIEST** [obs] stocky; stout; hearty

COBIA *n pl* **-S** or **COBIA** a large dark-striped tropical food and game fish related to perch and sea bass

COBLE *n pl* **-S** BRIT. a flat-bottomed fishing boat with a lug sail

COBRA *n pl* **-S** a venomous snake native to Asia and Africa that is capable of expanding the skin of the neck to form a flattened hood

COCCI *n pl of* **COCCUS** spherical microorganisms, especially bacteria

COCKS *v pr t of* **COCK** to tilt or slant to one side

COCKY *adj* **COCKIER, COCKIEST** overly self-confident or self-assertive

COCOA *n* a powder made from roasted and ground cacao seeds

COCOS *n pl of* **COCO** tall palm trees bearing coconut fruit

CODAS *n pl of* **CODA** closing sections of musical compositions

CODEC *n pl* **-S** an integrated circuit that converts analog to digital and vice versa

CODED *v p t of* **CODE** converted ordinary language into symbols or letters for security purposes

CODEN *n pl* **CODEN** a six character, alphanumeric bibliographic code that provides concise, unique and unambiguous identification of the titles of serial publications

CODER *n pl* **-S** a person who designs and writes and tests computer programs

CODES *v pr t of* **CODE** converts ordinary language into symbols or letters for security purposes

CODEX *n pl* **CODICES** a manuscript volume, especially of a classic work or of scripture

CODLE *v* **-D, CODLING, -S** to cook in water that is just below the boiling point; *also* **CODDLE**

CODON *n pl* **-S** a sequence of three adjacent nucleotides in DNA

COEDS *n pl of* **COED** women at a two-gender college

COFFS *v pr t of* **COFF** SCOT. buys

COGON *n* tall grass for thatching, fodder and erosion control

COGUE *n* SCOT. a small wooden vessel; a pail

COHOE *n pl* **-S** or **COHOE** a small salmon, originally of Pacific waters; *also* **COHO**

COHOG *n pl* **-S** an edible clam with a hard round shell; *also* **QUAHOG, QUAHAUG**

COHOS *n pl of* **COHO** small salmon, originally of Pacific waters; *also* **COHOES**

COIFS *v pr t of* **COIF** arranges or dresses the hair

OIGN *v* **-ED, -ING, -S** to build an outer corner of a wall using blocks that are different from those used to build the wall; *also* **QUOIN, COIGNE**

OILS *v pr t of* **COIL** winds in spirals

OINS *v pr t of* **COIN** invents a word or phrase

OIRS *n pl of* **COIR** the fiber obtained from the husk of the coconut, used in making rope and matting; *also* **KYARS**

OKED *v p t of* **COKE** changed into a carbon fuel

OKES *v pr t of* **COKE** changes into a carbon fuel

OLAS *n pl of* **COLA** carbonated beverages

OLBY *n* a moist mild cheese similar to cheddar

OLDS *n pl of* **COLD** viral infections, especially of the nose and throat

OLIC *n pl* **-S** excessive crying and irritability in infants, especially from stomach or intestinal discomfort

OLIN *n* any of several American quails

OLLA *n pl of* **COLLUM** necks; the parts between shoulders and heads

OLLY *v* **COLLIED, -ING** BRIT. to render black with or as if with soot

OLOG *n pl* **-S** the logarithm of the reciprocal of a number

OLON *n pl* **-S** or **COLA** a section of the large intestine

COLOR *v* **-ED, -ING, -S** to impart or change the color of; to change the property of an object that depends on the light that it reflects

COLTS *n pl of* **COLT** young male horses, donkeys, etc.

COLZA *n pl* **-S** an herb of the mustard family grown as forage and for its seeds that yield rapeseed oil

COMAE *n pl of* **COMA** tufts of silky hairs on seeds, as on a willow or milkseed

COMAL *n pl* **-S** a griddle made from sandstone or earthenware

COMAS *n pl of* **COMA** states of deep, often prolonged unconsciousness caused by injury or disease

COMBE *n pl* **-S** BRIT. a small valley with steep sides that seldom has water in it; *also* **COOMB, COOMBE**

COMBO *n pl* **-S** informal term for a small jazz band

COMBS *v pr t of* **COMB** straightens with an instrument that has teeth for arranging the hair

COMER *n pl* **-S** one who moves forward or draws near

COMES *v pr t of* **COME** moves forward or draws near

COMET *n pl* **-S** an astronomical object that is composed of ice and dust and has a long tail produced by vaporization when its orbit passes close to the Sun

COMFY *adj* **COMFIER, COMFIEST** informal term for comfortable; relaxed

COMIC *n pl* **-S** a comedian, a professional entertainer who amuses by engaging in humorous repartee

COMMA *n pl* **-S** a punctuation mark that represents a slight pause in a sentence

COMPO *n pl* **-S** a substance that is a mix of ingredients, such as cement or mortar

COMPS *v pr t of* **COMP** plays a jazz accompaniment, as on a piano or guitar

COMPT *v* [obs] to compute; to count

COMTE *n pl* **-S** a French nobleman equivalent in rank to an English earl

67

CONCH *n pl* **-S** or **-ES** a tropical invertebrate ocean animal with a large spiral shell

CONDO *n pl* **-S** a commonly used abbreviation for condominium; an individually owned unit in a complex

CONED *v p t of* **CONE** shaped like a cone, a pointed object with a round base

CONES *v pr t of* **CONE** shapes like a cone, a pointed object with a round base

CONEY *n pl* **-S** or **CONIES** a rabbit; *also* **CONY**

CONGA *v* **-ED, -ING, -S** to perform a Latin American dance where people form a line and, holding the waist of the person in front of them, take three steps forward and then kick out a leg

CONGE *n pl* **-S** a formal permission to depart; an abrupt dismissal; *also* **CONGEE**

CONGO *n* black tea grown in China, often called English breakfast tea; *also* **CONGOU**

CONIA *n* a powerful and very poisonous alkaloid, constituting the poison in hemlock; *also* **CONEINE, CONIINE, CONIN, CONINE**

CONIC *adj* having the form of, resembling, or pertaining to a cone, a pointed object with a round base

CONIN *n* a powerful and very poisonous alkaloid, constituting the poison in hemlock; *also* **CONIA, CONEINE, CONIINE, CONINE**

CONKS *v pr t of* **CONK** hits on the head; *also* **KONKS**

CONKY *adj* pertaining to the body of certain wood-decaying fungi

CONNS *v pr t of* **CONN** conducts or directs the steering of a vessel

CONNY *adj* **CONNIER, CONNIEST** BRIT. brave; fine; canny

CONTE *n pl* **-S** a short story

CONTO *n pl* **-S** a monetary unit of Portugal

CONUS *n pl* **CONI** a cone shaped structure, a pointed object with round bases

COOED *v p t of* **COO** cried softly, as a pigeon

COOEE *v* **-D, -ING, -S** AUS. to utter a prolonged shrill clear cry used as a signal by Australian Aborigines; *also* **COOEY**

COOER *n pl* **-S** one that cries softly, as a pigeon

COOEY *v* **-ED, -ING, -S** AUS. to utter a prolonged shrill clear cry used as a signal by Australian Aborigines; *also* **COOEE**

COOFS *n pl of* **COOF** SCOT. silly people; dolts

COOKS *v pr t of* **COOK** prepares food for eating by subjecting it to heat

COOKY *n pl* **COOKIES** a small, flat, crisp baked cake, especially one made from sweetened dough; *also* **COOKIE**

COOLS *v pr t of* **COOL** makes less warm

COOMB *n pl* **-S** BRIT. a small valley with steep sides that seldom has water in it; *also* **COMBE, COOMBE**

COOMS *n pl of* **COOM** SCOT. soot; coal dust

COONS *n pl of* **COON** informal term for raccoons

COOPS *n pl of* **COOP** enclosures for confining small animals

COOPT *v* [obs] to choose or elect in concert with another

COOTS *n pl of* **COOT** duck-like wading birds with lobed toes

COPAL *n* a brittle aromatic resin used in varnishes

COPAY *n pl* **-S** the amount an insured person is expected to pay for a medical expense at the time of the visit

COPED *v p t of* COPE dealt with or came to terms with

COPEN *n* a medium blue color

COPER *n pl* -S BRIT. a horse dealer

COPES *v pr t of* COPE deals with or comes to terms with

COPPS *n* [obs] a thicket of small trees or bushes; *also* COPSE, COPPICE

COPRA *n pl* -S the dried meat of the coconut, from which coconut oil is obtained

COPSE *n pl* -S a thicket of small trees or bushes; *also* COPPS, COPPICE

COPSY *adj* characterized by thickets of small trees or bushes

CORAL *n pl* -S a marine colonial polyp characterized by an external skeleton

CORBE *adj* [obs] crooked

CORBY *n pl* CORBIES [obs] a raven or crow; *also* CORBIE

CORDS *n pl of* CORD small ropes of several strands twisted together

CORED *v p t of* CORE removed the core or central part of

CORER *n pl* -S a device for removing the core from apples

CORES *v pr t of* CORE removes the core or central part of

CORIA *n pl of* CORIUM the deep vascular inner layer of the skin

CORKS *v pr t of* CORK seals a container with a cork, a stopper for bottles or casks

CORKY *adj* CORKIER, CORKIEST consisting of, or like, cork, which comes from the outer bark of an oak tree

CORMS *n pl of* CORM short thick solid food-storing underground stems, sometimes bearing papery scale leaves

CORNS *v pr t of* CORN preserves or pickles with salt or in brine

CORNU *n pl* -A any structure that resembles a horn in shape

CORNY *adj* CORNIER, CORNIEST unsophisticated and trite

COROL *n pl* -S the inner envelope of a flower; *also* COROLL, COROLLA

CORPS *n pl* CORPS a military force that carries out specialized duties

CORSE *n* [obs] the dead body, usually of a human being; *also* CORPSE

CORVE *n pl* -S a basket used to carry coal; *also* CORB, CORF

COSEC *n pl* -S the ratio of the hypotenuse to the opposite side of a right-angled triangle; *also* COSECANT

COSEN *v* -ED, -ING, -S to cheat; to defraud; *also* COZEN

COSES *n pl of* COS varieties of crisp, long-leafed lettuce

COSET *n pl* -S a mathematical subset

COSEY *n pl* -S a padded cloth covering to keep a teapot warm; *also* COSIE, COZIE

COSIE *n pl* -S a padded cloth covering to keep a teapot warm; *also* COSEY, COZIE

COSTA *n pl* -E a rib of an animal or a human being

COSTS *v pr t of* COST requires a specified payment

COTAN *n* a trigonometric function equal to the length of the side adjacent to the angle divided by that of the side opposite the angle

COTED *v p t of* COTE [obs] to pass by; to outrun and get before

COTES *n pl of* COTE small sheds or shelters for sheep or birds

COTTA *n pl* -E or -S a short surplice worn by clergy, acolytes and choristers

COUCH *v* -ED, -ING, -ES to phrase something in a particular way

COUDE *n pl* -S a set of auxiliary mirrors so arranged as to always direct light to a fixed position; a telescope that reflects light

COUGH *v* -ED, -ING, -S to expel air from the lungs through the windpipe and mouth sharply and noisily

COULD *v p t of* **CAN** used to indicate ability or permission in the past

COUNT *v* -ED, -ING, -S to number; to enumerate; to compute

COUPE *n pl* -S a closed two-door automobile

COUPS *n pl of* **COUP** sudden appropriations of leadership or power; takeovers

COURB *adj* [obs] curved, rounded

COURT *v* -ED, -ING, -S to try to win somebody's affection; to woo

COUTH *adj* very sophisticated; having very good manners

COVED *v p t of* **COVE** had or gave an inward curve

COVEN *n pl* -S an assembly witches, usually 13 in number

COVER *v* -ED, -ING, -S to place something over the whole or the upper surface of something

COVES *v pr t of* **COVE** has or gives an inward curve

COVET *v* -ED, -ING, -S to have a strong desire to possess something that belongs to somebody else

COVEY *n pl* -S a group of game birds such as partridge, grouse, quail, etc.

COVIN *n pl* -S a conspiracy of two or more people to defraud or injure another

COWAN *n* SCOT. one who works as a mason without having served a regular apprenticeship

COWED *v p t of* **COW** intimidated; frightened with threats or shows of force

COWER *v* -ED, -ING, -S to crouch or curl up

COWLS *n pl of* **COWL** draped necklines on women's garments

COWRY *n pl* **COWRIES** a marine gastropod mollusk with a smooth, glossy, domed shell; *also* **COWRIE**

COXAE *n pl of* **COXA** hips or hip joints

COXAL *adj* pertaining to hips or hip joints

COXED *v p t of* **COX** acted as a coxswain, a person who steers a boat

COXES *v pr t of* **COX** acts as a coxswain, a person who steers a boat

COYED *v p t of* **COY** [obs] caressed, pet; coaxed, enticed

COYER *adj* more shy; more reserved

COYLY *adv* in a coy, shy manner; with reserve

COYOL *n pl* -S a tropical American palm tree having edible nuts

COYPU *n* an aquatic beaver-like rodent, bred for its fur

COZEN *v* -ED, -ING, -S to cheat; to defraud; *also* **COSEN**

COZES *n pl of* **COZ** informal term for cousins; *also* **CUZES**

COZEY *v* COZIED, -ING or COZYING, COZIES to make more cozy, warm and comfortable

COZIE *n pl* -S a padded cloth covering to keep a tea pot warm; *also* **COSEY, COSIE**

CRAAL *v* -ED, -S to shut up in a kraal, an enclosure for cattle and other domestic animals in S. Africa; *also* **KRAAL**

CRABS *n pl* **CRAB** decapods having eyes on short stalks and broad flattened carapaces with small abdomens

CRACK *v* -ED, -ING, -S to break or burst, with or without entire separation of the parts

CRAFT *v* -ED, -ING, -S to make by hand and with much skill

CRAGS *n pl of* **CRAG** steep, rugged rocks; rough, broken cliffs

CRAIE *n pl* -S [obs] a slow unwieldy trading vessel; *also* **CRARE**

CRAIL *n pl* **-S** a wicker basket used by anglers to hold fish; *also* **CREEL**

CRAKE *n pl* **-S** a short-billed marsh bird with a harsh voice

CRAMP *v* **-ED, -ING, -S** to confine or contract; to restrain

CRAMS *v pr t of* **CRAM** stuffs; crowds or packs to capacity

CRANE *v* **-D, CRANING, -S** to stretch the neck in order to get a better view

CRANG *n pl* **-S** the carcass of a whale after the blubber has been removed; *also* **KRANG**

CRANK *v* **-ED, -ING, -S** to start, move, or operate something by turning a device consisting of an arm and a handle

CRANS *n pl of* **CRAN** SCOT. units of capacity formerly used for measuring fresh herring

CRAPE *v* **-D, CRAPING, -S** to cover or drape with or as with crepe, a light soft thin crinkled fabric

CRAPY *adj* resembling crape, a light soft thin crinkled fabric

CRARE *n pl* **-S** a slow unwieldy trading vessel; *also* **CRAIE**

CRASE *v* **-D, CRASING, -S** [obs] to break into pieces; to crack; *also* **CRAZE**

CRASH *v* **-ED, -ING, -ES** to come together with violent, direct impact

CRASS *adj* **-ER, -EST** so crude and unrefined as to be lacking in discrimination and sensibility

CRATE *v* **-ED, CRATING, -S** to put or pack into a large open sturdy box used to carry or store objects

CRAVE *v* **-D, CRAVING, -S** to desire strongly

CRAWL *v* **-ED, -ING, -S** to move slowly by drawing the body along the ground, as a worm

CRAWS *n pl of* **CRAW** stomachs of animals

CRAZE *v* **-D, CRAZING, -S** to break into pieces, to crack; *also* **CRASE**

CRAZY *adj* **CRAZIER, CRAZIEST** not showing good sense or practicality

CREAK *v* **-ED, -ING, -S** to make a prolonged sharp grating or squeaking sound

CREAM *v* **-ED, -ING, -S** to form foam or froth at the top

CREAT *n* an usher to a riding master

CREDO *n pl* **-S** a system of principles or beliefs; *also* **CREED**

CREDS *n/pl* a commonly used abbreviation for a law enforcement officer's badge and identification card

CREED *n pl* **-S** a system of principles or beliefs; *also* **CREDO**

CREEK *n pl* **-S** a stream, especially one that flows into a river

CREEL *n pl* **-S** a wicker basket used by anglers to hold fish; *also* **CRAIL**

CREEP *v* **CREPT** or **-ED, -ING, -S** to crawl

CRÈME *n pl* **-S** a sweet liquor

CREPE *n pl* **-S** a light fine fabric with a crinkled surface

CREPT *v p t of* **CREEP** crawled

CREPY *adj* **CREPIER, CREPIEST** like a light fine fabric with a crinkled surface; *also* **CREPEY**

CRESS *n pl* **-ES** an annual plant with small pungently flavored leaves, used in salads and as a garnish

CREST *v* **-ED, -ING, -S** to reach the summit of a hill or mountain ridge

CREWS *v pr t of* **CREW** serves as a member of a group of people who work on and operate a ship, boat, aircraft or train

CRIBS *n pl of* **CRIB** small enclosed beds for children

CRICK *v* **-ED, -ING, -S** to cause a painful stiffness or muscle spasm in the neck or back

CRIED *v p t of* **CRY** wept

CRIER *n pl* **-S** one who cries; one who makes proclamations

CRIES *v pr t of* **CRY** weeps

CRIME *n pl* **-S** any violation of law, either divine or human

CRIMP *v* **-ED, -ING, -S** to pinch and hold; to seize

CRISP *adj* **-ER, -EST** brittle; friable

CRITH *n* the weight of a liter of hydrogen

CRITS *n pl of* **CRIT** BRIT. the smallest or weakest pigs in litters

CROAK *v* **-ED -ING, -S** to make a low, hoarse noise in the throat

CROCI *n pl of* **CROCUS** spring-blooming colorful flowers

CROCK *n pl* **-S** a pot made of clay

CROCS *n pl of* **CROC** commonly used abbreviation for crocodiles

CROFT *n pl* **-S** SCOT. a small tenant farm

CROMA *n* [obs] a quaver; a shake

CRONK *adj* AUS. not reliable or sound

CRONY *n pl* **CRONIES** an intimate companion; a familiar friend

CROOK *v* **-ED, -ING, -S** to curve, or make something such as a finger take on a hooked or curved shape

CROON *v* **-ED, -ING, -S** to hum or sing in a low, gentle tone

CROPS *v pr t of* **CROP** cuts very short or trims the edges off of

CRORE *n pl* **-S** a monetary unit of India and Pakistan equal to ten million rupees

CROSS *v* **-ED, -ING, -ES** to intersect

CROUD *n pl* **-S** an ancient Celtic musical instrument, somewhat like a violin, but with a broad, shallow body; *also* **CROWTH, CRUTH, CRWTH**

CROUP *n pl* **-S** the hindquarter of a four-legged animal, especially a horse; *also* **CROUPE**

CROUT *n pl* **-S** commonly used abbreviation for sauerkraut, shredded cabbage fermented in brine; *also* **KRAUT, KROUT**

CROWD *v* **-ED, -ING, -S** to push, to press, to urge

CROWN *v* **-ED, -ING, -S** to confer royal status on somebody; to place a crown on a person's head to symbolize monarchy

CROWS *v pr t of* **CROW** shouts in exultation or defiance; brags

CROZE *n pl* **-S** a groove at the top of a barrel or cask into which the flat surface is fitted

CRUCK *n pl* **-S** BRIT. a curved wooden timber to support the end of the roof

CRUDE *adj* **-ER, -EST** unripe; not mature or perfect

CRUDY *adj* [obs] coagulated

CRUEL *adj* **-ER, -EST** lacking or showing kindness or compassion or mercy

CRUET *n pl* **-S** a glass bottle for holding wine, vinegar, oil, etc.

CRULL *adj* [obs] curly; curled

CRUMB *n pl* **-S** a small fragment or piece; a small piece of baked food

CRUMP *v* **-ED, -ING, -S** to make a crunching noise like the sound of footsteps in the snow

CRUNK *n* a style of hip-hop or rap music most commonly made by artists from the southern United States

CRUOR *n* coagulated blood, or the portion of the blood that forms the clot

CRURA *n pl of* **CRUS** parts of legs from knees to feet

CRUSE *n pl* **-S** a small earthenware container to hold liquids

CRUSH *v* **-ED, -ING, -ES** to press or bruise between two hard bodies; to squeeze

CRUST *n pl* **-S** the hard external coat or covering of anything

CRUTH *n pl* **-S** an ancient Celtic musical instrument, somewhat like a violin, but with a broad, shallow body; *also* **CROUD**, **CROWTH**, **CRWTH**

CRUTS *n pl of* **CRUT** the rough, shaggy parts of oak bark

CRWTH *n pl* **-S** an ancient Celtic musical instrument, somewhat like a violin, but with a broad, shallow body; *also* **CROUD**, **CROWTH**, **CRUTH**

CRYER *n* the female of the hawk; a falcon-gentil

CRYPT *n pl* **-S** a vault wholly or partly underground, used as a burial chamber or chapel, or for storing religious artifacts

CTENE *n pl* **-S** a comb-plate; a locomotor organ consisting of a row of strong cilia whose bases are fused

CUBBY *n pl* **CUBBIES** a small secluded room; any of a group of small boxlike enclosures

CUBEB *n pl* **-S** a small unripe brownish spicy berry of a climbing plant, formerly used to treat respiratory and urinary disorders

CUBED *v p t of* **CUBE** formed into a regular solid body with six equal square sides

CUBER *n pl* **-S** a machine that forms food into regular solid bodies with six equal square sides, especially a meat cuber

CUBES *v pr t of* **CUBE** forms into a regular solid body with six equal square sides

CUBIC *adj* having three dimensions; the shape of a cube

CUBIT *n pl* **-S** an ancient unit of length based on the length of the forearm

CUDDY *n pl* **CUDDIES** a small cabin or galley on a boat

CUFFS *v pr t of* **CUFF** fights; scuffles; boxes

CUFIC *adj* having an early angular style of Arabic writing used for Koranic manuscripts and inscriptions; *also* **KUFIC**

CUING *v p part of* **CUE** giving a signal to an actor; *also* **CUEING**

CUISH *n pl* **-ES** a piece of armor formerly worn in battle to protect the thigh; *also* **CUISSE**

CUKES *n pl of* **CUKE** cylindrical green fruits with thin green rinds and white flesh eaten as vegetables; cucumbers

CULCH *n* an oyster bed of rocks, crushed shells and sea detritus where oyster spawn can attach themselves; *also* **CULTCH**, **SCHULCH**, **SCULTCH**

CULET *n pl* **-S** the flat face at the base of a faceted gemstone

CULLS *v pr t of* **CULL** reduces the number of animals by selective slaughter

CULLY *v* **CULLIED, -ING, CULLIES** to trick; cheat, or impose on; to deceive

CULMS *n pl of* **CULM** the stalks or stems of grain and grasses, jointed and usually hollow

CULPA *n pl* **-E** negligence or fault

CULTI *n pl of* **CULTUS** groups of people who share religious or spiritual beliefs

CULTS *n pl of* **CULT** groups of people who share religious or spiritual beliefs, especially beliefs regarded by others as misguided, unorthodox, extremist or false

CUMIN *n* an annual Mediterranean plant of the carrot family long cultivated for its aromatic seeds, which are used in cooking

CUPEL *v* **-ED** or **-LED, -ING** or **-LING** to heat or refine in a shallow porous container

CUPPA *n* BRIT. a cup of tea

CUPPY *adj* **CUPPIER, CUPPIEST** cuplike; with the shape of a cup; full of shallow depressions

CURAT *n* [obs] a cuirass or corselet; defensive armor for the torso comprised of a breastplate and backplate

CURBS *n pl of* **CURB** edgeS between sidewalks and roadways; *also* **KERBS**

CURCH *n* SCOT. a kerchief for the head worn by Scottish women; *also* **COURCHE**

CURDS *n pl of* **CURD** soft white substances formed when milk coagulates, used as the basis for cheese

CURDY *adj* **CURDIER, CURDIEST** like curd; full of curd; coagulated

CURED *v p t of* **CURE** restored to health; healed

CURER *n pl* **-S** one who cures; a healer; a physician

CURES *v pr t of* **CURE** restores to health; heals

CURET *v* **-TED, -TING, -S** to scrape tissue from the inner surface of a body cavity using a spoon-shaped surgical instrument; *also* **CURETTE**

CURIA *n pl* **-E** a medieval monarch's court of justice

CURIE *n pl* **-S** a unit of radioactivity

CURIO *n pl* **-S** an object that is valued and often collected for its interest or rarity

CURLS *v pr t of* **CURL** twists or forms into ringlets

CURLY *adj* **CURLIER, CURLIEST** curling or tending to form ringlets

CURRY *v* **CURRIED, -ING, CURRIES** to prepare food in spicy sauce

CURSE *v* **-D, CURSING, -S** to wish harm upon; to invoke evil upon

CURST *v p t of* **CURSE** [obs] wished harm upon, invoked evil upon

CURVE *v* **-D, CURVING, -S** to move or bend in a line that bends smoothly and regularly from being straight or flat, like part of a sphere or circle

CURVY *adj* **CURVIER, CURVIEST** curved; bent; not straight

CUSEC *n pl* **-S** [obs] a volumetric unit for measuring the flow of liquids, equal to one cubic foot per second

CUSHY *adj* **CUSHIER, CUSHIEST** not burdensome or demanding; easy

CUSKS *n pl of* **CUSK** large, edible, marine; *also* **BURBOTS**

CUSPS *n pl of* **CUSP** sharp and rigid points

CUSSO *n* an Ethiopian tree of the rose family, the flowers of which have medicinal properties; *also* **KOSSO, KOUSSO**

CUTAN *n* one of the waxy polymers that forms the cuticle on the surface of a plant

CUTCH *n pl* **-ES** a hard, brown substance obtained from Asiatic acacia trees and shrubs used in medicine and dye; *also* **CATECHU**

CUTER *adj of* **CUTE** more pleasing; more attractive

CUTES *n pl of* **CUTIS** more than one of the layer of skin beneath the epidermis

CUTEY *n pl* **-S** a cute, attractive person; *also* **CUTIE**

CUTIE *n pl* **-S** a cute, attractive person; *also* **CUTEY**

CUTIN *n pl* **-S** one of the waxy polymers that forms the cuticle on the surface of a plant

CUTIS *n pl* **CUTES** the layer of skin beneath the epidermis

CUTTY *n pl* **CUTTIES** something cut short, such as a spoon or short-stemmed tobacco pipe

CUTUP *n pl* **-S** a mischievous person; a prankster

CUVEE *n pl* -**S** a single batch of wine

CUZES *n pl of* **CUZ** informal term for cousins; *also* **COZES**

CYANO *adj* related to or containing cyanogen, a colorless toxic gas with a pungent almond odor

CYCAD *n pl* -**S** a tropical fernlike plant

CYCLE *v* -**D**, **CYCLING**, -**S** to put something through or go through a series of events

CYCLO *n pl* -**S** a three-wheeled passenger vehicle which may be pedaled like a bicycle or be motorized

CYDER *n* -**S** BRIT. [obs] the expressed juice of apples used to make a beverage or other products such as vinegar; *also* **CIDER**

CYLIX *n* **CYLICES** an ancient Greek drinking vessel with two handles, a shallow bowl and lavish decoration; *also* **KYLIX**

CYMAE *n pl of* **CYMA** the moldings of a cornice, the profiles of which are wavelike in form; *also* **CYMAS**, **CYMES**

CYMAR *n pl* -**S** a 17th or 18th century loose, lightweight jacket or robe for women; *also* **SIMAR**

CYMAS *n pl of* **CYMA** flat-topped or convex flower clusters; *also* **CYMAE**, **CYMES**

CYMES *n pl of* **CYME** flat-topped or convex flower clusters; *also* **CYMAE**, **CYMAS**

CYNIC *n pl* -**S** someone who is critical of the motives of others

CYONS *n pl of* **CYON** detached shoots or twigs containing buds from a woody plant, used in grafting; *also* **CIONS**, **SCIONS**

CYPRE *n pl* -**S** a large tropical American tree with creamy white flowers and valuable wood

CYSTS *n pl of* **CYST** small sacs or bladder-like structures

CYTON *n pl* -**S** the body of a nerve cell

CYTTY *adj* SCOT. short; as, a cutty knife

CZARS *n pl of* **CZAR** male monarchs or emperors, especially the former emperors of Russia; *also* **TSARS**, **TZARS**

DE *prep* of or from (used in French, Spanish and Portuguese names, originally to indicate place of origin)

DO *v* **DID** or -**NE**, -**ING**, -**ES** to perform or execute

THREE LETTERS

DAB *v* -**BED**, -**BING**, -**S** to apply with short poking strokes

DAD *n pl* -**S** father

DAG *n pl* -**S** a decorative edging for garments, used especially in medieval times

DAH *n pl* -**S** a dash in Morse code

DAK *n* post; mail; *also* **DAUK**, **DAWK**

DAL *n* a dish of lentils and spices in India; *also* **DAHL**, **DHAL**

DAM *v* -**MED**, -**MING**, -**S** to build a barrier to obstruct water

DAN *n pl* -**S** a small buoy

DAP *v* -**PED**, -**PING**, -**S** to dip lightly or quickly into water

DAW *n pl* -**S** a common black-and-gray Eurasian bird; the jackdaw

DAY *n pl* -**S** the period of light between dawn and nightfall

DEB *n pl* -**S** commonly used abbreviation for a debutante

DEE *n pl* -**S** the letter "D"

DEF *adj* -**FER**, -**FEST** informal term for excellent; brilliant

DEN *v* -**NED**, -**NING**, -**S** to inhabit or hide in a lair or cave

DEV *n* a divine being; *also* **DEVA**

DEW *v* **-ED, -ING, -S** to wet with water droplets; to moisten

DEX *n* commonly used abbreviation for dextroamphetamine, a sulfate stimulant for the central nervous system

DEY *n pl* **-S** the title of the governor of Algiers before the French conquest in 1830

DIB *v* **-BED, -BING, -S** to dip bait into water

DID *v pt of* **DO** performed or executed

DIE *v* **-D, DYING, -S** to suffer death; to lose life

DIG *v* **DUG** or **-GED, -GING, -S** to excavate, turn over or remove earth

DIM *v* **-MED, -MING, -S** to make something less bright

DIN *v* **-NED, -NING, -S** to make a loud persistent noise

DIP *v* **-PED** or **DIPT, -PING, -S** to plunge or immerse

DIT *n pl* **-S** a spoken representation of a short sound used in Morse code

DOB *v* **-BED, -BING** SCOT., N.Z. to inform against; to betray

DOC *n pl* **-S** commonly used abbreviation for a doctor

DOE *n pl* **-S** a female deer or antelope

DOG *n pl* **-S** a domestic animal with a long muzzle, fur coat and tail

DOL *n* a unit for measuring the intensity of pain

DON *v* **-NED, -NING, -S** to put on a garment

DOO *n pl* **-S** SCOT. a dove

DOP *n* a tool for holding gemstones for cutting and polishing

DOR *n* any of several insects that make a buzzing noise in flight, such as the June bug; *also* **DORR; DORBEETLE**

DOT *v* **-TED, -TING, -S** to make a very small spot

DOW *n* a lateen-rigged sailing vessel; *also* **DHOW**

DRY *v* **DRIED, -ING, DRIES** to make free from moisture

DUB *v* **-BED, -BING, -S** to give a nickname to

DUD *n pl* **-S** a bomb or shell that fails to explode

DUE *adj* owed or owing as a debt or right

DUG *v pt of* **DIG** excavated, turned over, or removed earth

DUH *Interj* used to express annoyance at obviousness

DUN *v* **-NED, -NING, -S** to press for payment of a debt

DUO *n pl* **DUOS** a pair, a couple; an instrumental duet

DUP *v* [obs] to open

DUX *n pl* **-ES** SCOT. the pupil who is first in a class or school

DYE *v* **-D, DYING, -S** to give color to fabric, hair, etc.

DZO *n pl* **-S** or **DZO** a cross between a yak and a cow; *also* **ZHO, ZO**

FOUR LETTERS

DABS *v pr t of* **DAB** applies with short poking strokes

DACE *n pl* **-S** a small European freshwater fish with a slender bluish-green body

DADA *n* a nihilistic art movement of the early 20th century characterized by anarchy, irrationality and irreverence; *also* **DADAISM**

DADE *v* [obs] to walk unsteadily, as a child just learning to walk

DADO *n pl* **-ES** or **-S** the lower part of an interior wall when decorated differently from the upper part

DADS *n pl of* **DAD** fathers

DAFF *v* **-ED, -ING, -S** [obs] to cast aside; to take off; to doff

DAFT *adj* **-ER, -EST** foolish; idiotic

DAGS *n pl of* **DAG** decorative edgings for garments, used especially in medieval times

DAHL *n* a dish of lentils and spices in India; *also* **DAL, DHAL**

DAHS *n pl of* **DAH** dashes in Morse code

DAIS *n* a platform slightly raised above the floor of a hall, to give prominence to the person on it; *also* **DEIS**

DALE *n pl* **-S** a low place between hills; a valley

DALF *v* [obs] to dig into; to investigate; *also* **DELVE, DOLF**

DALO *n* an herb of the Pacific islands having an edible root and large glossy leaves

DAME *n pl* **-S** a mistress of a family; lady; woman in authority

DAMN *v* **-ED, -ING, -S** to condemn; to declare guilty; to doom

DAMP *v* **-ED, -ING, -S** to make somebody or something slightly wet

DAMS *v pr t of* **DAM** builds a barrier to obstruct water

DANG *interj* informal term expressing irritation

DANK *adj* **-ER, -EST** damp and cold; moist; wet

DANS *n pl of* **DAN** small buoys

DAPS *v pr t of* **DAP** dips lightly or quickly into water

DARE *v* **-D, DARING, -S** to challenge; to provoke; to defy

DARK *adj* **-ER, -EST** lacking light; of a deep shade; black or approaching black

DARN *v* **-ED, -ING, -S** to mend or repair by filling in with thread or yarn and a needle

DARR *n* the European black tern; a small slender gull

DART *v* **-ED, -ING, -S** to move swiftly or suddenly

DASE *v* [obs] to stupefy or bewilder, as by a glare of light or physical or mental shock; *also* **DAZE**

DASH *v* **-ED, -ING, -ES** to hurry off; to run, move or travel fast or hastily

DATA *n pl of* **DATUM** items of factual information derived from measurement or research

DATE *v* **-D, DATING, -S** to note or fix the time of, as of an event

DATO *n a* chief of a Muslim Moro tribe in the Philippine Islands; *also* **DATTO, DATU**

DATU *n a* chief of a Muslim Moro tribe in the Philippine Islands; *also* **DATO, DATTO**

DAUB *v* **-ED, -ING, -S** to paint in a coarse or unskillful manner

DAUK *n* post; mail; *also* **DAK, DAWK**

DAUN *n* [obs] a title of honor for a respected man, such as a cleric or a poet

DAUT *v* SCOT. to fondle; pet; caress

DAWK *n* post; mail; *also* **DAK, DAUK**

DAWN *v* **-ED, -ING, -S** to begin to grow light in the morning

DAWS *n pl of* **DAW** common black-and-gray Eurasian birds; jackdaws

DAYS *n pl of* **DAY** the periods of light between dawn and nightfall

DAZE *v* **-D, DAZING, -S** to stupefy or bewilder, as by a glare of light or physical or mental shock; *also* **DASE**

DEAD *adj* **-ER, -EST** deprived of life; *also* **DEDE**

DEAF *adj* lacking or deficient in the sense of hearing

DEAL *v* **DEALT, -ING, -S** to do business; to trade

DEAN *n pl* **-S** the head of a faculty

DEAR *adj* **-ER, -EST** beloved

DEBS *n pl of* **DEB** commonly used abbreviation for debutantes

DEBT *n pl* **-S** an obligation to pay or do something

DECK *v* **-ED, -ING, -S** to dress elegantly; to adorn; to embellish

DECO *n* a style of decorative art that used geometric designs and bold colors and outlines; art deco

DEDE *adj* [obs] deprived of life; *also* **DEAD**

DEED v **-ED, -ING, -S** to sign over or transfer something, especially real estate, to another person

DEEL n SCOT. the devil; *also* **DEIL, DEVEL**

DEEM v **-ED, -ING, -S** to decide; judge; consider; regard; believe

DEEP adj **-ER, -EST** extending far below the surface

DEER n pl **DEER** a ruminant animal distinguished by the branched antlers on the males

DEES n pl of **DEE** more than one of the letter "D"

DEET n a colorless, oily chemical that is the active ingredient in most insect repellents

DEFT adj apt; dexterous; clever; handy

DEFY v **DEFIED, -ING, DEFIES** to act in disregard of; resist openly or boldly

DEGU n a small South American rodent having long, smooth fur and a black-tipped, tufted tail

DEIL n SCOT. the devil; *also* **DEEL, DEVEL**

DEIS n a platform slightly raised above the floor of a hall, to give prominence to the person on it; *also* **DAIS**

DEKE v **-D, DEKING, -S** to deceive an opponent in hockey by a fake

DELE v **-D, -ING, -S** to mark a passage of printed material for deletion

DELF n [obs] a mine; a quarry; a pit dug; a ditch

DELI n pl **-S** commonly used abbreviation for delicatessen, a shop selling cooked meats, cheeses and unusual or foreign prepared foods

DELL n pl **-S** a small, secluded valley

DELT n pl **-S** commonly used abbreviation for deltoid, a thick triangular muscle that covers the shoulder joint

DEME n pl **-S** a population of related species

DEMO v **-ED, -ING, -S** to explain, describe or give a demonstration of how something works

DEMY n of standard paper size

DENE n pl **-S** BRIT. a narrow wooded valley

DENI n pl **DENI** a monetary unit of Macedonia

DENS v pr t of **DEN** inhabits or hides in a lair or cave

DENT v **-ED, -ING, -S** to cause a slight depression by striking or pressing

DENY v **DENIED, -ING, DENIES** to declare not to be true; to refuse to acknowledge

DERE v [obs] to hurt, to harm, to injure; *also* **DEARE**

DERF adj [obs] strong; powerful; fierce

DERM n the integument of animal; the skin

DERN v SCOT. to hide; to skulk; *also* **DEARN, DERNE**

DESK n pl **-S** a piece of furniture typically having a flat or sloping top for writing and often drawers or compartments

DEVA n a divine being; *also* **DEV**

DEWS v pr t of **DEW** wets with water droplets; moistens

DEWY adj moist; wet with dew; water droplets

DEYS n pl of **DEY** titles of the governors of Algiers before the French conquest in 1830

DHAK n an East Indian tree that yields a yellow dye

DHAL n a dish of lentils and spices in India; *also* **DAL, DAHL**

DHOW n a lateen-rigged sailing vessel; *also* **DOW**

DIAL v **-ED, -ING, -S** to call by turning a dial or using a keypad

DIBS v pr t of **DIB** dips bait into water

DICE v **-D, -ING, -S** to cut into small cubes

DICK n pl **-S** informal term for a detective

DIDO *n pl* **-S** or **-ES** a shrewd trick; an antic; a caper

DIED *v p t of* **DIE** suffered death; lost life

DIEL *adj* involving a full day

DIES *v pr t of* **DIE** suffers death; loses life

DIET *v* **-ED, -ING, -S** to eat and drink according to a prescribed selection of foods

DIGS *v pr t of* **DIG** excavates, turns over, or removes earth

DIKA *n* tropical African tree with fruit that resembles a mango

DIKE *v* **-D, -DIKING, -S** to drain with a ditch; *also* **DYKE**

DILL *n* an aromatic threadlike foliage used as seasoning

DIME *n pl* **-S** a ten-cent coin of the United States

DIMS *v pr t of* **DIM** makes something less bright

DINE *v* **-D, DINING, -S** to eat the principal regular meal of the day

DING *v* **-ED, -ING, -S** to make a ringing sound like that of a bell

DINK *n pl* **-S** a drop shot in racket games

DINO *n pl* **-S** commonly used abbreviation for a dinosaur

DINS *v pr t of* **DIN** makes a loud persistent noise

DINT *v* **-ED, -ING, -S** to drive something in with force

DIOL *n* a chemical compound containing two hydroxyl groups

DIPS *v pr t of* **DIP** plunges or immerses

DIPT *v p t of* **DIP** [obs] plunged or immersed; *also* **DIPPED**

DIRE *adj* evil in great degree; dreadful; dismal; horrible

DIRK *v* **-ED, -ING, -S** to stab with a dirk, a dagger formerly used by Scottish Highlanders

DIRL *v* SCOT. to vibrate or shake

DIRT *n* any foul of filthy substance, mud, dust

DISC *n pl* **-S** a thin, flat, circular object; *also* **DISK**

DISH *n pl* **-ES** a vessel, as a platter, a plate, a bowl, used for serving up food at the table

DISK *n pl* **-S** a thin, flat, circular object; *also* **DISC**

DISS *v* **-ED, -ING, -ES** to treat, mention or speak to rudely

DITA *n* an evergreen tree of eastern Asia and Philippines

DITE *n* BRIT. a bit; a trifle

DITS *n pl of* **DIT** spoken representations of short sounds used in Morse code

DIVA *n pl* **-S** an operatic prima donna; distinguished female singer

DIVE *v* **-D** or **DOVE, DIVING, -S** to plunge into water head foremost

DIZZ *v* [obs] to make dizzy; to astonish; to puzzle

DJIN *n pl* **-S** or **DJIN** in Islamic myth any class of spirits lower than angels, capable of assuming human or animal forms and influencing humankind; *also* **DJINN, DJINNI, JIN, JINN, JINNI**

DOAB *n* a tongue or tract of land included between two rivers

DOAT *v* to bestow or express excessive love or fondness habitually; *also* **DOTE**

DOCK *v* **-ED, -ING, -S** to haul into a dock, a wharf

DOCS *n pl of* **DOC** commonly used abbreviation for doctors

DODO *n pl* **-S** or **-ES** an extinct heavy flightless bird of Mauritius

DOER *n pl* **-S** a person who does something or acts in a specified manner

DOES *v pr t of* **DO** performs or executes

DOFF *v* **-ED, -ING, -S** to remove an item of clothing, especially a hat

DOGE *n pl* **-S** the elected chief magistrate in the former republics of Venice and Genoa

DOGS *n pl of* **DOG** domestic animals with a long muzzle, fur coat and tail

DOGY *n pl* **DOGIES** a motherless calf in a range herd of cattle; *also* **DOGEY, DOGIE**

DOIT *n* a small low-value Dutch coin used between the 15th and 17th centuries; *also* **DUIT**

DOJO *n pl* **-S** a school for training in Japanese arts of self-defense, such as judo and karate

DOKO *n* an eel-shaped ganoid fish that has both gills and lungs

DOLE *v* **-D, DOLING, -S** to distribute sparingly

DOLF *v* [obs] to dig into; to investigate; *also* **DALF, DELVE**

DOLL *n pl* **-S** a small replica of a person used as a toy

DOLT *n pl* **-S** a blockhead; a numskull

DOME *v* **-D, DOMING, -S** to form or rise into a hemispherical shape

DONA *n pl* **-S** AUS. a courtesy title for a Spanish lady

DONE *v p part of* **DO** performed or executed

DONG *v* **-ED, -ING, -S** to make a ringing sound like that of a bell

DONI *n* a clumsy craft, having one mast with a long sail, used for trading purposes on the coasts of Coromandel and Ceylon; *also* **DHONI**

DONS *v pr t of* **DON** puts on a garment

DOOM *v* **-S, -ING, -ED** to condemn to ruination or death

DOOP *n* a little copper cup in which a diamond is held while being cut

DOOR *n pl* **-S** a movable barrier used to open and close the entrance to a building

DOOS *n pl of* **DOO** SCOT. doves

DOPA *n* a natural precursor of epinephrine and dopamine; used in synthetic form to treat Parkinson's disease

DOPY *adj* **DOPIER, DOPIEST** sluggish or drowsy; *also* **DOPEY**

DORE *n* gold and silver bullion remaining in a cupeling furnace after removal of the oxidized lead

DORK *n pl* **-S** informal term for a foolish person

DORM *n pl* **-S** common abbreviation for a dormitory, a building used as living and sleeping quarters by college students

DORP *n pl* **-S** a village or small country town, sometimes perceived as backward

DORR *n* any of several insects that make a buzzing noise in flight, such as the June bug; *also* **DOR, DORBEETLE**

DORY *n pl* **DORIES** a small boat

DOSE *v* **-D, DOSING, -S** to give a specified quantity of medicine

DOSS *v* **-ED, -ING, -ES** to sleep on a makeshift bed

DOST *v* [obs] second person singular present of to do; does

DOTE *v* **-D, DOTING, -S** to bestow or express excessive love or fondness habitually; *also* **DOAT**

DOTH *v* [obs] a third person singular present tense of to do; does

DOTS *v pr t of* **DOT** makes a very small spot

DOTY *adj* **DOTIER, DOTIEST** half-rotten; as, decayed wood or timber

DOUC *n pl* **-S** a rare yellow-faced monkey of the langur family

DOUM *n pl* **-S** Egyptian palm tree with a divided trunk

DOUR *adj* hard; inflexible; obstinate; bold

DOUT *v* [obs] to put out, as a fire; to extinguish

DOUX *adj* very sweet, of champagne

DOVE *n pl* **-S** a small pigeon

DOWL *n* feathery or wool-like down; filament of a feather; *also* **DOWLE**

DOWN *v* **-ED, -ING, -S** to eat or drink something, especially quickly or greedily

DOWY *adj* SCOT., BRIT. dull; melancholy; dismal; *also* **DOWIE**

DOXY *n pl* **-IES** a set of beliefs, especially religious beliefs; *also* **DOXIE**

DOZE *v* **-D, DOZING, -S** to slumber; to sleep lightly

DOZY *adj* **DOZIER, DOZIEST** drowsy; inclined to doze; sleepy; sluggish

DRAB *adj* **-BER, -BEST** lacking brightness or color; dull

DRAG *v* **-GED, -GING, -S** to draw along with effort

DRAM *n pl* **-S** a minute quantity; a very small amount

DRAT *interj* used to express annoyance or frustration

DRAW *v* **DREW** or **DRAWN, -ING, -S** produce by making lines and marks on paper

DRAY *v* **-ED, -ING, -S** to haul by means of a low, heavy sideless cart

DREE *v* **-D, -ING** SCOT., BRIT. to endure; to suffer; *also* **DRIE**

DREG *n pl* **-S** a sediment in liquid

DREK *n* worthless items, especially inferior merchandise; *also* **DRECK**

DREW *v p t of* **DRAW** produced by making lines and marks on paper

DREY *n pl* **-S** the nest of a squirrel

DRIB *n* a small amount

DRIE *v* to endure; to suffer; *also* **DREE**

DRIP *v* **-PED** or **-T, -PING, -S** to fall in drops, a round-shaped amount of liquid

DROP *v* **-PED,** or **-T, -PING, -S** to let go of and cause to fall

DRUB *v* **-BED, -BING, -S** to defeat somebody

DRUG *v* **-GED, -GING, -S** to give someone or something a chemical which causes loss of feeling

DRUM *v* **-MED, -MING, -S** to play an instrument of percussion

DRYS *n pl of* **DRY** prohibitionists

DUAD *n* a union of two; duality; a pair

DUAL *adj* composed of two like or complementary parts

DUBS *v pr t of* **DUB** gives a nickname to

DUCE *n pl* **-S** or **DUCI** a leader or dictator

DUCI *n pl of* **DUCE** leaders or dictators; *also* **DUCES**

DUCK *v* **-ED, -ING, -S** to drop or lower suddenly

DUCT *n pl* **-S** an enclosed conduit through which something can flow or be carried

DUDE *v* **-ED, -ING, -S** informal term meaning to dress up in flashy clothes

DUDS *n pl of* **DUD** bombs or shells that fail to explode

DUEL *v* **-ED** or **-LED, -ING** or **-LING, -S** to oppose actively and forcefully

DUES *n/pl* official payments made to belong to an organization

DUET *n pl* **-S** a vocal and/or instrumental composition for two performers

DUFF *v* **-ED, -ING, -S** to play a bad shot in golf by hitting the ground behind the ball

DUIT *n* a small low-value Dutch coin used between the 15th and 17th centuries; *also* **DOIT**

DUKE *v* **-D, DUKING, -S** to fight especially with fists

DULL *v* **-ED, -ING, -S** to make blunt

DULY *adv* in a proper, correct or suitable way

DUMA *n* an official assembly in Russia during czarist times; *also* **DOUMA**

DUMB *v* **-ED, -ING, -S** to make or become less intellectual

DUMP *v* **-ED, -ING, -S** to deposit or dispose of

DUNE *n pl* **-S** a ridge of sand created by the wind

81

DUNG _v_ **-ED, -ING, -S** to cover land with manure

DUNK _v_ **-ED, -ING, -S** to plunge into liquid; immerse

DUNS _v pr t of_ **DUN** presses for payment of a debt

DUNT _v_ **-ED, -ING, -S** to hit somebody or something

DUOS _n pl of_ **DUO** pairs, couples; instrumental duets

DUPE _v_ **-D, DUPING, -S** to deceive

DURE _adj_ [obs] hard; severe

DURN _v_ **-ED, -ING, -S** informal term meaning to darn, to condemn somebody

DURO _n_ any of a breed of large vigorous red American hogs

DUSK _v_ **-ED, -ING, -S** to become or make dark

DUST _v_ **-ED, -ING, -S** to remove fine, dry particles by wiping, brushing or beating

DUTY _n pl_ **DUTIES** service morally obligatory

DYAD _n pl_ **-S** two units treated as one; a couple; a pair

DYED _v p t of_ **DYE** gave color to fabric, hair, etc.

DYER _n_ someone who gives color to fabric, hair, etc.

DYES _v pr t of_ **DYE** gives color to fabric, hair, etc.

DYKE _v_ **-D, DYKING, -S** to drain with a ditch; _also_ **DIKE**

DYNE _n pl_ **-S** a unit of force; the force that will accelerate a mass of one gram one centimeter per second

DZOS _n pl of_ **DZO** cross between a yak and a cow; _also_ **ZHOS, ZOS**

FIVE LETTERS

DACES _n pl of_ **DACE** small European freshwater fish with a slender bluish-green bodies

DACHA _n pl_ **-S** a Russian cottage

DADDY _n pl_ **-IES** father

DADOS _n pl of_ **DADO** the lower parts of an interior wall when decorated differently from the upper part

DAFFS _v pr t of_ **DAFF** [obs] casts aside; takes off; doffs

DAFFY _adj_ **DAFFIER, DAFFIEST** silly

DAGGA _n_ relatively nontoxic S. African herb smoked like tobacco

DAILY _adv_ every day; day by day

DAIRY _n pl_ **DARIES** a farm where milk products are produced

DAISY _n pl_ **DAISIES** a flowering plant with ray flowers

DAKER _n_ a measure of certain commodities by number; _also_ **DAKIR**

DAKIR _n_ a measure of certain commodities by number; _also_ **DAKER**

DALED _n pl_ **-S** the fourth letter of the Hebrew alphabet; _also_ **DALET, DALETH**

DALES _n pl of_ **DALE** low places between hills; valleys

DALET _n pl_ **-S** the fourth letter of the Hebrew alphabet; _also_ **DALED, DALETH**

DALLY _v_ **DALLIED, -ING, DALLIES** to delay unnecessarily; to while away

DAMAN _n_ a small herbivorous mammal

DAMAR _n_ a hard resin from Southeast Asian trees; _also_ **DAMMAR, DAMMER**

DAMES _n pl of_ **DAME** mistresses of families; ladies; women in authority

DAMNS _v pr t of_ **DAMN** condemns; declares guilty; dooms

DAMPS _v pr t of_ **DAMP** makes somebody or something slightly wet

DANCE _v_ **-D, DANCING, -S** to move with measured steps to the sound of music

DANDI _n_ a boatman; an oarsman

DANDY _adj_ **DANDIER, DANDIEST** fine

DANIO _n pl_ **-S** an aquarium fish

DARED *v p t of* **DARE** challenged; provoked; defied

DARER *n* one who challenges, provokes or defies

DARES *v pr t of* **DARE** challenges; provokes; defies

DARIC *n* a gold coin of ancient Persia

DARNS *v pr t of* **DARN** mends or repairs by filling in with thread or yarn and a needle; *also* **DURNS**

DAROO *n* a large Egyptian sycamore tree

DARTS *v pr t of* **DART** moves swiftly or suddenly

DASHI *n* a fish broth

DASHY *adj* **DASHIER, DASHIEST** ostentatiously fashionable; showy

DATED *v p t of* **DATE** noted or fixed the time of, as of an event

DATER *n pl* **-S** one who notes or fixes the time of, as of an event

DATES *v pr t of* **DATE** notes or fixes the time of, as of an event

DATTO *n* a chief of a Muslim Moro tribe in the Philippine Islands; *also* **DATO, DATU**

DATUM *n pl* **DATA** item of factual information derived from measurement or research

DAUBE *n pl* **-S** a braised meet stew

DAUBS *v pr t of* **DAUB** paints in a coarse or unskillful manner

DAUBY *adj* **DAUBIER, DAUBIEST** smeary; viscous; glutinous; adhesive

DAUNT *v* **-ED, -ING, -S** to overcome; to conquer

DAVEN *v* **-ED, -ING, -S** to recite Jewish liturgical prayers; *also* **DOVEN**

DAVIT *n pl* **-S** a crane-like device on a ship

DAWNS *v pr t of* **DAWN** begins to grow light in the morning

DAZED *v p t of* **DAZE** stupefied or bewildered, as by a glare of light or physical or mental shock

DAZES *v pr t of* **DAZE** stupefies or bewilders, as by a glare of light or physical or mental shock

DEALS *v pr t of* **DEAL** does business; trades

DEALT *v p t of* **DEAL** did business; traded

DEANS *n pl of* **DEAN** the heads of faculties

DEARE *v* [obs] to hurt, to harm, to injure; *also* **DERE**

DEARN *v* SCOT. to hide; to skulk; *also* **DERN, DERNE**

DEARS *n pl of* **DEAR** beloved persons

DEARY *n pl* **DEARIES** a dear, a darling

DEATH *n pl* **-S** end of life

DEAVE *v* **-D, DEAVING, -S** to stun or stupefy with noise; to deafen

DEBAG *v* **-GED, -GING** to remove trousers of someone as a joke

DEBAR *v* **-RED, -RING, -S** to prevent from entering; to keep out

DEBEL *v* [obs] to conquer

DEBIT *v* **-ED, -ING, -S** to remove a sum of money from an account

DEBTS *n pl of* **DEBT** obligations to pay or do something

DEBUG *v* **-GED, -GING, -S** to remove bugs, insects from

DEBUT *n pl* **-S** a beginning or first attempt

DEBYE *n* a unit of electric dipole moment

DECAF *n* coffee or tea with the caffeine removed

DECAL *n pl* **-S** a design fixed to some surface or a paper bearing the design to be transferred to the surface

DECAY *v* **-ED, -ING, -S** to waste away; to decline; to decompose

DECKS *v pr t of* **DECK** dresses elegantly; adorns; embellishes

DECOR *n pl* **-S** a style or scheme of interior decoration

DECOY *v* **-ED, -ING, -S** to lure or entrap with or as if with a decoy, a distractor

DECRY v DECRIED, -ING, DECRIES to express strong disapproval of

DEDAL adj skillful; ingenious; cleverly intricate; also DAEDAL

DEEDS v pr t of DEED signs over or transfers something, especially real estate, to another person

DEEDY adj DEEDIER, DEEDIEST BRIT. industrious; active

DEEMS v pr t of DEEM decides; judges; considers; regards; believes

DEESS n [obs] a goddess

DEFAT v -TED, -TING, -S to remove all or most of the fat of food

DEFER v -RED, -RING, -S to put off; to postpone to a future time

DEFIX v [obs] to fix; to fasten; to establish

DEFOG v -GED, -GING, -S to remove condensed water vapor from

DEGAS v -SED, -SING, -SES to remove gas from

DEGUM v -MED, -MING, -S to deprive of, or free from, gum

DEICE v -D, DEICING, -S to free of ice; prevent or remove ice

DEIFY v DEIFIED, -ING, DEIFIES to treat with supreme regard; godlike

DEIGN v -ED, -ING, -S to esteem worthy; to consider worth notice

DEISM n the doctrine or creed of a deist denying revelation

DEIST n a freethinker

DEITY n pl DIETIES a god or goddess; a heathen god

DEKED v p t of DEKE deceived an opponent in hockey by a fake

DEKES v pr t of DEKE deceives an opponent in hockey by a fake

DEKKO n pl -S BRIT. a quick look or glance

DELAY v -ED, -ING, -S to put off; to defer; to procrastinate

DELED v p t of DELE marked a passage of printed material for deletion

DELES v pr t of DELE marks a passage of printed material for deletion

DELFT n glazed earthenware

DELIS n pl of DELI commonly used abbreviation for delicatessens, shops selling cooked meats, cheeses and unusual or foreign prepared foods

DELLS n pl of DELL small, secluded valleys

DELOO n the duykerbok, a small South African antelope

DELPH n the drain on the land side of a sea embankment

DELTA n pl -S a low triangular area where a river divides before entering a larger body of water

DELTS n pl of DELT commonly used abbreviation for deltoids, thick triangular muscles that cover the shoulder joints

DELVE v -D, DELVING, -S to dig into; to investigate; also DALF, DOLF

DEMES n pl of DEME populations of related species

DEMIT v -TED, -TING, -S to resign; to relinquish; also DIMIT

DEMOB v -BED, -BING, -S to discharge from military service

DEMON n pl -S an evil supernatural being; a devil

DEMOS v pr t of DEMO explains, describes or gives a demonstration of how something works

DEMUR v -RED, -RING, -S to linger; to stay; to tarry

DENAR n pl -S or -I a monetary unit of Macedonia

DENAY n [obs] to deny

DENES n pl of DENE BRIT. narrow wooded valleys

DENIM n pl -S a coarse cotton drilling used for overalls; jeans

DENSE adj -ER, -EST closely crowded together

DENTS *v pr t of* **DENT** causes a slight depression by striking or pressing

DEOXY *adj* having less oxygen than the compound from which it is derived; *also* **DESOXY**

DEPOT *n pl* **-S** a place of deposit for the storing of goods

DEPTH *n pl* **-S** deepness, profoundness, abundance

DERAT *v* **-TED, -TING, -S** to rid of rats

DERAY *n* [obs] disorder; merriment

DERBY *n pl* **-IES** a stiff felt hat with a dome-shaped crown

DERMA *n pl* **-S** the deep vascular inner layer of the skin

DERNE *v* SCOT. to hide; to skulk; *also* **DEARN, DERN**

DERRY *n* a meaningless word often used in the chorus of old songs

DESEX *v* **-ED, -ING, -ES** to remove part or all of the reproductive organs of

DESKS *n pl of* **DESK** pieces of furniture typically having flat or sloping tops for writing and often drawers or compartments

DETER *v* **-RED, -RING, -S** to hinder or prevent from action by fear of consequences

DETOX *v* **-ED, -ING, -ES** to rid of toxic substances

DETUR *n* a present of books given to a meritorious undergraduate student as a prize

DEUCE *n pl* **-S** a tie in tennis or table tennis that requires winning two successive points to win the game

DEVEL *n* SCOT. the devil; *also* **DEEL, DEIL**

DEVEX *adj* [obs] bending down; sloping

DEVIL *n pl* **-S** an evil spirit; a demon

DEVON *n* one of a breed of small, long horned, hardy cattle

DEWAN *n pl* **-S** a government official in India; *also* **DIWAN**

DEWAR *n pl* **-S** an insulated container used to store liquefied gases

DEWAX *v* **-ED, -ING, -ES** to take wax off

DEWED *v p t of* **DEW** wetted with water droplets; moistened

DEVOW *v* [obs] to give up; to devote

DHOBI *n pl* **-S** a person who does laundry in India

DHOLE *n pl* **-S** a fierce, wild dog in the mountains of India

DHONI *n* a Ceylonese boat; *also* **DONI**

DHOTI *n pl* **-S** or **-ES** a loincloth worn by Hindu men in India; *also* **DHOOTI, DHOOTIE, DHUTI**

DHUTI *n pl* **-S** or **-ES** a loincloth worn by Hindu men in India; *also* **DHOOTI, DHOOTIE, DHOTI**

DIALS *v pr t of* **DIAL** calls by turning a dial or using a keypad

DIARY *n pl* **DIARIES** a personal daily journal

DIAZO *adj* relating to or containing a pair of bonded nitrogen atoms

DICED *v p t of* **DICE** cut into small cubes

DICER *n pl* **-S** a mechanical device used for cutting food into small cubes

DICES *v pr t of* **DICE** cuts into small cubes

DICEY *adj* **DICIER, DICIEST** dangerous or tricky

DICKS *n pl of* **DICK** informal term for detectives

DICKY *n pl* **DICKIES** a seat behind a carriage, for a servant

DICOT *n pl* **-S** a flowering plant having two floral organs

DICTA *n pl of* **DICTUM** an authoritative statement

DICTY *adj* **DICTIER, DICTIEST** high-class; stylish; fashionable

DIDAL *n* [obs] a kind of triangular spade

DIDOS *n pl of* **DIDO** shrewd tricks; antics; capers

DIDST *v p t of* **DO** [obs] second person present singular of did

DIENE *n pl* **-S** hydrocarbon with carbon double bonds	**DINOS** *n pl of* **DINO** commonly used abbreviation for dinosaurs
DIETS *v pr t of* **DIET** eats and drinks according to a prescribed selection of foods	**DINTS** *v pr t of* **DINT** drives something in with force
DIGHT *v* **-ED, -ING, -S** [obs] to dress; to adorn	**DIODE** *n pl* **-S** an electronic device that restricts current flow chiefly to one direction
DIGIT *n pl* **-S** a finger or toe in human beings	**DIOTA** *n* a vase or drinking cup having two handles or ears
DIGNE *adj* [obs] worthy; honorable; deserving	**DIPPY** *adj* **DIPPIER, DIPPIEST** not sensible; foolish
DIGUE *n* [obs] a bank; a dike	**DIRER** *adj* having more dreadful or terrible consequences
DIKED *v p t of* **DIKE** drained with a ditch; *also* **DYKED**	**DIRGE** *n pl* **-S** a funeral hymn
DIKER *n pl* **-S** one who builds stone walls; a ditcher	**DIRKS** *v pr t of* **DIRK** stabs with a dirk, a dagger formerly used by Scottish Highlanders
DIKES *v pr t of* **DIKE** drains with a ditch; *also* **DYKES**	**DIRLS** *v pr t of* **DIRL** to thrill; to vibrate; to penetrate
DILLY *n pl* **DILLIES** informal term for a person that is remarkable or outstanding	**DIRTY** *adj* **DIRTIER, DIRTIEST** defiled with dirt; foul; nasty; filthy
DIMER *n pl* **-S** a molecule consisting of two identical simpler molecules	**DISCI** *n pl of* **DISCUS** a quoit; a circular plate intended to be pitched
DIMES *n pl of* **DIME** ten-cent coins of the United States	**DISCO** *v* **-ED, -ING, -S** to dance to disco music, a steady-beat pop music
DIMIT *v* [obs] to resign; to relinquish	
DIMLY *adv* in a dim or obscure manner; not brightly or clearly	**DISCS** *n pl of* **DISC** thin, flat circular objects
DINAR *n pl* **-S** an ancient gold coin of the East	**DISHY** *adj* **DISHIER, DISHIEST** attractive, good looking
DINED *v p t of* **DINE** ate the principal regular meal of the day	**DISKS** *n pl of* **DISK** thin, flat circular objects
DINER *n pl* **-S** a person that dines or eats	**DISME** *n pl* **-S** a United States coin first minted in 1792, worth ten cents
DINES *v pr t of* **DINE** eats the principal regular meal of the day	**DITCH** *n pl* **-ES** a trench made in the earth by digging
DINGE *n* grime or squalor	**DITSY** *adj* **DITSIER, DITSIEST** eccentric; scatterbrained; silly; *also* **DITZY**
DINGO *n pl* **-ES** a wild, wolf-like dog of Australia	**DITTO** *n pl* **-S** the aforesaid thing; repeat an action or statement
DINGS *v pr t of* **DING** makes a ringing sound like that of a bell	**DITTY** *n pl* **-IES** a short simple song or poem
DINGY *adj* **DINGIER, DINGIEST** thickly covered with dirt or soot	
DINKS *n pl of* **DINK** drop shots in racket games	**DITZY** *adj* **DITZIER, DITZIEST** eccentric; scatterbrained; silly; *also* **DITSY**
DINKY *adj* **DINKIER, DINKIEST** of poor quality; shabby; small	

86

DIVAN *n pl* **-S** a long backless sofa or couch

DIVAS *n pl of* **DIVA** operatic prima donnas; distinguished female singers

DIVED *v p t of* **DIVE** plunged into water head foremost

DIVEL *v* [obs] to rend apart

DIVER *n pl* **-S** one who works under water, especially one equipped with breathing apparatus and weighted clothing

DIVES *v p t of* **DIVE** plunges into water head foremost

DIVOT *n pl* **-S** a piece of turf dug out of a lawn or fairway

DIVVY *v* **DIVVIED, -ING, DIVVIES** to divide

DIWAN *n* a government official in India; *also* **DEWAN**

DIXIE *n pl* **-S** BRIT. a large metal pot, gallon camp kettle, for cooking

DIXIT *n* a statement; a dictum

DIZEN *v* **-ED, -ING, -S** [obs] to deck out in fine clothes and ornaments

DIZZY *adj* **DIZZIER, DIZZIEST** having in the head a sensation of whirling

DJINN *n pl* **-S** or **DJINN** in Islamic myth any class of spirits lower than angels, capable of assuming human or animal forms and influencing humankind; *also* **DJIN, DJINNI, JIN, JINN, JINNI**

DOBBY *n pl* **-IES** a weaving tool

DOBIE *n* a playing marble made of clay

DOBLA *n* a medieval Spanish gold coin

DOBRA *n pl* **-S** the basic monetary unit of Sao Tome and Principe

DOCKS *v pr t of* **DOCK** hauls into a dock, a wharf

DODGE *v* **-D, DODGING, -S** to evade by a sudden shift of place

DODGY *adj* **DODGIER, DODGIEST** evasive

DODOS *n pl of* **DODO** extinct heavy flightless birds of Mauritius

DOERS *n pl of* **DOER** people who do something or act in a specified manner

DOEST *v p t of* **DO** does

DOETH *v pr t of* **DO** does

DOFFS *v pr t of* **DOFF** removes an article of clothing, especially a hat

DOGAL *adj* of or pertaining to a doge

DOGES *n pl of* **DOGE** elected chief magistrates in the former republics of Venice and Genoa

DOGEY *n pl* **-S** a motherless calf in a range herd of cattle; *also* **DOGIE, DOGY**

DOGGO *adv* BRIT. remain motionless and quiet to escape detection

DOGGY *n pl* **-IES** a small dog

DOGIE *n pl* **-S** a motherless calf in a range herd of cattle; *also* **DOGEY, DOGY**

DOGMA *n pl* **-S** or **-TA** a formally stated and authoritatively settled doctrine

DOILY *n pl* **DOILIES** a small round fringed piece of linen or paper placed under a dish or bowl; *also* **DOYLY**

DOING *n pl* **-S** anything done; a deed; an action

DOJOS *n pl of* **DOJO** schools for training in Japanese arts of self-defense, such as judo and karate

DOLCE *adv* gently, sweetly or softly

DOLED *v p t of* **DOLE** distributed sparingly

DOLES *v pr t of* **DOLE** distributes sparingly

DOLLS *n pl of* **DOLL** small replicas of people used as toys

DOLLY *n pl* **DOLLIES** a conveyance consisting of a wheeled platform for moving heavy objects

DOLMA *n pl* **-S** or **-DES** a grape or cabbage leaf stuffed with meat

87

DOLOR *n* pain; grief; distress; anguish

DOLTS *n pl of* **DOLT** blockheads; numskulls

DOLUS *n pl* an evil intent, embracing both malice and fraud

DOMAL *adj* pertaining to a dome

DOMED *v p t of* **DOME** formed or rose into a hemispherical shape

DOMES *v pr t of* **DOME** forms or rises into a hemispherical shape

DOMIC *adj* domelike, hemispherical in shape

DONAS *n pl of* **DONA** AUS. a courtesy title for a Spanish lady

DONEE *n pl* **-S** the person to whom a gift or donation is made

DONGA *n* a gully formed by erosion by water

DONGS *v pr t of* **DONG** makes a ringing sound like that of a bell

DONOR *n pl* **-S** one who gives or bestows; a benefactor

DONSY *adj* SCOT., BRIT. unfortunate; ill-fated; unlucky; *also* **DONSIE**

DONUT *n pl* **-S** a small ring-shaped cake; *also* **DOUGHNUT**

DOOLE *adj* [obs] sorrow; dole

DOODY *n pl* **-IES** solid bodily waste

DOOLY *n pl* **DOOLIES** a simple litter, often used to transport sick or wounded persons; *also* **DOOLIE, DHOOLY**

DOOMS *v pr t of* **DOOM** condemns to ruination or death

DOOMY *adj* **DOOMIER, DOOMIEST** doomful; ominous

DOORS *n pl of* **DOOR** movable barriers used to open and close the entrances to a building

DOOZY *n pl* **DOOZIES** informal term for an extraordinary one of its kind; *also* **DOOZER, DOOZIE**

DOPEY *adj* **DOPIER, DOPIEST** half-asleep or drowsy; *also* **DOPY**

DOREE *n* a European marine fish of yellow color

DORKS *n pl of* **DORK** informal term for a foolish people

DORKY *adj* **DORKIER, DORKIEST** foolish

DORMS *n pl of* **DORM** common abbreviation for dormitories, buildings used as living and sleeping quarters by college students

DORMY *adj* being ahead by as many holes in golf as remain to be played in match play; *also* **DORMIE**

DORPS *n pl of* **DORP** villages or small country towns, sometimes perceived as backward

DORSA *n pl of* **DORSUM** the back

DORSE *n* the back of a book

DORTY *adj* SCOT. sullen; sulky

DOSED *v p t of* **DOSE** gave a specified quantity of medicine

DOSER *n* one who doses

DOSES *v pr t of* **DOSE** gives a specified quantity of medicine

DOTAL *adj* pertaining to a dowry, property or money brought by a bride to her husband at marriage

DOTED *v p t of* **DOTE** bestowed or expressed excessive love or fondness habitually

DOTER *n* one who dotes, is excessively fond in love; *also* **DOATER**

DOTES *v pr t of* **DOTE** bestows or expresses excessive love or fondness habitually

DOTTY *adj* **DOTTIER, DOTTIEST** silly

DOUAR *n* a village composed of Arab tents arranged in streets

DOUBT *v* **-ED, -ING, -S** to waver in opinion or judgment

DOUCE *adj* BRIT. sweet; pleasant; sedate

DOUCS *n pl of* **DOUC** rare yellow-faced monkeys of the langur family

DOUGH *n pl* **-S** paste of bread

DOULA *n pl* **-S** a woman who assists another woman during and after childbirth

DOUMA *n* an official assembly in Russia during czarist times; *also* **DUMA**

DOUMS *n pl of* **DOUM** Egyptian palm trees with divided trunks

DOUPE *n* the carrion crow

DOURA *n* a cereal grain of Asia and northern Africa; *also* **DURRA, DOURAH**

DOUSE *v* **-D, DOUSING, -S** to plunge suddenly into water; to duck

DOVEN *v* to recite Jewish liturgical prayers; *also* **DAVEN**

DOVES *n pl of* **DOVE** small pigeons

DOWDY *adj* **DOWDIER, DOWDIEST** plain or unfashionable

DOWED *v p t of* **DOW** SCOT., BRIT. thrived; prospered

DOWEL *n pl* **-S** a pin, or block, of wood or metal for fastening

DOWER *n pl* **-S** a widow's inheritance

DOWIE *adj* SCOT., BRIT. dull; melancholy; dismal; *also* **DOWY**

DOWLE *n* feathery or wool-like down; filament of a feather; *also* **DOWL**

DOWNS *v pr t of* **DOWN** eats or drinks something, especially quickly or greedily

DOWNY *adj* **DOWNIER, DOWNIEST** as soft as down, soft fine feathers

DOWRY *n pl* **-IES** money or property brought by a woman to her husband at marriage; *also* **DOWERY**

DOWSE *v* **-D, DOWSING, -S** to plunge, or duck into water; to immerse; to douse

DOXIE *n pl* **-S** a set of beliefs, especially religious; *also* **DOXY**

DOYEN *n pl* **-S** the eldest man or senior member of a group

DOYLY *n pl* **-IES** a small round fringed piece of linen or paper to place under a dish or bowl; *also* **DOILY**

DOZED *v p t of* **DOZE** slumbered; slept lightly

DOZEN *n pl* **-S** a collection of twelve objects

DOZER *n pl* **-S** one who slumbers or sleeps lightly

DOZES *v pr t of* **DOZE** slumbers; sleeps lightly

DRABA *n* a low-growing cushion-forming flowering plant

DRACO *n* a luminous exhalation from marshy grounds

DRAFF *n* the residue of husks after fermentation of the grain used in brewing, used as food for cattle

DRAFT *n pl* **-S** a preliminary sketch of a design or picture

DRAGS *v pr t of* **DRAG** draws along with effort

DRAIL *v* [obs] to trail; to draggle

DRAIN *v* **-ED, -ING, -S** to cause to flow gradually out or off

DRAKE *n pl* **-S** an adult male of a wild or domestic duck

DRAMA *n pl* **-S** a dramatic work intended for performance by actors on a stage

DRAMS *n pl of* **DRAM** minute quantities; very small amounts

DRANK *v p t of* **DRINK** swallowed anything liquid

DRAPE *v* **-D, DRAPING, -S** to arrange in a particular way

DRAVE *v p t of* **DRIVE** [obs] to keep in motion; to conduct

DRAWL *v* **-ED, -ING, -S** to utter in a slow, lengthened tone

DRAWN *v p part of* **DRAW** produced by making lines and marks on paper

DRAWS *v pr t of* **DRAW** produces by making lines and marks on paper

DRAYS *n pl of* **DRAY** hauls by means of a low, heavy sideless cart

DREAD *v* **-ED, -ING, -S** to fear in a great degree

DREAM *n pl* **-S** a series of mental images and emotions occurring during sleep

DREAR *adj* melancholy

DRECK *n* worthless items, especially inferior merchandise; *also* **DREK**

DREED *v p t of* **DREE** SCOT. endured; suffered

DREGS *n pl of* **DREG** sediments in liquid

DRENT *v* [obs] drenched, drowned

DRESS *v* **-ED, DREST, -ING, -ES** to put on clothes

DREST *v p t of* **DRESS** to put on clothes

DREUL *v* [obs] to drool

DREYS *n pl of* **DREY** nests of squirrels

DRIED *v p t of* **DRY** made free from moisture

DRIER *n pl* **-S** one who, or that which, makes something free from moisture; *also* **DRYER**

DRIES *v pr t of* **DRY** makes free from moisture

DRIFT *v p part* **-ED, -ING** to change or develop gradually, or move slowly from one point or position to another

DRILL *v* **-ED, -ING, -S** to pierce or bore a hole

DRILY *adv* in a dry manner; *also* **DRYLY**

DRINK *v* **DRANK** or **DRUNK, -ING, -S** to swallow anything liquid

DRIPS *v pr t of* **DRIP** falls in drops, a round-shaped amount of liquid

DRIPT *v p t of* **DRIP** fell in drops, a round-shaped amount of liquid

DRIVE *v* **DROVE** or **-N, -ING, -S** to keep in motion; to conduct

DROCK *n* a water course

DROID *n pl* **-S** an intelligent robot; *also* **DROYD**

DROIL *v* [obs] to work sluggishly or slowly; to plod

DROIT *n pl* **-S** claim due to somebody

DROLL *v* **-ED, -ING, -S** to jest; to play the buffoon

DROME *n* a peculiar North African bird, allied to the oyster catcher

DRONE *v* **-D, DRONING, -S** to make a humming or deep murmuring sound

DRONY *adj* **DRONIER, DRONIEST** like a drone; sluggish; lazy

DROOL *v* **-ED, -ING, -S** to drivel

DROOP *v* **-ED, -ING, -S** to hang bending downward

DROPS *v pr t of* **DROP** lets go of and causes to fall

DROPT *v p t of* **DROP** let go of and caused to fall

DROSS *n pl* **-ES** waste matter; refuse

DROUK *v* SCOT. to drench

DROVE *v p t of* **DRIVE** to keep in motion; to conduct

DROVY *adj* turbid; muddy; filthy

DROWN *v* **-ED, -ING, -S** to cover with too much liquid

DRUBS *v pr t of* **DRUB** defeats somebody

DRUGS *v pr t of* **DRUG** gives someone or something a chemical which causes loss of feeling

DRUID *n pl* **-S** one of an order of Celtic priests in ancient times

DRUMS *v pr t of* **DRUM** plays an instrument of percussion

DRUNK *v p t of* **DRINK** swallowed anything liquid

DRUPE *n pl* **-S** a fleshy indehiscent fruit with a single seed

DRUSE *n* a cavity in a rock, having its interior surface studded with crystals; *also* **DRUZE**

DRUXY *adj* [obs] timber having decayed spots or streaks of a whitish color

DRUZE *n* a cavity in a rock, having its interior surface studded with crystals; *also* **DRUSE**

DRYAD *n pl* **-S** or **-ES** a deity or nymph of the woods

DRYAS *n/pl* a creeping plan of the rose family

DRYER *n pl* **-S** one who, or that which, makes something free from moisture; *also* **DRIER**

DRYLY *adj* in a dry manner; not succulently; *also* **DRILY**

DUCAL *adj* of or pertaining to a duke, a rank

DUCAT *n pl* **-S** formerly a gold coin of various European countries

DUCES *n pl of* **DUCE** leaders or dictators; *also* **DUCI**

DUCHY *n pl* **-IES** or **DUCHIES** the territory of a duke or duchess

DUCKS *v pr t of* **DUCK** drops or lowers suddenly

DUCKY *adj* **DUCKIER, DUCKIEST** excellent; fine

DUCTS *n pl of* **DUCT** enclosed conduits through which things can flow or be carried

DUDDY *adj* SCOT. ragged, tattered; *also* **DUDDIE**

DUDED *v p t of* **DUDE** informal term for dressed up in flashy clothes

DUDES *v pr t of* **DUDE** informal term for dresses up in flashy clothes

DUELO *n* [obs] a duel; also, the rules of dueling

DUELS *v pr t of* **DUEL** opposes forcefully and actively

DUETS *n pl of* **DUET** vocal and/or instrumental compositions for two performers

DUFFS *v pr t of* **DUFF** plays a bad shot in golf by hitting the ground behind the ball

DUFUS *n pl* **-ES** informal for a foolish person; *also* **DOOFUS**

DUKED *v p t of* **DUKE** fought, especially with fists

DUKES *v pr t of* **DUKE** fights, especially with fists

DULIA *n* veneration given to angels and saints

DULLS *v pr t of* **DULL** makes blunt

DULLY *adv* in a dull manner; stupidly; slowly; sluggishly

DULSE *n pl* **-S** or **DULSE** a seaweed of a reddish brown color

DUMAL *adj* pertaining to, or set with, briers or bushes; brambly

DUMBS *v pr t of* **DUMB** makes or becomes less intellectual

DUMKA *n pl* **DUMKY** an Eastern European folk ballad

DUMKY *n pl of* **DUMKA** an Eastern European folk ballad

DUMMY *v* **DUMMIED, -ING, DUMMIES** to make an imitation, substitute or copy of something

DUMPS *v pr t of* **DUMP** deposits or disposes of

DUMPY *adj* **DUMPIER, DUMPIEST** having a short and plump shape

DUNAM *n* a unit of land measure in Israel equal to about one acre

DUNCE *n pl* **-S** a person weak in intellect

DUNES *n pl of* **DUNE** ridges of sand created by the wind

DUNGS *v pr t of* **DUNG** covers land with manure

DUNGY *adj* full of dung; filthy; vile; low

DUNKS *v pr t of* **DUNK** plunges into liquid; immerses

DUNNY *n pl* **DUNNIES** AUS. toilet; *also* **DUNNAKIN**

DUNTS *v pr t of* **DUNT** hits somebody or something

DUOMI *n pl of* **DUOMO** cathedrals, especially in Italy

DUOMO *n pl* **-S** or **DUOMI** a cathedral, especially in Italy

DUPED *v p t of* **DUPE** deceived

DUPER *n pl* **-S** a person who deceives another

DUPES *v pr t of* **DUPE** deceives

DUPLE *adj* consisting of or involving two parts or components

DURAL *adj* relating to the dura mater, a brain membrane

DURNS *v pr t of* **DURN** informal term meaning to darn, to condemn somebody; *also* **DARNS**

DUROC *n* a large vigorous red American hog

DURRA _n_ a cereal grain of Asia and northern Africa; _also_ **DOURA, DOURAH**

DURST _v p t of_ **DARE** [obs] to have courage

DURUM _n_ a hardy wheat for making pasta

DUSKS _v pr t of_ **DUSK** makes something dark

DUSKY _adj_ **DUSKIER, DUSKIEST** partially dark or obscure; not luminous

DUSTS _v pr t of_ **DUST** removes fine, dry particles by wiping, brushing or beating

DUSTY _adj_ **DUSTIER, DUSTIEST** filled, covered, or sprinkled with fine, dry particles

DUVET _n pl_ **-S** a down-filled bed quilt

DUXES _n pl of_ **DUX** SCOT. the pupils who are first in their class or school

DWALE _n pl_ **-S** or **DWALE** a poisonous, deadly nightshade plant

DWARF _v_ **-ED, -ING, -S** to make or keep small; to stunt

DWEEB _n pl_ **-S** a boring person

DWELL _v_ **-ED** or **DWELT, -ING, -S** to inhabit; to reside

DWELT _v p t of_ **DWELL** inhabited; resided

DWINE _v_ [obs] to waste away; to pine; to languish; _also_ **DWINDLE**

DYADS _n pl of_ **DYAD** two units treated as one; a couple; a pair

DYING _adj_ about to die; drawing to an end

DYKED _v p t of_ **DYKE** drained with a ditch; _also_ **DIKED**

DYKES _v pr t of_ **DYKE** drains with a ditch; _also_ **DIKES**

DYNES _n pl of_ **DYNE** more than one of the unit of force that will accelerate a mass of one gram one centimeter per second

ED _n_ a commonly used abbreviation for education, knowledge or skill obtained by a learning process

EE _n pl_ **-N** SCOT. an eye

EF _n pl_ **-S** the letter "F"; _also_ **EFF**

EH _interj_ used to express surprise or doubt

EL _n pl_ **-S** an elevated railroad or train

EM _n pl_ **-S** the letter "M"

EN _n pl_ **-S** the letter "N"

ER _interj_ used to express hesitation

ES _n pl of_ **E** more than one of the letter "E"

ET _v p t of_ **EAT** [obs] consumed food

EW _n_ a military action involving electromagnetic energy

EX _v_ **-ED, -ING, -ES** to delete or cross out

EY _n pl_ **-S** an island; _also_ **AIT, AYT, EYET, EYGHT, EYOT**

THREE LETTERS

EAR _v_ **-ED, -ING, -S** to form the fruiting head of a cereal plant

EAT _v_ **ATE, -EN, -ING, -S** to consume food

EAU _n pl_ **EAUX** water

EBB _v_ **-ED, -ING, -S** to recede; to flow back

ECU _n pl_ **-S** an old French coin

EDH _n pl_ **-S** a character used in the runic alphabet to represent the "th" sound in the English words "this" and "other"; _also_ **ETH**

EEK _interj_ used to express sudden fright

EEL _n pl_ **-S** a snakelike fish

EEN _n pl of_ **EE** SCOT. eyes

EFF _n pl_ **-S** the letter "F"; _also_ **EF**

92

EFS *n pl of* **EF** more than one of the letter "F"; *also* **EFFS**

EFT *n pl* **-S** the common newt; *also* **EFFET, EVAT, EVET, EWT**

EGG *v* **-ED, -ING, -S** to incite or urge

EGO *n pl* **-S** a person's sense of self-esteem or self-importance

EIK *n pl* **-N** SCOT. an oak tree

EKE *v* **-D, EKING, -S** to obtain with great effort; *also* **EEKE**

ELD *n* old age

ELF *n pl* **ELVES** a small often mischievous fairy

ELK *n pl* **-S** a large deer

ELL *n pl* **-S** a building extension

ELM *n pl* **-S** a deciduous tree

ELS *n pl of* **EL** elevated railroads or trains

EME *n pl* **-S** SCOT. [obs] an uncle; *also* **EAME**

EMO *n* a music genre that features heavy, guitar-based sound and melodic, emotional tunes

EMS *pl of* **EM** more than one of the letter "M"

EMU *n pl* **-S** a large, flightless Australian bird; *also* **EMEU, EMEW**

END *v* **-ED, -ING, -S** to terminate

ENG *n* a large deciduous tree of Burma similar to Keruing and used for construction work

ENS *n pl of* **EN** more than one of letter "N"

EON *n pl* **-S** an indefinitely long period of time; *also* **AEON**

ERA *n pl* **-S** an epoch

ERD *n* the earth

ERE *prep* before; sooner than, previous

ERF *n pl* **-S, ERVEN** a garden plot in South Africa, usually about half an acre

ERG *n pl* **-S** a unit of work or energy

ERK *n pl* **-S** BRIT. a low-ranking member of the Royal Air Force

ERN *n pl* **-S** a bulky grayish-brown sea eagle; *also* **ERNE**

ERR *v* **-ED, -ING, -S** to be mistaken or incorrect; do wrong

ERS *n* a species of vetch; bitter vetch

ESE *n* [obs] ease; pleasure

ESS *n pl* **-ES** the letter "S"

EST *n* [obs] east

ETA *n pl* **-S** the 7th letter in the Greek alphabet

ETH *n pl* **-S** a character used in the runic alphabet to represent the "th" sound in the English words "this" and "other"; *also* **EDH**

EVE *n pl* **-S** the evening before an event or occasion

EWE *n pl* **-S** a female sheep; *also* **YOWE**

EWT *n* the common newt; *also* **EFFET, EFT, EVAT, EVET**

EYE *v* **-D, EYING, -S** to look at carefully

EYR *n* [obs] air

EYS *n pl of* **EY** islands; *also* **AITS, AYTS, EYETS, EYGHTS, EYOTS**

FOUR LETTERS

EACH *adj* every one of the two or more individuals composing a number of objects

EALE *n* [obs] an intoxicating liquor made from an infusion of malt; *also* **ALE**

EAME *n pl* **-S** SCOT. [obs] an uncle; *also* **EME**

EARL *n pl* **-S** a nobleman of England ranking below a marquis; a count

EARN *v* **-ED, -ING, -S** to merit or deserve, as by labor or service

EARS *v pr t of* **EAR** forms the fruiting head of a cereal plant

EASE *v* **-D, EASING, -S** to alleviate; to free from pain

EAST *n* toward the rising sun; directly opposite of west

EASY *adj* **EASIER, EASIEST** free from pain, trouble, or constraint

EATH *adj* SCOT. easy; *also* **ETHE**

EATS *v pr t of* **EAT** consumes food

EAUX *n pl of* **EAU** waters

EAVE *n pl* **-S** the projecting overhang at the lower edge of a roof

EBBS *v pr t of* **EBB** recedes; flows back

93

EBON *n pl* **-S** the color black; *also* **EBONY**

ECHE *v* **-D, ECHING, -S** [obs] to increase or enlarge

ECHO *v* **-ED, -ING, -ES** or **-S** to resound with repercussion

ECHT *adj* real; genuine

ECRU *n pl* **-S** unbleached; a beige color

ECUS *n pl of* **ECU** old French coins

EDDA *n pl* **-S** tropical starchy tuberous root

EDDO *n pl* **-ES** the edible starchy tuberous root of the taro

EDDY *v* **EDDIED, -ING, EDDIES** to move in a circular movement of water causing a small whirlpool

EDEN *n pl* **-S** a place of complete bliss, delight, and peace

EDGE *v* **-D, EDGING, -S** to provide with an edge; sharpen

EDGY *adj* **EDGIER, EDGIEST** easily irritated; sharp

EDHS *n pl of* **EDH** more than one of the characters used in the runic alphabet to represent the "th" sound in the English words "this" and "other"; *also* **ETHS**

EDIT *v* **-ED, -ING, -S** to select, correct, arrange for publishing

EEKE *v* to obtain with great effort; *also* **EKE**

EELS *n pl of* **EEL** a snakelike fish

EELY *adj* resembling a snakelike fish

EERY *adj* **EERIER, EERIEST** weird, very strange; *also* **EERIE**

EFFS *n pl of* **EFF** more than one of the letter "F"

EFTS *n pl of* **EFT** common newts; *also* **EFFETS, EVATS, EVETS, EWTS**

EGAD *interj* used to express exultation or surprise; *also* **EGADS**

EGAL *adj* [obs] equal; impartial

EGER *n pl* **-S** a high wave caused by tidal flow; *also* **EAGER, EAGRE, EYGRE**

EGGS *v pr t of* **EGG** incites or urges

EGGY *adj* **EGGIER, EGGIEST** containing eggs, the oval thin-shelled reproductive bodies of birds, used as food

EGIS *n* with the support or protection of somebody or something; *also* **AEGIS**

EGOS *n pl of* **EGO** people's senses of self-esteem or self-importance

EIDE *n pl of* **EIDOS** distinctive expressions of the cognitive or intellectual character of a culture or social group

EIKN *n pl of* **EIK** SCOT. oak trees

EILD *n* [obs] the whole duration of a being, a lifetime; *also* **AGE**

EJOO *n* the black gomuti fiber used for making cordage

EKED *v p t of* **EKE** obtained with great effort; *also* **EEKED**

EKES *v pr t of* **EKE** obtains with great effort; *also* **EEKES**

ELAN *n* ardor inspired by passion or enthusiasm

ELHI *adj* relating to, or designed for use in grades 1 to 12

ELIX *v* **-ED, -ING, -ES** to extract

ELKS *n pl of* **ELK** large deer

ELLS *n pl of* **ELL** building extensions

ELMS *n pl of* **ELM** deciduous trees

ELMY *adj* abounding with elm trees

ELSE *adv* other; in a different time, way or place

ELVE *n pl* **-S** a dim, short-lived, expanding disk of reddish light found above thunderstorms

EMES *n pl of* **EME** SCOT. [obs] an uncle; *also* **EAMES**

EMEU *n pl* **-S** a large, flightless Australian bird; *also* **EMEW, EMU**

EMEW *n pl* **-S** a large, flightless Australian bird; *also* **EMEU, EMU**

EMIC *adj* of or relating to the analysis of structural elements in a system, as in behavioral science or linguistics

EMIR *n pl* **-S** a ruler or nobleman of Asia or Africa; *also* **AMIR, AMEER, EMEER**

EMIT *v* **-TED, -TING, -S** to send forth; to throw or give out

EMOS *n pl of* **EMO** informal for young people who mainly wear black clothes and like emo music

EMUS *n pl of* **EMU** large, flightless Australian birds; *also* **EMEUS, EMEWS**

ENDS *v pr t of* **END** terminates

ENOL *n pl* **-S** an organic compound that has a hydroxyl group bonded to a carbon atom that is attached to another carbon atom by a double bond

ENOW *adj* [obs] enough

ENUF *adj* a sufficiency; simplified spelling of enough

ENVY *v* **ENVIED, -ING, ENVIES** to desire something possessed by another

EONS *n pl of* **EON** indefinitely long periods of time

EPEE *n pl* **-S** a fencing sword similar to a foil but with a heavier blade

EPHA *n pl* **-S** an ancient Hebrew unit of dry measure about equal to a bushel; *also* **EPHAH**

EPIC *n pl* **-S** a long narrative poem telling of a hero's deeds

EPOS *n* a body of poetry that conveys the traditions of society by treating some epic theme

ERAS *n pl of* **ERA** epochs

ERFS *n pl of* **ERF** garden plots in South Africa, usually about half an acre; *also* **ERVEN**

ERGO *conj* therefore; consequently; often used in a jocular way

ERGS *n pl of* **ERG** units of work or energy

ERIC *n* [obs] IRISH a recompense formerly given by a murderer to the relatives of the murdered person

ERKE *adj* [obs] slothful

ERKS *n pl of* **ERK** BRIT. low-ranking members of the Royal Air Force

ERNE *n pl* **-S** a bulky grayish-brown sea eagle; *also* **ERN**

ERNS *n pl of* **ERN** bulky grayish-brown sea eagles; *also* **ERNES**

EROS *n* a desire for love or intimacy

ERRS *v pr t of* **ERR** makes a mistake or is incorrect; does wrong

ERSH *n* the stubble of wheat or grass; a stubble field; *also* **ARISH, ARRISH, EARSH**

ERST *adv* [obs] previously; before; formerly; heretofore; first

ESNE *n* a laborer in Anglo-Saxon England

ESPY *v* **ESPIED, ESPING, ESPIES** to catch sight of; to perceive with the eyes

ETAS *n pl of* **ETA** more than one of the 7th letter in the Greek alphabet

ETCH *v* **-ED, -ING, -ES** to produce, as figures or designs, on metal or glass

ETHE *adj* [obs] easy; *also* **EATH**

ETHS *n pl of* **ETH** more than one of the characters used in the runic alphabet to represent the "th" sound in the English words "this" and "other"; *also* **EDHS**

ETIC *adj* relating to a type of linguistic analysis

ETNA *n pl* **-S** a gas burner used in laboratories

ETUI *n pl* **-S** a small ornamental case for one or several small articles; *also* **ETWEE**

EUGE *n* [obs] applause

EURO *n pl* **-S** the basic monetary unit of most countries of the European Union

EVAT *n pl* **-S** the common newt; *also* **EFFET, EFT, EVET, EWT**

EVEN *v* **-ED, -ING, -S** to make or become level or more equal

EVER *adv* at any time; at any period or point of time

EVES *n pl of* **EVE** evenings before events or occasions

EVET *n pl* **-S** the common newt; *also* **EFFET, EFT, EVAT, EWT**

EVIL *adj* **-ER, -EST** morally objectionable behavior; in a very bad manner

EWER *n pl* **-S** a kind of wide mouthed pitcher or jug

EWES *n pl of* **EWE** more than one female sheep; *also* **YOWES**

EXAM *n pl* **-S** commonly used abbreviation for examination; a test

EXEC *n pl* **-S** commonly used abbreviation for an executive, one who exercises administrative or managerial control

EXED *v p t of* **EX** deleted or crossed out

EXES *v pr t of* **EX** deletes or crosses out

EXIT *v* **-ED, -ING, -S** to leave something such as a room, building or gathering

EXON *n pl* **-S** a discontinuous sequence of DNA that carries the genetic code for the final messenger RNA molecule

EXPO *n pl* **-S** commonly used abbreviation for a public exhibition or trade fair

EYAS *n pl* **-ES** a young hawk or falcon; *also* **EYASS**

EYED *v p t of* **EYE** looked at carefully

EYEN *n pl of* **EYE** [obs] the organs of sight or vision; *also* **EYNE**

EYER *n pl* **-S** one who looks at another

EYES *v pr t of* **EYE** looks at carefully

EYET *n pl* **-S** an island; *also* **AIT, AYT, EY, EYGHT, EYOT**

EYLE *v* [obs] to ail

EYNE *n pl of* **EYE** [obs] organs of sight or vision; *also* **EYEN**

EYOT *n pl* **-S** an island; *also* **AIT, AYT, EY, EYGHT, EYET**

EYRA *n pl* **-S** a long-bodied, long-tailed tropical wildcat

EYRE *n pl* **EYRIES** the nest of a bird of prey; *also* **AERIE, AERY, AYRIE, AYRY, EYRIE, EYRY**

EYRY *n pl* **EYRIES** the nest of a bird of prey; *also* **AERIE, AERY, AYRIE, AYRY, EYRE, EYRIE**

EZED *n* the 26th letter of the Roman alphabet

FIVE LETTERS

EAGER *n pl* **-S** a high wave caused by tidal flow; *also* **EAGRE, EGER, EYGRE**

EAGLE *n pl* **-S** a golf score of two strokes under par on a hole

EAGRE *n pl* **-S** a high wave caused by tidal flow; *also* **EAGER, EGER, EYGRE**

EAMES *n pl of* **EAME** SCOT. [obs] uncles; *also* **EMES**

EARAL *adv* [obs] receiving by the ear

EARED *adj* having ears

EARLS *n pl of* **EARL** noblemen of England ranking below marquis; counts

EARLY *adv* **EARLIER, EARLIEST** in advance of the usual or appointed time

EARNS *v pr t of* **EARN** merits or deserves, as by labor or service

EARSH *n* the stubble of wheat or grass; a stubble field; *also* **ARISH, ARRISH, ERSH**

EARTH *v* **-ED, -ING, -S** to cover with dirt or mold; to bury

EASED *v p t of* **EASE** alleviated; freed from pain

EASEL *n pl* **-S** an upright tripod for displaying something

EASES *v pr t of* **EASE** alleviates; frees from pain

EATEN *v p part of* **EAT** to have consumed food

EATER *n pl* **-S** someone who consumes food

EAVED *adj* pertaining to the edges or lower borders of a roof

EAVES *n pl of* **EAVE** the projecting overhangs at the lower edge of a roof

EBBED *v p t of* **EBB** receded; flowed back

EBONS *n pl of* **EBON** black colors; *also* **EBONIES**

EBONY *n pl* **EBONIES** the color black; *also* **EBON**

EBOOK *n pl* **-S** an electronic version of a traditional print book

ECALL *n* European green woodpecker; *also* **EAQUALL, ECCLE, ECKLE, YAFFLE**

ECCLE *n* European green woodpecker; *also* **EAQUALL, ECALL, ECKLE, YAFFLE**

ECHED *v p t of* **ECHE** [obs] increased or enlarged

ECHES *v pr t of* **ECHE** [obs] increases or enlarges

ECHOS *v pr part of* **ECHO** resounds with repercussion; *also* **ECHOES**

ECKLE *n* European green woodpecker; *also* **EAQUALL, ECALL, ECCLE, YAFFLE**

ECLAT *n* brilliant success or effort

ECRUS *n pl of* **ECRU** unbleached; beige colors

ECTAD *adv* outward; toward the outside

ECTAL *adj* pertaining to, or situated near, the surface; outer

EDDAS *n pl of* **EDDA** tropical starchy tuberous roots

EDEMA *n pl* **-S** or **-TA** abnormal collecting of fluids in the cells, tissues, or body cavities; *also* **OEDEMA**

EDENS *n pl of* **EDEN** places of complete bliss, delight, and peace

EDGED *v p t of* **EDGE** provided with an edge; sharpened

EDGER *n pl* **-S** a tool used to trim the edges of a lawn

EDGES *v pr t of* **EDGE** provides with an edge; sharpens

EDICT *n pl* **-S** a formal or authoritative proclamation

EDIFY *v* **EDIFIED, EDIFING, EDIFIES** to instruct or improve morally or intellectually

EDILE *n pl* **-S** a magistrate in ancient Rome; *also* **AEDILE**

EDITS *v pr t of* **EDIT** selects, corrects, arranges for publishing

EDUCE *v* **-D, EDUCING, -S** to bring or draw out; to cause to appear

EDUCT *n pl* **-S** that which is drawn out, as by analysis

EEKED *v p t of* **EEKE** obtained with great effort; *also* **EKED**

EEKES *v pr t of* **EEKE** obtains with great effort; *also* **EKES**

EERIE *adj* **-R, -ST** weird, very strange; *also* **EERY**

EGADS *interj* used to express exultation or surprise; *also* **EGAD**

EGERS *n pl of* **EGER** high waves caused by tidal flow; *also* **EAGERS, EAGRES, EYGRES**

EGEST *v* **-ED, -ING, -S** to eliminate from the body; to excrete

EFFET *n pl* **-S** the common newt; *also* **EFT, EVAT, EVET, EWT**

EGGAR *n pl* **-S** a moth whose larvae are known as tent caterpillars; *also* **EGGER**

EGGED *v p t of* **EGG** incited or urged

EGGER *n pl* **-S** a moth whose larvae are known as tent caterpillars; *also* **EGGAR**

EGRET *n pl* **-S** a white wading bird

EIDER *n pl* **-S** a sea duck much valued for the fine soft down of the females

EIDOS *n pl* **EIDE** the distinctive expression of the cognitive or intellectual character of a culture or social group

EIGHT *n pl* **-S** a number; one greater than seven

EIGNE *n* a legal term meaning firstborn, eldest

EIKON *n pl* **-S** an image or effigy; *also* **ICON, IKON**

EJECT *v* -ED, -ING, -S to expel; to dismiss; to cast forth

EKING *v pr part of* **EKE** obtaining with great effort; *also* **EEKING**

ELAIN *n* a naturally occurring oil that is found in fats; *also* **OLEIN**

ELAND *n pl* -S a large African antelope with short twisted horns

ELATE *v* -ED, **ELATING,** -S to make somebody very happy

ELBOW *v* -ED, -ING, -S to push or hit somebody with the joint or bend of the arm

ELDER *n pl* -S one who is older; a superior in age; a senior

ELECT *v* -ED, -ING, -S to pick out; to select; to choose

ELEGY *n pl* **ELEGIES** a mournful or plaintive poem; a funereal song

ELEMI *n pl* -S a fragrant gum resin from tropical trees

ELFIN *adj* like a little elf or urchin; small and lively

ELIDE *v* -D, **ELIDING,** -S to omit or slur over in pronunciation

ELINT *n* the gathering of intelligence by monitoring with electronic equipment from airplanes, ships or satellites

ELITE *n pl* -S a group or class of persons enjoying superior intellectual, social or economic status

ELOGY *n pl* **ELOGIES** laudatory obituary notice; *also* **EULOGY**

ELOIN *v* -ED, -ING to remove to a distance, especially beyond the jurisdiction of a court; *also* **ELOIGN**

ELONG *v* [obs] to lengthen out; to prolong

ELOPE *v* -D, **ELOPING,** -S to run away, or escape privately to be married

ELUDE *v* -D, **ELUDING,** -S to avoid slyly, to escape

ELUTE *v* -D, **ELUTING,** -S to wash out with a solvent

ELVAN *adj* pertaining to elves; elvish

ELVER *n pl* -S a young conger or sea eel

ELVES *n pl of* **ELF** small often mischievous fairies

EMAIL *v* -ED, -ING, -S to send a message via computer

EMBAR *v* -RED, -RING to bar or shut in; to enclose securely

EMBAY *v* -ED, -ING, -S to put, shelter, or detain in, or as if in bay

EMBED *v* -DED, -DING, -S to lay in surrounding matter; to bed

EMBER *n pl* -S a lighted coal, smoldering amid ashes

EMBOW *v* -ED, -ING, -S to bend like a bow; to curve

EMBOX *v* -ED, -ING, -S to enclose, as in a box

EMCEE *v* -D, -ING, -S to serve as master of ceremonies

EMEER *n pl* -S a ruler or nobleman of Asia or Africa; *also* **AMIR, AMEER, EMIR**

EMEND *v* -ED, -ING, -S to edit text; to correct; *also* **EMENDATE**

EMERY *n pl* **EMERIES** a hard gray-black mineral, used as an abrasive

EMEUS *n pl of* **EMEU** large, flightless Australian birds; *also* **EMEWS, EMUS**

EMEWS *n pl of* **EMEW** large, flightless Australian birds; *also* **EMEUS, EMUS**

EMIRS *n pl of* **EMIR** rulers or noblemen of Asia or Africa; *also* **AMIRS, AMEERS, EMEERS**

EMITS *v pr t of* **EMIT** sends forth; throws or gives out

EMMER *n* a type of wheat grown as livestock feed

EMMET *n pl* -S [obs] an ant

EMMEW *v* [obs] to mew or coop up

EMOTE *v* -D, **EMOTING,** -S to express emotion, especially in an excessive or theatrical manner

EMPTY *v* **EMPTIED,** -ING, **EMPTIES** to remove the contents of

ENACT *v* -ED, -ING, -S to decree; to make into a law

ENATE *adv* related on one's mother's side; *also* **ENATIC**

ENDED *v p t of* **END** terminated

ENDER *n pl* -S one who, or that which, terminates something

ENDOW *v* -ED, -ING, -S to provide with something freely or naturally; *also* **INDOW**

ENDUE *v* -D, ENDUING, -S to provide with something; *also* **INDUE**

ENEMA *n pl* -S or -TA cleaning of the bowels by injection of a solution

ENEMY *n pl* **ENEMIES** one hostile to another; a foe

ENGLE *n* [obs] a favorite; a paramour

ENJOY *v* -ED, -ING, -S to take satisfaction; to live in happiness

ENNEW *v* [obs] to make new

ENNUI *n* a feeling of weariness and disgust

ENODE *v* [obs] to clear of knots; to make clear

ENOKI *n pl* -S a whitish cultivated mushroom

ENOLS *n pl of* **ENOL** organic compounds that have a hydroxyl group bonded to a carbon atom that is attached to another carbon atom by a double bond

ENORM *adj* [obs] enormous; huge

ENROL *v* -LED, -LING, -S to enroll; to register formally; *also* **ENROLL**

ENSKY *v* ENSKIED or -ED, -ING, -S to place in the sky or in heaven

ENSUE *v* -D, ENSUING, -S to follow; to pursue and overtake

ENTAD *adv* toward the inside or central part

ENTAL *adj* pertaining to or situated on the inside

ENTER *v* -ED, -ING, -S to come or go into

ENTIA *n pl of* **ENS** existing or real things; entities

ENTRY *n pl* **ENTRIES** the act of coming or going into

ENURE *v* -D, ENURING, -S over a period of time, to harden someone to something undesirable; *also* **INURE**

ENVIE *v* -D, ENVYING, -S [obs] to emulate; to strive; *also* **VIE**

ENVOI *n pl* -S [obs] closing of a poem or prose work; *also* **ENVOY**

ENVOY *n pl* -S closing of a poem or prose work; *also* **ENVOI**

ENZYM *n pl* -S a complex protein, *also* **ENZYME**

EOSIN *n pl* -S a yellow or brownish red dyestuff; *also* **EOSINE**

EPACT *n pl* -S the difference between the length of a solar and lunar year

EPEES *n pl of* **EPEE** fencing swords similar to foils but with heavier blades

EPHAH *n pl* -S an ancient Hebrew unit of dry measure about equal to a bushel; *also* **EPHA**

EPHAS *n pl of* **EPHA** ancient Hebrew units of dry measure about equal to a bushel; *also* **EPHAHS**

EPHOD *n pl* -S an ancient Hebrew vestment

EPHOR *n pl* -S or -I an ancient Greek magistrate

EPICS *n pl of* **EPIC** long narrative poems telling of a hero's deeds

EPOCH *n pl* -S a period marked by distinctive character

EPODE *n pl* -S the after song; the last part of a lyric ode or poem

EPOPT *n* one instructed in the mysteries of a secret system

EPOXY *n pl* **EPOXIES** a flexible synthetic resin

EPURE *n* a draught or model from which to build

EQUAL *n pl* **-S** someone or something that is the same in quantity, size, quality, degree or value of another

EQUID *n pl* **-S** an animal of the horse family

EQUIP *v* **-PED, -PING, -S** to supply with whatever is necessary

ERASE *v* **-D, ERASING, -S** to rub or scrape out; to efface

ERECT *v* **-ED, -ING, -S** to raise; to build; to construct

ERGOT *n pl* **-S** a fungus that infects rye and other cereals

ERNES *n pl of* **ERNE** bulky grayish-brown sea eagles; *also* **ERNS**

ERODE *v* **-D, ERODING, -S** to wear away by contact friction

EROSE *adj* irregular, as if gnawed away

ERRED *v p t of* **ERR** made a mistake or was incorrect; did wrong

ERROR *n pl* **-S** a mistake; an incorrectness

ERUCA *n* an insect in the larval state

ERUCT *v* **-ED, -ING, -S** to belch

ERUPT *v* **-ED, -ING, -S** to cause to burst forth

ERVEN *n pl of* **ERF** garden plots, usually about half an acre; *also* **ERFS**

ERVIL *n pl* **-S** a vetch grown in Europe, used mainly for forage

ESCAR *n* a mound or ridge of gravelly and sandy drift; *also* **ESCHAR, ESKAR, ESKER**

ESCOT *v* [obs] to pay the reckoning for; to support; to maintain

ESKAR *n* a mound or ridge of gravelly and sandy drift; *also* **ESCHAR, ESCAR, ESKER**

ESKER *n pl* **-S** a mound or ridge of gravelly and sandy drift; *also* **ESCHAR, ESKAR, ESCAR**

ESSAY *v* **-ED, -ING, -S** to make an effort or attempt; to try

ESSES *n pl of* **ESS** more than one of the letter "S"

ESTER *n pl* **-S** a type of chemical compound

ESTOP *v* **-PED, -PING, -S** to impede or prohibit by a legal restraint

ESTRE *n* [obs] the inward part of a building; the interior

ETAPE *n pl* **-S** a warehouse

ETHER *n pl* **-S** a colorless volatile highly inflammable liquid formerly used as an inhalation anesthetic

ETHIC *n pl* **-S** a system of principles governing morality and acceptable conduct

ETHOS *n* shared fundamental traits of a culture, era, or community

ETHYL *n* an alkyl radical derived from ethane

ETNAS *n pl of* **ETNA** gas burners used in laboratories

ETTIN *n* [obs] a giant

ETUDE *n pl* **-S** a short composition for a solo instrument

ETUIS *n pl of* **ETUI** small ornamental cases for one or several small articles; *also* **ETWEES**

ETWEE *n* a small ornamental case for one or several small articles; *also* **ETUI**

ETYMA *n pl of* **ETYMON** derivations of words; *also* **ETYMONS**

EUROS *n pl of* **EURO** more than one of the basic monetary unit of most countries of the European Union

EVADE *v* **-D, EVADING, -S** to attempt to escape; practice artifice

EVENS *v pr t of* **EVEN** makes or becomes level or more equal

EVENT *n pl* **-S** any incident, good or bad that happens

EVERT *v* **-ED, -ING, -S** to turn inside out or outward

EVERY *adj* used to indicate each member of a group without exception

EVICT *v* **-ED, -ING, -S** to expel by legal process

EVILS *n pl of* **EVIL** things that are morally objectionable or very bad

EVITE *v* [obs] **-D, EVITING, -S** to shun, to avoid

EVOKE *v* **-D, EVOKING, -S** to bring to mind a memory

EWERS *n pl of* **EWER** kind of wide-mouthed pitchers or jugs

EWERY *n pl* **EWERIES** [obs] a room for storing ewers, towels, napkins, etc.

EXACT *adj* precisely or definitely conceived or stated

EXALT *v* **-ED, -ING, -S** to raise high; to elevate; to lift up

EXAMS *n pl of* **EXAM** commonly used abbreviation for examinations; tests

EXCEL *v* **-LED, -LING, -S** to go beyond or surpass

EXCUR *v* [obs] to run out or forth; to extend

EXEAT *n pl* **-S** a license for absence from a college or a religious house

EXECS *n pl of* **EXEC** commonly used abbreviation for executives, those who exercises administrative or managerial control

EXERT *v* **-ED, -ING, -S** to put forth strenuous effort

EXILE *v* **-D, -ING, -S** to enforce removal from one's native country

EXINE *n pl* **-S** the outer layer of certain spores

EXING *v pr part of* **EX** deleting or crossing out

EXIST *v* **-ED, -ING, -S** to be

EXITS *v pr t of* **EXIT** leaves something such as a room, building or gathering

EXODE *n* the final chorus; the catastrophe

EXODY *n* [obs] exodus; withdrawal

EXONS *n pl of* **EXON** discontinuous sequences of DNA that carry the genetic code for final messenger RNA molecules

EXPAT *n pl* **-S** BRIT. informal term for a person who lives outside their native country

EXPEL *v* **-LED, -LING, -S** to keep out, off or away; to exclude

EXPOS *n pl of* **EXPO** commonly used abbreviation for public exhibitions or trade fairs

EXTOL *v* **-LED, -LING, -S** to place on high; to lift up; to elevate

EXTRA *n pl* **-S** something that is beyond what is due, usual, expected or necessary

EXUDE *v* **-D, EXUDING, -S** to discharge through pores or incisions

EXULT *v* **-ED, -ING, -S** to be in high spirits; to triumph

EXURB *n pl* **-S** a prosperous residential area beyond the suburbs of a city

EYASS *n pl* **-ES** a young hawk or falcon; *also* **EYAS**

EYERS *n pl of* **EYER** those who look at others

EYETS *n pl of* **EYET** islands; *also* **AITS, AYTS, EYOTS, EYGHTS, EYS**

EYGHT *n pl* **-S** islands; *also* **AIT, AYT, EYET, EYOT, EY**

EYGRE *n pl* **-S** a high wave caused by tidal flow; *also* **EAGER, EAGRE, EGER**

EYING *v pr part of* **EYE** looking at carefully

EYOTS *n pl of* **EYOT** islands; *also* **AITS, AYTS, EYETS, EYGHTS, EYS**

EYRAS *n pl of* **EYRA** long-bodied, long-tailed tropical wildcats

EYRIE *n pl* **-S** the nest of a bird of prey; *also* **AERIE, AERY, AYRIE, AYRY, EYRE, EYRY**

EYRIR *n pl* **AURAR** a monetary unit of Icelandic currency, equal to one hundredth of a krona

FA *n* the 4th musical note of a major scale

FY *interj* [obs] expressing disapproval or disgust; *also* **FIE**

THREE LETTERS

FAB *adj* commonly used abbreviation for fabulous

FAC *n* a large ornamental letter used by early printers

FAD *n pl* **-S** an interest with brief popularity

FAE *n pl* **-S** a fairy, a tiny being possessing magical powers; *also* **FAERIE, FAERY, FAIE, FAIRY, FAY, FEY**

FAG *v* **-GED, -GING, -S** to become weary; to tire

FAN *v* **-NED, -NING, -S** to blow on something

FAP *adj* [obs] fuddled; drunk

FAR *adj* distant in any direction; not near

FAT *n pl* **-S** nutritional component of food

FAX *v* **-ED, -ING, -ES** to transmit documents by electronic means

FAY *n pl* **-S** a fairy, a tiny being possessing magical powers; *also* **FAE, FAERIE, FAERY, FAIE, FAIRY, FEY**

FED *v p part* of **FEED** gave food to; supplied with nourishment

FEE *n pl* **-S** a fixed charge for a privilege or professional services

FEH *interj* used to express disgust, contempt or scorn

FEM *n* a commonly used abbreviation for feminine or female

FEN *n pl* **-S** low land overflowed, boggy land; moor; marsh

FER *adj* [obs] far

FET *v* [obs] to fetch

FEU *n pl* **-S** SCOT. a right to use land in return for an annual fee

FEW *adj* not many; small, limited or confined in number

FEY *n pl* **-S** a fairy, a tiny being possessing magical powers; *also* **FAE, FAERIE, FAERY, FAIE, FAIRY, FAY**

FEZ *n pl* **–ES** or **-ZES** a felt or cloth cap, usually red with a tassel

FIB *v* **-BED, -BING, -S** to speak falsely

FID *n pl* **-S** a conical wooden or metal bar or pin used to support or anything

FIE *interj* expressing disapproval or disgust; *also* **FY**

FIG *n pl* **-S** fleshy, sweet, pear-shaped fruit eaten fresh or preserved or dried

FIN *n pl* **-S** a stabilizing appendage meant to direct flight through water or air

FIR *n pl* **-S** an evergreen tree with needle-shaped leaves

FIT *v* **-TED, -TING, -S** satisfy a condition or restriction, make correspond or harmonize

FIX *v* **-ED, -ING, -ES** to make firm, to arrange, to repair

FLU *n pl* **-S** an acute febrile highly contagious viral disease

FLY *v* **FLEW** or **FLOWN, -ING, FLIES** move through the air

FOB *v* [obs] **-BED, -BING** to cheat or deceive

FOE *n pl* **-S** an enemy in war; a hostile army

FOG *v* **-GED, -ING, -S** to make or become obscured

FOH *interj* exclaiming abhorrence or contempt; *also* **FAUGH, FUGH**

FON *n* [obs] a fool; an idiot

FOP *v* **-PED, -PING** [obs] to deceive

FOR *prep* because; by reason that; in favor of

FOU *adj* SCOT. full of food or drink

FOX *v* -ED, -ING, -ES to act cunningly; to cheat

FOY *n* [obs] faith; loyalty

FRO *adv* from; away; back or backward

FRY *v* FRIED, -ING, FRIES to cook in a pan or on a griddle; cook in oil or fat

FUB *v* -BED, -BING [obs] to put off by trickery; to cheat

FUD *n* commonly used abbreviation for fuddy-duddy, an unimaginative person

FUG *v* -GED, -GING, -S BRIT. to make stuffy and odorous

FUM *v* [obs] to play upon a fiddle

FUN *adj* enjoyable

FUR *n pl* -S animal hair

FOUR LETTERS

FACE *v* -D, FACING, -S to oppose or meet defiantly

FACT *n pl* -S a piece of information about circumstances that exist or events that have occurred

FADE *v* -D, -DING, -S to grow weak; to lose strength; to wither

FADS *n pl of* FAD interests with brief popularity

FADY *adj* [obs] weak; lacking strength

FAES *n pl of* FAE fairies, tiny beings possessing magical powers; *also* FAERIES, FAIES, FAIRIES, FAYS, FEYS

FAGS *v pr t of* FAG becomes weary; tires

FAIE *n pl* -S a fairy, a tiny being possessing magical powers; *also* FAE, FAERIE, FAERY, FAIRY, FAY, FEY

FAIL *v* -ED, -ING, -S to fall short; to be found lacking

FAIN *adj* well-pleased; glad; apt; fond; inclined; *also* FAWE

FAIR *adj* free from favoritism or self-interest; without bias or deception

FAKE *v* -D, FAKING, -S to cheat; to swindle; to steal

FALL *v* FELL, -ING, -S to descend, either suddenly or gradually

FALX *n pl* FALCES a sickle-shaped anatomical structure

FAME *v* -D, FAMING, -S to become widely honored and acclaimed

FAND *v* [obs] to come upon, often by accident; to meet with; *also* FIND

FANE *n* a temple; a church

FANG *n pl* -S a long, sharp, pointed tooth, especially a canine tooth

FANS *v pr t of* FAN blows on something

FARD *v* [obs] to apply cosmetics to the face

FARE *v* -D, FARING, -S to get on in a particular way in doing something

FARL *n pl* -S SCOT. a triangular cake; a scone

FARM *n pl* -S any tract of land devoted to agricultural purposes

FARO *n* a card game in which the players lay wagers on the top card of the deck

FART *n pl* -S a boring, contemptible person

FASH *v* SCOT. to vex; to tease; to trouble; to upset

FAST *v* -ED, -ING, -S to abstain from food voluntarily for a time

FATE *v* -D, FATING, -S to destine; to predetermine the course of events

FATS *n pl of* FAT nutritional components of food

FAUN *n pl* -S a rural deity represented as having the body of a man and the horns, ears, tail and sometimes legs of a goat

FAUX *adj* not genuine or real; being an imitation

FAVA *n* the edible seed (bean) of a climbing vine

FAVE *n pl* -S informal term for favorite, something that is preferred above all others

103

FAWE *adj* [obs] well-pleased; glad; apt; fond; inclined; *also* **FAIN**

FAWN *v* **-ED, -ING, -S** seek favor by flattery

FAYS *n pl of* **FAY** fairies, tiny beings possessing magical powers; *also* **FAES, FEYS, FAIES, FAERIES**

FAZE *v* **-D, FAZING, -S** to disturb the composure of; *also* **FEAZE**

FEAL *adj* [obs] faithful; loyal

FEAR *v* **-ED, -ING, -S** to be afraid or scared of

FEAT *n pl* **-S** an act; a deed; an exploit

FEDS *n pl of* **FED** informal term for federal agents

FEED *v* **FED, -ING, -S** to give food to; to supply with nourishment

FEEL *v* **FELT, -ING, -S** to perceive by the touch; to handle

FEES *n pl of* **FEE** fixed charges for privileges or professional services

FEET *n pl of* **FOOT** the terminal parts of the leg of man or animal

FELE *adj* [obs] many

FELL *v p t of* **FALL** descended, either suddenly or gradually

FELT *v p t of* **FEEL** perceived by the touch; handled

FEME *n pl* **-S** a woman or wife; *also* **FEMME**

FEND *v* **-ED, -ING, -S** to keep off; to ward off

FENS *n pl of* **FEN** low land overflowed, boggy land; moor; marsh

FEOD *n* [obs] a feud; a contention or quarrel

FERE *n* [obs] a consort, husband or wife; a companion; *also* **FEERE**

FERM *n* [obs] a farm; an abode

FERN *n pl* **-S** a flowerless, seedless vascular plant

FERS *adj* [obs] furious; violent; unrestrained; *also* **FIERCE**

FESS *n pl* **-ES** a wide band forming the middle section of a shield; *also* **FESSE**

FEST *n pl* **-S** a gathering with emphasis on a particular activity

FETA *n* a white sheep or goat cheese popular in Greece

FETE *v* **-D, FETING, -S** to honor with an elaborate festival

FEUD *v* **-ED, -ING, -S** quarrelling between two or more parties

FEUS *n pl of* **FEU** SCOT. a right to use land in return for an annual fee

FEYS *n pl of* **FEY** fairies, tiny beings possessing magical powers; *also* **FAES, FAERIES, FAIES, FAIRIES, FAYS**

FIAR *n* SCOT. one in whom the property of an estate is vested, subject to the estate of a life renter

FIAT *n pl* **-S** an authoritative command or order

FIBS *v pr t of* **FIB** speaks falsely

FICE *n* [obs] a nervous belligerent little mongrel dog; *also* **FYCE, FEIST**

FICO *n pl* **-ES** [obs] obscene gesture of contempt

FIDO *n pl* **-S** a coin containing a minting error

FIDS *n pl of* **FID** conical wooden or metal bars or pins used to support things

FIEF *n pl* **-S** a piece of land held under the feudal system

FIFE *n* a small shrill pipe, resembling the piccolo flute

FIGS *n pl of* **FIG** fleshy sweet pear-shaped fruits eaten fresh or preserved or dried

FILA *n pl of* **FILUM** threadlike anatomical structures; filaments

FILE *v* **-D, -ING, -S** to store something in order

FILL *v* **-ED, -ING, -S** to make full

FILM *n pl* **-S** a thin skin; a pellicle; a membranous covering

FILO *n* very thin pastry dough; *also* **FILLO, PHYLLO**

FIND *v* **FOUND, -ING, -S** to come upon, often by accident; to meet with; *also* **FAND**

FINE *adj* **FINER, FINEST** excellent; of top quality

FINK *v* **-ED, -ING, -S** to inform against another person

FINO *n* a pale, very dry sherry

FINS *n pl of* **FIN** stabilizing appendages meant to direct flight through water or air

FIRE *v* **-D, FIRING, -S** to be discharged

FIRK *v* [obs] to beat; to strike; to chastise

FIRM *v* **-ED, -ING, -S** to fix; to settle; to confirm; to establish

FIRN *n* snow that did not melt in the previous summer

FIRS *n pl of* **FIR** evergreen trees with needle-shaped leaves

FISC *n* a public, royal or state treasury

FISH *v* **-ED, -ING, -ES** to catch or try to catch fish

FIST *n pl* **-S** the hand closed tightly

FITS *v pr t of* **FIT** satisfies a condition or restriction; makes correspond or harmonize

FIVE *n pl* **-S** a number; one more than four

FIXT *v p t of* **FIX** [obs] to make firm, to arrange

FIZZ *v* **-ED, -ING, -ES** to make a hissing sound, as a burning fuse

FLAB *n* a soft fatty body tissue

FLAG *n pl* **-S** a cloth bearing devices to indicate nationality

FLAK *n* the fire of antiaircraft guns

FLAM *n* a drumbeat of two strokes of which the first is a very quick grace note

FLAN *n pl* **-S** a tart with a filling of custard, fruit or cheese

FLAP *v* **-ED, -ING, -S** to move or sway repeatedly

FLAT *adj* **-TER, -EST** having an even and horizontal surface

FLAW *n pl* **-S** a crack or breach; a gap or fissure; a defect

FLAX *n* a fiber used to make linen

FLAY *v* **-ED, -ING, -S** to strip off the skin or surface of

FLEA *n pl* **-S** a wingless blood-sucking parasitic insect

FLED *v p t of* **FLEE** ran away

FLEE *v* **FLED, -ING, -S** to run away

FLET *v p part of* **FLEET** [obs] skimmed

FLEW *v p t of* **FLY** moved through the air

FLEX *v* **-ED, -ING, -ES** to bend, as to flex the arm

FLEY *v* **-ED, -ING, -S** SCOT. to frighten

FLIC *n pl* **-S** a police officer, especially in France

FLIP *v* **-PED, -PING, -S** to move with a flick or light motion

FLIT *v* **-TED, -TING, -S** to move with celerity through the air

FLOC *n pl* **-S** a flocculent mass formed in a fluid through precipitation

FLOE *n pl* **-S** a low, flat mass of floating ice

FLOG *v* **-GED, -GING, -S** to beat or strike with a rod or whip

FLOP *v* **-PED, -PING, -S** to fall or lie down heavily and noisily

FLOW *v* **-ED, -ING, -S** to glide along smoothly

FLUB *v* **-BED, -BING, -S** to botch; to bungle

FLUE *n pl* **-S** smoke or heat outlet

FLUS *n pl of* **FLU** acute febrile highly contagious viral diseases

FLUX *n pl* **-ES** the state of being liquid through heat; fusion

FOAL *n pl* **-S** a young horse

FOAM *v* **-ED, -ING, -S** to produce bubbles

FOBS *n pl* **FOB** ornaments on a key ring

FOCI *n pl of* **FOCUS** a central point; a point of concentration

FOES *n pl of* **FOE** enemies in war; hostile armies

FOGS *v p t of* **FOG** makes or becomes obscured

FOGY *n pl* **FOGIES** an old-fashioned person who resists change; *also* **FOGEY, FOGIE**

FOIL *v* **-ED, -ING, -S** prevent the success of

FOIN *v* [obs] to thrust with a sword or spear; to lunge

FOLD *v* **-ED, -ING, -S** to double or lay together

FOLK *n pl* **-S** people in general; a community; a tribe

FOND *adj* **-ER, -EST** feeling affection

FONE *n pl of* **FOE** [obs] an enemy in war; a hostile army

FONT *n pl* **-S** a specific size and style of type within a type family

FOOD *n pl* **-S** any solid substance that is used as a source of nourishment

FOOL *v* **-ED, -ING, -S** to infatuate; to make foolish; to deceive

FOOT *n pl* **FEET** the terminal part of the leg of man or an animal

FORA *n pl of* **FORUM** public facilities to meet for open discussion

FORB *n pl* **-S** any herbaceous plant that is not a grass

FORD *n pl* **-S** a shallow place in a body of water, such as a river, where one can cross by walking

FORE *n* the front of something, or something at the front

FORK *v* **-ED, -ING, -S** to divide into two

FORM *v* **-ED, -ING, -S** to give shape to something

FORT *n pl* **-S** a strong or fortified place; a defensive structure

FOSS *n* **-ES** a wide ditch, usually filled with water and used for defense; *also* **FOSSE**

FOUL *v* **-ED, -ING, -S** to act illegally in sport

FOUR *n pl* **-S** a number; one more than three; twice two

FOWL *n pl* **-S** any domesticated bird used as food, as a hen, turkey or duck

FOXY *adj* **FOXIER, FOXIEST** clever in a cunning or deceitful way

FOZY *adj* SCOT. spongy; soft; fat and puffy; also too ripe

FRAE *prep* SCOT. from

FRAG *v* **-GED, -GING, -S** to beat an opponent in a computer game

FRAP *v* **-PED, -PING, -S** to draw together; to tighten

FRAT *n pl* **-S** common abbreviation for fraternity, a social club for male undergraduates

FRAY *v* **-ED, -ING, -S** to alarm; frighten

FREE *v* **-D, -ING, -S** to make free, available

FREN *n* a stranger

FRET *v* **-TED, -TING, -S** to be agitated

FRIT *v* **-TED, -TING, -S** to fuse into a vitreous substance

FRIZ *v* **-ZED, -ZING, -ZES** to form into small tight curls; *also* **FRIZZ**

FROE *n pl* **-S** an iron cleaver or splitting tool; *also* **FROW**

FROG *n pl* **-S** any of various stout-bodied amphibians with long hind limbs for leaping

FROM *prep* starting at; to indicate the starting or focal point of an activity

FROW *n pl* **-S** an iron cleaver or splitting tool; *also* **FROE**

FRUG *v* **-GED, -GING, -S** to dance the frug, a twist variation

FUCI *n pl of* **FUCUS** seaweed

FUEL *v* **-ED, -ING, -S** to stimulate something

FUFF *n* a sudden and single emission of breath from the mouth, like a puff

FUGA *n* a musical form consisting of a theme repeated; *also* **FUGUE**

FUGH *interj* exclaiming abhorrence or contempt; *also* **FOH, FAUGH**

FUGO *n* a bomb carried by a balloon

FUGS *v pr t of* **FUG** BRIT. makes stuffy and odorous

FUGU *n pl* **-S** a poisonous pufferfish that is eaten

FUJI *n* a spun silk fabric in plain weave originally made in Japan

FULL *adj* **-ER, -EST** resembling something thickened, as cloth

FUME *v* **-D, FUMING, -S** to smoke; to throw off fumes

FUMY *adj* producing fumes, smoke

FUND *n pl* **-S** a reserve of money set aside for some purpose

FUNK *n pl* **-S** a state of melancholy

FUNS *v pr t of* **FUN** plays; frolics

FURL *v* **-ED, -ING, -S** to draw up or gather into close compass

FURS *n pl of* **FUR** animal hair

FURY *n pl* **-IES** violent anger; extreme wrath; rage

FUSE *v* **-D, FUSING, -S** to equip with an exploding device; *also* **FUZE**

FUSS *v* **-ED, -ING, -ES** to worry too much

FUTZ *v* **-ED, -ING, -ES** to waste time or effort on frivolities

FUZE *v* **-D, FUZING, -S** to equip with an exploding device; *also* **FUSE**

FUZZ *n* fine, light particles or fibers; loose, volatile matter

FYCE *n* [obs] a nervous belligerent little mongrel dog; *also* **FICE, FEIST**

FYKE *n pl* **-S** a long bag net distended by hoops, into which fish can pass easily

FYRD *n* the military force of the whole nation, consisting of all men able to bear arms

FIVE LETTERS

FABLE *n pl* **-S** a story about mythical or supernatural beings or events

FACED *v p t of* **FACE** opposed or met defiantly

FACER *n pl* **-S** one that faces

FACES *v pr t of* **FACE** opposes or meets defiantly

FACET *n pl* **-S** a little face; small, plane surface as of a diamond

FACIA *n pl* **-S** or **-E** a band, sash or fillet; in surgery, a bandage or roller; *also* **FASCIA**

FACTA *n pl of* **FACTUM** acts or deeds; things done

FACTO *adv* in fact; actually

FACTS *n pl of* **FACT** pieces of information about circumstances that exist or events that have occurred

FADDY *adj* **FADDIER, FADDIEST** intensely fashionable for a short time

FADED *v p t of* **FADE** grew weak; lost strength; withered

FADER *n pl* **-S** a device used to control sound volume

FADES *v pr t of* **FADE** grows weak; loses strength; withers

FADGE *v* [obs] to fit; to suit; to agree

FAENA *n pl* **-S** a series of final passes leading to the kill made by the matador in a bullfight

FAERY *n pl* **FAERIES** a fairy, a tiny being possessing magical powers; *also* **FAE, FAERIE, FAIE, FAIRY, FAY, FEY**

FAGIN *n* a person who instructs others in crime

FAGOT *v* **-ED, -ING, -S** to bind or tie together in bundles; *also* **FAGGOT**

FAIES *n pl of* **FAIE** fairies, tiny beings possessing magical powers; *also* **FAES, FAERIES, FAIRIES, FAYS, FEYS**

FAILS *v pr t of* **FAIL** falls short; is lacking

FAINT *v* **-ED, -ING, -S** to fall into an abrupt brief loss of consciousness

FAIRS *n pl of* **FAIR** gatherings of buyers and sellers

FAIRY *n pl* **FAIRIES** a tiny being possessing magical powers; *also* **FAE, FAERIE, FAERY, FAIE, FAY, FEY**

FAITH *n* belief or trust

FAKED *v p t of* **FAKE** cheated; swindled; stole

FAKER *n pl* **-S** a person who makes deceitful pretenses

107

FAKES *v pr t of* **FAKE** cheats; swindles; steals

FAKIR *n pl* **-S** a Hindu religious ascetic or begging monk; *also* **FAKEER, FAQIR, FAQUIR**

FALLS *v pr t of* **FALL** descends, either suddenly or gradually

FALSE *adj* **-ER, -EST** not faithful or loyal; not genuine or real

FAMED *v p t of* **FAME** became widely honored and acclaimed

FAMES *v pr t of* **FAME** becomes widely honored and acclaimed

FANAL *n* a lighthouse, or the apparatus placed in it for giving light

FANCY *adj* **FANCIER, FANCIEST** extravagant; above real value

FANGS *n pl of* **FANG** long, sharp, pointed teeth, especially canine teeth

FANNY *n pl* **FANNIES** the buttocks

FANON *n* a peculiar striped scarf worn by the pope at mass

FAQIR *n pl* **-S** a Hindu religious ascetic or begging monk; *also* **FAKEER, FAKIR, FAQUIR**

FARCE *n pl* **-S** a ridiculous situation in which everything goes wrong or becomes a sham

FARCI *adj* stuffed with mingled ingredients; *also* **FARCIE**

FARCY *n* a contagious disease of horses

FARED *v p t of* **FARE** got on in a particular way in doing something

FARER *n* a traveler

FARES *v pr t of* **FARE** gets on in a particular way in doing something

FARLS *n pl of* **FARL** SCOT. triangular cakes; scones

FARMS *n pl of* **FARM** tracts of land devoted to agricultural purposes

FARSE *adj* presumptuous and prone to interfering in other people's business

FARTS *n pl of* **FART** boring, contemptible people

FASTS *v pr t of* **FAST** abstains from food voluntarily for a time

FATAL *adj* foreboding great disaster

FATED *v p t of* **FATE** destined; predetermined the course of events

FATES *v pr t of* **FATE** destines; predetermine the course of events

FATLY *adv* ponderously; richly

FATTY *adj* **FATTIER, FATTIEST** containing or composed of fat, lard

FATWA *n pl* **-S** a legal opinion or ruling issued by an Islamic scholar; *also* **FATWAH**

FAUGH *interj* exclaiming abhorrence or contempt; *also* **FOH, FUGH**

FAULD *n* a piece of armor plate below the breastplate

FAULE *n* [obs] a fall or falling band

FAULT *v* **-ED, -ING, -S** to accuse; to blame

FAUNA *n pl* **-S** or **-E** all the animal life in a particular region

FAUNS *n pl of* **FAUN** rural deities represented as having the body of a man and the horns, ears, tail and sometimes the legs of a goat

FAUVE *n pl* **-S** a painter practicing fauvism, a movement in painting typified by the work of Matisse; *also* **FAUVIST**

FAVEL *n* a horse of a yellow or dun color

FAVES *n pl of* **FAVE** informal term for favorites, things that are preferred above all others

FAVOR *v* **-ED, -ING, -S** to regard with kindness; to support; to aid

FAVUS *n* a contagious fungal infection of the scalp

FAWNS *v pr t of* **FAWN** seeks favor by flattery

FAWNY *adj* **FAWNIER, FAWNIEST** of a light grayish brown

FAXED *v p t of* **FAX** transmitted documents by electronic means

FAXES *v pr t of* **FAX** transmits documents by electronic means

FAYED *v p t of* **FAY** fitted; joined; united closely

FAZED *v p t of* **FAZE** disturbed the composure of

FAZES *v pr t of* **FAZE** disturbs the composure of

FEARS *v pr t of* **FEAR** is afraid or scared of

FEAST *v* **-ED, -ING, -S** to eat a joyous meal

FEATS *n pl of* **FEAT** acts; deeds; exploits

FEAZE *v* **-D, FEAZING, -S** to disturb the composure of; *also* **FAZE**

FECAL *adj* pertaining to feces, solid waste matter

FECES *n/pl* solid waste matter

FEDEX *v* **-ED, -ING, -ES** informal term meaning to send by Federal Express

FEEDS *v pr t of* **FEED** gives food to; supplies with nourishment

FEELS *v pr t of* **FEEL** perceives by the touch; handles

FEERE *n* [obs] a consort, husband or wife; a companion; *also* **FERE**

FEESE *n* the short run before a leap

FEEZE *adj* a state of alarm or excitement

FEIGN *v* **-ED, -ING, -S** to pretend; to form and relate as if true; *also* **FEINE**

FEINE *v* [obs]to pretend; to form and relate as if true; *also* **FEIGN**

FEINT *v* **-ED, -ING, -S** to make a deceptive move

FEIST *n* a nervous belligerent little mongrel dog; *also* **FICE, FYCE**

FELID *n pl* **-S** a feline or cat

FELLA *n pl* **-S** a man or a boy

FELLY *n pl* **-IES** a rim into which spokes are inserted; *also* **FELLOE**

FELON *n pl* **-S** a person who has committed a felony, a crime

FELTS *v pr t of* **FELT** becomes matted

FEMES *n pl of* **FEME** women or wives; *also* **FEMMES**

FEMME *n pl* **-S** a woman or wife; *also* **FEME**

FEMUR *n pl* **-S** or **FEMORA** the thigh bone

FENCE *v* **-D, FENCING, -S** to practice the art of fencing, fighting with slender swords

FENDS *v pr t of* **FEND** keeps off; wards off

FENKS *n/pl* the refuse whale blubber, used as a manure

FENNY *adj* swampy; boggy

FEOFF *v* to invest with a fee or feud

FERAL *adj* gone wild; savage; *also* **FERINE**

FERIA *n pl* **-S** or **-E** a weekday on which no festival or holiday is celebrated in the Roman Catholic Church

FERIE *n* [obs] a holiday

FERLY *n pl* **FERLIES** something strange; *also* **FERLIE**

FERME *n* [obs] rent for a farm; a farm; also an abode

FERMI *n pl* **-S** a metric unit of length used for nuclear distances

FERNS *n pl of* **FERN** flowerless, seedless vascular plants

FERNY *adj* **FERNIER, FERNIEST** abounding in ferns, flowerless, seedless vascular plants

FERRY *v* **FERRIED, -ING, FERRIES** to pass over water in a boat or by ferry

FESSE *n pl* **-S** a wide band forming the middle section of a shield; *also* **FESS**

FESTS *n pl of* **FEST** gatherings with emphasis on particular activities

FETAL *adj* of or relating to a fetus, unborn offspring

FETCH *v* **-ED, -ING, -ES** to bring or get within reach by going

FETED *v p t of* **FETE** honored with an elaborate festival

109

FETES *v pr t of* **FETE** honors with an elaborate festival

FETID *adj* malodorous; having an offensive smell; stinking; *also* **FOETID**

FETIS *adj* [obs] neat; pretty; well made; graceful

FETOR *n pl* -S a strong, offensive smell; stench; *also* **FOETOR**

FETUS *n pl* -ES a developing and unborn vertebrate; *also* **FOETUS**

FEUAR *n pl* -S SCOT. one who pays an annual fee for the right to use land

FEUDS *v pr t of* **FEUD** quarrels between two or more parties

FEVER *n pl* -S a rise in the temperature of the body

FEWER *adj* not as many; smaller, more limited or confined in number

FEYLY *adv of* **FEY** SCOT. crazily

FEZES *n pl of* **FEZ** felt or cloth caps, usually red with a tassel

FIATS *n pl of* **FIAT** authoritative commands or orders

FIBER *n pl* -S a slender, elongated, threadlike object or structure; *also* **FIBRE**

FIBRE *n pl* -S a slender, elongated, threadlike object or structure; *also* **FIBER**

FICHE *n pl* -S a sheet of microfilm

FICHU *n pl* -S a lightweight triangular scarf worn by a woman

FICUS *n pl* -ES a tropical fig tree

FIDGE *v* -D, FIDGING, -S SCOT. to move uneasily one way and the other; *also* **FIDGET**

FIDOS *n pl of* **FIDO** coins containing a minting error

FIEFS *n pl of* **FIEF** land held under the feudal system

FIELD *n pl* -S cultivated ground; the open country

FIEND *n pl* -S an implacable or malicious foe; a demon

FIERY *adj* burning hot; parched; feverish

FIFER *n* one who plays on a fife, a small high-pitched flute

FIFTH *n pl* -S position five in a countable series of things; the ordinal of five

FIFTY *n pl* -IES the sum of five tens

FIGHT *v* -ED, -ING, -S to struggle or contest

FILAR *adj* pertaining to a thread or line

FILCH *v* -ED, -ING, -ES to steal

FILED *v p t of* **FILE** stored something in order

FILER *n pl* -S one that stores something in order

FILES *v pr t of* **FILE** stores something in order

FILET *n pl* -S a piece or slice of boneless meat or fish; *also* **FILLET**

FILLE *n* a young unmarried woman

FILLO *n* very thin pastry dough; *also* **FILO, PHYLLO**

FILLS *v pr t of* **FILL** makes full

FILLY *n pl* -IES a young female horse under the age of four

FILMI *adj* melodramatic or exaggerated

FILMS *n pl of* **FILM** thin skin; pellicles; membranous coverings

FILMY *adj* FILMIER, FILMIEST covered by a thin coating or film; blurry

FILTH *n* a foul matter; dirt; nastiness

FILUM *n pl* FILA a threadlike anatomical structure; a filament

FINAL *adj* conclusive in a process or progression

FINCA *n pl* -S a rural property, farm or ranch in Spanish-speaking countries

FINDS *v pr t of* **FIND** comes upon, often by accident; meets with

FINED *v p t of* **FINE** subjected to a fine, a monetary penalty

FINER *adj of* **FINE** greater in excellence or quality

FINES *v pr t of* **FINE** subjects to a fine, a monetary penalty

FINEW *n* moldiness

FINIS *n* the concluding part of any performance; the end

FINKS *v pr t of* FINK informs against another person

FINNY *adj* FINNIER, FINNIEST having, or abounding in, fins, as fishes

FIORD *n pl* -S a narrow inlet of the sea; *also* FJORD

FIRED *v p t of* FIRE discharged

FIRER *n* one who discharges something or someone

FIRES *v pr t of* FIRE is discharged

FIRMS *v pr t of* FIRM fixes; settles; confirms; establishes

FIRRY *adj* FIRRIER, FIRRIEST made of fir; abounding in firs, needle-shaped leaves of an evergreen tree

FIRST *n pl* -S that precedes all others of a series or kind

FIRTH *n* SCOT. a long, narrow inlet of the sea; *also* FRITH

FISHY *adj* FISHIER, FISHIEST arousing suspicion

FISTS *n pl of* FIST the hands closed tightly

FITCH *n pl* -ES the fur of a polecat; *also* FITCHET, FITCHEW

FITLY *adv* in an appropriate manner

FIVER *n pl* -S informal term for a five-dollar bill

FIVES *n pl of* FIVE numbers; one more than four

FIXED *v p t of* FIX made firm, arranged, repaired

FIXER *n pl* -S one that makes firm, arranges or repairs

FIXES *v pr t of* FIX makes firm, arranges, repairs

FIZZY *adj* FIZZIER, FIZZIEST making a hissing or sputtering sound

FJELD *n* a high, barren plateau in Scandinavian countries

FJORD *n pl* -S a narrow inlet of the sea; *also* FIORD

FLACK *v* -ED, -ING, -S informal for to publicize or promote

FLAGS *n pl of* FLAG cloth bearing devices to indicate nationality

FLAIL *v* -ED, -ING, -S to thrash about

FLAIR *n* a uniquely attractive quality

FLAKE *n pl* -S a crystal of snow; a small fragment; *also* FLEAK

FLAKY *adj* FLAKIER, FLAKIEST consisting of flakes, small, loose masses; *also* FLAKEY

FLAME *n pl* -S a stream of burning vapor or gas, emitting light and heat

FLAMY *adj* FLAMIER, FLAMIEST resembling a flame, a stream of burning vapor

FLANK *n pl* -S the fleshy or muscular part of the side of an animal

FLANS *n pl of* FLAN tarts with a filling of custard, fruit or cheese

FLAPS *v p t of* FLAP moves or sways repeatedly

FLARE *v* -D, FLARING, -S to burn with an unsteady, waving flame

FLASH *v* -ED, -ING, -ES to cause to burst forth with sudden flame or light

FLASK *n pl* -S a small bottle-shaped vessel for holding fluids

FLATS *n/pl* women's shoes without high heels

FLAWS *n pl of* FLAW cracks or breaches; gaps or fissures; defects

FLAXY *adj* like flax, a fiber used to make linen; *also* FLAXEN

FLAYS *v pr t of* FLAY to strip off the skin or surface of

FLEAK *n* [obs] a flake; a thread or twist; *also* FLAKE

FLEAM *n pl* -S the edge of a tooth on a saw

FLEAS *n pl of* FLEA wingless blood-sucking parasitic insects

FLECK *n pl* -S a spot; a streak; a speckle

FLEER *v* -ED, -ING, -S to laugh with contempt

FLEES *v pr t of* FLEE runs away

FLEET v -ED, -ING, -S to sail; to float swiftly

FLEME v [obs] to banish; to drive out; to expel

FLESH n the soft tissue of the body of a vertebrate

FLEWS n/pl the pendulous lateral parts of a dog's upper lip

FLEYS v pr t of **FLEY** SCOT. frightens

FLICK v -ED, -ING, -S to whip lightly or with a quick jerk; to flap

FLICS n pl of **FLIC** police officers, especially in France

FLIER n pl -S someone who travels by air; also **FLYER**

FLIES n pr t of **FLY** moves through the air

FLING v **FLUNG**, -ING, -S to throw from the hand; to hurl

FLINT n pl -S a hard kind of stone

FLIPE v SCOT. to turn inside out, as a stocking in pulling off or for putting on

FLIPS v pr t of **FLIP** moves with a flick or light motion

FLIRT v -ED, -ING, -S to talk or behave amorously, without serious intentions

FLISK v [obs] SCOT. to frisk; to skip; to caper

FLITE v -D, **FLITING**, -S BRIT. to scold; to quarrel; also **FLYTE**

FLITS v pr t of **FLIT** moves with celerity through the air

FLOAT v -ED, -ING, -S to remain on the surface of a liquid

FLOCK v -ED, -ING, -S to gather in companies or crowds

FLOCS n pl of **FLOC** flocculent masses formed in a fluid through precipitation

FLOES n pl of **FLOE** a low, flat masses of floating ice

FLOGS v pr t of **FLOG** beats or strikes with a rod or whip

FLONG n pl -S a compressed mass of paper sheets, forming a matrix or mold

FLOOD n pl -S a great flow or stream of any fluid substance

FLOOK n [obs] the triangular blades at the end of an anchor

FLOOR v -ED, -ING, -S to astonish somebody

FLOPS v pr t of **FLOP** falls or lies down heavily and noisily

FLORA n pl -S or -E all the plant life in a particular region

FLOSH n a trough in which tin ore is washed

FLOSS v -ED, -ING, -ES to use dental floss to clean the teeth

FLOTA n a fleet of Spanish ships

FLOTE v [obs] to fleet; to skim

FLOUR v -ED, -ING, -S to cover something with flour, the finely ground meal of wheat

FLOUT v -ED, -ING, -S to mock or insult; to treat with contempt

FLOWN v p t of **FLY** moved through the air

FLOWS v pr t of **FLOW** glides along smoothly

FLUBS v pr t of **FLUB** botches; bungles

FLUES n pl of **FLUE** smoke or heat outlets

FLUEY adj downy; fluffy

FLUFF v -ED, -ING, -S shake something to insert air

FLUID n pl -S a continuous amorphous substance that flows

FLUKE n pl -S accidental success

FLUKY adj **FLUKIER**, **FLUKIEST** subject to accident or chance or change; also **FLUKEY**

FLUME n pl -S a narrow gorge with a stream running through it

FLUMP v to fall heavily

FLUNG v p t of **FLING** to throw with violence

FLUNK v -ED, -ING, -S to fail, as on a lesson; to back out

FLUOR n a variously colored crystalline mineral consisting of calcium fluoride; also **FLOURITE**

FLUSH v **-ED, -ING, -ES** to flow and spread suddenly; to rush

FLUTE n pl **-S** a musical wind instrument

FLUTY adj **FLUTIER, FLUTIEST** soft and clear in tone, like a flute; also **FLUTEY**

FLYBY n pl **-S** a flight made by an aircraft or a spacecraft over a particular place to record details about it

FLYER n pl **-S** someone who travels by air; also **FLIER**

FLYTE v **-D, FLYTING, -S** SCOT. to scold; to quarrel; also **FLITE**

FOALS n pl of **FOAL** young horses

FOAMS v pr t of **FOAM** produces bubbles

FOAMY adj **FOAMIER, FOAMIEST** covered with foam or bubbles; frothy

FOCAL adj main and most important

FOCUS v **-ED, -ING, -ES** to adjust vision to see clearly

FOEHN n a warm, dry wind blowing down the side of a mountain

FOGEY n pl **-S** an old-fashioned person who resists change; also **FOGY, FOGIE**

FOGGY adj **FOGGIER, FOGGIEST** clouded or blurred

FOGIE n pl **-S** an old-fashioned person who resists change; also **FOGEY, FOGY**

FOILS v pr t of **FOIL** prevents the success of

FOIST v **-ED, -ING, -S** to impose something on someone surreptitiously

FOLDS v pr t of **FOLD** doubles or lays together

FOLEY n the process used to produce sound effects for a film

FOLIA n pl of **FOLIUM** thin leaf-like layers occurring in metamorphic rock

FOLIC adj derived from folic acid, a vitamin found in green vegetables and liver

FOLIE n a psychological disorder of thought or emotion

FOLIO n pl **-S** the page number of a book or manuscript

FOLKS n pl of **FOLK** people in general; a community; a tribe

FOLKY adj **FOLKIER, FOLKIEST** of or pertaining to folk singers or folk music, traditional songs and music

FOLLY n pl **-IES** a foolish idea or action; the state of being foolish

FONDE v [obs] to endeavor; to strive; to try

FONDU n pl **-S** a hot dish made of melted cheese and wine and eaten with bread; also **FONDUE**

FONTS n pl of **FONT** specific sizes and styles of type within a type family

FOODS n pl of **FOOD** any solid substances that are used as a source of nourishment

FOOLS v pr t of **FOOL** infatuates; makes foolish; deceives

FOOTY adj **FOOTIER, FOOTIEST** BRIT. paltry; lacking in importance or worth

FORAM n pl **-S** a seawater organism

FORAY v **-ED, -ING, -S** to pillage; to ravage

FORBS n pl of **FORB** any herbaceous plants that are not a grass

FORBY prep near; past; also **FORBYE**

FORCE v **-D, -ING, -S** impose or thrust urgently, importunately or inexorably

FORDO v **FORDID** or **-NE, -ING, -ES** to destroy; to ruin

FORDS n pl of **FORD** shallow places in a body of water, such as a river, where one can cross by walking

FORGE v **-ED, -ING, -S** to make an illegal copy of something

FORGO v **-NE** or **FORWENT, -ING, -ES** to refrain from

FORKS v p t of **FORK** divides into two

113

FORKY *adj* **FORKIER, FORKIEST** opening into two or more parts or shoots; forked; furcated

FORME *n* BRIT. a body of typographical elements assembled in a chase and ready for printing

FORMS *v pr t of* **FORM** gives shape to something

FORTE *n pl* **-S** the strong point

FORTH *adv* forward; onward in time, place, or order

FORTS *n pl of* **FORT** strong or fortified places; defensive structures

FORTY *n pl* **-IES** four times ten; a number

FORUM *n pl* **-S** or **FORA** a public facility to meet for open discussion

FOSSA *n pl* **-E** a pit, groove, cavity

FOSSE *n pl* **-S** a wide ditch, usually filled with water and used for defense; *also* **FOSS**

FOULS *v pr t of* **FOUL** acts illegally in sport

FOUND *v p t of* **FIND** came upon, often by accident; met with

FOUNT *n pl* **-S** a plumbing fixture that provides a flow of water; *also* **FOUNTAIN**

FOURS *n pl of* **FOUR** numbers; one more than three; twice two

FOUTY *adj* [obs] despicable

FOVEA *n pl* **-E** a slight depression or pit in a bone or organ

FOWLS *n pl of* **FOWL** domesticated birds used as food, as hens, turkeys or ducks

FOXED *v p t of* **FOX** acted cunningly; cheated

FOXES *v pr t of* **FOX** acts cunningly; cheats

FOXLY *adj* [obs] fox like

FOYER *n pl* **-S** a large entrance or reception room or area

FRACT *v* [obs] to break; to violate

FRAGS *v pr t of* **FRAG** beats an opponent in a computer game

FRAIL *adj* **-ER, -EST** fragile; weak; infirm

FRAME *v* **-D, FRAMING, -S** to construct by putting together various parts

FRANC *n pl* **-S** the monetary unit of many different countries

FRANK *adj* **-ER, -EST** honest in speech; evident

FRAPE *n* [obs] a crowd, a rabble

FRAPS *v pr t of* **FRAP** draws together; tightens

FRASS *n* debris made by insects

FRATS *n pl of* **FRAT** common abbreviation for fraternities, social clubs for male undergraduates

FRAUD *n pl* **-S** a trap or snare; a trickery

FRAYS *v pr t of* **FRAY** alarms; frightens

FREAK *v* **-ED, -ING, -S** to streak with color

FRECK *v* to checker; to diversify

FREED *v p t of* **FREE** made free, available

FREER *n* one who frees or makes available

FREES *v pr t of* **FREE** makes free, available

FREMD *adj* [obs] SCOT., BRIT. strange

FRENA *n pl of* **FRENUM** connecting folds of membrane

FRERE *n pl* **-S** a brother or member of any religious order; *also* **FRIAR**

FRESH *adj* **-ER, -EST** not yet used or soiled

FRETA *n pl of* **FRETUM** straits or arms of the sea

FRETS *v pr t of* **FRET** is agitated

FRETT *n* the worn side of the bank of a river

FRIAR *n pl* **-S** a brother or member of any religious order; *also* **FRERE**

FRIED *v p t of* **FRY** cooked in a pan or on a griddle; cooked in oil or fat

FRIER *n pl* **-S** one who cooks in oil or fat

FRIES *v pr t of* **FRY** cooks in a pan or on a griddle; cooks in oil or fat

FRILL *v* **-ED, -ING, -S** to provide or decorate with a ruffle

FRISK *v* -ED, -ING, -S to play boisterously

FRIST *v* to sell upon credit, as goods

FRITH *n* SCOT. a long, narrow inlet of the sea; *also* FIRTH

FRITS *v pr t of* FRIT fuses into a vitreous substance

FRITZ *n* informal for broken or nonfunctioning state

FRIZZ *v* -ED, -ING, -ES to form into small tight curls; *also* FRIZ

FROCK *v* -ED, -ING, -S to induct as a member of clergy

FROES *n pl of* FROE iron cleavers or splitting tools; *also* FROWS

FROGS *n pl of* FROG any of various stout-bodied amphibians with long hind limbs for leaping

FROND *n pl* -S a compound leaf of a fern or palm

FRONS *n pl* FRONTES the uppermost part of the head of an insect

FRONT *v* -ED, -ING, -S to give covering or appearance to something

FRORE *adj* [obs] extremely cold; frosty

FROSH *n pl* FROSH freshman

FROST *v* -ED, -ING, -S to produce a surface resembling frost upon, as upon cake, metals or glass

FROTE *v* [obs] to rub or wear by rubbing; to chafe

FROTH *v* -ED, -ING, -S to cause to foam

FROWN *v* -ED, -ING, -S to contract the brow in displeasure

FROWS *n pl of* FROW iron cleavers or splitting tools; *also* FROES

FROWY *adj* [obs] musty or rancid, as in frowy butter

FROZE *v p t of* FREEZE became congealed by cold

FRUGS *v pr t of* FRUG dance the frug, a twist variation

FRUIT *n pl* -S a product of plant growth

FRUMP *n pl* -S a drab, old-fashioned person

FRUSH *v* [obs] to batter; to break in pieces

FRYER *n pl* -S one that fries, cooks in fat

FUBBY *adj* BRIT. informal for plump and short; *also* FUBSY

FUBSY *adj* FUBSIER, FUBSIEST BRIT. informal for plump and short; *also* FUBBY

FUCUS *n pl* -ES or FUCI seaweed

FUDDY *n pl* -IES a fussy person

FUDGE *v* -D, FUDGING, -S to fake or falsify

FUELS *v pr t of* FUEL stimulates something

FUFFY *adj* light; puffy

FUGAL *adj* being in the style of a fugue, a musical form consisting of a theme repeated

FUGGY *adj* FUGGIER, FUGGIEST odorous and stuffy atmosphere

FUGLE *v* -D, FUGLING, -S to maneuver; to lead

FUGUE *n pl* -S a musical form consisting of a theme repeated; *also* FUGA

FUGUS *n pl of* FUGU poisonous pufferfish that are eaten

FULLY *adj* in a complete manner or degree

FUMED *v p t of* FUME smoked; threw off fumes

FUMER *n* one that throws off fumes or smoke

FUMES *v pr t of* FUME smokes; throws off fumes

FUMET *n pl* -S a reduced, seasoned fish, meat, vegetable stock

FUNDI *n pl* FUNDUS the portion of a hollow organ opposite its opening

FUNDS *n pl of* FUND reserves of money set aside for some purpose

FUNGE *n* [obs] a blockhead; a dolt; a fool

FUNGI *n pl of* FUNGUS any of large groups of plant-like living organisms

FUNGO *n pl* -ES a fly ball hit for fielding practice in baseball

FUNIC *adj* of, relating to, or originating in the umbilical cord

FUNIS *n* the umbilical cord

FUNKS *n pl of* **FUNK** states of melancholy

FUNKY *adj* **FUNKIER, FUNKIEST** informal term for offbeat, creative and novel

FUNNY *adj* **FUNNIER, FUNNIEST** droll; comical; amusing; laughable

FURAN *n* a colorless toxic flammable liquid

FURLS *v pr t of* **FURL** draws up or gathers into close compass

FUROR *n* a general commotion; public disorder or uproar

FURRY *adj* **FURRIER, FURRIEST** covered with fur, animal hair

FURZE *n* very spiny and dense evergreen shrub; *also* **GORSE**

FURZY *adj* bounding in or characterized by furze, a very spiny and dense evergreen shrub

FUSED *v p t of* **FUSE** equipped with an exploding device; *also* **FUZED**

FUSEE *n pl* **-S** a flare used as a warning device; *also* **FUZEE**

FUSEL *n* an oily liquid, accompanying many alcoholic liquors, as potato whiskey and corn whiskey

FUSES *v pr t of* **FUSE** equips with an exploding device; *also* **FUZES**

FUSIL *n pl* **-S** a light kind of flintlock musket

FUSSY *adj* **FUSSIER, FUSSIEST** exacting; choosy; nagging; annoying

FUSTY *adj* **FUSTIER, FUSTIEST** moldy; musty; ill-smelling; rank

FUTON *n pl* **-S** a thin mattress of tufted cotton batting for use as a bed

FUZED *v p t of* **FUZE** equipped with an exploding device; *also* **FUSED**

FUZEE *n pl* **-S** a flare used as a warning device; *also* **FUSEE**

FUZES *v pr t of* **FUZE** equips with an exploding device; *also* **FUSES**

FUZZY *adj* **FUZZIER, FUZZIEST** blurry

FYKES *n pl of* **FYKE** long bag nets distended by hoops, into which fish can pass easily

GI *n pl* **-S** a loose-fitting white suit worn in judo, karate and other martial arts; *also* **GIE**

GO *v* **-NE, -ING, ES** to move to or from a place

THREE LETTERS

GAB *v* **-BED, -BING, -S** to talk incessantly about trivial matters

GAD *v* **-DED, -DING, -S** moves about restlessly and with little purpose

GAE *v* **-D** or **GANE** or **GAEN, GAUN, -S** SCOT. to go

GAG *v* **-GED, -GING, -S** to prevent from speaking; *also* to choke

GAL *n pl* **-S** informal term for a girl or woman

GAM *v* **-MED, -MING, -S,** to visit with someone socially

GAN *v p t of* **GIN** [obs] began

GAP *v* **-PED, -PING, -S** to make an opening in

GAR *n pl* **–S** or **GAR** freshwater fish with long narrow jaws and an elongated body

GAS *v* **-SED, -SING, -ES** or **-SES** to release gas, a substance that is neither a solid nor a liquid at ordinary temperatures

GAT *n pl* **-S** a narrow passage of water

GAY *adj* **-ER, -EST** happy and excited, merry; *also* **GAYER**

GED *n pl* **–S** or **GED** SCOT., BRIT. any fish of the pike family; *also* **GEDD, GEDS**

GEE v -D, -ING, -S to give a command to a horse or other draft animal to turn away from the driver

GEL v -LED, -LING, -S to form or become a semisolid jellylike substance

GEM v -MED, -MING, -S to adorn with precious or semiprecious stones

GEN n BRIT. information about a particular subject

GET v GOT or GOTTEN, -TING, -S to receive, to acquire

GEY adv SCOT. considerably; very

GHI n clarified butter; also GHEE

GIB v -BED, -BING, -S to secure something with an adjustable piece of metal

GID n a disease of sheep, characterized by vertigo

GIE n a loose-fitting white suit worn in judo, karate and other martial arts; also GI

GIF conj BRIT. [obs] the old form of if

GIG v -GED, -ING, -S to catch a fish or frog with a pronged spear

GIM adj neat; spruce

GIN v -NED, -NING, -S to remove the seeds from with a cotton gin, a machine that separates the seeds from raw cotton fibers

GIP n BRIT. pain or discomfort; also GYP

GIS n pl of GI loose-fitting white suits worn in judo, karate and other martial arts

GIT v GOTTEN, -TING, -S informal term meaning to receive, to acquire

GNU n pl -S an African antelope also called wildebeest

GOA n a gazelle native to Tibet

GOB n pl -S a small mass or lump

GOD n pl -S a being or object believed to have more than natural attributes and powers

GOG n [obs] haste; ardent desire to go

GON n pl -S one hundredth of a right angle; a gradian

GOO n informal for any thick, messy, viscous substance; also GOOK, GOOP, GUCK, GUNK

GOR interj BRIT. used as a mild oath

GOT v p t of GET received, acquired

GRY n [obs] a measurement equal to one tenth of a line

GUE n [obs] a sharper; a rogue

GUL n pl -S a design in oriental carpets

GUM v -MED, -MING to smear, stiffen or stick together using a sticky viscid substance

GUN v -NED, -NING, -S to shoot; to open the throttle and accelerate an engine

GUT v -TED, TING, -S to remove the insides of an animal

GUV n pl -S BRIT. an informal term of address used to address a superior man

GUY n pl -S informal for a man

GYE v [obs] to guide

GYM n pl -S a large room used for various indoor athletic activities

GYN v [obs] to begin

GYP n BRIT. pain or discomfort; also GIP

FOUR LETTERS

GABS v pr t of GAB talks incessantly about trivial matters

GABY n pl GABIES BRIT. a person lacking in common sense

GADS v pr t of GAD moves about restlessly and with little purpose

GAED v p t of GAE SCOT. went

GAEN v p part of GAE SCOT. gone; also GANE

GAES v pr t of GAE SCOT. goes

GAFF v -ED, -ING, -S to catch fish with a hooked pole

GAGA adj silly; completely absorbed, infatuated or excited

GAGE v -D, GAGING, -S to place a bet on

GAGS v pr t of GAG prevents from speaking; also chokes

GAIN v -ED, -ING, -S to get; to obtain or acquire

GAIT n a manner of walking or moving on foot

GALA *n pl* **-S** a festive occasion; festival; celebration

GALE *n pl* **-S** a very strong wind

GALL *v* **-ED, -ING, -S** to make somebody angry

GALS *n pl of* **GAL** informal term for girls or women

GALT *n* BRIT. a heavy thick clay; *also* **GAULT**

GAMB *n* an animal's leg or shank, especially on a coat of arms; *also* **GAMBE**

GAME *n* **-D, GAMING, -S** to play a game, a competitive activity with rules

GAMP *n pl* **-S** BRIT. a large baggy umbrella

GAMS *v pr t of* **GAM** visits with someone socially

GAMY *adj* **GAMIER, GAMIEST** having the tangy flavor or odor of an animal hunted for food or sport; *also* **GAMEY**

GANE *v p part of* **GAE** SCOT. gone; *also* **GAEN**

GANG *v* **-ED, -ING, -S** act as an organized group

GAOL *n* BRIT. a jail or prison

GAPE *v* **-D, GAPING, -S** to stare with open mouth

GAPS *v pr t of* **GAP** makes an opening in

GARB *v* **-ED, -ING, -ES** to clothe

GARE *n* coarse wool on the legs of sheep

GARI *n* grated cassava, an edible root of a plant

GARS *n pl of* **GAR** freshwater fish with long narrow jaws and elongated bodies

GASH *n pl* **-ES** a deep and long cut

GASP *v* **-ED, -ING, -S** to strain for air

GAST *v* **-ED, -ING, -S** [obs] to make aghast; to frighten; to terrify

GATE *v* **-D, GATING, -S** to supply with a gate, a structure that can be swung to block a passageway

GATS *n pl of* **GAT** narrow passages of water

GAUD *n pl* **-S** a showy ornament or trinket

GAUM *v* **-ED, -ING, -S** informal term meaning to smear

GAUN *v pr part of* **GAE** SCOT. going

GAUR *n pl* **-S** a massive wild ox of Southeast Asia

GAVE *v p t of* **GIVE** bestowed without receiving a return

GAWK *v* **-ED, -ING, -S** to look at with amazement; *also* **GAWP**

GAWN *n* a small tub or lading vessel

GAWP *v* **-ED, -ING, -S** BRIT. to look at with amazement; *also* **GAWK**

GAZE *v* **-D, GAZING, -S** to view with attention

GEAL *v* SCOT. [obs] to congeal

GEAN *n pl* **-S** a wild or seedling sweet cherry used as stock for grafting

GEAR *v* **-ED, -ING, -S** to prepare or adjust

GEAT *n* the channel or spout through which molten metal runs into a mold in casting

GECK *v* to deride; to scorn; to mock

GEDD *n pl* **GEDS** or **GED** SCOT. , BRIT. any fish of the pike family; *also* **GED**

GEDS *n pl of* **GED** or **GEDS** SCOT., BRIT. any fish of the pike family; *also* **GED**

GEED *v p t of* **GEE** gave a command to a horse or other draft animal to turn away from the driver; *also* **JEED**

GEEK *n pl* **-S** a person regarded as foolish or clumsy

GEES *v pr t of* **GEE** gives a command to a horse or other draft animal to turn away from the driver; *also* **JEES**

GEEZ *interj* to express mild surprise of dissatisfaction or annoyance; *also* **JEEZ**

GEIC *adj* pertaining to earthy or vegetable mold

GELD *v* **-ED** or **GELT, -ING, -S** to deprive of strength or vigor

GELS *v pr t of* **GEL** to form or become a semisolid jellylike substance

118

GELT *v pt of* **GELD** deprived of strength or vigor; *also* **GELDED**

GEMS *v pr t of* **GEM** adorns with precious or semiprecious stones

GENA *n pl* **-E** the cheek or side region of the head

GENE *n pl* **-S** the basic physical unit of heredity

GENS *n pl* **GENTES** a clan of ancient Rome consisting of a group of families with the same name

GENT *n pl* **-S** a gentleman; man

GENU *n pl* **GENUA** the knee

GERM *n pl* **-S** that from which something can develop or grow

GERN *v* [obs] to grin or yawn

GERY *adj* [obs] changeable; fickle

GEST *n* a notable adventure or exploit; *also* **GESTE**

GETA *n pl* **–S** or **GETA** a high wooden clog fastened to the foot by a thong between the first and second toes

GETS *v pr t of* **GET** to receive, to acquire

GHAT *n pl* **-S** a flight of steps leading down to a river

GHEE *n pl* clarified butter; *also* **GHI**

GIBE *v* **-D**, **GIBING**, **-S** to jeer or taunt; scoff at

GIBS *v pr t of* **GIB** secures something with an adjustable piece of metal

GIFT *v* **-ED**, **-ING**, **-S** to offer something without compensation

GIGS *n pl of* **GIG** a performing engagement by a musical group

GILD *v* **-ED**, **-ING**, **-S** to overlay with a thin layer of gold

GILL *n pl* **-S** the respiratory organ of aquatic animals

GILT *n pl* **-S** a young female pig

GIMP *v* **-ED**, **-ING**, **-S** to walk with a limp

GING *n* [obs] a group or band of individuals

GINK *n pl* **-S** an awkward person, especially a man, who is considered clumsy

GINS *v pr t of* **GIN** removes the seeds from with a cotton gin, a machine that separates the seeds from raw cotton fibers

GIRD *v* **-ED** or **GIRT**, **-ING**, **-S** to surround, encircle or enclose; *also* **GIRT**

GIRE *n* [obs] a circular or spiral motion; *also* **GYRE**

GIRL *n pl* **-S** a female child

GIRN *v* **-ED**, **-ING**, **-S** to complain, whine or grumble; *also* **GURN**

GIRO *n pl* **-S** a system of electronic credit transfer

GIRT *v p t of* **GIRD** surrounded, encircled or enclosed; *also* **GIRD**

GISE *v* [obs] to feed or pasture

GIST *n* the main point

GITE *n pl* **-S** a simple, usually inexpensive rural vacation retreat, especially in France

GITH *n* the corn cockle, a weedy annual Mediterranean plant

GITS *v p t of* **GIT** informal term meaning receives, acquires; *also* **GETS**

GIVE *v* **GAVE** or **GIVEN**, **GIVING**, **-S** to bestow without receiving a return

GLAD *v* **-DED**, **-DING**, **-S** [obs] to make happy, to cheer

GLAM *v* **-MED**, **-MING**, **-S** to make somebody glamorous, having an air of allure, romance and excitement

GLEE *n pl* **-S** jubilant delight, joy

GLEG *adj* SCOT. quick of perception; alert; sharp

GLEI *n* a sticky, bluish-gray subsurface layer of clay found in some waterlogged soils; *also* **GLEY**

GLEN *n pl* **-S** a secluded and narrow valley between hills; a dale

GLEW *n* [obs] adhesive or viscous substances

GLEY *n* a sticky, bluish-gray subsurface layer of clay found in some waterlogged soils; *also* **GLEI**

GLIA *n* the major support cells of the brain, involved in the nutrition and maintenance of the nerve cells; *also* **NEUROGLIA**

GLIB *adj* BER, BEST smooth; slippery; fluent; voluble

GLIM *n* a source of light

GLOB *n pl* **-S** a soft, thick lump or mass

GLOM *n pl* **-MED**, **-MING**, **-S** to grab or steal

GLOP *n pl* **-S** a soft soggy mixture, as of food

GLOW *v* **-ED**, **-ING**, **-S** to shine with an intense or white heat

GLUE *v* **-D**, **GLUING**, **-ING**, **-S** to affix with an adhesive substance

GLUG *v* **-GED**, **-GING**, **-S** to make a gurgling sound

GLUM *adj* moody; silent; sullen

GLUT *v* **-TED**, **-TING**, **-S** to swallow greedily; to gorge; to fill to excess

GNAR *v* **-RED**, **-RING**, **-S** to gnarl; to snarl; to growl; *also* **GNARR**

GNAT *n pl* **-S** a small blood-sucking dipterous fly

GNAW *v* **-ED** or **-N**, **-ING**, **-S** to wear away or remove by persistent biting or nibbling; *also* **KNAW**

GNOF *n* a churl, curmudgeon

GNUS *n pl of* **GNU** African antelopes also called wildebeests

GOAD *n pl* **-ED**, **-DING**, **-S** prod or urge as if with a long stick

GOAF *n pl* **GOAVES** waste or barren material usually left in mines

GOAL *n pl* **-S** the final purpose or aim; target area

GOAR *n* [obs] dirt; mud

GOAT *n pl* **-S** a hollow-horned ruminant mammal

GOBO *n pl* **-S** or **-ES** a shield placed around a microphone to exclude unwanted sounds

GOBS *n pl of* **GOB** small masses or lumps

GOBY *n pl* **-IES** a small, spiny-finned fish of coastal waters

GODS *n pl of* **GOD** beings or objects believed to have more than natural attributes and powers

GODE *n* [obs] good

GOEL *adj* [obs] yellow

GOER *n pl* **-S** one who, or that which, goes; a runner or walker

GOES *v pr t of* **GO** moves to or from a place

GOFF *n pl* **-S** a silly clown

GOLD *n* a precious metallic element

GOLF *v* **-ED**, **-ING**, **-S** to play a game in which a small ball is driven with clubs through a series of 9 or 18 holes with the fewest possible strokes

GOLL *n* [obs] a hand, paw or claw

GOME *n* the black grease on the axle of a wagon wheel; *also* **GORM**

GONE *v p part of* **GO** moved to or from a place

GONG *v* **-ED**, **-ING**, **-S** to summon with a percussion instrument consisting of a metal plate that is struck with a soft-headed drumstick

GONS *n pl of* **GON** one hundredth of right angles; gradians

GOOD *adj* kind; benevolent; humane; merciful; gracious; polite

GOOF *v* **-ED**, **-ING**, **-S** to make a careless mistake; a slip

GOOK *n* informal for any thick, messy, viscous substance; *also* **GOO**, **GOOP**, **GUCK**, **GUNK**

GOON *n pl* **-S** informal term for a thug or oafish person

GOOP *n* informal for any thick, messy, viscous substance; *also* **GOO**, **GOOK**, **GOOP**, **GUCK**, **GUNK**

GOOT *n* [obs] a goat

GORD *n* any of numerous hard-rinded inedible fruits; *also* **GOURD**

GORE *v* **-D**, **GORING**, **-S** to pierce or wound, as with a horn

GORM *n* the black grease on the axle of a wagon wheel; *also* **GOME**

GORP *n* a mixture of nuts and dried fruit, eaten as a snack

GORY *adj* **GORIER, GORIEST** full of or characterized by blood

GOSH *interj* to express surprise

GOTE *n* a channel for water

GOTH *n pl* **-S** style of popular music that combines heavy metal with punk

GOUR *n* a fire worshiper; *also* **GIAOUR**

GOUT *n pl* **-S** disease marked by painful inflammation of the small joints

GOVE *n* [obs] a mow; a rick for hay

GOWD *n pl* **-S** SCOT. gold; wealth

GOWK *n pl* **-S** a simpleton; a fool

GOWN *n pl* **-S** a loose, long flowing upper garment

GRAB *v* **-BED, -BING, -S** to grip suddenly; to seize; to snatch

GRAD *n pl* **-S** informal term for a graduate of a school, college or university

GRAF *n pl* **-EN** a title of nobility in Germany, Austria and Sweden

GRAM *n pl* **-S** metric unit of mass

GRAN *n* BRIT. one's grandmother

GRAY *v* **-ED, -ING, -S** to make gray, a mixture of the colors black and white; *also* **GREY**

GREE *v* **-D, -ING** BRIT. to agree

GREW *v p t of* **GROW** increased in any way

GREY *v* **-ED, -ING, -S** to make gray, a mixture of the colors black and white; *also* **GRAY**

GRID *n pl* **-S** a grating of thin and vertical parallel bars

GRIG *n* a lively, animated person

GRIL *adj* harsh; hard; severe; stern; rough

GRIM *adj* **-MER, -MEST** fierce; stern; surly; cruel; frightful; horrible

GRIN *v* **-NED, -NING, -S** to smile broadly, usually showing teeth

GRIP *v* **-PED** or **-T, -PING, -S** to grasp or seize firmly

GRIS *n* [obs] the gray skin of the Siberian squirrel

GRIT *n pl* **-S** sand or gravel; rough, hard particles

GROG *n* a mixed drink of rum and hot water

GROK *v* **-KED, -KING, -S** to understand profoundly through intuition

GROS *n* a heavy silk with a dull finish

GROT *n* a small cave or cavern; *also* **GROTTO**

GROW *v* **GREW** or **-N, -ING, -S** to increase in any way

GRUB *v* **-BED, -BING, -S** to clear by digging roots

GRUE *v* **-D, GRUING** SCOT. to shiver or shudder

GRUM *adj* **-MER, -MEST** surly; glum; grim

GUAN *n pl* **-S** a large fruit-eating bird

GUAR *n pl* **-S** an annual leguminous plant native to India

GUCK *n* informal for any thick, messy, viscous substance; *also* **GOO, GOOK, GOOP, GUNK**

GUDE *interj* SCOT., BRIT. good

GUFF *n* nonsense; *also* insolent talk

GUHR *n* a loose, earthy deposit from water, found in the cavities or clefts of rocks, mostly white, but sometimes red or yellow, from a mixture of clay or ocher

GUIB *n* an antelope with white markings like a harness and twisted horns

GUID *n* [obs] a flower; the marigold

GULA *n pl* **-S** or **-E** the upper front of the neck, the upper throat or gullet

GULE *v* **-D, GULING, -S** to give the color of gules to, the color red

GULF *n pl* **-S** a deep chasm or abyss

GULL *v* **-ED, -ING, -S** to deceive, trick or cheat

GULP *v* **-ED, -ING, -S** to swallow eagerly, or in large draughts

GULS *n pl of* **GUL** designs in oriental carpets

GUMP *v* **-ED, -ING, -S** to muddle through

GUMS *n pl of* **GUM** firm pink tissue in mouths covering the bones and into which the teeth are fixed

GUNK *n* informal for any thick, messy, viscous substance; *also* **GOO, GOOK, GOOP, GUCK**

GUNS *v pr t of* **GUN** shoots; opens the throttle and accelerates an engine

GURN *v* **-ED, -ING, -S** to complain, whine or grumble; *also* **GIRN**

GURT *n* a gutter or channel for water, hewn out of the bottom of a working drift

GURU *n pl* **-S** a recognized leader in some field or movement

GUSH *v* **-ED, -ING, -ES** to flow rapidly and in large quantities

GUST *n pl* **-S** a sudden strong blast of wind

GUTS *v pr t of* **GUT** removes the insides of an animal

GUVS *n pl of* **GUV** BRIT. an informal term of address used to address superior men

GUYS *n pl of* **GUY** informal for men or a group of people of either sex

GUZE *n* a sanguine roundel on a heraldic shield or flag

GYBE *v* **-D, GYBING, -S** to shift from one side to other when running before the wind, as a fore-and-aft sail or its boom; *also* **JIB, JIBB, JIBE**

GYLE *n pl* **-S** fermented wort used for making vinegar

GYMS *n pl of* **GYM** large rooms used for various indoor athletic activities

GYRE *v* **-ED, -ING, -S** a to move in a circular motion or a turn or revolution; *also* **GIRE**

GYRI *n pl of* **GYRUS** convoluted ridges in the brain

GYRO *n pl* **-S** meat, usually lamb, roasted on a vertical spit, then thinly sliced, topped with onions and usually served in a sandwich of pita bread

GYSE *n* [obs] external appearance in manner or dress; *also* **GUISE**

GYTE *adj* SCOT. delirious; senselessly extravagant

GYVE *v* **-D, GYVING, -S** to shackle or fetter

FIVE LETTERS

GABBY *adj* **GABBIER, GABBIEST** talkative

GABEL *n* a rent, service, tribute, custom, tax, impost, duty

GABLE *n pl* **-S** the vertical triangular section of a wall between the sloping ends of a gable roof

GADDI *n* a cushion on a throne for a prince in India

GADID *n pl* **-S** a fish of the cod family; *also* **GADOID**

GADRE *v* [obs] to gather

GAFFE *n pl* **-S** a clumsy social error; a faux pas

GAFFS *v pr t of* **GAFF** catches fish with a hooked pole

GAGED *v p t of* **GAGE** placed a bet on

GAGER *n pl* **-S** a person or instrument that measures something; *also* **GAUGER**

GAGES *v pr t of* **GAGE** places a bet on

GAILY *adv* in a joyous manner; *also* **GAYLY**

GAINS *v pr t of* **GAIN** gets; obtains; acquires

GALAH *n pl* **-S** a pink-breasted Australian cockatoo

GALAS *n pl of* **GALA** festive occasions; festivals; celebrations

GALEA *n pl* **-E** a helmet-shaped part, especially of corolla or calyx

GALES *n pl of* **GALE** very strong winds

GALLS *n pl of* **GALL** makes somebody angry

GALLY *v* **GALLIED, -ING** informal term meaning to frighten

GALOP *n pl* **-S** a lively dance in two-four time; *also* **GALLOP**

GAMAY *n* a red grape used for making red wine, especially Beaujolais

122

GAMBA *n* a viola, a stringed instrument

GAMBE *n* an animal's leg or shank, especially on a coat of arms; *also* **GAMB**

GAMED *v p t of* **GAME** played a game, a competitive activity with rules

GAMER *n* one who plays competitive activities with rules

GAMES *v pr t of* **GAME** plays a game, a competitive activity with rules

GAMEY *adj* **GAMIER, GAMIEST** having the tangy flavor or odor of an animal hunted for food or sport; *also* **GAMY**

GAMIN *n pl* **-S** a homeless child who roams the streets

GAMMA *n* the 3rd letter of the Greek alphabet

GAMMY *adj* **GAMMIER, GAMMIEST** BRIT. injured or impaired

GAMPS *n pl of* **GAMP** BRIT. a large baggy umbrella

GAMUT *n* the entire scale of musical notes

GANCH *v* to drop from a high place upon sharp stakes or hooks

GANEF *n pl* **-S** informal term for a thief or a rascal; *also* **GANEV, GANIF, GANOF, GONOF**

GANEV *n pl* **-S** informal term for a thief or a rascal; *also* **GANEF, GANIF, GANOF, GONOF**

GANGS *v pr t of* **GANG** acts as an organized group

GANIF *n pl* **-S** informal term for a thief or a rascal; *also* **GANEF, GANEV, GANOF, GONOF**

GANIL *n* a kind of brittle limestone

GANOF *n pl* **-S** informal term for a thief or a rascal; *also* **GANEF, GANEV, GANIF, GONOF**

GANSA *n* a kind of wild goose by flock of which kind of wild goose, by a flock of which a virtuoso was fabled to be carried to the lunar world; *also* **GANZA**

GANZA *n* a kind of wild goose by flock of which kind of wild goose, by a flock of which a virtuoso was fabled to be carried to the lunar world; *also* **GANSA**

GAPED *v p t of* **GAPE** stared with open mouth

GAPER *n pl* **-S** a person who stares with open mouth

GAPES *v pr t of* **GAPE** stares with open mouth

GAPPY *adj* **GAPPIER, GAPPIEST** having many gaps

GARBS *n pl of* **GARB** clothing in general

GARDA *n pl* **-I** a police officer in Ireland

GARIS *n pl of* **GARI** grated cassava; cassava flour, or grated cassava mixed with water

GARNI *adj* garnished, having decorative additions

GARTH *n pl* **-S** a close; a yard; a croft; a garden

GASES *v pr t of* **GAS** releases gas, a substance that is neither a solid nor a liquid at ordinary temperatures

GASPS *v pr t of* **GASP** strains for air

GASSY *adj* **GASSIER, GASSIEST** of or resembling gas, a substance that is neither a solid nor a liquid at ordinary temperatures

GASTS *v pr t of* **GAST** [obs] makes aghast; frightens; terrifies

GATED *v p t of* **GATE** supplied with a gate, a structure that can be swung to block a passageway

GATER *n pl* **-S** informal term for an alligator; *also* **GATOR**

GATES *v pr t of* **GATE** supplies with a gate, a structure that can be swung to block a passageway

GATOR *n pl* **-S** informal term for an alligator; *also* **GATER**

GAUDS *n pl of* **GAUD** showy ornaments or trinkets

GAUDY *adj* **GAUDIER, GAUDIEST** tastelessly showy

GAUGE *v* **-D, GAUGING, -S** to measure precisely

GAULT *n* BRIT. a heavy thick clay; *also* **GALT**

GAUMS *v pr t of* **GAUM** informal term for smears

GAUNT *adj* **-ER, -EST** thin and bony; angular

GAURE *v* [obs] to gaze; to stare

GAURS *n pl* **-S** a massive wild ox of Southeast Asia

GAUSS *n pl* **-ES** or **GAUSSES** the centimeter-gram-second unit of magnetic flux density, equal to one maxwell per square centimeter

GAUZE *n pl* **-S** a surgical dressing of loosely woven fabric

GAUZY *adj* **GAUZIER, GAUZIEST** pertaining to, or resembling, gauze, a net of transparent fabric with a loose open weave

GAVEL *n* **-S** the mallet of the presiding officer in a legislative body, public assembly, court, etc.

GAVOT *n pl* **-S** a kind of difficult, old formal French dance in quadruple time

GAWKS *v pr t of* **GAWK** looks at with amazement; *also* **GAWPS**

GAWKY *adj* **GAWKIER, GAWKIEST** foolish and awkward; clumsy; clownish

GAWPS *v pr t of* **GAWP** looks at with amazement; *also* **GAWKS**

GAWSY *adj* SCOT., SCOT. well-dressed and of cheerful appearance; *also* **GAWSIE**

GAYAL *n pl* **-S** or **GAYAL** an ox of Southeast Asia and the Malay Archipelago, sometimes considered to be a domesticated breed of the guar

GAYER *adj* happier and more excited, merrier; *also* **GAY**

GAYLY *adv* in a joyous manner; *also* **GAILY**

GAZAR *n* a loosely woven silk with a crisp finish

GAZED *v p t of* **GAZE** viewed with attention

GAZER *n pl* **-S** one who gazes

GAZES *v pr t of* **GAZE** views with attention

GAZET *n* [obs] a Venetian coin worth about one and a half cents

GAZON *n* one of the pieces of sod used to line or cover parapets and the faces of earthworks

GEANS *n pl of* **GEAN** wild or seedling sweet cherries used as stock for grafting

GEARS *v of* **GEAR** prepares or adjusts

GECKO *n pl* **-S** or **-ES** any lizard of the Geckonidae

GECKS *v of* **GECK** to deride; to scorn; to mock

GEEKS *n pl of* **GEEK** people regarded as foolish or clumsy

GEEKY *adj* **GEEKIER, GEEKIEST** foolish or clumsy

GEESE *n pl of* **GOOSE** large edible water birds with short legs and webbed feet

GEEST *n* alluvial matter on the surface of land

GELDS *v pr t of* **GELD** deprives of strength or vigor

GELEE *n pl* **-S** a jellied substance, as cosmetic gel or a jellied food

GELID *adj* cold; very cold; frozen

GEMEL *adj* coupled; paired

GEMMA *n pl* **-E** an asexual bud-shaped structure that can detach from the parent and form a plant

GEMMY *adj* **GEMMIER, GEMMIEST** full of gems; bright

GEMOT *n pl* **-S** a judicial or legislative assembly in Anglo-Saxon England; *also* **GEMOTE**

GEMUL *n* a small South American deer with simple forked horns

GENAE *n pl of* **GENA** the cheeks or side regions of the head

GENES *n pl of* GENE the basic physical unit of heredity

GENET *n* a small size well-proportioned Spanish horse; *also* **JENNET**

GENIC *adj* relating to or produced by a gene or genes, basic physical units of heredity

GENIE *n pl* -S a magic spirit believed to take human form and serves the person who calls it

GENII *n pl of* GENIUS tutelary deities or guardian spirits of a person or place

GENIO *n* a man of a particular turn of mind

GENIP *n* a tropical American tree having small fragrant greenish-white flowers and small fruits

GENOA *n pl* -S a large jib used on cruising and racing yachts, overlapping the mainsail

GENOM *n* a full set of chromosomes; *also* **GENOME**

GENRE *n pl* -S a kind, or type, as of works of literature, art, etc.

GENRO *n pl* GENRO the elder statesmen of Japan

GENTS *n pl of* GENT gentlemen; men

GENTY *adj* SCOT. neat; trim

GENUA *n pl of* GENU the knees

GENUS *n pl* -ES or GENERA a kind, sort or class

GEODE *n* a hollow rock or nodule with the cavity usually lined with crystals

GEOID *n* a hypothetical surface of the earth that coincides with mean sea level

GERAH *n pl* -S an ancient Hebrew coin worth one twentieth of a shekel

GERBE *n* a kind of ornamental firework

GERMS *n pl of* GERM that from which something can develop or grow

GERMY *adj* GERMIER, GERMIEST full of germs or pathological microorganisms

GESSO *n pl* -ES a preparation of plaster of Paris and glue used as a base for low relief or as a surface for painting

GESTE *n* a notable adventure or exploit; *also* **GEST**

GETAS *n pl of* GETA high wooden clogs fastened to the foot by a thong between the first and second toes

GETUP *n* informal term for a set of clothing with accessories

GHAST *adj* [obs] shockingly frightful

GHATS *n pl of* GHAT flights of steps leading down to a river

GHAUT *n pl* -S a small valley

GHAZI *n pl* -S a Muslim warrior

GHOLE *n* an imaginary sylvan demon, supposed to devour men and animals; *also* **GHOUL**

GHOST *n pl* -S the visible disembodied soul of a dead person

GHOUL *n pl* -S an imaginary sylvan demon, supposed to devour men and animals; *also* **GHOLE**

GHYLL *n* a ravine

GIANT *n pl* -S a person or thing of great size

GIBED *v p t of* GIBE jeered or taunted; scoffed

GIBEL *n pl* -S a kind of carp

GIBER *n* one who utters gibes, scoffing words; *also* **JIBER**

GIBES *v pr t of* GIBE jeers or taunts; scoffs at

GIDDY *adj* GIDDIER, GIDDIEST dizzy

GIFTS *v pr t of* GIFT offers something without compensation

GIGOT *n* a leg of lamb or mutton

GIGUE *n* music in 3/4 time for dancing a jig

GILDS *v pr t of* GILD overlays with a thin layer of gold

GILLS *n pl of* GILL the respiratory organs of aquatic animals

GILLY *n pl* **GILLIES** SCOT. a professional hunting or fishing guide; *also* **GILLIE**

GILTS *n pl of* **GILT** young female pigs

GIMEL *n* the third letter of the Hebrew alphabet

GIMME *n pl* **-S** something easily gotten

GIMPS *v pr t of* **GIMP** to walk with a limp

GIMPY *adj* **GIMPIER, GIMPIEST** to walk with a limp

GINKS *n pl of* **GINK** awkward people, especially men, who are considered clumsy

GINNY *adj* having the characteristics of gin, a colorless alcoholic beverage

GIPON *n* a close-fitting tunic usually padded and bearing heraldic arms, worn over armor; *also* **JUPON, JUPE**

GIPSY *n pl* **GIPSIES** a member of a nomadic people originating in northern India; *also* **GYPSY**

GIRDS *n pl of* **GIRD** surrounds, encircles, or encloses

GIRLS *n pl of* **GIRL** female children

GIRNS *v pr t of* **GIRN** complains, whines or grumbles; *also* **GURNS**

GIRON *n pl* **-S** triangular part of shield; *also* **GYRON**

GIROS *n pl of* **GIRO** systems of electronic credit transfer

GIRSH *n* a monetary unit of Saudi Arabia; *also* **QIRSH, QURSH, GHIRSH, GURSH**

GIRTH *n* a band or strap which encircles the body

GIRTS *v pr t of* **GIRT** surrounds, encircles, or encloses

GISLE *n* [obs] a pledge

GISMO *n pl* **-S** a gadget or device; *also* **GIZMO**

GITES *n pl of* **GITE** simple, usually inexpensive rural vacation retreats, especially in France

GIVEN *v p part of* **GIVE** to have bestowed without receiving a return

GIVER *n pl* **-S** someone who bestows without receiving a return

GIVES *v pr t of* **GIVE** bestows without receiving a return

GIZMO *n pl* **-S** a gadget or device; *also* **GISMO**

GLACE *v* **-ED, -ING** to frost or ice, as cake

GLADE *n pl* **-S** an area in a wood or forest without trees or bushes

GLADS *v pr t of* **GLAD** [obs] makes happy, cheers

GLAIR *v* **-ED, -ING, -S** or **-ES** the white of an egg; *also* **GLAIRE**

GLAMS *v pr t of* **GLAM** makes somebody glamorous, having an air of allure, romance and excitement

GLAND *n pl* **-S** a cell or group of cells that secrete substances

GLARE *v* **-D, GLARING, -S** to shine with or reflect a very harsh, bright, dazzling light

GLARY *adj* **GLARIER, GLARIEST** of a dazzling luster; glaring; bright

GLASS *n pl* **-ES** a transparent solid substance

GLAUM *v* SCOT. to grope with the hands, as in the dark

GLAVE *n pl* **-S** [obs] a sword; *also* **GLAIVE**

GLASE *v* **-D, GLASEN** or **GLAZEN** to furnish with glass, a transparent solid substance; *also* **GLAZE**

GLAZE *v* **-D, GLAZING, -S** to furnish with glass, a transparent solid substance; *also* **GLASE**

GLAZY *adj* having a glazed, transparent, appearance

GLEAD *n* [obs] a live coal; *also* **GLEED**

GLEAM *v* **-ED, - ING, -S** to shine brightly and continuously

GLEAN *v* **-ED, -ING, -S** to collect with patient and minute labor

126

GLEBA *n pl* **-E** a spore-bearing mass in certain fungi, as in puffballs and stinkhorns

GLEBE *n* BRIT. the cultivable land owned by a parish church or ecclesiastical office

GLEDE *n* the common European kite or hawk

GLEED *n* [obs] a live coal; *also* **GLEAD**

GLEEK *n* [obs] a jest or scoff; a trick or deception

GLEES *n pl of* **GLEE** jubilant delights, joys

GLENS *n pl of* **GLEN** secluded and narrow valleys between hills; dales

GLIAL *adj* of or relating to neuroglia, tissues and fibers in the brain and spinal cord

GLIDE *v* **-D, -ING, -S** to move smoothly

GLIFF *n* a transient glance; an unexpected view of something that startles one

GLINT *n* SCOT. a glimpse, glance or gleam

GLITZ *v* **-ED, -ING, -ES** to invest with an ostentatiously showy quality

GLOAM *v* [obs] to begin to grow dark; to grow dusky

GLOAT *v* **-ED, -ING, -S** to feel or express great, often malicious, pleasure or self-satisfaction

GLOBE *n pl* **-S** a sphere on which a map is represented

GLOBS *n pl of* **GLOB** soft, thick lumps or masses

GLOGG *n* a hot punch made of red wine, brandy and sherry flavored with almonds, raisins and orange peel

GLOMS *n pl of* **GLOM** grabs or steals

GLOOM *v* **-ED, -ING, -S** to appear or become dark, dim or somber

GLORY *n pl* **-IES** great beauty and splendor

GLOSS *v* **-ED, -ING, -ES** to give a bright sheen or luster to

GLOST *n* the lead glaze used for pottery

GLOUT *v* [obs] to pout; to look sullen

GLOVE *n pl* **-S** a fitted covering for the hand with a separate sheath for each finger and the thumb

GLOWS *v pr t of* **GLOW** to shine with an intense or white heat

GLOZE *v* **-ED, -ING, -S** to explain away, extenuate, gloss over

GLUED *v p t of* **GLUE** affixed with an adhesive substance

GLUER *n pl* **-S** someone who affixes with adhesive

GLUES *v pr t of* **GLUE** affixes with an adhesive substance

GLUEY *adj* **GLUIER, GLUIEST** like glue; sticky

GLUGS *v pr t of* **GLUG** makes a gurgling sound

GLUME *n* the bracteal covering of the flowers or seeds of grain and grasses

GLUMS *n* BRIT. [obs] a state of being moody; the blues

GLUON *n pl* **-S** a theoretical elementary particle believed to mediate the strong interaction that binds quarks together

GLUTE *n pl* **-S** any one of three large skeletal muscles that form the buttock and move the thigh

GLUTS *v pr t of* **GLUT** swallows greedily; fills to excess

GLYPH *n pl* **-S** a symbol, such as a stylized figure or arrow on a public sign, that imparts information nonverbally

GNARL *v* **-ED, -ING, -S** to snarl or growl

GNARR *v* **-ED, -ING, -S** to gnarl; to snarl; to growl; *also* **GNAR**

GNARS *v pr t of* **GNAR** gnarls; snarls; growls; *also* **GNARRS**

GNASH *v* **-ED, -ING, -ES** to strike or grind (as the teeth) together

GNATS *n pl of* **GNAT** small blood-sucking dipterous flies

127

GNAWN *v p part of* **GNAW** wore away or removed by persistent biting or nibbling

GNAWS *v pr t of* **GNAW** to wear away or remove by persistent biting or nibbling; *also* **KNAWS**

GNOME *n pl* -**S** one of a fabled race of dwarf-like creatures who live underground and guard treasure hoards

GOADS *v pr t of* **GOAD** prods or urges as if with a long stick

GOALS *n pl of* **GOAL** the final purpose or aim; target area

GOATS *n pl of* **GOAT** a hollow-horned ruminant mammal

GOBAN *n* a Japanese game, played on a checkerboard in which the object of the game is to be the first in placing five pieces, or men, in a row in any direction; *also* **GOBANG**

GOBOS *n pl of* **GOBO** shields placed around microphones to exclude unwanted sounds; *also* **GOBOES**

GODET *n* a triangular piece of fabric, often rounded at the top, inserted in a garment to give fullness

GODLY *adj* **GODLIER, GODLIEST** having great reverence for God

GOERS *n pl of* **GOER** one who, or that which, goes; a runner or walker

GOFER *n pl* -**S** an employee whose duties include running errands

GOFFS *n pl of* **GOFF** silly clowns

GOING *v pr part of* **GO** moving to or from a place

GOLEM *n pl* -**S** in Jewish folklore, an artificially created human being that is given life by supernatural means

GOLFS *v pr t of* **GOLF** plays a game in which a small ball is driven with clubs through a series of 9 or 18 holes with the fewest possible strokes

GOLLY *interj* used to express surprise, amazement, or anxiety, or for emphasis

GOMBO *n pl* -**S** a soup or stew thickened with okra pods; *also* **GUMBO**

GOMER *n* an informal term for an undesirable hospital patient

GOMES *n pl of* **GOME** the black grease on the axle of a wagon wheel; *also* **GORM**

GONAD *n pl* -**S** a sex gland in which gametes, cells connected with sexual reproduction, are produced

GONER *n pl* -**S** a person or thing that is lost or past recovery

GONGS *v pr t of* **GONG** summons with a percussion instrument consisting of a metal plate that is struck with a soft-headed drumstick

GONIA *n pl of* **GONIUM** the germ cell during the phase marked by mitosis

GONOF *n pl* -**S** an informal term for a thief or rascal; *also* **GANEF, GANEV, GANIF, GANOF**

GONZO *adj* informal term for bizarre; unconventional

GOODS *n/pl* merchandise

GOODY *n pl* **GOODIES** something enjoyable or attractive, especially food; *also* **GOODIE**

GOOEY *adj* **GOOIER, GOOIEST** sticky and messy; *also* **GOOPY, GUNKY**

GOOFS *v pr t of* **GOOF** makes a careless mistake; a slip

GOOFY *adj* **GOOFIER, GOOFIEST** silly; ridiculous

GOONS *n pl of* **GOON** informal term for thugs or oafish people

GOONY *adj* **GOONIER, GOONIEST** foolish or awkward

GOOPY *adj* **GOOPIER, GOOPIEST** sticky and messy; *also* **GOOEY, GUNKY**

GOOSE *n pl* **GEESE** large edible water birds with short legs and webbed feed

GOOSY *adj* **GOOSIER, GOOSIEST** behaving in what is regarded as silly; *also* **GOOSEY**

GOPIK *n pl* **-S** old Azerbaijan currency

GORAL *n pl* **-S** an Indian goat antelope, resembling the chamois

GORED *v p t of* **GORE** pierced or wounded with a horn or tusk

GORES *v pr t of* **GORE** pierces or wounds, as with a horn

GORGE *v* **-D, GORGING** to swallow greedily

GORSE *n* a spiny bush with yellow flowers and black pods; *also* **FURZE**

GORSY *adj* having the characteristics of a gorse, a spiny bush with yellow flowers and black pods

GOTHS *n pl of* **GOTH** styles of popular music that combine heavy metal with punk

GOUGE *v* **-ED, GOUGING, -S** to cut or scoop a hole or groove in something, usually using a sharp tool

GOURD *n pl* **-S** any of numerous hard-rinded inedible fruits; *also* **GORD**

GOUTS *n pl of* **GOUT** diseases marked by painful inflammation of the small joints

GOUTY *adj* **GOUTIER, GOUTIEST** resulting from or causing gout, a disease marked by painful inflammation of the small joints

GOWAN *n pl* **-S** SCOT. a yellow or white wildflower

GOWDS *n pl of* **GOWD** SCOT. gold; wealth

GOWKS *n pl of* **GOWK** simpletons; fools

GOWNS *n pl of* **GOWN** loose, long flowing upper garments

GRAAL *n* any greatly desired and sought-after objective; *also* **GRAIL**

GRABS *v pr t of* **GRAB** grips suddenly; seizes; snatches

GRACE *v* **-D, GRACING, -S** to bring honor to

GRADE *v* **-D, GRADING, -S** assign a rank or rating to

GRADS *n pl of* **GRAD** informal term for graduates of a school, college or university

GRAFT *v* **-ED, -ING, -S** to become joined

GRAIL *n pl* **-S** any greatly desired and sought-after objective; *also* **GRAAL**

GRAIN *n pl* **-S** a small, dry, one-seeded fruit of a cereal grass, having the fruit and the seed walls united

GRAMA *n* a pasture grass that grows in western North America and South America; *also* **GRAMMA**

GRAME *n* [obs] anger; wrath; scorn

GRAMP *n pl* **-S** a grandfather

GRAMS *n pl of* **GRAM** metric units of mass

GRANA *n pl of* **GRANUM** one of the structural units of a chloroplast in vascular plants, consisting of layers of thylakoids

GRAND *adj* **-ER, -EST** large and impressive in size, scope, or extent

GRANT *v* **-ED, -ING, -S** to bestow or transfer formally

GRAPE *n pl* **-S** a well-known edible berry growing in pendent clusters or bunches on the grapevine

GRAPH *v* **-ED, -ING, -S** to represent by means of a diagram

GRAPY *adj* **GRAPIER, GRAPIEST** of, made of, or tasting of grapes, an edible berry

GRASP *v* **-ED, -ING, -S** to clasp firmly with or as if with the hand

129

GRASS *n pl* **-ES** herbage suitable or used for grazing animals

GRATE *v* **-D, GRATING, -S** to make a grinding sound by rubbing together

GRAVE *adj* **-R, -ST** of great gravity or crucial importance

GRAVY *n pl* **GRAVIES** liquid dressing for meat, fish, vegetables, etc.

GRAYS *v pr t of* **GRAY** makes gray, a mixture of the colors black and white; *also* **GREYS**

GRAZE *v* **-D, GRAZING, -S** to feed on growing grass

GREAT *adj* **-ER, -EST** very large in size

GREBE *n* any of a worldwide order of diving and swimming birds with broadly lobed toes an legs set far back on the body

GREED *n* excessive desire to acquire or possess more material wealth

GREEN *adj* **-ER, -EST** grass-colored

GREET *v* **-ED, -ING, -S** to express greetings upon meeting someone

GREGE *v* [obs] to make heavy, to increase; *also* **GREGGE**

GREGO *n pl* **-S** a short jacket or cloak, made of very thick, coarse cloth, with a hood attached, worn in the Levant

GREVE *n* [obs] a garden consisting of a small cultivated wood without undergrowth; *also* **GROVE**

GREYS *v pr t of* **GREY** makes gray, a mixture of the colors black and white; *also* **GRAYS**

GRICE *n* SCOT. a young suckling pig; *also* **GRISE**

GRIDE *v* **-D, GRIDING, -S** to pierce or cut; *also* **GRYDE**

GRIDS *n pl of* **GRID** gratings of thin and vertical parallel bars

GRIEF *n pl* **-S** intense sorrow generally caused by a loss of someone

GRIFF *n* a fabled monster usually have the head and wings of an eagle and the body of a lion; *also* **GRIFFIN**

GRIFT *v* **-ED, -ING, -S** to swindle

GRILL *v* **-ED, -ING, -S** to cook on a grill, a device on a cooker that radiates heat for cooking food

GRIME *v* **-D, GRIMING, -S** to sully or soil deeply; to dirt

GRIMY *adj* **GRIMIER, GRIMIEST** full of grime; begrimed; dirty; foul

GRIND *v* **GROUND** or **-ED, -ING, -S** to be polished or sharpened by friction

GRINS *v pr t of* **GRIN** smiles broadly, usually showing teeth

GRIOT *n* a storyteller in western Africa who perpetuates the oral tradition and history of a village or family

GRIPE *v* **-D, GRIPING, -S** to complain constantly; *also* **GRYPE**

GRIPS *v pr t of* **GRIP** grasps or seizes firmly

GRIPT *v p t of* **GRIP** grasped or seized firmly; *also* **GRIPPED**

GRIPY *adj* **GRIPIER, GRIPIEST** resembling or causing complaints; *also* **GRIPEY**

GRISE *n* SCOT. a young suckling pig; *also* **GRICE**

GRIST *n* ground grain

GRITH *n* SCOT. protection or asylum for a limited period of time, as under church or crown

GRITS *n pl of* **GRIT** sand or gravel; rough, hard particles

GROAN *v* **-ED, -ING, -S** to utter a deep sound expressing pain, distress, or disapproval

GROAT *n* an obsolete English silver coin worth four pence

GRODY *adj* **GRODIER, GRODIEST** repulsive; disgusting; nauseating

GROIN *n pl* **-S** the fold or hollow on either side of the front of the body where the thigh joins the abdomen

GROKS *v pr t of* **GROK** understands profoundly through intuition

GROOM *v* **-ED, -ING, -S** to care for the appearance of

GROPE *v* **-ED, -ING, -S** to feel with or use the hands; to handle

GROSS *v* **-ED, -ING, -ES** to earn before taxes, expenses

GROSZ *n pl* **GROSZY** a unit of currency in Poland

GROUP *v* **-ED, -ING, -S** to place or associate together in a group, as with others

GROUT *v* **-ED, -ING, -S** to fill up cracks with a thin mortar

GROVE *n pl* **-S** a garden consisting of a small cultivated wood without undergrowth; *also* **GREVE**

GROWL *v* **-ED, -ING, -S** to murmur or complain angrily; grumble

GROWN *v p t of* **GROW** increased in any way

GROWS *v pr t of* **GROW** increases in any way

GRUBS *v pr t of* **GRUB** to clear by digging roots

GRUEL *n* a thin porridge

GRUED *v p t of* **GRUE** SCOT. shivered or shuddered

GRUES *v pr t of* **GRUE** SCOT. shivers or shudders

GRUFF *adj* **-ER, -EST** brusque or stern in manner or appearance

GRUME *n* a thick, sticky fluid

GRUMP *n pl* **-S** a cranky, complaining person

GRUNT *v* **-ED, -ING, -S** to utter a deep, guttural sound

GRYDE *v* **-D, GRYDING, -S** to pierce or cut; *also* **GRIDE**

GRYPE *v* **-D, GRYPING, -S** to complain constantly; *also* **GRIPE**

GUACO *n* a plant of Carthagena used as an antidote to serpent bites

GUANO *n pl* **-S** a fertilizer containing the accumulated excrement of seabirds or bats

GUANS *n pl of* **GUAN** large fruit-eating birds

GUARA *n pl* **-S** a large-maned wild dog of South America

GUARD *v* **-ED, -ING, -S** to protect from danger

GUARS *n pl of* **GUAR** annual leguminous plants native to India

GUAVA *n pl* **-S** small tropical American shrubby tree

GUESS *v* **-ED, -ING, -S** to judge or form an opinion of, from reasons that seem preponderating, but are not decisive

GUEST *n pl* **-S** a visitor to whom hospitality is extended

GUIDE *v* **-D, GUIDING, -S** to direct in a way

GUILD *n pl* **-S** an association of people with similar interests or pursuits

GUILE *v* **-D, GUILING, -S** to disguise or conceal; to deceive or delude

GUILT *n* the state of having committed an offense

GUIRO *n pl* **-S** a Latin-American percussion instrument made of a hollow gourd with a grooved or serrated surface

GUISE *n pl* **-S** external appearance in manner or dress; *also* **GYSE**

GULAE *n pl of* **GULA** the upper fronts of the neck, the upper throats or gullets; *also* **GULAS**

GULAG *n* a forced labor camp or prison, especially for political dissidents

GULAR *adj* of, relating to, or located on the throat

GULAS *n pl of* **GULA** the upper fronts of the neck, the upper throats or gullets; *also* **GULAE**

GULCH *n* -ES a narrow gorge with a stream running through it

GULES *v pr t of* **GULE** to give the color of gules to, the color red

GULFS *n pl of* **GULF** deep chasms or abysses

GULFY *adj* **GULFIER, GULFIEST** full of whirlpools or gulfs

GULLS *v pr t of* **GULL** to deceive, trick or cheat

GULLY *n pl* **GULLIES** a channel or small valley, especially one carved out by persistent heavy rainfall

GULPS *v pr t of* **GULP** to swallow eagerly, or in large draughts

GUMBO *n pl* -S a soup or stew thickened with okra pods; *also* **GOMBO**

GUMMA *n pl* -S or -TA a kind of soft tumor

GUMMY *adj* **GUMMIER, GUMMIEST** having the properties of glue or gum

GUMPS *v pr t of* **GUMP** muddles through

GUNKY *adj* **GUNKIER, GUNKIEST** sticky and messy; *also* **GOOEY, GOOPY**

GUNNY *n pl* **GUNNIES** a coarse heavy fabric made of jute or hemp

GUPPY *n pl* **GUPPIES** a small bony, tropical fish

GURGE *v* -D, **GURGING** to swirl like a whirlpool

GURNS *v* -ED, -ING, -S complains, whines or grumbles; *also* **GIRNS**

GURRY *n* refuse from the processing of fish in a cannery

GURSH *n* a monetary unit of Saudi Arabia; *also* **QIRSH, QURSH, GIRSH, GHIRSH**

GURUS *n pl of* **GURU** recognized leaders in some field or movement

GUSHY *adj* **GUSHIER, GUSHIEST** marked by excessive displays of sentiment or enthusiasm

GUSSY *v* **GUSSIED, -ING, GUSSIES** to dress or decorate elaborately; adorn or embellish

GUSTO *n pl* -ES vigorous and enthusiastic enjoyment

GUSTS *n pl of* **GUST** sudden strong blasts of wind

GUSTY *adj* **GUSTIER, GUSTIEST** blowing in gusts

GUTSY *adj* **GUTSIER, GUTSIEST** marked by courage or daring

GUTTA *n pl* -E one of a series of ornaments shaped like drops that are attached to the underside of a Doric entablature

GUTTY *adj* **GUTTIER, GUTTIEST** having a vigorous challenging quality

GUYED *v p t of* **GUY** to ridicule

GUYOT *n pl* -S a flat-topped submarine mountain and considered to be an extinct volcano

GWINE *v pr part of* **GO** informal term for going, moving to or from a place

GYBED *v p t of* **GYBE** shifted from one side to other when running before the wind, as a fore-and-aft sail or its boom; *also* **JIBBED, JIBED**

GYBES *v pr t of* **GYBE** shifts from one side to other when running before the wind, as a fore-and-aft sail or its boom; *also* **JIBS, JIBBS, JIBES**

GYOZA *n* a pocket of dough stuffed with minced pork or shrimp, and fried

GYPSY *n pl* **GYPSIES** a member of a nomadic people originating in northern India; *also* **GIPSY**

GYRAL *adj* moving in a circular path or way

GYRED *v p t of* **GYRE** moved in a circular motion or a turn or revolution

GYRES *v pr t of* **GYRE** moves in a circular motion or a turn or revolution

GYRON *n pl* **-S** triangular part of shield; *also* **GIRON**

GYROS *n pl of* **GYRO** meat, usually lamb, roasted on a vertical spit, then thinly sliced, topped with onions and usually served in a sandwich of pita bread

GYRUS *n pl* **GYRI** a convoluted ridge in the brain

GYVED *v p t of* **GYVE** shackled or fettered

GYVES *v pr t of* **GYVE** shackles or fetters

HA *interj* used to express joy, surprise, wonder, puzzlement, triumph or scorn; *also* **HAH**

HE *pron* used to refer to a man, boy or male animal, either previously mentioned or easily identified

HI *interj* used as a friendly and informal greeting

HM *interj* a sound made when thinking or when one needs time to decide what to say; used typically to express thoughtful consideration, absorption, hesitation, doubt or perplexity; *also* **HMM**

HO *interj* used to draw or attract attention to something

THREE LETTERS

HAD *v p t of* **HAVE** no longer possessed, owned or held

HAE *v* **-D, -N, -ING, -S** SCOT. to have, to possess, own or hold

HAG *n pl* **-S** an old woman considered ugly, frightful or vicious

HAH *interj* used to express joy, surprise, wonder, puzzlement, triumph or scorn; *also* **HA**

HAJ *n pl* **-ES** a pilgrimage or religious journey to Mecca, which Muslims try to make at least once in their lifetime; *also* **HADJ, HAJJ**

HAM *v* **-MED, -MING, -S** to act with exaggerated speech or gestures; to overact a dramatic role

HAO *n pl* **HAO** a subunit of currency in Vietnam

HAP *v* **-PED, -PING, -S** to happen or occur by chance

HAS *v pr t of* **HAVE** possesses, owns or holds

HAT *v* **-TED, -TING, -S** to put on, wear, supply or provide a covering for the head

HAW *v* **-ED, -ING, -S** to fumble or make hesitative sounds while speaking; to vocalize a pause

HAY *v* **-ED, -ING, -S** to furnish animals with cut and dried plants, such as grass, clover or alfalfa

HEH *interj* a half laugh offered as a non-negative response

HEM *v* **-MED, -MING, -S** to turn under and sew down the edge of fabric or clothing

HEN *n pl* **-S** an adult female chicken

HEP *adj* **-PER, -PEST** informal for trendy; very fashionable; stylish; *also* **HIP**

HER *pron* used to refer to a woman, girl, or female animal previously mentioned or easily identified

HET *adj* made warm or hot

HEW *v* **-ED, -N, -ING, -S** to chop or cut with repeated heavy blows of an axe, pick, knife or other cutting tool

HEX *v* **-ED, -ING, -ES** to cast a spell on; to curse or bewitch; to practice witchcraft

HEY *interj* used to attract attention or to preface a remark; also used as an informal greeting

HIC *interj* used to imitate or represent the sound of a hiccup

HID *v p t of* **HIDE** concealed or withdrawn from sight; put or kept out of view; kept secret

HIE *v* **-D, -ING** or **HYING, -S** to go quickly; to hasten or hurry

HIM *pron* used to refer to a man, boy or male animal previously mentioned or easily identified

HIN *n pl* **-S** a liquid measurement used by the ancient Hebrews, equal to about one and a half gallons

HIP *adj* **-PER, -PEST** informal for trendy; very fashionable; stylish; *also* **HEP**

HIS *pron* used to refer to a thing belonging to or associated with a male person or animal; *also* **HISN**

HIT *v* **HIT, -TING, -S** to strike deliberately; to make contact forcefully or violently

HMM *interj* a sound made when thinking or when one needs time to decide what to say; used typically to express thoughtful consideration, absorption, hesitation, doubt or perplexity; *also* **HM**

HOB *v* **-BED, -BING, -S** to furnish something with hobnails, a short nail with a broad head

HOD *n pl* **-S** a v-shaped trough with a long pole handle, used for carrying bricks, mortar or building materials on the shoulder

HOE *v* **-D, -ING, -S** to weed, cultivate or dig up with a hoe, a flat bladed, long-handled garden tool

HOG *v* **-GED, -GING, -S** to take more than one's share or to keep something longer than is fair or polite

HON *n* an informal and affectionate term of address, short or slang for honey

HOO *interj* [obs] an exclamation of triumphant joy

HOP *v* **-PED, -PING, -S** to jump lightly or quickly, especially on one foot; to move by a quick springy leap

HOT *adj* **-TER, -TEST** very warm; at a high temperature

HOW *adv* in what manner; by what means

HOX *v* [obs] to disable by cutting the tendons of the hock, a joint in the hind limb of quadrupeds just above the foot

HOY *n pl* **-S** a small sloop-rigged coasting ship

HUB *n pl* **-S** the central part of a wheel, fan or propeller, rotating on or with the axel

HUE *n pl* **-S** the color or shade of color; tint

HUG *v* **-GED, -GING, -S** to put the arms around and hold closely; to embrace tightly and affectionately

HUH *interj* used to express surprise, disbelief, confusion or lack of interest

HUI *n pl* **HUI** N.Z. a ceremonial or social gathering in Maori culture

HUM *v* **-MED, -MING, -S** to sing with closed lips, without words; to make a low, prolonged murmuring sound, like that of a bee

HUN *n pl* **-S** a destructive person

HUP *interj* used to set a marching cadence and mark time

HUT *v* **-TED, -TING, -S** to shelter or take shelter in a small, single story, makeshift dwelling of simple construction

HYP *n pl* **-S** [obs] low spirits, melancholy, used with "the"

FOUR LETTERS

HAAF *n pl* **-S** a deep-sea fishing ground off the Shetland or Orkney Islands

HAAK *n* a marine food fish with an elongated body, related to and resembling the cod; *also* **HAKE**

HAAR *n pl* **-S** SCOT a thick, wet fog along the seacoast

HABU *n pl* **-S** a large venomous snake, native to Okinawa and other Ryukyu Islands in the Pacific

HACK *v* **-ED, -ING, -S** to cut or chop roughly with crude, irregular and repeated blows

HADE *v* **-D, HADING, -S** to incline from the vertical plane, as a fault, vein or lode

HADJ *n pl* **-ES** a pilgrimage or religious journey to Mecca, which Muslims try to make at least once in their lifetime; *also* **HAJ, HAJJ**

HAED *v p t of* **HAE** SCOT. had, possessed, owned or held

HAEM *n* BRIT. the deep red, non-protein portion of the hemoglobin that contains iron; *also* **HEME**

HAEN *v p part of* **HAE** SCOT. had, possessed, owned or held

HAES *v pr t of* **HAE** SCOT. has, possesses, owns or holds

HAET *n pl* **-S** SCOT. a small quantity or amount; a bit

HAFT *v* **-ED, -ING, -S** to equip a weapon or a tool with a hilt or handle

HAGS *n pl of* **HAG** old women considered ugly, frightful or vicious

HAIK *n pl* **-S** a large piece of cotton, silk or wool cloth, worn as a loose fitting outer garment by Arabs in Morocco and northern Africa; *also* **HAICK**

HAIL *v* **-ED, -ING, -S** to cheer, salute, greet or welcome

HAIR *n pl* **-S** any of the fine, threadlike, protein strands that grow from follicles in the skin or epidermis of a human or animal, especially those on the head

HAJI *n* **-S** a Muslim who has made the pilgrimage to Mecca; *also* **HAJJI, HADJI**

HAJJ *n pl* **-ES** a pilgrimage or religious journey to Mecca, which Muslims try to make at least once in their lifetime; *also* **HAJ, HADJ**

HAKE *n pl* **HAKE** or **-S** a marine food fish with an elongated body, related to and resembling the cod; *also* **HAAK**

HAKU *n pl* **-S** a Hawaiian term for a crown made of fresh flowers

HALE *v* **-D, HALING, -S** to compel or force someone to go somewhere, especially to court

HALF *n pl* **HALVES** one of two equal parts that together make a whole

HALK *n* [obs] a nook; a corner

HALL *n pl* **-S** a connecting corridor or passageway in a building

HALM *n pl* **-S** the stalks or stems of cultivated plants, such as peas, beans, potatoes or grasses, left after harvesting the crop; *also* **HAULM**

HALO *v* **-ED, -ING, -S** to encircle with a luminous ring of light

HALT *v* **-ED, -ING, -S** to cause or come to an abrupt stop

HAME *n pl* **-S** one of two curved supports attached to the collar of a draft horse to which the traces are fastened

HAMS *v pr t of* **HAM** exaggerates speech or gestures; overacts a dramatic role

HAND *v* **-ED, -ING, -S** to give, pass or transmit with the part of the arm below the wrist

HANG *v* **HUNG, -ING, -S** to suspend; to fasten to some elevated point without support from below

HANK *n pl* **-S** a coil or looped bundle of fiber, such as rope, wool or yarn

HANT *n pl* **-S** a dialectical variation, from the southern United States, of haunt, a ghost or other supernatural being; *also* **HAINT**

HAPS *v pr t of* **HAP** happens or occurs by chance

HARD *adj* **-ER, -EST** firm; stiff; resistant to pressure; not easily penetrated

HARE *v* **-D, HARING, -S** BRIT. to run or go very quickly

HARK *v* **-ED, -ING, -S** to listen to; to hearken

HARL *v* **-ED, -ING, -S** to cover the exterior walls of a building with lime and gravel or sand

HARM *n pl* **-S** injury; hurt; damage; detriment; misfortune

HARP *v* **-ED, -ING, -S** to talk or write about to an excessive degree

HART *n pl* **-S** a stag; the male of the red deer; *also* **HERT**

HARY *v* [obs] to draw; to drag; to carry off by violence

HASH *v* **-ED, -ING, -ES** to chop into small pieces; to mince

HASK *n* [obs] a basket made of rushes or flags, for carrying fish

HASP *v* **-ED, -ING, -S** to fasten with a hasp, a clasp for a door

HAST *v pr t of* **HAVE** [obs] possesses, owns or holds

HATE *v* **-D, HATING, -S** to dislike intensely; feel antipathy or aversion towards

HATH *v pr t of* **HAVE** [obs] possesses, owns or holds

HATS *v pr t of* **HAT** puts on, wears, supplies or provides a covering for the head

HAUL *v* **-ED, -ING, -S** to pull or draw with force; to drag

HAUT *adj* high-class; *also* **HAUTE**

HAVE *v* **HAD, HAVING, HAS** to possess, own or hold

HAWK *v* **-ED, -ING, -S** to hunt using a bird of prey

HAWM *v* **-ED, -ING, -S** to lounge; to loiter

HAWS *v pr t of* **HAW** fumbles or makes hesitative sounds while speaking; vocalizes a pause

HAYS *v pr t of* **HAY** furnishes animals with cut and dried plants, such as grass, clover or alfalfa

HAZE *v* **-D, HAZING, -S** to harass by imposing humiliating or painful tasks

HAZY *adj* **HAZIER, HAZIEST** obscure; confused; not clear

HEAD *n pl* **-S** the uppermost or forward most part of the body of a vertebrate, containing the brain and the eyes, ears, nose, mouth and jaws

HEAL *v* **-ED, -ING, -S** to provide a cure for, make healthy again

HEAM *n pl* **-S** the afterbirth or secundines of a beast

HEAP *v* **-ING, ED, -S** put things in a pile

HEAR *v* **-D, -ING, -S** to perceive sound by the ear

HEAT *v* **-ED, -ING, -S** to make warm or hot

HEBE *n pl* **-S** a shrub or tree having evergreen leaves and clusters or spikes of white, pink or purple flowers

HECK *n pl* **-S** a device that guides yarn onto the bobbin of a spinning wheel

HEED *v* **-ED, -ING, -S** to mind; to consider

HEEL *v* **-ED, -ING, -S** to follow closely when commanded

HEEP *n* [obs] the hip of the dog-rose

HEER *n pl* **-S** an old unit of measure for yarn

HEFT *v* **-ED, -ING, -S** to heave up; to raise aloft

HEHS *n pl of* **HEH** the fifth letter of the Hebrew alphabet

HEIL *v* **-ED, -ING, -S** to salute

HEIR *n pl* **-S** one who will legally receive money, property or a title from another person when that person dies

HELD *v p t of* **HOLD** grasped something

HELE *v* [obs] to hide; to cover; to roof

HELL *n pl* **-S** a place of punishment after death

HELM *v* **-ED, -ING, -S** to steer; to guide; to direct

HELO *n pl* **-S** informal for a helicopter, a rotary-winged aircraft

HELP *v* **-ED, -ING, -S** to assist someone

HEME *n* the deep red, non-protein portion of the hemoglobin that contains iron; *also* **HAEM**

HEMP *n pl* **-S** a plant used to make rope and strong, rough cloth

HEMS *v pr t of* **HEM** turns under and sews down the edge of fabric or clothing

HENS *n pl of* **HEN** adult female chickens

HENT *v* **-ED, -ING, -S** [obs] to seize; to take hold of

HERB *n pl* **-S** a low-growing aromatic plant used fresh or dried for seasoning, perfumes or medicinal properties

HERD *n pl* **-S** a group of animals assembled together

HERE *adv* in or at this place

HERL *n pl* **-S** the barb of a feather used for trimming an artificial fishing fly

HERM *n pl* **-S** a pillar with a bust on top usually of the Greek god Hermes; *also* **HERMA**

HERN *n pl* **-S** a heron

HERO *n pl* **-ES** a person distinguished by exceptional courage, nobility and strength

HERS *pron* something belonging to her

HERT *n pl* **-S** [obs] a stag; the male of the red deer; *also* **HART**

HERY *v* [obs] to worship; to glorify; to praise

HESP *n* SCOT. a measure of two hanks of linen thread

HEST *n pl* **-S** a command or directive

HETH *n pl* **-S** the eighth letter of the Hebrew alphabet; *also* **CHETH**

HEUK *n* [obs] an outer garment worn in Europe in the Middle Ages; *also* **HUKE, HYKE**

HEWE *n* [obs] a domestic servant

HEWN *v p part of* **HEW** has chopped or cut with repeated heavy blows of an axe, pick, knife or other cutting tool

HEWS *v pr t of* **HEW** chops or cuts with repeated heavy blows of an axe, pick, knife or other cutting tool

HICK *n pl* **-S** a person regarded as gullible or provincial

HIDE *v* **HID, HIDDEN, HIDING, -S** to conceal or withdraw from sight; to put or keep out of view; to keep secret

HIED *v p t of* **HIE** gone quickly; hastened or hurried

HIES *v pr t of* **HIE** goes quickly; goes in haste or hurries

HIGH *adj* **-ER, -EST** of great height

HIKE *v* **-D, HIKING, -S** to walk a long distance

HILA *n pl of* **HILUM** the scar on a seed, such as a bean, indicating the point of attachment to the ovule

HILI *n pl of* **HILUS** openings through which blood vessels and nerves enter or leave an organ

HILL *n pl* **-S** a well-defined natural elevation smaller than a mountain

HILT *n pl* **-S** the handle of a sword or dagger

HIMS *n pl of* **HIM** a male

HIND *n pl* **-S** a female red deer

HINE *n* [obs] a servant; a farm laborer; *also* **HYNE**

HINK *n* a reaping hook

HINS *n pl of* **HIN** liquid measurements used by the ancient Hebrews, equal to about one and a half gallons

HINT *v* **-ED, -ING, -S** to make an indirect suggestion

HIPS *n pl of* **HIP** the fruits of rosebushes

HIRE *v* -D, HIRING, -S to engage the services of a person for a fee

HISN *pron* [obs] used to refer to a thing belonging to or associated with a male person or animal; *also* **HIS**

HISS *v* -ED, -ING, -ES to make a sharp sibilant sound; *also* **HIZZ**

HIST *interj* a sibilant exclamation used to attract attention

HITS *v pr t of* **HIT** strikes deliberately; makes contact forcefully or violently

HIVE *v* -D, HIVING, -S to cause bees to gather in their shelter

HIZZ *v* -ED, -ING, -ES [obs] to make a sharp sibilant sound; *also* **HISS**

HOAR *adj* white or grayish in color, usually as a result of age or frost

HOAX *v* -ED, -ING, -ES to deceive or cheat

HOBO *n pl* -S or -ES a person without a job or a house, especially one who travelled looking for work during the depression

HOBS *v pr t of* **HOB** furnishes something with hobnails, a short nail with a broad head

HOCK *v* -ED, -ING, -S to pawn

HODS *n pl of* **HOD** v-shaped troughs with long pole handles, used for carrying bricks, mortar or building materials on the shoulder

HOED *v p t of* **HOE** weeded, cultivated or dug up with a hoe, a flat bladed, long-handled garden tool

HOER *n pl* -S a person who weeds or cultivates

HOES *v pr t of* **HOE** weeds, cultivates or digs up with a hoe, a flat bladed, long-handled garden tool

HOGG *n pl* -S BRIT. a domesticated swine

HOGH *n* [obs] a hill; a cliff

HOGO *n* [obs] a high flavor; strong scent

HOGS *v pr t of* **HOG** takes more than one's share or keeps something longer than is fair or polite

HOIT *v* -ED, -ING, -S [obs] to leap

HOKE *v* -D, HOKING, -S to give an impressive but artificial quality to

HOLD *v* HELD, -ING, -S to grasp something

HOLE *v* -D, HOLING, -S to make a hollow space in a solid object

HOLM *n pl* -S an island in a river or lake

HOLP *v p t of* **HELP** [obs] assisted someone

HOLS *n/pl* BRIT. informal for days spent on vacation, especially a school or annual vacation

HOLT *n pl* -S a wood or grove

HOLY *adj* HOLIER, HOLIEST having a spiritually pure quality

HOME *v* -D, HOMING to go or return to the place where one lives

HOMY *adj* HOMIER, HOMIEST like a home; pleasant, cozy; *also* **HOMEY**

HONE *v* -D, HONING, -S make more acute or effective over time

HONG *n pl* -S a commercial establishment or warehouse in China

HONK *v* -ED, -ING, -S to sound the horn of a car

HOOD *v* -ED, -ING, -S to furnish with a covering for the head

HOOF *v* -ED, -ING, -S to dance

HOOK *v* -ED, -ING, -S to fasten with a metal device that is curved or bent to suspend, hold or pull something

HOOP *v* -ED, -ING, -S to encircle; surround

HOOT *v* -ED, -ING, -S to make the peculiar cry of an owl

HOPE *v* -D, HOPING, -S to look forward to with desire

HOPS *v pr t of* **HOP** jumps lightly or quickly, especially on one foot; moves by a quick springy leap

HORA *n pl* **-S** a traditional round dance of Romania and Israel; *also* **HORAH**

HORN *v* **-ED, -ING, -S** to strike, butt or gore with the hard pointed part on the head of cows, goats and other animals

HOSE *v* **-D, HOSING, -S** to water, drench or wash with a tube connected to a water source

HOST *v* **-ED, -ING, -S** to entertain guests in a social or official capacity

HOTE *v* **HOTEN, HATTE, HOT** [obs] to be called; to be named

HOTS *adj* enamored with

HOUR *n pl* **-S** a division of time, one of twenty-four parts of a day

HOVE *v p t of* **HEAVE** to raise or haul up by means of a rope, line or cable, as an anchor

HOWE *n pl* **-S** SCOT. a hollow or valley

HOWF *n pl* **-S** SCOT. a familiar haunt or meeting place; *also* **HOWFF**

HOWL *v* **-ED, -ING, -S** to utter a loud, protracted, mournful sound or cry

HOWS *n/pl* a way or manner of doing things

HOYA *n pl* **-S** any flowering shrub or climbing vine of the milkweed family

HOYS *n pl of* **HOY** small sloop-rigged coasting ships

HUBS *n pl of* **HUB** the central part of wheels, fans, or propellers, rotating on or with the axle

HUCK *v* **-ED, -ING, -S** [obs] to haggle in trading

HUED *adj* having color or shades of color; tinted

HUER *n pl* **-S** a person stationed at the bow of a boat to watch the movements of the fish and direct the course of the boat accordingly

HUES *n pl of* **HUE** colors or shades of color; tints

HUFF *v* **-ED, -ING, -S** exhale noisily to show annoyance

HUGE *adj* **-R, -ST** very large; enormous; immense

HUGS *v pr t of* **HUG** puts the arms around and holds closely; embraces tightly and affectionately

HUGY *adj* [obs] vast

HUKE *n* [obs] an outer garment worn in Europe in the Middle Ages; *also* **HEUK, HYKE**

HULA *n pl* **-S** a native Hawaiian dance marked by flowing, pantomimic gestures

HULK *v* **-ED, -ING, -S** to appear as a large looming object

HULL *v* **-ED, -ING, -S** to remove the outer rind or shell from a fruit or vegetable

HULY *adj* SCOT. cautious; gentle; *also* **HOOLY**

HUMP *v* **-ED, -ING, -S** to bend or round into an arch

HUMS *v pr t of* **HUM** sings with closed lips, without words; makes a low, prolonged murmuring sound, like that of a bee

HUNG *v p t of* **HANG** suspended; fastened to some elevated point without support from below

HUNH *interj* used to ask a question

HUNK *n pl* **-S** a large piece of something; a chunk

HUNS *n pl of* **HUN** destructive people

HUNT *v* **-ED, -ING, -S** to search diligently after; to pursue; to follow

HURL *v* **-ED, -ING, -S** to send whirling or whizzing through the air; to fling

HURR *v* **-ED, -ING, -S** [obs] to make a rolling or burring sound

HURT *v* **-ING, -S** to wound or bruise painfully; to injure

HUSH *v* **-ED, -ING, -ES** to silence; to make quiet

HUSK v **-ED, -ING, -S** to remove the external covering of certain fruits or seeds

HUSO n pl **-S** a large European sturgeon; also **HAUSEN, BELUGA**

HUTS v pr t of **HUT** shelters or takes shelter in a small, single story, makeshift dwelling of simple construction

HUZZ v **-ING, -ES** [obs] to buzz; to murmur

HWAN n pl **HWAN** formerly, the basic monetary unit of North Korea and South Korea

HYKE n [obs] an outer garment worn in Europe in the Middle Ages; also **HEUK, HUKE**

HYLA n pl **-S** a small tree frog

HYMN n pl **-S** a song of praise

HYNE n [obs] a servant; a farm laborer; also **HINE**

HYPE v **-D, HYPING, -S** to stimulate; to promote extravagantly

HYPO n pl **-S** a chemical compound used as a fixing agent in photographic processing

HYPS n pl of **HYPE** [obs] low spirits, melancholies, used with "the"

HYTE adj SCOT. [obs] insane; mad

FIVE LETTERS

HAAFS n pl of **HAAF** deep-sea fishing grounds off the Shetland or Orkney Islands

HAARS n pl of **HAAR** SCOT thick, wet fogs along the seacoast

HABIT v **-ED, -ING, -S** to dress somebody in clothing distinctive to a particular position or office

HABUS n pl of **HABU** large venomous snakes, native to Okinawa and other Ryukyu Islands in the Pacific

HACEK n **-S** a diacritical mark (ˇ) placed above certain letters (such as the letter c) to indicate pronunciation

HACKS v pr t of **HACK** cuts or chops roughly with crude, irregular, and repeated blows

HADAL adj pertaining to the deepest trenches in the ocean

HADED v p t of **HADE** inclined from the vertical plane, as a fault, vein or lode

HADES v pr t of **HADE** inclines from the vertical plane, as a fault, vein or lode

HADJI n **-S** a Muslim who has made the pilgrimage to Mecca; also **HAJI, HAJJI**

HADST v [obs] a second person singular past tense of have

HAETS n pl of **HAET** SCOT. small quantities or amounts; bits

HAFIZ n pl **-ES** someone who knows the Koran by heart

HAFTS v pr t of **HAFT** equips a weapon or a tool with a hilt or handle

HAICK n pl **-S** a large piece of cotton, silk or wool cloth, worn as a loose fitting outer garment by Arabs in Morocco and northern Africa; also **HAIK**

HAIKS n pl of **HAIK** large pieces of cotton, silk or wool cloth, worn as a loose fitting outer garments by Arabs in Morocco and northern Africa; also **HAICKS**

HAIKU n pl **HAIKU** or **-S** a Japanese verse form, rendered in English as three unrhymed lines of 5, 7, and 5 syllables, respectively; also **HOKKU**

HAILS v pr t of **HAIL** cheers, salutes, greets or welcomes

HAINT n pl **-S** a dialectical variation, from the southern United States, of haunt, a ghost or other supernatural being; also **HANT**

HAIRS *n pl of* **HAIR** fine, threadlike, protein strands that grow from follicles in the skin or epidermis of a human or animal, especially those on the head

HAIRY *adj* having an abundance of hair

HAJES *n pl of* **HAJ** pilgrimages or religious journeys to Mecca, which Muslims try to make at least once in their lifetime; *also* **HADJES, HAJJES**

HAJIS *n pl of* **HAJI** Muslims who have made the pilgrimage to Mecca; *also* **HAJJIS, HADJIS**

HAJJI *n pl* **-S** a Muslim who has made the pilgrimage to Mecca; *also* **HAJI, HADJI**

HAKES *n pl of* **HAKE** marine fish with elongated bodies, related to and resembling the cod

HAKIM *n pl* **-S** a Muslim doctor who uses traditional remedies; *also* **HAKEEM**

HAKUS *n pl of* **HAKU** a Hawaiian term for crowns made of fresh flowers

HALAL *adj* used to describe meat prepared as prescribed by Muslim law

HALED *v p t of* **HALE** compelled or forced someone to go somewhere, especially to court

HALER *n pl* **-S** or **HALERU** a unit of currency in Bohemia, Moravia and Slovakia, equal to one-hundredth of a koruna; *also* **HELLER**

HALES *v pr t of* **HALE** compels or forces someone to go somewhere, especially to court

HALLO *v* **-ED, -ING, -S** or **-ES** to call out with a loud voice; shout; *also* **HALLOA, HALLOO, HILLO, HILLOA, HOLLO, HULLO, HULLOO**

HALLS *n pl of* **HALL** connecting corridors or passageways in a building or buildings

HALMA *n* a board game similar to Chinese checkers in which players try to move their pieces into their opponent's bases

HALMS *n pl of* **HALM** stalks or stems of cultivated plants, such as peas, beans, potatoes or grasses, left after harvesting the crop; *also* **HAULMS**

HALON *n* **-S** any of several halocarbons used as fire-extinguishing agents

HALOS *v pr t of* **HALO** encircles with a luminous ring of light

HALTS *v pr t of* **HALT** causes or comes to an abrupt stop

HALVA *n pl* **-S** a confection usually made from crushed sesame seeds and honey; *also* **HALVAH, HALAVAH**

HALVE *v* **-ED, -ING, -S** to divide into two equal parts

HAMAL *n pl* **-S** a porter or bearer in certain Muslim countries; *also* **HAMMAL**

HAMES *n pl of* **HAME** two curved supports attached to the collar of a draft horse to which the traces are fastened

HAMMY *adj* **HAMMIER, HAMMIEST** affectedly dramatic; overacted

HAMZA *n pl* **-H** or **-S** a sign (ˈ) used in the written Arabic language representing a glottal stop

HANCE *n pl* **-S** one of the sides of an arch, especially in architecture or ship design

HANDS *v pr t of* **HAND** gives, passes or transmits with the part of the arm below the wrist

HANDY *adj* **HANDIER, HANDIEST** within easy reach

HANGS *v pr t of* **HANG** suspends; fastens to some elevated point without support from below

HANKS *n pl of* **HANK** coils or looped bundles of fiber, such as rope, wool or yarn

HANKY *n pl* **HANKIES** a square piece of cloth used for wiping the eyes or nose; a handkerchief

HANSA *n pl* **-S** a medieval merchant guild or trading association; *also* **HANSE**

HANSE *n pl* **-S** a medieval merchant guild or trading association; *also* **HANSA**

HANTS *n pl of* **HANT** a dialectical variation, from the southern United States, of haunts, ghosts or other supernatural beings; *also* **HAINTS**

HAOLE *n pl* **-S** a non-Polynesian resident of Hawaii

HAPLY *adv* by chance; by accident; perhaps

HAPPY *adj* **HAPPIER, HAPPIEST** enjoying or showing joy or pleasure

HARDS *n/pl* the refuse or coarser parts of flax or hemp before spinning; *also* **HURDS**

HARDY *adj* **HARDIER, HARDIEST** able to survive under unfavorable conditions; capable of enduring fatigue, hardship

HARED *v p t of* **HARE** BRIT. to have run or gone very quickly

HAREM *n pl* **-S** a house or a section of a house reserved for women members of a Muslim household

HARES *v pr t of* **HARE** BRIT. runs or goes very quickly

HARKS *v pr t of* **HARK** listens to; hearkens

HARLS *v pr t of* **HARL** covers the exterior walls of a building with lime and gravel or sand

HARMS *n pl of* **HARM** injuries; hurts; damages; detriments; misfortunes

HARPS *v pr t of* **HARP** talks or writes about to an excessive degree

HARPY *n pl* **HARPIES** a predatory person

HARRY *v* **HARRIED, -ING, HARRIES** annoy continually or chronically

HARSH *adj* **-ER, -EST** disagreeable to the senses

HARTS *n pl of* **HART** stags; males of the red deer; *also* **HERTS**

HASPS *v pr t of* **HASP** fastens with a hasp, a clasp for a door

HASTE *n* quickness in motion

HASTY *adj* **HASTIER, HASTIEST** characterized by speed

HATCH *v* **-ED, -ING, -ES** to emerge from an egg

HATED *v p t of* **HATE** disliked intensely; felt antipathy or aversion towards

HATER *adj* one who feels antipathy or aversion toward something or somebody

HATES *v pr t of* **HATE** dislikes intensely; feels antipathy or aversion towards

HAUGH *n pl* **-S** SCOT. a stretch of alluvial land forming part of a river valley; bottom land

HAULM *n pl* **-S** the stalks or stems of cultivated plants, such as peas, beans, potatoes or grasses, left after harvesting the crop; *also* **HALM**

HAULS *v pr t of* **HAUL** pulls or draws with force; drags

HAUNT *v* **-ED, -ING, -S** to inhabit, visit or appear to in the form of a ghost or other supernatural being

HAUTE *adj* high-class; *also* **HAUT**

HAVEN *n pl* **-S** a place of refuge or safety; shelter

HAVER *v* **-ED, -ING, -S** BRIT. to talk foolishly; to chatter

HAVES *n pl of* **HAVE** a person who possesses great material wealth, as the haves and the have-nots

HAVOC *v* **-KED, -KING, -S** to destroy or pillage

HAWED *v p t of* **HAW** fumbled or made hesitative sounds while speaking; vocalized a pause

HAWKS *v pr t of* **HAWK** hunts using a bird of prey

HAWMS *v pr t of* **HAWM** lounges; loiters

HAWSE *n pl* **-S** the hole in a ship's bow that an anchor rope passes through

HAYED *v p t of* **HAY** furnished animals with cut and dried plants, such as grass, clover or alfalfa

HAYER *n pl* **-S** one who furnishes animals with cut and dried plants, such as grass, clover or alfalfa

HAZED *v p t of* **HAZE** harassed by imposing humiliating or painful tasks

HAZEL *n pl* **-S** a small tree with edible nuts

HAZER *n pl* **-S** one who harasses by imposing humiliating or painful tasks

HAZES *v pr t of* **HAZE** harasses by imposing humiliating or painful tasks

HEADS *n pl of* **HEAD** the uppermost or forward most part of the body of a vertebrate, containing the brain and the eyes, ears, nose, mouth and jaws

HEADY *adj* **HEADIER, HEADIEST** affecting the mind or senses greatly

HEALS *v pr t of* **HEALS** provides a cure for, makes healthy again

HEAPS *v pr t of* **HEAP** puts things in a pile

HEAPY *adj* gathered in heaps

HEARD *v p t of* **HEAR** perceived sound by the ear

HEARS *v pr t of* **HEAR** perceives sound by the ear

HEART *n pl* **-S** the muscular organ in your chest that pumps the blood around your body

HEATH *n pl* **-S** a tract of open, uncultivated land

HEATS *v pr t of* **HEAT** makes warm or hot

HEAVE *v* **-D, HEAVING, -S** to push, pull or lift something using great effort

HEAVY *adj* **HEAVIER, HEAVIEST** having great weight

HEBES *n pl of* **HEBE** shrubs and trees having evergreen leaves and clusters or spikes of white, pink or purple flowers

HECKS *n pl of* **HECK** devices that guide yarn onto the bobbins of spinning wheels

HEDER *n pl* **HADARIM** or **-S** a Jewish elementary school to teach children Hebrew, the Bible, and the fundamentals of Judaism

HEDGE *v* **-D, HEDGING, -S** to avoid making a clear, direct response or statement

HEDGY *adj* **HEDGIER, HEDGIEST** abounding in rows of closely planted shrubs that form a boundary

HEEDS *v pr t of* **HEED** minds; considers

HEELS *v pr t of* **HEEL** follows closely when commanded

HEERS *n pl of* **HEER** units of yarn, under an old measuring system

HEFTS *v pr t of* **HEFT** heaves up; raises aloft

HEFTY *adj* **HEFTIER, HEFTIEST** of considerable weight and size

HEIGH *interj* used to attract notice, give encouragement, etc.

HEILS *v pr t of* **HEIL** salutes

HEIRS *n pl of* **HEIR** those who will legally receive money, property or a title from another person when that person dies

HEIST	*v* -ED, -ING, -S to steal	**HERBY**	*adj* HERBIER, HERBIEST abounding in herbs or grass
HELIX	*n pl* HELICES or -ES an object with a spiral shape or form	**HERDS**	*n pl of* HERD groups of animals assembled together
HELLO	*v* -ED, -ING, -S to express a greeting by using the word "hello"	**HERES**	*n pl* HEREDES an heir; *also* HAERES
HELLS	*n pl of* HELL places of punishment after death	**HERLS**	*n pl of* HERL barbs of feathers used for trimming an artificial fishing fly
HELMS	*v pr t of* HELM steers; guides; directs	**HERMA**	*n pl* -E or -I a pillar with a bust on top usually of the Greek god Hermes; *also* HERM
HELOS	*n pl of* HELO informal for helicopters, rotary-winged aircrafts	**HERMS**	*n pl of* HERM pillars with a bust on top usually of the Greek god Hermes; *also* HERMAE, HERMAI
HELOT	*n pl* -S a serf, a slave		
HELPS	*v pr t of* HELP assists someone		
HELVE	*v* -D, HELVING, -S to furnish an ax, hatchet, hammer or the like with a handle	**HERNS**	*n pl of* HERN herons
HEMAL	*adj* relating to blood or blood vessels	**HERON**	*n pl* -S a freshwater wading bird which has long legs and a long beak, and which eats fish
HEMIC	*adj* relating to blood or blood vessels	**HERRY**	*v* SCOT. HERRIED, HERRYING to harass; annoy continually or chronically
HEMPS	*n pl of* HEMP plants used to make rope and strong, rough cloth	**HERTS**	*n pl of* HERT [obs] stags; males of the red deer; *also* HARTS
HEMPY	*adj* SCOT. mischievous; often in trouble for mischief	**HERTZ**	*n pl* HERTZ a unit of frequency; one hertz has a periodic interval of one second
HENCE	*adv* from this time; for this reason		
HENGE	*n* -S a prehistoric monument consisting of a circle of stone or wooden uprights	**HESTS**	*n pl of* HEST commands or directives
HENNA	*v* -ED, -ING, -S to dye using henna, a reddish or black dye obtained from the powdered leaves and young shoots of the mignonette tree	**HETHS**	*n pl of* HETH more than one of the eighth letter of the Hebrew alphabet
		HEUCH	*n pl* -S SCOT. cliff, ravine
		HEWED	*v p t of* HEW chopped or cut with repeated heavy blows of an axe, pick, knife or other cutting tool
HENRY	*n pl* HENRIES, -S a unit of inductance in which an induced electromotive force of one volt is produced when the current is varied at the rate of one ampere per second	**HEWER**	*n pl* -S one who hews, especially one who chops wood with an axe
		HEXAD	*n pl* -S a group or series of six
		HEXED	*v p t of* HEX casted a spell on; cursed or bewitched; practiced witchcraft
HENTS	*v pr t of* HENT [obs] seizes; takes hold of	**HEXER**	*n pl* -S one who places a spell
HERBS	*n pl of* HERB low-growing aromatic plants used fresh or dried for seasoning, perfumes or medicinal properties	**HEXES**	*v pr t of* HEX casts a spell on; curses or bewitches; practices witchcraft

HEXYL *adj* containing the hydrocarbon radical, C_6H_{13}

HICKS *n pl of* **HICK** people regarded as gullible or provincial

HIDED *v p t of* **HIDE** beat severely; flogged

HIDER *n pl* -**S** one who conceals things

HIDES *v pr t of* **HIDE** conceals or withdraws from sight; places or keeps out of view; keeps secret

HIGHS *adj* positive or happy feelings

HIGHT *adj* [obs] called or named

HIJAB *n* a headscarf worn by Muslim women

HIJRA *n* the flight of Muhammad from Mecca to Medina, marking the beginning of the Muslim Era; *also* **HEGIRA, HEJIRA**

HIKED *v p t of* **HIKE** to have walked a long distance

HIKER *n pl* -**S** a person who is going for a long walk

HIKES *v pr t of* **HIKE** walks a long distance

HILAR *adj* of or relating to the hilum, the scar on a seed where it was attached to the stalk

HILLO *v* -**ED, -ING, -S** to call out with a loud voice; shout; *also* **HALLO, HALLOA, HALLOO, HILLOA, HOLLO, HULLO, HULLOO**

HILLS *n pl of* **HILL** well-defined natural elevations smaller than a mountain

HILLY *adj* **HILLIER, HILLIEST** full of hills

HILTS *n pl of* **HILT** handles of swords or daggers

HILUM *n pl* **HILA** the scar on a seed, such as a bean, indicating the point of attachment to the ovule

HILUS *n pl* **HILI** an opening through which blood vessels and nerves enter or leave an organ

HINDS *n pl of* **HIND** more than one female red deer

HINGE *v* -**D, -ING** or **HINGING, -S** to depend on or be contingent upon

HINKY *adj* **HINKIER, HINKIEST** suspicious; strange, unusual

HINNY *n pl* **HINNIES** the offspring of a male horse and a female donkey

HINTS *v pr t of* **HINT** makes an indirect suggestion

HIPLY *adv* fashionably or stylishly

HIPPO *n pl* -**S** informal for hippopotamus, a massive thick-skinned herbivorous animal living in or around rivers of tropical Africa

HIPPY *adj* **HIPPIER, HIPPIEST** having large hips

HIRED *v p t of* **HIRE** engaged the services of a person for a fee

HIREE *n* -**S** someone who is engaged by another to provide a service in exchange for a fee

HIRER *n* -**S** someone who engages the services of another for a fee

HIRES *v pr t of* **HIRE** engages the services of a person for a fee

HISSY *n pl* **HISSIES** a fit of anger; temper tantrum

HITCH *v* -**ED, -ING, -ES** to connect to a vehicle

HIVED *v p t of* **HIVE** caused bees to gather in their shelter

HIVES *v pr t of* **HIVE** causes bees to gather in their shelter

HOAGY *n pl* **HOAGIES** sandwich made on a long bun; submarine sandwich; *also* **HOAGIE**

HOARD *v* -**ED, -ING, -S** to save or store things

HOARY *adj* **HOARIER, HOARIEST** gray or white with age

HOBBY *n pl* **HOBBIES** an activity followed regularly for pleasure

HOBOS *n pl of* **HOBO** people without jobs or houses, especially those who travelled looking for work during the depression

HOCKS *v pr t of* **HOCK** pawns

HOCUS *v* **-ED, -ING, -ES** or **-SES** to perpetrate a trick

HODAD *n pl* **-S** a non-surfer who spends time at the beach with surfers

HODDY *n pl* **HODDIES** the hooded or carrion crow; *also* **HOODY**

HOERS *n pl of* **HOER** people who weed or cultivate

HOGAN *n pl* **-S** a Navajo Indian dwelling

HOGGS *n pl of* **HOGG** BRIT. domesticated swine

HOICK *v* **-ED, -ING, -S** to change direction abruptly

HOISE *v* **-D, -ING, -S** [obs] to raise or haul up with or as with the help of a mechanical apparatus; *also* **HOIST**

HOIST *v* **-ED, -ING, -S** to raise or haul up with or as with the help of a mechanical apparatus; *also* **HOISE**

HOKED *v p t of* **HOKE** gave an impressive but artificial quality to

HOKES *v pr t of* **HOKE** gives an impressive but artificial quality to

HOKEY *adj* **HOKIER, HOKIEST** obviously contrived

HOKKU *n pl* **HOKKU** a Japanese verse form, rendered in English as three unrhymed lines of 5, 7, and 5 syllables, respectively; *also* **HAIKU**

HOKUM *n* nonsense

HOLDS *v pr t of* **HOLD** grasps something

HOLED *v p t of* **HOLE** made a hollow space in a solid object

HOLES *n pl of* **HOLE** makes a hollow space in a solid object

HOLEY *adj* full of hollow spaces

HOLLO *v* **-ED, -ING, -S** or **-ES** to call out with a loud voice; shout; *also* **HALLO, HALLOA, HALLOO, HILLO, HILLOA, HULLO, HULLOO**

HOLLY *n pl* **HOLLIES** an evergreen bush with red berries

HOLMS *n pl of* **HOLM** islands in rivers or lakes

HOLTS *n pl of* **HOLT** woods or groves

HOMED *v p t of* **HOME** went or returned to the place where one lives

HOMER *n pl* **-S** a home run

HOMES *n pl of* **HOME** places where people live; residences

HOMEY *adj* **HOMIER, HOMIEST** like a home; pleasant, cozy; *also* **HOMY**

HOMIE *n pl* **-S** informal for a friend; somebody one often hangs out with

HONAN *n* a pongee fabric made from the filaments of the wild silkworm

HONDA *n* an eye at one end of a lariat through which the other end is passed to form a lasso, noose, etc.

HONED *v p t of* **HONE** made more acute or effective over time

HONER *n pl* **-S** a whetstone made of fine gritstone; used for sharpening blades

HONES *v pr t of* **HONE** makes more acute or effective over time

HONEY *v* **HONIED** or **-ED, -ING, -S** to make sweet with or as with the fluid produced by bees from the nectar of flowers

HONGI *v* **-ED, -ING, -ES** N.Z. to greet each other in the traditional Maori fashion, by touching noses

HONGS *n pl of* **HONG** commercial establishments or warehouses in China

HONKS *v pr t of* **HONK** sounds the horn of a car

HONOR v -ED, -ING, -S to pay public respect to

HOOCH n illicitly made or obtained alcoholic liquor; also **HOOTCH**

HOODS v pr t of **HOOD** furnishes with a covering for the head

HOODY n pl **HOODIES** the hooded or carrion crow; also **HODDY**

HOOEY n silly talk or writing

HOOFS v pr t of **HOOF** dances

HOOKA n pl -S a tobacco smoking pipe designed with a long tube passing through an urn of water; also **HOOKAH**, **NARGHILE**

HOOKS v pr t of **HOOK** fastens with a metal device that is curved or bent to suspend, hold or pull something

HOOKY n unjustifiable absence from school, work, etc.; also **HOOKEY**

HOOLY adj SCOT. cautious; gentle; also **HULY**

HOOPS v pr t of **HOOP** encircles; surrounds

HOOTS v pr t of **HOOT** makes the peculiar cry of an owl

HOPED v p t of **HOPE** looked forward to with desire

HOPER n pl -S one who looks forward to something with desire

HOPES v pr t of **HOPE** looks forward to with desire

HOPPY adj HOPPIER, HOPPIEST having the taste or aroma of hops, a dried fruit used to make beer

HORAH n pl -S a traditional round dance of Romania and Israel; also **HORA**

HORAL adj of or pertaining to an hour or hours; hourly

HORAS n pl of **HORA** traditional round dances of Romania and Israel; also **HORAHS**

HORDE n -S a very large excited crowd

HORNS v pr t of **HORN** strikes, butts or gores with the hard pointed part on the head of cows, goats and other animals

HORNY adj HORNIER, HORNIEST consisting of or feeling hard like horn

HORSE v -D, HORSING, -S informal for to fool about or indulge in frivolous activity

HORST n pl -S a mass of the earth's crust that lies between two faults and is higher than the surrounding land

HORSY adj HORSIER, HORSIEST of, pertaining to, or characteristic of a horse

HOSED v p t of **HOSE** drenched or washed with a tube connected to a water source

HOSEL n pl -S the socket in the head of a golf club where the shaft is attached

HOSEN n pl of **HOSE** [obs] articles of clothing for the feet and lower parts of the legs

HOSER n one who drenches or washes with a tube connected to a water source

HOSES v pr t of **HOSE** drenches or washes with a tube connected to a water source

HOSEY v -ED, -ING, -S to choose sides, as in a children's game

HOSTA n pl -S a shade-tolerant plant with ornamental foliage

HOSTS v pr t of **HOST** entertains guests in a social or official capacity

HOTCH v -ED, -ING, -ES SCOT. to fidget

HOTEL n -S an establishment where travelers can pay for lodging and often food

HOTLY adv in an angry or hot manner

HOUND v -S, -ING, -ED to chase someone or refuse to leave them alone; harass

HOURI n pl -S one of the beautiful young female companions in the Muslim paradise

HOURS *n pl of* **HOUR** divisions of time, more than one of twenty-four parts of a day

HOUSE *v* **-D, HOUSING, -S** to provide living quarters for; lodge

HOVEL *n pl* **-S** a small crude shelter used as a dwelling

HOVER *v* **-S, -ING, -ED** to suspend or float in the air near one place

HOWDY *interj* greeting expression of hello; how do you do

HOWES *n pl of* **HOWE** SCOT. hollows or valleys

HOWFF *n pl* **-S** SCOT. a familiar haunt or meeting place; *also* **HOWF**

HOWFS *n pl of* **HOWF** SCOT. familiar haunts or meeting places; *also* **HOWFFS**

HOWLS *v p t of* **HOWL** utters a loud, protracted, mournful sounds or cries

HOYAS *n pl of* **HOYA** flowering shrubs or climbing vines of the milkweed family

HUBBY *n pl* **HUBBIES** informal term for a husband

HUCKS *v pr t of* **HUCK** [obs] haggles in trading

HUERS *n pl of* **HUER** people stationed at the bows of boats to watch the movements of the fish and direct the course of the boats accordingly

HUFFS *v pr t of* **HUFF** exhales noisily to show annoyance

HUFFY *adj* **HUFFIER, HUFFIEST** easily offended; touchy

HUGER *adj* larger; more enormous; more immense

HULAS *n pl of* **HULA** native Hawaiian dances marked by flowing, pantomimic gestures

HULKS *v pr t of* **HULK** appears as a large looming object

HULKY *adj* **HULKIER, HULKIEST** of great size and bulk

HULLO *v* **-ED, -ING, -S** or **-ES** to call out with a loud voice; shout; *also* **HALLO, HALLOA, HALLOO, HILLO, HILLOA, HOLLO, HULLOO**

HULLS *v pr t of* **HULL** removes the outer rind or shell from a fruit or vegetable

HUMAN *n pl* **-S** a person

HUMIC *adj* of or relating to the organic component of soil

HUMID *adj* containing or characterized by a great deal of water vapor

HUMOR *v* **-ED, -ING, -S** to do what someone wants in order to keep them happy

HUMPH *interj* used to indicate disbelief contempt

HUMPS *v pr t of* **HUMP** bends or rounds into an arch

HUMPY *adj* **HUMPIER, HUMPIEST** covered with or containing humps or bunches

HUMUS *n* the organic part of soil which consists of dead plants that have begun to decay

HUNCH *v* **-ED, -ING, -ES** to bend one's upper body forward

HUNKS *n pl of* **HUNK** large pieces of something; chunks

HUNKY *adj* **HUNKIER, HUNKIEST** with good physique; masculine, well built

HUNTS *v pr t of* **HUNT** searches diligently after; pursues; follows

HURDS *n/pl* the refuse or coarser parts of flax or hemp before spinning; *also* **HARDS**

HURLS *v pr t of* **HURL** sends whirling or whizzing through the air; flings

HURLY *n pl* **HURLIES** noise; confusion; uproar

HURRS *v pr t of* **HURR** [obs] makes a rolling or burring sound

HURRY *v* **HURRIED, -ING, HURRIES** to move quickly

HURST *n pl* **-S** a wood or grove

HURTS *v pr t of* **HURT** wounds or bruises painfully; injures

HUSKS *v pr t of* **HUSK** removes the external covering of certain fruits or seeds

HUSKY *adj* **HUSKIER, HUSKIEST** sounding deep and hoarse

HUSOS *n pl of* **HUSO** large European sturgeon; *also* **HAUSEN, BELUGA**

HUTCH *n pl* **-ES** a box or cage for keeping rabbits or small animals

HUZZA *v* **-ED, -ING, -S** to cheer; *also* **HUZZAH**

HYDRA *n pl* **-E** or **-S** a small tubular solitary freshwater polyp

HYDRO *n pl* **-S** informal for hydroelectric power

HYENA *n pl* **-S** a dog-like nocturnal mammal of Africa and southern Asia; *also* **HYAENA**

HYING *v pr part of* **HIE** going quickly; hasting or hurrying

HYLAS *n pl of* **HYLA** small tree frogs

HYMEN *n pl* **-S** a membranous fold of tissue that partly or completely occludes the external vaginal orifice

HYMNS *n pl of* **HYMN** songs of praise

HYPED *v p t of* **HYPE** stimulated; promoted extravagantly

HYPER *adj* having a very excitable or nervous temperament

HYPES *v pr t of* **HYPE** stimulates; promotes extravagantly

HYPHA *n pl* **-E** one of the threadlike elements of mycelium

HYPOS *n pl of* **HYPO** chemical compounds used as fixing agents in photographic processing

HYRAX *n pl* **-ES** or **HYRACES** any of several herbivorous mammals of the family Procaviidae

HYSON *n pl* **-S** a Chinese green tea dried and prepared from twisted leaves

ID *n pl* **-S** a small European freshwater cyprinoid fish

IF *n pl* **-S** an uncertain possibility

IN *prep* used to indicate location, state or period of time during or after

IO *n pl* **-S** a small, rare Hawaiian hawk, which is the only living indigenous bird of prey on the island of Hawaii

IS *v pr t of* **BE** the 3rd person singular of the substantive verb be

IT *pron* **-S** used to refer to that one previously mentioned

THREE LETTERS

ICE *v* **-D, ICING, -S** to cover or decorate with a sugar coating

ICH *n pl* **ICHS** a contagious disease of certain fishes

ICK *interj* an expression of distaste or repugnance

ICY *adj* **ICIER, ICIEST** pertaining to, resembling ice; cold; frosty

IDS *pl of* **ID** small European freshwater cyprinoid fish

IFF *conj* if and only if

IFS *n pl of* **IF** uncertain possibilities

IGG *v* **-ED, -ING, -S** to ignore or snub

ILE *n pl* **-S** [obs] an island

ILK *n* type or kind of person or thing

ILL *adj* **-ER, -EST** not healthy; sick

IMP *v* **-ED, -ING, -S** to repair the broken wing of a hawk or falcon by grafting on new feathers

INK *v* **-ED, -ING, -S** to mark, coat or stain with a colored liquid or paste used for writing, printing or drawing

INN *v* -ED, -ING, -S [obs] to house, to lodge

INS *n/pl* usually used with "and outs" to mean all the detailed facts and points about something

ION *n pl* -S an electrically charged atom or molecule

IOS *pl of* **IO** small, rare Hawaiian hawks, which are the only living indigenous birds of prey on the island of Hawaii

IRA *n* belligerence aroused by a real or supposed wrong

IRE *n* -FUL strong anger

IRK *v* -ED, -ING, -S to irritate, annoy or exasperate

IRP *n pl* -S [obs] a fantastic grimace or contortion of the body; *also* **IRPE**

ISM *n pl* -S a distinctive doctrine, system of belief or theory

ITS *pron* the possessive form of **IT**

IVY *n pl* **IVIES** a climbing vine of the genus Hedera

FOUR LETTERS

IAMB *n pl* -S, -USES or **IAMBI** a metrical foot with an unstressed then stressed syllable; *also* **IAMBUS**

IBEX *n pl* -ES or **IBICES** a wild mountain goat with large backward-curving horns

IBIS *n pl* -ES large wading bird having long, slender, downward-curved bill

ICED *v p t of* **ICE** covered or decorated with a sugar coating

ICES *v pr t of* **ICE** covers or decorates with a sugar coating

ICHS *n pl of* **ICH** contagious diseases of certain fishes

ICKY *adj* **ICKIER, ICKIEST** unpleasantly sticky; offensive; distasteful

ICON *n pl* -S an image or representation; *also* **IKON, EIKON**

IDEA *n pl* -S a thought, conception or notion

IDEM *adj* the same, especially a book, article or chapter previously mentioned

IDES *n pl* in the Roman calendar: the 15th of March, May, July or October or the 13th of any other month

IDLE *v* -D, -LING, -S to pass time without working or while avoiding work

IDLY *adv* ineffectually; vainly; lazily; carelessly

IDOL *n pl* -S an image or representation of anything

IDYL *n pl* -S a short poem or prose piece depicting a rural or pastoral scene, usually in idealized terms; *also* **IDYLL**

IFFY *adj* **IFFIER, IFFIEST** doubtful; uncertain

IGGS *v pr t of* **IGG** ignores or snubs

IGLU *n pl* -S an Eskimo house or hut, usually dome-shaped and built of blocks of packed snow; *also* **IGLOO**

IKAT *n* a craft in which one tie-dyes and weaves yarn to create an intricately designed fabric

IKON *n pl* -S an image or representation; *also* **ICON, EIKON**

ILEA *n pl of* **ILEUM** more than one of the third portion of the small intestine

ILES *n pl of* **ILE** [obs] islands; *also* **ISLES**

ILEX *n pl* -ES evergreen trees and shrubs, including holly

ILIA *n pl of* **ILIUM** the large broad bones forming the upper part of the pelvis

ILKA *adj* SCOT. each; every

ILLY *adv* not wisely or well; ill

IMAM *n pl* -S in Islam, a man who leads the prayers in a mosque; *also* **IMAN**

IMAN *n pl* -S in Islam, a man who leads the prayers in a mosque; *also* **IMAM**

IMID *n pl* **-S** an acidic derivative of ammonia; *also* **AMIDE, IMIDE**

IMMY *n pl* **IMMIES** a type of playing marble

IMPI *n pl* **-ES** or **IMPI** a group of Zulu warriors

IMPS *v pr t of* **IMP** repairs the broken wing of a hawk or falcon by grafting on new feathers

INBY *adv* away from the shaft or entrance to a mine and therefore toward the working face

INCH *v* **-ED, -ING, -ES** to move or cause to move slowly or by small degrees

INEE *n pl* **-S** a poison used to poison arrow heads or darts for the purposes of hunting; *also* **ONAYE**

INFO *n* commonly used abbreviation for information, collected facts and data about a specific subject

INKS *v pr t of* **INK** marks, coats or stains with a colored liquid or paste used for writing, printing or drawing

INKY *adj* **INKIER, INKIEST** consisting of, or resembling a colored liquid or paste used for writing, printing or drawing

INLY *adv* inwardly; with thorough knowledge or understanding

INNS *v pt t of* **INN** [obs] houses, lodges

INRO *n pl* **INRO** or **-S** a small, usually ornamented box that is hung from the waist sash of a Japanese kimono

INST *adj* in or of the present month

INTI *n pl* **-S** a former monetary unit of Peru

INTO *prep* to the inside or interior of; within

IONS *n pl of* **ION** electrically charged atoms or molecules

IOTA *n pl* **-S** a very small quantity or degree

IRID *n pl* **-S** a plant of the iris family

IRIS *n pl* **IRISES** or **IRIDES** a part of the eye

IRKS *v pr t of* **IRK** to irritate, annoy or exasperate

IRON *v* **-ED, -ING, -S** to remove creases by pressing with a tool made of heated iron or steel

IRPE *n pl* **-S** [obs] a fantastic grimace or contortion of the body; *also* **IRP**

IRPS *n pl of* **IRP** [obs] a fantastic grimace or contortion of the body; *also* **IRPES**

ISBA *n pl* **-S** the traditional log house of rural Russia; *also* **IZBA**

ISLE *v* **-D, ISLING** to place on or as if on an small island

ISMS *n pl of* **ISM** distinctive doctrines, systems, or theories

ITCH *v* **-ED, -ING, -ES** to have a desire to scratch

ITEM *n pl* **-S** an individual article or unit

ITER *n pl* **-S** a passage; especially, between the 3rd and 4th ventricles in the brain

IWIS *adv* [obs] certainly; indeed; truly; *also* **YWIS**

IZAR *n pl* **-S** a long, white cotton outer garment traditionally worn by Muslim women

IZBA *n pl* **-S** the traditional log house of rural Russia; *also* **ISBA**

FIVE LETTERS

IAMBI *n pl of* **IAMB** a metrical foot with an unstressed then stressed syllable; *also* **IAMBS, IAMBUSES**

IAMBS *n pl of* **IAMB** a metrical foot with an unstressed then stressed syllable; *also* **IAMBI, IAMBUSES**

ICIER *adj* colder; frostier; covered in more ice

ICILY *adv* in an icy manner; very coldly

ICING *v pr t of* **ICE** covering or decorating with a sugar coating

ICKER *n pl* **-S** SCOT. the fruit-bearing spike of any cereal plant, esp. an ear of corn

ICONS *n pl of* **ICON** images or representations; *also* **IKONS**

ICTIC *adj* of or relating to a seizure or convulsion

ICTUS *n pl* **-ES** or **ICTUS** a sudden stroke or seizure

IDEAL *n pl* **-S** a conception of something in its perfection

IDEAS *n pl of* **IDEA** thoughts, conceptions or notions

IDIOM *n pl* **-S** a construction or expression peculiar to a language

IDIOT *n pl* **-S** an utterly foolish or senseless person

IDLED *v p t of* **IDLE** passed time without working or while avoiding work

IDLER *n pl* **-S** lazy person

IDLES *v pr t of* **IDLE** passes time without working or while avoiding work

IDOLS *n pl of* **IDOL** images or representations of anything

IDYLL *n pl* **-S** a short poem or prose piece depicting a rural or pastoral scene, usually in idealized terms; *also* **IDYL**

IDYLS *n pl of* **IDYL** short poems or prose pieces depicting a rural or pastoral scene, usually in idealized terms; *also* **IDYLLS**

IGGED *v p t of* **IGG** ignored or snubbed

IGLOO *n pl* **-S** an Eskimo house or hut, usually dome-shaped and built of blocks of packed snow; *also* **IGLU**

IGLUS *n pl of* **IGLU** Eskimo houses or huts, usually dome-shaped and built of blocks of packed snow; *also* **IGLOOS**

IHRAM *n pl* **-S** the sacred dress of Muslim pilgrims, consisting of two lengths of white cotton, one wrapped around the loins and the other thrown over the left shoulder

IKONS *n pl of* **IKON** images or representations; *also* **ICONS**

ILEAC *adj* of or pertaining to the ileum; *also* **ILIAC**

ILEAL *adj* of or pertaining to the ileum; *also* **ILIAL**

ILEUM *n pl* **ILEA** the third portion of the small intestine

ILEUS *n* a medical condition caused by an intestinal obstruction, often accompanied by extreme pain and vomiting

ILIAC *adj* of or pertaining to the ileum; *also* **ILEAC**

ILIAL *adj* of or pertaining to the ileum; *also* **ILEAL**

ILIUM *n pl* **ILIA** the large broad bone forming the upper part of each half of the pelvis

ILLER *adj* comparatively speaking, less healthy; sicker

IMAGE *n pl* **-S** a reproduction of the form of a person or object

IMAGO *n pl* **-ES** or **IMAGINES** an insect in its sexually mature adult stage after metamorphosis

IMAMS *n pl of* **IMAM** in Islam, men who lead the prayers in mosques; *also* **IMANS**

IMANS *n pl of* **IMAN** in Islam, men who lead the prayers in mosques; *also* **IMAMS**

IMBED *v* **-DED, -DING, -S** to fix firmly in a surrounding mass

IMBUE *v* **-D, IMBUING, -S** to permeate or saturate

IMIDE *n pl* **-S** an acidic derivative of ammonia; *also* **IMID, AMIDE**

IMIDO *adj* of or relating to an imide, an acidic derivative of ammonia

IMIDS *n pl of* **IMID** acidic derivatives of ammonia; *also* **AMIDES, IMIDES**

IMINE *n pl* **-S** a nonacidic derivative of ammonia; *also* **AMINE**

IMINO *adj* of or relating to an imine, an acidic derivative of ammonia

IMMIX *v* **-ED, -ING, -ES** to commingle; blend

IMPED *v p part of* **IMP** repaired the broken wing of a hawk or falcon by grafting on new feathers

IMPEL *v* **-LED, -LING, -S** to drive forward; propel

IMPLY *v* **IMPLIED, -ING, IMPLIES** to express or indicate indirectly

INANE *adj* silly; stupid

INAPT *adj* not suitable; inappropriate

INCOG *adv* in disguise; colloquial for incognito

INCUR *v* **-RED, -RING, -S** to become liable for; to bring upon oneself

INCUS *n pl* **INCUDES** a small anvil-shaped bone in the middle ear of mammals

INDEX *n pl* **-ES** or **INDICES** a sequential arrangement of material; an indicator

INDIE *n pl* **-S** an artistic work produced by an independent group or company

INDOL *n pl* **-S** a chemical compound obtained from blue indigo; *also* **INDOLE**

INDOW *v* **-ED, -ING, -S** to give qualities or abilities to; *also* **ENDOW**

INDRI *n pl* **-S** a short-tailed lemur of Madagascar

INDUE *v* **-D, -ING, -S** to provide with a quality or trait; endow; *also* **ENDUE**

INEPT *adj* not suitable to the purpose; unfit

INERT *adj* lacking the ability or strength to move

INFER *v* **-RED, -RING, -S** to derive by reasoning; speculate

INFIX *v* **-ED, -ING, -ES** implant or insert firmly in something

INFRA *adv* below; used in an explanatory note to refer a reader to a point later in a text

INGLE *n pl* **-S** SCOT. a domestic fire or fireplace; *also* **ENGHLE**

INGOT *n pl* **-S** a block of metal, typically oblong in shape

INION *n* the projecting part of the occipital bone at the base of the skull

INKED *v p t of* **INK** marked, coated or stained with a colored liquid or paste used for writing, printing or drawing

INKER *n* one who, or that which, inks; especially in printing, the pad or roller which applies ink to the type

INKLE *n pl* **-S** a kind of braided linen tape

INLAW *v* **-ED** [obs] BRIT. to restore (an outlaw) to the benefits and protection of the law

INLAY *v* **INLAID, -ING, -S** to decorate an object with shaped pieces of contrasting material set in its surface

INLET *v* **-TING, -S** to inlay or insert

INNED *v p t of* **INN** [obs] to house, to lodge

INNER *adv* located farther within; interior; internal

INPUT *v* **-TED, -TING, -S** to put data into a computer

INROS *n pl of* **INRO** small, usually ornamented boxes that are hung from the waist sash of a Japanese kimono

INRUN *n pl* **-S** the approach ramp of a ski jump

INSET *v* **-TED, -TING, -S** to set into something; insert

INTER *v* **-RED, -RING, -S** to put into the earth; bury

INTIS *n pl of* **INTI** former monetary units of Peru

INTRO *n pl* **-S** commonly used abbreviation for introduction

INURE *v* **-D, INURING, -S** to habituate to something undesirable; accustom

INURN *v* **-ED, -ING, -S** to put into an urn, especially ashes after cremation

153

INVAR *n pl* **-S** an alloy of iron and nickel having a low coefficient of thermal expansion

IODIC *adj* pertaining to, or containing, iodine

IODIN *n pl* **-S** a nonmetallic element belonging to the halogens; *also* **IODINE**

IONIC *adj* of, relating to, or using ions

IOTAS *n pl of* **IOTA** very small quantities or degrees

IRADE *n pl* **-S** a written decree of the Turkish Sultan

IRATE *adj* angry; enraged

IRIDS *n pl of* **IRID** plants of the iris family

IRKED *v p t of* **IRK** irritated, annoyed or exasperated

IROKO *n pl* **-S** a hard African wood often used instead of teak

IRONE *n pl* **-S** a fragrant liquid substance used in perfumery for its odor of violets

IRONS *v pr t of* **IRON** removes creases by pressing with a tool made of heated iron or steel

IRONY *n pl* **IRONIES** the use of words to convey a meaning that is the opposite of its literal meaning

IRPES *n pl of* **IRPE** [obs] a fantastic grimace or contortion of the body; *also* **IRPS**

ISBAS *n pl of* **ISBA** Russian log huts; *also* **IZBAS**

ISLED *v p t of* **ISLE** to have placed on or as if on an isle

ISLES *n pl of* **ISLE** small islands; *also* **ILES**

ISLET *n pl* **-S** a small island

ISSEI *n pl* **-S** a first generation Japanese immigrant to the United States

ISSUE *v* **-D, ISSUING, -S** to supply or distribute something

ISTLE *n pl* **-S** a fiber from agave or yucca plants, used to make bags, carpets and nets; *also* **IXTLE**

ITCHY *adj* having or causing a need to scratch

ITEMS *n pl of* **ITEM** more than one individual article or unit

ITERS *n pl of* **ITER** passages; esp., between the 3rd and 4th ventricles in the brain

IVIED *adj* covered or overgrown with a climbing vine of the genus *Hedera*

IVIES *n pl of* **IVY** climbing vines of the genus Hedera

IVORY *n pl* **IVORIES** a hard, creamy-white substance composing the main part of the tusks of an elephant, walrus, or narwhal

IXIAS *n pl of* **IXIA** South African bulbous plants of the Iris family, remarkable for the brilliancy of their flowers

IXTLE *n pl* **-S** a fiber from agave or yucca plants, used to make bags, carpets and nets; *also* **ISTLE**

IZARS *n pl of* **IZAR** long, white cotton outer garments traditionally worn by Muslim women

IZBAS *n pl of* **ISBA** Russian log huts; *also* **ISBAS**

J

JO *n pl* **-ES** SCOT. a sweetheart; a darling

THREE LETTERS

JAB *v* **-BED, -BING, -S** to poke abruptly with a sharp object; to stab; to punch with quick blows

JAG *v* **-GED, -GING, -S** to notch; to cut unevenly; *also* **JAGG**

JAK *n pl* **-S** immense East Indian fruit resembling breadfruit; *also* **JACK**

JAM *v* **-MED, -MING, -S** to wedge forcibly into a tight position

JAR *v* **-RED, -RING, -S** to disturb, to shake abruptly

JAW *v* **-ED, -ING, -S** talk socially without exchanging too much information

JAY *n pl* **-S** a crested, largely blue bird, of the crow family

JEE *v* **-D, -ING, -S** to turn to the right

JET *v* **-TED, -TING, -S** to travel by aircraft; to move quickly

JEU *n pl* **JEUX** a game; a diversion

JIB *v* **-BED, -BING, -S** to shift or swing a sail from one side of the ship to the other when sailing; *also* **GYBE, JIBB, JIBE**

JIG *v* **-GED, -GING, -S** to dance or move up and down in a quick, jerking fashion

JIN *n pl* **-S** or **JIN** in Islamic myth any class of spirits lower than angels, capable of assuming human or animal forms and influencing humankind; *also* **DJIN, DJINN, DJINNI, JINN, JINNI**

JOB *v* **-BED, -BING, -S** to work casually or occasionally; to do odd or occasional work for hire

JOE *n pl* **-S** an ordinary man

JOG *v* **-GED, -GING, -S** to run at a slow steady pace

JOT *v* **-TED, -TING, -S** to write quickly; to make a brief note of

JOW *v* SCOT. to toll a bell

JOY *v* **-ED, -ING, -S** [obs] to take great pleasure in something

JUB *n* [obs] a vessel for holding ale or wine; a jug

JUG *n pl* **-S** a container for liquids; a pitcher

JUN *n pl* **JUN** a North Korean coin, equal to one hundredth of a won

JUS *n pl* **JURA** a legal principle, right or power

JUT *v* **-TED, -TING, -S** to project or stick out

FOUR LETTERS

JABS *v pr t of* **JAB** pokes abruptly with a sharp object; stabs; punches with quick blows

JACK *n pl* **-S** immense East Indian fruit resembling breadfruit; *also* **JAK**

JADE *v* **-D, JADING, -S** to weary or tire through overuse or great strain or stress

JAGG *v* [obs] to notch; to cut unevenly; *also* **JAG**

JAGS *v pr t of* **JAG** notches; cuts unevenly; *also* **JAGGS**

JAIL *v* **-ED, -ING, -S** to imprison

JAKE *n pl* **-S** a male wild turkey under two years old

JAKO *n* an African parrot commonly kept as a caged bird; gray parrot

JAKS *n pl of* **JAK** more than one of an immense East Indian fruit resembling breadfruit; *also* **JACKS**

JAMB *n pl* **-S** one of a pair of vertical posts that form the side of a window frame or door; *also* **JAMBE**

JAMS *v pr t of* **JAM** wedges forcibly into a tight position

JANE *n* informal for a girl or a woman

JAPE *v* **-D, JAPING, -S** to jest; to joke; to mock

JARL *n pl* **-S** a chieftain or nobleman in medieval Scandinavia

JARS *v pr t of* **JAR** disturbs; shakes abruptly

JATO *n pl* **-S** an auxiliary jet or rocket that aids aircraft engines during takeoff

JAUK *v* **-ED, -ING, -S** SCOT. to dally; to dawdle

JAUP *n* SCOT., BRIT. a splash or spurt of water or mud; *also* **JAWP**

JAVA *n* brewed coffee, as opposed to instant

JAWP *n* SCOT., BRIT. a splash or spurt of water or mud; *also* **JAUP**

JAWS *v pr t of* **JAW** talks socially without exchanging too much information

JAWY *adj* relating to the bones of the mouth

JAYS *n pl of* **JAY** crested, largely blue birds, of the crow family

JAZZ *v* **-ED, -ING, -ES** to make more lively; to excite; to exaggerate

JEAN *n* a heavy twilled cotton cloth used especially for clothing; denim

JEED *v p t of* **JEE** turned to the right; *also* **GEED**

JEEP *n pl* **-S** a small, sturdy motor vehicle with four wheel drive, suitable for traveling over rough terrain, first used by U.S. forces during World War II

JEER *v* **-ED, -ING, -S** to make rude, derisive, mocking remarks

JEES *v pr t of* **JEE** turns to the right; *also* **GEES**

JEEZ *interj* used to express surprise, enthusiasm, anger, annoyance; *also* **GEEZ**

JEFE *n pl* **-S** chief; leader; boss

JEHU *n pl* **-S** [obs] a driver of a coach or cab, especially one who drives recklessly

JELL *v* **-ED, -ING, -S** to become gelatinous; to congeal; to become set and firm

JEON *n pl* **JEON** a monetary unit of South Korea; *also* **CHON**

JERK *v* **-ED, -ING, -S** move suddenly; to move with a quick abrupt motion

JESS *v* **-ED, -ING, -ES** to fasten a short strap, usually with a ring for attaching a leash, around the leg of a hawk, falcon or trained bird of prey

JEST *v* **-ED, -ING, -S** to speak, act or write in a playful, joking manner

JETÉ *n pl* **-S** a step in which a ballet dancer springs from one leg and lands on the other

JETS *v pr t of* **JET** travels by aircraft; moves quickly

JEUX *n pl of* **JEU** games; diversions

JIAO *n pl* **JIAO** a unit of currency in the People's Republic of China; *also* **CHIAO**

JIBB *v* **-ED, -ING, -S** to shift or swing a sail from one side of the ship to the other when sailing; *also* **GYBE, JIB, JIBE**

JIBE *v* **-D, JIBING, -S** to shift or swing a sail from one side of the ship to the other when sailing; *also* **GYBE, JIB JIBB**

JIBS *v pr t of* **JIB** shifts or swings a sail from one side of the ship to the other when sailing; *also* **GYBES, JIBBS, JIBES**

JIFF *n* a moment; a very short time; *also* **JIFFY**

JIGS *v pr t of* **JIG** dances or moves up and down in a quick, jerking fashion

JILL *n pl* **-S** a young woman; a sweetheart

JILT *v* **-ED, -ING, -S** to abruptly break off a relationship; to leave or deceive (a lover) suddenly or callously

JIMP *adj* SCOT. neat; handsome; elegant

JINK *v* **-ED, -ING, -S** to change direction suddenly and nimbly; to make a quick, evasive turn

JINN *n pl* **-S** or **JINN** in Islamic myth any class of spirits lower than angels, capable of assuming human or animal forms and influencing humankind; *also* **DJIN, DJINN, DJINNI, JIN, JINNI**

JINX *v* **-ED, -ING, -ES** to bring bad luck to someone or something

JIRD *n* a small burrowing rodent found in the deserts and dry regions of Asia and northern Africa that is popular as a pet; a tamarisk gerbil

JIVE *v* **-D, JIVING, -S** to play or dance in a lively, uninhibited manner related to jazz or swing music

JIVY *adj* **JIVIER, JIVIEST** lively, uninhibited and artistically hip; *also* **JIVEY**

JOBS *v pr t of* **JOB** works casually or occasionally; does odd or occasional work for hire

JOCK *n pl* **-S** an athlete, especially a male college or high school athlete

JOES *n pl of* **JOE** ordinary men

JOEY *n pl* **-S** AUS. a young animal, especially a baby kangaroo

JOGS *v pr t of* **JOG** runs at a slow steady pace

JOHN *n pl* **-S** informal for a toilet

JOIN *v* **-ED, -ING, -S** to bring together, literally or figuratively

JOKE *v* **-D, JOKING, -S** to say or do something to evoke laughter or amusement

JOKY *adj* **JOKIER, JOKIEST** amusing; good-humored; lacking in seriousness; comical; *also* **JOKEY**

JOLE *n pl* **-S** a fold of flesh hanging from the jaw; *also* **JOLL, JOUL, JOWL**

JOLL *n pl* **-S** a fold of flesh hanging from the jaw; *also* **JOLE, JOUL, JOWL**

JOLT *v* **-ED, -ING, -S** to roughly shake, move or dislodge in an abrupt and jarring manner

JOOK *v* **-ED, -ING, -S** to deceive or outmaneuver a defender by a feint; *also* **JOUK, JUKE**

JOSH *v* **-ED, -ING, -ES** to tease in a friendly, good-natured way

JOSO *n* a small freshwater fish

JOSS *n pl* **-ES** an image or statue representing a Chinese deity

JOTA *n pl* **-S** a fast Spanish dance performed with castanets

JOTS *v pr t of* **JOT** writes quickly; makes a brief note of

JOUK *v* **-ED, -ING, -S** to deceive or outmaneuver a defender by a feint; *also* **JOOK, JUKE**

JOUL *n pl* **-S** a fold of flesh hanging from the jaw; *also* **JOLE, JOLL, JOWL**

JOWL *n pl* **-S** a fold of flesh hanging from the jaw; *also* **JOLE, JOLL, JOUL**

JOYS *v pr t of* **JOY** [obs] takes great pleasure in something

JUBA *n pl* **-S** a group dance characterized by lively, rhythmic clapping, practiced by African Americans on southern plantations in the 18th and 19th centuries

JUBE *n pl* **-S** ornamental screen separating the choir from the church nave and often supporting a crucifix

JUDO *n* a sport derived from jujitsu; a Japanese martial art

JUGA *n pl of* **JUGUM** yoke-like structure of some insects that joins the forewings to the hind wings, keeping them together during flight; *also* **JUGUMS**

JUGS *n pl of* **JUG** containers for liquids; pitchers

JUJU *n pl* **-S** an object used, especially in West Africa, as a magical charm or fetish

JUKE *v* **-D, JUKING, -S** to deceive or outmaneuver a defender by a feint; *also* **JOOK, JOUK**

JUKU *n pl* **JUKU** a Japanese school that prepares students for college or university entrance exams

JUMP *v* **-ED, -ING, -S** to spring from the ground or other surface using the feet and leg muscles

JUNK *v* **-ED, -ING, -S** to discard as worthless or useless

JUPE *n* a medieval tunic worn under or over armor; *also* **GIPON, JUPON**

JURA *n pl of* **JUS** legal principles, rights or powers

JURY *v* **JURIED, -ING, JURIES** to judge or evaluate

JUST *adv* a very short time ago

JUTE *n* a plant fiber used in making rope or sacks

JUTS *v pr t of* **JUT** projects or sticks out

JYNX *n* in superstition and folklore, a curse placed on a person that makes them prey to many minor misfortunes and other forms of bad luck

FIVE LETTERS

JABOT *n pl* **-S** an ornamental cascade of ruffles, frills or lace falling from the neckline of a shirt or blouse

JACAL *n pl* **-S** a hut of Mexico and the southwestern United States having a thatched roof with walls made of poles or sticks covered with mud or clay

JACKS *n pl of* **JACK** more than one of an immense East Indian fruit resembling breadfruit; *also* **JAKS**

JACKY *n pl* **JACKIES** a sailor

JADED *v p t of* **JADE** wearied or tired through overuse or great strain or stress

JADES *v pr t of* **JADE** wearies or tires through overuse or great strain or stress

JAGED *v p t of* **JAG** notched; cut unevenly; *also* **JAGGED**

JAGER *n* a hunter; a sharpshooter; *also* **JAEGER, YAGER**

JAGGS *v pr t of* **JAG** notches; cuts unevenly; *also* **JAGS**

JAGGY *adj* **JAGGIER, JAGGIEST** sharply or unevenly notched; serrated; *also* **JAGGED**

JAILS *v pr t of* **JAIL** imprisons

JAKES *n pl of* **JAKE** male wild turkeys under two years old

JALAP *n pl* **-S** the dried root of a Mexican vine, part of the morning-glory family, used medicinally as a purgative; *also* **JALOP**

JALOP *n pl* **-S** the dried root of a Mexican vine, part of the morning-glory family, used medicinally as a purgative; *also* **JALAP**

JAMBE *n pl* **-S** one of a pair of vertical posts that form the side of a window frame or door; *also* **JAMB**

JAMBS *n pl of* **JAMB** a pair of vertical posts that form the sides of a window frame or door; *also* **JAMBES**

JAMMY *adj* **JAMMIER, JAMMIEST** covered, filled or resembling jam, fruit boiled and thickened with sugar

JAPAN *v* **-NED, -NING, -S** to lacquer or varnish with japan, a hard, glossy black enamel

JAPED *v p t of* **JAPE** jested; joked; mocked

JAPER *n* one who jests, jokes or mocks

JAPES *v pr t of* **JAPE** jests; jokes; mocks

JARLS *n pl of* **JARL** chieftains or noblemen in medieval Scandinavia

JATOS *n pl of* **JATO** auxiliary jets or rockets that aid aircraft engines during takeoff

JAUKS *v pr t of* **JAUK** SCOT. dallies; dawdles

JAUNT *v* **-ED, -ING, -S** to make a short trip for fun or pleasure

JAWAN *n pl* **-S** a private soldier or police constable in South Asia

JAWED *v p t of* **JAW** talked socially without exchanging too much information

JAZZY *adj* **JAZZIER, JAZZIEST** lively; bright; colorful; showy

JEANS *n/pl* casual pants with raised seams made from denim

JEBEL *n pl* **-S** a hill or mountain: often used as part of a place name in Arabic speaking countries; *also* **DJEBEL**

JEEPS *n pl of* **JEEP** small, sturdy motor vehicles with four wheel drive, suitable for traveling over rough terrain, first used by U.S. forces during World War II

JEERS *n pr t of* **JEER** makes rude, derisive, mocking remarks

JEFES *n pl of* **JEFE** chiefs; leaders; bosses

JEHAD *n pl* **-S** an Islamic campaign against nonbelievers; *also* **JIHAD**

JEHUS *n pl of* **JEHU** [obs] drivers of coaches or cabs; especially those who drive recklessly

JELLO *n* fruit-flavored dessert made from a commercially prepared gelatin powder

JELLS *v pr t of* **JELL** becomes gelatinous; congeals; becomes set and firm

JELLY *n pl* **JELLIES** a fruit preserve made by cooling boiled fruit juice, sugar, and pectin or gelatin until it has a semisolid consistency

JEMMY *v* **JEMMIES, -ING, JEMMIED** BRIT. to pry or force open with a short crowbar; *also* **JIMMY**

JENNY *n pl* **JENNIES** the female of certain animals, especially the donkey and the wren

JERID *n pl* **-S** a blunt javelin used in mock fights and games played on horseback in countries in the Middle East; *also* **JEREED, JERREED, JERRID**

JERKS *v pr t of* **JERK** moves suddenly; moves with a quick abrupt motion

JERKY *adj* **JERKIER, JERKIEST** having an irregular jolting motion

JESTS *v pr t of* **JEST** speaks, acts, or writes in a playful, joking manner

JETÉS *n pl of* **JETE** a series of steps in which a ballet dancer springs from one leg and lands on the other

JETON *n pl* **-S** an inscribed counter or token; *also* **JETTON**

JETTY *n pl* **JETTIES** a barrier or structure, such as a pier, built out into a body of water to protect a harbor or shoreline from erosion or storms

JEWEL *v* **-ED** or **LED, -ING** or **-LING, -S** to adorn or decorate with precious stones or gems

JIBBS *v pr t of* **JIBB** shifts or swings a sail from one side of the ship to the other when sailing; *also* **GYBES, JIBES, JIBS**

JIBED *v p t of* **JIBE** shifted or swung a sail from one side of the ship to the other when sailing; also **GYBED, JIBBED**

JIBER *n* one who taunts, mocks or derides; *also* **GIBER**

JIBES *v pr t of* **JIBE** shifts or swings a sail from one side of the ship to the other when sailing; *also* **GYBES, JIBBS, JIBS**

JIFFY *n pl* **JIFFIES** a moment; a very short time; *also* **JIFF**

JIHAD *n pl* **-S** an Islamic campaign against nonbelievers; *also* **JEHAD**

JILLS *n pl of* **JILL** young women; sweethearts

JILTS *v pr t of* **JILT** abruptly breaks off a relationship; leaves or deceives (a lover) suddenly or callously

JIMMY *v* **JIMMIED, -ING, JIMMIES** to pry or force open with a crowbar; *also* **JEMMY**

JINGO *n pl* **-ES** a person who boasts of his or her patriotism and advocates an aggressively hostile, warlike foreign policy; a chauvinistic patriot

JINKS *v pr t of* **JINK** changes direction suddenly and nimbly; makes a quick, evasive turn

JINNI *n pl* **JINN** in Islamic myth any class of spirits lower than angels, capable of assuming human or animal forms and influencing humankind; *also* **DJIN, DJINN, DJINNI, JIN, JINN**

JIVED *v p t of* **JIVE** played or danced in a lively, uninhibited manner related to jazz or swing music

JIVER *n pl* **-S** one who plays or dances to jazz or swing music, or lives in an uninhibited manner

JIVES *v pr t of* **JIVE** plays or dances in a lively, uninhibited manner related to jazz or swing music

JIVEY *adj* **JIVIER, JIVIEST** lively, uninhibited and artistically hip; *also* **JIVY**

JOCKO *n pl* **-S** a chimpanzee or a monkey

JOCKS *n pl of* **JOCK** athletes, especially male college or high school athletes

JOEYS *n pl of* **JOEY** AUS. young animals, especially baby kangaroos

JOHNS *n pl of* **JOHN** informal for toilets

JOINS *v pr t of* **JOIN** brings together, literally or figuratively

JOINT *v* **-ED, -ING, -S** to unite by a joint; to fasten, attach or fit two or more things together

JOIST *v* **-ED, -ING, -S** to construct or support a floor or ceiling with wood, steel or concrete beams set parallel from wall to wall or across or abutting girders

JOKED *v p t of* **JOKE** to have said or done something to evoke laughter or amusement

JOKER *n* **-S** one who frequently jests, teases or lacks in seriousness

JOKES *v pr t of* **JOKE** says or does something to evoke laughter or amusement

JOKEY *adj* **JOKIER, JOKIEST** amusing; good-humored; lacking in seriousness; comical; *also* **JOKY**

JOLES *n pl of* **JOLE** folds of flesh hanging from the jaw; *also* **JOLLS, JOULS, JOWLS**

JOLLS *n pl of* **JOLL** folds of flesh hanging from the jaw; *also* **JOLES, JOULS, JOWLS**

JOLLY *v* **JOLLIED, -ING, JOLLIES** to attempt to put or keep in good spirits by attention and flattery

JOLTS *v pr t of* **JOLT** roughly shakes, moves, or dislodges in an abrupt and jarring manner

JOLTY *adj* **JOLTIER, JOLTIEST** jarring, bumpy

JOMON *adj* of or pertaining to the early Neolithic period of Japanese culture

JONES *v* **-ED, -ING, -ES** to have a strong compulsion or craving for something

JOOKS *v pr t of* **JOOK** to deceives or outmaneuvers a defender by a feint; *also* **JOUKS**

JORAM *n pl* **-S** [obs] a large drinking bowl or its contents; *also* **JORUM**

JORUM *n pl* **-S** a large drinking bowl or its contents; *also* **JORAM**

JOTAS *n pl of* **JOTA** a fast Spanish dance performed with castanets

JOUAL *n* a dialect of Canadian French containing many English words

JOUKS *v pr t of* **JOUK** deceives or outmaneuvers a defender by a feint; *also* **JOOKS**

JOULE *n pl* **-S** the International System unit of energy equal to the work done when one newton of force acts through a distance of one meter

JOULS *n pl of* **JOUL** folds of flesh hanging from the jaw; *also* **JOLES, JOLLS, JOWLS**

JOUST *v* **-ED, -ING, -S** to engage in combat with lances while on horseback

JOWAR *n* a drought resistant cereal crop grown in warm dry regions such as India; sorghum

JOWLS *n pl of* **JOWL** folds of flesh hanging from the jaw; *also* **JOLES, JOLLS, JOULS**

JOWLY *adj* **JOWLIER, JOWLIEST** having heavy, sagging folds of flesh from the lower jaw or beneath the chin

JOYED *v p t of* **JOY** [obs] to have taken great pleasure; enjoyed

JUBAS *n pl of* **JUBA** group dances characterized by lively, rhythmic clapping, practiced by African Americans on southern plantations in the 18th and 19th centuries

JUBES *n pl of* **JUBES** ornamental screens separating choirs from church naves and often supporting a crucifix

JUDAS *n pl* **-ES** a peephole or very small window

JUDGE *v* **-D, JUDGING, -S** to form or give an opinion; to determine the verdict in a court of law

JUGAL *adj* pertaining to or in the region of the upper cheek or cheekbone

JUGUM *n pl* **JUGA** *or* **JUGUMS** the yoke-like structure of some insects that joins the forewings to the hind wings, keeping them together during flight

JUICE *v* **-D, JUICING, -S** to extract the liquid part from a plant, fruit or vegetable

JUICY *adj* **JUICIER, JUICIEST** succulent; moist and tasty; rich in flavor

JUJUS *n pl of* **JUJU** objects used, especially in West Africa, as magical charms or fetishes

JUKED *v p t of* **JUKE** deceived or outmaneuvered a defender by a feint; *also* **JOOKED, JOUKED**

JUKES *v pr t of* **JUKE** deceives or outmaneuvers a defender by a feint; *also* **JOOKS, JOUKS**

JULEP *n pl* **-S** a sweet, syrupy drink, often with bourbon and mint

JUMBO *n pl* **-S** an extremely large person, animal or thing

JUMPS *v pr t of* **JUMP** springs from the ground or other surface using the feet and leg muscles

JUMPY *adj* **JUMPIER, JUMPIEST** on edge; jittery; anxious

JUNKS *v pr t of* **JUNK** discards as worthless or useless

JUNKY *adj* **JUNKIER, JUNKIEST** worthless; useless; trashy

JUNTA *n pl* **-S** a group of military officers ruling a country after seizing power by violent means; *also* **JUNTO**

JUNTO *n pl* **-S** a group of military officers ruling a country after seizing power by violent means; *also* **JUNTA**

JUPON *n pl* **-S** a medieval tunic worn under or over armor; *also* **GIPON, JUPE**

JURAL *adj* relating to law or the administration of justice

JURAT *n pl* **-S** a closing statement or certification added to an affidavit

JUREL *n pl* **-S** various edible carangoid or jack fishes

JUROR *n pl* **-S** a jury member; one who takes an oath

JUTTY *v* **JUTTIED, -ING, JUTTIES** [obs] to project beyond

KA *n pl* **-S** the soul, in ancient Egyptian religion

KI *n pl* **-S** the circulating life energy that in Chinese philosophy is thought to be inherent in all things; *also* **QI, CHI**

KO *n* a commonly used abbreviation for knockout, a victory in boxing in which one's opponent is unable to rise from the canvas within a specified time after being knocked down; *also* **KAYO**

KY *n* domesticated bovine animals as a group; *also* **KEE, KIE, KINE, COWS**

THREE LETTERS

KAB *n pl* **-S** an ancient Hebrew unit of measure

KAE *n pl* **-S** a jay, a crow-like bird

KAF *n* the 11th letter of the Hebrew alphabet; *also* **KHAF, KAPH, CAPH**

KAI *n pl* **-S** N.Z. food

KAM *adj* [obs] crooked; awry

KAN *v* [obs] to know; to ken

KAS *n pl of* **KA** the soul, in ancient Egyptian religion

KAT *n pl* **-S** an Arabian shrub whose leaves are chewed as a stimulant or made into a tea; *also* **KHAT, QAT**

KAW *v* **-ED, -ING, -S** to cry like a crow, rook or raven; *also* **CAW**

KAY *n pl* **-S** the letter "K"

KEA *n pl* **-S** a mountain-dwelling New Zealand parrot

KED *n pl* **-S** an insect that is a parasite of sheep; sheep tick

KEE *n* domesticated bovine animals as a group; *also* **COWS, KIE, KINE, KY**

KEF *n pl* **-S** a state of dreamy tranquility, especially one induced by narcotics; *also* **KAIF, KEEF, KEIF, KIF, KIEF**

KEG *n pl* **-S** a small cask or barrel

KEN *v* **-NED** or **-T, -NING, -S** to know; to recognize

KEP *v* **-PED, -PING, -S** [obs] to catch

KEX *n pl* **KAXES, KECKS, KECKSIES** a dry, hollow stalk of a jointed plant; *also* **KECKSY**

KEY *v* **-ED, -ING, -S** to lock or adjust something with a device that operates a door or lock

KHI *n pl* **-S** the 22nd letter of the Greek alphabet

KID *v* **-DED, -DING, -S** to tease

KIE *n* domesticated bovine animals as a group; *also* **COWS, KEE, KINE, KY**

KIF *n pl* **-S** a state of dreamy tranquility, especially one induced by narcotics; *also* **KAIF, KEEF, KEF, KEIF, KIEF**

KIN *n* a group of persons of common ancestry

KIP *v* **-PED, -PING, -S** to sleep or nap

KIR *n* a drink made from dry white wine and cassis

KIS *n pl of* **KI** the circulating life energies that in Chinese philosophy are thought to be inherent in all things; *also* **QIS, CHIS**

KIT *n pl* **-S** a set of articles or implements used for a specific purpose

KOA *n pl* **-S** or **KOA** an acacia tree native to Hawaii

KOB *n pl* **-S** or **KOB** any one of several species of African antelopes of the genus *Kobus*; *also* **KOBA**

KOI *n pl* **KOI** a carp bred especially in Japan for large size and a variety of colors

KON *v* [obs] to know; *also* **CAN, CON**

KOP *n pl* **-S** BRIT. a high bank of terracing at a soccer ground

KOR *n* an ancient Hebrew unit of capacity; *also* **COR**

KOS *n pl* **KOS** a unit of linear land measurement in South Asia; *also* **COSS, KOSS**

KRA *n* a long-tailed ape of India and Sumatra

KYE *n pl* **-S** a private Korean-American banking club to which members pay contributions and from which they may take out loans, usually to start a small business

KYU *n pl* **-S** a metric unit of distance used in typography and graphic design equal to ¼ of a millimeter or 0.71 point

FOUR LETTERS

KABS *n pl of* **KAB** an ancient Hebrew unit of measure

KADI *n pl* **-S** a judge in a Muslim community, whose decisions are based on Islamic religious law; *also* **CADI, QADI**

KAES *n pl of* **KAE** jays, crow-like birds

KAFS *n pl of* **KAF** the 11th letter of the Hebrew alphabet; *also* **KHAFS**

KAGE *n pl* **-S** a chantry chapel enclosed with lattice work

KAGU *n pl* **-S** a large grayish flightless bird native to New Caledonia

KAIF *n pl* **-S** a state of dreamy tranquility, especially one induced by narcotics; *also* **KEEF, KEF, KEIF, KIF, KIEF**

KAIL *n pl* **-S** a hearty cabbage with dark green leaves and no heart; *also* **KALE, COLE**

KAIN *n* SCOT. a tax required by a property lease to be paid in produce or livestock; *also* **KANE**

KAIS *n pl of* **KAI** N.Z. food

KAKA *n pl* **-S** a brownish-green New Zealand parrot

KAKI *n pl* **-S** a Chinese tree with edible, orange to reddish fruit; also called Japanese persimmon

KALE *n pl* **-S** a hearty cabbage with dark green leaves and no heart; *also* **KAIL, COLE**

KALI *n pl* **-S** a plant, the ashes of which are used in making glass

KAME *n pl* **-S** a ridge of sand and gravel left by a melting glacier

KAMI *n pl* **KAMI** a divine power or aura in Shintoism

KANA *n pl* **-S** or **KANA** the Japanese syllabic writing/script; *also* **KANAS**

KAND *n* in mining, a fluorite or fluor spar

KANE *n* SCOT. a tax required by a property lease to be paid in produce or livestock; *also* **KAIN**

KAON *n pl* **-S** an unstable elementary particle produced as a result of a high-energy particle collision

KAPA *n* a kind of cloth made from the inner bark of the paper mulberry

KAPH *n* the 11th letter of the Hebrew alphabet; *also* **KAF, KHAF, CAPH**

KARN *n* a pile of rocks

KART *n pl* **-S** a miniature car used in racing, also called a go-cart

KATA *n pl* **-S** a sequence of movements in martial arts

KATE *n* the brambling finch

KATS *n pl of* **KAT** Arabian shrubs whose leaves are chewed as a stimulant or made into a tea; *also* **KHATS, QATS**

KAVA *n pl* **-S** an herbal medicine made from the roots of a bush of the pepper family

KAWN *n pl* **-S** a Turkish or central Asian inn

KAWS *v pr t of* **KAW** cries like a crow, rook, or raven; *also* **CAWS**

KAYO *v* **-ED, -ING, -S** to knock someone out, especially in boxing; *also* **KO**

KAYS *n pl of* **KAY** more than one of the letter "K"

KBAR *n pl* **-S** commonly used abbreviation for a kilobar, a unit of pressure equal to 1,000 bars

KEAS *n pl of* **KEA** mountain-dwelling New Zealand parrots

KECK *v* **-ED, -ING, -S** to heave or retch, as if about to vomit

KEDS *n pl of* **KED** insects that are parasites of sheep; sheep ticks

KEEF *n pl* **-S** a state of dreamy tranquility, especially one induced by narcotics; *also* **KAIF, KEF, KEIF, KIF, KIEF**

KEEK *v* **-ED, -ING, -S** to peek at something, usually in a quick, furtive way

KEEL *v* **-ED, -ING, -S** to capsize a vessel

KEEN *v* **-ED, -ING, -S** to lament, especially for the dead

KEEP *v* **KEPT, -ING, -S** to have or retain possession of

KEET *n pl* **-S** a young guinea fowl

KEFS *n pl of* **KEF** states of dreamy tranquility, especially those induced by narcotics; *also* **KAIFS, KEEFS, KEIFS, KIFS, KIEFS**

KEGS *n pl of* **KEG** small casks or barrels

KEKE *v* **-D, KEKING, -S** [obs] to look steadfastly; to gaze; *also* **KYKE**

KEIF *n pl* **-S** a state of dreamy tranquility, especially one induced by narcotics; *also* **KAIF, KEF, KEEF, KIF, KIEF**

KEIR *n pl* **-S** a large tub or vat to hold liquid; *also* **KIVE, KEEVE, KIER**

KELD *adj* [obs] having a kell or covering

KELE *v* **-D, KELING, -S** [obs] to cool

KELL *n pl* **-S** the cocoon or chrysalis of an insect

KELP *n pl* **-S** or **KELP** a brown seaweed with broad fronds; *also* **KELPS**

KELT *n pl* **-S** a salmon that has recently spawned

KEMB *v* **-ED, KEMPT, -ING, -S** [obs] to comb

KEMP *n pl* **-S** a coarse hair or fiber, especially of wool

KENO *n* a game of chance in which players wager on a set of numbers to be drawn at random

KENS *v pr t of* **KEN** knows; recognizes

KENT *v p t of* **KEN** knew; recognized; *also* **KENNED**

KEPI *n pl* **-S** a French military cap with a flat circular top and a visor

KEPS *v pr t of* **KEP** [obs] catches

KEPT *v p t of* **KEEP** had or retained possession of

KERB *n pl* **-S** BRIT. an edge between a sidewalk and a roadway; *also* **CURB**

KERF *n pl* **-S** a groove or notch made by a cutting tool, such as a saw

KERL *n pl* **-S** [obs] a rude, rustic man; a churl; *also* **CARL, CARLE**

KERN *v* **-ED, -ING, -S** to adjust the spacing between characters

KETO *adj* pertaining to a ketone, a class of organic compounds characterized by a carbonyl group and two carbon atoms

KEYS *v pr t of* **KEY** locks or adjusts something with a device that operates a door or lock

KHAF *n* the 11th letter of the Hebrew alphabet; *also* **KAF, KAPH, CAPH**

KHAN *n pl* **-S** a Turkish or central Asian inn; *also* **KAWN, CHAM**

KHAT *n pl* **-S** an Arabian shrub whose leaves are chewed as a stimulant or made into a tea; *also* **KAT, QAT**

KHIS *n pl of* **KHI** more than one of the 22nd letter of the Greek alphabet

KIBE *n pl* **-S** a chapped or inflamed area on the skin, especially on the heel, caused by exposure to cold

KICK *v* **-ED, -ING, -S** to strike with the foot or feet

KIDS *v pr t of* **KID** teases

KIEF *n pl* **-S** a state of dreamy tranquility, especially one induced by narcotics; *also* **KAIF, KEF, KEEF, KEIF, KIF**

KIER *n pl* **-S** a large tub or vat to hold liquid; *also* **KIVE, KEEVE, KEIR**

KIFS *n pl of* **KIF** states of dreamy tranquility, especially those induced by narcotics; *also* **KAIFS, KEFS, KEEFS, KEIFS, KIEFS**

KILL *v* **-ED, -ING, -S** to cause the death of a living thing

KILN *n pl* **-S** a furnace or oven for burning, baking or drying, especially one for firing pottery

KILO *n pl* **-S** a commonly used abbreviation for kilogram or kilometer, metric units of measure

KILT *v* **-ED, -ING, -S** SCOT. to tuck up; to truss, as the clothes

KINA *n pl* **-S** a monetary unit of Papua New Guinea

KIND *adj* **-ER, -EST** having or showing a friendly, generous and considerate nature

KINE *n* domesticated bovine animals as a group; *also* **COWS, KEE, KIE, KY**

KING *v* **-ED, -ING, -S** to crown a piece in the game of checkers

KINK *v* -ED, -ING, -S to form or cause to form a sharp twist or curve

KINO *n pl* -S a reddish resin obtained from several Old World trees, used variously in tanning, dyeing, and as an astringent

KIPE *n* BRIT. an osier basket used for catching fish

KIPS *v pr t of* KIP sleeps or naps

KIRK *n pl* -S SCOT. a church

KIRN *v* -ED, -ING, -S SCOT. to churn

KISS *v* -ED, -ING, -ES to touch with the lips as a sign of love, reverence or greeting

KIST *n pl* -S a stone-lined grave; *also* CIST

KITE *v* -D, KITING, -S to soar or glide; to fly like a kite, a light frame covered with thin material to be flown in the wind at the end of a long string

KITH *n* one's friends, acquaintances

KITS *n pl of* KIT sets of articles or implements used for a specific purpose

KIVA *n pl* -S an underground chamber in a Pueblo village, used by the men especially for ceremonies or councils

KIVE *n pl* -S a large tub or vat to hold liquid; *also* KEIR, KEEVE, KIER

KIWI *n pl* -S a flightless bird native to New Zealand

KLIK *n pl* -S slang for a kilometer, 1,000 meters or 0.621 miles; *also* KLICK

KNAB *v* -BED, -BING, -S [obs] to seize with the teeth; to gnaw

KNAP *v* -PED, -PING, -S to break or chip stone with sharp blows

KNAR *n pl* -S a knot or burl on a tree or in wood; *also* KNAUR

KNAW *v* -ED, -ING, -S [obs] to bite off little by little, with effort; *also* GNAW

KNEE *v* -D, -ING, -S to strike with the part of the leg where the femur and tibia meet

KNEW *v p t of* KNOW had a clear perception or understanding of

KNIT *v* -TED, -TING, -S to interlock loops of yarn with long needles

KNOB *n pl* -S a rounded protuberance

KNOP *n pl* -S a small decorative knob; *also* KNOSP

KNOR *n pl* -S a bump or knot, as on a tree trunk; a gnarl; *also* KNUR

KNOT *v* -TED, -TING, -S to fasten by looping a piece of string, rope, etc. on itself and tightening

KNOW *v* KNEW, KNOWN, -ING, -S to have a clear perception or understanding of

KNUR *n pl* -S a bump or knot, as on a tree trunk; a gnarl; *also* KNOR

KOAN *n pl* -S or KOAN a Zen Buddhist riddle used to focus the mind during meditation and to develop intuitive thinking; *also* KOAN

KOAS *n pl of* KOA acacia trees native to Hawaii

KOBA *n* any one of several species of African antelopes; *also* KOB

KOBO *n pl* -S or KOBO a monetary unit of Nigeria

KOBS *n pl of* KOB reddish brown African antelopes

KOEL *n pl* -S any of various large cuckoos of India, the East Indies and Australia

KOFF *n* a two-masted Dutch vessel

KOHL *n* a dark powder used as an eyeliner or eyeshadow

KOJI *n* a fungus used to initiate fermentation in the making of soy sauce

KOLA *n pl* -S a type of nut produced by a tropical evergreen tree of the genus *Cola*

KOLO *n pl* **-S** a central European folk dance performed in a circle

KONK *n pl* **-S** a blow, hit on the head; *also* **CONK**

KOOK *n pl* **-S** a person regarded as strange, eccentric or crazy

KOPH *n pl* **-S** the 19th letter of the Hebrew alphabet; *also* **QOPH**

KOPS *n pl of* **KOP** BRIT. high banks of terracing at a soccer ground

KORA *n pl* **-S** a West African musical instrument shaped like a lute and played like a harp

KORE *n pl* **KORAI** an ancient Greek statue of a clothed young woman standing with feet together

KOSS *n pl* **KOSS** a unit of linear land measurement in South Asia; *also* **COSS, KOS**

KOTO *n pl* **-S** a Japanese musical instrument similar to a zither

KRIS *n pl* **-ES** a Malay or Indonesian dagger with a wavy two-edged blade; *also* **CREESE**

KSAR *n* an emperor or king; *also* **CZAR, TSAR, TZAR**

KUDA *n pl* **-S** the East Indian tapir

KUDO *n pl* **-S** a statement of praise or approval; accolade; compliment

KUDU *n pl* **-S** a striped African antelope, the male of which has long spirally curved horns; *also* **KOODOO**

KUFI *n pl* **-S** a brimless, short, rounded cap customarily worn by African men

KUNA *n pl of* **KUNE** more than one of the basic monetary unit of Croatia

KUNE *n pl* **KUNA** the basic monetary unit of Croatia

KURU *n* a fatal neurological disease occurring in New Guinea and spread by cannibalism

KUZU *n* a white Japanese food thickener that also has medicinal properties, made from kudzu vine root

KVAS *n pl* **-ES** a Russian fermented beverage similar to beer; *also* **KVASS, QUAS, QUASS**

KWAI *n* the basic monetary unit of China; *also* **YUAN**

KYAK *v* **-ED, -ING, -S** to travel in a lightweight plastic or fiberglass covered canoe propelled by a double-bladed paddle; *also* **KAIAK, KAYAK**

KYAR *n* a cocoanut fiber, or the cordage made from it; *also* **COIR**

KYAT *n pl* **-S** the basic monetary unit of Myanmar

KYAW *n pl* **-S** SCOT. a daw, a bird of the crow family known for stealing things

KYES *n pl of* **KYE** private Korean-American banking clubs to which members pay contributions and from which they may take out loans, usually to start a small business

KYKE *v* **-D, KYKING, -S** [obs] to look steadfastly; to gaze; *also* **KEKE**

KYTE *n pl* **-S** SCOT. the paunch; stomach; belly

KYUS *n pl of* **KYU** metric units of distance used in typography and graphic design, each one being equal to ¼ of a millimeter or 0.71 point

FIVE LETTERS

KABAB *n pl* **-S** a dish of pieces of meat, fish or vegetables roasted or grilled on a skewer or spit; *also* **KABOB, KEBAB, KEBOB, CABOB**

KABOB *n pl* **-S** a dish of pieces of meat, fish or vegetables roasted or grilled on a skewer or spit; *also* **KABAB, KEBAB, KEBOB, CABOB**

KADIS *n pl of* **KADI** judges in Muslim communities, whose decisions are based on Islamic religious law; *also* **CADIS, QADIS**

KAGES *n pl of* **KAGE** chantry chapels enclosed with lattice work

KAGUS *n pl of* **KAGU** large, grayish, flightless birds native to New Caledonia

KAIAK *v* **-ED, -ING, -S** to travel in a lightweight plastic or fiberglass covered canoe propelled by a double-bladed paddle; *also* **KAYAK, KYAK**

KAIFS *n pl of* **KAIF** states of dreamy tranquility, especially those induced by narcotics; *also* **KEFS, KEEFS, KEIFS, KIFS, KIEFS**

KAILS *n pl of* **KAIL** a hearty cabbage with dark green leaves and no heart; *also* **KALES**

KAINS *n pl of* **KAIN** SCOT. taxes required by a property lease to be paid in produce or livestock; *also* **KANES**

KAKAS *n pl of* **KAKA** brownish-green New Zealand parrots

KAKIS *n pl of* **KAKI** a Chinese tree with edible, orange to reddish fruit; also called Japanese persimmons

KALAM *n pl* **-S** a school of philosophical theology in Islam

KALES *n pl of* **KALE** hearty cabbages with dark green leaves and no heart; *also* **KAILS**

KALIF *n pl* **-S** a title taken by Islamic rulers that asserts religious authority to rule; *also* **CALIF, CALIPH, KHALIF, KALIPH**

KALIS *n pl of* **KALI** plants, the ashes of which are used in making glass

KALPA *n pl* **-S** in Hindu philosophy, an immeasurably long period of time

KAMES *n pl of* **KAME** ridges of sand and gravel left by a melting glacier

KAMIK *n pl* **-S** a traditional Inuit boot made of caribou hide or sealskin

KANAS *n pl of* **KANA** Japanese syllabic writing/script; *also* **KANA**

KANAT *n* an ancient irrigation system of deep underground tunnels and wells used in the Middle East to channel water from the mountains to dry, lower regions; *also* **QANAT**

KANES *n pl of* **KANE** SCOT. taxes required by a property lease to be paid in produce or livestock; *also* **KAINS**

KANJI *n pl* **-S** or **KANJI** a Japanese system of writing based on borrowed or modified Chinese characters

KANZU *n pl* **-S** a long, usually white garment worn by men in Africa

KAONS *n pl of* **KAON** unstable elementary particles produced as a result of a high-energy particle collision

KAPAS *n* unginned cotton, which is sold as a commodity

KAPOK *n pl* **-S** a silky fiber obtained from the seed covering of a tropical tree, used for insulation and as padding

KAPPA *n pl* **-S** the tenth letter of the Greek alphabet

KAPUT *adj* informal for ruined; done for; demolished; *also* **KAPUTT**

KARAT *n pl* **-S** a unit of measure for the fineness of gold

KARMA *n pl* **-S** in Hindu and Buddhist philosophy, action seen as bringing upon oneself inevitable results, either in this life or in a reincarnation

KAROO *n pl* **-S** an arid plateau of southern Africa; *also* **KARROO**

KARST *n pl* **-S** a limestone landscape, characterized by caves, fissures and underground streams

KARTS *n pl of* **KART** miniature cars used in racing, also called go-carts

167

KASHA n pl -S a dish of cooked buckwheat resembling oatmeal, originally from eastern Europe

KATAS n pl of KATA sequences of movements in martial arts

KAUDI n pl -S a tall evergreen native to New Zealand; also KAURI, KAURY, COWDIE, COWRIE

KAURI n pl -S a tall evergreen native to New Zealand; also KAUDI, KAURY, COWDIE, COWRIE

KAURY n pl KAURIES a tall evergreen native to New Zealand; also KAUDI, KAURI, COWDIE, COWRIE

KAVAS n pl of KAVA herbal medicines made from the roots of a bush of the pepper family

KAWED v p t of KAW cried like a crow, rook, or raven; also CAWED

KAWNS n pl of KAWN Turkish or central Asian inns; also KHANS

KAXES n pl of KEX dry, hollow stalks of jointed plants; also KECKS, KECKSIES

KAYAK v -ED, -ING, -S to travel in a lightweight plastic or fiberglass covered canoe propelled by a double-bladed paddle; also KAIAK, KYAK

KAYOS v pr t of KAYO knocks someone out, especially in boxing

KAZOO n pl -S a toy musical instrument that makes a buzzing sound

KBARS n pl of KBAR commonly used abbreviation for kilobars, units of pressure equal to 1,000 bars each

KEBAB n pl -S a dish of pieces of meat, fish or vegetables roasted or grilled on a skewer or spit; also KABAB, KABOB, KEBOB, CABOB

KEBOB n pl -S a dish of pieces of meat, fish or vegetables roasted or grilled on a skewer or spit; also KABAB, KABOB, KEBAB, CABOB

KECKS n pl KEX dry, hollow stalks of jointed plants; also KAXES, KECKSIES

KEDGE v -D, KEDGING, -S to move a ship by pulling on a rope fastened to a dropped anchor

KEEFS n pl of KEEF states of dreamy tranquility, especially those induced by narcotics; also KAIFS, KEFS, KEIFS, KIFS, KIEFS

KEEKS v pr t of KEEK peeks at something, usually in a quick, furtive way

KEELS v pr t of KEEL capsizes a vessel

KEENS v pr t of KEEN laments, especially for the dead

KEEPS v pr t of KEEP has or retains possession of

KEETS n pl of KEET young guinea fowls

KEEVE n pl -S a large tub or vat to hold liquid; also KIVE, KEIR, KIER

KEFIR n pl -S a beverage of fermented cow's milk

KEIFS n pl of KEIF states of dreamy tranquility, especially those induced by narcotics; also KAIFS, KEFS, KEEFS, KIFS, KIEFS

KEIRS n pl of KEIR large vats or tubs that hold liquid; also KIERS, KEEVES, KIVES

KEKED v p t of KEKE [obs] looked steadfastly; gazed; also KYKED

KEKES v pr t of KEKE [obs] looks steadfastly; gazes; also KYKES

KELED v p t of KELE [obs] cooled

KELEP n pl -S a Central American carnivorous ant

KELES v pr t of KELE [obs] cools

KELIM n pl -S a carpet or rug woven without a pile, made in Turkey, Kurdistan, and neighboring areas; also KILIM

KELLS *n pl of* **KELL** cocoons or chrysalises of an insect

KELLY *n pl* **-S** or **KELLIES** informal for a man's stiff hat, as a derby or straw skimmer

KELPS *n pl of* **KELP** brown seaweeds with broad fronds; *also* **KELP**

KELPY *n pl* **KELPIES** SCOT. in Scottish folklore, a malicious water spirit that takes the form of a horse and lures people to death by drowning; *also* **KELPIE**

KELTS *n pl of* **KELT** salmon that have recently spawned

KEMBS *v pr t of* **KEMB** [obs] to comb

KEMPS *n pl of* **KEMP** coarse hairs or fibers, especially of wool

KEMPT *adj* neat; tidy; well-groomed

KEMPY *adj* of or like coarse hairs or fibers, especially of wool

KENAF *n pl* **-S** a tropical Asiatic hibiscus

KENCH *n pl* **-ES** a box or bin in which fish or skins are salted

KENDO *n* a Japanese form of fencing using bamboo sticks

KENTE *n* a patterned ceremonial cloth of the Ashanti

KEPIS *n pl of* **KEPI** French military caps with a flat circular top and visor

KERBS *n pl of* **KERB** BRIT. edges between sidewalks and roadways; *also* **CURBS**

KERFS *n pl of* **KERF** grooves or notches made by a cutting tool, such as a saw

KERLS *n pl of* **KERL** [obs] rude, rustic men; churls; *also* **CARLS, CARLES**

KERNE *n pl* **-S** a medieval foot soldier

KERNS *v pr t of* **KERN** adjusts the spacing between characters

KERRY *n pl* **KERRIES** any of a breed of small black Irish dairy cattle

KETCH *n pl* **-ES** a small two-masted sailing vessel

KETOL *n pl* **-S** an organic compound containing a ketone group and an alcohol group in the molecule

KEVEL *n pl* **-S** a sturdy belaying pin for the heavier cables of a ship

KEYED *v p t of* **KEY** locked or adjusted something with a device that operates a door or lock

KHADI *n pl* **-S** homespun cotton cloth made in India; *also* **KHADDAR**

KHAFS *n pl of* **KHAF** the 11th letter of the Hebrew alphabet; *also* **KAFS**

KHAKI *n pl* **-S** a cotton or wool fabric of a dull brownish-yellow color, used especially in military clothing

KHANS *n pl of* **KHAN** Turkish or central Asian inns; *also* **KAWNS**

KHATS *n pl of* **KHAT** Arabian shrubs whose leaves are chewed as a stimulant or made into a tea; *also* **KATS, QATS**

KHEDA *n pl* **-S** an enclosure constructed to ensnare wild elephants; *also* **KEDDAH, KHEDAH**

KHOUM *n pl* **-S** a monetary unit of Mauritania

KIANG *n pl* **-S** a large wild ass native to the Tibetan plateau and the Himalayan region

KIBBE *n pl* **-S** a Near Eastern dish of ground lamb and bulgur; *also* **KIBBI, KIBBEH**

KIBBI *n pl* **-S** a Near Eastern dish of ground lamb and bulgur; *also* **KIBBE, KIBBEH**

KIBES *n pl of* **KIBE** chapped or inflamed areas on the skin, especially on the heel, caused by exposure to cold

KIBLA *n pl* **-S** the direction toward which Muslims face while praying; *also* **KIBLAH, QIBLA, QIBLAH**

KICKS *v pr t of* **KICK** strikes with the foot or feet

KICKY *adj* **KICKIER, KICKIEST** exciting; providing a thrill

KIDDO *n pl* **-S** used as a term of address, especially to a young person

KIDDY *n pl* **KIDDIES** informal for a small child; *also* **KIDDIE**

KIEFS *n pl of* **KIEF** states of dreamy tranquility, especially those induced by narcotics; *also* **KAIFS, KEFS, KEEFS, KEIFS, KIFS**

KIERS *n pl of* **KIER** large vats or tubs that hold liquid; *also* **KEIRS, KEEVES, KIVES**

KILIM *n pl* **-S** a carpet or rug woven without a pile, made in Turkey, Kurdistan, and neighboring areas; *also* **KELIM**

KILLS *v pr t of* **KILL** causes the death of a living thing

KILNS *n pl of* **KILN** furnaces or ovens for burning, baking or drying, especially ones for firing pottery

KILOS *n pl of* **KILO** a commonly used abbreviation for kilograms or kilometers, metric units of measure

KILTS *v pr t of* **KILT** SCOT. tucks up; trusses (the clothes)

KILTY *n pl* **KILTIES** a shoe having a fringed tongue that flaps over the instep; *also* **KILTIE**

KINAS *n pl of* **KINA** monetary units of Papua New Guinea

KINDA *adv* an informal way of saying "kind of"

KINDS *n pl of* **KIND** a class of similar or related objects

KINGS *v pr t of* **KING** crowns a piece in the game of checkers

KININ *n pl* **-S** a polypeptide hormone that causes dilation in blood vessels and contraction of smooth muscle

KINKS *v pr t of* **KINK** forms or causes to form a sharp twist or curve

KINKY *adj* **KINKIER, KINKIEST** tightly twisted or curled

KINOS *n pl of* **KINO** reddish resins obtained from several Old World trees, used variously in tanning, dyeing and as an astringent

KIOSK *n pl* **-S** a small structure with one or more open sides that is used to vend merchandise or services

KIRKS *n pl of* **KIRK** SCOT. churches

KIRNS *v pr t of* **KIRN** SCOT. churns

KISSY *adj* inclined to kiss

KISTS *n pl of* **KIST** stone-lined graves; *also* **CISTS**

KITED *v p t of* **KITE** soared or glided; flew like a kite, a light frame covered with thin material to be flown in the wind at the end of a long string

KITER *n pl* **-S** a person who flies kites

KITES *v pr t of* **KITE** soars or glides; flies like a kite, a light frame covered with thin material to be flown in the wind at the end of a long string

KITHE *v* **-D, KITHING, -S** SCOT. to make or become known; *also* **KYTHE**

KITTY *n pl* **KITTIES** informal for a kitten or cat

KIVAS *n pl of* **KIVA** underground chambers in a Pueblo village, used by the men especially for ceremonies or councils

KIVES *n pl of* **KIVE** large vats or tubs that hold liquid; *also* **KIERS, KEEVES, KEIRS**

KIWIS *n pl of* **KIWI** flightless birds native to New Zealand

KLICK *n pl* **-S** slang for a kilometer, 1,000 meters or 0.621 miles; *also* **KLIK**

KLIKS *n pl of* **KLIK** slang for kilometers; *also* **KLICKS**

KLONG *n pl* **-S** a type of canal in Thailand; *also* **KHLONG**

KLOOF *n pl* **-S** a deep ravine, usually wooded, in South Africa

KLUGE *n pl* **-S** a clumsy or inelegant software or hardware configuration that provides a solution to a problem; *also* **KLUDGE**

KLUTZ *n pl* **-ES** a clumsy person

KNABS *v pr t of* **KNAB** [obs] seizes with the teeth; gnaws

KNACK *n* a clever, expedient way of doing something

KNAPS *n pl of* **KNAP** breaks or chips stone with sharp blows

KNARS *n pl of* **KNAR** knots or burls on a tree or in wood; *also* **KNAURS**

KNAUR *n pl* **-S** a knot or burl on a tree or in wood; *also* **KNAR**

KNAVE *n pl* **-S** a playing card that shows the figure of a servant or soldier and ranks below a queen

KNAWE *n pl* **-S** a low-growing, weedy Eurasian annual having narrow leaves and inconspicuous green flowers; *also* **KNAWEL**

KNAWS *v pr t of* **KNAW** [obs] bites off little by little, with effort; *also* **GNAWS**

KNEAD *v* **-ED, -ING, -S** to work into a smooth, uniform mass with the hands

KNEED *v p t of* **KNEE** struck with the part of the leg where the femur and tibia meet

KNEEL *v* **-ED, KNELT, -ING, -S** to rest on one or both knees

KNEES *v pr t of* **KNEE** strikes with the part of the leg where the femur and tibia meet

KNELL *v* **-ED, -ING, -S** to ring a bell slowly

KNELT *v p t of* **KNEEL** rested on, or got down on, one or both knees

KNIFE *v* **-D, KNIFING, -S** to stab or cut with a tool used for cutting, slicing or spreading

KNISH *n pl* **-ES** a piece of thin rolled dough folded over a filling of meat, cheese or potato

KNITS *v pr t of* **KNIT** interlocks loops of yarn with long needles

KNOBS *n pl of* **KNOB** rounded protuberances

KNOCK *v* **-ED, -ING, -S** to strike loudly against something in order to attract attention

KNOLL *n pl* **-S** a small hill or mound

KNOPS *n pl of* **KNOP** small decorative knobs; *also* **KNOSPS**

KNORS *n pl of* **KNOR** bumps or knots, as on a tree trunk; gnarls; *also* **KNURS**

KNOSP *n pl* **-S** a small decorative knob; *also* **KNOP**

KNOTS *v pr t of* **KNOT** fastens by looping a piece of string, rope, etc. on itself and tightening

KNOUT *n pl* **-S** a whip used for flogging

KNOWN *n pl* **-S** a fact or piece of information that is certain

KNOWS *v pr t of* **KNOW** has a clear perception or understanding of

KNURL *v* **-ED, -ING, -S** to make grooves or ridges in; *also* **NURL**

KNURS *n pl of* **KNUR** bumps or knots, as on a tree trunk; gnarls; *also* **KNORS**

KOALA *n pl* **-S** a bear-like tree-dwelling Australian marsupial; *also* **COALA**

KOANS *n pl of* **KOAN** Zen Buddhist riddles used to focus the mind during meditation and to develop intuitive thinking; *also* **KOAN**

KOBOS *n pl of* **KOBO** monetary units of Nigeria

KOELS *n pl of* **KOEL** various large cuckoos of India, the East Indies and Australia

KOINE *n pl* **-S** a regional dialect or language that has become the common language of a larger area

KOLAS *n pl of* **KOLAS** nuts produced by a tropical evergreen tree of the genus *Cola*

KOLOS *n pl of* **KOLO** central European folk dances performed in a circle

KOMBU *n pl* **-S** a sun-dried kelp used in Japanese cooking; *also* **KONBU**

KONBU *n pl* **-S** a sun-dried kelp used in Japanese cooking; *also* **KOMBU**

KONKS *n pl of* **KONK** blows, hits on the head; *also* **CONKS**

KOOKS *n pl of* **KOOK** people regarded as strange, eccentric or crazy

KOOKY *adj* **KOOKIER, KOOKIEST** strange in one's appearance or behavior

KOPEK *n pl* **-S** a monetary unit of Russia, equal to 1/100 of a ruble; *also* **COPECK, KOPECK**

KOPHS *n pl of* **KOPH** more than one of the 19th letter of the Hebrew alphabet; *also* **QOPHS**

KOPJE *n pl* **-S** a small usually rocky hill especially on the African veld; *also* **KOPPIE**

KOPPA *n pl* **-S** the 17th letter of the ancient Greek alphabet

KORAI *n pl of* **KORE** ancient Greek statues of a clothed young woman standing with feet together

KORAS *n pl of* **KORAS** West African musical instruments shaped like lutes and played like harps

KORAT *n pl* **-S** any of a breed of domestic cat having a shiny bluish coat and large greenish eyes

KORMA *n pl* **-S** an Indian dish of meat or vegetables in a creamy sauce

KORUN *n pl of* **KORUNA** a monetary unit of the Czech Republic and Slovakia; *also* **KORUNAS, KORUNNY**

KOSSO *n* an Ethiopian tree, the flowers of which have medicinal properties; *also* **CUSSO, KOUSSO**

KOTOS *n pl of* **KOTO** Japanese musical instruments similar to zithers

KOTOW *v* **-ED, -ING, -S** to show servile deference; *also* **KOWTOW**

KRAAL *v* **-ED, -ING, -S** to drive livestock into a type of enclosure, especially in southern Africa; *also* **CRAAL**

KRAFT *n* strong wrapping paper, usually brown

KRAIT *n pl* **-S** a venomous snake native to Southeast Asia

KRANG *n pl* **-S** the carcass of a whale after the blubber has been removed; *also* **CRANG**

KRAUT *n pl* **-S** informal for sauerkraut; *also* **CROUT, KROUT**

KREWE *n pl* **-S** any of several private social clubs in New Orleans that participate in the Mardi Gras festivities

KRILL *n pl* **KRILL** shrimp-like crustacean eaten by baleen whales

KRONA *n pl* **KRONOR** the basic monetary unit of Sweden

KRONE *n pl* **KRONER** the basic monetary unit of Denmark and Norway

KROON *n pl* **-S** or **-I** the basic monetary unit of Estonia

KROUT *n pl* **-S** informal for sauerkraut; *also* **CROUT, KRAUT**

KRUBI *n pl* **-S** tropical plant having a bad odor and a spathe that resembles the corolla of a morning glory and attains a diameter of several feet

KUDAS *n pl of* **KUDA** East Indian tapirs

KUDOS *n pl of* **KUDO** statements of praise or approval; accolades; compliments

KUDUS *n pl of* **KUDU** striped African antelopes, the males of which have long spirally curved horns; *also* **KOODOOS**

KUDZU *n pl* **-S** a hardy Asian vine

KUFIC *adj* having an early angular style of Arabic writing used for Koranic manuscripts and inscriptions; *also* **CUFIC**

KUFIS *n pl of* **KUFI** brimless, short, rounded caps customarily worn by African men

KUGEL *n pl* **-S** in Jewish cooking, a casserole often made of noodles or potatoes

KUKRI *n pl* **-S** a long curved knife used as a weapon by the Gurkhas of Nepal

KULAK *n pl* **-S** a wealthy landowning peasant in 19th century Russia

KUMIS *n pl* **-ES** fermented mare or camel milk, used as a beverage by Asian nomads; *also* **KOUMISS, KOUMYSS, KUMYS, KUMISH, KUMYSS**

KUMYS *n pl* **-ES** fermented mare or camel milk, used as a beverage by Asian nomads; *also* **KOUMISS, KOUMYSS, KUMIS, KUMISH, KUMYSS**

KURTA *n pl* **-S** a long loose collarless shirt worn by some men and women in or from South Asia

KURUS *n pl* **KURUS** a monetary unit of Turkey

KVASS *n* a Russian fermented beverage similar to beer; *also* **KVAS, QUAS, QUASS**

KVELL *v* **-ED, -ING, -S** to exclaim joyfully or proudly

KYACK *n pl* **-S** a double packsack to be slung on either side of a packsaddle

KYAKS *v pr t of* **KYAK** travels in a lightweight plastic or fiberglass covered canoe propelled by a double-bladed paddle; *also* **KAIAKS, KAYAKS**

KYARS *n pl of* **KYAR** coconut fibers, or the cordage made from them; *also* **COIRS**

KYATS *n pl of* **KYAT** more than one of the basic monetary unit of Myanmar

KYAWS *n pl of* **KYAW** SCOT. daws, birds of the crow family known for stealing things

KYKED *v p t of* **KYKE** [obs] looked steadfastly; gazed; *also* **KEKED**

KYKES *v pr t of* **KYKE** [obs] looks steadfastly; gazes; *also* **KEKES**

KYLIX *n pl* **KYLICES** or **KYLIKES** an ancient Greek shallow, two-handled, stemmed cup; *also* **CYLIX**

KYRIE *n pl* **-S** a religious petition for mercy

KYTES *n pl of* **KYTE** SCOT. paunches; stomachs; bellies

KYTHE *v* **-D, KYTHING, -S** SCOT. to make or become known; *also* **KITHE**

L

LA *n* a syllable representing the 6th note in a musical scale; *also* **LAH**

LI *n pl* **LI** a Chinese measure of distance equivalent to 500 meters

LO *interj* used to express wonder, surprise or to call attention to something; look!

THREE LETTERS

LAB *n pl* **-S** informal for a laboratory

LAC *n pl* **-S** one hundred thousand, used especially for referring to sums of rupees; *also* **LAKH**

LAD *n pl* **-S** a boy; a young man

LAG *v* **-GED, -GING, -S** to fall behind; to fail to keep up in pace; to straggle

LAH *n* a syllable representing the 6th note in a musical scale; *also* **LA**

LAM *v* **-MED, -MING, -S** [obs] to hit or beat hard; to thrash; *also* **LAMM**

LAP *v* **-PED, -PING, -S** to overtake a competitor in a race by completing at least one more circuit than he or she has

LAR *n pl* **-ES** in ancient Rome, a guardian spirit, especially the spirit of one's ancestors, that protected the family and watched over the household

LAS *n* [obs] a lace; a string; a cord; *also* **LAAS**

LAT *n pl* **-I** or **-S** the basic monetary unit of Latvia

LAV *n pl* **-S** BRIT. a lavatory; a room equipped with toilet facilities

LAW *v* **-ED, -ING, -S** [obs] to litigate; to take legal action; to sue or prosecute

LAX *adj* **-ER, -EST** lacking in firmness; not strict or careful

LAY *v* **LAID, -ING, -S** to put or set down, often gently or carefully

LEA *n pl* **-S** a meadow or grassy field; *also* **LEY**

LED *v p t of* **LEAD** showed or guided the way by going in advance

LEE *n* an area sheltered from the wind

LEG *v* **-GED, -GING, -S** to travel by foot; to walk or run

LEI *n pl* **-S** a garland of flowers, especially one worn around the neck

LEK *n pl* **-E** or **-S** the basic monetary unit of Albania

LEP *v* **-T, -PING, -S** [obs] to spring or move suddenly; to bound; *also* **LEAP**

LES *n* [obs] a leash

LET *v* **LET, -TING, -S** to allow; to give permission or permit

LEU *n pl* **LEI** the basic monetary unit of Romania and Moldova

LEV *n pl* **-A** the basic monetary unit of Bulgaria

LEW *adj* [obs] lukewarm; tepid

LEX *n pl* **LEGES** a named law or set of laws

LEY *n* a meadow or grassy field; *also* **LEA**

LIB *n* informal for liberation; the act or process of seeking or securing equal rights

LID *n pl* **-S** a removable or hinged cover for a container

LIE *v* **LAY, LAIN, LYING, -S** to recline; to be in or assume a horizontal, resting position

LIF *n* [obs] the fiber by which the petioles of the date palm are bound together

LIG *v* **-GED, GING, -S** BRIT. to do nothing; to be habitually lazy, often at the expense of others generosity

LIM *n* [obs] a limb, an appendage such as a leg, arm, wing or a large tree branch

LIN *v* **-NED, -NING, -S** BRIT. to cease; stop; rest

LIP *v* **-PED, -PING, -S** to touch with the lips, to kiss

LIT *v pt of* **LIGHT** ignited; illuminated; *also* **LIGHTED**

LOB *v* **-BED, -BING, -S** to hit, throw or propel in a high arc

LOG *v* **-GED, -GING, -S** to cut and haul trees for lumber

LOO *n pl* **-S** BRIT. a toilet

LOP *v* **-PED, -PING, -S** to cut off something cleanly

LOS *n* [obs] praise;

LOT *v* **-TED, TING, -S** to divide into specified segments, such as a piece of land

LOW *v* **-ED, -ING, -S** to make the calling sound of cows and other bovine animals; to moo

LOX *n pl* **LOX** smoked salmon

LOY *n* [obs] a long, narrow spade for stony lands

LUD *n* BRIT. used with *my* to address a judge in court

LUG *v* **-GED, -GING, -S** to pull, drag, or carry with great effort

LUM *n pl* **-S** SCOT., BRIT. informal for a chimney

LUO *n* any of several sizes and styles of Chinese gong

LUV *n* BRIT. love; sweetheart; an affectionate term of address

LUX *n pl* **LUX, -ES** or **LUCES** a basic unit of illumination equal to one lumen per square meter

LUZ *n* [obs] a bone of the human body which was supposed by Rabbinical scholars to be indestructible

LYE *n* a strong alkaline substance used in making soap and as a chemical cleaning agent

LYN *n pl* **-S** SCOT. a waterfall, a torrent of rushing water; *also* **LINN**

FOUR LETTERS

LAAS *n* [obs] a lace; a string; a cord; *also* **LAS**

LABS *n pl of* **LAB** informal for laboratories

LACE *v* **-D, -ING, -S** to thread a cord or ribbon through eyelets or around hooks

LACK *v* **-ED, -ING, -S** to be in need; to be deficient

LACS *n pl of* **LAC** one hundred thousand, used especially for referring to sums of rupees; *also* **LAKHS**

LACY *adj* **LACIER, LACIEST** containing a fine netting of delicate fabric woven in an ornamental design; *also* **LACEY**

LADE *v* **-D, -N, LADING, -S** to load heavily; to place cargo on a ship

LADS *n pl of* **LAD** boys; young men

LADY *n pl* **LADIES** a woman, especially one polite and well-mannered

LAGS *v pr t of* **LAG** falls behind; fails to keep up in pace; straggles

LAIC *adj* involving laypersons or followers of a church who are not clergy; *also* **LAICAL**

LAID *v p t of* **LAY** put or set down, often gently or carefully

LAIN *v p part of* **LIE** to have reclined; to have assumed a horizontal, resting position

LAIR *v* **-ED, -ING, -S** to take or drive a wild animal to its resting place or den

LAKE *n pl* **-S** a large body of usually fresh water surrounded by land

LAKH *n pl* **LAKH** or **-S** one hundred thousand, used especially for referring to sums of rupees; *also* **LAC**

LAKY *adj* **LAKIER, LAKIEST** the color of a purplish red pigment called lake

LALL *v* **-ED, -ING, -S** to speak with an imperfect pronunciation of the letter *r* or *l* or both

LALO *n* the powdered leaves of the baobab tree, added to soups

LAMA *n pl* **-S** a title for a Tibetan teacher of the Dharma, used to designate a level of spiritual attainment and authority to teach

LAMB *v* **-ED, -ING, -S** to give birth to a baby sheep

LAME *v* **-D, LAMING, -S** to cause or make unable to walk

LAMM *v* **-ED, -ING, -S** [obs] to hit or beat hard; to thrash; *also* **LAM**

LAMP *n pl* **-S** a device or mechanism for producing light by electricity

LAMS *v pr t of* **LAM** [obs] hits or beats hard; thrashes

LAND *v* **-ED, -ING, -S** to come down onto solid ground or water

175

LANE *n pl* **-S** a narrow path, road, or street

LANG *adj* SCOT. long

LANK *adj* **-ER, -EST** limp and straight

LAPS *v pr t of* **LAP** overtakes a competitor in a race by completing at least one more circuit than he or she has

LARD *v* **-ED, -ING, -S** to cover or coat with fat; to grease

LARE *v* **-D, -ING, -S** [obs] to feed; to fatten

LARI *n pl* **LARI** or **-S** a subunit of currency in the Maldives; *also* **LAARI, LAREE**

LARK *v* **-ED, -ING, -S** to be mischievous or irresponsible

LARY *n* [obs] a guillemot; a northern seabird; *also* **LAVY**

LASE *v* **-D, LASING, -S** to emit single-wavelength radiation

LASH *v* **-ED, -ING, -ES** to strike with force or violence, as if with a whip

LASK *v* **-ED, -ING, -S** [obs] to sail with wind abeam or on the quarter

LASS *n pl* **-ES** SCOT., BRIT. a girl; a young woman; *also* **LASSIE**

LAST *v* **-ED, -ING, -S** to continue or endure for a period of time

LATE *adj* **-R, -ST** tardy; coming after the time when due

LATH *v* **-ED, -ING, -S** to attach a narrow strip of wood or metal to rafters, studs or floor beams as a substructure for plaster, tiles or shingles

LATI *n pl of* **LAT** more than one of the basic monetary unit of Latvia; *also* **LATS**

LATS *n pl of* **LAT** more than one of the basic monetary unit of Latvia; *also* **LATI**

LAUD *v* **-ED, -ING, -S** to highly commend or praise; to extol

LAVA *n* molten rock that reaches the earth's surface through a volcano or fissure

LAVE *v* **-D, LAVING, -S** to lap or wash against, as waves on the shore

LAVS *n pl of* **LAV** BRIT. lavatories; rooms equipped with toilet facilities

LAVY *n* a guillemot; a northern seabird; *also* **LARY**

LAWN *n pl* **-S** an area of cultivated and mowed grass

LAWS *v pr t of* **LAW** [obs] litigates; takes legal action; sues or prosecutes

LAYS *v pr t of* **LAY** puts or sets down, often gently or carefully

LAZE *v* **-D, LAZING, -S** to be lazy or idle; to do very little

LAZY *adj* **LAZIER, LAZIEST** disinclined to activity or exertion

LEAD *v* **LED, -ING, -S** to show or guide the way by going in advance

LEAF *v* **-ED, -ING, -S** turn over pages of written material, especially to browse or to skim

LEAK *v* **-ED, -ING, -S** to escape through a breach or flaw

LEAL *adj* SCOT. faithful; loyal; true

LEAM *n* [obs] a ray or glimmer of light; *also* **LEME**

LEAN *v* **-ED, -ING, -S** to bend or slant away from the vertical

LEAP *v* **-ED** or **LEAPT, -ING, -S** to spring or move suddenly; to bound; *also* **LEP**

LEAR *n* SCOT., BRIT. learning, instruction, lesson

LEAS *n pl of* **LEA** meadows or grassy fields; *also* **LEYS**

LEAT *n pl* **-S** BRIT. a trench or open watercourse that conducts water to a mill or factory

LECH *v* **-ED, -ING, -ES** [obs] to lick

LEEK *n pl* **-S** an edible perennial plant with a white, slender bulb and flat, dark-green leaves

LEER *v* **-ED, -ING, -S** to cast a sidelong glance

LEES *n/pl* sediment of wine or other alcoholic beverages that settles during fermentation; the dregs

LEET *n pl* **-S** SCOT. a list of people, especially candidates for office

LEFT *v p t of* **LEAVE** went away; departed

LEGS *n pr t of* **LEG** travels by foot; walks or runs

LEHR *n pl* **-S** an oven used to anneal glass

LEIS *n pl of* **LEI** garlands of flowers, especially ones worn around the neck

LEKE *n pl of* **LEK** more than one of the basic monetary unit of Albania; *also* **LEKS**

LEKS *n pl of* **LEK** more than one of the basic monetary unit of Albania; *also* **LEKE**

LEME *n* [obs] a ray or glimmer of light; *also* **LEAM**

LEND *v* **LENT, -ING, -S** to give or allow the use of temporarily

LENE *adj* smooth, as an unaspirated consonant, *p*, *k*, or *t*

LENO *n pl* **-S** an open weave textile in which warp yarns are paired and twisted

LENS *v* **-ED, -ING, -ES** to record a motion picture on film

LENT *v p t of* **LEND** gave or allowed the use of temporarily

LEOD *n* [obs] a people; a nation

LEPS *v pr t of* **LEP** [obs] springs or moves suddenly; bounds; *also* **LEAPS**

LEPT *v p t of* **LEP** and **LEAP** sprung or moved suddenly; bounded; *also* **LEAPT**

LESS *adj* **-ER, LEAST** a smaller amount or proportion of something

LEST *conj* for fear that; to avoid the risk of

LETS *v pr t of* **LET** allows; gives permission or permits

LEUD *n pl* **-S** or **-ES** a vassal or tenant in the early Middle Ages

LEVA *n pl of* **LEV** more than one of the basic monetary unit in Bulgaria

LEVO *adj* of or relating to an optically active chemical that rotates the plane of polarized light to the left; *also* **LEVOROTARY**

LEVY *v* **LEVIED, -ING, LEVIES** to impose or collect a tax

LEWD *adj* **-ER, -EST** [obs] evil, wicked

LEYS *n pl of* **LEY** meadows or grassy fields; *also* **LEAS**

LIAR *n pl* **-S** a person who knowingly utters falsehood

LICE *n pl of* **LOUSE** wingless, flat-bodied insects that are parasitic on warm-blooded animals

LICH *n* BRIT. a dead body; a corpse; *also* **LYCH**

LICK *v* **-ED, -ING, -S** to pass the tongue over something

LIDO *n pl* **-S** BRIT. a public, open-air swimming pool or bathing beach

LIDS *n pl of* **LID** removable or hinged covers for containers

LIED *v p t of* **LIE** knowingly told a falsehood; deceived

LIEF *adv* **-ER, -EST** [obs] readily; willingly; gladly; *also* **LIEVE**

LIEN *n pl* **-S** a legal claim; a right to keep the real or personal property of another for the satisfaction of some debt

LIER *n pl* **-S** one who lies down; one who reclines or assumes a horizontal, resting position

LIES *v pr t of* **LIE** reclines; is in or assumes a horizontal, resting position

LIEU *n* in place of; instead

LIFE *n pl* **LIVES** the entire period during which somebody is, has been, or will be alive

LIFT *v* **-ED, -ING, -S** to raise; to elevate

LIGE *v* [obs] to lie; to tell lies

LIGS *v pr t of* **LIG** BRIT. does nothing; is habitually lazy, often at the expense of others' generosity

LIKE *v* **-D, LIKING, -S** to find pleasant or attractive; to enjoy

LILL *v* [obs] to loll

177

LILT *v* -ED, -ING, -S to speak, sing or play in a cheerful, rhythmic manner

LILY *n pl* LILIES a perennial, bulbous plant with large, trumpet shaped flowers on a tall, slender stem

LIMB *n pl* -S an appendage such as a leg, arm, wing or a large tree branch

LIME *v* -D, -LIMING, -S to treat, mix or spread with calcium oxide

LIMN *v* -ED, -ING, -S to depict by painting or drawing, especially in outline

LIMO *n pl* -S commonly used abbreviation for a limousine; a large luxurious car, usually driven by a chauffeur

LIMP *v* -ED, -ING, -S to walk lamely, favoring one leg

LIMY *adj* LIMIER, LIMIEST of, like, or containing a form of calcium oxide; *also* LIMEY

LINE *v* -D, LINING, -S to mark, draw or trace with a very thin, thread-like mark, long in proportion to its breadth

LING *n pl* LING or -S an edible marine fish related to or resembling cod

LINK *v* -ED, -ING, -S to join or connect things together

LINN *n pl* -S SCOT. a waterfall, a torrent of rushing water; *also* LYN

LINO *n pl* -S BRIT. informal for linoleum; a tough, smooth, washable floor covering

LINS *v pr t of* LIN BRIT. ceases; stops; rests

LINT *n* clinging bits of fiber, thread or fluff

LINY *adj* LINIER, LINIEST thin or thread-like; long in proportion to breadth; *also* LINEY

LION *n pl* -S a large, powerful and carnivorous wildcat

LIPA *n pl* LIPA, -S, or LIPE a subunit of currency in Croatia; *also* LIPE, LIPAS

LIPE *n pl* LIPA more than one of a subunit of currency in Croatia; *also* LIPA, LIPAS

LIPS *v pr t of* LIP touches with the lips, kisses

LIRA *n pl* -S or LIRE the basic monetary unit of Turkey

LIRE *n pl of* LIRA more than one of the basic monetary unit of Turkey; *also* LIRAS

LISP *v* -ED, -ING, -S to mispronounce the sounds 's' and 'z' with a soft "th" sound

LISS *v* [obs] to free, as from care or pain; to relieve

LIST *v* -ED, -ING, -S to record a series of items in a meaningful grouping or sequence for a given purpose

LITE *adj* low in alcohol, calories, sugar or fat, used especially in food labeling

LITH *n* BRIT. an arm or leg; a limb

LITU *n pl of* LITAS formerly, more than one of the basic monetary unit in Lithuania; *also* LITAI, LITAS

LIVE *v* -D, LIVING, -S to be alive; to exist

LIZA *n* a mullet or fish found in the tropical Atlantic Ocean

LOAD *v* -ED, -ING, -S to put something into a machine or onto a vehicle for transport

LOAF *v* -ED, -ING, -S to pass time idly

LOAM *v* -ED, -ING, -S to fill, coat or cover with an earthy mixture of clay, silt, sand and some organic matter

LOAN *v* -ED, -ING, -S to grant permission for temporary use or allow one to borrow, often for a specified period repayable with interest

LOBE *n pl* -S a rounded projection that is part of a larger structure

LOBO *n pl* -S the gray wolf

LOBS *v pr t of* LOB hits, throws or propels in a high arc

LOCH *n pl* **-S** SCOT. a lake; a long, narrow arm of the sea; *also* **LOUGH**

LOCI *n pl of* **LOCUS** particular positions, points or places

LOCK *v* **-ED, -ING, -S** to fasten and secure; to make safe

LOCO *v* **-ED, -ING, -S** to poison with locoweed, a plant found in the Southwest United States that is deadly to horses and cattle

LODE *n pl* **-S** a vein-like deposit of metal ore that fills a fissure in a rock formation

LOFT *v* **-ED, -ING, -S** to kick, hit, throw or propel in a high arc

LOGE *n pl* **LOGES** a private box in a theater

LOGO *n pl* **-S** a symbol, trademark or graphic used by an organization or company, designed for easy and immediate recognition

LOGS *v pr t of* **LOG** cuts and hauls trees for lumber

LOGY *adj* **LOGIER, LOGIEST** sluggish; without energy or enthusiasm; *also* **LOGGY**

LOID *v* to force open a door by sliding a thin piece of celluloid or plastic between the door edge and doorframe

LOIN *n pl* **-S** the area of a human or animal, between the lowest ribs and hip bones on both sides of the spine

LOIR *n* [obs] a large European dormouse

LOKE *n* [obs] a private path or road

LOLL *v* **-ED, -ING, -S** to move, stand or recline in a lazy, relaxed manner

LOMA *n pl* **-S** a rounded hill or ridge with a broad top

LONE *adj* without accompaniment or companionship; solitary

LONG *v* **-ED, -ING, -S** to desire strongly; to yearn

LOOB *n* the clay or slimes washed from tin ore

LOOF *n* SCOT., BRIT. the palm of the hand

LOOK *v* **-ED, -ING, -S** to direct one's gaze in a given direction or towards a given object

LOOL *n* in mining, a receptacle for ore-washings

LOOM *v* **-ED, -ING, -S** to come into view as a massive, indistinct or distorted image

LOON *n pl* **-S** a large diving bird that feeds on fish, has a sharp bill, short tail, webbed feet and a weird, laughing cry

LOOP *v* **-ED, -ING, -S** to wind or coil around something

LOOS *n pl of* **LOO** BRIT. toilets

LOOT *v* **-ED, -ING, -S** to plunder; to pillage; to steal during a time of disorder and confusion

LOPE *v* **-D, LOPING, -S** to move, ride or run with a long bounding stride and easy gait

LOPS *v pr t of* **LOP** cuts off something cleanly

LORD *v* **-ED, -ING, -S** to behave as if you are better than others; to domineer

LORE *n pl* **-S** the part on each side of a bird's head between its eyes and the base of the beak

LORI *n pl* **-ES** or **LORY** a small brightly colored parrot native to Australia, New Guinea and Indonesia; *also* **LORY**

LORN *adj* forsaken; abandoned; solitary; bereft

LORY *n pl* **LORIES** or **LORY** a small brightly colored parrot native to Australia, New Guinea and Indonesia; *also* **LORI**

LOSE *v* **LOST, LOSING, -S** to misplace; to no longer have possession of

LOSS *n pl* **-ES** the fact of no longer having something or someone

LOST *v p t of* **LOSE** misplaced; no longer has possession of

LOTA *n pl* **-S** a small, round water container made of brass or copper and used in South Asia; *also* **LOTAH**

LOTE *n* a large hard wood tree of Southern Europe, with cherry-like fruit, also called a nettle tree

LOTH *adj* reluctant; unwilling; disinclined; *also* **LOATH**

LOTI *n pl* **MALOTI** basic unit of currency in Lesotho

LOTS *v pr t of* **LOT** divides into specified segments, such as a piece of land

LOUD *adj* **-ER, -EST** high in volume and intensity; noisy; clamorous

LOUK *n* [obs] an accomplice; a pal

LOUP *v* **-S, -ING, -ED** SCOT. to leap or jump over an obstacle; *also* **LOWP**

LOUR *v* **-ED, -ING, -S** to look angry, sullen, or threatening

LOUT *v* **-ED, -ING, -S** to bow or curtsy; to bend or stoop

LOVE *v* **-D, LOVING, -S** to feel deep devotion, affection and attachment

LOWE *v* **-D, LOWING, -S** BRIT. to burn; to blaze

LOWN *adj* SCOT. calm; quiet; peaceful

LOWP *v* **-S, -ING, -ED** SCOT. to leap or jump over an obstacle; *also* **LOUP**

LOWS *v pr t of* **LOW** makes the calling sound of cows and other bovine animals; moos

LUAU *n pl* **-S** an elaborate Hawaiian feast featuring traditional foods and entertainment

LUBE *v* **-D, LUBING, -S** to lubricate; to make slippery or smooth

LUCE *n pl* **LUCE** a pike, especially when full grown

LUCK *v* **-ED, -ING, -S** to gain something by chance or good fortune

LUFF *v* **-ED, -ING, -S** to steer a sailing vessel toward the wind, or too close to the wind so that the sail flaps

LUGE *v* **-D, -ING, -S** to race on a sled for one or two people that is ridden with the rider or riders lying supine

LUGS *v pr t of* **LUG** pulls, drags or carries with great effort

LUKE *adj* [obs] moderately warm; not hot; tepid

LULL *v* **-ED, -ING, -S** to soothe or calm; to send to sleep with soothing sounds or movements

LULU *n pl* **-S** informal for an outstanding example of a person, object or idea

LUMA *n pl* **LUMA** or **-S** a unit of currency in Armenia; *also* **LOUMA**

LUMP *v* **-ED, -ING, -S** to put together and consider alike despite differences; to group together carelessly

LUMS *n pl of* **LUM** SCOT., BRIT. informal for chimneys

LUNA *n* [obs] in alchemy, a designation for silver

LUNE *n pl* **-S** a crescent shaped area on the surface of a plane or sphere

LUNG *n pl* **-S** an organ for aerial respiration

LUNK *n pl* **-S** a fool; a blockhead

LUNT *v* **-ED, -ING, -S** SCOT. to kindle or light a fire

LUNY *adj* **LUNIER, LUNIEST** extremely foolish or silly; crazy; insane; *also* **LOONY, LOONEY**

LURE *v* **-D, LURING, -S** to draw; to attract; to entice; to tempt

LURG *n* a large marine worm, inhabiting the sandy shores of Europe and America

LURK *v* **-ED, -ING, -S** to lie in wait, behave in a secretive and sneaky manner

LUSH *adj* **-ER, -EST** abundant and thriving

LUSK *adj* [obs] lazy; slothful

LUTE *v* **-D, LUTING, -S** to coat, pack or seal with clay or cement

LUTZ *n pl* -**ES** a backward jump in figure skating

LUXE *adj* luxurious; sumptuous; elegantly opulent

LWEI *n pl* **LWEI** or -**S** a subunit of currency in Angola

LYAM *n* [obs] a leash; a cord or strap for leading a dog

LYCH *n* BRIT. [obs] a dead body, a corpse; *also* **LICH**

LYNS *n pl of* **LYN** SCOT. waterfalls, torrents of rushing water; *also* **LINNS**

LYNX *n pl* **LYNX** or -**ES** a short-tailed wildcat with tufted ears and a mottled coat

LYRE *n pl* -**S** an ancient harp-like instrument with a U-shaped frame

LYSE *v* -**D**, **LYSING**, -**S** to cause the process of cell destruction

FIVE LETTERS

LAARI *n pl* **LAARI** or **LAARIS** a subunit of currency in the Maldives; *also* **LARI**, **LAREE**

LABEL *v* -**ED**, -**ING**, -**S** to assign a category; to apply a sticker with identifying information

LABOR *v* -**ED**, -**ING**, -**S** to work hard; to toil

LABRA *n pl of* **LABRUM** the projecting upper mouthpart of some insects

LACED *v p t of* **LACE** threaded a cord or ribbon through eyelets or around hooks

LACER *n* one who laces or binds objects such as shoes, footballs or books

LACES *v pr t of* **LACE** threads a cord or ribbon through eyelets or around hooks

LACEY *adj* **LACIER**, **LACIEST** containing a fine netting of delicate fabric woven in an ornamental design; *also* **LACY**

LACKS *v pr t of* **LACK** is in need; deficient

LADED *v p t of* **LADE** loaded heavily; placed cargo on a ship

LADEN *v p part of* **LADE** to have loaded heavily; to have placed cargo on a ship

LADES *v pr t of* **LADE** loads heavily; places cargo on a ship

LADLE *v* -**ED**, -**ING**, -**S**, to lift out and serve with a long-handled, cup-like spoon

LAGAN *n* cargo or goods cast overboard with a buoy attached, so as to make them recoverable; *also* **LAGEND**, **LIGAN**

LAGER *n pl* -**S** a light-colored beer that contains a relatively small amount of hops

LAHAR *n pl* -**S** flowing mass or landslide of volcanic debris

LAIGH *adj* SCOT. low, of little height or elevation

LAIRD *n pl* -**S** SCOT. the landowner, especially of a large estate

LAIRS *v pr t of* **LAIR** to take or drive a wild animal to its resting place or den

LAITH *adj* SCOT. loath; unwilling; reluctant; disinclined

LAITY *n/pl* lay people, the followers of a church who are not clergy

LAKER *n pl* -**S** a fish living in a lake rather than the sea

LAKES *n pl of* **LAKE** large bodies of usually fresh water surrounded by land

LAKHS *n pl of* **LAKH** multiples of one hundred thousand, used especially for referring to sums of rupees; *also* **LACS**

LALLS *v pr t of* **LALL** speaks with an imperfect pronunciation of the letter *r* or *l* or both

LAMAS *n pl of* **LAMA** titles for Tibetan teachers of the Dharma, used to designate a level of spiritual attainment and authority to teach

LAMBS *v pr t of* **LAMB** to give birth to a baby sheep

LAMBY *adj* resembling a lamb or baby sheep

LAMED *v p t of* **LAME** caused or made unable to walk

LAMER *adj* a person who is more out of touch with modern fads or trends than the person they are being compared to

LAMES *v pr t of* **LAME** causes or makes unable to walk

LAMIA *n pl* -S, -E a female vampire

LAMMS *v pr t of* **LAMM** [obs] hits or beats hard; thrashes

LAMPS *n pl of* **LAMPS** devices or mechanisms for producing light by electricity

LANAI *n pl* -S a veranda or roofed patio often used as an open-sided living room in Hawaii

LANCE *v* -D, LANCING, -S to pierce, incise or cut open with a sharp instrument

LANDS *v pr t of* **LAND** comes down onto solid ground or water

LANES *n pl of* **LANE** narrow paths, roads, or streets

LANKY *adj* LANKIER, LANKIEST tall and thin in a bony, angular way

LAPEL *n pl* -S the fold on the front of a coat or jacket that extends from the collar

LAPIN *n pl* -S rabbit fur, especially when sheared and dyed

LAPIS *n pl* LAPIDES Latin word for stone, used especially in chemistry and in the names of minerals, gems, etc.

LAPSE *v* -D, LAPSING, -S to fall from a previous level or standard; to deviate from an accepted way

LARCH *n pl* LARCH or -ES a deciduous tree of the pine family

LARDS *v pr t of* **LARD** covers or coats with fat; greases

LARDY *adj* LARDIER, LARDIEST consisting of lard; fat

LARED *v p t of* **LARE** [obs] fed; fattened

LAREE *n pl* **LAREE** or **LAREES** a subunit of currency in the Maldives; *also* LARI, LAARI

LARES *n pl of* **LAR** in ancient Rome, guardian spirits, especially the spirits of ones' ancestors, that protect the family and watch over the household

LARGE *adj* -ER, -EST of greater than average size; very big

LARGO *n pl* -S a slow musical movement or passage

LARIS *n pl of* **LARI** more than one of a subunit of currency in the Maldives; *also* LARI, LAARI, LAARIS, LAREE, LAREES

LARKS *v pr t of* **LARK** is mischievous or irresponsible

LARKY *adj* LARKIER, LARKIEST playful, high-spirited, foolish

LARUM *n* [obs] any sound, outcry or information intended to warn of approaching danger

LARVA *n pl* -E, -S newly hatched, wingless, worm-like form of many insects before metamorphosis

LASED *v p t of* **LASE** emitted single-wavelength radiation

LASER *n pl* -S a device that generates a highly focused beam of single-wavelength radiation

LASES *v pr t of* **LASE** emits single-wavelength radiation

LASKS *v pr t of* **LASK** [obs] sails with wind abeam or on the quarter

LASSI *n pl* -S a South Asian drink made from yogurt

LASSO *v* -ED, -ING, -ES or -S to catch or capture using a long, stiff rope with a sliding noose at one end

LASTS *v pr t of* **LAST** continues or endures for a period of time

LATCH *v* -ED, -ING, -ES to close or lock with a fastening device such as a notched bar lifted by a lever

LATED *adj* poetic for too late

LATEN *v* -ED, -ING, -S to make or become late

LATER *adv* subsequently; afterward; after some time

LATEX *n pl* **-ES, LATICES** a milky fluid found in many plants, including the rubber tree, which coagulates when exposed to air

LATHE *v* **-D, LATHING, -S** to cut or shape with a machine that rotates the object or material along the edge of a cutting tool

LATHI *n pl* **-S** in India, a heavy stick of iron and bamboo used as a weapon, especially by the police

LATHS *v pr t of* **LATH** attaches a narrow strip of wood or metal to rafters, studs or floor beams as a substructure for plaster, tiles or shingles

LATHY *adj* **LATHIER, LATHIEST** like a lath, long and slender

LATKE *n pl* **-S** a pancake made of grated potatoes and egg

LATTE *n pl* **-S** an espresso drink made with steamed milk

LAUAN *n pl* **-S** wood from a type of tropical tree found in Southeast Asia, also called Philippine mahogany

LAUDS *v pr t of* **LAUD** highly commends or praises; extols

LAUGH *v* **ED, -ING, -S** to smile while making sounds with your voice that show you are happy; to chuckle

LAURA *n pl* **-S** a monastery of an Eastern church

LAVED *v p t of* **LAVE** lapped or washed against, as waves on the shore

LAVER *n pl* **-S** a vessel used for ancient Hebrew ceremonial washings

LAVES *v pr t of* **LAVE** laps or washes against, as waves on the shore

LAWED *v p t of* **LAW** [obs] litigated; took legal action; sued or prosecuted

LAWNS *n pl of* **LAWN** areas of cultivated and mowed grass

LAWNY *adj* consisting of resembling cut grass

LAXER *adj* less firm; less strict or careful

LAXLY *adv* in a loose, careless, unconcerned manner

LAYER *v* **-ED, -ING, -S** to apply or form things as separate thicknesses

LAYUP *n pl* **-S** a type of shot in basketball made just under the basket, and typically, off the backboard

LAZAR *n pl* **-S** [obs] a person affected with leprosy; *also* **LEPER**

LAZED *v p t of* **LAZE** was lazy or idle; did very little

LAZES *v pr t of* **LAZE** is lazy or idle; does very little

LEACH *v* **-ED, -ING, -ES** to cause a liquid to filter through something

LEADS *v pr t of* **LEAD** shows or guides the way by going in advance

LEADY *adj* **LEADIER, LEADIEST** resembling lead, a heavy, comparatively soft, malleable, bluish-gray metal

LEAFS *v pr t of* **LEAF** turns over pages of written material, especially browses or skims

LEAFY *adj* **LEAFIER, LEAFIEST** covered with leaves, heavy with foliage

LEAKS *v pr t of* **LEAK** escapes through a breach or flaw

LEAKY *adj* **LEAKIER, LEAKIEST** tending to escape through a breach or flaw

LEANS *v pr t of* **LEAN** bends or slants away from the vertical

LEANT *v p t of* **LEAN** BRIT. bent or slanted away from the vertical

LEAPS *v pr t of* **LEAP** springs or moves suddenly; bounds; *also* **LEPS**

LEAPT *v p t of* **LEAP** sprung or moved suddenly; bounded; *also* **LEPT**

LEARN *v* **-ED** or **LEARNT, -ING, -S** to gain knowledge by experience, instruction, or study

LEARY *adj* **LEARIER, LEARIEST** regarding with suspicion; wary; *also* **LEERY**

LEASE *v* **-D, LEASING, -S** to grant temporary use of property in exchange for rent, under the terms of a contract

LEASH *v* **-ED, -ING, -S** to control or restrain an animal with a chain, rope or strap attached to a collar or harness

LEAST *adj* the smallest in size or proportion

LEATS *n pl of* **LEAT** trenches or open watercourses that conduct water to a mill or factory

LEAVE *v* **LEFT, LEAVING, -S** to go away; to depart

LEAVY *adj* [obs] **LEAVIER, LEAVIEST** covered with leaves, heavy with foliage

LEDGE *n pl* **-S** a narrow, shelf-like projection

LEDGY *adj* **LEDGIER, LEDGIEST** having a raised or projecting, shelf-like edge

LEECH *v* **-ED, -ING, -ES** to cling to and feed upon; to drain the essence or exhaust the resources

LEEKS *n pl of* **LEEK** edible perennial plants with white, slender bulbs and flat, dark-green leaves

LEERS *v pr t of* **LEER** casts a sidelong glance

LEERY *adj* **LEERIER, LEERIEST** regarding with suspicion; wary; also **LEARY**

LEETS *n pl of* **LEET** SCOT. lists of people, especially candidates for office

LEFTY *n pl* **LEFTIES** informal for a left-handed person

LEGAL *adj* relating to law or the courts of law

LEGER *n* a type of bait and sinker system used to catch fish; *also* **LEDGER**

LEGES *n pl of* **LEX** named laws or sets of laws

LEGGY *adj* **LEGGIER, LEGGIEST** having very long legs

LEGIT *adj* informal for legitimate; honest and truthful

LEHRS *n pl of* **LEHR** ovens for annealing glass

LEHUA *n pl* **-S** a flowering hard-wood tree that grows in Hawaii and other Pacific Islands; *also* **OHIA**

LEMAN *n pl* **-S** [obs] a sweetheart; a lover; a beloved

LEMMA *n pl* **-S, -TA** an assumption for the sake of an argument

LEMON *n pl* **-S** a small, oval-shaped citrus fruit with a pale yellow rind

LEMUR *n pl* **-S** a tree-dwelling, mostly nocturnal primate, found in Madagascar, having large eyes and a long tail

LENDS *v pr t of* **LEND** gives or allows the use of temporarily

LENES *n pl of* **LENIS** unaspirated consonants; *p*, *k*, and *t*

LENIS *n pl* **LENES** an unaspirated consonant; *p*, *k*, or *t*

LENOS *n pl of* **LENO** open weave textiles in which warp yarns are paired and twisted

LENTO *n pl* **-S** a piece of music to be played at a slow tempo

LEONE *n pl* **LEONE** or **-S** the basic monetary unit in Sierra Leone

LEPER *n pl* **-S** [obs] a person affected with leprosy; *also* **LAZAR**

LEPTA *n pl of* **LEPTON** small coins, formerly used as currency in Greece

LETHE *n* a dreamy state of forgetfulness; oblivion

LETUP *n* informal for a pause, especially during something unpleasant

LEUDS *n pl of* **LEUD** vassals or tenants in the early Middle Ages

LEVEE *v* **-D, -ING, -S** to build an embankment on a river to prevent flooding

LEVEL *v* **-ED, -ING, -S** to make even, flat or perfectly horizontal

LEVER *v* -ED, -ING, -S to move, lift or pry with a simple device, such as a straight bar pivoted on a fixed point

LEVIN *n* [obs] lightning, a discharge of atmospheric electricity

LEWIS *n pl* -ES a hoisting device for heavy stones

LEXES *n pl of* LEXIS the total stock of words in languages

LEXIS *n pl* LEXES the total stock of words in a language

LIANA *n pl* -S a woody climbing tropical vine; *also* LIANE

LIANE *n pl* -S a woody climbing tropical vine; *also* LIANA

LIANG *n pl* LIANG or -S a Chinese unit of weight equal to about 11/3 ounces

LIARS *n pl of* LIAR people who knowingly utter falsehoods

LIBEL *v* -ED, -ING, -S to make a false, malicious statement that damages a reputation; to defame

LIBER *n pl* LIBRI a book of public records

LIBRI *n pl of* LIBER books of public records

LICHI *n pl* -S the small, nut-like fruit of a Chinese tree, with a single large seed and sweet pulp; *also* LEECHEE, LICHEE, LITCHI, LYCHEE

LICHT *v* SCOT. [obs] to ignite; to illuminate

LICIT *adj* permitted by law; legal

LICKS *v pr t of* LICK passes the tongue over something

LIDAR *n pl* -S an electronic locating device used to study the weather and atmospheric conditions

LIDOS *n pl of* LIDO BRIT. public, open-air swimming pools or bathing beaches

LIEGE *n pl* -S a feudal lord entitled to allegiance and service

LIENS *n pl of* LIEN legal claims; rights to keep the real or personal property of others for the satisfaction of debts

LIERS *n pl of* LIER those who lie down; recline or assume a horizontal, resting position

LIEVE *adv* readily; willingly; gladly; *also* LIEF

LIFER *n* -S informal for a prisoner serving a life sentence

LIFTS *v pr t of* LIFT raises; elevates

LIGAN *n* cargo or goods cast overboard with a buoy attached, so as to make them recoverable; *also* LAGAN, LAGEND

LIGER *n* the offspring of a male lion and a female tiger

LIGHT *v* -ED or LIT, -ING, -S to ignite; to illuminate

LIKED *v p t of* LIKE found pleasant or attractive; enjoyed

LIKEN *v* -ED, -ING, -S to represent as similar; to compare

LIKES *v pr t of* LIKE finds pleasant or attractive; enjoys

LILAC *n pl* -S a shrub or small tree with fragrant flowers of violet, white or pink

LILTS *v pr t of* LILT speaks, sings or plays in a cheerful, rhythmic manner

LIMAN *n* a muddy lagoon near the mouth of a river

LIMBA *n* a large West African tree with straight-grained wood

LIMBI *n pl of* LIMBUS distinctive borders or edges of various body parts

LIMBO *n pl* -S an uncertain period when awaiting a decision or resolution

LIMBS *n pl of* LIMB appendages such as legs, arms, wings or large tree branches

LIMED *v p t of* LIME treated, mixed or spread with calcium oxide

LIMEN *n pl* **-S** or **LIMINA** the threshold of a physiological or psychological response

LIMES *v pr t of* **LIME** treats, mixes or spreads with calcium oxide

LIMEY *adj* **LIMIER, LIMIEST** of, like, or containing a form of calcium oxide; *also* **LIMY**

LIMIT *v* **-ED, ING, -S** to confine or restrict within boundaries

LIMNS *v pr t of* **LIMN** depicts by painting or drawing, especially in outline

LIMOS *n pl of* **LIMO** commonly used abbreviation for limousines; large luxurious cars, usually driven by chauffeurs

LIMPA *n* rye bread made with molasses or brown sugar

LIMPS *v pr t of* **LIMP** walks lamely, favoring one leg

LINAC *n pl* **-S** linear accelerator, a device that propels charged particles in a straight line by successive impulses from a series of electric fields

LINDY *n pl* **LINDIES** a lively swing dance for couples, similar to the jitterbug

LINED *v p t of* **LINE** marked, drew or traced with very thin, thread-like marks, long in proportion to their breadth

LINEN *n pl* **-S** fabric or cloth woven from flax

LINER *n pl* **-S** a passenger ship or airplane run by a large commercial company

LINES *v pr t of* **LINE** marks, draws, or traces with a very thin, thread-like mark, long in proportion to its breadth

LINEY *adj* **LINIER, LINIEST** thin or thread-like; long in proportion to breadth; *also* **LINY**

LINGO *n pl* **-ES** specialized vocabulary of a group or profession; jargon

LINGS *n pl of* **LING** edible marine fish related to or resembling cod

LININ *n* a connective material in the nucleus of a cell

LINKS *v pr t of* **LINK** joins or connects things together

LINNS *n pl of* **LINN** SCOT. waterfalls, torrents of rushing water; *also* **LYNS**

LINOS *n pl of* **LINO** BRIT. informal for linoleum floors; tough, smooth, washable floor coverings

LINTY *adj* **LINTIER, LINTIEST** covered with clinging bits of fiber, thread or fluff

LIONS *n pl of* **LION** large, powerful and carnivorous wildcats

LIPAS *n pl of* **LIPA** more than one of a subunit of currency in Croatia; *also* **LIPE, LIPA**

LIPID *n pl* **-S** any of a class of fatty substances that are insoluble in water

LIPIN *n pl* **-S** a complex lipid

LIPPY *adj* **LIPPIER, LIPPIEST** impudent; sassy; showing no respect in the way that one talks to others

LIRAS *n pl of* **LIRA** more than one of the basic monetary unit of Turkey; *also* **LIRE**

LISLE *n* a fine, tightly twisted cotton thread

LISPS *v pr t of* **LISP** mispronounces the sounds 's' and 'z' with soft "th" sounds

LISTS *v pr t of* **LIST** records a series of items in a meaningful grouping or sequence for a given purpose

LITAI *n pl of* **LITAS** formerly, the basic monetary unit in Lithuania; *also* **LITAS, LITU**

LITAS *n pl* **LITAI, LITAS, LITU** formerly, the basic monetary unit in Lithuania

LITER *n pl* **-S** a metric unit of volume a little larger than a liquid quart; *also* **LITRE**

LITHE *adj* **-R, -ST** bending easily or gracefully

186

LITHO *v* -ED, -ING, -S to make prints by lithography, in which only the image to be printed takes up ink, the rest of the page is treated to repel ink

LITRE *n pl* -S a metric unit of volume a little larger than a liquid quart; *also* **LITER**

LIVED *v p t of* **LIVE** was alive; existed

LIVEN *v* -ED, -ING, -S to make lively, cheerful or interesting

LIVER *n pl* -S a large organ in the abdomen that secretes bile and neutralizes toxins

LIVES *v pr t of* **LIVE** to be alive; to exist

LIVID *adj* extremely angry; furious; enraged

LIVRE *n pl* -S the basic monetary unit of Lebanon

LLAMA *n pl* -S a South American animal, related to the camel but without a hump, used as a beast of burden and valued for its wool

LLANO *n pl* -S a flat, grassy plain, especially in Latin America

LOACH *n pl* -ES small, bottom-dwelling freshwater fish related to carp and native to Europe and Asia

LOADS *v pr t of* **LOAD** puts something into a machine or onto a vehicle for transport

LOAFS *v pr t of* **LOAF** passes time idly

LOAMS *v pr t of* **LOAM** fills, coats or covers with an earthy mixture of clay, silt, sand and some organic matter

LOAMY *adj* resembling loam, an earthy mixture of clay, silt, sand and some organic matter

LOANS *v pr t of* **LOAN** grants permission for temporary use or allows one to borrow, often for a specified period repayable with interest

LOATH *adj* reluctant; unwilling; disinclined; *also* **LOTH**

LOBAR *adj* relating to a lobe, especially a lobe of a lung

LOBBY *v* **LOBBIED**, -ING, **LOBBIES** to attempt to influence legislators for or against a specific cause

LOBED *adj* having lobes or rounded projections

LOBES *n pl of* **LOBE** rounded projections that are part of a larger structure

LOBOS *n pl of* **LOBO** gray wolves

LOCAL *n pl* -S a native or long-term resident of a town or city

LOCHS *n pl of* **LOCH** lakes; long, narrow arms of the sea; *also* **LOUGHS**

LOCKS *v pr t of* **LOCK** fastens and secures; makes safe

LOCOS *v pr t of* **LOCO** to poison with locoweed, a plant found in the Southwest United States that is deadly to horses and cattle

LOCUM *n pl* -S BRIT. a temporary substitute, especially for a doctor or member of the clergy

LOCUS *n pl* **LOCI** a particular position, point or place

LODEN *n* a thick, waterproof, woolen fabric often used for coats

LODES *n pl of* **LODES** vein like deposits of metal ore that fill fissures in rock formations

LODGE *v* -ED, **LODGING**, -S to provide or rent temporary quarters, especially for sleeping

LOESS *n* fine-grained, wind-blown soil deposits

LOFTS *v pr t of* **LOFT** kicks, hits, throws or propels in a high arc

LOFTY *adj* **LOFTIER**, **LOFTIEST** having great or imposing height; towering

LOGES *n pl of* **LOGE** private boxes in a theater

LOGGY *adj* **LOGIER**, **LOGIEST** sluggish; without energy or enthusiasm; *also* **LOGY**

LOGIA *n pl of* **LOGION** collections of sayings, maxims and doctrines ascribed to a religious leader, especially sayings attributed to Jesus

LOGIC *n* a system of reasoning and inference

LOGIN *n pl* **-S** the process of identifying oneself to a computer, usually by entering a username and password; *also* **LOGON**

LOGON *n pl* **-S** the process of identifying oneself to a computer, usually by entering a username and password; *also* **LOGIN**

LOGOS *n pl of* **LOGO** symbols, trademarks or graphics used by an organization or company, designed for easy and immediate recognition

LOINS *n pl of* **LOIN** more than one of the area in humans or animals, between the lowest ribs and hip bones on both sides of the spine

LOLLS *v pr t of* **LOLL** moves, stands or reclines in a lazy, relaxed manner

LOLLY *n pl* **LOLLIES** BRIT. a lollipop; a piece of hard candy

LOMAS *n pl of* **LOMA** rounded hills or ridges with broad tops

LONER *n pl* **-S** a person who prefers to be alone

LONGE *v* **-D, -ING, -S** to train a horse using a lunge or long rope; *also* **LUNGE**

LONGS *v pr t of* **LONG** desires strongly; yearns

LOOBY *n pl* **LOOBIES** an awkward, clumsy person; a lubber

LOOEY *n* informal for a lieutenant in the armed forces; *also* **LOOIE, LOUIE**

LOOFA *n pl* **-S** a natural sponge made of the dried fibrous interior of an oblong fruit of a tropical gourd; *also* **LOOFAH, LUFFA**

LOOIE *n* informal for a lieutenant of the armed forces; *also* **LOOEY, LOUIE**

LOOKS *v pr t of* **LOOK** directs one's gaze in a given direction or towards a given object

LOOMS *v pr t of* **LOOM** to come into view as a massive, indistinct or distorted image

LOONS *n pl of* **LOON** large diving birds that feed on fish, have sharp bills, short tails, webbed feet and a weird, laughing cry

LOONY *adj* **LOONIER, LOONIEST** extremely foolish or silly; crazy; insane; *also* **LOONEY, LUNY**

LOOPS *v pr t of* **LOOP** winds or coils around something

LOOPY *adj* **LOOPIER, LOOPIEST** crazy; irrational; bizarre

LOOSE *v* **-D, LOOSING, -S** to release; undo; set free

LOOTS *v pr t of* **LOOT** plunders; pillages; and steals during a time of disorder and confusion

LOPED *v p t of* **LOPE** moved, rode or ran with a long bounding stride and easy gait

LOPER *n pl* **-S** one who moves with a slow, steady, bounding stride and easy gait

LOPES *v pr t of* **LOPE** moves, rides or runs with a long bounding stride and easy gait

LOPPY *adj* **LOPPIER, LOPPIEST** hanging limp; pendulous

LORAL *adj* pertaining to the space between the eye and the bill of a bird

LORAN *n* a long-range navigational system by which the position of a ship or aircraft can be determined by the time interval between radio signals from two or more stations

LORDS *v pr t of* **LORD** behaves as if better than others; domineers

LORES *n pl of* **LORE** the parts on each side of birds' heads between their eyes and the base of their beaks

LORIS *n pl* **LORIS** or **-ES** a small, slow-moving nocturnal primate, related to lemurs and found in South Asia

LORRY *n pl* **LORRIES** BRIT. a large, heavy vehicle for transporting goods, cargo or troops

LOSEL *adj* worthless, useless

LOSER *n pl* **-S** a defeated contestant

LOSES *v pr t of* **LOSE** misplaces; no longer has possession of

LOSSY *adj* causing appreciable loss of energy

LOTAH *n pl* **-S** a small, round water container made of brass or copper and used in South Asia; *also* **LOTA**

LOTAS *n pl of* **LOTA** small, round water containers made of brass or copper and used in South Asia; *also* **LOTAHS**

LOTIC *adj* living in swift-flowing water

LOTOS *n* an aquatic plant related to the water lily, having large leaves and fragrant pinkish flowers; *also* **LOTUS**

LOTTE *n* a monkfish, a fish having a large mouth and a wormlike filament for luring prey

LOTTO *n pl* **-S** a game of chance in which numbers are called at random and players try to be the first to cover all the corresponding numbers on their cards, similar to bingo

LOTUS *n* an aquatic plant related to the water lily, having large leaves and fragrant pinkish flowers; *also* **LOTOS**

LOUGH *n pl* **-S** SCOT. a lake; a long, narrow arm of the sea; *also* **LOCH**

LOUIE *n* informal for a lieutenant of the armed forces; *also* **LOOEY**, **LOOIE**

LOUIS *n pl* **LOUIS** a gold coin formerly used as currency in France

LOUMA *n pl* **LOUMAS** a subunit of currency in Armenia; *also* **LUMA**

LOUPE *n pl* **-S** a small magnifying glass usually set in an eyepiece used by watchmakers and jewelers

LOUPS *v pr t of* **LOUP** SCOT. to leap or jump over an obstacle; *also* **LOWPS**

LOURS *v pr t of* **LOUR** looks angry, sullen or threatening; *also* **LOWERS**

LOURY *adj* overcast; dark and threatening; gloomy; *also* **LOWERY**

LOUSE *v* **-D, LOUSING, -S** to ruin, spoil, bungle or foul up

LOUSY *adj* **LOUSIER, LOUSIEST** painful or in bad health

LOUTS *v pr t of* **LOUT** bows or curtsies; bends or stoops

LOVAT *n* a muted green color mixture in fabrics, especially in tweed and woolen garments

LOVED *v p t of* **LOVE** felt deep devotion, affection and attachment

LOVER *n pl* **-S** one who loves another

LOVES *v pr t of* **LOVE** feels deep devotion, affection and attachment

LOWED *v p t of* **LOW** made the calling sound of cows and other bovine animals; mooed

LOWER *v pr t of* **LOWE** BRIT. to burn; to blaze

LOWES *v pr t of* **LOWE** BRIT. burns; blazes

LOWLY *adj* **LOWLIER, LOWLIEST** humble or low in rank, position or status

LOWPS *v pr t of* **LOWP** SCOT. to leap or jump over an obstacle; *also* **LOUPS**

LOWSE *v* **-D, LOWSING, -S** SCOT., BRIT. loose; to release; undo; set free

189

LOYAL *adj* faithful, constant or steadfast in one's allegiance

LUAUS *n pl of* **LUAU** elaborate Hawaiian feasts featuring traditional foods and entertainment

LUBED *v p t of* **LUBE** lubricated; made slippery or smooth

LUBES *v pr t of* **LUBE** lubricates; makes slippery or smooth

LUCES *n pl of* **LUX** units of illumination equal to one lumen per square meter; *also* **LUXES**

LUCID *adj* easily understood; rational; clear; mentally sound

LUCKS *v pr t of* **LUCK** gains something by chance or good fortune

LUCKY *adj* **LUCKIER, LUCKIEST** having good fortune; fortunate or fortuitous

LUCRE *n* money, wealth or profits

LUDIC *adj* spontaneous; aimlessly playful

LUFFA *n pl* **-S** a natural sponge made of the dried fibrous interior of an oblong fruit of a tropical gourd; *also* **LOOFA, LOOFAH**

LUFFS *v pr t of* **LUFF** steers a sailing vessel toward the wind, or too close to the wind so that the sail flaps

LUGED *v p t of* **LUGE** raced on a sled for one or two people that is ridden with the rider or riders lying supine

LUGER *n pl* **-S** one who races on a sled for one or two people that is ridden with the rider or riders lying supine

LUGES *v pr t of* **LUGE** races on a sled for one or two people that is ridden with the rider or riders lying supine

LULLS *v pr t of* **LULL** soothes or calms; sends to sleep with soothing sounds or movements

LULUS *n pl of* **LULU** informal for outstanding examples of a person, object or idea

LUMAS *n pl of* **LUMA** more than one of a subunit of currency in Armenia

LUMEN *n pl* **-S, LUMINA** the space inside any tubular structure in the body, such as a blood vessel or intestine

LUMPS *v pr t of* **LUMP** puts together and considers alike despite differences; groups together carelessly

LUMPY *adj* **LUMPIER, LUMPIEST** full of irregular shapes; raised and bumpy

LUNAR *adj* involving, caused by, or affecting the moon

LUNCH *v* **-ED, -ING, -ES** to eat a mid-day meal

LUNES *n pl of* **LUNE** crescent shaped areas on the surfaces of planes or spheres

LUNET *n* [obs] a little moon or satellite; *also* **LUNETTE**

LUNGE *v* **-D, LUNGING, -S** to train a horse using a lunge or long rope; *also* **LONGE**

LUNGI *n pl* **-S** or **LUNGYIS** a length of cloth worn as a loincloth or skirt in India, Pakistan and Myanmar; *also* **LUNGEE, LUNGYI**

LUNGS *n pl of* **LUNG** organs for aerial respiration

LUNKS *n pl of* **LUNK** fools; blockheads

LUNTS *v pr t of* **LUNT** SCOT. kindles or lights a fire

LUPIN *n pl* **-S** any of several plants in the pea family; *also* **LUPINE**

LUPUS *n* an inflammatory disease affecting connective tissue

LURCH *v* **-ED, -ING, -ES** to make a sudden unsteady movement; stagger

LURED *v p t of* **LURE** drew; attracted; enticed; tempted

LURER *n* one who draws, attracts, entices or tempts

LURES *v pr t of* **LURE** draws; attracts; entices; tempts

LURID *adj* causing shock or horror; sensational; gruesome

LURKS *v pr t of* **LURK** lies in wait, behaves in a secretive and sneaky manner

LUSTY *adj* **LUSTIER, LUSTIEST** full of health and vigor; robust; hearty; energetic

LUTED *v p t of* **LUTE** coated, packed or sealed with clay or cement

LUTES *v pr t of* **LUTE** coats, packs or seals with clay or cement

LUXES *n pl of* **LUX** units of illumination equal to one lumen per square meter; *also* **LUCES**

LWEIS *n pl of* **LWEI** more than one of a subunit of currency in Angola

LYARD *adj* SCOT. streaked with grey; *also* **LYART**

LYART *adj* SCOT. streaked with grey; *also* **LYARD**

LYASE *n pl* **-S** an enzyme that acts as a catalyst in chemical reactions involving double bonds

LYCEA *n pl of* **LYCEUM** halls in which lectures, concerts and other public programs are presented; *also* **LYCEUMS**

LYCEE *n pl* **-S** a secondary school in France funded by the state

LYING *v pr part of* **LIE** reclining; assuming a horizontal, resting position

LYMPH *n* a body fluid containing white cells that can transport bacteria, viruses and cancer cells

LYNCH *v* **-ED, -ING, -ES** to put to death by mob action without legal sanction

LYRES *n pl of* **LYRE** ancient harp-like instruments with U-shaped frames

LYRIC *n pl* **-S** a short poem that expresses the personal thoughts and feelings of the author

LYSED *v p t of* **LYSE** caused the process of cell destruction

LYSES *v pr t of* **LYSE** causes the process of cell destruction

LYSIN *n pl* **-S** an antibody capable of destroying cells

LYSIS *n* the disintegration of cells by rupture of the cell wall or membrane

LYSSA *n* an acute viral disease of the nervous system of warm-blooded animals, transmitted by the bite of an infected animal; *also* **RABIES**

LYTIC *adj* pertaining to lysis or the disintegration of cells

LYTTA *n pl* **-S, -E** a band of cartilage lying along the underside of the tongue of dogs and certain other carnivorous mammals

MA *n pl* **-S** commonly used abbreviation for mama or mother

ME *pron* the objective case of "I"; used to refer to the speaker, the writer or one's self

MI *n* the 3rd note of a major scale; the syllable given to the 3rd tone of the diatonic scale

MO *n* BRIT. a moment or short while

MU *n* the 12th letter of the Greek alphabet corresponding to the English letter "m"

MY *adj* the possessive form of "I"; belonging to or associated with the speaker or writer

THREE LETTERS

MAC *n pl* **-S** BRIT. a mackintosh, a waterproof raincoat made of rubberized fabric; *also* **MACK**

MAD *v* **-DED, -DING, -S** to make or become insane; to drive someone crazy; to enrage

MAE *adj* SCOT. more

MAG *n pl* **-S** commonly used abbreviation for a magazine

MAM *n* BRIT. mum; mama; mother

MAN *v* **-NED, -NING, -S** to furnish with a labor force; to provide personnel; to supply with workers

MAP *v* **-PED, -PING, -S** to create a geographic diagram or visual representation of a specific area or place

MAR *v* **-RED, -RING, -S** to inflict disfiguring damage; to spoil; to ruin

MAS *n pl of* **MA** commonly used abbreviation for mamas or mothers

MAT *v* **-TED, -TING, -S** to place a stiff material or border around a picture, as a decorative edge or simple frame

MAW *n* **-S** the jaw, gullet or throat of a fierce carnivore; the mouth of a voracious animal

MAX *v* **-ED, -ING, -ES** to reach the upper limit

MAY *v* **MIGHT** to be allowed or permitted

MED *n pl* **-S** commonly used abbreviation for a medication or dose of medication

MEG *n pl* **-S** commonly used abbreviation for a megabyte, a unit of computer data or storage space equal to 1,048,576 bytes

MEL *n* honey, especially in the pure, clarified form, used in pharmacies

MEM *n* the 13th letter in the Hebrew alphabet

MEN *n pl of* **MAN** adult human males

MET *v p t of* **MEET** came together or came across someone at a specific place and time by arrangement or accident; encountered

MEU *n* a European plant with aromatic leaves and small white flowers found in mountain pastures; the spignel or spicknel plant

MEW *v* **-ED, -ING, -S** to cry with a soft, high-pitched sound, most often by a kitten or cat; *also* **MEAW, MEOW, MIAOU, MIAOW, MIAUL**

MHO *n pl* **-S** formerly, a unit of electrical conductance equal to one ampere per volt, now known by the term siemen

MIB *n pl* **-S** a type of playing marble

MIC *n pl* **-S** commonly used abbreviation for a microphone

MID *adj* in the middle, center or halfway through something

MIG *n pl* **-S** a type of playing marble

MIL *n* commonly used abbreviation for a million

MIM *adj* BRIT., SCOT. primly quiet and demure; affectedly shy and modest

MIN *n* BRIT. a minute or a short while

MIR *n* in Czarist Russia, before the Revolution, a village community of peasant farmers

MIX *v* **-ED** or **-T, -ING, -ES** to combine or blend into a new substance

MOA *n pl* **-S** an extinct flightless bird of New Zealand

MOB *v* **-BED, -BING, -S** to crowd about and jostle noisily from curiosity or anger

MOC *n pl* **-S** commonly used abbreviation for a moccasin

MOD *n pl* **-S** one who is boldly stylish

MOE *n* [obs] a wry face or mouth

MOG *v* **-GED, -GING, -S** to plod along steadily; to move on; depart

MOI *pron* me; used by a writer or speaker to refer to himself or herself, often facetiously

MOL *n pl* **-S** the quantity of a chemical substance having a weight in grams numerically equal to its molecular weight

MOM *n pl* **-S** commonly used abbreviation for mother

MON *n pl* **MON** Japanese heraldic symbols that serve roughly similar functions to badges, crests and coats of arms in European heraldry

MOO *v* **-ED, -ING, -S** to make a deep, moaning sound like a cow; to low

MOP *v* **-PED, -PING, -S** to clean or clear away; to wash or remove; to rub or wipe

MOR *n* a layer of humus, typically compact or matted, that gathers on the surface of cool, moist soil

MOT *n pl* **-S** an incisive or witty remark; a pithy saying

MOW *v* **-ED, -N, -ING, -S** to cut down grass, grain, or plant growth with a device or machine

MUD *v* **-DED, -ING, -S** to cover, spatter or soil with wet, soft, sticky earth

MUE *v* [obs] to mew; to molt

MUG *v* **-GED, -GING, -S** to attack and rob a pedestrian in a public place

MUM *v* **-MED, -MING, -S** to call for silence; to say "mum"; *also* **MUMM**

MUN *v* SCOT., BRIT. must; to be compelled or obliged; *also* **MAUN**

MUX *v* [obs] to make a mess of; to mix in an untidy way

FOUR LETTERS

MAAR *n pl* **-E** or **-S** a flat-bottomed volcanic crater, formed by an explosion and often filled with water

MAAT *adj* [obs] dejected; sorrowful; downcast

MACE *v* **-D, MACING, -S** to attack with a chemical compound, typically sprayed from an aerosol container, that temporarily stuns its victims

MACH *n* a measurement of speed, calculated by dividing the speed of an object by the speed of sound

MACK *n pl* **-S** BRIT. a mackintosh, a waterproof raincoat made of rubberized fabric; *also* **MAC**

MACS *n pl of* **MAC** BRIT. mackintoshes, waterproof raincoats made of rubberized fabric; *also* **MACKS**

MADE *v p t of* **MAKE** caused to exist; brought into being; formed; produced

MADS *v pr t of* **MAD** makes or becomes insane; drives someone crazy; enrages

MAGE *n pl* **-S** a magician, sorcerer or wizard

MAGI *n pl of* **MAGUS** in ancient Media and Persia, Zoroastrian priests from a hereditary caste

MAGS *n pl of* **MAG** commonly used abbreviation for magazines

MAHA *n* the wanderoo; a kind of baboon or large monkey

MAID *n pl* **-S** a female domestic servant

MAIL *v* **-ED, -ING, -S** to send a letter or package by post

MAIM *v* **-ED, -ING, -S** to mutilate; to cripple; to injure; to disable

MAIN *n pl* **-S** a large, principle pipe or cable that carries water, gas or electricity from one place to another

MAIR *adj* SCOT., BRIT. more

MAKE *v* **MADE, MAKING, -S** to cause to exist; to bring into being; to form; to produce

MAKI *n* rolled sushi, a type of Japanese cuisine

MAKO *n pl* **-S** a large, powerful, mackerel shark with a deep blue back and white underbelly

MALA *n pl* **-S** in South Asia, a garland of flowers given as sign of welcome

MALE *n pl* **-S** in humans, a man or a boy

MALL *n pl* **-S** a large enclosed shopping area or retail complex with a variety of stores and eateries

MALM *n* BRIT. a soft, crumbly, grayish white limestone

MALT *v* **-ED**, **-ING**, **-S** to process or convert cereal grains into malt by soaking in water, drying in a kiln and forcing germination

MAMA *n pl* **-S** mother, often used with tenderness and familiarity; *also* **MAMMA, MOMMA**

MANA *n* a dynamic, supernatural force or magical power believed to dwell in a person or sacred object, capable of great good or evil; power; authority

MANE *n pl* **-S** the long, coarse hair growing from the head and neck of a horse, lion and other mammals

MANO *n pl* **-S** a hand-held stone or roller for grinding corn and other grains, used on metates or stone blocks

MANS *v pr t of* **MAN** furnishes with a labor force; provides personnel; supplies with workers

MANY *adj* **MORE, MOST** consisting of a great number; numerous

MAPS *v pr t of* **MAP** creates a geographic diagram or visual representation of all or part of specific area or place

MARA *n pl* **-S** a long-eared, long-legged, hare-like rodent, found in the scrub desert and grasslands of Argentina; Patagonian hare

MARC *n* the skins, pulpy residue and remains left after juice has been pressed from grapes, apples and other fruits

MARE *n pl* **-S** or **MARIA** one of several large, dark, flat areas on the Moon, Mercury or Mars

MARK *v* **-ED**, **-ING**, **-S** to make or leave a visible sign, impression, scratch, dent or symbol

MARL *v* **-ED**, **-ING**, **-S** to fertilize or add to soil an earthy mixture of carbonate of lime, clay, sand and shells

MARS *v pr t of* **MAR** inflicts disfiguring damage; spoils; ruins

MART *n pl* **-S** a market or trading center

MASA *n pl* **-S** flour or dough made from dried corn, soaked in limewater, rinsed and ground, and used to make tortillas, tamales, and other foods

MASH *v* **-ED**, **-ING**, **-ES** to beat, crush or smash ingredients to a reduced, soft pulpy state

MASK *v* **-ED**, **-ING**, **-S** to disguise; to cover, conceal, or hide

MASS *v* **-ED**, **-ING**, **-ES** to gather, collect, or form into a large, unified body with no specific shape

MAST *v* **-ED**, **-ING**, **-S** to furnish or assemble a pole, or long, strong, round piece of metal or timber, vertically from the deck of a vessel, to support sails, yards, and other types of nautical equipment

MATE *v* **-D, MATING, -S** to join as a pair, couple

MATH *n pl* **-S** mathematics; the study of relationships among numbers, shapes, and quantities using signs, symbols, reason, and proofs

MATS *v pr t of* **MAT** places a stiff material or border around a picture, as a decorative edge or simple frame

MATT *adj* BRIT. lacking highlights or gloss; surface or color that is not shiny; flat and dull; *also* **MATTE**

MATY *n* [obs] a native house servant in India

MAUD *n* a wrap, shawl or rug, made of gray, woolen plaid and worn in Scotland

MAUL *v* **-ED, -ING, -S** to treat savagely or roughly; to injure by beating; to batter, abuse or manhandle

MAUN *v* SCOT., BRIT. must; to be compelled or obliged; *also* **MUN**

MAUT *n* SCOT. malt

MAWK *n* SCOT. a maggot

MAWS *n pl of* **MAW** the jaws, gullets or throats of fierce carnivores; the mouths of voracious animals

MAXI *n pl* **-S** a long skirt, coat or dress, that extends to or just past the ankles

MAYA *n* in Hinduism, the ability to create illusion through supernatural, magical or sacred power

MAYO *n* commonly used abbreviation for mayonnaise; a creamy dressing or condiment spread made with egg yolks, oil, lemon juice or vinegar, and flavorings

MAZE *v* **-D, MAZING, -S** to daze or stupefy; to bewilder or astonish

MAZY *adj* **MAZIER, MAZIEST** perplexed with turns and intricate windings; tangled and interwoven like a maze

MEAD *n* an alcoholic beverage made of fermented honey and water to which malt, yeast and spices are added

MEAK *n* [obs] a hook with a long handle

MEAL *n pl* **-S** food served or eaten regularly at a certain time during the day, such as breakfast, lunch or dinner

MEAN *v* **-T, -ING, -S** to intend; to indicate; to signify

MEAR *n* BRIT. [obs] a boundary or boundary marker

MEAT *n* the flesh of animals used as food

MEAW *v* to cry with a soft, high-pitched sound, most often by a kitten or cat; *also* **MEOW, MEW, MIAOU, MIAOW, MIAUL**

MEDS *n pl of* **MED** commonly used abbreviation for medications or doses of medications

MEED *n* a deserved merit; reward; recompense

MEEK *adj* **-ER, -EST** patient and mild of temper; not easily provoked or irritated; submissive or compliant

MEET *v* **MET, -ING, -S** to come together or come across someone at a specific place and time by arrangement or accident; to encounter

MEGA *adj* surpassing other examples of its kind; extraordinary in size; great; large; powerful

MEGS *n pl of* **MEG** megabytes, units of computer data or storage space

MELD *v* **-ED, -ING, -S** blend or combine; to cause to merge

MELL *v* **-ED, -ING, -S** [obs] to mingle or mix; to meddle

MELT *v* **-ED, -ING, -S** to reduce from a solid to a liquid state, generally by heat; to liquefy or dissolve

MEME *n pl* **-S** an idea, behavior, style or usage that spreads from person to person within a culture

MEMO *n pl* **-S** commonly used abbreviation for memorandum, a brief written note written as a reminder

MEND *v* **-ED, -ING, -S** to repair; to restore; to improve

MENO *adv* a musical direction indicating "less"

MENU *n pl* **-S** a list of food or dishes available at a restaurant

MEOW *v* **-ED, -ING, -S** to cry with a soft, high-pitched sound, most often by a kitten or cat; *also* **MEAW, MEW, MIAOU, MIAOW, MIAUL**

MERD *n* [obs] ordure; dung; excrement

195

MERE *adj* **-ST** being nothing more than what is specified; small; slight

MERK *n* [obs] an old Scotch silver coin

MERL *n* the European black thrush or blackbird; *also* **MERLE**

MESA *n pl* **-S** a high, broad, flat tableland with steep sides, more extensive than a butte but less than a plateau

MESH *v* **-ED, -ING, -ES** to become entangled or entwined; to catch or ensnare; to be in harmony or coordinate

MESS *v* **-ED, -ING, -ES** to make untidy, disorderly or dirty; to bungle; to behave in a silly, playful way; to meddle

META *n pl* **-E** in ancient Rome, a column or post placed at each end of a racetrack to mark the turning places

METE *v* **-D, METING, -S** to allot, apportion or distribute by measure

METH *n* commonly used abbreviation for methamphetamine, a stimulant drug

MEVE *v* [obs] to move

MEWL *v* **-ED, -ING, -S** to whimper or cry weakly, as a baby or infant

MEWS *v pr t of* **MEW** cries with a soft, high-pitched sound, like a kitten or cat; *also* **MEAWS, MEOWS, MIAOUS, MIAOWS**

MEZE *n pl* **MEZE** or **-S** an appetizer, snack or light meal in Greek or Middle Eastern cuisine; *also* **MEZZE**

MHOS *n pl of* **MHO** formerly, units of electrical conductance, now known by the term siemens

MIBS *n pl of* **MIB** playing marbles

MICA *n* mineral silicates that form into flexible sheets or very thin leaves and are resistant to heat and electricity

MICE *n pl of* **MOUSE** small rodents having pointed snouts and long, thin, almost hairless tails

MICS *n pl of* **MIC** commonly used abbreviation for microphones

MIDA *n* [obs] the larva of the bean fly

MIDI *n pl* **-S** a skirt, dress or coat, that extends to the middle of the calf

MIEN *n pl* **-S** aspect; air; manner; demeanor; carriage; bearing

MIFF *v* **-ED, -ING, -S** to offend slightly; to annoy

MIGO *v* [obs] to go astray

MIGS *n pl of* **MIG** playing marbles

MIKE *v* **-D, MIKING, -S** to amplify, record or transmit by use of a microphone

MILD *adj* **-ER, -EST** gentle, moderate or temperate in disposition, action or affect

MILE *n pl* **-S** a measure of distance equal to 5,280 feet

MILK *v* **-ED, -ING, -S** to draw or extract a white, nutritious liquid from female mammals

MILL *v* **-ED, -ING, -S** to grind, pulverize or process grain with a machine or device

MILO *n pl* **-S** an early-growing, drought-resistant grain sorghum that resembles millet

MILT *v* **-ED, -ING, -S** to fertilize fish roe with the seminal fluid of male fishes

MIME *v* **-D, MIMING, -S** to mimic or imitate; to play a part with actions and gestures and not words

MINA *n pl* **-E** or **-S** a unit weight or currency used in ancient Greece and Asia Minor

MIND *v* **-ED, -ING, -S** to heed or obey; to pay attention to; to remember

MINE *v* **-D, MINING, -S** to dig, excavate or extract valuable minerals from the earth

MINI *n pl* **-S** something that is distinctively smaller than other members of its type or class

MINK _n pl_ **-S** a slender-bodied, semi-aquatic, carnivorous mammal with highly valued, soft, thick, lustrous fur

MINT _v_ **-ED, -ING, -S** to produce or make money; to invent or fabricate

MINX _n pl_ **-ES** a pert, saucy, bold and flirtatious girl, who knows how to control other people to her advantage

MINY _adj_ [obs] abounding with or resembling large, cavernous excavations in the earth

MIRE _v_ **-D, MIRING, -S** to soil or splatter with mud or muck; to sink or get stuck in deep, soggy earth

MIRK _n_ partial or total darkness; gloomy darkness caused by fog, mist, clouds or smoke; _also_ **MURK**

MIRY _adj_ **MIRIER, MIRIEST** abounding with deep mud; very muddy or boggy; swampy

MISE _n_ an agreement, pact or settlement; the issue in obsolete writ of right

MISO _n_ a thick, brown, salty paste, made from soy beans, salt and fermented grain, used especially in Japanese soups and sauces

MISS _v_ **-ED, -ING, -ES** to fail to hit, reach, meet, catch, accomplish, understand or hear

MIST _v_ **-ED, -ING, -S** to rain in a very fine shower; to spray obscure, or blur with a visible, watery vapor

MISY _n_ an impure yellow sulphate of iron; yellow copperas or copiapite

MITE _n pl_ **-S** tiny, sometimes microscopic arachnid, often parasitic, and occasionally disease carrying

MITT _n pl_ **-S** a large, padded protective leather glove used in baseball by the catcher and first basemen

MITU _n_ [obs] a South American long-tailed game bird; a curassow

MITY _adj_ [obs] having or abounding with mites, very tiny arachnids

MIXT _v p t of_ **MIX** combined or blended into a new substance; _also_ **MIXED**

MOAN _v_ **-ED, -ING, -S** to make a low, sustained, mournful cry of grief, pain or misery; to lament

MOAS _n pl of_ **MOA** extinct, flightless birds of New Zealand

MOAT _v_ **-ED, -ING, -S** to surround or fortify with a deep, water-filled trench, either as protection from attack or a barrier to escape

MOBS _v pr t of_ **MOB** crowds about and jostles noisily, from curiosity or anger

MOCK _v_ **-ED, -ING, -S** to treat with scorn or contempt; to deride; to ridicule and imitate

MOCO _n_ [obs] a South American rodent, related to the guinea pig, but larger

MOCS _n pl of_ **MOC** commonly used abbreviation for moccasins

MODE _n pl_ **-S** a method, manner or way of living or behaving; a prevailing popular custom or fashion

MODI _n pl of_ **MODUS** modes; manners; ways of living or behaving

MODS _n pl of_ **MOD** those who are boldly stylish

MODY _adj_ [obs] fashionable

MOFF _n_ [obs] a thin silk made in the Caucasus mountains between the Caspian and Black seas

MOGS _v pr t of_ **MOG** plods along steadily; moves on; departs

MOHA _n_ [obs] a kind of millet or small cereal grain; German millet

MOHO *n* the boundary layer between the earth's crust and the mantle

MOHR *n* a West African gazelle, having horns with eleven or twelve very prominent rings; *also* **MHORR**

MOIL *v* **-ED, -ING, -S** to toil; to slave; to churn or swirl in continuous confusion or agitation

MOJO *n pl* **-S** or **-ES** a magical charm, amulet or spell; supernatural power; personal magnetism

MOKE *n pl* **-S** BRIT. a donkey

MOKY *adj* [obs] misty; dark; murky

MOLA *n pl* **-S** a large, bony, silvery fish, found in tropical and temperate seas; an ocean sunfish

MOLD *v* **-ED, -ING, -S** to form or cast an object out of a malleable substance; to form or give shape; *also* **MOULD**

MOLE *n pl* **-S** a small, permanent, slightly protruding, dark spot on the human skin

MOLL *n pl* **-S** the girlfriend or female accomplice of a gangster or gunman

MOLT *v* **-ED, -ING, -S** to periodically or seasonally shed an old coat of feathers, hair or skin, to make way for new growth; *also* **MOULT**

MOLY *n pl* **MOLIES** a legendary, mythical herb, said to have black roots, white blossoms, and magical powers

MOME *n* [obs] a dull, silent person; a blockhead; a fool; a lout

MOMI *n pl of* **MOMUS** fault finders or carping critics

MOMS *n pl of* **MOM** commonly used abbreviation for mothers

MONA *n pl* **-S** a small, West American monkey, with a dark back and a white or yellow belly

MONE *n* [obs] the moon

MONK *n pl* **-S** a man living in a monastery or part of a religious order, devoted to contemplation and prayer, under vows of chastity, poverty and obedience

MONO *n* commonly used abbreviation for mononucleosis, an acute infectious disease

MONS *n pl of* **MON** people native to the Pegu region of Myanmar, east of Yangon

MONY *adj* SCOT., BRIT. many

MOOD *n pl* **-S** a state of mind or feeling, especially a temporary one

MOOL *n* SCOT., BRIT. soft, crumbly soil, rich in mold or humus

MOON *v* **-ED, -ING, -S** to be idle in a listless or dreamy way

MOOR *v* **-ED, -ING, -S** to fix or secure a boat, ship or aircraft in a particular place by casting cables, ropes, chains or anchor

MOOS *v pr t of* **MOO** makes a deep, moaning sound like a cow; lows

MOOT *v* **-ED, -ING, -S** to put forward for discussion; to bring up as subject for debate

MOPE *v* **-D, MOPING, -S** to be gloomy, dejected, listless, apathetic and sulky

MOPS *v pr t of* **MOP** cleans or clears away; washes or removes; rubs or wipes

MORA *n pl* **-S** or **-E** the minimal unit of metrical time in quantitative verse, equal to the short syllable

MORE *adj* greater in quantity, extent, or degree

MORN *n* commonly used abbreviation for morning; dawn; the first part of the day

MORO *n pl* **MORO** or **MORROS** a member of any of the various Muslim Malay tribes in the southern Philippines

MORT *n* a note sounded on a hunting horn, signifying the death of a hunted animal

MOSH *v* -ED, -ING, -ES to intentionally knock against others in a violent and frenzied way while dancing at a rock concert; to slam dance

MOSS *v* -ED, -ING, -ES to cover with a growth of tiny leafy-stemmed flowerless plants that grow in velvety clusters on rocks, trees and moist ground

MOST *adj* greatest in quantity, extent or degree

MOTE *n pl* -S a minute particle or tiny speck, especially of dust

MOTH *n pl* -S a nocturnal, winged insect, resembling the butterfly, but smaller, stouter, with duller coloring

MOTO *n pl* -S one of the heats in a motocross race

MOTS *n pl of* **MOT** incisive or witty remarks; pithy sayings

MOTT *n* a small grove of trees on a prairie; *also* **MOTTE**

MOUE *n pl* -S a disdainful or pouting grimace; a wry face

MOVE *v* -D, MOVING, -S to change place or position; to stir or shift; to go, in any manner

MOWN *v p part of* **MOW** to have cut grass, grain or plant growth with a device or machine

MOWS *v pr t of* **MOW** cuts grass, grain or plant growth with a device or machine

MOXA *n* a soft, downy substance, obtained from the dried leaves of an Asian plant, burnt on the skin as a counterirritant or cauterizing agent in Eastern medicine

MOYA *n* [obs] mud poured out from volcanoes during eruptions

MOZO *n pl* -S a man who helps with a pack train or serves as a porter; a waiter or male household servant

MUCH *adj* great in amount or degree

MUCK *v* -ED, -ING, -S to fertilize with manure or compost

MUDS *v pr t of* **MUD** covers, spatters or soils with wet, soft, sticky earth

MUFF *v* -ED, -ING, -S to perform or handle clumsily; to do something badly or awkwardly; to botch or bungle

MUGS *v pr t of* **MUG** attacks and robs a pedestrian in a public place

MULE *n* -S the sterile, hybrid offspring of a male donkey and a female horse

MULL *v* -ED, -ING, -S to ponder or consider at length

MUMM *v* -ED, -ING, -S to call for silence; to say "mum"; *also* **MUM**

MUMP *v* BRIT. to mumble or mutter

MUMS *v pr t of* **MUM** calls for silence; says "mum"; *also* **MUMMS**

MUMU *n pl* -S a long, loose, shapeless, Hawaiian dress made of brightly colored fabric; *also* **MUUMUU**

MUNG *n pl* -S a round green bean

MUNI *n pl* -S a municipal bond or security, issued by a state or local government

MUON *n pl* -S an elementary, subatomic particle, similar to the electron, but unstable

MURE *v* -D, MURING, -S to enclose within walls

MURK *n* partial or total darkness; gloomy darkness caused by fog, mist, clouds or smoke; *also* **MIRK**

MURR *n* [obs] a catarrh, an inflammation of mucous membranes

MUSE *v* -D, MUSING, -S to think deeply or consider at length; to meditate; to ponder

MUSH *v* -ED, -ING, -ES to mash or crush into a soft pulpy mass

MUSK *n* a substance with a strong, penetrating odor, used in perfumes

MUSS *v* **-ED, -ING, -ES** to make messy or untidy; to rumple

MUST *v* to be obliged, required, commanded or compelled by morality, law or custom

MUTE *v* **-D, MUTING, -S** to soften, muffle, or deaden the sound of something

MUTT *n pl* **-S** a mixed breed dog; a dog of unknown breed

MUXY *adj* [obs] soft, sticky and dirty

MYNA *n* an Asian starling; *also* **MYNAH**

MYTH *n pl* **-S** an ancient or traditional story concerning the early history of a people or explaining a natural or social phenomenon

MYXA *n* [obs] part of the jaw of a bird

FIVE LETTERS

MAARE *n pl* of **MAAR** flat-bottomed, volcanic craters, formed by explosions and often filled with water; *also* **MAARS**

MAARS *n pl* of **MAAR** flat-bottomed, volcanic craters, formed by explosions and often filled with water; *also* **MAARE**

MACAW *n pl* **-S** a large, bright-colored, long-tailed parrot, native to Central and South America

MACED *v p t* of **MACE** attacked with a chemical compound, typically sprayed from an aerosol container, that temporarily stuns its victims

MACER *n* SCOT. an official who carries a ceremonial staff and keeps order in the Scottish courts

MACES *v pr t* of **MACE** attacks with a chemical compound, typically sprayed from an aerosol container, that temporarily stuns its victims

MACHE *n* corn salad, a Eurasian herb with edible leaves

MACHO *n pl* **-S** an overly assertive, domineering man

MACKS *n pl* of **MACK** BRIT. mackintoshes, waterproof raincoats made of rubberized fabric; *also* **MACS**

MACLE *n pl* **-S** a twinned crystal, often of a diamond

MACON *n* a wine produced in the region near Macon, a city in east central France

MACRO *n pl* **-S** in computing, a single instruction that expands automatically into a set of instructions to perform a particular task

MADAM *n pl* **-S** a woman or lady; a polite form of address

MADLY *adv* insanely; wildly; frantically; intensely

MADRE *n pl* **-S** Spanish for mother, commonly used in the Southwestern United States

MAFIA *n* a tightly knit group of trusted associates, as of a political leader; *also* **MAFFIA**

MAFIC *adj* pertaining to minerals and igneous rocks rich in magnesium and iron

MAGES *n pl* of **MAGE** magicians, sorcerers or wizards

MAGIC *v* **-KED, -KING, -S** to cause, change, make or influence by spells, charms or supernatural forces

MAGMA *n pl* **-S, -TA** liquid or molten rock within the earth

MAGOT *n pl* **-S** a Barbary ape, a tailless monkey native to northwestern Africa

MAGUS *n pl* **MAGI** in ancient Media and Persia, a Zoroastrian priest from a hereditary caste

MAHOE *n* **-S** a tropical hibiscus tree that produces a wood used for cabinetry

MAIDS *n pl* of **MAID** female domestic servants

MAILE *n* a Pacific Island vine, traditionally used to make Hawaiian leis

MAILL *n* SCOT. a monetary payment, especially rent or tax

MAILS *v pr t of* **MAIL** sends a letter or package by post

MAIMS *v pr t of* **MAIM** mutilates; cripples; injures; disables

MAINS *n pl of* **MAIN** large, principle pipes, or cables that carry water, gas or electricity from one place to another

MAIST *adj* SCOT. most

MAIZE *n* BRIT. corn; also the yellow color of ripe corn

MAJOR *v* **-ED, -ING, -S** to pursue a specific course of study

MAKAR *n* SCOT. a writer, especially a poet

MAKER *n pl* **-S** a person who creates or produces

MAKES *v pr t of* **MAKE** causes to exist; brings into being; forms; produces

MAKOS *n pl of* **MAKO** large, powerful, mackerel sharks with deep blue backs and white underbellies

MALAR *n* the zygomatic bone, the cheekbone

MALAS *n pl of* **MALA** in South Asia, garlands of flowers given as signs of welcome

MALES *n pl of* **MALE** in humans, men or boys

MALIC *adj* pertaining to, or derived from apples

MALLS *n pl of* **MALL** large, enclosed shopping areas or retail complexes with a variety of stores and eateries

MALTS *v pr t of* **MALT** processes or converts cereal grains into malt by soaking in water, drying in a kiln, and forcing germination

MALTY *adj* **MALTIER, MALTIEST** of, like, or containing malt

MAMAS *n pl of* **MAMA** mothers, often used with tenderness and familiarity; *also* **MAMMAS, MOMMAS**

MAMBA *n pl* **-S** a long, agile, highly venomous, African tree snake

MAMBO *v* **-ED, -ING, -S** to perform a rhythmic, Caribbean ballroom dance, resembling the rumba

MAMEY *n pl* **-S, -ES** a tall, tropical, American tree, bearing large, edible fruit; *also* **MAMMEE**

MAMMA *n pl* **-S** mother, often used with tenderness and familiarity; *also* **MAMA, MOMMA**

MAMMY *n pl* **MAMMIES** a child's word for mother

MANAS *n* in Hinduism and Buddhism, the rational faculty of the mind

MANAT *n pl* **MANAT** or **-S** a basic form of currency in Azerbaijan and Turkmenistan

MANED *adj* having a mane, having long course hair growing from the head and neck

MANES *n pl of* **MANE** long coarse hair growing from the heads and necks of horses, lions and other mammals

MANGA *n pl* **MANGA** a Japanese style or genre of comic book, cartoon, graphic novel or animated film

MANGE *n* an infectious skin disease of domestic animals caused by parasitic mites, causing severe itching and hair loss

MANGO *n pl* **-S, -ES** an edible tropical fruit

MANGY *adj* **MANGIER, MANGIEST** affected with mange, an itchy skin disease; shabby and filthy; squalid

MANIA *n pl* **-S** a mental illness characterized by excessive intensity and periods of delusions, over activity, excitement and impulsive behavior

MANIC *n pl* **-S** one that is affected by mania and thinks or behaves with excessive intensity or frantic excitement

MANLY *adj* **MANLIER, MANLIEST** having conventionally idealized masculine attributes, especially in regards to courage and physical strength

MANNA *n* divinely supplied food

MANOR *n pl* **-S** a landed estate; the main house on an estate; a mansion

MANOS *n pl of* **MANO** hand-held stones or rollers for grinding corn and other grains, used on metates or stone blocks

MANSE *n* a clergyman's house; the residence provided to a minister by the church

MANTA *n pl* **-S** a coarse cotton cloth used for blankets, cloaks and shawls in Latin American and the southwestern United States

MANUS *n pl* **MANUS** the wrist and hand in humans and the corresponding part in vertebrates, such as the claw, forefoot or hoof

MAPLE *n pl* **-S** a hardwood tree with syrupy sap

MAQUI *n pl* **-S** a Chilean evergreen shrub and ornamental plant with edible purple berries

MARAS *n pl of* **MARA** long-eared, long-legged, hare-like rodents found in the scrub desert and grasslands of Argentina; Patagonian hares

MARCH *v* **-ED, -ING, -ES** to walk with steady pacing, in a formal military formation

MARES *n pl of* **MARE** large, dark, flat areas on the Moon, Mercury or Mars; *also* **MARIA**

MARGE *n* BRIT. commonly used abbreviation for margarine

MARIA *n pl of* **MARE** large, dark, flat areas on the Moon, Mercury or Mars; *also* **MARES**

MARKA *n pl* **MARKA** or **-S** a form of currency in Bosnia and Herzegovina

MARKS *v pr t of* **MARK** makes or leaves a visible sign, impression, scratch, dent or symbol

MARLS *v pr t of* **MARL** fertilizes or adds to the soil an earthy mixture of carbonate of lime, clay, sand and shells

MARLY *adj* earthy, limey, sandy

MARRY *v* **MARRIED, -ING, MARRIES** to enter the union of marriage, a committed, legal partnership between two people

MARSH *n pl* **-ES** a tract of low, wet, soft land, with aquatic, grassy vegetation, often a transition area between water and land

MARTS *n pl of* **MART** markets or trading centers

MARVY *adj* very good; fine; marvelous

MASAS *n pl of* **MASA** flour or dough made from dried corn, soaked in limewater, rinsed and ground, and used to make tortillas, tamales and other foods

MASHY *n pl* **MASHIES** a five iron club used in golf; *also* **MASHIE**

MASKS *v pr t of* **MASK** disguises; covers, conceals or hides

MASON *v* **-ED, -ING, -S** to build or strengthen with stone or brick

MASSE *n* a type of shot or stroke in billiards where the cue ball is hit to make it curve around one ball and hit another

MASSY *adj* **MASSIER, MASSIEST** weighty; bulky; massive

MASTS *v pr t of* **MAST** furnishes or assembles poles, or long, strong, round pieces of metal or timber, vertically from the deck of a vessel, to support sails, yards and other types of nautical equipment

MATCH *v* **-ED, -ING, -ES** to be exactly alike

MATED *v p t of* **MATE** joined as a pair, coupled

MATER *n pl* **-S** BRIT. mother

MATES *v pr t of* **MATE** joins as a pair, couples

MATEY *n* BRIT. friend; an informal form of address

MATHS *n* BRIT. mathematics; the study of relationships among numbers, shapes and quantities

MATIN *adj* related to the morning or to matins, the first of the seven canonical hours

MATTE *adj* lacking highlights or gloss; surface or color that is not shiny; flat and dull; also **MATT**

MATZO *n pl* **-S, -T, -TH** a flat, thin, crisp type of unleavened bread, traditionally eaten at Passover; also **MATZAH, MATZOH**

MAULS *v pr t of* **MAUL** treats savagely or roughly; injures by beating; batters, abuses or manhandles

MAUND *n pl* **-S** a unit of weight used in India and parts of Asia

MAUVE *n pl* **-S** a color that ranges in shade from grayish violet to a rosy, reddish purple

MAVEN *n pl* **-S** an expert or connoisseur; also **MAVIN**

MAVIN *n pl* **-S** an expert or connoisseur; also **MAVEN**

MAVIS *n* a song thrush, a small songbird

MAXED *v p t of* **MAX** reached the upper limit

MAXES *v pr t of* **MAX** reaches the upper limit

MAXIM *n pl* **-S** a brief statement of a general truth

MAXIS *n pl of* **MAXI** long skirts, coats or dresses, that extend to or just past the ankles

MAYAN *adj* in Hinduism, related to the ability to create illusion through supernatural, magical or sacred power

MAYBE *adv* perhaps; possibly

MAYOR *n pl* **-S** the chief executive official in a city, town or borough

MAZED *v p t of* **MAZE** dazed or stupefied; bewildered or astonished

MAZER *n pl* **-S** a large drinking bowl or goblet

MAZES *v pr t of* **MAZE** dazes or stupefies; bewilders or astonishes

MBIRA *n pl* **-S** an African musical instrument consisting of a hollow gourd or wooden resonator

MEALS *n pl of* **MEAL** food served or eaten regularly at certain times during the day, such as breakfast, lunch or dinner

MEALY *adj* **MEALIER, MEALIEST** powdery; dry; crumbly, coarse, or granular

MEANS *v pr t of* **MEAN** intends; indicates; signifies

MEANT *v p t of* **MEAN** intended; indicated; signified

MEANY *n pl* **MEANIES** a small-minded, bad-tempered, nasty person; also **MEANIE**

MEATY *adj* **MEATIER, MEATIEST** full of substance; fleshy or muscular; stout

MEAWS *v pr t of* **MEAW** cries with a soft, high-pitched sound, like a kitten or cat; also **MEOWS, MEWS, MIAOUS, MIAOWS**

MECCA *n pl* **-S** a place or attraction visited by many people; a place regarded as an important center for a specified group, activity or interest

MEDAL *v* **-ED** or **-LED**, **-ING** or **-LING**, **-S** to win a medal, a metal disc awarded for achievement

MEDIA *n pl of* **MEDIUM** the means of mass communication collectively

MEDIC *n pl* **-S** a medical practitioner or student; a member of the military medical corps

MEDII *n pl of* **MEDIUS** in anatomy, third or middle fingers

MEETS *v pr t of* **MEET** comes together or comes across someone at a specific place and time by arrangement or accident; encounters

MEINY *n pl* **MEINIES** SCOT. a crowd; a multitude; a group of people; *also* **MEINIE**

MELDS *v pr t of* **MELD** blends or combines; causes to merge

MELEE *n* confused, hand-to-hand fighting in a pitched battle

MELIC *adj* suitable for singing or meant to be sung; lyric

MELON *n pl* **-S** a large, juicy fruit, of the gourd family, with a sweet taste, a thick outer skin and many seeds

MELTS *v pr t of* **MELT** reduces from a solid to a liquid state, generally by heat; liquefies or dissolves

MEMOS *n pl of* **MEMO** commonly used abbreviation for memoranda, brief written notes, written as reminders

MENAD *n* a frenzied or raging woman, unnaturally excited or distraught; *also* **MAENAD**

MENDS *v pr t of* **MEND** repairs; restores; improves

MENSA *n pl* **-S** or **-E** the flat stone forming the top of an altar

MENSE *v* **-D, MENSING, -S** BRIT. to adorn; bring honor to; to grace

MENSH *n pl* **-ES** or **-EN** a good, decent, honorable person; an admirable person; *also* **MENSCH**

MENTA *n pl of* **MENTUM** part of an insect's lip or mouth

MENUS *n pl of* **MENU** lists of food or dishes available at a restaurant

MEOWS *v pr t of* **MEOW** cries with a soft, high-pitched sound, like a kitten or cat; *also* **MEAWS, MEWS, MIAOUS, MIAOWS**

MERCY *n pl* **MERCIES** compassion shown to an enemy or to those with less power; clemency

MERGE *v* **-ED, MERGING, -S** to combine or blend

MERIT *v* **-ED, -ING, -S** to earn; to deserve

MERLE *n* the European black thrush or blackbird; *also* **MERL**

MERRY *adj* **MERRIER, MERRIEST** full of fun and laughter; lively and high-spirited; jolly

MESAS *n pl of* **MESA** high, broad, flat tablelands with steep sides, more extensive than buttes but less than plateaus

MESHY *adj* **MESHIER, MESHIEST** netted or screen-like

MESIC *adj* requiring moderate amounts of moisture

MESNE *adj* legal term for middle, intermediate, or intervening, generally used with assignments of property

MESON *n pl* **-S** an unstable, subatomic particle composed of a quark and an antiquark

MESSY *adj* **MESSIER, MESSIEST** untidy; disordered, dirty

METAE *n pl of* **META** in ancient Rome, columns or posts placed at each end of racetracks to mark the turning places

METAL *v* **-ED** or **-LED**, **-ING** or **-LING**, **-S** to cover, fit, or supply with metal, a chemical element, that can be melted, fused and hammered into thin sheets

METED *v p t of* **METE** allotted, apportioned or distributed by measure

METER *v* **-ED**, **-ING**, **-S** to measure the quantity, variation or flow rate of something

METES *v pr t of* **METE** allots, apportions or distributes by measure

METHS *n* BRIT. methylated spirits, alcohol used as solvents or fuels

METIS *n pl* **METIS** a person whose parents are from different countries or of different races

METOL *n* a colorless, soluble powder, used as a photographic developer

METRE *n pl* **-S** BRIT. the basic unit of length in the metric system, equivalent to 100 centimeters and 39.37 inches

METRO *n pl* **-S** an underground railway system or subway

MEWED *v p t of* **MEW** cried with a soft, high-pitched sound, most often by a kitten or cat; *also* **MEOWED**

MEWLS *v pr t of* **MEWL** whimpers or cries weakly, as a baby or infant

MEZES *n pl of* **MEZE** appetizers, snacks, or light meals in Greek or Middle Eastern cuisine; *also* **MEZZES**

MEZZE *n pl* **MEZZE** or **-S** an appetizer, snack, or light meal in Greek or Middle Eastern cuisine; *also* **MEZE**

MEZZO *n* **-S** a mezzo soprano, a singer with a moderately high range, between a soprano and a contralto

MHORR *n pl* **-S** a West African gazelle, having horns with eleven or twelve very prominent rings; *also* **MOHR**

MIAOU *v* **-ED**, **-ING**, **-S** to cry with a soft, high-pitched sound of a kitten or cat; *also* **MEAW, MEOW, MEW, MIAOW, MIAUL**

MIAOW *v* **-ED**, **-ING**, **-S** to cry with a soft, high-pitched sound of a kitten or cat; *also* **MEAW, MEOW, MEW, MIAOU, MIAUL**

MIASM *n pl* **-S** a predisposition to a particular disease

MIAUL *v* **-ED**, **-ING**, **-S** to cry with a soft, high-pitched sound of a kitten or cat; *also* **MEAW, MEOW, MEW, MIAOU, MIAOW**

MICHE *v* **-D**, **MICHING**, **-S** BRIT. to skulk, to lurk out of sight

MICRA *n pl of* **MICRON** units of linear measure used in the metric system; units of one millionth of a meter; *also* **MIKRA**

MICRO *n pl* **-S** commonly used abbreviation for a microprocessor

MIDDY *n pl* **MIDDIES** a student in training at a naval academy

MIDGE *n pl* **-S** gnat-like flies that form swarms near water

MIDIS *n pl of* **MIDI** skirts, dresses or coats that extend to the middle of the calf

MIDST *n* the middle or central part of something

MIENS *n pl of* **MIEN** aspects; airs; manners; demeanors; carriages; bearings

MIFFS *v pr t of* **MIFF** offends slightly; annoys

MIFFY *adj* **MIFFIER, MIFFIEST** easily offended; touchy

MIGHT *v pr t of* **MAY** used to express possibility, probability, permission or liberty

MIKED *v p t of* **MIKE** amplified, recorded or transmitted by use of a microphone

MIKES *v pr t of* **MIKE** amplifies, records or transmits by use of a microphone

MIKRA *n pl of* **MICRON** units of linear measure used in the metric system; units of one millionth of a meter; *also* **MICRA**

MILCH *adj* giving or kept for milk, as a domestic animal

MILER *n pl* **-S** one who competes in a one-mile

MILES *n pl of* **MILE** more than one unit of distance equal to 5,280 feet

MILIA *n pl of* **MILIUM** whiteheads, small, secretion-filled, whitish bumps on the surface of the skin

MILKS *v pr t of* **MILK** draws or extracts a white, nutritious liquid from female mammals

MILKY *adj* **MILKIER, MILKIEST** resembling milk in color or consistency

MILLE *n pl* **-S** the Latin word for 1,000, sometimes used in English in very learned or literary contexts

MILLS *v pr t of* **MILL** grinds, pulverizes or processes grain with a machine or device

MILOS *n pl of* **MILO** early-growing, drought-resistant grain sorghums, resembling millet

MILPA *n pl* **-S** a small field or tract of land, cleared and cultivated, and then abandoned after a few seasons

MILTS *v pr t of* **MILT** fertilizes fish roe with the seminal fluid of male fishes

MIMED *v p t of* **MIME** mimicked or imitated; played a part with actions and gestures and not words

MIMEO *v* **-ED, -ING, -S** to make copies with a mimeograph, a duplicating device that reproduces by means of a stencil and an ink-filled rotary drum

MIMER *n pl* **-S** one who communicates entirely by gestures and facial expression

MIMES *v pr t of* **MIME** mimics or imitates; plays a part with actions and gestures and not words

MIMIC *v* **-KED, -KING, -S** to imitate in order to entertain or ridicule; to copy or imitate closely

MINAE *n pl of* **MINA** units of weight or currency used in ancient Greece and Asia Minor; *also* **MINAS**

MINAS *n pl of* **MINA** units of weight or currency used in ancient Greece and Asia Minor; *also* **MINAE**

MINCE *v* **-D, MINCING, -S** to cut up into very small pieces

MINDS *v pr t of* **MIND** heeds or obeys; pays attention to; remembers

MINED *v p t of* **MINE** dug, excavated or extracted valuable minerals from the earth

MINER *n pl* **-S** a person whose work is digging coal, ore or other minerals in a mine

MINES *v pr t of* **MINE** digs, excavates or extracts valuable minerals from the earth

MINGY *adj* **MINGIER, MINGIEST** small and meager; mean and stingy

MINIM *n* the smallest liquid measure; a tiny drop

MINIS *n pl of* **MINI** objects that are distinctively smaller than other members of its type or class

MINKE *n* a small whale that grows up to 33 feet in length

MINKS *n pl of* **MINK** slender-bodied, semi-aquatic, carnivorous mammals with highly valued, soft, thick, lustrous fur

MINNY *n pl* **MINNIES** a minnow, a small freshwater fish

MINOR *v* **-ED, -ING, -S** to pursue or study as a subsidiary subject or second specialization

MINTS *v pr t of* **MINT** produces or makes money; invents or fabricates

MINTY *adj* **MINTIER, MINTIEST** having the flavor of mint, an aromatic plant and culinary herb

MINUS *prep* reduced by the subtraction of; diminished by

MIRED *v p t of* **MIRE** soiled or splattered with mud or muck; sunk or stuck in deep, soggy earth

MIRES *v pr t of* **MIRE** soils or splatters with mud or muck; sinks or gets stuck in deep, soggy earth

MIREX *n* a banned insecticide, formerly used to kill fire ants

MIRIN *n* a sweet Japanese rice wine used especially in cooking

MIRKY *adj* **MIRKIER, MIRKIEST** dark and gloomy; *also* **MURKY**

MIRTH *n* joyfulness, gaiety or merriment, especially when expressed by laughter

MIRZA *n* a Persian title of honor

MISDO *v* **MISDID, MISDONE, MISDOING, -ES** to do wrongly or awkwardly; to botch

MISER *n pl* **-S** a greedy, stingy person, who hoards money, even at the expense of their own comfort

MISSY *n pl* **MISSIES** a familiar term used to address a young girl, both affectionately or as a reprimand

MISTS *v pr t of* **MIST** rains in a very fine shower; sprays obscures, or blurs with a visible, watery vapor

MISTY *adj* **MISTIER, MISTIEST** consisting, resembling or obscured by mist, a fine, visible, watery vapor

MITER *v* **-ED, -ING, -S** to join where two points of wood or other material meet at an angle of 90 degrees and the line of the joint bisects this angle; *also* **MITRE**

MITES *n pl of* **MITE** tiny, sometimes microscopic arachnids, often parasitic, and occasionally disease carrying

MITIS *n* a malleable form of iron, made by adding aluminum

MITRE *v* **-ED, -ING, -S** BRIT. to join where two points of wood or other material meet at an angle of 90 degrees and the line of the joint bisects this angle; *also* **MITER**

MITTS *n pl of* **MITT** mittens; large, padded protective leather gloves used in baseball by the catcher and first basemen

MIXED *v p t of* **MIX** combined or blended into a new substance; *also* **MIXT**

MIXER *n pl* **-S** an electronic appliance, machine or device for beating or blending substances

MIXES *v pr t of* **MIX** combines or blends into a new substance

MIZEN *n* a triangular, fore-and-aft sail set on the mizzenmast, the third mast from the bow; *also* **MIZZEN**

MOANS *v pr t of* **MOAN** makes a low, sustained, mournful cry of grief, pain, or misery; laments

MOATS *v pr t of* **MOAT** surrounds or fortifies with a deep, water-filled trench, either as protection from attack or a barrier to escape

MOCHA *n pl* **-S** a coffee drink flavored with milk, sugar, cocoa or chocolate

MOCKS *v pr t of* **MOCK** treats with scorn or contempt; derides; ridicules and imitates

MODAL *n pl* **-S** a kind of verb used with other verbs to express such ideas as permission, possibility and necessity

MODEL *v* **-ED** or **-LED**, **-ING** or **-LING**, **-S** to make, construct or fashion according to a preliminary work that serves as a plan

MODEM *n* **-S** a device that converts data to a form that can be transmitted; a device that allows a computer to receive data through a standard telephone line

MODES *n pl of* **MODE** methods, manners or ways of living or behaving; prevailing popular customs or fashions

MODUS *n pl* **MODI** mode; manner; way of living or behaving

MOGGY *n pl* **MOGGIES** a cat; *also* **MOGGIE**

MOGUL *n pl* **-S** an important, powerful or influential person; a magnate

MOHUR *n* a gold coin used in British India in the 19th and early 20th centuries

MOILS *v pr t of* **MOIL** toils; slaves; churns or swirls in continuous confusion or agitation

MOIRA *n pl* **-I** in ancient Greek mythology, fate, destiny or the personification of fate

MOIRÉ *n pl* **-S** a fabric, especially silk or rayon, treated to have an appearance like that of rippled water

MOIST *adj* **-ER, -EST** slightly wet or damp

MOJOS *n pl of* **MOJO** magical charms, amulets, or spells; supernatural powers; personal magnetism; *also* **MOJOES**

MOLAL *adj* a solution containing one mole of dissolved substance solute per 1,000 grams of solvent

MOLAR *n pl* **-S** a large tooth with a broad crown, used for grinding and chewing, located at the back of a mammal's mouth

MOLAS *n pl of* **MOLA** large, bony, silvery fishes found in tropical and temperate seas; ocean sunfishes

MOLDS *v pr t of* **MOLD** forms or casts an object out of a malleable substance; forms or gives shape; *also* **MOULDS**

MOLDY *adj* **MOLDIER, MOLDIEST** covered or overgrown with mold, a downy or furry growth caused by fungi, especially in warm, moist places; *also* **MOULDY**

MOLES *n pl of* **MOLE** small, permanent, slightly protruding dark spots on the human skin

MOLLY *n pl* **MOLLIES** any of several tropical, live-bearing fish, commonly kept in aquariums; *also* **MOLLIE**

MOLTO *adv* used for emphasis before or after a musical direction -- very; much

MOLTS *v pr t of* **MOLT** periodically or seasonally sheds an old coat of feathers, hair or skin to make way for new growth; *also* **MOULTS**

MOMMA *n pl* **-S** mother, often used with tenderness and familiarity; *also* **MAMA, MAMMA**

MOMMY *n pl* **MOMMIES** a child's word for mother, often used with tenderness or familiarity

MOMUS *n pl* **-ES** or **MOMI** a fault finder or carping critic

MONAD *n pl* **-S** a microorganism consisting of just one cell, especially a flagellate protozoan

MONAS *n pl of* **MONA** small, West American monkeys, with dark backs and white or yellow bellies

MONDE *n* the world; society

MONDO *adj* enormous; huge

MONEY *n pl* **-S** or **MONIES** the official currency, coins and negotiable paper notes issued by a government

MONGO *n pl* **MONGO** or **-S** a unit of currency in Mongolia

MONKS *n pl of* **MONK** men living in a monastery or part of a religious order, devoted to contemplation and prayer, under vows of chastity, poverty and obedience

MONTE *n* a gambling game of Spanish origin, played with a special deck of forty cards

MONTH *n pl* **-S** one of the twelve, named divisions in a calendar year; a period of time lasting approximately 30 days or one cycle of the moon's phases

MOOCH *v* **-ED**, **-ING**, **-ES** to obtain something without paying or working for it; to sponge off others; *also* **MOUCH**

MOODS *n pl of* **MOOD** states of mind or feelings, especially temporary ones

MOODY *adj* **MOODIER**, **MOODIEST** given to changing moods, particularly gloomy, sullen or morose ones

MOOED *v p t of* **MOO** made a deep, moaning sound like a cow; lowed

MOOLA *n* money; *also* **MOOLAH**

MOONS *v pr t of* **MOON** idles in a listless or dreamy way

MOONY *adj* **MOONIER**, **MOONIEST** in a distracted, listless, dreamy state

MOORS *v pr t of* **MOOR** fixes or secures a boat, ship or aircraft in a particular place by casting cables, ropes, chains or anchors

MOORY *n* [obs] resembling the moors, a marshy, boggy landscape of rolling, peat covered hills

MOOSE *n pl* **MOOSE** a large, heavily built mammal of the deer family whose males have large antlers

MOOTS *v pr t of* **MOOT** puts forward for discussion; brings up as subject for debate

MOPED *v p t of* **MOPE** behaved in a gloomy, dejected, listless, apathetic or sulky manner

MOPER *n pl* **-S** one who mopes, sulks or broods

MOPES *v pr t of* **MOPE** behaves in a gloomy, dejected, listless, apathetic or sulky manner

MOPEY *adj* **MOPIER**, **MOPIEST** sulky and gloomy; brooding; languishing

MORAE *n pl of* **MORA** minimal units of metrical time in quantitative verse, equal to short syllables; *also* **MORAS**

MORAL *adj* relating to issues of right and wrong and how individuals should behave

MORAS *n pl of* **MORA** minimal units of metrical time in quantitative verse, equal to short syllables; *also* **MORAE**

MORAY *n pl* **-S** a brightly colored, voracious eel, found in warm seas and frequently coral reefs

MOREL *n pl* **-S** an edible mushroom with a sponge like cap

MORES *n/pl* the established, traditional customs or conventions of a social group or community

MORON *n pl* **-S** a very foolish or stupid person; a dolt

MORPH *v* **-ED, -ING, -S** to change smoothly and gradually from one image to another

MORRO *n pl* **-S** a rounded hill, headland or promontory point

MORSE *n pl* **-S** a clasp or brooch for fastening garments in front

MOSEY *v* **-ED, -ING, -S** to saunter, stroll or shuffle along; to move in a leisurely way

MOSSO *adv* a musical direction meaning with motion or animation

MOSSY *adj* covered or resembling moss, tiny, leafy-stemmed, flowerless plants that grow in velvety clusters

MOTEL *n pl* **-S** a hotel, usually close to the highway, typically for traveling motorists, where the rooms have direct access to an open parking area

MOTES *n pl of* **MOTE** minute particles or tiny specks, especially of dust

MOTET *n pl* **-S** a vocal composition with parts for different voices, usually based on a sacred text

MOTHS *n pl of* **MOTH** nocturnal, winged insects, resembling butterflies but smaller, stouter, with duller coloring

MOTHY *adj* **MOTHIER, MOTHIEST** damaged, moth-eaten or infested by moths, small winged insects

MOTIF *n pl* **-S** an underlying, recurrent theme in a literary, musical or artistic work

MOTOR *v* **-ED, -ING, -S** to travel by automobile

MOTOS *n pl of* **MOTO** heats in a motocross race

MOTTE *n pl* **-S** a small grove of trees on a prairie; *also* **MOTT**

MOTTO *n pl* **-ES, -S** a word or phrase capturing a belief or ideal, or chosen as a principle of behavior; a maxim

MOUCH *v* **-ED, -ING, -ES** to obtain something without paying or working for it; to sponge off others; *also* **MOOCH**

MOUES *n pl of* **MOUE** disdainful or pouting grimaces; wry faces

MOULD *v* **-ED, -ING, -S** BRIT. to form or cast an object out of a malleable substance; to form or give shape; *also* **MOLD**

MOULT *v* **-ED, -ING, -S** BRIT. to periodically or seasonally shed an old coat of feathers, hair or skin to make way for new growth; *also* **MOLT**

MOUND *v* **-ED, -ING, -S** to heap or pile; to fortify

MOUNT *v* **-ED, -ING, -S** to climb or ascend; to get up on

MOURN *v* **-ED, -ING, -S** to feel or express grief or sorrow following the death or loss of something

MOUSE *n pl* **MICE** a small rodent having a pointed snout and a long, thin, almost hairless tail

MOUSY *adj* **MOUSIER, MOUSIEST** quiet, timid, shy or drab; *also* **MOUSEY**

MOUTH *v* **-ED, -ING, -S** to speak in a forceful, affected or oratorical manner

MOVED *v p t of* **MOVE** changed place or position; stirred or shifted; left or went, in any manner

MOVER *n pl* **-S** someone whose work or business involves moving furniture, etc. for those changing residences

MOVES *v pr t of* **MOVE** changes place or position; stirs or shifts; goes, in any manner

MOVIE *n pl* **-S** a motion picture

MOWED *v p t of* **MOW** cut down grass, grain, or plant growth with a device or machine

MOWER *n pl* **-S** a machine for cutting, especially grass

MOXIE *n* courage, pep, perseverance and inventiveness

MOZOS *n pl of* **MOZO** men who help with pack trains or serve as porters; waiters or male household servants

MUCHO *adj* a lot of; much or many

MUCID *adj* [obs] moldy; musty; slimy

MUCIN *n pl* **-S** a complex protein present in mucus

MUCKS *v pr t of* **MUCK** fertilizes with manure or compost

MUCKY *adj* **MUCKIER, MUCKIEST** foul; nasty; filthy

MUCRO *n pl* **-NES** an abrupt, sharp, terminal point, projecting from an organ or the tip of a plant

MUCUS *n pl* **-ES** the thick, slimy secretion of the mucous membranes

MUDDY *v* **MUDDIED, -ING, MUDDIES** to splatter, soil or stain with wet, sticky dirt

MUDRA *n* a series of symbolic body postures and hand movements used in East Indian classical dancing, Hindu rituals and yoga

MUFFS *v pr t of* **MUFF** performs or handles clumsily; does something badly or awkwardly; botches or bungles

MUFTI *n pl* **-S** ordinary clothes worn by someone who usually wears a uniform

MUGGY *adj* **MUGGIER, MUGGIEST** hot and damp with little or no stirring of air; unpleasantly warm and humid

MUJIK *n* a Russian peasant, especially during the tsarist era; *also* **MOUJIK, MUZHIK, MUZJIK**

MULCH *v* **-ED, -ING, -ES** to cover plants with leaves, compost, peat moss, etc., to help them retain moisture and protect them from frost and erosion

MULCT *v* **-ED, -ING, -S** to penalize by fining

MULES *n pl of* **MULE** sterile, hybrid offspring of a male donkey and a female horse

MULEY *n pl* **-S** a hornless animal, especially a cow

MULLA *n* a Muslim scholar or teacher, trained in Islamic theology and sacred law; *also* **MULLAH**

MULLS *v pr t of* **MULL** ponders or considers at length

MUMMS *v pr t of* **MUM** calls for silence; says "mum"; *also* **MUMS**

MUMMY *n pl* **MUMMIES** a body embalmed, preserved for burial and wrapped in cloth, especially as was the custom of the ancient Egyptians

MUMPS *n/pl* an acute, inflammatory, contagious disease, mainly affecting children, prevented by vaccination

MUMUS *n pl of* **MUMU** long, loose, shapeless, Hawaiian dresses, made of brightly colored fabric; *also* **MUUMUUS**

MUNCH *v* **-ED, -ING, -ES** to chew steadily with a crunching noise

MUNGO *n pl* **-S** the waste of milled wool, used to make cheap cloth of the same name

MUNGS *n pl of* **MUNG** round green beans

MUNIS *n pl of* **MUNI** municipal bonds or securities issued by a state or local government

MUONS *n pl of* **MUON** elementary, subatomic particles, similar to electrons, but unstable

MURAL *n pl* **-S** a large picture painted on a wall or ceiling

MURED *v p t of* **MURE** enclosed within walls

MURES *v pr t of* **MURE** encloses within walls

MUREX *n pl* **-ES** *or* **MURICES** flesh-eating snails found in tropical waters

MURKY *adj* **MURKIER, MURKIEST** dark and gloomy; *also* **MIRKY**

MURRA *n* a mineral or stone used in ancient Rome for making fine vases; *also* **MURRHA**

MURRE *n pl* **MURRE** *or* **-S** a North American diving shorebird

MUSED *v p t of* **MUSE** thought deeply or considered at length; meditated; pondered

MUSER *n* a reflective thinker who ponders at length

MUSES *v pr t of* **MUSE** thinks deeply or considers at length; meditates; ponders

MUSHY *adj* **MUSHIER, MUSHIEST** thick, soft, and yielding

MUSIC *n* the art of arranging sounds to form a composition

MUSKY *adj* **MUSKIER, MUSKIEST** having a sweet, pungent smell

MUSSY *adj* **MUSSIER, MUSSIEST** disordered, untidy, rumpled

MUSTH *n* a frenzied state of aggressiveness occurring periodically in male elephants and camels

MUSTY *adj* **MUSTIER, MUSTIEST** stale, damp or moldy

MUTCH *n* BRIT., SCOT. a close-fitting linen cap worn by infants and elderly women

MUTED *v p t of* **MUTE** softened, muffled or deadened the sound of something

MUTER *adj* more silent, comparatively

MUTES *v pr t of* **MUTE** softens, muffles or deadens the sound of something

MUTON *n pl* **-S** the smallest unit of DNA that can produce a mutation

MUTTS *n pl of* **MUTT** mixed breed dogs; dogs of unknown breed

MUZZY *adj* **MUZZIER, MUZZIEST** confused; muddled; befuddled

MYNAH *n* an Asian starling; *also* **MYNA**

MYOID *adj* resembling muscle

MYOMA *n pl* **-S** *or* **-TA** a tumor composed of muscle tissue

MYOPE *n pl* **-S** a nearsighted person

MYOPY *n* a visual defect of the eyes, resulting in nearsightedness; *also* **MYOPIA**

MYRRH *n* a fragrant gum resin, found in certain shrubs and trees, used in incense, perfume and medicinally

MYSID *n* small, shrimp-like crustaceans

MYTHS *n pl of* **MYTH** ancient or traditional stories, concerning the early history of a people or explaining a natural or social phenomenon, typically involving the supernatural

NA *adv* SCOT., BRIT. no; not; *also* **NAE**

NE *adj* born as, used to introduce a man's former or original name

NO *n pl* **-S, -ES** a negative reply; a refusal or denial

NU *n pl* **-S** the thirteenth letter of the Greek alphabet

THREE LETTERS

NAB *v* **-BED, -BING, -S** to seize or snatch suddenly; to capture or arrest

NAD *v* [obs] had not; *also* **NADDE**

NAE *adv* SCOT., BRIT. no; not; *also* **NA**

NAG v **-GED, -GING, -S** to remind or urge constantly; to continually find fault; to harass

NAH interj same as no, a negative reply

NAN n pl **-S** a flat, leavened bread of India made of white flour and traditionally baked in a clay oven; also **NAAN**

NAP v **-PED, -PING, -S** to sleep for a short while, often during the day

NAS v [obs] was not, has not

NAT v [obs] not at; nor at

NAW interj no, a negative reply

NAY n pl **-S** a negative vote or voter; a denial or refusal

NEB n pl **-S** BRIT. the beak or bill of a bird; the snout or nose of an animal

NEE adj born as, used to introduce a woman's former or maiden name

NEF n pl **-S** a silver or gold table furnishing, in the form of a ship

NEG n pl **-S** informal for a photographic negative

NEK n pl **-S** a low point in a ridge of mountains, between two peaks, often the site of a pass in South Africa

NEP n pl **-S** [obs] catnip, an aromatic herb attractive to cats

NER adv [obs] nearer

NET v **-TED, -TING, -S** to catch or cover with a net; to capture or ensnare

NEW adj **-ER, -EST** existing only a short time; recent

NIB n pl **-S** the writing point of a pen; the projecting, pointed part of something; the tip

NIL n pl **-S** a quantity of no value; nothing; zero; also **NIHIL**

NIM v **-MED, -MING, -S** to steal, pilfer or filch

NIN adj [obs] not in

NIP v **-PED, -PING, -S** to bite, pinch or clip sharply

NIS v [obs] is not

NIT n pl **-S** the egg or young form of a parasitic insect, especially a louse

NIX v **-ED, -ING, -ES** to forbid, refuse, prevent or veto something

NOB n pl **-S** BRIT. somebody rich or socially powerful

NOD v **-DED, -DING, -S** to lower and raise the head briefly as a sign of acknowledgement, agreement or assent

NOF adv [obs] not of; nor of

NOG v **-GED, -GING, -S** to fill a wall or partition with small stones or bricks

NOH n a type of traditional Japanese theatre or classical drama, with music, dance, and a heroic theme, performed in a highly stylized manner with elaborate costumes; also **NOGAKU**

NOM n pl **-S** names

NOO adv SCOT. now

NOR conj and not; or not; not either

NOS n pl of **NO** negative replies; refusals or denials; also **NOES**

NOT adv in no way or no manner; expresses negation, prohibition, denial, or refusal

NOW adv at once; at the present time; at this moment

NOY v [obs] to annoy; to vex

NTH adj relating to an unspecified ordinal number; relating to something as the last in a series

NUB n pl **-S** a knob or protuberance; a small lump or chunk

NUN n pl **-S** a woman devoted to a religious life, often in a convent, living under vows of poverty, chastity and obedience

NUR n [obs] a hard knot in wood

NUS n pl of **NU** the thirteenth letter of the Greek alphabet

NUT n pl **-S** a hard-shelled dry fruit or seed with a separable rind or shell and interior kernel

NYE n/pl [obs] a brood or flock of pheasants

FOUR LETTERS

NAAN *n pl* **-S** a flat, leavened bread of India made of white flour and traditionally baked in a clay oven; *also* **NAN**

NABE *n pl* **-S** a neighborhood movie theater

NABK *n/pl* the edible berries of the Zizyphys Lotus, a tree found in North Africa, and southwestern Europe; *also* **NUBK, NEBAK**

NABS *v pr t of* **NAB** seizes or snatches suddenly; captures or arrests

NADA *n* nothing; none

NAFF *v* **-ED, -ING, -S** BRIT. to fool around

NAGA *n pl* **-S** in Indian mythology, a semi-divine serpent associated with water and fertility; *also* **NAGI**

NAGI *n pl* **-S** in Indian mythology, a semi-divine serpent associated with water and fertility; *also* **NAGA**

NAGS *v pr t of* **NAG** reminds or urges constantly; continually finds fault; harasses

NAIF *n pl* **-S** a naïve or inexperienced person

NAIK *n pl* **-S** a chief; a leader; a rank in the Indian army equal to a corporal

NAIL *v* **-ED, -ING, -S** to fasten or fix in place with a thin, tapered piece of metal, pointed at one end and broadened at the other for driving into wood, etc.

NAKE *v* [obs] to make naked; unveil; expose

NALE *n* [obs] ale; an alehouse

NALL *n* [obs] an awl, a small, pointed tool for making holes in leather or wood for shoe and collar makers

NAME *v* **-D, NAMING, -S** to give someone or something a word, phrase, or title by which they are referred to and known

NANA *n pl* **-S** a grandmother, used familiarly, chiefly by children; *also* **NANNA**

NANS *n pl of* **NAN** flat, leavened breads of India, made of white flour and traditionally baked in a clay oven; *also* **NAANS**

NAOI *n pl of* **NAOS** the inner rooms or sanctuaries in ancient temples containing a shrine or statue of a god; *also* **CELLAE**

NAOS *n pl* **NAOI** the inner room or sanctuary in an ancient temple, containing a shrine or statue of a god; *also* **CELLA**

NAPA *n* a soft leather made from sheep or kid's skin; *also* **NAPPA**

NAPE *n pl* **-S** the back of the neck; *also* **NUCHA**

NAPS *v pr t of* **NAP** sleeps for a short while, often during the day

NAPU *n* a very small, hornless deer native to south Asia

NARC *n pl* **-S** a narcotics officer, especially an undercover drug agent

NARD *n pl* **-S** an aromatic ointment used in ancient times

NARK *v* **-ED, -ING, -S** to act as an informer, especially to the police

NARY *adj* not one; not any

NASH *adj* [obs] firm; stiff; hard

NAVE *n pl* **-S** the central area of a church

NAVY *n pl* **NAVIES** a nation's entire military organization for sea warfare and defense

NAYS *n pl of* **NAY** negative votes or voters; denials or refusals

NAYT *v* [obs] to refuse; to deny

NAZE *n pl* **-S** [obs] a promontory or headland

NAZI *n pl* **-S** an advocate or supporter of the policies of the German fascist political party, led by Adolf Hitler during World War II

NEAL *v* **-ED, -ING, -S** [obs] to be tempered by heat

214

NEAP *n pl* **-S** a less than average tide occurring at the first and third quarters of the moon

NEAR *v* **-ED, -ING, -S** to approach; to come close or closer to

NEAT *adj* **-ER, -EST** orderly, trim, tidy, clean

NEBS *n pl of* **NEB** BRIT. the beaks or bills of birds; the snouts or noses of animals

NECK *n pl* **-S** the part of an organism that connects the head to the rest of the body

NEED *v* **-ED, -ING, -S** to want and lack; to require urgently

NEEM *n pl* **-S** a large, tropical, semi-evergreen tree of south Asia, widely cultivated for its timber, resin, bitter bark and aromatic seed oil, used medicinally and as an insecticide

NEEP *n pl* **-S** SCOT., BRIT. a turnip, a round root with white or cream flesh, eaten as a vegetable

NEFS *n pl of* **NEF** silver or gold table furnishings, in the form of ships

NEGS *n pl of* **NEG** photographic negatives

NEIF *n pl* **-S** [obs] the fist or hand; *also* **NIEVE**

NEKS *n pl of* **NEK** a low point in a ridge of mountains, between two peaks, often the site of a pass in South Africa

NENE *n pl* **NENE** or **NENES** a rare, wild goose native to the Hawaiian Islands

NEON *n pl* **-S** a small iridescent blue and red fish, often kept in aquariums

NEPS *n pl of* **NEP** [obs] catnips, aromatic herbs attractive to cats

NERD *n pl* **-S** a person enthusiastically or obsessively single-minded, often accomplished in scientific and technical subjects, but felt to be socially inept; *also* **NURD**

NESH *adj* BRIT. sensitive to cold temperatures

NESS *n pl* **-ES** a promontory, cape or headland; a section of coastline that projects into the sea

NEST *n pl* **-S** the structure made or place chosen by a bird for laying her eggs and for sheltering and rearing her young

NETS *v pr t of* **NET** catches or covers with a net; captures or ensnares

NETT *v* **-ED, -ING, -S** BRIT. to acquire or clear as a profit

NEUK *n pl* **-S** SCOT. a nook; a corner

NEUM *n pl* **-S** a notational sign used in medieval church music and Gregorian chants; *also* **NEUME**

NEVE *n pl* **-S** granular snow, found at the top of a glacier or high mountain, that has not yet become ice

NEVI *n pl of* **NEVUS** or **NAEVUS** congenital growths on the skin, such as moles or birthmarks; *also* **NAEVI**

NEWS *n/pl* newly received or noteworthy information about recent events; previously unknown information

NEWT *n pl* **-S** a small, slender, semi-aquatic salamander, often brightly colored with a long tail

NEXT *adj* immediately following or succeeding in time, order or sequence

NIAS *n* [obs] a young fledgling; untrained hawk; eyas

NIBS *n pl of* **NIB** the writing points of pens; the projecting, pointed parts of something; the tips

NICE *adj* **-R, -ST** pleasing and agreeable; kind and courteous

NICK *v* **-ED, -ING, -S** to make a slight cut, chip or notch into something

NIDE *n pl* **-S** a nest or brood, especially of pheasants

NIDI *n pl of* **NIDUS** nests in which spiders, insects or small animals deposit their eggs also **NIDUSES**

NIFF *n pl* **-S** BRIT. an unpleasant smell or odor

215

NIGH v -ED, -ING, -S to approach or draw near

NILL v -ED, -ING, -S [obs] to be unwilling; to refuse to act

NILS n pl of **NIL** quantities of no value; zeroes

NIMS v pr t of **NIM** steals, pilfers or filches

NINE n pl -S a number, the sum of eight and one; the cardinal number between eight and ten

NIPS v pr t of **NIP** bites, pinches or clips sharply

NISI adj taking effect at a specified date unless cause is shown for modification or nullification

NITE n pl -S an informal, simplified spelling of night, the period from sunset to sunrise; also **NIGHT**

NITS n pl of **NIT** eggs or young forms of parasitic insects, especially lice

NIXY n pl **NIXIES** a misaddressed or illegibly addressed piece of mail, therefore undeliverable; also **NIXIE**

NOBS n pl of **NOB** BRIT. people who are rich or socially powerful

NOCK v -ED, -ING, -S to make a groove in a bow, or a notch in an arrow: to fit an arrow to a bowstring

NODE n pl -S a knob, knot or swelling; a protuberance

NODI n pl of **NODUS** difficult situations or problems; complications

NODS v pr t of **NOD** lowers and raises the head briefly as a sign of acknowledgement, agreement or assent

NOËL n pl -S a Christmas carol; also **NOWEL**

NOES n pl of **NO** negative replies; refusals or denials; also **NOS**

NOGG n BRIT. a strong ale

NOGS v pr t of **NOG** fills a wall or partition with small stones or bricks

NOIL n pl -S a short fiber combed from long fibers during the preparation of textile yarns

NOIR adj relating to a genre of film and crime literature featuring tough, cynical characters and bleak settings

NOLE n [obs] the head; also **NOLL**

NOLL n [obs] the head; also **NOLE**

NOMA n pl -S a severe gangrenous inflammation of the mouth or genitals, usually occurring in children who are malnourished or otherwise debilitated

NOME n pl -S any of the provinces of Ancient Egypt

NOMS n pl of **NOM** names

NONE pron not one; no one

NOOK n pl -S an alcove or narrow place, especially in a large room; a corner; a small recess or secluded spot

NOON n pl -S the middle of the day, 12 p.m.

NOPE adv no, a negative reply

NORI n pl -S an edible preparation of dried pressed seaweed, often used to wrap sushi or as a seasoning

NORM n pl -S a rule, model or standard regarded as typical or usual in society

NOSE v -D, NOSING, -S to sniff, touch or rub with the nose

NOSH v -ED, -ING, -ES to eat a snack or light meal

NOSY adj NOSIER, NOSIEST given to prying into the affairs of others; intrusively inquisitive; curious; also **NOSEY**

NOTA n pl of **NOTUM** hard protective coverings found on the back of the thorax in insects, the segment between the head and the abdomen to which the legs are attached

NOTE v -D, NOTING, -S to notice or observe; to write down

NOTT v [obs] to shear

NOUN *n pl* **-S** the part of speech that is used to name a person, place, thing, quality or action, and can function as the subject or object of a verb, or the object of a preposition

NOUS *n pl* **-ES** mind; intellect; rational thought and reason

NOVA *n pl* **-E, -S** a variable star that suddenly becomes much brighter and then gradually fades to its original luminosity

NOWD *n pl* **-S** [obs] a European gray gurnard, a marine fish

NOWT *pron* BRIT. nothing

NUBK *n/pl* the edible berries of the Zizyphus Lotus, a tree found in Northern Africa, and Southwestern Europe; *also* **NABK, NEBAK**

NUBS *n pl of* **NUB** knobs or protuberances; small lumps or chunks

NUDE *n pl* **-S** a figure drawn, sculpted or painted without clothing or covering; a naked person

NUKE *v* **-D, NUKING, -S** to attack or destroy with nuclear weapons

NULL *v* **-ED, -ING, -S** to reduce to nothing; to make void or invalid

NUMB *v* **-ED, -ING, -S** to eliminate sensation; to deaden feeling

NUNS *n pl of* **NUN** women devoted to a religious life, often in a convent, living under vows of poverty, chastity and obedience

NURD *n pl* **-S** a person enthusiastically or obsessively single-minded, often accomplished in scientific and technical subjects, but felt to be socially inept; *also* **NERD**

NURL *v* **-ED, -ING, -S** [obs] to cut with reeding or fluting on the edge of, as coins, screws, etc.; *also* **KNURL**

NUTS *n pl of* **NUT** a hard-shelled dry fruit or seed with a separable rind or shell and interior kernel

FIVE LETTERS

NAANS *n pl of* **NAAN** flat, leavened breads of India, made of white flour and traditionally baked in a clay oven; *also* **NANS**

NABES *n pl of* **NABE** neighborhood movie theaters

NABOB *n pl* **-S** a person of great wealth, prominence and influence

NACHO *n pl* **-S** a tortilla chip covered with melted cheese, chilis and other savory toppings

NACRE *n pl* **-S** the iridescent internal layer of a mollusk shell

NADDE *v* [obs] had not; *also* **NAD**

NADIR *n pl* **-S** the lowest possible point

NAEVI *n pl of* **NAEVUS** or **NEVUS** BRIT. congenital growths on the skin, such as moles or birthmarks; *also* **NEVI**

NAFFS *v pr t of* **NAFF** BRIT. fools around

NAGAS *n pl of* **NAGA** in Indian mythology, semi-divine serpents associated with water and fertility; *also* **NAGIS**

NAGGY *adj* tending to nag, scold, find fault

NAGIS *n pl of* **NAGI** in Indian mythology, semi-divine serpents associated with water and fertility; *also* **NAGAS**

NAIAD *n pl* **-S, -ES** a water nymph in Greek mythology

NAIFS *n pl of* **NAIF** naïve or inexperienced persons

NAIKS *n pl of* **NAIK** chiefs; leaders; officers in the Indian army of the rank equal to a corporal

NAILS *v pr t of* **NAIL** fastens or fixes in place with thin, tapered pieces of metal, pointed at one end and broadened at the other for driving into wood, etc.

NAIRA *n pl* **NAIRA** a basic unit of currency in Nigeria

NAÏVE *adj* lacking worldly experience, simple, guileless and extremely trusting

NAKED *adj* completely unclothed; nude; bare

NAKFA *n pl* **NAKFA** or **-S** the main unit of currency in Eritrea, a region or territory north of Ethiopia

NALED *n* a non-persistent insecticide used to control crop pests and mosquitoes

NAMED *v p t of* **NAME** gave someone or something a word, phrase or title by which they are referred to and known

NAMER *n pl* **-S** one that names, gives a person or object an identifying label or moniker

NAMES *v pr t of* **NAME** gives someone or something a word, phrase or title by which they are referred to and known

NANAS *n pl of* **NANA** grandmothers, used familiarly, chiefly by children; *also* **NANNAS**

NANNA *n pl* **-S** a grandmother, used familiarly, chiefly by children; *also* **NANA**

NANNY *n pl* **NANNIES** a person employed to care for a family's children, often in their home

NAPES *n pl of* **NAPE** the back part of the neck; *also* **NUCHAS**

NAPPA *n* a soft leather made from sheep or kid's skin; *also* **NAPA**

NAPPE *n pl* **-S** a sheet of water flowing over a dam, spillway or similar structure

NAPPY *n pl* **NAPPIES** BRIT. a diaper

NARCO *n pl* **-S** drug trafficker

NARCS *n pl of* **NARC** narcotics officers, especially undercover drug agents

NARDS *n pl of* **NARD** aromatic ointments used in ancient times

NARES *n pl of* **NARIS** openings into the nasal cavities, especially the nostrils

NARIS *n pl* **NARES** an opening into the nasal cavities, especially a nostril

NARKS *v pr t of* **NARK** informers, especially to the police

NARKY *adj* **NARKIER, NARKIEST** BRIT. irritable, easily annoyed

NASAL *adj* forming part or relating to the nose

NASTY *adj* **NASTIER, NASTIEST** disgusting, offensive, repellent

NATAL *adj* relating to or accompanying birth

NATCH *adv* naturally, of course

NATES *n/pl* the buttocks

NATTY *adj* **NATTIER, NATTIEST** neat, trim and smart in appearance; smartly or fashionably dressed; dapper

NAVAL *adj* part of or characteristic of the navy, including its ships, personnel, procedures, etc.

NAVEL *n pl* **-S** the small scar, usually a small hollow, in the middle of the abdomen caused by the detachment of the umbilical cord

NAVES *n pl of* **NAVE** the central areas of churches

NAVVY *n pl* **NAVVIES** BRIT. a laborer, especially one who constructs railways, roads or canals

NAWAB *n pl* **-S** a governor in India during the Mogul Empire

NAZES *n pl of* **NAZE** [obs] promontories or headlands

NAZIS *n pl of* **NAZI** advocates or supporters of the German fascist political party, led by Adolf Hitler during World War II

NEALS *v pr t of* **NEAL** [obs] tempers by heat

NEAPS *n pl of* **NEAP** less than average tides occurring at the first and third quarters of the moon

NEARS *v pr t of* **NEAR** approaches; comes close or closer to

NEATH *prep* poetic variation of beneath

NEBAK *n/pl* [obs] the edible berries of the Zizyphys Lotus, a tree found in northern Africa, and southwestern Europe also **NUBK, NABK**

NECKS *n pl of* **NECK** the part of organisms that connects the head to the rest of the body

NEDDY *n pl* **NEDDIES** BRIT. a donkey

NEEDS *v pr t of* **NEED** wants and lacks; requires urgently

NEEDY *adj* **NEEDIER, NEEDIEST** not having enough to live on; very poor

NEEMS *n pl of* **NEEM** large, tropical, semi-evergreen trees of south Asia, widely cultivated for their timber, resin, bitter bark, and aromatic seed oil, used medicinally and as an insecticide

NEEPS *n pl of* **NEEP** SCOT., BRIT. turnips, round roots with white or cream flesh, eaten as vegetables

NEGUS *n pl* **-ES** a hot beverage made from wine, water and lemon juice, sweetened and flavored with spices

NEIFS *n pl of* **NEIF** [obs] fists or hands; also **NIEVES**

NEIGH *v* **-ED, -ING, -S** to utter the long, high-pitched cry of a horse; to whinny

NENES *n pl of* **NENE** a rare, wild geese native to the Hawaiian Islands

NEONS *n pl of* **NEON** small iridescent blue and red fish, often kept in aquariums

NERDS *n pl of* **NERD** persons who are enthusiastically or obsessively single-minded, often accomplished in scientific and technical subjects, but felt to be socially inept; also **NURDS**

NERDY *adj* **NERDIER, NERDIEST** obsessively single-minded and socially awkward

NEROL *n pl* **-S** a colorless, liquid alcohol used in perfumes

NERTS *interj* dated informal term used to express disgust, contempt, or refusal

NERVE *v* **-D, NERVING, -S** to muster courage; to brace one's self for a demanding situation

NERVY *adj* **NERVIER, NERVIEST** bold and fearless; brazen and brash

NESTS *n pl of* **NEST** the structures made or places chosen by birds for laying their eggs and for sheltering and rearing their young

NETTS *v pr t of* **NETT** BRIT. acquires or clears as a profit

NETTY *adj* resembling a net, resembling an open-meshed fabric twisted, knotted or woven together at regular intervals

NEUKS *n pl of* **NEUK** SCOT. nooks; corners

NEUME *n pl* **-S** notational signs used in medieval church music and Gregorian chants; also **NEUM**

NEUMS *n pl of* **NEUM** a notational sign used in medieval church music and Gregorian chants; also **NEUMES**

NEVER *adv* not ever; not at any time

NEVES *n pl of* **NEVE** granular snows, found at the tops of a glaciers or high mountains, that have not yet become ice

NEVUS *n pl* **NEVI** or **NAEVI** congenital growth on the skin, such as a mole or birthmark; also **NAEVUS**

NEWEL *n pl* **-S** the vertical support at the center of a circular or spiral staircase

NEWER *adj* existing only a very short time; very recent

NEWLY *adv* recently; lately; not long ago

NEWSY *adj* **NEWSIER, NEWSIEST** full of news; informative

NEWTS *n pl of* **NEWT** small, slender, semi-aquatic salamanders, often brightly colored with a long tail

NEXUS *n pl* **NEXUS** or **-ES** a connection, tie or link between people or things

NGWEE *n pl* **NGWEE** a form of currency in Zambia

NICER *adj* pleasing and agreeable; kind and courteous

NICHE *v* **-D, NICHING, -S** to place something in a hollow or recess; to fill a specified need or function in a specialized area

NICKS *v pr t of* **NICK** makes a slight cut, chip or notch into something

NICOL *n pl* **-S** a pair of prisms used to produce and analyze plane-polarized light in a polarizing microscope

NIDES *n pl of* **NIDE** nests or broods, especially of pheasants

NIDUS *n pl* **NIDI** or **-ES** a nest, especially one in which spiders, insects or small animals deposit their eggs

NIECE *n pl* **-S** the daughter of one's brother or sister, or the daughter of one's brother-in-law or sister-in-law

NIEVE *n pl* **-S** SCOT., BRIT. the fist or hand; *also* **NEIF**

NIFFS *n pl of* **NIFF** BRIT. unpleasant smells or odors

NIFTY *adj* **NIFTIER NIFTIEST** very good; pleasing; smart

NIGHS *v pr t of* **NIGH** approaches or draws near

NIGHT *n pl* **-S** the period from sunset to sunrise; *also* **NITE**

NIHIL *n* nothing; nil; *also* **NIL**

NILLS *v pr t of* **NILL** [obs] is unwilling; refuses to act

NIMBI *n pl of* **NIMBUS** according to mythology, luminous clouds said to surround gods and goddesses appearing on earth

NINES *n pl of* **NINE** numbers, several of the cardinal number between eight and ten

NINJA *n pl* **NINJA** or **-S** a feudal Japanese warrior, highly skilled in ancient martial arts and employed as a spy, saboteur or assassin

NINNY *n pl* **NINNIES** a fool; a simpleton; a silly person

NINON *n pl* **-S** a sturdy, sheer fabric, sometimes synthetic, used chiefly for curtains

NINTH *n pl* **-S** one of nine equal parts; the one following the eighth

NIPPY *adj* **NIPPIER, NIPPIEST** sharp or biting, as cold weather

NISEI *n pl* **NISEI** or **-S** a person born and raised in the United States or Canada whose parents emigrated from Japan

NISUS *n pl* **NISUS** an effort or endeavor to realize a goal

NITER *n pl* **-S** BRIT. potassium or sodium nitrate, a chemical salt; saltpeter; *also* **NITRE**

NITES *n pl of* **NITE** an informal, simplified spelling of nights, the periods from sunset to sunrise; *also* **NIGHTS**

NITID *adj* bright with a steady but subdued shining

NITON *n pl* **-S** an old term for radon; symbol Nt

NITRE *n pl* **-S** BRIT. potassium or sodium nitrate, a chemical salt; saltpeter; *also* **NITER**

NITRO *adj* designating certain compounds containing nitrogen and produced by the action of nitric or nitrous acid

NITTY *adj* **NITTIER, NITTIEST** full of lice or lice eggs

NIVAL *adj* growing in or under the snow

NIXED *v p t of* **NIX** forbade, refused, prevented or vetoed something

NIXES *v pr t of* **NIX** forbids, refuses, prevents or vetoes something

NIXIE *n pl* **-S** a misaddressed or illegibly addressed piece of mail, therefore undeliverable; *also* **NIXY**

NIZAM *n pl* **NIZAM** or **-S** a soldier in the Turkish army

NOBBY *adj* **NOBBIER, NOBBIEST** BRIT. elegant or stylish; chic and smart

NOBLE *adj* **-R, -ST** possessing high ideals or excellent moral character

NOBLY *adv* with courage and spirit; gallantly

NOCKS *v pr t of* **NOCK** makes a groove in a bow, or a notch in an arrow; fits an arrow to a bowstring

NODAL *adj* of, relating to, resembling, being, or situated near or at a node

NODDY *n pl* **NODDIES** a silly or foolish person; a simpleton

NODES *n pl of* **NODE** knobs, knots or swellings; protuberances

NODUS *n pl* **NODI** a difficult situation or problem; a complication

NOËLS *n pl of* **NOEL** Christmas carols; *also* **NOWELS**

NOHOW *adv* in no manner; not by any means

NOILS *n pl of* **NOIL** short fibers combed from long fibers during the preparation of textile yarns

NOISE *n pl* **-S** any sound or combination of sounds

NOISY *adj* **NOISIER, NOISIEST** loud; clamorous

NOMAD *n pl* **-S** a member of a tribe having no permanent home who moves from place to place in search of food, water, and shelter

NOMAS *n pl of* **NOMA** severe gangrenous inflammations of the mouth or genitals, usually occurring in children who are malnourished or otherwise debilitated

NOMEN *n pl* **NOMINA** in ancient Rome, a citizen's second name, which indicated to which clan he or she belonged

NOMES *n pl of* **NOME** several provinces of Ancient Egypt

NONCE *n pl* **-S** the present time or particular occasion; the time being

NONES *n/pl* the ninth day before the ides, according to the ancient Roman calendar, the seventh day of March, May, July, and October, and the fifth day of any other month

NONET *n pl* **-S** a combination of nine instruments or voices, also a music composition for such a combination

NONYL *n pl* **-S** a monovalent alkyl radical; symbol C_9H_{19}

NOOKS *n pl of* **NOOK** alcoves or narrow places, especially in large rooms; corners; small recesses or secluded spots

NOONS *n pl of* **NOON** many middles of the day

NOOSE *v* **-D, NOOSING, -S** to capture or secure with a rope or cord, tied into a loop with a running knot which tightens as the rope is pulled

NOPAL *n pl* **-S, -ES** a cactus of Mexico and Central America

NORIA *n pl* **-S** a series of buckets on a water wheel, used for raising water from a stream

NORIS *n pl of* **NORI** edible preparations of dried pressed seaweed, often used to wrap sushi or as a seasoning

NORMS *n pl of* **NORM** rules, models or standards, regarded as typical or usual in society

NORTH *n* the cardinal point on the mariner's compass, located at 0°; the direction which goes towards the part of the Earth above the equator, opposite to the south

NOSED *v p t of* **NOSE** sniffed, touched or rubbed with the nose

NOSES *v pr t of* **NOSE** sniffs, touches or rubs with the nose

NOSEY *adj* **NOSIER, NOSIEST** given to prying into the affairs of others; intrusively inquisitive; curious; *also* **NOSY**

NOTAL *adj* of or pertaining to the back; dorsal

NOTCH *v* **-ED, -ING, -ES** to make an angular or v-shaped cut into a surface

NOTED *v p t of* **NOTE** noticed or observed; wrote down

NOTER *n pl* **-S** one who takes notice

NOTES *v pr t of* **NOTE** notices or observes; writes down

NOTUM *n pl* **NOTA** the back portion and hard protective covering of an insect's thorax, the segment between the head and abdomen to which its legs are attached

NOUNS *n pl of* **NOUN** parts of speech that are used to name a person, place, thing, quality or action, and can function as the subject or object of a verb, or the object of a preposition

NOVAE *n pl of* **NOVA** variable stars that suddenly become much brighter and then gradually fade to their original luminosity; *also* **NOVAS**

NOVAS *n pl of* **NOVA** variable stars that suddenly become much brighter and then gradually fade to their original luminosity; *also* **NOVAE**

NOVEL *n pl* **-S** a fictional prose narrative of book length

NOWAY *adv* in no manner; by no means; not at all

NOWDS *n pl of* **NOWD** [obs] European gray gurnards, marine fish

NOWEL *n pl* **-S** [obs] an archaic spelling of Noel, a Christmas carol; *also* **NOËL**

NUBBY *adj* **NUBBIER, NUBBIEST** knobby or lumpy; having a rough, knotted surface

NUBIA *n pl* **-S** a light, knitted, woolen head scarf for women

NUCHA *n pl* **-E** the nape of the neck; *also* **NAPE**

NUDER *adj* more naked or unclothed, as a person or body

NUDES *n pl of* **NUDE** figures drawn, sculpted, or painted without clothing or covering; naked people

NUDGE *v* **-D, NUDGING, -S** to touch or push gently; to prod with one's elbow to attract attention

NUDZH *n pl* **-ES** a persistent complainer, a nag, a whiner

NUKED *v p t of* **NUKE** attacked or destroyed with nuclear weapons

NUKES *v pr t of* **NUKE** attacks or destroys with nuclear weapons

NULLS *v pr t of* **NULL** reduces to nothing; makes void or invalid

NUMBS *v pr t of* **NUMB** eliminates sensation; deadens feeling

NUMEN *n pl* **NUMINA** a local divinity or presiding spirit, in ancient Roman religion, often identified with a natural object or place

NURDS *n pl of* **NURD** persons who are enthusiastically or obsessively single-minded, often accomplished in scientific and technical subjects, but felt to be socially inept; *also* **NERDS**

NURLS *v pr t of* **NURL** [obs] cuts with reeding or fluting on the edges of, as coins, screws, etc.; *also* **KNURLS**

NURSE *v* **-D, NURSING, -S** to care for the sick, injured or infirm

NUTSY *adj* **NUTSIER, NUTSIEST** silly or ridiculous; eccentric; insane

NUTTY *adj* **NUTTIER, NUTTIEST** containing or tasting like nuts, a dry, one-seeded fruit consisting of a kernel in a hard shell

NYALA *n pl* **NYALA** or **-S** a African antelope with vertical white stripes on the sides of the body and large spiral horns on the males

NYLON *n pl* **-S** a tough, lightweight, elastic, synthetic material, used especially in textiles and plastics

NYLONS *n/pl* stockings or hosiery made from nylon

NYMPH *n pl* **-S** according to Greek and Roman mythology, a female spirit dwelling in scenes of natural beauty, such as groves, forests, rivers, fountains, etc.

OD *n* [obs] an alleged force or natural power, formerly thought to pervade all nature and to manifest itself in magnetism, hypnotism, light, etc.; *also* **ODYL, ODYLE**

OF *prep* expressing the relationship between a part and a whole; derived or coming from; belonging to

OH *interj* used to express a strong, emotional reaction such as surprise, joy, disappointment, shock or pain

OI *interj* used to express dismay, pain, annoyance, grief or worry; *also* **OY**

OK *interj* commonly used abbreviation to express approval or agreement

OM *n* a mystic syllable used in meditation, affirmations or blessings; *also* **AUM**

ON *prep* used as a function word to indicate position above, in contact with, or supported by; upon

OO *n* a beautiful bird of the Hawaiian Islands with two tufts of brilliant yellow feathers, also called the yellow-tufted honey sucker

OP *n* a commonly used abbreviation for a surgical operation

OR *conj* used to indicate and link alternatives; used to connect different possibilities; used to express approximation or uncertainty

OS *n pl* **ORA** a mouth or similar opening in an organism

OU *n* informal term for a man, bloke or chap, used in South Africa

OW *interj* used to express sudden pain, often an automatic or involuntary expression

OX *n pl* **-EN** a domesticated, bovine mammal, usually an adult bull, a male cow, often used on farms in the past as a draft animal for pulling plows and heavy loads; *also* **OWSE**

OY *interj* used to express dismay, pain, annoyance, grief or worry; *also* **OI**

THREE LETTERS

OAF *n pl* **-S** a clumsy, awkward or uncultured person

OAK *n pl* **OAK** or **-S** a shrub, bush or large hardwood tree of rich color bearing acorns as fruit, whose wood is often used in flooring and furniture

OAR *v* **-ED, -ING, -S** to row, propel or steer a boat, raft, watercraft, etc. with an oar, a pole with a flat blade, often used in pairs

OAT *n pl* **-S** a hardy cereal grass widely cultivated for its edible grain

OBA *n pl* **-S** a hereditary chief or tribal ruler among various peoples in the Benin region of western Africa

OBE *n* [obs] a magical charm, object or fetish used in obeah, a form of religious belief involving sorcery, practiced especially in the Caribbean; *also* **OBI, OBY, OBEAH**

OBI *n pl* **-S** a magical charm, object or fetish used in obeah, a form of religious belief involving sorcery, practiced especially in the Caribbean; *also* **OBE, OBY, OBEAH**

OBY *n* [obs] a magical charm, object or fetish used in obeah, a form of religious belief involving sorcery, practiced especially in the Caribbean; *also* **OBE, OBI, OBEAH**

OCA *n* a South American wood sorrel, grown in the high Andes, cultivated for its edible tubers; *also* **OKA**

OCH *interj* SCOT. exclamation to express surprise, regret, exasperation, disapproval or disbelief

ODD *adj* **-ER, -EST** strange, peculiar or unusual; deviating from what is ordinary or expected

ODE *n pl* **-S** a lyric poem of serious nature and elevated style, expressing noble feelings in a complex scheme of rhyme and meter, often addressed to a person or celebrating an event

ODS *interj* [obs] corruption of God's, formerly used in oaths and exclamatory phrases

OFF *v* **-ED, -ING, -S** to go away; to leave or depart

OFO *n* a Siouan language spoken by the Ofo people, living in the Yazoo river valley of Mississippi

OFT *adv* poetic or literary spelling of often, now chiefly used in compound words; frequently; many times

OHM *n pl* **-S** a unit of electrical resistance

OHO *interj* used to express surprise, triumph, astonishment

OIK *n pl* **-S** BRIT. a person regarded as ill-mannered and socially inferior

OIL *v* **-ED, -ING, -S** to grease, to lubricate

OJO *n* [obs] a spring, surrounded by rushes or rank grass; an oasis

OKA *n* a South American wood sorrel, grown in the high Andes, cultivated for its edible tubers; *also* **OCA**

OKE *n* a unit of weight used in Turkey, Egypt and other countries in the Near East

OLA *n* a leaf or strip from the Talipot palm used in India for writing paper

OLD *adj* **-ER** or **ELDER, -EST** or **ELDEST** living or existing for many years; aged; from an earlier time

OLE *interj* a shout of approval, triumph, joy, etc.; bravo

OLM *n pl* **-S** a blind, cave-dwelling, aquatic salamander with permanent external gills, found in southeastern Europe

OMY *adj* mellow, soft, easily crumbled or pulverized

ONE *n pl* **-S** informal term for a one-dollar bill

OOH *v* **-ED, -ING, -S** to exclaim in surprise, pleasure, satisfaction, or amazement

OOM *n pl* **-S** a title of respect used to address an elderly man in South Africa, literally, uncle

OON *adj* [obs] one

OOP *v* [obs] SCOT. to bind with a thread or cord; to join; to unite

OPE *v* **-D, OPING, -S** to open, unclose, unfasten, or remove obstructions from

OPT *v* **-ED, -ING, -S** to make a choice or decision; to choose or select in preference to other alternatives

ORA *pl of* **OS** mouths or similar openings in an organism

ORB *v* **-ED, -ING, -S** to form into a circle or sphere

ORC *n* a killer whale or other aquatic mammal, such as the grampus, a playful black and white dolphin, identified by early writers as sea monsters; *also* **ORK**

ORD *n* [obs] an edge or point; also a beginning

ORE *n pl* **-S** a solid, naturally occurring mineral from which metal can be profitably mined or extracted

ORF *n* an infectious, viral disease affecting sheep, sometimes goats and cattle, and transmittable to humans

ORK *n* [obs] a killer whale or other aquatic mammal, such as the grampus, a playful black and white dolphin, identified by early writers as sea monsters; *also* **ORC**

ORN *v* [obs] to ornament; to adorn

ORT *n pl* **-S** a small scrap of food left after a meal

OSS *v* [obs] to prophesy; to presage

OST *n* [obs] a kiln for drying hops, malt, and tobacco; *also* **OAST**

OUD *n pl* **-S** a stringed musical instrument of North Africa and the Middle East, resembling a lute or mandolin

OUL *n* [obs] an awl, a small pointed tool for making holes

OUR *adj* belonging to or associated with the speaker or writer and one or more others; belonging to us; the possessive form of we

OUT *v* **-ED, -ING, -S** to cause to be out, to eject, expel, or oust

OVA *n pl of* **OVUM** eggs, female reproductive cells; female gametes

OWE *v* **-D, OWING, -S** to be indebted, to be obligated to pay or repay in return for something received

OWL *n pl* **-S** a nocturnal bird of prey with hawk-like beak and claws, a large head with front-facing eyes, and a loud hooting call

OWN *v* **-ED, -ING, -S** to hold as property; to have a legal or rightful title to; to possess

OWT *pron* BRIT. anything

OXO *adj* containing oxygen

FOUR LETTERS

OAFS *n pl of* **OAF** clumsy, awkward or uncultured people

OAKS *n pl of* **OAK** shrubs, bushes or large hardwood trees of rich color, bearing acorns as fruit, whose wood is often used in flooring and furniture

OAKY *adj* used to describe wine which has a slightly woody flavor from the barrel in which it was aged

OARS *v pr t of* **OAR** rows, propels or steers a boat, raft, watercraft, etc. with an oar, a pole with a flat blade, often used in pairs

OAST *n pl* **-S** a kiln for drying hops, malt and tobacco; *also* **OST**

OATH *n pl* **-S** a solemn promise, formal declaration or legally binding pledge, often made by naming God or a loved one as witness

OATS *n pl of* **OAT** hardy cereal grasses widely cultivated for their edible grain

OBAS *n pl of* **OBA** hereditary chiefs or tribal rulers among various peoples in the Benin region of western Africa

OBEY *v* **-ED, -ING, -S** to carry out or follow a command or order; to comply; to be obedient; to submit to authority

OBIS *n pl of* **OBI** magical charms, objects or fetishes used in obeah, a form of religious belief involving sorcery, practiced especially in the Caribbean; *also* **OBEAHS**

OBIT *n pl* **-S** commonly used abbreviation for an obituary, a notice of a person's death, usually with a short, biographical account

OBOE *n pl* **-S** a slender, woodwind instrument with a double-reed mouthpiece, a range of nearly three octaves, and a high, penetrating, melancholy tone

OBOL *n pl* **-S** or **-I** a silver alloy coin issued during the Middle Ages; *also* **OBOLE, OBOLUS**

ODDS *n/pl* the chance or probability that something will or will not occur, sometimes expressed as a ratio; the difference in favor of one side over the other

ODEA *n pl of* **ODEON** or **ODEUM** small buildings used for public performances of music and poetry in ancient Greece and Rome

ODES *n pl of* **ODE** lyric poems of serious nature and elevated style, expressing noble feelings in a complex scheme of rhyme and meter, often addressed to a person or celebrating an event

ODIC *adj* relating or similar to a lyric poem of some length

ODOR *n pl* **-S** any scent or smell, whether fragrant or offensive; *also* **ODOUR**

ODYL *n* an alleged force or natural power, formerly thought to pervade all nature and to manifest itself in magnetism, hypnotism, light, etc.; *also* **OD, ODYLE**

OFFS *v pr t of* **OFF** goes away; leaves or departs

OGAM *n* an ancient British and Irish alphabet, consisting of 20 characters, using notches for vowels and lines for consonants, found inscribed on memorial stones; *also* **OGHAM**

OGEE *n* a decorative molding, having a S-curve in profile

OGLE *v* **-D, OGLING, -S** to stare at, with obvious interest

OGRE *n pl* **-S** a hideous creature or giant of fairy tales and folklore

OHIA *n* a red flowering hardwood tree that grows in Hawaii and other Pacific Islands; *also* **LEHUA**

OHMS *n pl of* **OHM** units of electrical resistance

OIKS *n pl of* **OIK** BRIT. people regarded as ill-mannered and socially inferior

OILS *v pr t of* **OIL** greases, lubricates

OILY *adj* **OILIER, OILIEST** relating to, consisting of, or covered with oil, a greasy substance soluble in alcohol or ether, but not in water

OINK *v* **-ED, -ING, -S** to utter the characteristic nasal grunt of a hog

OINT *v* [obs] to anoint

OKAY *v* **-ED, -ING, -S** to approve; to agree to

OKEH *n* approval or endorsement

OKRA *n* an annual tropical plant whose long, ridged, seed pods are eaten as a vegetable and often used in soups and stews

OLAY *n/pl* [obs] palm leaves, prepared for being written upon with a style pointed with steel

OLDY *n pl* **OLDIES** an old joke, saying, song, film that was popular in the past; *also* **OLDIE**

OLEA *n pl of* **OLEUM** heavy, oily, strongly oxidizing solutions of sulfur trioxide in sulfuric acid

OLEO *n* a spread made chiefly from vegetable oils and used as a substitute for butter; margarine

OLIO *n pl* **-S** a highly spiced stew consisting of various kinds of meat, vegetables and chickpeas

OLLA *n pl* **-S** a round, large-mouthed, earthenware pot or jar used for food storage, cooking or containing water

OLMS *n pl of* **OLM** blind, cave-dwelling, aquatic salamanders with permanent external gills, found in southeastern Europe

OLPE *n* [obs] an earthenware vase or pitcher without a spout

OMEN *n pl* **-S** a phenomenon, event or incident regarded as a prophetic sign of future good or evil; an augury

OMER *n* an ancient Hebrew unit of dry measure

OMIT *v* **-TED, -TING, -S** to leave out; to fail to include

ONCE *adv* one time, without repetition; one time only

ONDE *n* [obs] hatred; fury; envy

ONES *n pl of* **ONE** informal term for one dollar bills

ONLY *adj* alone in a class or category; by itself; sole

ONTO *prep* on the top of; to a position on; to and upon

ONUS *n* a burden or responsibility; an obligation; a difficult or unpleasant task

ONYX *n* a kind of quartz with alternating colored layers, used as a semiprecious gemstone, especially in cameos

OOHS *v pr t of* **OOH** exclaims in surprise, pleasure, satisfaction or amazement

OOMS *n pl of* **OOM** title of respect used to address elderly men in South Africa, literally, uncles

OOPS *interj* a natural exclamation used in recognition of a blunder, mistake or minor accident; used to express mild apology, surprise or dismay; whoops

OOZE *v* **-D, OOZING, -S** to flow or leak out slowly, through small holes or openings; to seep

OOZY *adj* **OOZIER, OOZIEST** exuding moisture or leaking fluid; gently dripping; slimy

OPAH *n* a large, elliptical, brightly colored, deep-sea fish of the Atlantic, Pacific and Mediterranean

OPAL *n pl* **-S** a translucent mineral of hydrated silica, softer and less dense than quartz, with shifting color, including some iridescent varieties valued as semiprecious gemstones

OPED *v p t of* **OPE** opened, unclosed, unfastened or removed obstructions from

OPEN *v* **-ED, -ING, -S** to release from a closed or fastened position; to allow access; to make available for entry or passage

OPES *v pr t of* **OPE** opens, uncloses, unfastens or removes obstructions from

OPTS *v pr t of* **OPT** makes a choice or decision; chooses or selects in preference to other alternatives

OPUS *n pl* **OPERA** or **OPUSES** a creative work, especially a musical composition, numbered in order of composition or publication

ORAD *adv* toward the mouth or oral region

ORAL *n pl* **-S** an academic examination in which the questions and answers are spoken rather than written

ORBS *v pr t of* **ORB** forms into a circle or sphere

ORBY *adj* [obs] having the circular or spherical course of an orb; revolving

ORCA *n pl* **-S** a large, black and white, predatory whale that feeds on large fish, squid, seals, etc.; a killer whale

ORDO *n pl* **-S** or **ORDINES** an annual calendar in the Catholic Church containing instructions for the Mass and office to be celebrated on each day of the year

ORES *n pl of* **ORE** solid, naturally occurring minerals from which metal can be profitably mined or extracted

ORFE *n* a small, brightly colored and silvery, fresh water fish of the carp family

ORLE *n* a border that follows the inside and parallel edge of the shield in a coat of arms

ORLO *n* [obs] a wind instrument used in Spain

ORRA *adj* SCOT. extra, occasional, odd, or miscellaneous

ORTS *n pl of* **ORT** small scraps of food left after a meal

ORZO *n* a small type of pasta shaped like grains of rice

OSAR *n pl of* **OS** long, narrow ridges of coarse gravel either in or under decaying glacial ice sheets, deposited by sub-glacial streams of melting water

OSSA *n pl of* **OS** bones

OSSE *n* [obs] a prophetic or ominous utterance

OTIC *adj* pertaining to or in the region of the ear; auricular

OTTO *n* a fragrant essential oil or perfume obtained from flowers, especially rose petals; *also* **ATAR, ATHAR, ATTAR, OTTAR**

OUCH *interj* a natural exclamation used to express sudden physical pain

OUDS *n pl of* **OUD** stringed musical instruments of North Africa and the Middle East, resembling a lute or mandolin

OURS *pron* belonging to or associated with the speaker or writer and one or more others; belonging to us; the possessive form of we

OUST *v* **-ED, -ING, -S** to force or drive out; to remove from a position or office; to eject or expel

OUTS *v pr t of* **OUT** causes to be out, ejects, expels or ousts

OUZO *n pl* **-S** a colorless Greek liqueur, flavored with anise

OVAL *n pl* **-S** an elliptical or egg-shaped figure or object

OVEN *n pl* **-S** an enclosed chamber or compartment, typically a kitchen appliance, in which food is heated, cooked, baked or roasted

OVER *v* **-ED, -ING, -S** to pass, leap or jump above and across

OVUM *n pl* **OVA** an egg, the female reproductive cell; a female gamete

OWED *v p t of* **OWE** was indebted, was obligated to pay or repay in return for something received

OWES *v pr t of* **OWE** is indebted, is obligated to pay or repay in return for something received

OWLS *n pl of* **OWL** nocturnal birds of prey with hawk-like beaks and claws, large heads with front-facing eyes and loud hooting calls

OWNS *v pr t of* **OWN** holds as property; has a legal or rightful title to; possesses

OWRE *n* [obs] the aurochs, an extinct European ox

OWSE *n pl* **-N** SCOT., BRIT. a domesticated, bovine mammal, usually an adult bull, a male cow, often used on farms in the past as a draft animal for pulling plows and heavy loads; *also* **OX**

OXEN *n pl of* **OX** domesticated, bovine mammals, usually adult bulls, male cows, often used on farms in the past as draft animals for pulling plows and heavy loads; *also* **OWSEN**

OXER *n pl* **-S** a type of horse jump with two or more rails

OYER *n* a hearing in open court involving the production of some document pleaded by one party and demanded by the other

OYES *interj* a cry issued from a court officer, usually three times, to command silence and attention before a court begins session; *also* **OYEZ**

OYEZ *interj* a cry issued from a court officer, usually three times, to command silence and attention before a court begins session; *also* **OYES**

FIVE LETTERS

OAKEN *adj* consisting of or made from wood of the oak tree

OAKUM *n* loose, stringy hemp fiber obtained by untwisting old rope, treated with tar and used as a caulking material

OARED *v p t of* **OAR** rowed, propelled or steered a boat, raft, watercraft, etc. with an oar, a pole with a flat blade, often used in pairs

OASES *n pl of* **OASIS** areas in the desert made green or fertile by groundwater or irrigation

OASIS *n pl* **OASES** an area in the desert made green or fertile by groundwater or irrigation

OASTS *n pl of* **OAST** kilns for drying hops, malt, and tobacco

OATEN *adj* containing or made of oats, oatmeal, or oat straw

OATER *n* informal term for a movie about frontier or cowboy life; a western

OATHS *n pl of* **OATH** solemn promises, formal declarations, or legally binding pledges, often made by naming God or a loved one as witness

OBEAH *n pl* **-S** a magical charm, object or fetish used in obeah, a form of religious belief involving sorcery, practiced especially in the Caribbean; also **OBE, OBI, OBY**

OBELI *n pl of* **OBELUS** critical marks used in ancient manuscripts to indicate words or passages of spurious or doubtful nature

OBESE *adj* very fat; extremely overweight; corpulent

OBEYS *v pr t of* **OBEY** carries out or follows a command or order; complies; is obedient; submits to authority

OBITS *n pl of* **OBIT** commonly used abbreviation for obituaries, reports of a person's death, usually with short, biographical accounts

OBOES *n pl of* **OBOE** slender, woodwind instruments with double-reed mouthpieces, a range of nearly three octaves, and a high, penetrating, melancholy tone

OBOLE *n pl* **OBOLS** or **OBOLI** a silver alloy coin issued during the Middle Ages; also **OBOL, OBOLUS**

OBOLI *n pl of* **OBOL** or **OBOLUS** silver alloy coins issued during the Middle Ages; also **OBOLS**

OBOLS *n pl of* **OBOL** or **OBOLE** silver alloy coins issued during the Middle Ages; also **OBOLI**

OCCUR *v* **-RED, -RING, -S** to take place; to happen; to come about

OCEAN *n pl* **-S** a great body of salt water that covers more than 70% of the earth's surface

OCHER *n* an earthy mineral clay, colored yellow or reddish brown by iron oxides, and used as a pigment in paint; also **OCHRE**

OCHRE *n* BRIT. an earthy mineral clay, colored yellow or reddish brown by iron oxides and used as a pigment in paint; also **OCHER**

OCKER *n* AUS. informal term for a rough, boorish or uncultivated person

OCREA *n pl* **-E** a tube-like covering around some plant stems

OCTAD *n* a group or series of eight

OCTAL *adj* using or having a number system based on eight

OCTAN *adj* occurring every eighth day

OCTET *n* a group of eight musicians performing together; a composition for eight musical performers

OCTYL *n* a univalent hydrocarbon radical

OCULI *n pl of* **OCULUS** round or circular windows

ODDER *adj* stranger, very peculiar, or highly unusual; deviating from what is ordinary or expected

ODDLY *adv* in a strange, peculiar or surprising way

ODEON *n pl* **ODEA** a small building used for public performances of music and poetry in ancient Greece and Rome; *also* **ODEUM**

ODEUM *n pl* **ODEA** a small building used for public performances of music and poetry in ancient Greece and Rome; *also* **ODEON**

ODIST *n* a poet who writes odes, long, complex, lyric poems

ODIUM *n* hatred, condemnation, repugnance or contempt towards a person or thing regarded as loathsome

ODORS *n pl of* **ODOR** scents or smells, whether fragrant or offensive; *also* **ODOURS**

ODOUR *n pl* **-S** BRIT. any scent or smell, whether fragrant or offensive; *also* **ODOR**

ODYLE *n* an alleged force or natural power, formerly thought to pervade all nature and to manifest itself in magnetism, hypnotism, light, etc.; *also* **OD, ODYL**

OFFAL *n* something thrown away

OFFED *v p t of* **OFF** went away; left or departed

OFFER *v* **-ED, -ING, -S** to present for acceptance or rejection

OFTEN *adv* frequently or repeatedly; many times

OFTER *adv* [obs] often, frequently or repeatedly; many times

OGHAM *n* an ancient British and Irish alphabet, consisting of 20 characters, using notches for vowels and lines for consonants, found inscribed or memorial stones; *also* **OGAM**

OGIVE *n pl* **-S** a pointed arch

OGLED *v p t of* **OGLE** stared at, with obvious interest

OGLER *n pl* **-S** one who stares with obvious interest

OGLES *v pr t of* **OGLE** stares at, with obvious interest

OGRES *n pl of* **OGRE** hideous creatures or giants of fairy tales and folklore

OHMIC *adj* relating to or measured in ohms, units of electrical resistance

OILED *v p t of* **OIL** greased, lubricated

OILER *n pl* **-S** a person who greases or lubricates engines, machinery, etc.

OINKS *v pr t of* **OINK** utters the characteristic nasal grunt of a hog

OKAPI *n pl* **-S** or **OKAPI** a large mammal native to the Congo basin in central Africa, related to the giraffe, but smaller with a short neck, a chestnut brown coat and white stripes on its hindquarters

OKAYS *v pr t of* **OKAY** approves; agrees to

OLDEN *adj* belonging to a time long past; relating to a bygone era; from a distant past

OLDER *adj* living or existing for a relatively long time; aged; from an earlier time

OLDIE *n pl* **-S** an old joke, saying, song, film, that was popular in the past; *also* **OLDY**

OLEIC *adj* related to or derived from oil

OLEIN *n* an oily yellow liquid occurring naturally in most fats and oils; *also* **ELAIN**

LEUM *n pl* **OLEA** or **OLEUMS** a heavy, oily, strongly corrosive solution of sulfur trioxide in sulfuric acid

LIOS *n pl of* **OLIO** highly spiced stews consisting of various kinds of meat, vegetables and chickpeas

LIVE *n pl* **-S** an evergreen tree native to the Mediterranean which is widely cultivated for olives, the small, oval fruit, green or black, bitter in taste, pressed to produce olive oil and an important food source

LLAS *n pl of* **OLLA** round, large-mouthed, earthenware pots or jars used for food storage, cooking, or containing water

LOGY *n pl* **OLOGIES** an informal term for a branch of learning; a science or academic field

MASA *n pl of* **OMASUM** third stomach chambers of ruminant animals, such as cattle, buffalo, goat, etc.

MBER *n* a gambling game played with forty cards and three players, popular in the 17th and 18th century; *also* **OMBRE**

MBRE *n* a gambling game played with forty cards and three players, popular in the 17th and 18th century; *also* **OMBER**

MEGA *n* the 24th and final letter in the Greek alphabet

MENS *n pl of* **OMEN** phenomena, events or incidents regarded as prophetic signs of future good or evil; auguries

MITS *v pr t of* **OMIT** leaves out; fails to include

NAYE *n* a poison used to poison arrow heads or darts for the purposes of hunting; *also* **INEE**

NCET *adv* once, one time, without repetition; one time only

ONION *n pl* **-S** an herb of the lily family with a round, edible bulb of close, concentric layers, with a sharp, pungent taste, cultivated widely and cooked as a vegetable

ONLAY *v* **ONLAID, -ING, -S** to apply something to a surface so it stands in relief, for decorative purposes

ONSET *n* the beginning of something, especially something unpleasant or difficult

ONTIC *adj* having the status of real and ultimate existence

OOHED *v p t of* **OOH** exclaimed in surprise, pleasure, satisfaction or amazement

OOMPH *n* spirited vigor; energy or enthusiasm; power

OOTID *n* a haploid cell produced at the second meiotic division, that quickly becomes an egg cell or ovum

OOZED *v p t of* **OOZE** flowed or leaked out slowly, through small holes or openings; seeped

OOZES *v pr t of* **OOZE** flows or leaks out slowly, through small holes or openings; seeps

OPALS *n pl of* **OPAL** translucent minerals of hydrated silica, softer and less dense than quartz, with shifting colors, including some iridescent varieties valued as semiprecious gemstones

OPENS *v pr t of* **OPEN** releases from a closed or fastened position; allows access; makes available for entry or passage

OPERA *n pl* **-S** a highly stylized play or dramatic work having all of its text set to music and sung to orchestral accompaniment

OPINE *v* **-D, OPINING, -S** to hold or state as an opinion

OPING *v pr part of* **OPE** opening, unclosing, unfastening or removing obstructions from

OPIUM *n* a narcotic made from the extract of unripe poppy seeds

OPSIN *n* a protein of the retina, that makes up one of the visual, light-sensitive, pigments of the eye

OPTED *v p t of* **OPT** made a choice or decision; chose or selected in preference to other alternatives

OPTIC *adj* relation to vision or the eye

ORACH *n* an herb of the goosefoot family, some with edible leaves, eaten as a vegetable; *also* **ORACHE**

ORALS *n pl of* **ORAL** academic examinations in which the questions and answers are spoken rather than written

ORANG *n* an orangutan, a great ape with shaggy hair, long, powerful arms, small ears and a hairless face

ORATE *v* **-D, ORATING, -S** to make a long, formal, ceremonial speech

ORBED *v p t of* **ORB** formed into a circle or sphere

ORBIT *v* **-ED, -ING, -S** to move or revolve around an astronomical object in a circular path

ORCAS *n pl of* **ORCA** large, black and white, predatory whales that feed on large fish, squid, seals, etc.; killer whales

ORCIN *n* a colorless crystalline substance obtained from lichens and produced synthetically; *also* **ORCINOL**

ORDER *v* **-ED, -ING, -S** to give a command or instruction to

ORDOS *n pl of* **ORDO** annual calendars in the Catholic church containing instructions for the Mass and office to be celebrated on each day of the year; *also* **ORDINES**

OREAD *n* a mountain nymph in Greek or Roman mythology

ORGAN *n pl* **-S** a large wind instrument controlled by a keyboard, in which pipes of various size and length are sounded by compressed air, producing different tones

ORIBI *n pl* **ORIBI** or **-S** a small African antelope having slender, straight horns

ORIEL *n* a bay window, projecting from a wall or an upper floor, supported from below by a bracket or corbel

ORLOP *n* the lowest deck of a ship with four or more decks

ORMER *n* BRIT. an abalone with an edible sea mollusk with an oval, spiral shell, especially those from the Channel Islands

ORNIS *n* avifauna, birds of a specified region, considered as a whole

ORPIN *n* a succulent, flowering plant; *also* **ORPINE**

ORRIS *n* an iris with fragrant roots that are dried and used in medicine and perfume

OSIER *n* a willow whose long, flexible branches are used in baskets and furniture

OSMIC *adj* designating or containing osmium, a hard, metallic, chemical element of the platinum family, especially in a high valence state

OSMOL *n* a unit of osmotic pressure based on a one molal concentration of an ion in a solution; *also* **OSMOLE**

OSSIA *conj* a notation used to indicate an alternate version of a musical score; or else

OSTIA *n pl of* **OSTIUM** small openings or orifices in a bodily organ or passage

OTHER *pron* a different person or additional thing

232

OTTAR *n* a fragrant essential oil or perfume obtained from flowers, especially rose petals; *also* ATAR, ATHAR, ATTAR, OTTO

OTTER *n* -S a semi-aquatic, fish-eating mammal of the weasel family, with dense fur, webbed feet and a long, flat tail

OUGHT *v* to be compelled by obligation or duty

OUNCE *n* pl -S a unit of weight

OUPHE *n* [obs] an elf or goblin

OUSEL *n* a European thrush, a bird; *also* OUZEL

OUSTS *v* pr t of OUST forces or drives out; removes from a position or office; ejects or expels

OUTDO *v* OUTDID or -NE, -ING, -ES to exceed others or one's self in performance; to surpass or excel

OUTED *v* p t of OUT caused to be out, ejected, expelled, or ousted

OUTER *adj* exterior; external

OUTGO *v* OUTWENT or -NE, -ING, -ES to go beyond; to exceed or surpass

OUTRE *adj* deviating from convention; strikingly odd; exaggerated; eccentric; bizarre

OUZEL *n* a European thrush, a bird; *also* OUSEL

OUZOS *n* pl of OUZO colorless Greek liqueurs, flavored with anise

OVALS *n* pl of OVAL elliptical or egg-shaped figures or objects

OVARY *n* pl OVARIES one in a pair of female reproductive organs producing ova or eggs

OVATE *adj* oval or egg-shaped

OVENS *n* pl of OVEN enclosed chambers or compartments, typically kitchen appliances, in which food is heated, cooked, baked or roasted

OVERS *v* pr t of OVER passes, leaps or jumps above and across

OVERT *adj* open and observable without any attempt of concealment; apparent; manifest

OVINE *adj* of or pertaining to sheep; sheep-like

OVOID *adj* egg-shaped

OVOLI *n* pl of OVOLO rounded, convex, architectural moldings, often a quarter section of a circle or ellipse

OVOLO *n* pl OVOLI a rounded, convex, architectural molding, often a quarter section of a circle or ellipse

OVULE *n* a small egg or seed, especially one in the early stages of development

OWING *v* pr part of OWE being indebted, being obligated to pay or repay in return for something received

OWLET *n* pl -S a young or small owl

OWNED *v* p t of OWN held as property; had a legal or rightful title to; possessed

OWNER *n* pl -S one who has the legal title or right to possession of a thing; possessor; proprietor

OWSEN *n* pl of OWSE SCOT., BRIT. domesticated, bovine mammals, usually adult bulls, male cows, often used on farms in the past as draft animals for pulling plows and heavy loads; *also* OXEN

OXBOW *n* pl -S the U-shaped part of an ox yoke which passes under and around the neck of the animal

OXEYE *n* a perennial plant similar to a daisy or sunflower

OXIDE *n* -S any binary compound of oxygen with another element or with a radical

OXIME *n* an organic chemical compound containing a hydroxyl group bonded to a nitrogen atom

233

OXLIP *n pl* **-S** a perennial plant of the primrose family with yellow flowers clustered to one side

OXTER *n* SCOT., BRIT. a person's armpit

OZONE *n* a gaseous, very reactive form of oxygen with three oxygen atoms per molecule, beneficial to the upper atmosphere, but a pollutant to the lower atmosphere

PA *n pl* **-S** informal term for father

PE *n* the 17th letter of the Hebrew alphabet; *also* **PEH**

PI *v* **-ED, -ING** or **PIEING, -ES** to spill or throw type or type matter into disorder

THREE LETTERS

PAC *n* a moccasin or soft shoe designed to be worn inside a boot

PAD *v* **-DED, -DING, -S** to line or stuff with soft material

PAH *interj* used to express disgust, contempt or irritation; *also* **BAH, PAU**

PAL *v* **-LED, -LING, -S** to be or become friends

PAM *n pl* **-S** the jack of clubs

PAN *v* **-NED, -NING, -S** to move so as to follow a moving object, as a camera

PAP *n pl* **-S** a soft food for infants or invalids

PAR *v* **-RED, -RING, -S** to score the standard number of strokes set for each hole in golf

PAS *n pl* **PAS** a pace; a step, as in a dance

PAT *v* **-TED, -TING, -S** to stroke lightly; to tap gently

PAU *interj* used to express disgust, contempt, or irritation; *also* **BAH, PAH**

PAW *v* **-ED, -ING, -S** strikes out with the paws or feet, or touches somebody clumsily

PAX *n* the kiss of peace, in the Christian Church

PAY *v* **-ED** or **PAID, -ING, -S** to give money, usually in exchange for goods or services

PEA *n pl* **-S** the seed of a pea plant, used as a vegetable

PEC *n pl* **-S** a commonly used abbreviation for pectoral muscle, located in the chest

PED *n pl* **-S** a natural soil aggregate

PEE *v* **-D, -ING, -S** to urinate

PEG *v* **-GED, -GING, -S** to fix, attach or mark with a short projecting pin or bolt

PEH *n* the 17th letter of the Hebrew alphabet; *also* **PE**

PEL *n* in computer science, the smallest discrete component of an image or picture on a CRT screen

PEN *v* **-NED, -NING, -S** to write or compose

PEP *v* **-PED, -PING, -S** to fill with energy; invigorate

PER *prep* by; for; for each; as per annum, per capita

PES *n pl* **PEDES** a foot or foot-like part

PET *v* **-TED, -TING, -S** to stroke or caress gently

PEW *n pl* **-S** a long bench with a back, as in a church

PHI *n* the 21st letter of the Greek alphabet

PIA *n pl* **-S** a membrane around the brain and spine

PIC *n pl* **-S** informal for a picture, photograph or film

PIE *n pl* **-S** a baked dish of savory or sweet ingredients encased in or topped with pastry

PIG *n pl* **-S** any swine, especially domesticated hogs when young or of comparatively small size

PIN *v* **-NED, -NING, -S** to attach or fasten with a small, slender, often pointed piece of wood or metal

PIP *v* **-PED, -PING, -S** to cry or chirp, as a chicken; to peep

PIS *n pl of* **PI** the 16th letter of the Greek alphabet

PIT *v* **-TED, -TING, -S** to mark with cavities, depressions or scars

PIU *adv* a little more; as piu allegro, a little more briskly

PIX *n pl* **PIXES** in the Christian Church, the container in which the consecrated bread of the Eucharist is kept; *also* **PYX**

PLU *n* a beaver skin; *also* **PLEW**

PLY *v* **PLIED, -ING, PLIES** to use something such as a tool or weapon in a diligent or skillful way

POD *v* **-DED, -DING, -S** to strip peas or beans out of their long narrow outer case so that they can be eaten or cooked

POH *interj* an exclamation expressing contempt, disgust or disdain; *also* **POOH**

POI *n pl* **-S** a ball used in Maori dances

POL *n pl* **-S** informal term for a politician

POO *v* **-ED, -ING, -S** to defecate

POP *v* **-PED, -PING, -S** to make a short, sharp, explosive sound or report

POT *v* **-TED, -TING, -S** to place or plant in a container that is usually rounded or cylindrical

POW *n pl* **-S** a sound of a blow or explosion

POX *v* **-ED, -ING, -ES** to infect with a viral disease characterized by pustules or eruptions, such as smallpox or syphilis

POY *n* [obs] a long boat hook by which barges are propelled against the stream; *also* **PUY**

PRO *n pl* **-S** an argument or vote in favor of something

PRY *v* **PRIED, -ING, PRIES** to look or inquire closely

PSI *n* the 23rd letter of the Greek alphabet

PUB *n pl* **-S** an establishment where alcoholic beverages are sold and consumed

PUD *n pl* **-S** BRIT. informal for pudding

PUE *v* **-D, PUING** [obs] to make a low whistling sound; to chirp, as birds

PUG *v* **-GED, -GING, -S** to mix clay with water to make it pliable enough to form bricks or pottery

PUH *interj* an exclamation of disgust, as at an offensive odor; *also* **PUGH**

PUL *n pl* **PULS, PULI** a unit of currency in Afghanistan

PUN *v* **-NED, -NING, -S** to make a play on words that involves a word or phrase with more than one possible meaning

PUP *v* **-PED, -PING, -S** to give birth to puppies

PUR *v* **-RED, -RING, -S** to utter a low, murmuring, continued sound, as a cat does when pleased; *also* **PURR**

PUS *n* a viscous fluid produced by infection

PUT *v* **-S, -TING** to move something into a particular place or position

PUY *n* [obs] a long boat hook by which barges are propelled against the stream; *also* **POY**

PYA *n pl* **-S** a unit of currency in Myanmar

PYE *n pl* **-S** a book of ecclesiastical rules for finding the particulars of the service for the day

PYX *n pl* **PYXES** in the Christian Church, the container in which the consecrated bread of the Eucharist is kept; *also* **PIX**

FOUR LETTERS

PACA *n pl* **-S** a large burrowing rodent of South America

PACE *v* **-D, PACING, -S** to walk back and forth within a restricted area

PACK v -ED, -ING, -S to put into a receptacle for transporting or storing

PACO n pl -S a South American freshwater fish; also **PACU**

PACT n pl -S an agreement

PACU n pl -S a South American freshwater fish; also **PACO**

PACY adj PACIER, PACIEST BRIT. with fast-moving action or a fast-moving exciting plot; also **PACEY**

PADI n pl -S wet field in which rice is grown; also **PADDY**

PADS v pr t of **PAD** lines or stuffs with soft material

PAGE v -D, PAGING, -S to summon or call a person by name

PAHI n pl -S a large war canoe of the Society Islands

PAID v p t of **PAY** gave money, usually in exchange for goods or services

PAIK v -ED, -ING, -S SCOT. to beat or drub

PAIL n pl -S a bucket

PAIN v -ED, -ING, -S to make suffer or cause distress to

PAIR v -ED, -ING, -S to arrange in sets of two; couple

PAIS n in law, the people from among whom a jury is taken

PALE v -D, PALING, -S to become whiter or lose brilliance

PALI n pl of **PALUS** several upright slender processes which surround certain corals

PALL v -ED, -ING, -S to become insipid, boring or wearisome

PALM v -ED, -ING, -S to hide something in the hand, especially as part of a trick

PALP v -ED, -ING, -S [obs] to have a distinct touch or feeling of; to feel

PALS v pr t of **PAL** is or becomes friends

PALY adj PALIER, PALIEST [obs] somewhat pale; pallid

PAMS n pl of **PAM** the jacks of clubs

PANE n pl -S a single sheet of glass in a window or door

PANG v -ED, -ING, -S to cause to feel a sudden sharp spasm of pain; distress acutely

PANS v pr t of **PAN** moves so as to follow a moving object, as a camera

PANT v -ED, -ING, -S to breathe with short, quick breaths, typically from exertion or excitement

PAPA n pl -S an informal term for a father; also **POPPA**

PAPS n pl of **PAP** soft foods for infants or invalids

PARA n pl -S or **PARA** a unit of currency of Bosnia-Herzegovina, Montenegro and Serbia

PARD n pl -S [obs] a large cat, especially a leopard or a panther

PARE v -D, PARING, -S to trim by cutting away the outer edges

PARK v -ED, -ING, -S to stop and leave a vehicle temporarily

PARR n pl –S or **PARR** a young salmon or trout up to two years old

PARS v pr t of **PAR** scores the standard number of strokes set for each hole in golf

PART v -ED, -ING, -S to divide; to separate into distinct sections

PASE n pl -S a movement of a matador's cape

PASH v -ED, -ING, -ES [obs] to strike; to crush; to smash

PASS v -ED, -ING, -ES to move on or ahead; to proceed

PAST n pl -S the time before the present or the events that happened during that time

PATE n pl -S [obs] the top or crown of the head

PATH n pl -S a trodden way; a footway; a track

PATS v pr t of **PAT** strokes lightly; taps gently

PATY *adj* in heraldry, having arms of a cross of equal length, each expanding outward from the center

PAUM *v* [obs] to palm off by fraud; to cheat at cards

PAVE *v* **-D, PAVING, -S** to lay or cover with material, as asphalt or concrete, that forms a firm level surface for travel

PAWK *n* a small lobster

PAWL *n pl* **-S** a hinged catch that fits into a notch of a ratchet to prevent reverse motion

PAWN *v* **-ED, -ING, -S** to borrow and leave an article as security for repayment of the loan

PAWS *v pr t of* **PAW** strikes out with the paws or feet, or touches somebody clumsily

PAYN *n* bread

PAYS *v pr t of* **PAY** gives money, usually in exchange for goods or services

PEAG *n pl* **-S** wampum, small cylindrical beads made from polished shells; *also* **PEAGE; WAMPUM**

PEAK *v* **-ED, -ING, -S** to reach a highest point or maximum

PEAL *v* **-ED, -ING, -S** to sound loudly and sonorously

PEAN *n pl* **-S** a fervent expression of joy or praise; *also* **PAEAN**

PEAR *n pl* **-S** a teardrop shaped sweet juicy fruit with firm white flesh

PEAS *n pl of* **PEA** the seeds of a pea plant, used as a vegetable

PEAT *n pl* **-S** partially carbonized vegetable matter, usually mosses, found in bogs and used as fertilizer and fuel

PEBA *n pl* **-S** a type of armadillo

PECH *n pl* **-S** a short, fast and forceful breath

PECK *v* **-ED, -ING, -S** to strike with the beak or a pointed instrument

PECS *n pl of* **PEC** a commonly used abbreviation for pectoral muscles, located in the chest

PEDS *n pl of* **PED** natural soil aggregates

PEED *v p t of* **PEE** urinated

PEEK *v* **-ED, -ING, -S** to look quickly or furtively

PEEL *v* **-ED, -ING, -S** to strip off an outer layer of

PEEN *v* **-ED, -ING, -S** to hammer, bend or shape with the round-edged end to the head of a hammer; *also* **PEIN**

PEEP *v* **-ED, -ING, -S** to make high-pitched sounds; to chirp

PEER *v* **-ED, -ING, -S** to look intently, searchingly or with difficulty

PEES *v pr t of* **PEE** urinates

PEGM *n* [obs] a sort of moving machine employed in the old pageants; a moveable stage

PEGS *v pr t of* **PEG** fixes, attaches or marks with a short projecting pin or bolt

PEIN *v* **-ED, -ING, -S** to hammer, bend or shape with the round-edged end to the head of a hammer; *also* **PEEN**

PELE *n* a medieval fortified tower

PELF *n pl* **-S** [obs] money or wealth, especially when gained dishonestly

PELL *n pl* **-S** a skin or hide

PELT *v* **-ED, -ING, -S** to bombard with many blows or missiles

PEND *v* **-ED, -ING, -S** to be undecided; in process of adjustment

PENK *n* a minnow, a small fish

PENS *v pr t of* **PEN** writes or composes

PENT *adj* penned or shut up; confined; often with up

PEON *n pl* **-S, -ES** a laborer who is obliged to do menial work

PEPO *n pl* **-S** any fleshy gourd fruit with a hard rind and many seeds, as the melon or squash

PEPS *v pr t of* **PEP** fills with energy; invigorates

PERE *n pl* **-S** [obs] a Middle English form of pear

PERI *n pl* **-S** in Persian mythology, a beautiful supernatural being descended from the fallen angels

PERK *v* **-ED, -ING, -S** to prepare coffee

PERM *v* **-ED, -ING, -S** to give hair a permanent wave

PERN *v* **-ED, -ING, -S** [obs] to take profit of; to make profitable

PERP *n pl* **-S** informal for one who perpetrates a crime

PERS *adj* [obs] light blue; grayish blue

PERT *adj* **-ER, -EST** saucily free and forward; flippantly cocky and assured

PERY *n* [obs] a pear tree; *also* **PIRIE, PYRIE**

PESE *n pl* **-S** [obs] a pea, a green seed eaten as a vegetable; *also* **PEASE, PEASEN, PESES**

PESO *n pl* **-S** a unit of currency in several Spanish speaking countries

PEST *n pl* **-S** an annoying person or thing; a nuisance

PETS *v pr t of* **PET** strokes or caresses gently

PEWS *n pl of* **PEW** long benches with backs, as in a church

PFFT *interj* a sound indicating a sudden disappearance or failure of something

PFUI *interj* used to express contempt, disgust, or mocking disagreement; *also* **PHOOEY**

PHAT *adj* **-TER, -TEST** informal term for excellent; first-rate

PHEW *interj* used to express relief, fatigue, surprise or disgust

PHIZ *n pl* **-ES** or **PHIZOG** informal for a face or facial expression; short for physiognomy

PHON *n pl* **-S** a unit of apparent loudness

PHOT *n pl* **-S** a unit of illumination

PHUT *n pl* **-S** a sound like a small explosion or a sudden expulsion of air

PIAL *adj* pertaining to the pia mater, the innermost membrane enveloping the brain and spinal cord

PIAN *n pl* **-S** a highly infectious disease of tropical climates; *also* **FRAMBESIA**

PIAS *n pl of* **PIA** membranes around the brain and spine

PICA *n pl* **-S** a unit of measurement for printing type size and line length

PICE *n pl* **PICE** a former unit of currency in India

PICK *v* **-ED, -ING, -S** to select carefully from a group

PICS *n pl of* **PIC** informal for pictures, photographs, or films

PIED *v p t of* **PI** spilled or thrown type or type matter into disorder

PIER *n pl* **-S** a projecting wharf or landing place

PIES *n pl of* **PIE** baked dishes of savory or sweet ingredients encased in or topped with pastry

PIET *n pl* **-S** a magpie; dipper or water ouzel; *also* **PYET**

PIGS *n pl of* **PIG** any swine, especially domesticated hogs when young or of comparatively small size

PIKA *n pl* **-S** a small short-eared burrowing mammal that is related to the rabbit

PIKE *v* **-D, PIKING, -S** to pierce or wound with a sharp point or spike

PIKI *n* commonly used abbreviation for piki bread, a bread made from blue cornmeal and baked in thin sheets

PILE *v* **-D, PILING, -S** to heap or stack things one on top of the other

PILI *n pl* **-S** a Philippine tree and its edible nut

PILL *v* **-ED, -ING, -S** to become covered in small balls of matted fiber because of rubbing fabrics

PILY *adj* like pile or wool

PINE *v* -D, PINING, -S to yearn intensely and persistently, especially for something unattainable

PING *v* -ED, -ING, -S to make a sharp, high-pitched, metallic sound

PINK *v* -ED, -ING, -S to cut fabric with pinking shears to make a zigzag edge that will not easily fray

PINS *v pr t of* PIN attaches or fastens with a small, slender, often pointed piece of wood or metal

PINT *n pl* -S a unit of liquid and dry measure

PINY *adj* PINIER, PINIEST relating to or resembling pine trees; *also* PINEY

PION *n pl* -S a subatomic particle

PIPE *v* -D, PIPING, -S to convey through a tube

PIPS *v pr t of* PIP cries or chirps, as a chicken; peeps

PIPY *adj* PIPIER, PIPIEST like a pipe; hollow-stemmed; shrill

PIRL *v* to twist or twine, as hair in making fishing lines

PIRN *n pl* -S the bobbin or spool of a weaver's shuttle

PISH *interj* used to express contempt, annoyance or impatience

PISO *n pl* -S a unit of currency in the Philippines

PITA *n pl* -S flat hollow unleavened bread which can be split open to hold a filling

PITH *v* -ED, -ING, -S to remove the soft central cylinder of the stems from most flowering plants

PITS *v pr t of* PIT marks with cavities, depressions or scars

PITY *v* PITIED, -ING, PITIES to feel sorrow and compassion for the sufferings of others

PIXY *n pl* PIXIES a fairy or elf; *also* PIXIE

PLAN *v* -NED, -NING, -S to work out in advance how something is to be done or organized

PLAT *v* -TED, -TING, -S to braid or interweave the strands or locks of; *also* PLAIT

PLAY *v* -ED, -ING, -S to engage in sport or amusing activities

PLEA *n pl* -S an urgent, often emotional, request

PLEB *n pl* -S a commoner; a plebeian

PLED *v p t of* PLEAD to have appealed earnestly, begged

PLEW *n pl* -S a beaver skin; *also* PLU

PLEX *n pl* -ES informal for a multiplex

PLIE *n pl* -S a ballet movement in which the knees are bent while the back is held straight

PLIM *v* [obs] to swell, as grain or wood with water

PLOD *v* -DED, -DING, -S to walk heavily or slowly; to trudge

PLOP *v* -PED, -PING, -S to fall with a sound like that of an object falling into water without splashing

PLOT *v* -TED, -TING, -S to make a secret plan, especially to do something illegal or subversive with others

PLOW *v* -ED, -ING, -S to break up soil and turn it over into furrows

PLOY *n pl* -S a cunning maneuver to gain an advantage

PLUG *v* -GED, -GING, -S to close up a hole or gap

PLUM *n pl* -S a round or oval smooth-skinned fruit, usually red or purple, containing a flattened pit

PLUS *n pl* -ES or -SES a positive quantity, or something advantageous

POAK *n* [obs] waste matter from the preparation of skins, consisting of hair, lime, oil; *also* POAKE

POCK *v* -ED, -ING, -S to mark with scars left in the skin by pustules caused by eruptive diseases; pit

POCO *adv* a little or slightly, used in musical directions

PODS *v pr t of* POD strips peas or beans out of their long narrow outer case so that they can be eaten or cooked

POEM *n pl* -S a composition in verse, usually written in certain measures

POET *n pl* -S a writer of poetry, compositions in verse

POGY *n pl* POGY or POGIES a sea fish of the herring family; *also* MENHADEN

POIS *n pl of* POI balls used in Maori dances

POKE *v* -D, POKING, -S to jab or prod with a finger or a sharp object

POKY *adj* POKIER, POKIEST dull; tedious; uninteresting; slow

POLE *v* -D, POLING, -S to propel with a long slender usually cylindrical object

POLL *v* -ED, -ING, -S to sample the opinions or attitudes of a group of people systematically

POLO *n pl* -S a game played by teams of players on horseback using long-handled mallets to drive a wooden ball through goalposts

POLS *n pl of* POL informal term for politicians

POLT *n* [obs] a blow or thump

POLY *n pl* -S informal for a polymerized plastic or something made of this, especially a polyester fabric

POME *n pl* -S a fleshy fruit that has a central core typically containing five seeds, such as an apple or pear

POMO *n pl* -S informal for a postmodernist or Postmodernism

POMP *n pl* -S a display of great splendor and magnificence, sometimes ostentatious

POND *n pl* -S a fairly small body of still water

PONE *n pl* -S a cake of cornbread baked on a griddle or in hot ashes; *also* CORNPONE, JOHNNYCAKE

PONG *v* -ED, -ING, -S BRIT. to stink

PONS *n pl* PONTES a slender tissue joining two parts of an organ

PONT *n pl* -S a flat-bottomed ferryboat, in South Africa

PONY *v* PONIED, -ING, PONIES to pay money owed or due

POOD *n pl* -S a Russian unit of weight

POOF *interj* used to express disdain or dismissal, or to suggest instantaneous occurrence

POOH *interj* an exclamation expressing contempt, disgust or disdain; *also* POH

POOL *v* -ED, -ING, -S to put together; to contribute to a common fund

POON *n pl* POON or -S an East Indian tree

POOP *v* -ED, -ING, -S informal for to become fatigued; tire

POOR *adj* -ER, -EST lacking money or material possessions

POOS *v pr t of* POO defecates

POPE *n pl* -S the head of the Roman Catholic Church; one who resembles a pope (in authority)

POPS *v pr t of* POP makes a short, sharp, explosive sound or report

PORE *v* -D, PORING, -S to read or study carefully and attentively

PORK *v* -ED, -ING, -S to eat ravenously; gorge oneself

PORT *v* -ED, -ING, -S to move or turn (the helm) to the left-hand side of a ship, boat or airplane as one faces forward

PORY *adj* porous; easily crossed or penetrated

POSE *v* -D, POSING, -S to assume a fixed position or posture

POSH *adj* -ER, -EST luxurious and fashionable; elegant

POSS *v* -ED, -ING, -ES [obs] to push; to dash; to throw

POST *v* -ED, -ING, -S to mail (a letter or package)

POSY *n pl* POSIES a blooming flower; a small bouquet

POTS *v pr t of* **POT** places or plants in a container that is usually rounded or cylindrical

POTT *n* [obs] a size of paper

POUF *n pl* **-S** a bouffant or fluffy part of a garment or accessory; *also* **POUFFE**

POUR *v* **-ED, -ING, -S** to cause to flow in a stream

POUT *v* **-ED, -ING, -S** to show displeasure by thrusting out the lips or wearing a sullen expression

POWS *n pl of* **POW** sound of blows or explosions

POXY *adj* **POXIER, POXIEST** BRIT. informal for bad, unpleasant, annoying or generally worthless

PRAD *n pl* **-S** AUS. informal for a horse

PRAM *n pl* **-S** a flat-bottomed fishing boat or barge; *also* **PRAAM**

PRAO *n pl* **-S** a swift Malayan sailboat; *also* **PRAU, PROA, PRAHU**

PRAT *n pl* **-S** informal term for the buttocks

PRAU *n pl* **-S** a swift Malayan sailboat; *also* **PRAO, PROA, PRAHU**

PRAY *v* **-ED, -ING, -S** to make a fervent request or entreaty

PREE *v* **-D, -ING** SCOT. to taste tentatively; sample; *also* **PRIE**

PREP *v* **-PED, -PING, -S** prepare; make ready

PREX *n pl* **-ES** or **-IES** informal for a president, especially of a college or university; *also* **PREXY**

PREY *v* **-ED, -ING, -S** to take advantage of; to exploit

PREZ *n pl* **-ES or -ZES** informal for president

PRIE *v* SCOT. to taste tentatively; sample; *also* **PREE**

PRIG *n pl* **-S** a person who is annoyingly smug about his or her moral behavior, attitudes

PRIM *v* **-MED, -MING, -S** to make precise or proper to the point of affectation, as in facial expression or dress

PROA *n pl* **-S** a swift Malayan sailboat; *also* **PRAO, PRAU, PRAHU**

PROD *v* **-DED, -DING, -S** to poke with a finger or pointed object

PROF *n pl* **-S** informal for a professor

PROG *v* **-GED, -GING, -S** to prowl about, as in search of food or plunder; forage

PROM *n pl* **-S** a formal dance for high-school or college students, usually held at the end of the school year

PROP *v* **-PED, -PING, -S** to support by placing something beneath or against; shore up

PROS *n pl of* **PRO** arguments or votes in favor of something

PROW *n pl* **-S** the front part of a vessel; the bow

PSST *interj* used to attract someone's attention

PTUI *interj* used to express the sound of spitting; *also* **PTOOEY**

PUBS *n pl of* **PUB** establishments where alcoholic beverages are sold and consumed

PUCE *n pl* **-S** a dark red or purple-brown color

PUCK *v* **-ED, -ING, -S** in the Irish sport of hurling, to strike the ball

PUDS *n pl of* **PUD** BRIT. informal for puddings

PUDU *n pl* **-S** a very small deer native to the Chilean Andes

PUED *v p t of* **PUE** [obs] made a low whistling sound; chirped, as birds

PUER *n* [obs] the droppings of dogs

PUFF *v* **-ED, -ING, -S** to blow quickly in short blasts

PUGH *interj* an exclamation of disgust, as at an offensive odor; *also* **PUH**

PUGS *v pr t of* **PUG** mixes clay with water to make it pliable enough to form bricks or pottery

PUIT *n pl* **-S** [obs] a well; a small stream; a fountain; a spring

PUJA *n pl* **-S** a Hindu ceremonial offering; *also* **POOJA, PUJAH,** or **POOJAH**

PUKA *n pl* **-S** a small white shell found on Pacific, especially Hawaiian, beaches and strung in clusters to make necklaces

PUKE *v* **-D, PUKING, -S** to vomit

PUKU *n pl* **-S** an African antelope related to the waterbuck

PULA *n pl* **PULA** a unit of currency in Botswana

PULE *v* **-D, PULING, -S** to whine, whimper or cry plaintively

PULI *n pl of* **PUL** units of currency in Afghanistan, *also* **PULS**

PULL *v* **-ED, -ING, -S** to apply force so as to draw or tend to draw a person or thing toward the origin of the force

PULP *v* **-ED, -ING, -S** to reduce to a soft moist shapeless mass of matter

PULS *n pl of* **PUL** units of currency in Afghanistan, *also* **PULI**

PULU *n* a Hawaiian vegetable substance consisting of soft, elastic, yellowish brown chaff

PUMA *n pl* **-S** a large American wild cat; mountain lion

PUME *n* a stint, one of several species of small sandpipers

PUMP *v* **-ED, -ING, -S** to force a liquid or gas to flow

PUMY *adj* [obs] large and rounded

PUNA *n pl* **-S** a cold, arid plateau high in the Andes

PUNG *n pl* **-S** a low boxlike sleigh drawn by one horse

PUNK *n pl* **-S** informal for a young person, especially a member of a rebellious counterculture group

PUNS *v pr t of* **PUN** makes plays on words that involves a word or a phrase with more than one possible meaning

PUNT *v* **-ED, -ING, -S** to travel or convey in a long flat-bottomed boat used in shallow waters and propelled by a long pole

PUNY *adj* **PUNIER, PUNIEST** of inferior size, strength or significance; weak

PUPA *n pl* **-S, -E** an insect at the stage between a larva and an adult in metamorphosis during which it is in a cocoon or case, and undergoes internal changes

PUPS *v pr t of* **PUP** gives birth to puppies

PUPU *n pl* **-S** hot or cold usually bite-size Hawaiian appetizer

PURE *adj* **-R, -ST** free from mixture or contamination

PURI *n pl* **PURI, -S** a puffy fried wheat cake of India; *also* **POORI**

PURL *v* **-ED, -ING, -S** to knit with a purl stitch, usually made with the yarn at the front of the work by inserting the right needle into the front of a loop on the left needle

PURR *v* **-ED, -ING, -S** to utter a low, murmuring, continued sound, as a cat does when pleased; *also* **PUR**

PURS *v pr t of* **PUR** utters a low, murmuring, continued sound, as a cat does when pleased; *also* **PURRS**

PUSH *v* **-ED, -ING, -ES** to press against with force

PUSS *n pl* **-ES** a cat

PUTS *v pr t of* **PUT** moves something into a particular place or position

PUTT *v* **-ED, -ING, -S** to strike a golf ball gently so that it rolls into or near a hole

PUTZ *v* **-ED, -ING, -ES** to behave in an idle manner; putter

PUYS *n pl of* **PUY** small, remnant volcanic cones

PYAS *n pl of* **PYA** units of currency in Myanmar

PYES *n pl of* **PYE** books of ecclesiastical rules for finding the particulars of the service for the day

PYET *n pl* **-S** a magpie; dipper or water ouzel; *also* **PIET**

PYIC *adj* pertaining to or discharging pus

PYIN *n pl* **-S** an albuminous constituent of pus

PYLA *n pl* **-S** the passage between the iter and optocoele in the brain

PYRE *n pl* **-S** a heap of combustible material

PYRO *n pl* **-S** informal for a person who has a compulsion to set fires; a pyromaniac

FIVE LETTERS

PACAS *n pl of* **PACA** large burrowing rodents of South America

PACED *v p t of* **PACE** walked back and forth within a restricted area

PACER *n pl* **-S** one who paces, walks back and forth within a restricted area

PACES *v pr t of* **PACE** walks back and forth within a restricted area

PACEY *adj* **PACIER, PACIEST** BRIT. with fast-moving action or a fast-moving exciting plot; *also* **PACY**

PACHA *n pl* **-S** the title of a Turkish officer of high rank; *also* **PASHA**

PACKS *v pr t of* **PACK** puts into a receptacle for transporting or storing

PACOS *n pl of* **PACO** South American freshwater fish; *also* **PACUS**

PACTS *n pl of* **PACT** agreements

PACUS *n pl of* **PACU** South American freshwater fish; *also* **PACOS**

PADDY *n pl* **PADDIES** wet field in which rice is grown; *also* **PADI**

PADIS *n pl of* **PADI** wet lands in which rice is grown; *also* **PADDIES**

PADRE *n pl* **-S** or **PADRI** a Christian priest or chaplain

PAEAN *n pl* **-S** a fervent expression of joy or praise; *also* **PEAN**

PAEON *n pl* **-S** a foot of three short syllables and one long syllable occurring in any order

PAGAN *n pl* **-S** a follower of an ancient polytheistic or pantheistic religion

PAGED *v p t of* **PAGE** summoned or called a person by name

PAGER *n pl* **-S** a beeper

PAGES *v pr t of* **PAGE** summons or calls a person by name

PAGOD *n pl* **-S** a Hindu or Buddhist temple or other sacred building, typically having a many-tiered tower; *also* **PAGODA**

PAHIS *n pl of* **PAHI** large war canoes of the Society Islands

PAIKS *v pr t of* **PAIK** SCOT. beats or drubs

PAILS *n pl of* **PAIL** buckets

PAINS *v pr t of* **PAIN** makes suffer or causes distress to

PAINT *v* **-ED, -ING, -S** to apply color or pigment to a surface, in order to decorate or protect it

PAIRS *v pr t of* **PAIR** arranges in sets of two; couples

PAISA *n pl* **PAISA** or **PAISE** a unit of currency in some South Asian countries

PAISE *n pl of* **PAISA** units of currency in some South Asian countries

PALEA *n pl* **-E** a small chafflike bract enclosing the flower of a grass; *also* **PALET**

PALED *v p t of* **PALE** became whiter or lost brilliance

PALER *adj* more deficient in color or intensity of color; pallid

PALES *v pr t of* **PALE** becomes whiter or loses brilliance

PALET *n pl* **-S** a small chafflike bract enclosing the flower of a grass; *also* **PALEA**

PALLS *v pr t of* **PALL** becomes insipid, boring or wearisome

PALLY *adj* **PALLIER, PALLIEST** having a close, friendly relationship

PALMS *v pr t of* **PALM** hides something in the hand, especially as part of a trick

PALMY *adj* **PALMIER, PALMIEST** prosperous or flourishing, especially formerly

PALPI *n pl of* **PALPUS** a sensory organ of an arthropod

PALPS *v pr t of* **PALP** [obs] has a distinct touch or feeling; feels

PALSY *v* **PALSIED, -ING, PALSIES** to paralyze

PALUS *n pl* **PALI** one of several upright slender processes which surround certain corals

PAMPA *n pl* **-S** an extensive grassland of South America

PANDA *n pl* **-S** a rare bear-like mammal with distinctive black and white markings

PANDY *v* **PANDIED, -ING, PANDIES** BRIT. to punish a student by striking the open palm of the hand

PANED *adj* having panes, sheets of glass in windows or doors

PANEL *v* **-ED, -ING, -S** to furnish, cover or decorate something with flat rectangular pieces of hard material that serve as part of a door or wall

PANES *n pl of* **PANE** sheets of glass in windows or doors

PANGA *n pl* **-S** a long knife used in Africa as a tool or weapon; machete

PANGS *v pr t of* **PANG** causes to feel a sudden sharp spasm of pain; distresses acutely

PANIC *v* **-ED, -ING, -S** to be overwhelmed by fear

PANNE *n* a shining fabric resembling velvet, with a flattened pile

PANSY *n pl* **PANSIES** a plant of the viola family, with flowers in rich colors

PANTO *n pl* **-S** BRIT. informal for a pantomime, a dramatic performance or performer using only bodily and facial movements

PANTS *v pr t of* **PANT** breathes with short, quick breaths, typically from exertion or excitement

PANTY *n pl* **PANTIES** short underpants for women or children; *also* **PANTIE**

PAPAL *adj* relating to the pope or the papacy, authority or government in the Roman Catholic Church

PAPAS *n pl of* **PAPA** an informal term for fathers; *also* **POPPAS**

PAPAW *n pl* **-S** a tree of the custard-apple family; papaya; *also* **PAWPAW**

PAPER *v* **-ED, -ING, -S** to cover, wrap or line with paper

PAPPI *n pl of* **PAPPUS** a tuft of bristles on the achene of certain plants, as the dandelion and the thistle

PAPPY *adj* **PAPPIER, PAPPIEST** mushy; like pap

PARAE *n pl of* **PARA** a woman's status regarding the number of live born children she has delivered

PARAS *n pl of* **PARA** units of currency of Bosnia-Herzegovina, Montenegro and Serbia

PARCH *v* **-ED, -ING, -ES** to make very dry

PARDE *interj* [obs] indeed; *also* **PARDI, PARDY, PERDY, PARDIE, PERDIE**

PARDI *interj* [obs] indeed; *also* **PARDE, PARDY, PERDY, PARDIE, PERDIE**

PARDS *n pl of* **PARD** [obs] large cats, especially leopards or panthers

PARDY *interj* [obs] indeed; *also* **PARDE, PARDI, PERDY, PARDIE, PERDIE**

PARED *v p t of* **PARE** trimmed by cutting away the outer edges

PAREO *n pl* **-S** a rectangular printed cloth worn by Polynesians as a wraparound skirt; *also* **PAREU**

PARER *n pl* **-S** one who, or that which, trims by cutting away the outer edges; an instrument for paring

PARES *v pr t of* **PARE** trims by cutting away the outer edges

PAREU *n* a rectangular printed cloth worn by Polynesians as a wraparound skirt; *also* **PAREO**

PARGE *v* **-D, PARGING, -S** to apply ornamental or waterproofing plaster to; *also* **PARGET**

PARKA *n pl* **-S** a hooded jacket, often with a warm lining

PARKS *v pr t of* **PARK** stops and leaves a vehicle temporarily

PARLE *v* **-D, PARLING** to confer with another; to discuss terms with an enemy; *also* **PARLEY**

PAROL *n pl* **-S** a legal contract that is made orally only

PARRS *n pl of* **PARR** young salmon or trout up to two years old

PARRY *v* **PARRIED, -ING, PARRIES** to ward off a blow

PARSE *v* **-D, PARSING, -S** to describe the form, part of speech and function of a word in a sentence

PARTS *v pr t of* **PART** divides; separates into distinct sections

PARTY *v* **PARTIED, -ING, PARTIES** to attend or hold a social gathering

PARVE *adj* without either meat or milk products; *also* **PAREVE**

PARVO *n pl* **-S** a contagious disease of dogs and other animals; a parvovirus

PASEO *n pl* **-S** a leisurely walk in the evening; stroll

PASES *n pl of* **PASE** movements of a matador's cape

PASHA *n* the title of a Turkish officer of high rank; *also* **PACHA**

PASSE *adj* out-of-date; old-fashioned

PASTA *n pl* **-S** dough formed into various shapes, cooked as part of a dish or in boiling water and served with a savory sauce

PASTE *v* **-D, PASTING, -S** to cause to adhere with a sticky mixture

PASTS *n pl of* **PAST** the times before the present or the events that happened during that time

PASTY *adj* **PASTIER, PASTIEST** pale and unhealthy in appearance; pallid

PATCH *v* **-ED, -ING, -ES** to cover or mend a hole in something or to strengthen a weak place using cloth or a pasty substance

PATED *adj* having a pate, or head

PATEN *n pl* **-S** a metal disk or plate used to carry the bread at the celebration of the Christian Communion; *also* **PATIN**

PATER *n pl* **-S** BRIT. father

PATES *n pl of* **PATE** [obs] the tops or crowns of heads

PATHS *n pl of* **PATH** trodden ways; footways; tracks

PATIN *n pl* **-S** a metal disk or plate used to carry the bread at the celebration of the Christian Communion; *also* **PATEN**

PATIO *n pl* **-S** a paved outdoor area adjoining a house

PATLY *adv* fitly; seasonably

PATSY *n pl* **PATSIES** a person upon whom the blame for something falls

PATTY *n pl* **PATTIES** a small flat individual cake made from ground or chopped meat, vegetables or other food

PAUSE *v* **-D, PAUSING, -S** to stop temporarily

PAVAN *n pl* **-ES** a slow, stately dance popular in the 16th and 17th centuries; *also* **PAVIN**

PAVED *v p t of* **PAVE** laid or covered with material, as asphalt or concrete, that formed a firm level surface for travel

PAVER *n pl* **-S** one who paves, lays or covers asphalt or concrete

PAVES *v pr t of* **PAVE** lays or covers with material, as asphalt or concrete, that forms a firm level surface for travel

PAVID *adj* fearful; afraid; timid

PAVIN *n* a slow, stately dance popular in the 16th and 17th centuries; *also* **PAVAN**

PAVIS *n pl* **-ES** a large medieval shield; *also* **PAVISE, PAVISSE**

PAWED *v p t of* **PAW** to have struck out with the paws or feet, or touched somebody clumsily

PAWER *n pl* **-S** one who strikes out with the paws or feet, or touches somebody clumsily

PAWKY *adj* BRIT. witty or shrewd in a dry or sly manner

PAWLS *n pl of* **PAWL** hinged catches that fit into a notch of a ratchet to prevent reverse motion

PAWNS *v pr t of* **PAWN** borrows and leaves an article as security for repayment of the loan

PAYED *v p part of* **PAY** gave money, usually in exchange for goods or services

PAYEE *n pl* **-S** one to whom money is paid

PAYER *n pl* **-S** one that pays; *also* **PAYOR**

PAYOR *n pl* **-S** one that pays; *also* **PAYER**

PEACE *v* **-D, PEACING, -S** [obs] to be or become silent

PEACH *v* **-ED, -ING, -ES** to inform against someone; turn informer

PEAGE *n* wampum, small cylindrical beds made from polished shells; *also* **PEAG, WAMPUM**

PEAGS *n pl of* **PEAG** wampum, small cylindrical beads made from polished shells

PEAKS *v pr t of* **PEAK** reaches a highest point or maximum

PEAKY *adj* **PEAKIER, PEAKIEST** slightly ill, often looking pale; *also* **PEAKED**

PEALS *v pr t of* **PEAL** sounds loudly and sonorously

PEANS *n pl of* **PEAN** fervent expressions of joy or praise; *also* **PAEANS**

PEARL *v* **-ED, -ING, -S** to adorn with pearls, small spheres that form some mollusks and are used as gems

PEARS *n pl of* **PEAR** teardrop shaped sweet juicy fruits with firm white flesh

PEART *adj* **-ER, -EST** lively and brisk

PEASE *n pl* **-S, -N** [obs] a pea, a green seed eaten as a vegetable; *also* **PESE, PEASES, PEASEN**

PEATS *n pl of* **PEAT** partially carbonized vegetable matter, usually mosses, found in bogs and used as fertilizer and fuel

PEATY *adj* of or pertaining to peat, partially carbonized vegetable matter

PEAVY *n pl* **PEAVIES** a lever used to move logs; *also* **PEAVEY**

PEBAS *n pl* **-S** types of armadillos

PECAN *n pl* **-S** a nut-bearing hickory tree

PECHS *n pl of* **PECH** short, fast and forceful breaths

PECKS *v pr t of* **PECK** strikes with the beak or a pointed instrument

PECKY *adj* marked by decay caused by fungi

PEDAL *v* **-ED** or **-LED, -ING** or **-LING, -S** to operate by means of foot levers

PEDES *n pl of* **PES** feet or foot-like parts

PEDRO *n pl* **-S** the five of trumps in certain card games

PEEKS *v pr t of* **PEEK** looks quickly or furtively

PEELS *v pr t of* **PEEL** strips off an outer layer of

PEENS *v pr t of* **PEEN** hammers, bends or shapes with the round-edged end to the head of a hammer; *also* **PEINS**

PEEPS *v pr t of* **PEEP** makes high-pitched sounds; chirps

PEERS *v pr t of* **PEER** looks intently, searchingly, or with difficulty

PEEVE *v* **-D, PEEVING, -S** to annoy, irritate

PEINS *v pr t of* **PEIN** hammers, bends or shapes with the round-edged end to the head of a hammer; *also* **PEENS**

PEISE *v* **-D, PEISING** [obs] to weigh

PEKAN *n pl* **-S** a fisher, a carnivorous North American mammal with thick, dark-brown fur; *also* **WEJACK**

PEKIN *n* a striped silk material

PEKOE *n pl* **-S** a high-quality black tea

PELFS *n pl of* **PELF** [obs] money or wealth, especially when gained dishonestly

PELLS *n* skins or hides; pelts

PELTS *v pr t of* **PELT** bombards with many blows or missiles

PENAL *adj* pertaining to punishment, penalties or punitive institutions

PENCE *n pl of* **PENNY** coins that are worth one cent in the United States and Canada

PENDS *v pr t of* **PEND** is undecided; is in process of adjustment

PENES *n pl of* **PENIS** external male organs of copulation

PENGO *n pl* **-S** a former monetary unit of Hungary

PENIS *n pl* **-ES** or **PENES** the external male organs of copulation

PENNA *n pl* **-E** a contour feather of a bird

PENNE *n/pl* short tubular pasta cut diagonally at the ends

PENNI *n pl* **-S, -A** a formerly used Finnish coin

PENNY *n pl* **PENNIES** or **PENCE** a coin that is worth one cent in the United States and Canada

PEONS *n pl of* **PEON** laborers who are obliged to do menial work; *also* **PEONES**

PEONY *n pl* **PEONIES** a flowering plant

PEPLA *n pl of* **PEPLUM** a short section attached to the waistline of a garment; *also* **PEPLUMS**

PEPOS *n pl of* **PEPO** any fleshy gourd fruits with a hard rind and many seeds, as melons or squash

PEPPY *adj* **PEPPIER, PEPPIEST** full of or characterized by energy and high spirits; lively

PERCH *v* **-ED, -ING, -ES** to sit or rest on an elevated place

PERDU *n* [obs] a soldier sent on an especially dangerous mission; *also* **PERDUE**

PERDY *interj* [obs] indeed; *also* **PARDE, PARDI, PARDY, PARDIE, PERDIE**

PERES *n pl of* **PERE** [obs] a Middle English form of pears

PERIL *v* **-ED** or **-LED, -ING** or **-LING, -S** to expose to danger or the chance of injury; imperil

PERIS *n pl of* **PERI** in Persian mythology, beautiful supernatural beings descended from the fallen angels

PERKS *v pr t of* **PERK** prepares coffee

PERKY *adj* **PERKIER, PERKIEST** self-confident; sprightly or lively;

PERMS *v pr t of* **PERM** gives hair a permanent wave

PERNS *v pr t of* **PERN** [obs] takes profit of; makes profitable

PERPS *n pl of* **PERP** informal for ones who perpetrate a crime

PERRY *n pl* **PERRIES** fermented pear juice often made sparkling

PERSE *n* dark grayish blue or purple

PESES *n pl of* **PESE** [obs] peas, green seeds eaten as vegetables; *also* **PEASE, PEASEN, PESE**

PESKY *adj* **PESKIER, PESKIEST** troublesome; annoying

PESOS *n pl of* **PESO** units of currency in several Spanish speaking countries

PESTO *n pl* **-S** a sauce of basil, garlic and olive oil

PESTS *n pl of* **PEST** annoying people or things; nuisances

PESTY *adj* annoying

PETAL *n pl* **-S** one of the often brightly colored leaves of the corolla of a flower

PETER *v* **-ED, -ING, -S** diminish or come to an end gradually

PETIT *adj* lesser; minor; petty

PETTI *n pl* **-S** a woman's petticoat; a light, loose undergarment in the form of a skirt or dress

PETTO *n* the breast

PETTY *adj* **PETTIER, PETTIEST** of little importance; narrow-minded in nature

PEWEE *n pl* **-S** small fly-catching birds; *also* **PEEWEE**

PEWIT *n pl* **-S** a lapwing, a long-legged bird that is noted for its shrill cry and erratic flight; *also* **PEEWIT**

PHAGE *n pl* **-S** a kind of virus which acts as a parasite of bacteria, infecting them and reproducing inside them; bacteriophage

PHASE *v* **-D, PHASING, -S** to plan or carry out in gradual stages

PHIAL *n pl* **-S** a small glass bottle; *also* **VIAL**

PHLOX *n pl* **-S** a plant with dense clusters of colorful scented flowers

PHONE *v* **-D, PHONING, -S** to telephone; to call

PHONO *n pl* **-S** a record player

PHONS *n pl of* **PHON** units of apparent loudness

PHONY *adj* **PHONIER, PHONIEST** not genuine; *also* **PHONEY**

PHOTO *v* **-ED, -ING, -S** to photograph or take pictures

PHOTS *n pl of* **PHOT** units of illumination

PHUTS *n pl of* **PHUT** sounds like small explosions or sudden expulsions of air

PHYLA *n pl of* **PHYLON** or **PHYLUM** principal taxonomic categories in biology that ranks above class and below kingdom

PHYLE *n pl* **PHYLAE** a political subdivision in ancient Greece

PIANO *n pl* **-S** a musical instrument with a manual keyboard

PIANS *n pl of* **PIAN** highly infectious diseases of tropical climates; *also* **FRAMBESIAS**

PIBAL *n* observation by means of pilot balloon, a small balloon sent up to determine the direction and velocity of the wind

PICAS *n pl of* **PICA** units of measurement for printing type sizes and line lengths

PICKS *v pr t of* **PICK** selects carefully from a group

PICKY *adj* **PICKIER, PICKIEST** excessively fussy or fastidious

PICOT *v* **-ED, -ING, -S** to trim with small embroidered loops

PICUL *n pl* **-S** unit of weight used in southeast Asia and China

PIECE *v* **-D, PIECING, -S** to assemble from individual parts

PIERS *n pl of* **PIER** projecting wharves or landing places

PIETA *n pl* **-S** a representation of the Virgin Mary mourning over the dead body of Jesus

PIETS *n pl of* **PIET** magpies; dippers, or water ouzels; *also* **PYETS**

PIETY *n pl* **PIETIES** the quality or state of being pious or reverent

PIGGY *n pl* **PIGGIES** a small pig

PIGMY *n pl* **PIGMIES** a small person; *also* **PYGMY**

PIING *v pr t of* **PI** spilling or throwing type or type matter into disorder

PIKAS *n pl of* **PIKA** small short-eared burrowing mammals that are related to the rabbit

PIKED *v p t of* **PIKE** pierced or wounded with a sharp point or spike

PIKER *n pl* **-S** a stingy person; a gambler who makes only small bets

PIKES *v pr t of* **PIKE** pierces or wounds with a sharp point or spike

PILAF *n pl* **-S** a seasoned rice dish; *also* **PILAU, PILAW, PILAFF**

PILAR *adj* of, relating to, or covered with hair

PILAU *n pl* **-S** a seasoned rice dish; *also* **PILAF, PILAW, PILAFF**

PILAW *n pl* **-S** a seasoned rice dish; *also* **PILAF, PILAU, PILAFF**

PILEA *n pl of* **PILEUM** the top of a bird's head

PILED *v p t of* **PILE** heaped or stacked things one on top of the other

PILEI *n pl of* **PILEUS** the top cap-shaped part of a mushroom or other fungus

PILES *v pr t of* **PILE** heaps or stacks things one on top of the other

PILIS *n pl of* **PILI** Philippine trees and their edible nuts

PILLS *v pr t of* **PILL** becomes covered in small balls of matted fiber because of rubbing fabrics

PILOT *v* **-ED, -ING, -S** to control the course of; guide

PILUS *n pl* **PILI** a hair or hair-like structure

PINCH *v* **-ED, -ING, -ES** to squeeze between two surfaces

PINED *v p t of* **PINE** yearned intensely and persistently, especially for something unattainable

PINES *v pr t of* **PINE** yearns intensely and persistently, especially for something unattainable

PINEY *adj* **PINIER, PINIEST** relating to or resembling pine trees; *also* **PINY**

PINGO *n* a mound of soil-covered ice forced up by the pressure of water in permafrost

PINGS *v pr t of* **PING** makes a sharp, high-pitched, metallic sound

PINKS *v pr t of* **PINK** cuts fabric with pinking shears to make a zigzag edge that will not easily fray

PINKY *n pl* **PINKIES** the little finger; *also* **PINKIE**

PINNA *n pl* **-S, -E** a feather, wing, fin or similarly shaped appendage

PINNY *n pl* **PINNIES** informal for a pinafore; apron

PINON *n pl* **-S, -ES** a small sweet nut produced by a pine tree

PINOT *n pl* **-S** a red or white grape; wine made from these grapes

PINTA *n* a contagious skin disease of the tropics

PINTO *n pl* **-S, -ES** a horse with patchy markings of white and another color

PINTS *n pl of* **PINT** units of liquid and dry measure

PINUP *n pl* **-S** something intended to be affixed to a wall

PIONS *n pl of* **PION** subatomic particles

PIOUS *adv* **-LY, -NESS** marked by religious reverence; devout

PIPAL *n pl* **-S** a fig tree native to India; bo tree; *also* **PEEPUL**

PIPED *v p t of* **PIPE** conveyed through a tube

PIPER *n pl* **-S** a person who plays on a pipe or bagpipes

PIPES *v pr t of* **PIPE** conveys through a tube

PIPET *v* **-TED, -TING, -S** to pour or draw off liquid with a calibrated tube; *also* **PIPETTE**

PIPIT *n pl* **-S** small long-tailed songbird; *also* **TITLARK**

PIQUE *v* **-D, PIQUING, -S** to stimulate interest or curiosity

PIRIE *n* [obs] a pear tree; *also* **PERY, PYRIE**

PIRNS *n pl of* **PIRN** bobbins or spools of weavers' shuttles

PIROG *n pl* **-I** a large rectangular pie filled with meat, vegetables

PISCO *n pl* **-S** a brandy made in Peru

PISOS *n pl of* **PISO** units of currency in the Philippines

PISTE *n pl* **-S** a downhill ski trail

249

PITAS *n pl of* **PITA** flat hollow unleavened bread which can be split open to hold a filling

PITCH *v* **-ED, -ING, -ES** to throw, usually with a particular objective or toward a particular point

PITHS *v pr t of* **PITH** removes the soft central cylinder of the stems from most flowering plants

PITHY *adj* **PITHIER, PITHIEST** brief and to the point, often with an element of wit

PITON *n pl* **-S** a peg or spike driven into a crack to support a climber or a rope

PITTA *n pl* **-S** a perching bird of Asia, Australia, and Africa

PIVOT *v* **-ED, -ING, -S** to cause to rotate, revolve or turn

PIXEL *n pl* **-S** the basic unit of a video screen image

PIXIE *n pl* **-S** fairies or elves; *also* **PIXY**

PIXES *n pl of* **PIX** in the Christian Church, the containers in which the consecrated bread of the Eucharist are kept; *also* **PYXES**

PIZZA *n pl* **-S** a flat round piece of bread dough baked with a variety of toppings, often including tomato sauce and cheese

PLACE *v* **-D, PLACING, -S** to put in a particular position or situation

PLACK *n pl* **-S** a former coin of Scotland

PLAGE *n pl* **-S** a sandy beach at a seaside resort

PLAID *n pl* **-S** cloth with a tartan or checked pattern

PLAIN *adj* **-ER, -EST** free from obstructions; open; clear

PLAIT *v* **-ED, -ING, -S** to braid or interweave the strands or locks of; *also* **PLAT**

PLANE *v* **-D, PLANING, -S** to make smooth or even; level

PLANK *v* **-ED, -ING, -S** to broil and serve on a wooden board

PLANS *v pr t of* **PLAN** works out in advance how something is to be done or organized

PLANT *v* **-ED, -ING, -S** to put into soil to grow

PLASH *v* **-ED, -ING, -ES** to move in or through something liquid, scattering drops and making light splashing sounds

PLASM *n pl* **-S** the clear, yellowish portion of blood, lymph or milk; *also* **PLASMA**

PLATE *v* **-D, PLATING, -S** to coat with a thin layer of metal

PLATS *v pr t of* **PLAT** braids or interweaves the strands or locks of; *also* **PLAITS**

PLATY *n pl* **-S, PLATIES** brightly colored freshwater fish

PLAYA *n pl* **-S** the bottom of an undrained desert basin

PLAYS *v pr t of* **PLAY** engages in sport or amusing activities

PLAZA *n pl* **-S** a public square or marketplace

PLEAD *v* **-ED** or **PLED, -ING, -S** to appeal earnestly, beg

PLEAS *n pl of* **PLEA** urgent, often emotional, requests

PLEAT *v* **-ED, -ING, -S** to press or fold in an even manner

PLEBE *n pl* **-S** a freshman at a military or naval academy

PLEBS *n pl of* **PLEB** commoners; plebeians

PLENA *n pl* **-S** a Puerto Rican song style that features duple meter and syncopation with narrative, often satirical lyrics

PLEON *n pl* **-S** the abdomen of a crustacean

PLEWS *n pl of* **PLEW** beaver skins

PLICA *n pl* **-E** a fold or ridge, as of skin, membrane or shell

PLIED *v p t of* **PLY** used something such as a tool or weapon in a diligent or skillful way

PLIER *n pl* **-S** one who plies a trade; *also* **PLYER**

LIES *v pr t of* **PLY** uses something such as a tool or weapon in a diligent or skillful way

LINK *v* **-ED, -ING, -S** to make a tinkling sound

LODS *v pr t of* **PLOD** walks heavily or slowly; trudges

LONK *v* **-ED, -ING, -S** to strum or pluck; *also* **PLUNK**

LOPS *v pr t of* **PLOP** falls with a sound like that of an object falling into water without splashing

LOTS *v pr t of* **PLOT** makes a secret plan, especially to do something illegal or subversive with others

PLOTZ *v* **-ED, -ING, -ES** to be overcome with emotion

PLOWS *v pr t of* **PLOW** breaks up soil and turns it over into furrows

PLOYS *n pl of* **PLOY** cunning maneuvers to gain an advantage

PLUCK *v* **-ED, -ING, -S** to remove or detach by grasping and pulling abruptly with the fingers; pick

PLUGS *v pr t of* **PLUG** closes up a hole or gap

PLUMB *v* **-ED, -ING, -S** to determine the depth of

PLUME *v* **-D, PLUMING, -S** to decorate or cover with feathers

PLUMP *v* **-ED, -ING, -S** to make well-rounded, full in form

PLUMS *n pl of* **PLUM** round or oval smooth-skinned fruit, usually red or purple, containing a flattened pit

PLUMY *adj* **PLUMIER, PLUMIEST** having or resembling plumes; feathery

PLUNK *v* **-ED, -ING, -S** to strum or pluck; *also* **PLONK**

PLUSH *adj* **-ER, -EST** made of or covered with a fabric with a soft, thick, deep pile; luxurious

PLYER *n pl* **-S** one who plies a trade; *also* **PLIER**

POACH *v* **-ED, -ING, -ES** to cook by simmering in a small amount of liquid

POAKE *n pl* **-S** [obs] waste matter from the preparation of skins, consisting of hair, lime, oil; *also* **POAK**

POBOY *n pl* **-S** a large sandwich on a long split roll

POCKS *v pr t of* **POCK** marks with scars left in the skin by pustules caused by eruptive diseases; pits

POCKY *adj* of, like, or covered with pocks

PODGY *adj* **PODGIER, PODGIEST** BRIT. short and plump; chubby; *also* **PUDGY**

PODIA *n pl of* **PODIUM** elevated platforms; lecterns; *also* **PODIUMS**

POEMS *n pl of* **POEM** compositions in verse, usually written in certain measures

POESY *n pl* **POESIES** [obs] poetry; the art or skill of writing poetry

POETS *n pl of* **POET** writers of poetry, compositions in verse

POGEY *n pl* **-S, POGIES** informal for unemployment insurance, in Canada

POILU *n pl* **-S** informal for a French soldier, especially in World War I

POIND *v* **-ED, -ING, -S** SCOT. to seize the goods of a debtor so that they can be sold to pay a debt

POINT *v* **-ED, -ING, -S** to indicate direction with one's finger

POISE *v* **-D, POISING, -S** to balance; keep steady

POKED *v p t of* **POKE** jabbed or prodded with a finger or a sharp object

POKER *n pl* **-S** a rod, usually of iron, for stirring a fire

POKES *v pr t of* **POKE** jabs or prods with a finger or a sharp object

POKEY *n pl* **-S, POKIES** informal for a jail; *also* **POKY**

POLAR *adj* directly opposite in character or tendency

POLED *v p t of* **POLE** propelled with a long slender usually cylindrical object

POLER *n pl* **-S** somebody who uses a pole to move a boat along

POLES *v pr t of* **POLE** propels with a long slender usually cylindrical object

POLIO *n pl* **-S** an infectious viral disease that can cause paralysis; poliomyelitis

POLKA *v* **-ED, -ING, -S** to perform a lively dance in couples consisting of three quick steps and a hop

POLLS *v pr t of* **POLL** samples the opinions or attitudes of a group of people systematically

POLOI *n pl of* **POLOS** tall, cylindrical headdresses worn by women in ancient Greece

POLOS *n pl* **POLOI** a tall, cylindrical headdress worn by women in ancient Greece

POLYP *n pl* **-S** a coelenterate having a cylindrical body and an oral opening usually surrounded by tentacles, as the sea anemone

POLYS *n pl of* **POLY** informal for polymerized plastics or something made of them, especially polyester fabrics

POMES *n pl of* **POME** fleshy fruits that have a central core typically containing five seeds, such as an apple or pear

POMOS *n pl of* **POMO** informal for postmodernists or Postmodernism

POMPS *n pl of* **POMP** displays of great splendor and magnificence, sometimes ostentatious

PONDS *n pl of* **POND** fairly small bodies of still water

PONES *n pl of* **PONE** cakes of cornbread baked on a griddle or in hot ashes; *also* **CORNPONES, JOHNNYCAKES**

PONGS *v pr t of* **PONG** BRIT. stinks

PONTS *n pl of* **PONT** flat-bottomed ferryboats, in South Africa

POOCH *v* **-ED, -ING, -ES** to bulge; protrude

POODS *n pl of* **POOD** Russian units of weight

POOED *v p t of* **POO** defecated

POOJA *n pl* **-S** a Hindu ceremonial offering; *also* **PUJA, PUJAH,** or **POOJAH**

POOLS *v pr t of* **POOL** puts together; contributes to a common fund

POONS *n pl of* **POON** East Indian trees

POOPS *v pr t of* **POOP** informal term meaning becomes fatigued; tires

POORI *n pl* **-S** a puffy fried wheat cake of India; *also* **PURI**

POPES *n pl of* **POPE** the heads of the Roman Catholic Church; ones who resemble a pope, an authority

POPPA *n pl* **-S** an informal term for a father; *also* **PAPA**

POPPY *n pl* **POPPIES** a flowering plant

POPSY *n pl* **POPSIES** BRIT. a girl or young woman

PORCH *n pl* **-ES** a covered entrance to a building

PORED *v p t of* **PORE** read or studied carefully and attentively

PORES *v pr t of* **PORE** reads or studies carefully and attentively

PORGY *n pl* **PORGIES** a marine food fish

PORKS *v pr t of* **PORK** eats ravenously; gorges oneself

PORKY *adj* **PORKIER, PORKIEST** fat or corpulent

PORTS *v pr t of* **PORT** moves or turns to the left-hand side of a ship, boat or airplane as one faces forward

OSED *v p t of* **POSE** assumed a fixed position or posture

OSER *n pl* **-S** one who behaves affectedly in order to impress; *also* **POSEUR**

OSES *v pr t of* **POSE** assumes a fixed position or posture

OSEY *adj* **POSIER, POSIEST** informal for pretentious

OSIT *v* **-ED, -ING, -S** to assume the existence of; postulate

OSSE *n pl* **-S** a group of people summoned by a sheriff to aid in law enforcement

OSTS *v pr t of* **POST** mails a letter or package

OTSY *n pl* **POTSIES** a children's game, similar to hopscotch

OTTO *n pl* **-S** a nocturnal slow-moving arboreal African lemur

OTTY *adj* **POTTIER, POTTIEST** of little importance

OUCH *v* **-ED, -ING, -ES** to put something into a small soft bag

OUFS *n pl of* **POUF** bouffant or fluffy parts of a garment or accessory; *also* **POUFFES**

OULT *n pl* **-S** any young fowl, especially a turkey

OUND *v* **-ED, -ING, -S** to strike repeatedly and forcefully

OURS *v pr t of* **POUR** causes to flow in a stream

OUTS *v pr t of* **POUT** shows displeasure by thrusting out the lips or wearing a sullen expression

OUTY *adj* **POUTIER, POUTIEST** sulky; expressive of displeasure

OWER *v* **-ED, -ING, -S** to supply with the energy needed to operate

OXED *v p t of* **POX** infected with a viral disease characterized by pustules or eruptions, such as smallpox or syphilis

OXES *v pr t of* **POX** infects with a viral disease characterized by pustules or eruptions, such as smallpox or syphilis

POYOU *n pl* **-S** a South American armadillo

PRAAM *n pl* **-S** a flat-bottomed fishing boat or barge; *also* **PRAM**

PRADS *n pl of* **PRAD** AUS. informal for horses

PRAHU *n pl* **-S** a swift Malayan sailboat; *also* **PRAO, PRAU, PROA**

PRAMS *n pl of* **PRAM** flat-bottomed fishing boats or barges; *also* **PRAAMS**

PRANG *v* **-ED, -ING, -S** BRIT. to crash a motor vehicle or aircraft

PRANK *v* **-ED, -ING, -S** to dress or adorn gaily or showily

PRAOS *n pl of* **PRAO** swift Malayan sailboats; *also* **PRAUS, PROAS, PRAHUS**

PRASE *n pl* **-S** a translucent, greenish variety of quartz

PRATE *v* **-D, PRATING, -S** to talk idly and at length; chatter

PRATS *n pl of* **PRAT** informal term for buttocks

PRAUS *n pl of* **PRAU** swift Malayan sailboats; *also* **PRAOS, PROAS, PRAHUS**

PRAWN *v* **-ED, -ING, -S** to fish for prawns, crustaceans resembling large shrimp

PRAYS *v pr t of* **PRAY** makes a fervent request or entreaty

PREED *v p t of* **PREE** SCOT. tasted tentatively; sampled

PREEN *v* **-ED, -ING, -S** to dress or groom with elaborate care; primp

PREPS *v pr t of* **PREP** prepares; makes ready

PRESA *n pl* **PRESE** a sign showing where each successive voice enters in a musical canon

PRESE *n pl of* **PRESA** signs showing where each successive voice enters in a musical canon

PRESS *v* **-ED, -ING, -ES** to exert steady weight or force against

PREST *v* [obs] to give as a loan; to lend

253

PREXY *n pl* **PREXIES** informal for a president, especially of a college or university; *also* **PREX**

PREYS *v pr t of* **PREY** takes advantage of; exploits

PRICE *v* **-D, PRICING, -S** to decide how much something costs

PRICK *v* **-ED, -ING, -S** to puncture lightly

PRICY *adj* **PRICIER, PRICIEST** costly; expensive; *also* **PRICEY**

PRIDE *v* **-D, PRIDING, -S** to be proud of something

PRIED *v p t of* **PRY** looked or inquired closely

PRIER *n pl* **-S** one who pries; an inquisitive person; *also* **PRYER**

PRIES *v pr t of* **PRY** looks or inquires closely

PRIGS *n pl of* **PRIG** people who are annoyingly smug about their moral behavior, attitudes

PRILL *v* **-ED, -ING, -S** to make a solid into granules or pellets that flow freely and do not clump together

PRIMA *adj* indicating the most important performer or role

PRIME *v* **-D, PRIMING, -S** to make ready; prepare

PRIMI *n pl of* **PRIMO** the principal parts in duets or ensemble compositions; *also* **PRIMOS**

PRIMO *n pl* **PRIMI, -S** the principal part in a duet or ensemble composition

PRIMP *v* **-ED, -ING, -S** to dress or groom oneself with elaborate care; preen

PRIMS *v pr t of* **PRIM** makes precise or proper to the point of affectation, as in facial expression or dress

PRINK *v* **-ED, -ING, -S** to adorn in a showy manner

PRINT *v* **-ED, -ING, -S** to press onto or into a surface

PRION *n pl* **-S** a microscopic protein particle

PRIOR *n pl* **-S** an officer in a monastery of a rank below abbot

PRISE *v* **-D, PRISING, -S** to press, force or move with a lever; pry; *also* **PRIZE**

PRISM *n pl* **-S** a piece of glass or other transparent material of regular shape, used to separate white light into a spectrum of colors

PRISS *n pl* **-ES** someone who behaves in a very prudish and proper way

PRIVY *n pl* **PRIVIES** an outdoor toilet; outhouse

PRIZE *v* **-D, PRIZING, -D** to press, force, or move with a lever; pry; *also* **PRISE**

PROAS *n pl of* **PROA** swift Malayan sailboats; *also* **PRAOS, PRAUS, PRAHUS**

PROBE *v* **-D, PROBING, -S** to delve into; investigate

PRODS *v pr t of* **PROD** pokes with a finger or pointed object

PROEM *n pl* **-S** an introduction; a preface

PROFS *n pl of* **PROF** informal for professors

PROGS *v pr t of* **PROG** prowls about, as in search of food or plunder; forages

PROLE *n pl* **-S** a member of the working class; proletariat

PROMO *n pl* **-S** a promotional presentation or personal appearance

PROMS *n pl of* **PROM** formal dances for high-school or college students, usually held at the end of the school year

PRONE *adj* lying with the front or face downward

PRONG *v* **-ED, -ING, -S** to pierce with something sharp

PROOF *v* **-ED, -ING, -S** to make something capable of resisting harm, injury or damage

PROPS *v pr t of* **PROP** supports by placing something beneath or against; shores up

PROSE *v* **-D, PROSING, -S** to speak or write in a dull, tiresome style

PROSO *n pl* **-S** a cereal grass; *also* **MILLET**

PROST *interj* to your health; used as a toast; *also* **PROSIT**

PROSY *adj* **PROSIER, PROSIEST** matter of fact and dry; prosaic

PROUD *adj* **-ER, -EST** feeling pleased and satisfied

PROVE *v* **-D** or **-N, PROVING, S** to establish the truth of something

PROWL *v* **-ED, -ING, -S** to roam an area stealthily for prey

PROWS *n pl of* **PROW** front parts of vessels; the bows

PROXY *n pl* **PROXIES** a person authorized to act for another

PRUDE *n pl* **-S** one who is excessively concerned with being or appearing to be proper, modest or righteous

PRUNE *v* **-D, PRUNING, -S** to reduce something by removing unwanted material

PRUTA *n pl* **PRUTOT, PRUTOTH** a former monetary unit of Israel; *also* **PRUTAH**

PRYER *n pl* **-S** one who pries; an inquisitive person; *also* **PRIER**

PSALM *n pl* **-S** a sacred song or poem of praise

PSEUD *n pl* **-S** BRIT. a pretentious person; a poseur

PSHAW *interj* used to indicate disbelief, impatience or contempt

PSOAE *n pl of* **PSOAS** loin muscles that rotate the hip joint and flex the spine; *also* **PSOAI**

PSOAI *n pl of* **PSOAS** loin muscles that rotate the hip joint and flex the spine; *also* **PSOAE**

PSOAS *n pl* **PSOAE, PSOAI** either of two loin muscles that rotate the hip joint and flex the spine

PSYCH *v* **-ED, -ING, -S** to cause to be disturbed mentally or excited emotionally

PUBES *n pl of* **PUBIS** the pair of bones forming the two sides of the pelvis

PUBIC *adj* pertaining to the pubes or pubis

PUBIS *n pl* **PUBES** either of a pair of bones forming the two sides of the pelvis

PUCES *n pl of* **PUCE** dark red or purple-brown colors

PUCKA *adj* genuine; authentic; *also* **PUKKA**

PUCKS *v pr t of* **PUCK** in the Irish sport of hurling, strikes the ball

PUDGY *adj* **PUDGIER, PUDGIEST** short and plump; chubby; *also* **PODGY**

PUDIC *adj* of or relating to the external human genitalia

PUDUS *n pl of* **PUDU** very small deer native to the Chilean Andes

PUFFS *v pr t of* **PUFF** blows quickly in short blasts

PUFFY *adj* **PUFFIER, PUFFIEST** swollen

PUGGY *adj* **PUGGIER, PUGGIEST** N.Z. sticky; claylike

PUING *v pr part* of **PUE** [obs] making a low whistling sound; chirping, as birds

PUITS *n pl of* **PUIT** [obs] wells; small streams; fountains; springs

PUJAH *n pl* **-S** a Hindu ceremonial offering; *also* **PUJA, POOJA, or POOJAH**

PUJAS *n pl of* **PUJA** Hindu ceremonial offerings; *also* **POOJAS, PUJAHS, or POOJAHS**

PUKAS *n pl of* **PUKA** small white shells found on Pacific, especially Hawaiian, beaches and strung in clusters to make necklaces

PUKED *v p t of* **PUKE** vomited

PUKES *v pr t of* **PUKE** vomits

PUKKA *adj* genuine; authentic; *also* **PUCKA**

PUKUS *n pl of* **PUKU** African antelopes related to the waterbuck

PULED *v p t of* **PULE** whined, whimpered or cried plaintively

PULER *adj* one who whines or complains; a weak person

PULES *v pr t of* **PULE** whines, whimpers or cries plaintively

PULLS *v pr t of* **PULL** applies force so as to draw or tend to draw a person or thing toward the origin of the force

PULPS *v pr t of* **PULP** reduces to a soft moist shapeless mass of matter

PULPY *adj* **PULPIER, PULPIEST** of or like pulp; soft; fleshy

PULSE *v* **-D, PULSING, -S** to beat rhythmically

PUMAS *n pl of* **PUMA** large American wild cats; mountain lions

PUMPS *v pr t of* **PUMP** forces a liquid or gas to flow

PUNAS *n pl of* **PUNA** cold, arid plateaus high in the Andes

PUNCH *v* **-ED, -ING, -ES** to hit with a sharp blow or fist

PUNGS *n pl of* **PUNG** low boxlike sleighs drawn by one horse

PUNJI *n pl* **-S** a very sharp bamboo stake

PUNKA *n pl* **-S** a fan used especially in India; *also* **PUNKAH**

PUNKS *n pl of* **PUNK** informal for young people, especially members of a rebellious counterculture group

PUNKY *n pl* **PUNKIES** minute, biting flies; *also* **PUNKIE**

PUNNY *adj* **PUNNIER, PUNNIEST** constituting or involving a pun, a play on words that involves a word or phrase with more than one possible meaning

PUNTO *n pl* **-S** a point or hit in fencing

PUNTS *v pr t of* **PUNT** travels or conveys in a long flat-bottomed boat used in shallow waters and propelled by a long pole

PUNTY *n pl* **PUNTIES** an iron rod on which molten glass is handled when being shaped and worked; *also* **PONTIL**

PUPAE *n pl of* **PUPA** insects at the stage between a larva and an adult in metamorphosis during which they are in a cocoon or case, and undergo internal changes; *also* **PUPAS**

PUPAL *adj* of the insects in the chrysalis or post larval stage

PUPAS *n pl of* **PUPA** insects at the stage between a larva and an adult in metamorphosis during which they are in a cocoon or case, and undergo internal changes; *also* **PUPAE**

PUPIL *n pl* **-S** a person who is taught by another; a schoolchild

PUPPY *n pl* **PUPPIES** a young dog

PUPUS *n pl of* **PUPU** hot or cold usually bite-size Hawaiian appetizers

PURDA *n* the Hindu and Islamic custom of keeping women fully covered with clothing and apart from the rest of society; *also* **PARDAH, PURDAH**

PUREE *v* **-D, -ING, -S** to crush food into a thick, soft sauce

PURER *adj* more free from mixture or contamination

PURGE *v* **-D, PURGING, -S** to free from impurities; purify

PURIS *n pl of* **PURI** puffy fried wheat cakes of India; *also* **POORIS**

PURLS *v pr t of* **PURL** knits with a purl stitch, usually made with the yarn at the front of the work by inserting the right needle into the front of a loop on the left needle

PURRS *v pr t of* **PURR** utters a low, murmuring, continued sound, as a cat does when pleased; *also* **PURS**

PURSE *v* **-D, PURSING, -S** to gather into wrinkles or folds; pucker

PURSY *adj* **PURSIER, PURSIEST** short-winded, especially from being obese

PURTY *adj* **PURTIER, PURTIEST** variant of pretty

PUSHY *adj* **PUSHIER, PUSHIEST** disagreeably aggressive or forward

PUSSY *n pl* **PUSSIES** informal for a cat or kitten

PUTTI *n pl of* **PUTTO** representations of a small child, used especially in the art of the European Renaissance

PUTTO *n pl* **PUTTI** a representation of a small child, used especially in the art of the European Renaissance

PUTTS *v pr t of* **PUTT** strikes a golf ball gently so that it rolls into or near a hole

PUTTY *v* **PUTTIED, -ING, PUTTIES** to fill, cover or secure with putty, a dough-like cement

PYETS *n pl of* **PYET** magpies; dippers, or water ouzels; *also* **PIETS**

PYGMY *n pl* **PYGMIES** a small person; *also* **PIGMY**

PYINS *n pl of* **PYIN** albuminous constituents of pus

PYLAS *n pl of* **PYLA** passages between the iter and optocoele in the brain

PYLON *n pl* **-S** a steel tower supporting high-tension wires

PYOID *adj* of or like pus, a viscous fluid produced by infection

PYRAN *n pl* **-S** either of two cyclic compounds

PYRES *n pl of* **PYRE** heaps of combustible material

PYRIC *adj* of, relating to, or resulting from burning

PYRIE *n* [obs] a pear tree; *also* **PERY, PIRIE**

PYROS *n pl of* **PYRO** informal for people who have a compulsion to set fires; pyromaniacs

PYXES *n pl of* **PYX** in the Christian Church, the containers in which the consecrated bread of the Eucharist is kept; *also* **PIXES**

PYXIE *n pl* **-S** a creeping evergreen shrub

PYXIS *n pl* **PYXIDES** a seed capsule with a cap that falls off to release the seeds

QI *n pl* **-S** the energy or vital life force of the universe that in Chinese medicine and philosophy is thought to be present and inherent in all living things; *also* **CHI, KI**

THREE LETTERS

QAT *n pl* **-S** a shrub found in Africa and the Middle East, whose leaves are chewed as a stimulant or used in tea; *also* **KAT, KHAT**

QIS *n pl of* **QI** the energy or vital life forces of the universe that in Chinese medicine and philosophy is thought to be present and inherent in all living things; *also* **CHIS, KIS**

QUA *prep* in the capacity or character of; as

QUE *n* [obs] a half farthing; a coin of very little value, used in Great Britain in the 19ᵗʰ century

FOUR LETTERS

QADI *n pl* **-S** a judge of Islamic religious law; *also* **CADI, KADI**

QAID *n* a Muslim tribal chief, judge or senior official; *also* **CAID**

QATS *n pl* **QAT** shrubs found in Africa and the Middle East, whose leaves are chewed as a stimulant or used in tea; *also* **KATS, KHATS**

QOPH *n pl* **-S** the 19th letter of the Hebrew alphabet; *also* **KOPH**

QUAB *n* [obs] an unfledged bird; also something immature or unfinished

QUAD *n pl* **-S** a quadrangle; a square or rectangular green space that has buildings on all four sides, especially in a school or college campus

QUAG *n* a quagmire; a soft wet area of low-lying land that sinks underfoot; a marshy, boggy place

QUAI *n pl* **-S** a structure built parallel to the bank of a waterway as a landing place; a wharf; *also* **QUAY**

QUAP *v* [obs] to quaver; tremble; shake

QUAS *n* [obs] a thin, sour, Russian beer, made by pouring warm water on rye or barley meal and letting it ferment; *also* **QUASS, KVAS, KVASS**

QUAT *n* a shrub found in Africa and the Middle East, whose leaves used in tea

QUAY *n pl* **-S** a structure built parallel to the bank of a waterway as a landing place; a wharf; *also* **QUAI**

QUET *n* [obs] a common guillemot, a black and white diving seabird with a long, narrow beak, found in the northern Atlantic and Pacific

QUEY *n pl* **-S** SCOT., BRIT. a heifer, a young cow, especially one that has not borne a calf

QUIB *n* [obs] a quip, a clever, sarcastic or witty remark often made in the spur of the moment; *also* **QUIP**

QUID *n pl* **-S** a piece of chewing tobacco

QUIN *n* one of five children born at the same time from the same pregnancy; *also* **QUINT**

QUIP *v* **-PED, -PING, -S** to make a clever, sarcastic or witty remark in the spur of the moment

QUIT *v* **-TED, -TING, -S** to leave permanently; to give up or resign from a position; to stop doing something

QUIZ *v* **-ZED, -ZING, -ZES** to test or examine someone's knowledge; to question closely or repeatedly

QUOB *v* [obs] to throb; to quiver; *also* **QUOP**

QUOD *n pl* **-S** BRIT. informal term for a jail or prison

QUOP *v* [obs] to throb; to quiver; *also* **QUOB**

FIVE LETTERS

QADIS *n pl of* **QADI** judges of Islamic religious law; *also* **CADIS, KADIS**

QANAT *n* an ancient irrigation system of deep underground tunnels and wells used in the Middle East to channel water from the mountains to dry, lower regions; *also* **KANAT**

QIBLA *n pl* **-S** the direction toward which Muslims face while praying; *also* **KIBLA, KIBLAH, QIBLAH**

QIRSH *n* a form coin and fractional monetary unit of several Middle Eastern and North African countries; *also* **GIRSH, GURSH, GHIRSH, QURSH**

QOPHS *n pl of* **QOPH** more than one of the 19th letter of the Hebrew alphabet; *also* **KOPHS**

QUACK *v* **-ED, -ING, -S** to utter the characteristic cry of a duck

QUADS *n pl of* **QUAD** quadrangles, square or rectangular green spaces that have buildings on all four sides, especially in a school or college campus

QUAFF *v* **-ED, -ING, -S** to drink deeply or heartily in large gulps or with great enjoyment

QUAIL *v* **-ED, -ING, -S** to cower; to shrink back in fear

QUAIS *n pl of* **QUAI** structures built parallel to the bank of a waterway as landing places; wharves; *also* **QUAYS**

QUAKE *v* **-D, QUAKING, -S** to shake, tremble or vibrate from instability, fear or shock

QUAKY *adj* **QUAKIER, QUAKIEST** shaky or tremulous

QUALE *n pl* **QUALIA** a property or quality of something, its feel or appearance, rather than the thing itself

QUALM *n pl* **-S** a feeling of doubt or unease, uncertainty or apprehension; misgiving

QUANT *n pl* **-S** informal term for an expert in quantitative data, measurements of quantity

QUARK *n pl* **-S** any of a group of elementary, subatomic particles having electric charges of a magnitude one-third or two-thirds that of the electron

QUART *n pl* **-S** a liquid measure of capacity

QUASH *v* **-ED, -ING, -ES** to reject as invalid by legal procedure; to annul or nullify by judicial action

QUASI *adj* resembling; almost, but not quite the same; similar

QUASS *n* a thin, sour, Russian beer, made by pouring warm water on rye or barley meal and letting it ferment; *also* **QUAS, KVAS, KVASS**

QUAYS *n pl of* **QUAY** structures built parallel to the bank of a waterway as landing places; wharves; *also* **QUAIS**

QUBIT *n* a quantum bit; a physical structure for information storage in a quantum computer that is capable of existing in either of two quantum states, and hence can represent two different binary values simultaneously

QUEAN *n* SCOT. a girl or a young, unmarried woman

QUEEN *v* **-ED, -ING, -S** to make a girl or woman a ruler or sovereign in a monarchy

QUEER *adj* **-ER, -EST** eccentric; unconventional; odd; strange; deviating from expectation; singular

QUELL *v* **-ED, -ING, -S** to put an end to or stop forcibly; to subdue or suppress

QUERN *n pl* **-S** a simple hand-turned mill for grinding grain

QUERY *v* **QUERIED, -ING, QUERIES** to question or to express doubt or uncertainty; to ask about; to inquire

QUEST *v* **-ED, -ING, -S** to seek or pursue something

QUEUE *v* **-D, QUEUING, -S** to line up and wait one's turn; to wait in line

QUEYS *n pl of* **QUEY** SCOT., BRIT. heifers, young cows, especially ones that have not borne calves

QUICK *adj* **-ER, -EST** acting or capable of acting with speed; fast; rapid; swift

QUIDS *n pl of* **QUID** pieces of chewing tobacco

QUIET *v* **-ED, -ING, -S** to subdue; to calm; to hush; to pacify

QUIFF *n pl* **-S** BRIT. a hairstyle where the hair at the front of the head is brushed upward and backward, away from the forehead

QUILL *v* **-ED, -ING, -S** to wind thread or yarn on a bobbin or spindle

QUILT *v* **-ED, -ING, -S** to stitch together two layers of fabric with padding in between, using a decorative pattern

QUINT *n* one of five children born at the same time from the same pregnancy; *also* **QUIN**

QUIPS *v pr t of* **QUIP** makes a clever, sarcastic, or witty remark in the spur of the moment

QUIPU *n* a record-keeping device of the Inca empire using knotted strings of various colors

QUIRE *n* **-S** a set of twenty-four or twenty-five sheets of uniform paper, of the same size or quality

QUIRK *n* **-S** a peculiarity; an idiosyncrasy; a strange and unexpected turn of events

QUIRT *n* a riding whip with a braided leather lash

QUITE *adv* completely; entirely

QUITS *v pr t of* **QUIT** leaves permanently; gives up or resigns from a position; stops doing something

QUODS *n pl of* **QUOD** BRIT. informal term for jails or prisons

QUOIN *v* **-ED, -ING, -S** to build an exterior corner of a wall with distinctive blocks of stone masonry; *also* **COIGN, COIGNE**

QUOIT *n pl* **-S** a ring of iron, rope, etc. tossed in a game to encircle or land as close as possible to a peg

QUOLL *n* a catlike, carnivorous marsupial of Australia

QUOTA *n pl* **-S** a fixed, limited quantity; a proportional part or share; an official allotment

QUOTE *v* **-D, QUOTING, -S** to repeat the exact words of another

QUOTH *v* [obs] said; uttered

QURSH *n* a former coin and fractional monetary unit of several Middle Eastern and North African countries; *also* **GIRSH, GURSH, GHIRSH, QIRSH**

RE *n* a syllable that represents the second musical note of a major scale or the second tone of a diatonic scale

RO *n* an artificial language for international use that rejects all existing words and is based instead on an abstract analysis of ideas

THREE LETTERS

RAD *adj* **-DER, -DEST** cool; excellent; radical

RAG *v* **-GED, -GING, -S** to tease, taunt or torment persistently; to scold, criticize or nag

RAH *interj* used to cheer on a team of player; an exclamation of encouragement or approval; hurrah

RAI *n* a style of popular Algerian music, fusing traditional Arabic folk music with elements of western pop or rock, often with outspoken or controversial lyrics

RAJ *n* the period of British rule of the south Asian Indian subcontinent which ended in 1947

RAM *v* **-MED, -MING, -S** to strike or drive against with great force and violent impact

RAN *v p t of* **RUN** moved swiftly and steadily on foot at a fast pace so that both feet left the ground for an instant with each springing step

RAP *v* **-PED, -PING, -S** to hit swiftly and forcibly; to strike with a quick sharp blow

RAT *v* **-TED, -TING, -S** to hunt, catch or kill rats, long-tailed rodents similar to but larger than a mouse

RAW *adj* **-ER, -EST** uncooked

RAX *v* **-ED, -ING, -ES** SCOT. to stretch out

RAY *v* **-ED, -ING, -S** to emit light; to beam; to radiate

REB *n pl* **-S** informal for a Confederate soldier in the U.S. Civil War

REC *n* a commonly used abbreviation for recreation, as in parks and rec

RED *adj* **-DER, -DEST** having the color or hue of a ripe tomato, cherry or strawberry; crimson

REE *v* **-D, -ING** BRIT. to sift or separate objects such as grain, peas or beans

REF *v* **-FED, -FING, -S** to referee a sport or game, enforcing the rules and ensuring they are followed

REG *n pl* **-S** informal for a regulation, a rule, ordinance or law

REI *n pl* **-S** [obs] a former unit of currency in Portugal

REM *n pl* **-S** a measured dosage of ionizing radiation

REN *n* [obs] a run

REP *v* **-PED, -PING, -S** to work as a sales representative, to act and negotiate in place of or for another party

RES *n pl* **RES** in law, a particular thing or legal matter

RET *v* **-TED, -TING, -S** to soak or dampen plants, such as hemp, flax, etc., in order to soften, loosen, and separate the plant fiber from the woody tissue

REV *v* **-VED, -VING, -S** to increase a vehicle's engine speed by pressing down on the gas pedal or advancing the throttle, especially while the vehicle is stationary

REW *n* [obs] a row, a linear series

REX *n pl* **REGES** a king

RHO *n* the 17th letter of the Greek alphabet, represented as "r"

RIA *n pl* **-S** a long, funnel-shaped estuary, or coastal inlet, which widens and deepens toward the sea, formed by the partial submergence of a river valley

RIB *v* **-BED, -BING, -S** to shape, form or strengthen with curved supports

RID *v* **-DED, -DING, -S** to free, clear, relieve or disencumber, from something undesirable

RIF *v* **-FED, -FING, -S** to dismiss an employee, especially from a government job, due to budget reductions.

RIG *v* **-GED, -GING, -S** to fit or equip for future function, especially a boat or ship with sails, shrouds, etc.

RIM *v* **-MED, -MING, -S** to furnish with or form a raised edge along the edge of something curved or circular

RIN *n pl* **RIN** a form of Japanese currency

RIP *v* **-PED, -PING, -S** to tear or pull away roughly or forcibly; to split apart or split open

RIS *n* [obs] a bough or branch; a twig

ROB *v* **-BED, -BING, -S** to take illegally by force, threats, or violence; to steal; to plunder

ROC *n* according to Arabian legends, a gigantic, mythological bird of prey with incredible strength

ROD *n pl* **-S** a long, narrow, usually cylindrical length of wood, metal, plastic or other material, often having a particular function or use

ROE *n* a mass of mature fish eggs, especially when still inside the ovarian sac, often eaten as food

ROM *n pl* **-S** a male Gypsy

RON *n* a Chadic language spoken in northern Nigeria

ROO *n pl* **-S** AUS. informal for a kangaroo, a large leaping marsupial with powerful hind legs, short forelegs and a long tail

ROT *v* **-TED, -TING, -S** to decompose by the action of bacteria or fungi; to decay organically; to spoil

ROW *v* **-ED, -ING, -S** to propel a boat or canoe, along the surface of water by paddling with oars

ROY *n* [obs] a king

RUB *v* **-BED, -BING, -S** to move over a surface with pressure, friction and repeated motion

RUD *n* ruddle, a red iron ore or red ocher used in dyeing

RUE *v* **-D, RUING, -S** to feel sorrow, remorse or regret

RUG *n pl* **-S** a think, heavy fabric or small carpet used as a covering or decoration for a section of floor

RUM *adj* **-MER, -MEST** BRIT. odd, strange, peculiar; bizarre

RUN *v* **RAN, RUN, -NING, -S** to move swiftly and steadily on foot at a fast pace so that both feet leave the ground for an instant with each springing step

RUT *v* **-TED, -TING, -S** to hollow out a sunken track, groove, or channel in the ground with the passage of a vehicle, a tool or by a natural process like erosion

RYA *n pl* **-S** a hand woven Scandinavian rug with thick texture and a colorful pattern

RYE *n pl* **-S** a hardy cereal grass widely cultivated for its grain and seeds

RYS *n* [obs] a branch

FOUR LETTERS

RACE *v* **-D, RACING, -S** to compete in a contest of speed

RACK *v* **-ED, -ING, -S** to cause pain, suffering, or stress

RACY *adj* **RACIER, RACIEST** mildly shocking or indecent

RADE *n* SCOT. a raid, a sudden, surprise attack

RAFF *n* riffraff, people regarded as worthless, disreputable

RAFT *v* **-ED, -ING, -S** to travel or transport something by raft, a collection of logs, boards, pieces of timber, fastened together to float on water

RAGA *n* a traditional melodic and rhythmic pattern in types of Indian music, used as the basis for improvisation and to evoke different moods

RAGE *v* **-D, RAGING, -S** to act or speak with violent anger

RAGG *adj* comprised of a sturdy yarn with multiple light and dark strands, producing a flecked pattern

RAGI *n* a tropical cereal grass and staple food of India and parts of Africa; *also* **RAGEE, RAGGEE**

RAGS *v pr t of* **RAG** teases, taunts, or torments persistently; scolds, criticizes, or nags

RAIA *n* a Christian or non-Muslim subject of the Ottoman Empire; *also* **RAYA, RAYAH**

RAID *n pl* **-S** a sudden surprise attack attempting to seize, arrest or destroy something

RAIL *v* **-ED, -ING, -S** to complain or protest strongly; to object or criticize with bitter, harsh or abusive language

RAIN *v* **-ED, -ING, -S** to descend or fall from clouds in the sky, as droplets of water

RAIP *n* SCOT. a rope

RAJA *n pl* **-S** a king or prince in India and parts of South Asia; *also* **RAJAH**

RAKE *v* **-D, RAKING, -S** to move or gather with a long-handled, toothed implement

RAKI *n pl* **-S** an anise flavored brandy distilled from grapes or plums, made in Turkey, the Balkans, and the Middle East.; *also* **RAKEE**

RAKU *n* a type of earthenware and a special technique for firing and glazing pottery

RALE *n pl* **-S** an abnormal cracking or rattling sound in the lungs, caused by fluid, congestion, or disease, generally heard through a stethoscope

RAMI *n pl of* **RAMUS** biological branches, found in plants, nerves, blood vessels, bones, etc

RAMP *v* **-ED, -ING, -S** to increase something gradually

RAMS *v pr t of* **RAM** strikes or drives against with great force and violent impact

RAND *n pl* **RAND** the main unit of currency in South Africa

RANG *v p t of* **RING** gave forth a clear, resonant sound, like the sound of a bell

RANI *n pl* **-S** the wife of a Rajah, a queen or princess; *also* **RANEE**

RANK *v* **-ED, -ING, -S** to have a particular rating, position, or importance relative to others

RANT *v* **-ED, -ING, -S** to erupt verbally in an exaggerated, angry, uncontrolled or aggressive way; to rave

RAPS *v pr t of* **RAP** hits swiftly and forcibly; strikes with a quick sharp blow

RAPT *adj* enraptured; deeply moved or delighted; completely engrossed

RARE *v* **-D, RARING, -S** to be enthusiastic and eager

RASE *v* **-D, RASING, -S** to completely destroy a building, town, etc; to demolish or level; *also* **RAZE**

RASH *adj* **-ER, -EST** hasty, reckless, careless, impetuous

RASP *v* **-ED, -ING, -S** to rub or grate with a rough file

RATA *n* a forest tree with hard red wood and crimson flowers, native to New Zealand

RATE *v* **-D, RATING, -S** to judge value or character according to a particular scale

RATH *n pl* **-S** a circular enclosure built in ancient Ireland, surrounded by an earthen wall and used as a fort or dwelling place

RATS *v pr t of* **RAT** hunts, catches or kills rats, long-tailed rodents similar to but larger than mice

RAVE *v* **-D, RAVING, -S** to give high praise

RAYA *n* a Christian or non-Muslim subject of the Ottoman Empire; *also* **RAIA, RAYAH**

RAYS *v pr t of* **RAY** emits light; beams; radiates

RAZE *v* **-D, RAZING, -S** to completely destroy a building, town, etc; to demolish or level; *also* **RASE**

RAZZ *v* **-ED, -ING, -ES** to deride, heckle, or tease playfully

READ *v* **READ, -ING, -S** to examine, interpret, and grasp meaning and understanding from written or printed words

REAK *n* [obs] a prank

REAL *n pl* **-S** or **-ES** a silver coin formally used as currency in Spain and Latin America

REAM *v* **-ED, -ING, -S** to form, shape or widen an opening with a reamer, a tool designed to form holes

REAP *v* **-ED, -ING, -S** to cut and collect crops for harvest

REAR *v* **-ED, -ING, -S** to care for and raise a child

REBS *n pl of* **REB** informal for Confederate soldiers in the U.S. Civil War; rebels

RECK *v* **-ED, -ING, -S** to have care or concern for something

REDD *v* **–ED** or **REDD, -ING, -S** to clear; to put in order; to tidy

REDE *v* **-D, REDING, -S** to advise; to counsel

REDO *v* **REDID, -NE, -ING, -ES** to do over again, in order to correct mistakes

REDS *n pl of* **RED** the color or hues of a ripe tomato, cherry or strawberry; crimson

REED *n pl* **-S** a tall and slender perennial grass which grows in marshes and other wetland areas

REEF *v* **-ED, -ING, -S** to reduce the size of a boat's sail by gathering, folding and tying part of the sail in

REEK *v* **-ED, -ING, -S** to have and give off a very strong and unpleasant smell

REEL *v* **-ED, -ING, -S** to wind something onto or off of a reel, a cylindrical spool or wheel-shaped storage device

REFS *v pr t of* **REF** referees a sport or game, enforces the rules and ensures they are followed

REFT *v p t of* **REAVE** plundered; seized and carried off forcibly; took away by violence

REGS *n pl of* **REG** informal for regulations, rules, ordinances or laws

REIF *n* [obs] SCOT. plunder, booty or loot

REIM *n* a strip of pliable hairless ox hide that is twisting into ropes, etc.

REIN *v* **-ED, -ING, -S** to guide, direct, or control; to check or restrain

REIS *n pl of* **REI** [obs] former units of currency in Portugal

REIT *n* [obs] sedge; seaweed

RELY *v* **RELIED, -ING, RELIES** to be dependent on someone or something

REMS *n pl of* **REM** measured dosages of ionizing radiation

REND *v* **RENT** or **-ED, -ING, -S** to tear off forcibly; to pull or split apart violently

RENG *n pl* **-ES** [obs] a rank; a row

RENT *v* **-ED, -ING, -S** to obtain temporary use of something in return for compensation or regular payments

REPO *n pl* **-S** property that is repossessed due to lack of payment

REPP *n pl* **-S** a ribbed or corded fabric

REPS *v pr t of* **REP** works as a sales representative, acts and negotiates in place of or for another party

RESE *v* [obs] to shake; to quake; to tremble

RESH *n* the 20th letter in the Hebrew alphabet, represented as "r" in the English alphabet

REST *v* **-ED, -ING, -S** to cease motion, work or activity; to lie down and relax

RETE *n pl* **RETIA** an anatomical mesh or network, as of veins, arteries, or nerves

RETS *v pr t of* **RET** soaks or dampens plants, such as hemp, flax, etc., in order to soften, loosen and separate the plant fibers from the woody tissue

REVS *v pr t of* **REV** increases a vehicle's engine speed by pressing down on the gas pedal or advancing the throttle, especially while the vehicle is stationary

RIAL *n pl* **-S** the main unit of currency in Iran, Oman and Yemen

RIAS *n pl of* **RIA** long, funnel-shaped estuaries, or coastal inlets, which widen and deepen toward the sea, formed by the partial submergence of a river valley

RIBS *v pr t of* **RIB** shapes, forms or strengthens with curved supports

RICE *v* **-D, RICING, -S** to push food through a sieve or ricer to make it the consistency of a coarse purée

RICH *adj* **-ER, -EST** having an abundance of money, material wealth or possessions; wealthy

RICK *v* **-ED, -ING, -S** to stack or pile grain, straw or hay into an ordered shape, and then cover or thatch to protect from the weather

RIDE *v* **RODE, RIDDEN, RIDING, -S** to sit and travel on the back of an animal, such as a horse, while controlling or directing the animal's movements

RIDS *v pr t of* **RID** frees, clears, relieves or disencumbers, from something undesirable

RIEF *n* [obs] a robbery

RIEL *n pl* **-S** the basic unit of currency in Cambodia

RIFE *adj* prevailing; prevalent; abounding

RIFF *v* **-ED, -ING, -S** to play a riff, a short, rhythmic phrase, that forms a distinctive part or basic theme of a musical piece

RIFS *v pr t of* **RIF** dismisses an employee, especially from a government job, due to budget reductions, etc

RIFT *v* **-ED, -ING, -S** to split open; to break apart; to cleave

RIGS *v pr t of* **RIG** fits or equips for future function, especially a boat or ship with sails, shrouds, etc

RILE *v* **-D, RILING, -S** to agitate and anger; to irritate or annoy to the point of provoking anger

RILL *n pl* **-S** a small brook; a rivulet

RIMA *n pl* **-E** a narrow and elongated aperture; an anatomical cleft or fissure

RIME *v* **-D, RIMING, -S** to cover or coat with frost or ice

RIMS *v pr t of* **RIM** furnishes with or forms a raised edge along the edge of something curved or circular

RIMY *adj* **RIMIER, RIMIEST** frosty

RIND *n pl* **-S** a tough outer skin or layer, such as bark on trees, the skin of some fruits, or the coating of cheese

RING *v* **RANG, RUNG, -ING, -S** to give forth a clear, resonant sound, like the sound of a bell

RINK *n pl* **-S** a sheet of smooth ice, often prepared artificially, used for skating, hockey or curling

RIOT *v* **-ED, -ING, -S** to act in unruly, violent and destructive way

RIPE *adj* **-R, -EST** fully grown or developed; mature; ready to harvest or eat

RIPS *v pr t of* **RIP** tears or pulls away roughly or forcibly; splits apart or splits open

RISE *v* **ROSE, RISEN, RISING, -S** to assume an upright or vertical position after lying or sitting

RISH *n* [obs] a rush, the plant

RISK *v* **-ED, -ING, -S** to expose to potential danger, loss or hazards

RITE *n pl* **-S** a solemn, ceremonial practice, customary to a community, performed according to ritualistic rules

RITZ *n pl* **-ES** an elegant, often ostentatious display of luxury and glamour

RIVE *v* **-D, -N, RIVING, -S** to tear or wrench apart

ROAD *n pl* **-S** a long, generally public, hard surface for the passage and travel of people, vehicles, etc.

ROAM *v* **-ED, -ING, -S** to wander aimlessly; to move about without purpose or plan

ROAN *n pl* **-S** a horse or other animal having a red, brown or black coat, thickly sprinkled with white or gray hairs

ROAR *v* **-ED, -ING, -S** to cry with a full, loud, prolonged rumbling sound; to shout with a deep, growling voice

ROBE *v* **-D, ROBING, -S** to cover or dress in a long, loose, flowing garment

ROBS *v pr t of* **ROB** takes illegally by force, threats or violence; steals; plunders

ROCK *v* **-ED, -ING, -S** to move or sway back and forth or side to side, especially gently or rhythmically

RODE *v p t of* **RIDE** sat and traveled on the back of an animal, such as a horse, while controlling or directing the animal's movements

RODS *n pl of* **ROD** long, narrow, usually cylindrical lengths of wood, metal, plastic or other material, often having particular functions or uses

ROED *adj* filled with roe

ROIL *v* **-ED, -ING, -S** to make a liquid turbid, cloudy or muddy by stirring up the sediments

ROIN *n* [obs] a scab; a scurf, or scurfy spot

ROKE *n* mist; smoke; damp

ROKY *adj* misty; foggy; cloudy

ROLE *n pl* **-S** a part or character, played by a performer, actor or singer in a play, film, opera, etc.

ROLF *v* to practice a type of massage

ROLL *v* **-ED, -ING, -S** to move, impel forward, and cause to revolve by turning over and over

ROMP *v* **-ED, -ING, -S** to play roughly and energetically

ROMS *n pl of* **ROM** male Gypsies

ROOD *n pl* **-S** a crucifix symbolizing the cross on which Jesus died, specifically one mounted at the entrance to the choir or chancel of a church

ROOF *n pl* **-S** the protective exterior surface and its supporting structures on the top of a building

ROOK *v* **-ED, -ING, -S** to cheat, defraud or swindle

ROOM *v* **-ED, -ING, -S** to lodge, rent or occupy a room in a boarding house or other shared living situation

ROON *adj* vermilion or red

ROOP *n* SCOT. a sale of goods by auction

ROOS *n pl of* **ROO** AUS. informal for kangaroos, large leaping marsupials with powerful hind legs, short forelegs and a long tail

ROOT *v* **-ED, -ING, -S** to grow or develop roots, the underground portion of a plant that draws nutrients and water from the soil

ROPE *v* **-D, ROPING, -S** to catch, fasten or secure with a length of stout cord made of braided fibers

ROPY *adj* **ROPIER, ROPIEST** resembling a rope, a length of stout cord made of braided fibers; long and strong; *also* **ROPEY**

RORY *adj* dewy; *also* **ROARY**

ROSE *n pl* **-S** a garden plant with thorny stems and pleasant smelling, showy flowers

ROSS *n pl* **-ES** the rough, scaly matter on the surface of the bark of trees

ROSY *adj* **ROSIER, ROSIEST** the reddish pink color of roses

ROTA *n pl* **-S** BRIT. a roster of names showing the order in which people should perform certain duties

ROTE *n pl* **-S** a mechanical or habitual repetition; a fixed routine

ROTI *n pl* **-S** a round, flat, unleavened bread

ROTL *n pl* **-S** or **ARTAL** a unit of weight in Muslim countries

ROTO *n pl* **-S** a printing made by a rotogravure, a type of printing process using a photomechanical process and copper cylinders

ROTS *v pr t of* **ROT** decomposes by the action of bacteria or fungi; decays organically; spoils

ROTY *v* [obs] to make rotten

ROUÉ *n pl* **-S** a person, especially a man of society, who overindulges in physical pleasures to the point that's considered immoral or harmful

ROUN *v* [obs] to whisper; *also* **ROWN**

ROUP *n pl* **-S** a disease in poultry

ROUT *v* **-ED, -ING, -S** to disperse in defeat and disorderly flight

ROUX *n pl* **ROUX** a mixture of flour and fat, usually butter, used in preparing sauces and as a thickener for soups and gravies

ROVE *v* **-D, ROVING, -S** to travel aimlessly over a wide area; to wander; to roam

ROWN *v* [obs] to whisper; *also* **ROUN**

ROWS *v pr t of* **ROW** propels a boat or canoe along the surface of water by paddling with oars

RUBE *n pl* **-S** a naïve or unsophisticated person, especially one from the country who is not used to city ways

RUBS *v pr t of* **RUB** moves over a surface with pressure, friction and repeated motion

RUBY *n pl* **RUBIES** a highly valued translucent gemstone found in shades of red

RUCK *v* **-ED, -ING, -S** to fold, crease or wrinkle

RUDD *n pl* **-S** a European freshwater fish with red fins

RUDE *adj* **-R, -ST** ill-mannered; discourteous; offensive; crude

RUED *v p t of* **RUE** felt sorrow, remorse or regret

RUER *n* one who feels sorrow, remorse or regret

RUES *v pr t of* **RUE** feels sorrow, remorse or regret

RUFF *v* **-ED, -ING, -S** to play a trump card, in bridge or whist, on a card of a different suit

RUFT *n* [obs] an eructation; a belching

RUGA *n pl* **-E** an anatomical fold, wrinkle or crease

RUGS *n pl of* **RUG** thick, heavy fabrics or small carpets used as a covering or decoration for sections of floor

RUIN *v* **-ED, -ING, -S** to destroy; to demolish; to devastate

RULE *v* **-D, RULING, -S** to exert control and authority over

RULY *adj* **RULIER, RULIEST** neat and tidy; orderly

RUMP *n pl* **-S** the upper hindquarters of a four-legged mammal

RUNE *n pl* **-S** any character from an ancient Germanic alphabet

RUNG *v p part of* **RING** had given forth a clear, resonant sound, like the sound of a bell

RUNS *v pr t of* **RUN** moves swiftly and steadily at a fast pace, so that both feet leave the ground for an instant with each springing step

RUNT *n pl* **-S** an undersized animal, especially the smallest or weakest in the litter

RUSE *n pl* **-S** a clever trick or plot used to deceive others; a subterfuge; a wily stratagem

RUSH *v* **-ED, -ING, -ES** to move or act with urgent haste; to hurry

RUSK *n pl* **-S** a biscuit or a piece of crisp bread, dried and toasted or baked for a second time

RUST *v* **-ED, -ING, -S** to corrode with rust, a reddish-brown coating of iron oxide that forms on metal exposed to moist air

RUTH *n* sorrow for the misery of another; pity; compassion

RUTS *v pr t of* **RUT** hollows out a sunken track, groove or channel in the ground with the passage of a vehicle, a tool or by a natural process like erosion

RYAS *n pl of* **RYA** hand woven Scandinavian rugs with thick texture and a colorful pattern

RYES *n pl of* **RYE** hardy cereal grasses widely cultivated for grain and seeds

RYND *n* a piece of iron running across an upper millstone as a support

RYOT *n pl* **-S** in South Asia, a peasant and subsistence farmer who owns or rents a small piece of land

RYSH *n* [obs] a plant

RYTH *n* [obs] a ford, a shallow place in a body of water where one may cross

FIVE LETTERS

RABAT *n pl* -**S** a plain black dickey worn with a clerical collar especially by Roman Catholic and Anglican clergy

RABBI *n pl* -**S** the ordained spiritual leader of a Jewish congregation or synagogue; a scholar, teacher and leader in Jewish law, ritual and tradition

RABIC *adj* characterized by or relating to rabies, an infectious disease of animals transmitted to humans by the bite of an infected animal

RABID *adj* violent; raging; furious

RACED *v p t of* **RACE** competed in a contest of speed

RACER *n pl* -**S** one that races or takes part in a race

RACES *v pr t of* **RACE** competes in a contest of speed

RACKS *n pr t of* **RACK** causes pain, suffering or stress

RACON *n pl* -**S** a ground based, fixed position, radar receiver and transmitter whose signals help a ship or aircraft determine bearing and range

RADAR *n pl* -**S** a method of detecting distant objects and determining their position, direction and speed by analyzing reflected radio waves

RADII *n pl of* **RADIUS** line segments that join the center of a circle with any point on its circumference; *also* **RADIUSES**

RADIO *v* -**ED**, -**ING**, -**S** to communicate or transmit messages by radio, an electronic device used to send and receive signals encoded in electromagnetic waves

RADIX *n pl* -**ES**, **RADICES** the base of a number or logarithmic system

RADON *n* a radioactive, gaseous chemical, formed by the radioactive decay of radium

RAFTS *v pr t of* **RAFT** travels or transports something by raft, a collection of logs, boards, pieces of timber, fastened together to float on water

RAGED *v p t of* **RAGE** acted or spoke with violent anger

RAGEE *n* a tropical cereal grass and staple food of India and parts of Africa; *also* **RAGI**, **RAGGEE**

RAGES *v pr t of* **RAGE** acts or speaks with violent anger

RAGGY *adj* **RAGGIER**, **RAGGIEST** ragged, old and torn

RAIDS *n pl of* **RAID** sudden surprise attacks attempting to seize, arrest or destroy something

RAILS *v pr t of* **RAIL** complains or protests strongly; objects or criticizes with bitter, harsh or abusive language

RAINS *v pr t of* **RAIN** descends or falls from clouds in the sky, as droplets of water

RAINY *adj* **RAINIER**, **RAINIEST** long or recurring periods of rainfall; wet with rain, water falling from the sky

RAISE *v* -**D**, **RAISING**, -**S** move to a higher level or positions: elevate; lift

RAITA *n pl* -**S** a spiced yogurt, often with cucumber, eaten as a condiment, sauce or dip with Indian food

RAJAH *n pl* -**S** a king or prince in India and parts of South Asia; *also* **RAJA**

RAJAS *n pl* **RAJA** kings or princes in India and parts of South Asia; *also* **RAJAHS**

RAKED *v p t of* **RAKE** moved or gathered with a long-handled, toothed implement

RAKEE *n pl* **-S** an anise flavored brandy distilled from grapes or plums, made in Turkey, the Balkans and the Middle East; *also* **RAKI**

RAKER *n pl* **-S** a person or thing that moves or gathers objects with a long-handled, toothed implement

RAKES *v pr t of* **RAKE** moves or gathers with a long-handled, toothed implement

RAKIS *n pl of* **RAKI** anise flavored brandies distilled from grapes or plums, made in Turkey, the Balkans, and the Middle East; *also* **RAKEES**

RALES *n pl of* **RALE** an abnormal cracking or rattling sound in the lungs, caused by fluid, congestion or disease, generally heard through a stethoscope

RALLY *v* **RALLIED, -ING, RALLIES** to call together or unite for a common purpose or cause; to assemble

RALPH *v* **-ED, -ING, -S** to vomit

RAMAL *adj* of or pertaining to a ramus, branch-like

RAMEE *n* [obs] a tall, perennial herb of tropical Asia with fibrous, woody stems, used in textiles; *also* **RAMIE**

RAMEN *n* a Japanese noodle dish, served in a strong broth with pieces of meat and vegetables

RAMET *n pl* **-S** an individual member of a clone

RAMIE *n* a tall, perennial herb of tropical Asia with fibrous, woody stems, used in textiles; *also* **RAMEE**

RAMMY *n* SCOT. a noisy argument or fight; a brawl

RAMPS *v pr t of* **RAMP** increases something gradually

RAMUS *n pl* **RAMI** a biological branch, found in plants, nerves, blood vessels, bones, etc

RANCE *n* SCOT. a wooden prop or support, such as the lower cross bar which joins legs of a chair

RANCH *v* **-ED, -ING, -ES** to manage or work on large farm on which cattle, sheep or horses are raised on large tracts of open land

RANDY *adj* **RANDIER, RANDIEST** SCOT. coarse, crude or vulgar

RANEE *n pl* **-S** the wife of a Rajah, a queen or princess; *also* **RANI**

RANGE *v* **-D, RANGING, -S** to vary between a specified upper and lower limit

RANGY *adj* **RANGIER, RANGIEST** tall and slim; having long slender limbs

RANID *n* a long-legged frog with extensively webbed feet; a true frog

RANIS *n pl of* **RANI** wives of Rajahs, queens or princesses; *also* **RANEES**

RANKS *v pr t of* **RANK** has a particular rating, position or importance, relative to others

RANTS *v pr t of* **RANT** erupts verbally in an exaggerated, angry, uncontrolled or aggressive way; raves angrily

RAPHE *n pl* **RAPHAE** a seam like joining of the two lateral halves of an organ

RAPID *adj* **-ER, -EST** moving, acting or occurring with great speed; swift

RARED *v p t of* **RARE** was enthusiastic and eager

RARER *adj* infrequently occurring; uncommon; unusual

RARES *v pr t of* **RARE** is enthusiastic and eager

RASED *v p t of* **RASE** completely destroyed a building, town, etc; demolished or leveled; *also* **RAZED**

269

RASES *v pr t of* **RASE** completely destroys a building, town, etc; demolishes or levels; *also* **RAZES**

RASPS *v pr t of* **RASP** rubs or grates with a rough file

RASPY *adj* grating; rough; harsh

RATAL *n* BRIT. the amount on which rates or taxes are assessed

RATAN *n pl* **-S** [obs] a tropical palm with long, tough, flexible stems, used in wickerwork, canes, and furniture; *also* **RATTAN**

RATCH *n* a ratchet, mechanism with a toothed wheel that allows motion on one direction only

RATED *v p t of* **RATE** judged value or character according to a particular scale

RATEL *n pl* **-S** a carnivorous mammal of Asia and Africa, similar in appearance to a badger, with short legs and a thick furry coat that is dark below and whitish above

RATER *n pl* **-S** one who establishes or determines a rating; a judge

RATES *v pr t of* **RATE** judges value or character according to a particular scale

RATHE *adj* quick; prompt; early; eager

RATHS *n pl of* **RATH** circular enclosures built in ancient Ireland, surrounded by earthen walls and used as forts or dwelling places

RATIO *n pl* **-S** the quantitative relationship between two amounts showing the number of times one value contains or is contained within the other

RATTY *adj* **RATTIER, RATTIEST** resembling or infested with rats, large, long-tailed rodents

RAVED *v p t of* **RAVE** given high praise

RAVEL *v* **-ED, -ING, -S** to separate the threads of; untangle

RAVEN *v* **-ED, -ING, -S** to devour greedily; to eat voraciously

RAVER *n pl* **-S** a person who lives a wild, exciting and uninhibited social life, often one who attends underground, all-night, dance parties

RAVES *v pr t of* **RAVE** gives high praise

RAVIN *n* the act of violent seizure; plunder; pillage

RAWER *adj* more uncooked

RAWIN *n* a method of measuring upper air currents made by tracking a balloon with radar or a radio direction finder

RAWLY *adv* vulgar, course, crude

RAXED *v p t of* **RAX** SCOT. stretched out

RAXES *v pr t of* **RAX** SCOT. stretches out

RAYAH *n* a Christian or non-Muslim subject of the Ottoman Empire; *also* **RAIA, RAYA**

RAYED *v p t of* **RAY** emitted light; beamed; radiated

RAYON *n pl* **-S** a synthetic textile fiber made from cellulose

RAZED *v p t of* **RAZE** completely destroyed a building, town, etc; demolished or leveled; *also* **RASED**

RAZEE *n* a wooden warship reduced in height by the removal of the upper deck

RAZER *n* a person or thing that demolishes or destroys

RAZES *v pr t of* **RAZE** completely destroys a building, town, etc; demolishes or levels; *also* **RASES**

RAZOR *v* **-ED, -ING, -S** to shave or cut hair with a sharp-bladed instrument

REACH *v* **-ED, -ING, -ES** to extend or stretch out

REACT *v* **-ED, -ING, -S** to respond to a stimulus or prompting

READS *v pr t of* **READ** examines, interprets, and grasps meaning and understanding from written or printed words

READY *v* **READIED, -ING, -READIES** to prepare

REALM *n pl* **-S** a kingdom; a community or territory over which a sovereign rules

REALS *n pl of* **REAL** silver coins, formally used as currency in Spain and Latin America

REAMS *v pr t of* **REAM** forms, shapes or widens an opening with a reamer, a tool designed to form holes

REAPS *v pr t of* **REAP** cuts and collects crops for harvest

REARS *v pr t of* **REAR** cares for and raises a child

REATA *n pl* **-S** a lasso, a lariat; *also* **RIATA**

REAVE *v* **-D** or **REFT, REAVING, -S** to plunder; to seize and carry off forcibly; to take away by violence

REBAR *n pl* **REBAR** or **-S** a rod or bar used for reinforcement in the pouring of concrete or asphalt

REBBE *n pl* **-S** a rabbi, an ordained spiritual leader specifically for a Hasidic Jewish community

REBEC *n pl* **-S** a pear-shaped medieval instrument with two or three strings, played with a bow; *also* **REBECK**

REBEL *v* **-LED, -LING, -S** to refuse allegiance and resist conforming to those in authority or control;

REBOP *n* an early version of the term bebop, a modern style of Jazz popularized by Dizzie Gillespie, Charlie Parker, and others

REBUS *n pl* **-ES** a puzzle in which words or syllables are presented as pictures or symbols whose images have the same sounds as the puzzle word

REBUT *v* **-TED, -TING, -S** to refute or contradict

RECCE *n pl* **-S** reconnaissance, an exploratory military survey of enemy territory

RECKS *v pr t of* **RECK** has care or concern for something

RECON *n* reconnaissance, an exploratory military survey of enemy territory

RECTA *n pl of* **RECTUM** terminal portions of large intestines

RECTI *n pl of* **RECTUS** straight muscles found in the abdomen, eye, neck and thigh

RECTO *n pl* **-S** any right-hand page of a book; the front side of a printed sheet

RECUR *v* **-RED, -RING, -S** to happen again or occur repeatedly

REDAN *n pl* **-S** V-shaped parapets, usually projecting from a wall or other fortified point, as a line of defense

REDDS *v pr t of* **REDD** clears; puts in order; tidies

REDED *v p t of* **REDE** advised; counseled

REDES *v pr t of* **REDE** advises; counsels

REDIA *n pl* **-E** a larva produced by a saclike group of cells in certain parasitic flatworms

REDID *v p t of* **REDO** did over again, in order to correct mistakes

REDLY *adv* with a red color or glow

REDOX *n* oxidation reduction, a type of chemical reaction

REDUB *v* [obs] to refit; to repair

REDUX *adj* brought back; restored to former prominence or importance; revived

REEDS *n pl of* **REED** tall and slender perennial grasses which grow in marshes and other wetland areas

REEDY *adj* **REEDIER, REEDIEST** composed of or abounding with tall, slender, wetland grasses

REEFS *v pr t of* **REEF** reduces the size of a boat's sail by gathering, folding and tying part of the sail in

271

REEFY *adj* characterized by ridges of rock, sand or coral

REEKS *v pr t of* **REEK** has and gives off a very strong and unpleasant smell

REEKY *adj* smelly or stinky

REELS *v pr t of* **REEL** winds something onto or off of a reel, a cylindrical spool or wheel-shaped storage device

REEST *v* SCOT. to balk, to stop and refuse to go

REEVE *v* **ROVE, ROVEN, -D, REEVING, -S** to thread or pass something through a hole, a ring or other opening

REFEL *v* **-LED, -LING, -S** [obs] to refute; to reject; to disprove

REFER *v* **-RED, -RING, -S** to direct to a source for help or information

REFIT *v* **-TED, -TING, -S** to prepare, equip and make ready for further or additional use

REFIX *v* **-ED, -ING, -ES** to fix again or establish anew

REGAL *adj* royal; suitable for a king or queen; with grandeur and magnificence

REGES *n pl of* **REX** kings

REGMA *n pl* **-TA** a dry fruit, consisting of three or more carpels or segments that separate from the center when ripe

REGNA *n pl of* **REGNUM** kingdoms

REHAB *v* **-BED, -BING, -S** to rehabilitate, to restore to a good condition or state of health

REIFY *v* **REIFIED, -ING, REIFIES** to treat or regard an abstraction as a real, concrete, tangible object

REIGN *v* **-ED, -ING, -S** to exercise sovereign power; to rule

REINS *v pr t of* **REIN** guides, directs, or controls; checks or restrains

REIVE *v* **-D, REIVING, -S** SCOT. to raid; to plunder; to take away by violence

REJIG *v* **-GED, -GING, -S** to readjust or rearrange

REKEY *v* **-ED, -ING, -S** to reenter lost text or data into a computer

RELAX *v* **-ED, -ING, -ES** to loosen or lessen tension

RELAY *v* **-ED, -ING, -S** to receive and pass on

RELIC *n pl* **-S** an object, custom, etc. that has survived the passage of time, either wholly or partially

REMAN *v* **-NED, -NING, -S** to furnish with a fresh supply of men or new personnel

REMEX *n pl* **REMIGES** a quill or flight feather of a bird's wing

REMIT *v* **-TED, -TING, -S** to send money in payment

RENAL *adj* relating to or affecting the kidneys

RENDS *v pr t of* **REND** tears off forcibly; pulls or splits apart violently

RENEW *v* **-ED, -ING, -S** to restore; to revive

RENIN *n pl* **-S** a proteolytic enzyme or proteinase released by the kidneys, that helps regulate blood pressure

RENTE *n pl* **-S** annual income under French law

RENTS *v pr t of* **RENT** obtains temporary use of in return for compensation or regular payments

REPAY *v* **REPAID, -ING, -S** to settle or reimburse a debt; to compensate

REPEL *v* **-LED, -LING, -S** to drive or force back; to ward off

REPLY *v* **REPLIED, -ING, REPLIES** to answer; to respond

REPOS *n pl of* **REPO** items repossessed due to lack of payment

REPPS *n pl of* **REPP** ribbed or corded fabrics

REPRO *n pl* **-S** reproduction, a copy or duplicate

ERAN *v p t of* **RERUN** rebroadcasted, performed over or done again; repeated

ERUN *v* **RERAN, -NING, -S** to rebroadcast, perform over or do again; to repeat

ESAT *v p t of* **RESIT** BRIT. took an examination again after failing the first time

ESET *v* **RESET, -TING, -S** to place in the correct position; to return to proper order or working condition

ESEW *v* **-N, -ED, -ING, -S** to stitch again; to repair with needle and thread

ESID *n* residual oil, the low grade oil that remains after petroleum is distilled

ESIN *n* SCOT. a resin made from pine trees or synthetically from oil of turpentine; *also* **ROSIN, ROSET**

ESIT *v* **RESAT, -TING, -S** BRIT. to take an examination again after failing the first time

ESOW *v* **-ED** or **-N, RESOWING, RESOWS** to scatter or plant seed again

ESTS *v pr t of* **REST** ceases motion, work or activity; lies down and relaxes

ETCH *v* **-ED, -ING, -ES** to make an effort to vomit; to experience the spasm or straining action, without producing vomit

ETEM *n* a desert shrub with small white flowers; juniper

ETIA *n pl of* **RETE** anatomical networks, as of veins, arteries or nerves

ETIE *v* **-D, RETYING** or **-ING, -S** to fasten or secure again

ETRO *adj* modeled on or reminiscent of fashions of the past and styles of an earlier time

ETRY *v* **RETRIED, -ING, RETRIES** to make another effort; to attempt again

REUSE *v* **-D, REUSING, -S** to utilize again, often by finding an additional function for something, as an alternative to throwing it out

REVEL *v* **-ED, -LED, -ING, -LING, -S** to make merry; be noisily festive; to carouse or celebrate with boisterous pleasure

REVET *v* **-TED, -TING, -S** to protect or reinforce a wall or embankment with a facing of sandbags, masonry, etc.

REVUE *n pl* **-S** a musical variety show consisting of skits, songs, dances and jokes

REWET *n* a gunlock, the mechanism or device for igniting the charge of a firearm

REWIN *v* **REWON, -NING, -S** to triumph again; to gain back in victory

REWON *v p t of* **REWIN** triumphed again; gained back in victory

RHEME *n pl* **-S** the part of a sentence that adds the greatest amount of new information

RHEUM *n pl* **-S** a watery discharge from the mucous membranes

RHINO *n pl* **-S** a rhinoceros, a very large herbivorous animal with thick skin and one or two upright horns

RHOMB *n pl* **-S** a rhombus, an oblique-angled parallelogram, whose four sides are of equal length

RHUMB *n* an imaginary line used to chart a ships course; the path of a ship that maintains a fixed compass point

RHYME *v* **-D, RHYMING, -S** to compose verse with corresponding terminal sounds

RHYTA *n pl of* **RHYTON** ancient Greek drinking horns

RIALS *n pl of* **RIAL** units of currency in Iran, Oman and Yemen

RIANT *adj* laughing; smiling; cheerful; full of mirth

RIATA	*n pl* **-S** a lasso, a lariat; *also* **REATA**
RIBBY	*adj* **RIBBIER, RIBBIEST** marked by prominent, equally spaced, curved ridges
RICED	*v p t of* **RICE** pushed food through a sieve or ricer to make it the consistency of a coarse purée
RICER	*n pl* **-S** a kitchen utensil consisting of a container perforated with small holes through which food is pressed and reduced to the size of rice grains
RICES	*v pr t of* **RICE** pushes food through a sieve or ricer to make it the consistency of a coarse purée
RICIN	*n pl* **-S** an extremely toxic protein found in the castor bean
RICKS	*v pr t of* **RICK** stacks or piles grain, straw or hay into an ordered shape, and then covers or thatches to protect it from the weather
RIDER	*n pl* **-S** a person who travels on the back of an animal on a bike, or in a vehicle
RIDES	*v pr t of* **RIDE** sits and travels on the back of an animal, such as a horse, while controlling or directing the animal's movements
RIDGE	*v* **-D, RIDGING, -S** to form into long narrow elevations
RIDGY	*adj* **RIDGIER, RIDGIEST** having long, narrow, crest like elevations
RIELS	*n pl of* **RIEL** basic units of currency in Cambodia
RIFFS	*v pr t of* **RIFF** plays a riff, a short, rhythmic phrase, that forms a distinctive part or basic theme to a piece of music
RIFLE	*v* **-D, RIFLING, -S** to search through something hurriedly in order to find and possibly take
RIFTS	*v pr t of* **RIFT** splits open; breaks apart; cleaves
RIGHT	*v* **-ED, -ING, -S** to put into proper order or condition
RIGID	*adj* not bending or flexible; stiff; firm; unyielding; fixed
RIGOR	*n pl* **-S** harshness or severity; strictness; toughness
RILED	*v p t of* **RILE** agitated and angered; irritated or annoyed to the point of provoking anger
RILES	*v pr t of* **RILE** agitates and angers; irritates or annoys to the point of provoking anger
RILEY	*adj* emotional; upset; angry; vexed
RILLE	*n pl* **-S** a long, narrow valley on the moon's surface
RILLS	*n pl of* **RILL** small brooks; rivulets
RIMAE	*n pl of* **RIMA** narrow and elongated apertures; anatomical clefts or fissures
RIMED	*v p t of* **RIME** covered or coated with frost or ice
RIMER	*n* a writer of rhymes or poems; *also* **RHYMER**
RIMES	*v pr t of* **RIME** covers or coats with frost or ice
RINDS	*n pl of* **RIND** tough outer skins or layers, such as bark on trees, the skins of some fruits or the coatings of some cheeses
RINDY	*adj* [obs] having a tough outer skin or thick external layer
RINGS	*v pr t of* **RING** gives forth a clear, resonant sound, like the sound of a bell
RINKS	*n pl of* **RINK** sheets of smooth ice, often prepared artificially, used for skating, hockey or curling
RINSE	*v* **-D, RINSING, -S** to cleanse with clean water
RIOJA	*n pl* **-S** a wine from the Rioja region in northern Spain, especially a dry red wine from this area

IOTS *v pr t of* **RIOT** acts in an unruly, violent and destructive way

IPEN *v* **-ED, -ING, -S** to become ripe; to mature

IPER *adj* fully grown or developed; mature; ready to harvest or eat

ISEN *v p part of* **RISE** had assumed an upright or vertical position after lying down or sitting

ISER *n pl* **-S** a person who awakens from sleep and gets up at a particular time

ISES *v pr t of* **RISE** assumes an upright or vertical position after lying down or sitting

ISHI *n pl* **-S** a divinely inspired poet or sage in India

ISKS *v pr t of* **RISK** exposes to potential danger, loss or hazard

ISKY *adj* **RISKIER, RISKIEST** hazardous; dangerous

ITES *n pl of* **RITE** solemn, ceremonial practices, customary to a community, performed according to ritualistic rules

RITZY *adj* **RITZIER, RITZIEST** ostentatiously luxurious, glamorous and elegant

RIVAL *v* **-ED, -LED, -ING, -LING, -S** to strive to equal or surpass

RIVED *v p t of* **RIVE** tore or wrenched apart

RIVEN *v p part of* **RIVE** torn or wrenched apart

RIVER *n pl* **-S** a natural stream of water, larger than a creek, that empties into an ocean, a lake or larger river

RIVES *v pr t of* **RIVE** tears or wrenches apart

RIVET *v* **-ED, -TED, -ING, -TING, -S** to fasten and secure with a rivet, a metal bolt or pin with a head on one end

RIYAL *n pl* **-S** the basic unit of currency in Saudi Arabia and Qatar

ROACH *v* **-ED, -ING, -ES** to cut or shave the mane of a horse so that the remainder stands upright in a short bristle

ROADS *n pl of* **ROAD** long, generally public, hard surfaces for the passage and travel of people, vehicles, etc.

ROAMS *v pr t of* **ROAM** wanders aimlessly; moves about without purpose or plan

ROANS *n pl of* **ROAN** horses or other animals having red, brown or black coats, thickly sprinkled with white or gray hairs

ROARS *v pr t of* **ROAR** cries with a full, loud, prolonged rumbling sound; shouts with a deep, growling voice

ROARY *adj* dewy; *also* **RORY**

ROAST *v* **-ED, -ING, -S** to cook with dry heat and little or no moisture, as in an oven, over an open fire, in hot embers, etc.

ROBED *v p t of* **ROBE** covered or dressed in a long, loose, flowing garment

ROBES *v pr t of* **ROBE** covers or dresses in a long, loose, flowing garment

ROBIN *n pl* **-S** a thrush with a dull-red breast and belly

ROBLE *n pl* **-S** a Californian oak tree with leathery leaves and slender, tapered acorns

ROBOT *n pl* **-S** a mechanical device programmed to carry out complex directions, performing tasks usually done by humans

ROCKS *v pr t of* **ROCK** moves or sways back and forth or side to side, especially gently or rhythmically

ROCKY *adj* **ROCKIER, ROCKIEST** full of large pieces of natural stone or broken boulders; rough and gravelly

RODEO *n pl* **-S** an exhibition and contest in which cowboys show their skill at roping calves, riding broncos, etc.

ROGER *interj* used in radio communication and signaling to indicate that a transmitted message has been received and understood

ROGUE *v* **-D, ROGUING, -S** to cheat; to defraud

ROILS *v pr t of* **ROIL** makes a liquid turbid, cloudy, or muddy by stirring up the sediments

ROILY *adj* **ROILIER, ROILIEST** muddy or cloudy; turbid, full of sediment or dregs

ROLES *n pl of* **ROLE** parts or characters, played by a performer, actor or singer in a play, film, opera, etc.

ROLLS *v pr t of* **ROLL** moves, impels forward, and causes to revolve by turning over and over

ROMAN *n pl* **-S** a novel or book of fiction, especially a French one or one in a French genre

ROMEO *n pl* **-S** a romantic and passionate man, devoted to the pursuit of love

ROMPS *v pr t of* **ROMP** plays roughly and energetically

RONDO *n pl* **-S** a musical form with a recurring theme, repeated in contrasting sections, often found in the final movement of a sonata or concerto

ROODS *n pl of* **ROOD** crucifixes symbolizing the cross on which Jesus died, specifically ones mounted at the entrance to the choir or chancel of a church

ROOFS *n pl of* **ROOF** protective exterior surfaces and their supporting structures on top of buildings

ROOKS *v pr t of* **ROOK** cheats, defrauds or swindles

ROOKY *adj* full or inhabited by rooks, large birds of the Crow family, that nest in colonies near the tops of trees

ROOMS *v pr t of* **ROOM** lodges, rents, or occupies a room in a boarding house or other shared living situation

ROOMY *adj* **ROMMIER, ROOMIEST** having plenty of space in which to move around; spacious

ROOSE *v* **-D, ROOSING, -S** SCOT. to praise, to express favorable opinion

ROOST *v* **-ED, -ING, -S** to rest or sleep on

ROOTS *v pr t of* **ROOT** grows or develops roots, the underground portion of a plant that draws nutrients and water from the soil

ROOTY *adj* **ROOTIER, ROOTIEST** consisting of or abounding in roots, the underground portion of plants

ROPED *v p t of* **ROPE** caught, fastened or secured with a length of stout cord made of braided fibers

ROPER *n pl* **-S** a cowboy who uses rope or a craftsman who makes rope, stout cords of braided fibers

ROPES *v pr t of* **ROPE** catches, fastens or secures with a length of stout cord made of braided fibers

ROPEY *adj* resembling a rope, a length of stout cord made of braided fibers; long and strong; *also* **ROPY**

ROQUE *n* a version of croquet played with short-handled mallets on a hard court with a low, walled border

ROSES *n pl of* **ROSE** garden plants with thorny stems and pleasant smelling, showy flowers

ROSET *n* SCOT. a resin made from pine trees or synthetically from oil of turpentine; *also* **ROSIN, RESIN**

ROSHI *n pl* **-S** the spiritual leader of a group of Zen Buddhists

ROSIN *n* SCOT. a resin made from pine trees or synthetically from oil of turpentine; *also* **ROSET, RESIN**

ROTAS *n pl of* **ROTA** BRIT. rosters of names showing the order in which people should perform certain duties

ROTCH *n* a very small arctic sea bird; *also* **ROTCHE**

ROTES *n pl of* **ROTE** mechanical or habitual repetitions; fixed routines

ROTIS *n pl of* **ROTI** found, flat, unleavened breads

ROTLS *n pl of* **ROTL** units of weight in Muslim countries

ROTOR *n pl* **-S** any of various rotating mechanical parts

ROTOS *n pl of* **ROTO** printings made by a rotogravure, a type of printing process using a photomechanical process and copper cylinders

ROUEN *n pl* **-S** a common domestic duck, descended from and resembling the mallard

ROUÉS *n pl of* **ROUÉ** people, especially the men of society, who overindulge in physical pleasures to the point that it is considered immoral or harmful

ROUGE *v* **-D, ROUGING, -S** to color the cheeks or lips with a powder or cream cosmetic, typically red or pink

ROUGH *v* **-ED, -ING, -S** to treat brutally with physical violence

ROUND *v* **-ED, -ING, -S** to make round, circular, or spherical

ROUPS *n pl of* **ROUP** disease in poultry

ROUSE *v* **-D, ROUSING, -S** to awake or arouse from sleep, apathy, unconsciousness, etc.

ROUST *v* **-ED, -ING, -S** to arouse, stir or force one to take action, especially in an abrupt or rough manner

ROUTE *v* **-D, ROUTING, -S** to direct, transport or send along a specified course

ROUTH *n pl* **-S** SCOT. abundance; plenty

ROUTS *v pr t of* **ROUT** disperses in defeat and disorderly flight

ROVED *v p t of* **ROVE** traveled aimlessly over a wide area; wandered; roamed

ROVEN *v p part of* **REEVE** had thread or passed something through a hole, a ring or other opening

ROVER *n pl* **-S** a person who spends their time wandering from place to place, never settling anywhere for long

ROVES *v pr t of* **ROVE** travels aimlessly over a wide area; wanders; roams

ROWAN *n pl* **-S** a European tree with white flowers and red berries

ROWDY *adj* **ROWDIER, ROWDIEST** loud, coarse and disorderly; rough and quarrelsome

ROWED *v p t of* **ROW** propelled a boat or canoe, along the surface of water by paddling with oars

ROWEL *v* **-ED, -ING, -S** to urge or goad a horse forward by kicking it with a spiked wheel attached to the spur

ROWEN *n pl* **-S** the second crop of grass or hay in one season

ROWER *n pl* **-S** an oarsman; a person who propels a boat with oars

ROYAL *n pl* **-S** a member of a monarch's family

RUANA *n pl* **-S** a type of cape or poncho, originally worn in Columbia and Peru

RUBEL *n pl* **-S** a basic unit of currency in Belarus

RUBES n pl of **RUBE** naïve or unsophisticated people, especially those from the country who are not used to city ways

RUBLE n pl **-S** a basic unit of currency in Russia and some other former republics of the Soviet Union; also **ROUBLE**

RUCHE n pl **-S** a flute, pleat or ruffle of lace, ribbon, muslin, etc., used as trimming on women's clothing

RUCKS v pr t of **RUCK** folds, creases or wrinkles

RUDDY adj **RUDDIER, RUDDIEST** having a healthy, reddish color or glow

RUDDS n pl of **RUDD** European freshwater fish with red fins

RUDER adj ill-mannered; discourteous; offensive; crude

RUFFE n a small freshwater perch

RUFFS v pr t of **RUFF** plays a trump card, in bridge or whist, on a card of a different suit

RUGAE n pl of **RUGA** anatomical folds, wrinkles or creases

RUGBY n a kind of football with continuous play, a forerunner of the American game

RUING v pr part of **RUE** feeling sorrow, remorse, regret

RUINS v pr t of **RUIN** destroys; demolishes; devastates

RULED v p t of **RULE** exerted control and authority over

RULER n pl **-S** a person who exerts control and authority over a nation or people; a sovereign

RULES v pr t of **RULE** exerts control and authority over

RUMBA v **-ED, -ING, -S** to dance the rumba, a dance of Cuban origin with a complex rhythm and pronounced hip movements; also **RHUMBA**

RUMEN n pl **-S, RUMINA** the first chamber of a three or four chambered ruminant stomach

RUMMY adj **RUMMIER, RUMMIEST** BRIT. odd; strange; queer

RUMOR v **-ED, -ING, -S** to spread gossip, hearsay or unsubstantiated information

RUMPS n pl of **RUMP** upper hindquarters of four-legged mammals

RUNES n pl of **RUNE** characters from an ancient Germanic alphabet

RUNGS n pl of **RUNG** crosspieces forming steps of a ladder

RUNIC adj related to or written in runes, characters from an ancient Germanic alphabet

RUNNY adj **RUNNIER, RUNNIEST** more liquid than usual; inclined to run or flow

RUNTS n pl of **RUNT** undersized animals, especially the smallest or weakest in their litter

RUNTY adj **RUNTIER, RUNTIEST** small; stunted; puny

RUPEE n pl **-S** a basic unit of currency in India, Pakistan, Sri Lanka, Nepal, Mauritius and the Seychelles

RURAL adj of, related to, or characteristic of the countryside; rustic

RUSES n pl of **RUSE** clever tricks or plots used to deceive others; subterfuges; wily stratagems

RUSHY adj **RUSHIER, RUSHIEST** resembling, made of, or covered with rushes, a plant found in marshy and wetland areas

RUSKS n pl of **RUSK** biscuits or a pieces of crisp bread, dried and toasted or baked for a second time

RUSTS v pr t of **RUST** corrodes with rust, a reddish-brown coating of iron oxide that forms on metal exposed to moist air

RUSTY adj **RUSTIER, RUSTIEST** coated with iron oxide; corroded

RUTIN *n* a yellowish, powdery bioflavonoid, found in many plants, especially buckwheat and tobacco

RUTTY *adj* **RUTTIER, RUTTIEST** full of deep tracks, groves or furrows

RYOTS *n pl* of **RYOT** in South Asia, peasants and subsistence farmers who own or rent small pieces of land

SH *interj* used to urge silence; *also* **SHA, SHH**

SI *n* the 7th note in a scale; *also* **TI**

SO *n pl* **-S** the 5th (dominant) note of any musical scale; *also* **SOH, SOL**

SY *v p t of* **SEE** [obs] saw

THREE LETTERS

SAB *v* **-BED, -BING, -S** SCOT. to sob

SAC *n pl* **-S** a pouch-like structure in an animal or a plant

SAD *adj* **-DER, -DEST** unhappy

SAE *adv* SCOT. so

SAG *v* **-GED, -GING, -S** to bend or sink downward from weight or pressure

SAI *n pl* **-S** a capuchin monk who wears a cowl

SAL *n pl* **-S** pharmacy salt

SAM *adv* [obs] same

SAO *n* any marine annelid which inhabits a transparent movable tube

SAP *v* **-PED, -PING, -S** to gradually diminish the supply or intensity of

SAT *v p t of* **SIT** to rest on the buttocks; to be seated

SAU *n pl* **SAU** xu; a Vietnamese coin

SAV *n pl* **-S** BRIT. informal for saveloy, a spicy smoked pork sausage

SAW *v* **-ED** or **SAWN, -ING, -S** to cut or divide with a tool that has a toothed blade

SAX *n pl* **-ES** informal for saxophone

SAY *v* **SAID, -ING, -S** to utter or express in words; to tell; to speak; to declare

SAZ *n pl* **-ES** a stringed instrument of N. Africa; a baglama

SEA *n pl* **-S** a body of salt or fresh water which covers a large part of the globe

SEC *n* **-S** informal for a short period of time; a second

SEE *v* **SAW, SEEN, -ING, -S** to examine, look at, or watch with the eye

SEG *n pl* **-S** a castrated animal

SEI *n pl* **-S** a coalfish, a whale, a kind of rorqual

SEL *n* SCOT. variation of self

SEN *n pl* **SEN** units of currency in Indonesia, Cambodia and Malaysia

SER *n pl* **-S** a unit of weight of India and South Asia

SES *n pl of* **SUS** the type genus of pigs; hogs; boars

SET *v* **SET, -TING, -S** to put or place in position; also a wonderful family game by the makers of Quiddler

SEW *v* **-ED, -N, -ING, -S** to fasten with needle and thread

SEX *v* **-ED, -ING, -ES** to determine the gender of

SEY *v* [obs] to say

SHA *interj* used to urge silence; *also* **SH, SHH**

SHE *n pl* **-S** a female person or thing

SHH *interj* used to urge silence; *also* **SH, SHA**

SHY *v* **SHIED, SHYING, SHIES** to move suddenly, as if startled; start

SIB *n pl* **-S** a blood relation; sibling; *also* **SYB**

SIC *v* **-CED** or **-KED, -CING** or **-KING, -S** to urge a dog to attack; *also* **SICKS**

SIM *n pl* **-S** informal for a video game that simulates an activity

279

SIN *v* -NED, -NING, -S to commit an offense against religious or moral law

SIP *v* -PED, -PING, -S to drink in small mouthfuls

SIR *n pl* -S a respectful term of address to a man

SIS *n pl* -ES informal for sister

SIT *v* SAT, -TING, S to rest on the buttocks

SIX *n pl* -ES a cardinal number equal to 5 + 1

SKA *n pl* -S a popular music of Jamaica

SKI *v* -ED, -ING, -S to travel or glide on skis, a pair of long flat runners for traveling over slow

SKY *v* SKIED or SKYED, -ING, SKIES to hit or throw a ball very high

SLE *v* [obs] to slay

SLY *adj* SLIER or -ER, SLIEST or -EST artfully cunning; secretly mischievous; wily

SNY *n pl* SNIES an upward bend in a piece of timber; the sheer of a vessel

SOB *v* -BED, -BING, -S to cry uncontrollably

SOC *n pl* -S the liberty or privilege of tenants excused from customary burdens

SOD *v* -DED, -DING, -S to cover with sod, ground or soil

SOE *n pl* -S a large wooden vessel for holding water; a cowl

SOG *v* -GED, -GING, -S BRIT. informal for soak

SOH *n pl* -S the 5th (dominant) note of any musical scale; *also* SO, SOL

SOL *n pl* -S the 5th (dominant) note of any musical scale; *also* SOH, SO

SOM *n pl* SOM the basic monetary unit of Kyrgyzstan

SON *n pl* -S a male descendant

SOP *v* -PED, -PING, -S to steep or dip in or as if in liquid; to wet thoroughly

SOS *n* an urgent appeal for help

SOT *n pl* -S a habitual drunkard

SOU *n pl* -S an old French copper coin

SOV *n pl* -S BRIT. a sovereign (gold coin)

SOW *v* -ED, -N, -ING, -S to scatter over land for growth, as seed

SOX *n pl of* SOCK short stockings reaching a point between the ankle and the knee; *also* SOCKS

SOY *n pl* -S soybean; *also* SOJA, SOYA

SPA *n pl* -S a spring or mineral water; also a spa resort

SPY *n pl* SPIES secret watchers

SRI *n pl* -S used in India as a title of respect for a man; *also* SHRI

STY *n pl* STIES a pen or enclosure for swine

SUB *v* -BED, -BING, -S to be a substitute

SUD *n pl* -S froth of soapy water

SUE *v* -D, SUING, -S to take legal action against somebody to obtain something, usually compensation for a wrong

SUG *n pl* -S a kind of worm or larva

SUK *n pl* -S a marketplace in North Africa and the Middle East; *also* SUQ, SOOK, SOUK, SUKH

SUM *v* -MED, -MING, -S to add; to give a summary of

SUN *v* -NED, -NING, -S to expose to the sun's rays, as for warming, drying, or tanning

SUP *v* -PED, -PING, -S to eat or drink in swallows or gulps

SUQ *n pl* -S a marketplace in North Africa and the Middle East; *also* SUK, SOOK, SOUK, SUKH

SUS *n pl* SES the type genus of pigs; hogs; boars

SWA *adv* [obs] so

SWY *n pl* SWIES Australian two-up game

SYB *n pl* -S [obs] a blood relation; sibling; *also* SIB

SYE *v p t of* SEE [obs] looked at, viewed

FOUR LETTERS

SABS *v pr t of* **SAB** SCOT. sobs

SACK *v* **-ED, -ING, -S** to tackle a quarterback behind the line of scrimmage in football

SACS *n pl of* **SAC** pouch-like structures in animals or plants

SADE *n pl* **-S** the 18th Hebrew letter; *also* **SADI, SADHE, TSADE, TSADI**

SADI *n pl* **-S** the 18th Hebrew letter; *also* **SADE, SADHE, TSADE, TSADI**

SAFE *adj* **-R, -ST** free from harm, injury or risk

SAGA *n pl* **-S** a narrative telling the adventures of a hero or a family

SAGE *n pl* **-S** an aromatic herb used as seasoning

SAGO *n pl* **-S** a powdery starch from certain sago palms

SAGS *v pr t of* **SAG** bends or sinks downward from weight or pressure

SAGY *adj* **SAGIER, SAGIEST** flavored with sage

SAIC *n pl* **-S** a kind of ketch very common in the Levant

SAID *v p t of* **SAY** uttered or expressed in words; told; spoken; declared

SAIL *v* **-ED, -ING, -S** to set sail; to begin a voyage by boat

SAIM *n pl* **-S** lard; grease

SAIN *v* **-ED, -ING, -S** [obs] to sanctify; to bless so as to protect from evil influence

SAIS *n pl of* **SAI** capuchin monks who wear a cowl

SAKE *n pl* **-S** a purpose; a motive

SAKI *n pl* **-S** a Japanese liquor made from rice

SALE *n pl* **-S** the exchange of a commodity for money

SALL *v* [obs] shall

SALP *n pl* **-S** a minute floating marine tunicate having a transparent body with an opening at each end; *also* **SALPA**

SALS *n pl of* **SAL** pharmacy salts

SALT *v* **-ED, -ING, -S** to treat with salt, a crystalline compound used as a seasoning or preservative

SAME *adj* not different or other; identical

SAMP *n pl* **-S** an article of food consisting of maize broken or bruised

SAND *v* **-ED, -ING -S** to rub with sand paper; to spread sand

SANE *v* **-D, SANING, -S** to sain; to make the sign of the cross

SANG *v p t of* **SING** uttered sweet melodious sounds

SANK *v p t of* **SINK** fell or retired beneath or below the surface

SANS *prep* without; deprived or destitute of

SAPO *n pl* **-S** a large toadfish; *also* **SARPO**

SAPS *v pr t of* **SAP** gradually diminishes the supply or intensity of

SARD *n pl* **-S** a deep orange-red variety of quartz; *also* **SARDINE, SARDIUS**

SARI *n pl* **-S** a draped garment worn primarily by Hindu women; *also* **SAREE**

SARK *n pl* **-S** SCOT. a shirt

SARN *n pl* **-S** a pavement or stepping-stone

SASH *n pl* **-ES** a scarf or band worn around the waist

SASS *v* **-ED, -ING, -ES** to talk impudently to

SATE *v* **-D, SATING, -S** to satisfy the desire or appetite of; to satiate

SATI *n pl* **-S** the now illegal act or practice of a Hindu widow's cremating herself on her husband's funeral pyre; *also* **SUTTEE**

SAUF *prep* [obs] save; except

SAUL *n pl* **-S** [obs] a soul

SAVE *v* **-D, SAVING, -S** to procure the safety of; to preserve from injury

SAVS *n pl of* **SAV** BRIT. informal for saveloys, spicy smoked pork sausages

SAWN *v p t of* **SAW** cut or divided with a tool that has a toothed blade

SAWS *v pr t of* **SAW** cuts or divides with a tool that has a toothed blade

SAYS *v pr t of* **SAY** utters or expresses in words; tells; speaks; declares

SCAB *v* **-BED, -BING, -S** to become covered with a crust discharged from and covering a healing wound

SCAD *n pl* **-S** the cigar fish, or round robin

SCAM *v* **-MED, -ING -S** to commit a fraudulent business scheme; to swindle

SCAN *v* **-NED, -NING, -S** to examine closely; to look at

SCAR *v* **-RED, -RING, -S** to leave somebody or something with a physical or emotional mark after damage

SCAT *v* **-TED, -TING, -S** to leave hastily

SCOP *n pl* **-S** [obs] a bard or minstrel

SCOT *n pl* **-S** [obs] a tax or contribution; a fine

SCOW *n pl* **-S** a large flat bottomed boat

SCRY *v* **SCRIED, -ING SCRIES** to predict the future using a crystal ball

SCUD *v* **-DED, -DING, -S** to move swiftly as if driven forward by something

SCUG *n pl* **-S** a place of shelter; the declivity of a hill

SCUM *n pl* **-S** a film layer on the surface of a liquid

SCUP *n pl* **-S** a marine food fish

SCUR *v* **-RED, -RING, -S** [obs] to move hastily; to scour

SCUT *n pl* **-S** a short erect tail

SEAH *n pl* **-S** a Jewish dry measure

SEAK *n pl* **-S** a soap prepared for use in milling cloth

SEAL *v* **-ED, -ING, -S** to close something firmly

SEAM *v* **-ED, -ING, -S** to join things along an edge

SEAR *v* **-ED, -ING, -S** to wither; to dry up

SEAS *n pl of* **SEA** bodies of salt or fresh water that cover a large part of the globe

SEAT *v* **-ED, -ING, -S** to place someone in a chair or other seat

SECK *adj* barren; unprofitable

SECS *n pl of* **SEC** informal for short periods of time; seconds

SECT *n pl* **-S** a subdivision of a larger religious group

SEED *v* **-ED, -ING, -S** to plant in soil; sow

SEEK *v* **SOUGHT, -ING, -S** to go in search of; to look for

SEEL *v* **-ED, -ING, -S** to shut or close, as the eyes; to blind

SEEM *v* **-ED, -ING, -S** to give a certain impression or have a certain outward aspect

SEEN *v p part of* **SEE** examined, looked at, or watched with the eye

SEEP *v* **-ED, -ING, -S** to pass gradually or leak through or as if through small openings; *also* **SIPE**

SEER *n pl* **-S** a person who foresees events; a prophet

SEES *v pr t of* **SEE** examines, looks at, or watches with the eye

SEGO *n pl* **-S** the edible succulent bulb of the sego lily

SEGS *n pl of* **SEG** castrated animals

SEIF *n pl* **-S** a sharp-crested longitudinal sand dune

SEIS *n pl of* **SEI** coalfish, whales, kinds of rorquals

SELD *prep* [obs] rare; uncommon; unusual

SELF *n pl* **SELVES** the same; particular; very; identical

SELL *v* **SOLD, -ING, -S** to transfer to another for an equivalent value

SELY *adj* [obs] silly

282

ŞEME *n pl* **-S** a sprinkled or sown pattern

ŞEMI *n pl* **-S** informal for a semi-trailer; a tractor-trailer truck

ŞEND *v* **SENT, -ING, -S** to cause somebody or something to go

ŞENE *n pl* **SENE** a monetary unit of Western Samoa

ŞENT *v p t of* **SEND** caused somebody or something to go

ŞEPT *n pl* **-S** tribal people descended from a common ancestor

ŞERA *n pl of* **SERUM** the watery fluids left after blood has clotted

ŞERE *adj* withered; dry

ŞERF *n pl* **-S** a feudal servant or slave employed in husbandry

ŞERR *v* **-ED, -ING, -S** [obs] to crowd, press, drive together

ŞERS *n pl of* **SER** units of weight of India and South Asia

ŞETA *n pl* **-E** a stiff hair or bristle

ŞETS *v pr t of* **SET** puts or places in position

ŞETT *n pl* **-S** a badger's burrow; *also* **SET**

ŞEWE *v* **-D, SEWING, -S** [obs] to perform the duties of a sewer, an upper servant who set on and removed the dishes at a feast

ŞEWN *v p part of* **SEW** fastened with needle and thread

ŞEWS *v pr t of* **SEW** fastens with needle and thread

ŞEXT *n pl* **-S** the fourth of the seven canonical hours; about noon

ŞEXY *adj* **SEXIER, SEXIEST** sexually suggestive or stimulating

ŞHAB *v* **-BED, -BING, -S** [obs] to scratch; to rub

ŞHAD *n pl* **-S** a herring-like food fish

ŞHAG *v* **-GED, -GING, -S** to chase and bring back; fetch

ŞHAH *n pl* **-S** a former hereditary monarch of Iran

ŞHAM *v* **-MED, -MING, -S** to trick; to cheat; to deceive or delude with false pretenses

SHAW *n pl* **-S** [obs] a thicket; a small wood or grove

SHAY *n pl* **-S** a chaise lounge

SHEA *n pl* **-S** a tropical African tree

SHED *n pl* **-S** a temporary structure built to shelter something

SHES *n pl of* **SHE** female persons or things

SHET *v* **SHET, -TING, -S** [obs] to shut; *also* **SHETTE**

SHEW *v* **-ED, -N, -ING, -S** [obs] to show

SHIM *v* **-MED, -MING, -S** to fill in, level or adjust by using a thin wedge or spacer material

SHIN *v* **-NED, -NING, -S** to climb quickly up or down by gripping with one's arms and legs

SHIP *v* **-PED, -PING, -S** to transport something by water, overland or by air; to send

SHIV *v* **-ED, -ING, -S** informal for stabbing with a knife

SHMO *n pl* **-ES** informal for a stupid or obnoxious person; *also* **SCHMO, SCHMOE**

SHOD *v p t of* **SHOE** to provide with coverings for the feet

SHOE *v* **SHOD** or **-D, SHODDEN, -ING, -S** to provide with a covering for the feet

SHOG *v* **-GED, -GING -S** to shake, jolt or jostle

SHOO *v* **-ED, -ING, -S** to frighten or drive away

SHOP *v* **-PED, -PING, -S** to look for something with the intention of acquiring it

SHOT *v p t of* **SHOOT** fired a projectile from a weapon

SHOW *v* **-ED, -N, -ING, -S** to exhibit or present to view

SHRI *n pl* **-S** used in India as a title of respect for a man; *also* **SRI**

SHUG *v* **-GED, -GING, -S** [obs] to crawl; to sneak

SHUL *n pl* **-S** or **-N** a synagogue; *also* **SCHUL**

SHUN *v* **-NED, -NING, -S** to avoid; to keep clear of

SHUT v SHUT, -TING, -S to close

SHWA n pl -S a neutral middle vowel; occurs in unstressed syllables; *also* SCHWA

SIAL n pl -S a granite-like rock

SIBS n pl of SIB blood relations; siblings; *also* SYBS

SICE n pl -S the number six at dice; *also* SISE

SICH adj [obs] such

SICK adj -ER, -EST affected with disease of any kind; ill

SICS v pr t of SIC urges a dog to attack

SIDE v -D, SIDING, -S to align oneself in a disagreement

SIDH n pl -E a mound or hill in which fairies live

SIFT v -ED, -ING, -S to separate or part as if with a sieve

SIGH v -ED, -ING, -S to exhale audibly in a long deep breath, as in weariness or relief

SIGN v -ED, -ING, -S to mark with one's signature

SIKA n pl -S a small deer of Japan with slightly forked antlers

SIKE n pl -S a gutter; a stream; *also* SYKE

SILD n pl -S a young herring; *also* SYLE

SILE v -D, SILING, -S to drop; to flow; to fall

SILK n pl -S a fabric made from the fine threads produced by silkworms

SILL n pl -S the threshold beneath a window or door; *also* CILL

SILO n pl -S a cylindrical tower used for storage

SILT v -ED, -ING, -S to clog up

SIMA n pl -S a rock that forms the continuous lower layer of the earth's crust

SIMP n pl -S an informal for a simple or foolish person

SIMS n pl of SIM informal for video games that simulate activities

SINE n pl -S the ratio of the opposite side to the hypotenuse of a right-angled triangle

SING v SANG, SUNG, -ING, -S to utter sweet melodious sounds

SINH n pl -S in mathematics, a hyperbolic sine

SINK v SANK, SUNK, -ING, -S to fall or retire beneath or below the surface

SINS v pr t of SIN commits an offense against religious or moral law

SION n pl -S an imaginary place considered to be perfect or ideal

SIPE v -D, SIPING, -S to pass slowly through small openings or pores; ooze; *also* SEEP

SIPS v pr t of SIP drinks in small mouthfuls

SIPY adj oozy; land under cultivation that is not well drained; *also* SEEPY

SIRE v -D, SIRING, -S to father; beget

SIRS n pl of SIR a respectful term of address to men

SIRT n pl -S [obs] quicksand; a bog; *also* SYRT

SISE n pl -S the number six at dice; *also* SICE

SISS n pl -ES a hissing noise

SIST v -ED, -ING, -S to stay, as judicial proceedings; to delay or suspend; to stop

SITE v -D, SITING, -S to fix or build in a particular place

SITH adv [obs] afterwards; seeing that

SITS v pr t of SIT resting on the buttocks

SIZE v -D, SIZING, -S to arrange, classify, or distribute according to the physical dimensions, magnitude, or extent of an object; *also* CIZE

SIZY adj SIZIER, SIZIEST viscous; glutinous

SIZZ v -ED, -ING, -ES to make a sharp hissing disapproving sound

KAS *n pl of* **SKA** popular music of Jamaica

KAT *n pl* **-S** a card game for three persons

KEE *v* **-D, -ING, -S** to ski

KEG *n pl* **-S** an additional piece fastened to the keel of a boat to prevent lateral motion

KEN *v* **-NED, -NING, -S** [obs] to squint, to look obliquely

KEP *n pl* **-S** a coarse round farm basket; a beehive

KEW *v* **-ED, -ING, -S** to turn or place at an angle

KID *v* **-DED, -DING, -S** to slide without control

KIM *v* **-MED, -MING, -S** to remove floating matter from a liquid

KIN *v* **-NED, -NING, -S** to remove the outside layer of something

KIP *v* **-PED, -PING, -S** to move by hopping on one foot and then the other

KIS *v pr t of* **SKI** travels or glides on skis, a pair of long flat runners for traveling over slow

KIT *n pl* **-S** a short comic sketch

KUA *n pl* **-S** a large predatory sea bird

LAB *n pl* **-S** a broad, flat, thick piece, as of stone or cheese

LAG *n pl* **-S** the waste material from smelting

LAM *v* **-MED, -MING, -S** to shut with force and a loud noise

LAP *v* **-PED, -PING, -S** to give a blow, especially with the open hand

LAT *v* **-TED, -TING, -S** to add slats, narrow strips of metal or wood, to something

LAW *n pl* **-S** sliced cabbage served as a salad, cooked or uncooked

LAY *v* **SLEW** or **-ED, SLAIN, -ING, -S** to kill violently

LED *v* **-DED, -DING, -S** to move over the snow or ice by conveyance with runners

LEW *v p t of* **SLAY** killed violently

LEY *n pl* **-S** a guide way in a knitting machine

SLID *v p t of* **SLIDE** moved over a surface while maintaining smooth continuous contact

SLIK *adj* [obs] such

SLIM *v* **-MED, -MING, -S** to lose or cause to lose weight, as by dieting or exercise

SLIP *v* **SLIPT** or **-PED, -PING, -S** to move obliquely or sideways, usually in an uncontrolled manner

SLIT *v* **-TED, -TING, -S** to make a long, narrow cut into

SLOB *n pl* **-S** a lazy and untidy person

SLOE *n pl* **-S** a small, sour dark purple plum fruit

SLOG *v* **-GED, -GING, -S** to walk or progress with great effort

SLOP *v* **-PED, -PING, -S** to spill liquids

SLOT *v* **-TED, -TING, -S** to assign a place to something

SLOW *v* **-ED, -ING, -S** to reduce the speed or progress of something

SLUB *n pl* **-S** a lump in yarn or fabric that is sometimes an imperfection, but is often made to provide a knotty effect

SLUE *v* **-D, SLUING, -S** to turn about; to turn from the course; to slip

SLUG *v* **-GED, -GING, -S** to hit very hard

SLUM *v* **-MED, -MING, -S** to accept a lower standard than usual

SLUR *v* **-RED, -RING, -S** to soil; to sully; to contaminate; to disgrace

SLUT *n pl* **-S** an untidy woman; a slattern

SMEE *n pl* **-S** the pintail duck

SMEW *n pl* **-S** the smallest merganser and most expert diver

SMIT *v p part of* **SMITE** [obs] to have strike; inflicted a blow

SMOG *n pl* **-S** fog that has become mixed and polluted with smoke

SMUG *adj* **-GER, -GEST** very pleased with oneself; self-satisfied

SMUT *v* **-TED, -TING, -S** to become affected with smut, a fungus causing disease in plants

SNAG *v* **-GED, -GING, -S** to catch on or collide with a sharp projection

SNAP *v* **-PED, -PING, -S** to strike, to hit or to shut with a sharp sound

SNAW *n pl* **-S** [obs] snow

SNEB *v* **-BED, -BING, -S** [obs] to reprimand; *also* **SNEAP**

SNED *v* **-DED, -DING, -S** to lop; to prune

SNET *n pl* **-S** the fat of a deer

SNEW *v* **-ED, -ING, -S** [obs] to snow; to abound

SNIB *v* **-BED, -BING, -S** to operate or fasten the bolt on a door or lock

SNIG *v* **-GED, -GING, -S** to drag something heavy along; used in Canada

SNIP *v* **-PED, -PING, -S** to cut with small strokes

SNIT *n pl* **-S** a state of agitation or irritation

SNOB *n pl* **-S** a vulgar person who affects to be better, richer or more fashionable

SNOD *adj* smooth, sleek

SNOG *v* **-GED, -GING, -S** BRIT. to kiss and cuddle someone

SNOT *n pl* **-S** mucus from the nose

SNOW *v* **-ED, -ING, -S** to fall like snow (precipitation in the form of small white ice crystals)

SNUB *v* **-BED, -BING, -S** to treat with contempt or neglect

SNUG *v* **-GED, -GING, -S** to curl up in a cozy way

SNYE *n pl* **-S** a side channel of a river; used in Canada

SOAK *v* **-ED, -ING, -S** to drench; to wet thoroughly

SOAL *n pl* **-S** the sole of a shoe

SOAM *n pl* **-S** a chain by which a leading horse draws a plow

SOAP *v* **-ED, -ING, -S** to put soap on something or somebody

SOAR *v* **-ED, -ING, -S** to fly aloft, as a bird; to mount upward on wings

SOBA *n pl* **-S** a Japanese noodle made with buckwheat flour

SOBS *v pr t of* **SOB** cries uncontrollably

SOCA *n pl* **-S** a blend of Caribbean soul and calypso music

SOCK *v* **-ED, -ING, -S** to hit something or somebody hard, usually with a fist

SOCS *n pl of* **SOC** liberties or privileges of tenants excused from customary burdens

SODA *n pl* **-S** a sweet drink of carbonated water and flavoring

SODS *v pr t of* **SOD** covers with sod, ground or soil

SOES *n pl of* **SOE** large wooden vessels for holding water; cowls

SOFA *n pl* **-S** an upholstered seat for more than one person

SOFT *adj* **-ER, -EST** smooth; delicate; fine

SOGS *v pr t of* **SOG** BRIT. informal for soaks

SOIL *v* **-ED, -ING, -S** to make dirty or unclean on the surface

SOJA *n pl* **-S** an erect bushy hairy annual herb that produces soybeans; *also* **SOY, SOYA**

SOKE *n pl* **-S** BRIT. [obs] the right of local jurisdiction

SOKO *n pl* **-S** an African chimpanzee

SOLA *n pl of* **SOLUM** the upper layer of soil profiles

SOLD *v p t of* **SELL** transferred to another for an equivalent value

SOLE *n pl* **-S** the bottom of a foot, shoe or boot

SOLI *n pl of* **SOLO** activities that are performed alone without assistance; *also* **SOLOS**

SOLO *n pl* **SOLI, -S** any activity that is performed alone without assistance

SOLS *n pl of* **SOL** a monetary unit of Peru; *also* **SOLES**

SOMA *n pl* **-TA, -S** the entire body of an organism, exclusive of the germ cells

SOME *adj* an unspecified number or quantity

SONE *n pl* **-S** a unit of perceived loudness

SONG *n pl* **-S** a lyrical poem adapted to vocal music

SONS *n pl of* **SON** male descendants

SOOK *n pl* **-S** a marketplace in North Africa and the Middle East; *also* **SUK, SUQ, SOUK, SUKH**

SOON *adv* **-ER, -EST** in a short time

SOOT *v* **-ED, -ING, -S** to cover or coat with soot, a black dust given off by fire

SOPH *n pl* **-S** informal for sophomore

SOPS *v pr t of* **SOP** steeps or dips in or as if in liquid; wets thoroughly

SORA *n pl* **-S** a marsh bird

SORB *v* **-ED, -ING, -S** take up a liquid or a gas either by adsorption or by absorption

SORD *n pl* **-S** a flight or flock of mallards

SORE *v* **-D, SORING, -S** to mutilate the legs or feet of (a horse) in order to induce a particular gait in the animal.

SORI *n pl of* **SORUS** spore-producing structures in certain lichens and fungi

SORN *v* **-ED, -ING, -S** SCOT. to impose one's self on another for bed and board

SORT *v* **-ED, -ING, -S** to arrange or order by classes or categories

SORY *n* green vitriol, or some earth impregnated with it

SOSS *v* **-ED, -ING, -ES** to fall at once into a chair or seat; to sit lazily

SOTS *n pl of* **SOT** habitual drunkards

SOUK *n pl* **-S** a marketplace in North Africa and the Middle East; *also* **SUK, SUQ, SOOK, SUKH**

SOUL *n pl* **-S** the spiritual nature of humans

SOUP *n pl* **-S** a liquid food of many kinds

SOUR *v* **-ED, -ING, -S** to make or become somebody dissatisfied; to make or become something tart or sharp-tasting

SOUS *n pl of* **SOU** old French copper coins

SOUT *n* [obs] variant of **SOOT**

SOVS *n pl of* **SOV** BRIT. a sovereign, gold coin

SOWN *v p part of* **SOW** to have scattered over land for growth, as seed

SOWS *v pr t of* **SOW** scatters over land for growth, as seed

SOYA *n pl* **-S** soybeans; *also* **SOY, SOJA**

SOYS *n pl of* **SOY** soybeans; *also* **SOJAS, SOYAS**

SPAE *v* **-D, -ING, -S** to foretell; to divine

SPAM *v* **-MED, -MING, -S** to send unsolicited emails

SPAN *v* **-NED, -NING, -S** to extend across or over

SPAR *v* **-RED, -RING, -S** to make boxing or fighting motions without hitting one's opponent

SPAS *n pl of* **SPA** springs or mineral waters; also spa resorts

SPAT *v* **-TED, -TING, -S** to quarrel briefly over a petty matter

SPAY *v* **-ED, -ING, -S** to remove or extirpate the ovaries of

SPAZ *n pl* **-ZES** a clumsy or inept person; *also* **SPAZZ**

SPEC *v* **-CED, -CING, -S** to write or supply specifications for

SPED *v p t of* **SPEED** moved quickly; *also* **SPEEDED**

SPET *v* **-TED, -TING, -S** [obs] to spit; to throw out

SPEW *v* **-ED, -ING, -S** to eject forcefully; *also* **SPUE**

SPIN *v* **SPUN, -NING, -S** to draw out tediously and twist into threads

SPIT *v* **SPAT** or **SPIT, -TING, -S** to eject from the mouth

SPIV *n pl* **-S** BRIT. one, usually unemployed, who lives by one's wits

SPOT *v* **-TED, -TING, -S** to become stained with a blemish

SPRY *adj* **-ER** or **SPRIER, -EST** or **SPRIEST** nimble; active

SPUD *n pl* **-S** a sharp hand shovel for digging

SPUE *v* **-D, SPUING, -S** to eject forcefully; *also* **SPEW**

SPUN *v p t of* **SPIN** drawn out tediously and twisted into threads

SPUR *v* **-RED, -RING, -S** to give incentive to; encourage

SPUT *n pl* **-S** a thimble or annular plate used to reinforce a hole in a boiler

SRIS *n pl of* **SRI** used in India as titles of respect for men; *also* **SHRIS**

STAB *v* **-BED, -BING, -S** to pierce with a pointed weapon

STAG *n pl* **-S** the adult male of the red deer

STAR *v* **-RED, -RING, -S** to be the leading performer

STAT *adv* with no delay; at once

STAW *v* **-ED, -ING, -S** SCOT. to be fixed or set; to stay

STAY *v* **-ED** or **STAID, -ING, -S** to stop doing something; cease

STEE *n pl* **-S** [obs] a ladder; *also* **STEY**

STEG *n pl* **-S** [obs] a gander; a male goose

STEM *v* **-MED, -MING, -S** to derive, originate or be caused by something

STEP *v* **-PED, -PING, -S** to move the foot in walking

STET *v* **-TED, -TING, -S** in printing: to cancel, as of a correction or deletion

STEW *v* **-ED, -ING, -S** to be upset

STEY *n pl* **-S** [obs] a ladder; *also* **STEE**

STIR *v* **-RED, -RING, -S** to mix ingredients

STOA *n pl* **-E, STOAI, -S** an ancient Greek covered walk or colonnade

STOB *n pl* **-S** a short straight piece of wood, such as a stake

STOP *v* **-PED, -PING, -S** to obstruct; to render impassable

STOR *adj* **-ER, -EST** [obs] strong; powerful; hardy; bold; audacious

STOT *v* **-TED, -TING, -S** to run with a springing gait; *also* **STOTT**

STOW *v* **-ED, -ING, -S** to put away in some place; to hide; to lodge

STUB *v* **-BED, -BING, -S** to bang a toe against something accidentally

STUD *v* **-DED, -DING, -S** to set, mark or decorate conspicuously and often at intervals

STUM *v* **-MED, -MING, -S** to ferment wine by adding partly fermented grape juice to it while in the cask or vat

STUN *v* **-NED, -NING, -S** to astonish; to overpower; to bewilder

STYE *n pl* **STIES** or **-S** an infection of the sebaceous gland of the eyelid

SUBS *v pr t of* **SUB** to be a substitute

SUCH *adj* of that kind; of the like kind; like

SUCK *v* **-ED, -ING, -S** to draw liquid from, by the action of the mouth

SUDD *n pl* **-S** a floating mass of vegetation

SUDS *n pl of* **SUD** froths of soapy water

SUED *v p t of* **SUE** took legal action against somebody to obtain something, usually compensation for a wrong

SUER *n pl* **-S** a person that sues

SUES *v pr t of* **SUE** takes legal action against somebody to obtain something, usually compensation for a wrong

SUET *n pl* **-S** the hard white fat found on the kidneys and loins of sheep and cattle

SUGH *v* **-ED, -ING, -S** SCOT. [obs] to make a soft moaning or sighing sound; *also* **SOUGH**

SUGI *n pl* **-S** a tall evergreen of Japan and China yielding valuable soft wood

288

SUGS *n pl of* **SUG** kinds of worms or larvae

SUIT *v* **-ED, -ING, -S** to be appropriate to

SUJI *n* an Indian wheat, granulated but not pulverized; *also* **SOOJEE**

SUKH *n pl* **-S** a marketplace in North Africa and the Middle East; *also* **SUK, SUQ, SOOK, SOUK**

SUKS *n pl of* **SUK** marketplaces in North Africa and the Middle East; *also* **SUQS, SOOKS, SOUKS, SUKHS**

SULA *n pl* **-S** a sea bird, including the booby

SULK *v* **-ED, -ING, -S** to be angrily silent

SULL *n pl* **-S** [obs] a plow; a farm implement

SULU *n pl* **-S** a sarong-like garment, worn by Melanesians, as in the Fiji Islands

SUMO *n pl* **-S** a Japanese form of wrestling; a wrestler of sumo

SUMP *n pl* **-S** a reservoir for liquid

SUMS *v pr t of* **SUM** adds; gives a summary of

SUNG *v p part of* **SING** to have uttered sweet melodious sounds

SUNK *v p part of* **SINK** to have fallen or retired beneath or below the surface

SUNN *n pl* **-S** an East Indian leguminous plant

SUNS *v pr t of* **SUN** exposes to the sun's rays, as for warming, drying or tanning

SUPE *n pl* **-S** an actor without a speaking part; a supernumerary

SUPS *v pr t of* **SUP** eats or drinks in swallows or gulps

SUQS *n pl of* **SUQ** marketplaces in North Africa and the Middle East; *also* **SUKS, SOOKS, SOUKS, SUKHS**

SURA *n pl* **-S** any of the 114 chapters or sections of the Koran

SURD *n pl* **-S** a voiceless speech sound

SURE *adj* **-R, -ST** in a sure manner; safely; certainly

SURF *v* **-ED, -ING, -S** to ride the swells of the sea which break upon the shore with a board or body

SUSS *v* **-ED, -ING, -ES** BRIT. to infer or discover; figure out

SUSU *n pl* **-S** a dolphin; *also* **SOOSOO**

SWAB *v* **-BED, -BING, -S** to clean with a mop or swab; *also* **SWOB**

SWAD *n pl* **-S** [obs] a clown; a country bumpkin

SWAG *v* **-GED, -GING, -S** to hang or move; to sway; to swing

SWAM *v p t of* **SWIM** moved progressively in water by means of strokes with the hands and feet

SWAN *v* **-NED, -NING, -S** to declare or affirm solemnly and formally as true

SWAP *v* **-PED, -PING, -S** to exchange; to trade; *also* **SWOP**

SWAT *v* **-TED, -TING, -S** to strike or slap with a sharp blow; *also* **SWOT**

SWAY *v* **-ED, -ING, -S** to move or wield with the hand; to swing

SWIG *v* **-GED, -GING, -S** to drink in long draughts; to gulp

SWIM *v* **SWAM, SWUM, -MING, -S** to move progressively in water by means of strokes with the hands and feet

SWOB *n pl* **-S** a cleaning implement consisting of absorbent material fastened to a handle; *also* **SWAB**

SWOP *v* **-PED, -PING, -S** to exchange; to trade; *also* **SWAP**

SWOT *v* **-TED, -TING, -S** to strike or slap with a sharp blow; *also* **SWAT**

SWUM *v p t of* **SWIM** moved progressively in water by means of strokes with the hands and feet

SYBO *n pl* **-ES** or **-WS** SCOT. a spring onion; *also* **SYBOE, SYBOW**

SYBS *n pl of* **SYB** [obs] blood relations; siblings; *also* **SIBS**

SYCE *n pl* **-S** a stableman or groom, especially in India; *also* **SAICE**

SYKE *n pl* **-S** a small stream; a gutter; *also* **SIKE**

SYLE *n pl* **-S** [obs] a young herring; *also* **SILD**

SYLI *n pl* **-S** a former monetary unit of Guinea

SYNC *v* **-ED, -ING, -S** to cause to harmonize and operate in unison; *also* **SYNCH**

SYND *v* **-ED, -ING, -S** to rinse something, usually with water; *also* **SYNE**

SYNE *v* **-D, SYNING, -S** to rinse something, usually with water; *also* **SYND**

SYRT *n pl* **-S** [obs] quicksand; a bog; *also* **SIRT**

FIVE LETTERS

SABAL *n pl* **-S** a palmetto

SABER *n pl* **-S** a stout sword with a curved blade and thick back; *also* **SABRE**

SABIN *n pl* **-S** a unit of sound absorption

SABIR *n pl* **-S** a French-based pidgin language

SABLE *n pl* **-S** a carnivorous mammal

SABOT *n pl* **-S** a shoe carved from a single block of wood

SABRA *n pl* **-S** a native-born Israeli

SABRE *n pl* **-S** a stout sword with a curved blade and thick back; *also* **SABER**

SACKS *v pr t of* **SACK** tackles a quarterback behind the line of scrimmage in football

SACRA *n pl of* **SACRUM** bones of the pelvis

SADDA *n pl* **-S** a sacred Persian book

SADES *n pl of* **SADE** the 18th Hebrew letter; *also* **SADIS, SADHES, TSADES, TSADIS**

SADHE *n pl* **-S** the 18th Hebrew letter; *also* **SADE, SADI, TSADE, TSADI**

SADHU *n pl* **-S** an ascetic holy Hindu man

SADIS *n pl of* **SADI** the 18th Hebrew letter; *also* **SADES, SADHES, TSADES, TSADIS**

SADLY *adv* with sadness; affected with or expressive of grief or unhappiness

SAFER *adj of* **SAFE** more free from harm, injury, or risk

SAFES *n pl of* **SAFE** strong, lockable and fireproof receptacles for valuables

SAGAS *n pl of* **SAGA** narratives telling the adventures of a hero or a family

SAGER *adj* more wise through reflection and experience

SAGES *n pl of* **SAGE** aromatic herbs used as seasoning

SAGGY *adj* **SAGGIER, SAGGIEST** hang down loosely or unevenly

SAGOS *n pl of* **SAGO** powdery starches from certain sago palms

SAGUM *n pl* **-S** the military cloak of the Roman soldiers

SAHEB *n pl* **-S** sir; master, formerly a term of respect in colonial India; *also* **SAHIB**

SAHIB *n pl* **-S** sir; master, formerly a term of respect in colonial India; *also* **SAHEB**

SAHUI *n pl* **-S** a marmoset; a small squirrel monkey

SAICE *n pl* **-S** a stableman or groom, especially in India; *also* **SYCE**

SAICS *n pl of* **SAIC** kinds of ketches very common in the Levant

SAIDS *n pl of* **SAID** Islamic titles of respect for a man; *also* **SAYEDS, SAYIDS, SAYYIDS**

SAIGA *n pl* **-S** a goat-like antelope

SAILS *v pr t of* **SAIL** sets sail; begins a voyage by boat

SAILY *adj* like a sail

SAIMS *n pl of* **SAIM** lards; greases

SAINS *v pr t of* **SAIN** [obs] sanctifies; blesses so as to protect from evil influence

SAINT *n pl* **-S** a person sanctified; a holy or godly person

SAITH *v pr t of* **SAY** [obs] archaic third person singular present of **SAY**

SAJOU *n pl* **-S** a capuchin ringtail monkey; *also* **SAPAJOU**

SAKER *n pl* **-S** a Eurasian falcon

SAKES *n pl of* **SAKE** purposes; motives

SAKIS *n pl of* **SAKI** Japanese liquors made from rice; *also* **SAKES**

SAKTI *n pl* **-S** the divine energy; the female principle

SALAD *n pl* **-S** a dish of greens; raw vegetables

SALAL *n pl* **-S** a small evergreen shrub

SALAM *v* **-ED, -ING, -S** to greet with or perform a ceremonious act of deference or obeisance; *also* **SALAAM**

SALEB *n pl* **-S** the dried tubers of various species of Orchids; a nutritious beverage; *also* **SALEP**

SALEP *n pl* **-S** the dried tubers of various species of Orchids; a nutritious beverage; *also* **SALEB**

SALES *n pl of* **SALE** exchanges of commodities for money

SALIC *adj* pertaining to igneous rocks

SALIX *n pl* **SALICES** a tree or shrub of willow

SALLY *v* **SALLIED, -ING, SALLIES** to rush out suddenly

SALMI *n pl* **-S** a highly spiced dish consisting of roasted game birds

SALOL *n* a white crystalline substance

SALON *n pl* **-S** an elegant sitting room where guests are received

SALPA *n pl* **-S** or **-E** a free-swimming oceanic tunicate; *also* **SALP**

SALPS *n pl of* **SALP** minute floating marine tunicates having transparent bodies

SALSA *n pl* **-S** a spicy sauce of tomatoes, onions and hot peppers

SALSE *n pl* **-S** a mud volcano impregnated with salts

SALTS *v pr t of* **SALT** treats with salt, a crystalline compound used as a seasoning or preservative

SALTY *adj* **SALTIER, SALTIEST** of, containing, or seasoned with salt

SALUE *v* [obs] to salute

SALVE *n pl* **-S** a soothing remedy or antidote

SALVO *n pl* **-S, -ES** a simultaneous discharge of firearms

SAMAJ *n* in India: a society; a congregation; a worshiping assembly; *also* **SOMAJ**

SAMBA *n pl* **-S** a Brazilian ballroom dance of African origin

SAMEK *n pl* **-S** the 15th letter in the Hebrew alphabet; *also* **SAMEKH**

SAMPS *n pl of* **SAMP** articles of food consisting of maize broken or bruised

SANDS *v pr t of* **SAND** rubs with sand paper; spreads sand

SANDY *adj* **SANDIER, SANDIEST** consisting of or resembling sand

SANED *v p t of* **SANE** sained; made the sign of the cross

SANER *adj* more mentally healthy

SANES *v pr t of* **SANE** sains; makes the sign of the cross

SANGA *n pl* **-S** a type of draft cattle with a small hump and long horns; *also* **SANGU**

SANGH *n pl* **-S** an association or union, particularly between different groups in Hinduism

SANGU *n pl* **-S** a type of draft cattle with a small hump and long horns; *also* **SANGA**

SANTO *n pl* **-S** a painted or carved wooden image of a saint

SAPID *adj* possessing savor, or flavor; *also* **SIPID**

SAPOR *n pl* **-S** savor; flavor; taste

SAPOS *n pl of* **SAPO** large toadfishes; *also* **SARPOS**

SAPPY *adj* **SAPPIER, SAPPIEST** abounding with sap; juicy; succulent

SARAN *n pl* **-S** a thermoplastic resin

SARDS *n pl of* **SARD** deep orange-red varieties of quartz; *also* **SARDINES, SARDIUSES**

SAREE *n pl* **-S** a draped garment worn primarily by Hindu women; *also* **SARI**

SARGE *n pl* **-S** informal for sergeant

SARGO *n pl* **-S** a silvery marine fish; *also* **SARGU, SARGON**

SARGU *n pl* **-S** a silvery marine fish; *also* **SARGO, SARGON**

SARIN *n pl* **-S** a very toxic gas

SARIS *n pl of* **SARI** draped garments worn primarily by Hindu women; *also* **SAREES**

SARKS *n pl of* **SARK** SCOT. shirts

SARKY *adj* **SARKIER, SARKIEST** sarcastic

SARNS *n pl of* **SARN** pavements or stepping-stones

SAROD *n pl* **-S** a many-stringed lute of northern India

SAROS *n* the eclipse cycle of the sun and moon

SARPO *n pl* **-S** a large toadfish; *also* **SAPO**

SARSE *n pl* **-S** [obs] a fine sieve; *also* **SEARCE, SEARSE**

SASIN *n pl* **-S** an antelope of India

SASSE *n pl* **-S** [obs] a sluice or lock on a river

SASSY *adj* **SASSIER, SASSIEST** bold and spirited; impudent

SATAY *n pl* **-S** an Asian dish consisting of strips of marinated meat, poultry or seafood grilled on skewers; *also* **SATE**

SATED *v p t of* **SATE** satisfied the desire or appetite of; satiated

SATEM *adj* denoting or belonging to the group of Indo-European languages

SATES *v pr t of* **SATE** satisfies the desire or appetite of; satiates

SATIN *n pl* **-S** a smooth fabric with a smooth, glossy surface

SATIS *n pl of* **SATI** the now illegal acts or practices of Hindu widows cremating themselves on their husbands' funeral pyres; *also* **SUTTEES**

SATYR *n pl* **-S** in Greek mythology, a woodland creature with the head and body of a man and the ears, horns and legs of a goat

SAUCE *v* **-D, SAUCING, -S** to cause to relish anything

SAUCH *n pl* **-ES** SCOT. a willow tree; *also* **SAUGH**

SAUCY *adj* **SAUCIER, SAUCIEST** insolent, impudent

SAUGH *n pl* **-S** SCOT. a willow tree; *also* **SAUCH**

SAULS *n pl of* **SAUL** [obs] souls

SAULT *n pl* **-S** a rapids or a waterfall

SAUNA *n pl* **-S** a dry heat bath

SAURY *n pl* **SAURIES** a slender marine fish

SAUTE *v* **-ED, -ING, -S** to fry quickly in a little fat

SAVED *v p t of* **SAVE** procured the safety of; preserved from injury

SAVER *n pl* **-S** one who saves

SAVES *v pr t of* **SAVE** procures the safety of; preserves from injury

SAVIN *n pl* **-S** a juniper shrub; *also* **SAVINE**

SAVOR *v* **-ED, -ING, -S** to taste or smell with pleasure; to delight in; to relish

SAVOY *n pl* **-S** a variety of cabbage with curled leaves

SAVVY *v* **SAVVIED, -ING, SAVVIES** to understand; comprehend

SAWED *v p t of* **SAW** cut or divided with a tool that has a toothed blade

SAWER *n pl* **-S** one who saws

SAXES *n pl of* **SAX** informal for saxophones

SAYED	*n pl* **-S** an Islamic title of respect for a man; *also* **SAYID, SAYYID**
SAYER	*n pl* **-S** one who says; an utterer
SAYID	*n pl* **-S** an Islamic title of respect for a man; *also* **SAYED, SAYYID**
SAYST	*v pr t of* **SAY** [obs] archaic second person singular of **SAY**
SAZES	*n pl of* **SAZ** stringed instruments of N. Africa; baglamas
SCABS	*v pr t of* **SCAB** becomes covered with a crust discharged from and covering a healing wound
SCADS	*n pl of* **SCAD** cigar fishes, or round robins
SCALA	*n pl* **-E** a term applied to any one of the three canals of the cochlea
SCALD	*v* **-ED, -ING, -S** to burn with hot liquid or steam
SCALE	*v* **-D, SCALING, -S** to reach the highest point
SCALL	*n* a scaly eruption of the skin or scalp; *also* **SCALD**
SCALP	*v* **-ED, -ING, -S** to remove the skin of the head
SCALY	*adj* **SCALIER, SCALIEST** covered with scales
SCAMP	*n pl* **-S** a rascal; a swindler; a rogue
SCAMS	*v pr t of* **SCAM** commits fraudulent business schemes; swindles
SCANS	*v pr t of* **SCAN** examines closely; looks at
SCANT	*adj* **-ER, -EST** sparing; parsimonious; chary
SCAPE	*v* **-D, SCAPING, -S** [obs] to escape
SCARD	*n pl* **-S** [obs] a shard or fragment
SCARE	*v* **-D, SCARING, -S** to frighten
SCARF	*n pl* **-S** or **SCARVES** a garment worn around the head or neck or shoulders for warmth or decoration
SCARP	*v* **-ED, -ING, -S** to create a steep artificial slope
SCARS	*v pr t of* **SCAR** leaves somebody or something with a physical or emotional mark after damage
SCART	*v* **-ED, -ING, -S** SCOT. to scratch, scrape, mark or scar
SCARY	*adj* **SCARIER, SCARIEST** frightening
SCATH	*n pl* **-S** harm; damage; injury; hurt, *also* **SCATHE**
SCATS	*v pr t of* **SCAT** leaves hastily
SCATT	*n pl* **-S** a tribute, a tax
SCAUP	*n pl* **-S** a sea duck
SCAUR	*n pl* **-S** SCOT. a precipitous bank or rock; a scar
SCENA	*n pl* **-E** an elaborate solo vocal composition
SCEND	*v* **-ED, -ING, -S** to heave upward on a wave or swell
SCENE	*n pl* **-S** the context and environment in which something is set
SCENT	*v* **-ED, -ING, -S** to imbue or fill with odor; to perfume
SCERN	*v* **-ED, -ING, -S** to discern; to perceive
SCHAV	*n pl* **-S** a chilled soup made from sorrel or spinach
SCHMO	*n pl* **-S** or **-ES** informal for a stupid or obnoxious person; *also* **SHMO, SCHMOE**
SCHUL	*n pl* **-S** or **-N** a synagogue; *also* **SHUL**
SCHWA	*n pl* **-S** a neutral middle vowel; occurs in unstressed syllables; *also* **SHWA**
SCION	*n pl* **-S** a child or descendant
SCISE	*v* **-D, SCISING, -S** [obs] to cut; to penetrate
SCOAT	*v* **-ED, -ING, -S** to prop; to scotch
SCOBS	*n/pl* raspings of ivory, hartshorn, metals or others
SCOFF	*v* **-ED, -ING, -S** to show insolent ridicule or mockery
SCOKE	*n pl* **-S** a tall coarse perennial herb; pokeweed

293

SCOLD v **-ED, -ING, -S** to censure severely or angrily

SCOMM n pl **-S** a buffoon; a clown

SCONE n pl **-S** a flat cake, a small biscuit

SCOOP v **-ED, -ING, -S** to create a shallow hole in something with a scoop (utensil with a short handle and deep rounded sides) or a cupped hand

SCOOT v **-ED, -ING, -S** to walk fast; to go quickly

SCOPE v **-ED, -ING, -S** to examine or investigate

SCOPS n pl of **SCOP** [obs] bards or minstrels

SCORE v **-D, SCORING, -S** to assign a number or letter indicating performance

SCORN v **-ED, -ING, -S** to treat with extreme contempt

SCOTS n pl of **SCOT** [obs] taxes or contributions; fines

SCOUR v **-ED, -ING, -S** to pass swiftly over; to brush along

SCOUT v **-ED, -ING, -S** explore with the goal of finding something or somebody

SCOWL v **-ED, -ING, -S** to wrinkle the brows; to look sour, sullen, severe or angry

SCOWS n pl of **SCOW** large flat bottomed boats

SCRAG n pl **-S** a bony neckpiece of meat; the neck

SCRAM v **-MED, -MING, -S** to leave a scene at once, go abruptly

SCRAP v **-PED, -PING, -S** to dispose of worthless material

SCRAT v **-TED, -TING, -S** [obs] to scratch, to rake; to search

SCRAW n pl **-S** [obs] turf

SCRAY n pl **-S** a tern; the sea swallow

SCREE n pl **-S** a heap of stones or rocky debris

SCREW v **-ED, -ING, -S** to turn or twist

SCRID n pl **-S** a screed; a shred; a fragment

SCRIM n pl **-S** a light cotton or linen fabric

SCRIP n pl **-S** a piece of paper having recognized monetary value

SCRIT n pl **-S** a writing; a document; a scroll

SCROD n pl **-S** a young Atlantic cod or haddock

SCROG n pl **-S** a stunted shrub, bush or branch

SCROW n pl **-S** [obs] a scroll

SCRUB v **-BED, -BING, -S** to rub hard; to wash with rubbing

SCRUM v **-MED, -MING, -S** to engage a particular team in Rugby

SCUBA n pl **-S** a portable apparatus containing compressed air and used for breathing under water

SCUDI n pl of **SCUDO** former Italian silver coins

SCUDO n pl **SCUDI** a former Italian silver coin

SCUDS v pr t of **SCUD** moves swiftly as if driven forward by something

SCUFF v **-ED, -ING, -S** to walk without lifting the feet

SCUGS n pl of **SCUG** places of shelter; declivities of hills

SCULK v **-ED, -ING, -S** to hide, or get out of the way; also **SKULK**

SCULL v **-ED, -ING, -S** to impel a boat with a pair of oars

SCULP v **-S** to carve; to engrave; also **SCULPT**

SCUMS n pl of **SCUM** film layers on the surfaces of liquids

SCUPS n pl of **SCUP** marine food fishes

SCURF n thin dry scales or scabs upon the body

SCURS v pr t of **SCUR** [obs] moves hastily; scours

SCUTA n pl of **SCUTUM** horny plates or scales; also **SCUTE**

SCUTE n pl of **SCUTUM** horny plates or scales; also **SCUTA**

SCUTS n pl of **SCUT** short erect tails

SCUZZ n pl **-ES** a dirty or contemptible person

SEAHS *n pl of* **SEAH** Jewish dry measures

SEAKS *n pl of* **SEAK** soaps prepared for use in milling cloth

SEALS *v pr t of* **SEAL** closes something firmly

SEAMS *v pr t of* **SEAM** joins things along an edge

SEAMY *adj* **SEAMIER, SEAMIEST** morally degraded

SEARS *v pr t of* **SEAR** withers; dries up

SEATS *v pr t of* **SEAT** places someone in a chair or other seat

SEAVY *adj* overgrown with rushes

SEBUM *n/pl* an oily substance produced by certain glands in the skin

SECCO *n pl* **-S** the art or an example of painting on dry plaster

SECTS *n pl of* **SECT** subdivisions of a larger religious group

SEDAN *n pl* **-S** a type of automobile usually a 4-door

SEDER *n pl* **-S** or **SEDARIM** the feast commemorating the exodus of the Jews from Egypt

SEDGE *n pl* **-S** a perennial marsh plant

SEDGY *adj* **SEDGIER, SEDGIEST** overgrown with sedge (a perennial marsh plant)

SEDUM *n pl* **-S** a perennial flowering plant with fleshy leaves

SEEDS *n pl of* **SEED** the propagative parts of a plant or animal

SEEDY *adj* **SEEDIER, SEEDIEST** shabby, dirty-looking and often disreputable

SEEKS *v pr t of* **SEEK** goes in search of; looks for

SEELS *v pr t of* **SEEL** shuts or closes, as the eyes; blinds

SEELY *adj* frail; weak

SEEMS *v pr t of* **SEEM** gives a certain impression or has a certain outward aspect

SEEPS *v pr t of* **SEEP** passes gradually or leaks through or as if through small openings; *also* **SIPES**

SEEPY *adj* **SEEPIER, SEEPIEST** oozy; not well drained land; *also* **SIPY**

SEERS *n pl of* **SEER** people who foresee events; prophets

SEGGE *n pl* **-S** a hedge sparrow

SEGNI *n pl of* **SEGNO** musical signs

SEGNO *n pl* **SEGNI** a musical sign

SEGOS *n pl of* **SEGO** the edible succulent bulbs of the sego lily

SEGUE *v* **-D, -ING, -S** to move smoothly and unhesitatingly from one state, condition, situation or element to another

SEIFS *n pl of* **SEIF** sharp-crested longitudinal sand dunes

SEINE *n pl* **-S** a large fishnet that hangs vertically

SEISE *v* **-D, SEISING, -S** to put (someone) into possession of something

SEISM *n pl* **-S** an earthquake

SEIZE *v* **-D, SEIZING, -S** to fall or rush upon suddenly and lay hold of; to grasp suddenly

SEKES *n/pl* a place in a pagan temple in which the images of the deities were enclosed; a shrine

SELAH *n pl* **-S** a word of doubtful meaning, occurring frequently in the Psalms

SELCH *n pl* **-S** a seal

SELLE *n pl* **-S** a saddle

SELLS *v pr t of* **SELL** transfers to another for an equivalent value

SELVA *n pl* **-S** a dense tropical rain forest

SEMEN *n pl* **-S** a viscous whitish secretion of the male reproductive organs

SEMES *n pl of* **SEME** sprinkled or sown patterns

SEMIS *n pl of* **SEMI** informal for semi-trailers; tractor-trailer trucks

SENDS *v pr t of* **SEND** causes somebody or something to go

SENGI *n pl* **SENGI** a monetary unit of Zaire

SENNA *n pl* **-S** a medicinal plant

SENOR *n pl* **-S** or **-ES** a Spanish term of address for a man

SENSA *n pl of* **SENSUM** the faculties of perceiving by means of sense organs; *also* **SENSES**

SENSE *n pl* **-S** the faculty of perceiving by means of sense organs; *also* **SENSUM**

SENTE *n pl* **LISENTE** a monetary unit of Lesotho

SENTI *n pl of* **SENT** a monetary unit of Estonia

SENZA *adv* without something indicated by a following Italian noun

SEPAL *n pl* **-S** a leaf or division of the calyx

SEPIA *n pl* **-S** a shade of brown with a tinge of red

SEPIC *adj* of or pertaining to sepia; done in sepia

SEPON *n pl* **-S** a boiled Indian meal; hasty pudding; mush; *also* **SUPAWN**

SEPOY *n pl* **-S** a native of India employed as a soldier in the service of the British army

SEPTA *n pl of* **SEPTUM** dividing walls, membranes or partitions

SEPTS *n pl of* **SEPT** tribal peoples descended from a common ancestor

SERAC *n pl* **-S** a sharp ridge or pinnacle of ice among the crevasses of a glacier

SERAI *n pl* **-S** a palace; a seraglio; a caravansary

SERAL *adj* pertaining to successive changes in flora and fauna

SERFS *n pl of* **SERF** feudal servants or slaves employed in husbandry

SERGE *v* **-D, SERGING, -S** to overcast (the raw edges of a fabric) to prevent unraveling

SERIF *n pl* **-S** any of the short lines stemming from and at an angle to the upper and lower ends of the strokes of a letter

SERIN *n pl* **-ES** a Mediterranean finch

SEROW *n pl* **-S** a short-horned dark-coated goat antelope of Asian mountain areas

SERRS *v pr t of* **SERR** [obs] crowds, presses, drives together

SERRY *v* **SERRIED, -ING, SERRIES** [obs] to crowd together

SERUM *n pl* **-S** or **SERA** the watery fluid left after blood has clotted

SERVE *v* **-D, SERVING, -S** to be subordinate to

SERVO *n pl* **-S** an automatic device used to control another mechanism

SESSA *interj* [obs] hurry, run

SETAE *n pl of* **SETA** stiff hairs or bristles

SETAL *adj* pertaining to a stiff hair or bristle

SETON *n pl* **-S** a type of surgical thread

SETTS *n pl of* **SETT** badger's burrows

SETUP *n pl* **-S** the way something is arranged or organized

SEVEN *n pl* **-S** a number; one more than six

SEVER *v* **-ED, -ING, -S** to set or keep apart; divide or separate

SEWAN *n pl* **-S** shells used as money by the Algonquian Indians; *also* **SEAWAN**

SEWAR *n pl* **-S** a medieval servant

SEWED *v p t of* **SEW** fastened with needle and thread

SEWER *n pl* **-S** one that sews

SEWES *v pr t of* **SEWE** [obs] performs the duties of a sewer, an upper servant who set on and removed the dishes at a feast

SEXED *v p t of* **SEX** determined the gender of

SEXES *v pr t of* **SEX** determines the gender of

SEXLY *adj* pertaining to sex

SEXTO *n pl* **-S** the size of a piece of paper cut six from a sheet; *also* **SIXMO**

SEXTS *n pl of* **SEXT** the fourth of the seven canonical hours; about noon

HABS *v pr t of* **SHAB** [obs] scratches; rubs

HACK *v* **-ED, -ING, -S** to make one's home or live in

HADD *n/pl* rounded stones containing tin ore, indicating a vein

HADE *v* **-D, -ING, -S** to screen from light or heat

HADS *n pl of* **SHAD** herring-like food fishes

HADY *adj* **SHADIER, SHADIEST** of or pertaining to shade or darkness

HAFT *v* **-ED, -ING, -S** to push or propel with a pole

HAGS *v pr t of* **SHAG** chases and brings back; fetches

HAIK *n pl* **-S** the head of an Arab family; *also* **SHEIK**

HAHS *n pl of* **SHAH** former hereditary monarchs of Iran

HAIL *v* **-ED, -ING, -S** to walk sidewise

HAKE *v* **SHOOK, -N, SHAKING, -S** to move rapidly one way and the other

HAKO *n pl* **-S** or **-ES** a kind of military cap or headdress

HAKY *adj* **SHAKIER, SHAKIEST** easily shaken; tottering; unsound

HALE *n pl* **-S** a sedimentary rock formed by the deposition of successive layers of clay

HALL *v* **SHOULD, SHALL** used to express future determination or promise

HALT *v pr t of* **SHALL** [obs] archaic second person singular of SHALL

HALY *adj* **SHALIER, SHALIEST** resembling shale in structure

HAMA *n pl* **-S** a saxicoline singing bird of India

HAME *v* **-D, SHAMING, -S** to cover with ignominy or reproach; disgrace

HAMS *v pr t of* **SHAM** tricks; cheats; deceives or deludes

SHANK *v* **-ED, -ING, -S** to hit a poor golf stroke in which the heel of the club hits the ball

SHAPE *v* **-D, SHAPING, -S** to form or create; to mold

SHARD *n pl* **-S** a piece or fragment, especially of earthen ware

SHARE *v* **-D, SHARING, -S** to part among two or more; to divide

SHARK *v* **-ED, -ING, -S** to live by shifts and trickery

SHARN *n pl* **-S** SCOT. cow dung

SHARP *adj* **-ER, -EST** having a very thin edge or fine point

SHASH *n pl* **-ES** [obs] the scarf of a turban

SHAVE *v* **-D, SHAVING, -S** to remove hair with a razor

SHAWL *n pl* **-S** a square or oblong cloth of wool, cotton, silk

SHAWM *n pl* **-S** a medieval oboe

SHAWS *n pl of* **SHAW** [obs] thickets; small woods or groves

SHAYS *n pl of* **SHAY** chaise lounges

SHEAF *v* **-ED, -ING, -S** to gather and bind into a bundle

SHEAL *n pl* **-S** a shell or pod

SHEAR *v* **-ED** or **SHORE, SHORN, -ING, -S** to cut the wool from; to cut with shears

SHEAS *n pl of* **SHEA** tropical African trees

SHEDS *n pl of* **SHED** temporary structures built to shelter something

SHEEN *n pl* **-S** a shiny or glistening surface

SHEEP *n pl* **SHEEP** a woolly usually horned ruminant mammal

SHEER *adj* **-ER, -EST** of very thin or transparent fabric

SHEET *v* **-ED, -ING, -S** to cover with a sheet, as if by wrapping

SHEIK *n pl* **-S** the head of an Arab family; *also* **SHAIK**

SHELD *adj* [obs] variegated; spotted; speckled; piebald

SHELF *n pl* **SHELVES** a support that consists of a horizontal surface for holding objects

SHELL *n pl* **-S** a hard outside covering, as of a fruit or an animal

SHEND *v* **SHENT, -ING, -S** [obs] to degrade; to disgrace

SHENT *v p t of* **SHEND** degraded; disgraced

SHEOL *n pl* **-S** the place of departed spirits; hell

SHERD *n pl* **-S** a broken piece of a brittle artifact

SHETS *v pr t of* **SHET** [obs] shuts; *also* **SHETTES**

SHEWN *v p part of* **SHEW** [obs] has shown

SHEWS *v pr t of* **SHEW** [obs] shows

SHIED *v p part of* **SHY** moved suddenly, as if startled; started

SHIEL *n pl* **-S** a mountain hut used as a shelter; a shieling

SHIER *adj* more timid; *also* **SHYER**

SHIES *v pr t of* **SHY** moves suddenly, as if startled; starts

SHIFF *v* **-ED, -ING, -S** [obs] to divide; to distribute

SHIFT *v* **-ED, -ING, -S** to change the place of; to move

SHILF *n pl* **-S** [obs] straw

SHILL *v* **-ED, -ING, -S** to put under cover; to act as a decoy

SHILY *adj* in a shy or timid manner; not familiarly; *also* **SHYLY**

SHIMS *v pr t of* **SHIM** fills in, levels or adjusts by using a thin wedge or spacer material

SHINE *v* **-D** or **SHONE, SHINING, -S** to emit rays of light

SHINS *v pr t of* **SHIN** climbs quickly up or down by gripping with one's arms and legs

SHINY *adj* **SHINIER, SHINIEST** bright; luminous; clear; unclouded

SHIPS *v pr t of* **SHIP** transports something by water, overland or by air; sends

SHIRE *n pl* **-S** a large powerful draft horse of Britain

SHIRK *v* **-ED, -ING, -S** to avoid responsibility

SHIRL *adj* shrill

SHIRR *v* **-ED, -ING, -S** to gather fabric into 2 or more parallel rows for decoration

SHIRT *n pl* **-S** a garment worn on the upper half of the body

SHIST *n pl* **-S** a rock that splits into parallel layers; *also* **SCHIST**

SHIVA *n pl* **-S** a seven-day period of formal mourning observed after the funeral of a close relative; *also* **SHIVE, SHIBAH, SHIVAH**

SHIVE *n pl* **-S** a seven-day period of formal mourning observed after the funeral of a close relative; *also* **SHIVA, SHIBAH, SHIVAH**

SHIVS *v pr t of* **SHIV** informal for stabs with a knife

SHLEP *v* **-PED, -PING, -S** to carry clumsily or with difficulty; *also* **SCHLEP, SCHLEPP**

SHLUB *n pl* **-S** a person regarded as clumsy, stupid or unattractive; *also* **ZHLUB, SCHLUB**

SHOAL *v* **-ED, -ING, -S** to become shallow

SHOAT *n pl* **-S** a young hog; *also* **SHOTE**

SHOCK *v* **-ED, -ING, -S** to strike with surprise, terror or horror

SHODE *n pl* **-S** [obs] the parting of the hair on the head

SHOED *v p t of* **SHOE** provided with coverings for the feet

SHOER *n pl* **-S** a person who shoes horses

SHOES *v pr t of* **SHOE** provides with coverings for the feet

SHOGI *n pl* **-S** a form of chess played on a board of 81 square where each player has 20 pieces

SHOGS *v pr t of* **SHOG** shakes, jolts or jostles

HOJI *n pl* **-S** a translucent sliding panel of rice paper on a wooden frame, used in Japanese homes as a partition or door

HOLE *n pl* **-S** a plank fixed beneath an object for protection

HONE *v p t of* **SHINE** emitted rays of light

HOOK *v p t of* **SHAKE** moved rapidly one way and the other

HOOL *v* **-ED, -ING, -S** BRIT., SCOT. to shovel

HOON *n pl of* **SHOE** BRIT. external coverings for human feet

HOOS *v pr t of* **SHOO** frightens or drives away

HOOT *v* **SHOT, -ING, -S** to fire a projectile from a weapon

HOPS *v pr t of* **SHOP** looks for something with the intention of acquiring it

HORE *n pl* **-S** the land bordering a usually large body of water

HORL *n pl* **-S** a mineral; *also* **SCHORL**

HORN *v p part of* **SHEAR** to have cut the wool from; to cut with shears

ORT *adj* **-ER, -EST** not long; a brief length or linear extension

HORY *adj* lying near the shore

HOTE *n pl* **-S** a young hog; *also* **SHOAT**

HOTS *n pl of* **SHOT** the firing or discharging of weapons

HOTT *n pl* **-S** a shallow saline lake or marsh

HOUT *v* **-ED, -ING, -S** to utter a sudden and loud outcry

HOVE *v* **-D, SHOVING, -S** to push along, aside or away

HOWN *v p part of* **SHOW** has exhibited or presented to view

HOWS *v pr t of* **SHOW** exhibits or presents to view

HOWY *adj* **SHOWIER, SHOWIEST** making a show; attracting attention

HOYU *n pl* **-S** soy sauce

SHRAG *n pl* **-S** [obs] a twig of a tree cut off

SHRAM *v* **-MED, -MING, -S** BRIT. [obs] to cause to shrink or shrivel with cold; to benumb

SHRED *v* **-DED, -DING, -S** to cut or tear into small pieces

SHREW *n pl* **-S** a small mammal with a pointed nose

SHRIS *n pl of* **SHRI** used in India as titles of respect for men; *also* **SRIS**

SHROW *n pl* **-S** [obs] a **SHREW**

SHRUB *n pl* **-S** a low woody perennial plant

SHRUG *v* **-GED, -GING, -S** to raise or draw up the shoulders

SHTIK *n pl* **-S** an entertainment routine or gimmick; *also* **SCHTICK**

SHUCK *v* **-ED, -ING, -S** to remove the husk or shell from

SHUDE *n pl* **-S** the husks and other refuse of rice mills

SHUGS *v pr t of* **SHUG** [obs] crawls; sneaks

SHULN *n pl of* **SHUL** synagogues; *also* **SHULS, SCHULS**

SHULS *n pl of* **SHUL** synagogues; *also* **SHULN, SCHULS**

SHUNS *v pr t of* **SHUN** avoids; keeps clear of

SHUNT *v* **-ED, -ING, -S** transfer to another track or path

SHUSH *v* **-ED, -ING, -ES** to command someone to be silent

SHUTE *n pl* **-S** a channel or trough

SHUTS *v pr t of* **SHUT** closes

SHWAS *n pl of* **SHWA** neutral middle vowels that occur in unstressed syllables; *also* **SCHWAS**

SHYER *adj* more timid; *also* **SHIER**

SHYLY *adj* in a shy or timid manner; not familiarly; *also* **SHILY**

SIALS *n pl of* **SIAL** granite-like rocks

SIBYL *n pl* **-S** a female fortune teller; a prophetess

SICES	*n pl of* **SICE** the number sixes at dice; *also* **SISES**	**SIKES**	*n pl of* **SIKE** gutters; streams; *also* **SYKES**
SICKS	*v pr t of* **SICK** to urge to attack; *also* **SIC**	**SILDS**	*n pl of* **SILD** young herrings
SICLE	*n pl* **-S** a shekel, a Hebrew unit of weight and currency	**SILED**	*v p t of* **SILE** dropped; flowed; fell
SIDED	*v p t of* **SIDE** aligned oneself in a disagreement	**SILES**	*v pr t of* **SILE** drops; flows; falls
SIDER	*n pl* **-S** [obs] one who takes a side	**SILEX**	*n pl* **-ES** a pure form of finely ground silica
SIDES	*v pr t of* **SIDE** aligns oneself in a disagreement	**SILKS**	*n pl of* **SILK** fabrics made from the fine threads produced by silkworms
SIDHE	*n pl of* **SIDH** a mound or hill in which fairies live	**SILKY**	*adj* **SILKIER, SILKIEST** of or pertaining to smoothness of silk
SIDLE	*v* **-D, SIDLING, -S** to move sidewise	**SILLS**	*n pl of* **SILL** thresholds beneath a window or door
SIEGE	*v* **-D, SIEGING, -S** to surround an enemy's fortifications with troops and cut off all outside access to force surrender	**SILLY**	*adj* **SILLIER, SILLIEST** weak in intellect; foolish
		SILOS	*n pl of* **SILO** large cylindrical towers used for storage
SIEUR	*n pl* **-S** sir; a title of respect used by the French	**SILTS**	*v pr t of* **SILT** clogs up
SIEVA	*n pl* **-S** a kind of Lima bean	**SILTY**	*adj* **SILTIER, SILTIEST** full of silt; resembling silt
SIEVE	*v* **-D, SIEVING, -S** to put something through a sifter or strainer	**SILVA**	*n pl* **-S** or **-E** the forest trees of an area; *also* **SYLVA**
SIFTS	*v pr t of* **SIFT** separates or parts as if with a sieve	**SIMAR**	*n pl* **-S** a woman's long dress or robe; light covering; a scarf
SIGHS	*v pr t of* **SIGH** exhales audibly in a long deep breath, as in weariness or relief	**SIMAS**	*n pl of* **SIMA** rocks that form the continuous lower layer of the earth's crust
SIGHT	*v* **-ED, -ING, -S** to observe or notice; to gain view of	**SIMPS**	*n pl of* **SIMP** informal for simple or foolish people
SIGIL	*n pl* **-S** an official seal; a signature	**SINCE**	*adv* from then until now; ago
SIGLA	*n pl of* **SIGLUM** abbreviations, symbols, etc. used in the scholarly edition of a text as to indicate manuscript sources	**SINES**	*n pl of* **SINE** the ratio of the opposite side to the hypotenuse of right-angled triangles
SIGMA	*n pl* **-S** the 18th letter of the Greek alphabet	**SINEW**	*v* **-ED, -ING, -S** to strengthen the muscles
SIGNA	*v* to mark or write on label; used imperatively, in prescriptions	**SINGE**	*v* **-D, -ING, -S** to burn slightly or superficially
SIGNS	*v pr t of* **SIGN** marks with one's signature	**SINGS**	*v pr t of* **SING** utters sweet melodious sounds
SIKAS	*n pl of* **SIKA** small deer of Japan with slightly forked antlers	**SINHS**	*n pl of* **SINH** in mathematics, hyperbolic sines
SIKER	*adj* secure	**SINKS**	*v pr t of* **SINK** falls or retires beneath or below the surface
		SINUS	*n pl* **-ES** a cavity in facial bones in skull

300

IONS *n pl of* **SION** imaginary places considered to be perfect or ideal

IPED *v p t of* **SIPE** to pass slowly through small openings or pores; ooze; *also* **SEEPED**

IPES *v pr t of* **SIPE** passes slowly through small openings or pores; oozes; *also* **SEEPS**

IPID *adj* having a pleasing taste or flavor; *also* **SAPID**

IRED *v p t of* **SIRE** fathered; begat

IREE *n pl* **-S** sir; for emphasis after yes or no; *also* **SIRREE**

IREN *n pl* **-S** a warning signal that is a loud wailing sound; *also* **SYREN**

IRES *v pr t of* **SIRE** fathers; begets

IRRA *n pl* **-S** [obs] a form of address used to inferior persons; *also* **SIRRAH**

IRTS *n pl of* **SIRT** [obs] quicksand; bogs; *also* **SYRTS**

IRUP *n pl* **-S** a thick sweet sticky liquid; *also* **SYRUP**

ISAL *n pl* **-S** a strong white fiber used for rope and twine

ISES *n pl of* **SISE** the number sixes at dice; *also* **SICES**

ISSY *n pl* **SISSIES** a timid or cowardly person

ISTS *v pr t of* **SIST** stays, as judicial proceedings; delays or suspends; stops

ITAR *n pl* **-S** a stringed instrument of India

ITED *v p t of* **SITE** fixed or built in a particular place

ITES *v pr t of* **SITE** fixes or builds in a particular place

ITHE *n pl* **-S** a single bladed cutting implement; *also* **SCYTHE**

ITUP *n pl* **-S** a conditioning exercise performed from a supine position by raising the torso to a sitting position

ITUS *n pl* **-ES** a position, or location of an organ

IVER *v* **-ED, -ING, -S** [obs] to simmer

SIXER *n pl* **-S** a leader of six in scouting

SIXES *n pl of* **SIX** cardinal numbers equal to 5 + 1

SIXMO *n pl* **-S** the size of a piece of paper cut six from a sheet; *also* **SEXTO**

SIXTE *n pl* **-S** a fencing parry

SIXTH *n pl* **-S** one of six equal parts

SIXTY *n pl* **SIXTIES** the sum of six times ten

SIZAR *n pl* **-S** a body of students exempted from paying college fees

SIZED *v p t of* **SIZE** arranged, classified or distributed according to the physical dimensions, magnitude or extent of an object

SIZER *n pl* **-S** an instrument or contrivance to size articles

SIZES *v pr t of* **SIZE** arranges, classifies or distributes according to the physical dimensions, magnitude or extent of an object

SKALD *n pl* **-S** a medieval Scandinavian poet or traveling minstrel

SKALL *v* **-ED, -ING, -S** [obs] to scale; to mount

SKANK *v* **-ED, -ING, -S** to dance to reggae

SKARE *adj* BRIT., SCOT. wild; timid; shy

SKART *n pl* **-S** a shag; coarse hair or nap

SKATE *v* **-D, SKATING, -S** to slide smoothly along a surface

SKATS *n pl of* **SKAT** card games for three people

SKEAN *n pl* **-S** a knife or short dagger; *also* **SKEEN, SKENE**

SKEED *v p t of* **SKEE** skied

SKEEL *n pl* **-S** BRIT., SCOT. a shallow wooden vessel for holding milk or cream

SKEEN *n pl* **-S** a knife or short dagger; *also* **SKEAN, SKENE**

SKEES *v pr t of* **SKEE** skis

SKEET *n pl* **-S** the sport of shooting at clay pigeons

SKEGS *n pl of* **SKEG** additional pieces fastened to the keel of a boat to prevent lateral motion

SKEIN *n pl* **-S** bundles of yarn

SKELL *n pl* **-S** a homeless person who lives on the street

SKELM *n pl* **-S** a rascal; rogue; scamp; *also* **SKELLUM**

SKELP *n pl* **-S** a blow; a smart stroke

SKENE *n pl* **-S** a knife or short dagger; *also* **SKEAN, SKEEN**

SKENS *v pr t of* **SKEN** [obs] squints, looks obliquely

SKEPS *n pl of* **SKEP** coarse round farm baskets; beehives

SKEWS *v pr t of* **SKEW** turns or places at an angle

SKIDS *v pr t of* **SKID** slides without control

SKIED *v p t of* **SKI** traveled or glided on skis, a pair of long flat runners for traveling over slow

SKIER *n pl* **-S** someone who skis

SKIES *v pr t of* **SKY** hits or throws a ball very high

SKIEY *adj* like the sky; ethereal; *also* **SKYEY**

SKIFF *n pl* **-S** a small, open boat

SKILL *n pl* **-S** knowledge; understanding

SKIMP *v* **-ED, -ING, -S** to deal with inadequately or superficially

SKIMS *v pr t of* **SKIM** removes floating matter from a liquid

SKINK *n pl* **-S** a small smooth insect eating lizard

SKINS *v pr t of* **SKIN** removes the outside layer of something

SKINT *adj* lacking funds; having no money

SKIPS *v pr t of* **SKIP** to move by hopping on one foot and then the other

SKIRL *v* **-ED, -ING, -S** to utter in a shrill tone; to scream

SKIRR *v* **-ED, -ING, -S** to ramble over in order to clear; to scour

SKIRT *v* **-ED, -ING, -S** to pass around or about; to move along the border

SKITE *v* **-D, SKITING, -S** to slip on a slippery surface

SKITS *n pl of* **SKIT** short comic sketches

SKIVE *v* **-D, SKIVING, -S** to pare or shave off the rough or thick parts of leather

SKOAL *interj* to your health; used as a drinking toast

SKORT *n pl* **-S** a pair of shorts made to resemble a skirt

SKOSH *n pl* **-ES** informal for a small amount

SKUAS *n pl of* **SKUA** large predatory sea birds

SKULK *v* **-ED, -ING, -S** to hide, or get out of the way; *also* **SCULK**

SKULL *n pl* **-S** the bony framework of the head, enclosing the brain

SKUNK *v* **-ED, -ING, -S** to defeat overwhelmingly

SKYED *v p t of* **SKY** hit or threw a ball very high

SKYER *n pl* **-S** a ball hit high in the air in cricket

SKYEY *adj* like the sky; ethereal; *also* **SKIEY**

SLABS *n pl of* **SLAB** broad, flat, thick pieces, as of stone or cheese

SLACK *v* **-ED, -ING, -S** to make less active or intense

SLADE *n pl* **-S** a little dell or valley

SLAGS *n pl of* **SLAG** the waste materials from smelting

SLAIN *v p part of* **SLAY** to have killed violently

SLAKE *v* **-D, SLAKING, -S** to allay, to quench

SLAMS *v pr t of* **SLAM** shuts with force and a loud noise

SLANG *v* **-ED,-ING,-S** belonging to, expressed in or containing casual speech or language that is used by a particular group of people

SLANK *v p t of* **SLINK** moved stealthily

SLANT *v* **-ED, -ING, -S** to incline or bend from a vertical position

SLAPS *n pl of* **SLAP** give blows, especially with the open hand

SLASH *v* **-ED, -ING, -S** to strike violently and at random

SLATE *v* **-D, SLATING, -S** to choose or schedule someday or something for a particular job or time

SLATS *v pr t of* **SLAT** adds slats (narrow strips of metal or wood) to something

SLATT *n pl* **-S** slabs of stone used as a veneer for coarse masonry

SLATY *adj* resembling slate

SLAVE *n pl* **-S** a person who is owned by someone

SLAWS *n pl of* **SLAW** sliced cabbage served as salads, cooked or raw

SLAYS *v pr t of* **SLAY** kills violently

SLEDS *v pr t of* **SLED** moves over the snow or ice by conveyance with runners

SLEEK *adj* **-ER, -EST** having a smooth surface; glossy

SLEEP *v* **SLEPT, -ING, -S** to be in a natural and periodic state of rest

SLEET *v* **-ED, -ING, -S** to snow or hail with a mixture of rain

SLEPT *v p t of* **SLEEP** was in a natural and periodic state of rest

SLEWS *n pl of* **SLEW** *a* great deal or lots of

SLEYS *n pl of* **SLEY** guide ways in a knitting machine

SLICE *v* **-D, SLICING, -S** to cut into thin pieces

SLICK *adj* **-ER, -EST** smooth and slippery

SLIDE *v* **SLID, SLIDING, -S** to move over a surface while maintaining smooth continuous contact

SLIER *adj* more artfully cunning; secretly mischievous; wily

SLILY *adv* in a sly manner; shrewdly; craftily; *also* **SLYLY**

SLIME *n pl* **-S** a soft, moist, slippery substance that is unpleasant to the touch

SLIMS *v pr t of* **SLIM** loses or causes to lose weight, as by dieting or exercise

SLIMY *adj* **SLIMIER, SLIMIEST** of or pertaining to slime

SLING *v* **SLUNG, -ING, -S** to throw with force

SLINK *v* **SLANK** or **SLUNK, -ED, -ING, -S** to move stealthily

SLIPE *v* **-D, SLIPING, -S** to peel

SLIPS *v pr t of* **SLIP** moves obliquely or sideways, usually in an uncontrolled manner

SLIPT *v p t of* **SLIP** [obs] moved obliquely or sideways, usually in an uncontrolled manner; *also* **SLIPPED**

SLITS *v pr t of* **SLIT** makes long, narrow cuts into

SLOBS *n pl of* **SLOB** lazy and untidy people

SLOES *n pl of* **SLOE** small, sour dark purple plum fruits

SLOGS *v pr t of* **SLOG** walks or progresses with great effort

SLOID *n pl* **-S** a woodcarving manual training system originating in Sweden; *also* **SLOJD, SLOYD**

SLOJD *n pl* **-S** a woodcarving manual training system originating in Sweden; *also* **SLOID, SLOYD**

SLOOP *n pl* **-S** a sailing vessel with a single mast

SLOPE *v* **-D, SLOPING, -S** to diverge from the vertical or horizontal; incline

SLOPS *v pr t of* **SLOP** spills liquids

SLOPY adj **SLOPIER, SLOPIEST** sloping; inclined

SLOSH v **-ED, -ING, -S** to make a splashing sound

SLOTH n pl **-S** a slow-moving arboreal mammal

SLOTS v pr t of **SLOT** assigns a place to something

SLOWS v pr t of **SLOW** reduces the speed or progress of something

SLOYD n pl **-S** a woodcarving manual training system originating in Sweden; also **SLOID, SLOJD**

SLUBS n pl of **SLUB** lumps in yarn or fabrics that are sometimes an imperfection, but are often made to provide a knotty effect

SLUED v p t of **SLUE** turned about; turned from the course

SLUES v pr t of **SLUE** turns about; turns from the course

SLUFF n pl **-S** the cast-off skin of a snake; also **SLOUGH**

SLUGS v pr t of **SLUG** hits very hard

SLUMP v **-ED, -ING, -S** to fall or sink suddenly through or in

SLUMS v pr t of **SLUM** accepts a lower standard than usual

SLUNG v p t of **SLING** thrown with force

SLUNK v p t of **SLINK** moved stealthily

SLURB n pl **-S** informal for a suburban area with poor housing; a contraction of slum and suburb

SLURP v **-ED, -ING, -S** to eat or drink noisily

SLURS v pr t of **SLUR** soils; sullies; contaminates

SLUSH n **-ES** partially melted snow or ice

SLUTS n pl of **SLUT** untidy women; slatterns

SLYER adj more artfully cunning; secretly mischievous; wily

SLYLY adv in a sly manner; shrewdly; craftily; also **SLILY**

SLYPE n pl **-S** a covered passage between the transept and chapter house of a cathedral

SMACK v **-ED, -ING, -S** to kiss noisily

SMALL adj **-ER, -EST** having little size; not great

SMALT n pl **-S** a blue pigment

SMARM n pl **-S** excessive but superficial compliments given with affected charm

SMART adj **-ER, -EST** intelligent, alert, clever, witty

SMASH v **-ED, -ING, -ES** to break an object into pieces suddenly, noisily and violently; to shatter

SMAZE n pl **-S** an atmospheric mixture of smoke and haze

SMEAR v **-ED, -ING, -S** to spread or daub with a sticky, greasy or dirty substance

SMEEK v **-ED, -ING, -S** SCOT. to smoke

SMEES n pl of **SMEE** pintail ducks

SMEIR n pl **-S** a salt glaze on pottery

SMELL v **SMELT** or **-ED, -ING, -S** to detect or perceive, the scent of something by means of olfactory nerves.

SMELT v p t of **SMELL** detected or perceived the scent of something by means of olfactory nerves

SMERK v **-ED, -ING, -S** to smile in an affected or conceited manner; also **SMIRK**

SMEWS n pl of **SMEW** the smallest mergansers and most expert divers

SMIFT n pl **-S** a match for firing a charge of powder

SMILE v **-D, SMILING, -S** to express pleasure by turning up the corners of the mouth

SMIRK v **-ED, -ING, -S** to smile in an affected or conceited manner; also **SMERK**

SMITE v **SMOTE, SMIT** or **SMITTEN, SMITING, -S** to strike; to inflict a blow

SMITH *n pl* **-S** one who forges metals with a hammer

SMITT *n pl* **-S** fine clay or ocher made up into balls

SMOCK *n pl* **-S** a blouse; a smock frock

SMOGS *n pl of* **SMOG** fogs that have become mixed and polluted with smoke

SMOKE *v* **-D, SMOKING, -S** to draw in and exhale smoke from a cigarette, cigar or pipe

SMOKY *adj* **SMOKIER, SMOKIEST** filled with smoke, or with a vapor, or tasting of smoke

SMOLT *n pl* **-S** a young salmon of two or three years

SMOOR *v* **-ED, -ING, -S** to suffocate or smother; *also* **SMORE**

SMORE *v* **-ED, -ING, -S** to suffocate or smother; *also* **SMOOR**

SMOTE *v p t of* **SMITE** struck; inflicted a blow

SMUSH *v* **-ED, -ING, -ES** to smash and mush

SMUTS *v pr t of* **SMUT** becomes affected with smut, a fungus causing disease in plants

SNACK *n pl* **-S** a small quantity of food; light meal or refreshment taken between regular meals

SNAFU *v* **-ED, -ING, -S** to cause a situation or process to become confused or delayed

SNAGS *v pr t of* **SNAG** catches on or collides with a sharp projection

SNAIL *n pl* **-S** any mollusk having a spirally coiled shell

SNAKE *v* **-D, SNAKING, -S** to move or lie like a snake, with many beds or twists

SNAKY *adj* **SNAKIER, SNAKIEST** of or pertaining to a snake or snakes

SNAPS *v pr t of* **SNAP** strikes, hits or shuts with a sharp sound

SNARE *v* **-D, SNARING, -S** to trap

SNARF *v* **-ED, -ING, -S** to eat or drink rapidly or eagerly; to devour

SNARK *n pl* **-S** an imaginary animal

SNARL *v* **-ED, -ING, -S** to growl viciously while baring the teeth

SNASH *n pl* **-ES** SCOT. insolence; impertinence; abusive language

SNATH *n pl* **-S** the handle of a scythe; *also* **SNATHE**

SNAWS *n pl of* **SNAW** [obs] snows

SNEAK *v* **-ED** or **SNUCK, -ING, -S** to pass on stealthily

SNEAP *v* **-ED, -ING, -S** to check; to reprimand; to chide; *also* **SNEB**

SNEBS *v pr t of* **SNEB** [obs] reprimands; *also* **SNEAPS**

SNECK *v* **-ED, -ING, -S** to fasten by a hatch; to latch

SNEDS *v pr t of* **SNED** lops; prunes

SNEER *v* **-ED, -ING, -S** to smile or speak in a contemptuous or mocking manner

SNELL *adj* **-ER, -EST** active; brisk; nimble; quick; sharp

SNETS *n pl of* **SNET** the fats of a deer

SNEWS *v pr t of* **SNEW** [obs] snows; abounds

SNIBS *v pr t of* **SNIB** operates or fastens the bolt on a door or lock

SNICK *v* **-ED, -ING, -S** to make a small cut or mark

SNIDE *adj* **-R, -ST** tricky; deceptive; contemptible

SNIES *n pl of* **SNY** upward bend in pieces of timber; the sheer of vessels

SNIFF *v* **-ED** or **SNIFT, -ING, -S** to draw air audibly up the nose

SNIFT *v p t of* **SNIFF** drew air audibly up the nose

SNIGG *n pl* **-S** a small eel

SNIGS *v pr t of* **SNIG** drags something heavy along; used in Canada

SNIPE *v* **-D, SNIPING, -S** to make a gunshot from a concealed location

SNIPS *v pr t of* **SNIP** cuts with small strokes

SNITS *n pl of* **SNIT** states of agitation or irritation.

SNOBS *n pl of* **SNOB** vulgar persons who affect to be better, richer and more fashionable

SNOFF *n pl* **-S** a short candle end used for igniting a fuse

SNOGS *v pr t of* **SNOG** BRIT. kisses and cuddles someone

SNOOD *n pl* **-S** an ornamental net in the shape of a bag that confines a woman's hair

SNOOK *v* **-ED, -ING, -S** to lurk; to lie in ambush

SNOOL *v* **-ED, -ING, -S** to yield meekly

SNOOP *v* **-ED, -ING, -S** to look or pry especially in a sneaking or meddlesome manner

SNOOT *n pl* **-S** a snout or nose; *also* **SNOUT**

SNORE *v* **-D, SNORING, -S** to breathe during sleep with harsh, snorting noises

SNORT *v* **-ED, -ING, -S** to breathe noisily and forcefully through the nostrils

SNOTS *n pl of* **SNOT** mucus from the nose

SNOUT *n pl* **-S** a snout or nose; *also* **SNOOT**

SNOWL *n pl* **-S** the hooded merganser bird

SNOWS *v pr t of* **SNOW** falls like snow (precipitation in the form of small white ice crystals)

SNOWY *adj* **SNOWIER, SNOWIEST** abounding in snow

SNUBS *v pr t of* **SNUB** treats with contempt or neglect

SNUCK *v p t of* **SNEAK** passed on stealthily

SNUFF *v* **-ED, -ING, -S** to abruptly put an end to; extinguish

SNUGS *v pr t of* **SNUG** curls us in a cozy way

SNYES *n pl of* **SNY** upward bends in a piece of timber; the sheers of a vessel.

SNYPY *adj* like a snipe

SOAKS *v pr t of* **SOAK** drenches; wets thoroughly

SOAKY *adj* **SOAKIER, SOAKIEST** wet, drenched

SOALS *n pl of* **SOAL** the soles of a shoe

SOAMS *n pl of* **SOAM** chains by which a leading horse draws a plow

SOAPS *v pr t of* **SOAP** puts soap on somebody or something

SOAPY *adj* **SOAPIER, SOAPIEST** pertaining to or resembling soap

SOARS *v pr t of* **SOAR** flies aloft, as a bird; mounts upward on wings

SOAVE *n pl* **-S** a dry white Italian table wine

SOBAS *n pl of* **SOBA** Japanese noodles made with buckwheat flour

SOBER *adj* **-ER, -EST** temperate in the use of spirituous liquors

SOCAS *n pl of* **SOCA** blends of Caribbean soul and calypso music

SOCKO *adj* informal for strikingly impressive

SOCKS *n pl of* **SOCK** short stockings reaching a point between the ankle and the knee; *also* **SOX**

SOCKY *adj* **SOCKIER, SOCKIEST** bold; strong; clever, impressive, as in advertising

SOCLE *n pl* **-S** a plain block or plinth forming a low pedestal

SODAS *n pl of* **SODA** sweet drinks of carbonated water and flavoring

SODDY *n pl* **SODDIES** houses built of sod or adobe

SODIC *adj* of or pertaining to sodium

SODOM *n pl* **-S** any location known for vice and corruption

SOFAR *n pl* **-S** a system for locating an underwater explosion at sea by triangulation

SOFAS *n pl of* **SOFA** upholstered seats for more than one person

SOFTA *n pl* **-S** a student of the higher branches of theology in a mosque school

SOFTS *n pl of* **SOFT** persons regarded as weak or sentimental

SOFTY *n pl* **-IES** a person regarded as weak or sentimental

SOGGY *adj* **SOGGIER, SOGGIEST** soaked with moisture

SOILS *v pr t of* **SOIL** makes dirty or unclean on the surface

SOJAS *n pl of* **SOJA** erect bushy hairy annual herbs that produce soybeans; *also* **SOYS, SOYAS**

SOKES *n pl of* **SOKE** BRIT. [obs] rights of local jurisdiction

SOKOL *n pl* **-S** an international organization promoting physical health

SOKOS *n pl of* **SOKO** African chimpanzees

SOLAN *n pl* **-S** a gannet

SOLAR *adj* pertaining to the sun

SOLDI *n pl of* **SOLDO** former Italian coins

SOLDO *n pl* **SOLDI** a former Italian coin

SOLED *v p t of* **SOLE** to furnish with a sole

SOLEI *n pl of* **SOLEUS** broad flat muscles of the calf of the leg

SOLEN *n pl* **-S** a cradle, as for a broken limb

SOLES *n pl of* **SOLE** bottoms of feet, shoes or boots

SOLID *adj* **-ER, -EST** firm; compact; strong; stable

SOLON *n pl* **-S** a wise lawgiver; a legislator

SOLOS *n pl of* **SOLO** activities that are performed alone without assistance; *also* **SOLI**

SOLUM *n pl* **SOLA** the upper layer of a soil profile

SOLUS *adj* alone on stage

SOLVE *v* **-D, SOLVING, -S** to explain; to resolve; to unfold

SOMAJ *n* in India: a society; a congregation; a worshiping assembly; *also* **SAMAJ**

SOMAN *n pl* **-S** a toxic chemical warfare agent

SOMAS *n pl of* **SOMA** entire bodies of organisms, exclusive of germ cells; *also* **SOMATA**

SOMEN *n pl* **-S** thin, white Japanese noodles

SONAR *n pl* **-S** an underwater locating device

SONCY *adj* **SONCIER, SONCIEST** lucky; fortunate; thriving; *also* **SONSY**

SONDE *n pl* **-S** a device for testing meteorological conditions

SONES *n pl of* **SONE** units of perceived loudness

SONGS *n pl of* **SONG** lyrical poems adapted to vocal music

SONIC *adj* pertaining to sound

SONLY *adj* pertaining to a son

SONNY *n pl* **SONNIES** a small boy

SONSY *adj* **SONSIER, SONSIEST** lucky; fortunate; thriving; *also* **SONCY**

SOOEY *interj* a shout used in calling pigs

SOOKS *n pl of* **SOOK** marketplaces in North Africa and the Middle East; *also* **SUKS, SUQS, SOUKS, SUKHS**

SOOTH *adj* **-ER, -EST** true

SOOTS *v pr t of* **SOOT** covers or coats with soot, a black dust given off by fire

SOOTY *adj* **SOOTIER, SOOTIEST** pertaining to soot; covered with soot

SOPHS *n pl of* **SOPH** informal for sophomores

SOPHY *n pl* **SOPHIES** a sovereign of Persia

SOPOR *n pl* **-S** a profound sleep from which a person can be roused only with difficulty

SOPPY *adj* **SOPPIER, SOPPIEST** very wet or sloppy

SOPRA *adv* above; before; over; upon (in music)

SORAS *n pl of* **SORA** marsh birds

SORBS *v pr t of* **SORB** takes up a liquid or a gas either by adsorption or by absorption

SORDS *n pl of* **SORD** flights or flocks of mallards

SORED v p t of **SORE** mutilated the legs or feet of (a horse) in order to induce a particular gait in the animal.

SOREL n pl **-S** a young buck in the third year

SORER adj more painful to the touch; tenderer

SORES v pr t of **SORE** mutilates the legs or feet of (a horse) in order to induce a particular gait in the animal.

SORGO n pl **-S** a variety of millet; also **SORGHUM**

SORNS v pr t of **SORN** SCOT. imposes one's self on another for bed and board

SORRY adj **SORRIER, SORRIEST** feeling or expressing sorrow or pity

SORTA adv informal for sort of; somewhat

SORTS v pr t of **SORT** arranges or orders by classes or categories

SORUS n pl **SORI** a spore-producing structure in certain lichens and fungi

SOTHS n pl of **SOTH** sooths, truths

SOTOL n pl **-S** a flowering plant

SOUGH v **-ED, -ING, -S** to make a soft murmuring or rustling sound; also **SUGH**

SOUKE v **-D, SOUKING, -S** [obs] to suck

SOUKS n pl of **SOUK** marketplaces in North Africa and the Middle East; also **SUKS, SUQS, SOOKS, SUKHS**

SOULS n pl of **SOUL** the spiritual natures of humans

SOUND v **-ED, -ING, -S** to make known; proclaim

SOUPS n pl of **SOUP** liquid foods of many kinds

SOUPY adj **SOUPIER, SOUPIEST** resembling soup; soup like

SOURS v pr t of **SOUR** makes or becomes somebody dissatisfied; makes or becomes something tart or sharp-tasting

SOUSE v **-D, SOUSING, -S** to plunge into water

SOUTH v **-ED, -ING, -ES** to move toward the south

SOWAR n pl **-S** a mounted soldier in India

SOWED v p t of **SOW** scattered over land for growth, as seed

SOWER n pl **-S** one who, or that which, sows

SOWLE v **-D, SOWLING, -S** [obs] to pull by the ears; to drag about

SOYAS n pl of **SOYA** soybeans; also **SOYS, SOJAS**

SOYLE v **-D, SOYLING, -S** to solve, to clear up

SOYUZ n pl **-ES** a series of Soviet manned spacecraft capable of docking in space

SOZIN n pl **-S** a type of protein

SPAAD n pl **-S** a kind of spar; earth flax

SPACE v **-D, SPACING, -S** to set some distance apart

SPACY adj **SPACIER, SPACIEST** eccentric; also **SPACEY**

SPADE v **-D, SPADING, -S** to dig with a spade, a tool for digging

SPADO n pl **-S** an impotent person

SPAED v p t of **SPAE** foretold; divined

SPAES v pr t of **SPAE** foretells; divines

SPAHI n pl **-S** a Turkish cavalryman; also **SPAHEE**

SPAIL n pl **-S** a splinter or chip; also **SPALE**

SPAIT n pl **-S** a flood or state of overflowing; also **SPATE**

SPAKE v p t of **SPEAK** [obs] archaic past tense of SPEAK

SPALE n pl **-S** a splinter or chip; also **SPAIL**

SPALL n pl **-S** a small fragment or chip especially of stone

SPAMS v pr t of **SPAM** sends unsolicited emails

SPANG adv precisely; squarely

SPANK v **-ED, -ING, -S** to slap on the buttocks

SPANS *v pr t of* **SPAN** extends across or over

SPARE *v* **-D, SPARING, -S** to refrain from treating harshly

SPARK *v* **-ED, -ING, -S** to stimulate or incite something

SPARS *v pr t of* **SPAR** makes boxing or fighting motions without hitting one's opponent

SPARY *adj* **SPARIER, SPARIEST** sparing; parsimonious

SPASM *n pl* **-S** a sudden, involuntary contraction of a muscle or group of muscles

SPATE *n pl* **-S** a flood or state of overflowing; *also* **SPAIT**

SPATS *v pr t of* **SPAT** quarrels briefly over a petty matter

SPAWL *n pl* **-S** a splinter or fragment, as of wood or stone

SPAWN *v* **-ED, -ING, -S** to generate or give rise to something

SPAYS *v pr t of* **SPAY** removes or extirpates the ovaries of

SPAZZ *n pl* **-ES** one who is considered clumsy or inept; *also* **SPAZ**

SPEAK *v* **SPOKE, -ING, -S** to utter words or articulate sounds

SPEAN *v* **-ED, -ING, -S** to wean

SPEAR *v* **-ED, -ING, -S** to pierce or strike with a pointed object

SPECK *n pl* **-S** a small spot, mark or discoloration

SPECS *v pr t of* **SPEC** writes or supplies specifications for

SPEED *v* **SPED** or **-ED, -ING, -S** to move quickly

SPEEL *v* **-ED, -ING, -S** to climb; *also* **SPEIL**

SPEER *v* **-ED, -ING, -S** to inquire; *also* **SPEIR**

SPEIL *v* **-ED, -ING, -S** to climb; *also* **SPEEL**

SPEIR *v* **-ED, -ING, -S** to inquire; *also* **SPEER**

SPELL *v* **SPELT** or **-ED, -ING, -S** to name the letters of a word in order

SPELT *v p t of* **SPELL** named the letters of a word in order

SPEND *v* **SPENT, -ING, -S** to use up or put out; expend

SPENT *v p t of* **SPEND** used up or put out; expended

SPERM *n pl* **-S** a male reproductive cell

SPETS *v pr t of* **SPET** [obs] spits; throws out

SPEWS *v pr t of* **SPEW** ejects forcefully; *also* **SPUES**

SPICA *n pl* **-E** or **-S** a bandage that is applied in V-shaped crossings

SPICE *v* **-D, -ING, -S** to season with aromatic plant substances; to make something more exciting

SPICK *adj* very neat or tidy

SPICY *adj* **SPICIER, SPICIEST** having flavor, aroma, piquant

SPIED *v p t of* **SPY** to observe secretly with hostile intent

SPIEL *v* **-ED, -ING, -S** to talk volubly or extravagantly

SPIER *n pl* **-S** someone who spies

SPIES *v pr t of* **SPY** observes secretly with hostile intent

SPIFF *v* **-ED, -ING, -S** to make attractive, stylish or up-to-date

SPIKE *v* **-D, SPIKING, -S** to impale on or pierce with or as with a thin, pointed piece of metal or wood

SPIKY *adj* **SPIKIER, SPIKIEST** resembling a spike

SPILE *n pl* **-S** a column of wood or steel or concrete

SPILL *v* **-ED** or **SPILT, -ING, -S** to cause or allow (a substance) to run or fall out of a container

SPILT *v p t of* **SPILL** caused or allowed (a substance) to run or fall out of a container

SPINE *n pl* **-S** the spinal column of a vertebrate

SPINS *v pr t of* **SPIN** draws out tediously and twists into threads

SPINY	*adj* **SPINIER, SPINIEST** bearing or covered with spines or thorns	**SPOTS**	*v pr t of* **SPOT** becomes stained with blemishes
SPIRE	*n pl* **-S** a top part or point that tapers upward; a pinnacle	**SPOUT**	*v* **-ED, -ING, -S** to gush forth in a rapid stream or in spurts
SPIRT	*v* **-ED, -ING, -S** to spurt	**SPRAG**	*n pl* **-S** a chock or bar wedged under a wheel
SPIRY	*adj* **SPIRIER, SPIRIEST** of or pertaining to a spire; tall; slender	**SPRAT**	*n pl* **-S** a small marine food fish
SPITE	*v* **-D, SPITING, -S** to treat with malice	**SPRAY**	*v* **-ED, -ING, -S** to disperse in small particles
SPITS	*v pr t of* **SPIT** ejects from the mouth	**SPREE**	*n pl* **-S** a carefree, lively outing
		SPRIG	*n pl* **-S** a small shoot or twig of a tree or other plant
SPITZ	*n pl* **-ES** a dog belonging to a breed that has a pointed muzzle, erect pointed ears and a tightly curled tail	**SPRIT**	*n pl* **-S** a ship's light spar pivoted at the mast
		SPRUE	*n pl* **-S** a tropical disease
		SPRUG	*v* [obs] to make smart
SPIVS	*n pl of* **SPIV** BRIT. people, usually unemployed, who live by their wits	**SPUDS**	*n pl of* **SPUD** sharp hand shovels for digging
SPLAT	*n pl* **-S** a slat of wood, as one in the middle of a chair back	**SPUED**	*v p t of* **SPUE** ejected forcefully; *also* **SPEWED**
SPLAY	*v* **-ED, -ING, -S** spread or be spread out or further apart	**SPUES**	*v pr t of* **SPUE** ejects forcefully; *also* **SPEWS**
SPLIT	*v* **SPLIT, -TING, -S** to divide from end to end by a sharp blow	**SPUME**	*v* **-D, SPUMING, -S** to foam or froth a liquid
SPOIL	*v* **-ED** or **SPOILT, -ING, -S** to impair the value or quality of	**SPUMY**	*adj* **SPUMIER, SPUMIEST** foamy, frothy, lathery or spumous
SPOKE	*v p t of* **SPEAK** uttered words or articulated sounds	**SPUNK**	*n* courage, spirit, bravery
SPOOF	*n pl* **-S** nonsense; tomfoolery; a hoax	**SPURN**	*v* **-ED, -ING, -S** to reject with contempt
SPOOK	*v* **-ED, -ING, -S** to frighten or become frightened	**SPURS**	*v pr t of* **SPUR** gives incentive to; encourages
SPOOL	*v* **-ED, -ING, -S** to wind or be wound onto a cylindrical device	**SPURT**	*n pl* **-S** a sudden forcible gush or jet
SPOON	*v* **-ED, -ING, -S** to lift, scoop up or carry with or as if with a spoon (a utensil with a small, shallow bowl on a handle)	**SPUTA**	*n pl of* **SPUTUM** spews; salivas
		SPUTS	*n pl of* **SPUT** thimbles or annular plates used to reinforce holes in a boiler
SPOOR	*n pl* **-S** a track, a trail, a scent or droppings especially of a wild animal	**SQUAB**	*n pl* **-S** a fledgling pigeon about four weeks old
		SQUAD	*n pl* **-S** a small group of people organized in a common endeavor or activity
SPORE	*n pl* **-S** a small, usually single-celled reproductive body	
SPORT	*v* **-ED, -ING, -S** to frolic; to engage in a physical activity	**SQUAT**	*v* **-TED, -TING, -S** to sit in a crouching position with knees bent and the buttocks on or near the heels

SQUEG *v* **-GED, -GING, -S** to oscillate in an irregular manner

SQUIB *n pl* **-S** a short journalistic piece

SQUID *n pl* **-S** marine mollusk with 10 arms

STABS *v pr t of* **STAB** pierces with a pointed weapon

STACK *v* **-ED, -ING, -S** to arrange in an orderly pile

STADE *n pl* **-S** an ancient Greek unit of length

STAFF *n pl* **-S** or **STAVES** a stick or cane carried as an aid in walking or climbing

STAGE *v* **-ED, -ING, -S** to organize a performance or event

STAGS *n pl of* **STAG** the adult males of the red deer

STAGY *adj* **STAGIER, STAGIEST** having a theatrical, especially an artificial or affected, character or quality

STAID *adj* **-ER, -EST** sober, grave, serious

STAIG *n pl* **-S** a colt

STAIN *v* **-ED, -ING, -S** to discolor, soil or spot

STAIR *n pl* **-S** a series or flight of steps

STAKE *v* **-D, -ING, -S** to support, strengthen, or tether something to a stake, thin pointed posts driven into the ground

STALE *adj* **-R, -EST** having lost freshness, effervescence

STALK *v* **-ED, -ING, -S** to pursue quarry or prey stealthily

STALL *v* **-ED, -ING, -S** to delay with hesitation or evasion

STAMP *v* **-ED, -ING, -S** to bring down the foot forcibly

STAND *v* **STOOD, -ING, -S** to rise to an upright position

STANE *v* **-D, STANING, -S** to stone

STANG *v* **-ED, -ING, -S** [obs] to sting

STANK *v p t of* **STINK** emitted a strong, offensive smell

STAPH *n pl* **-S** a spherical gram-positive parasitic bacterium

STARE *v* **-D, STARING, -S** to look directly and fixedly

STARK *adj* **-ER, -EST** harsh in appearance

STARS *v pr t of* **STAR** to be the leading performer

START *v* **-ED, -ING, -S** to begin an activity or a movement

STASH *v* **-ED, -ING, -S** to hide or store away in a secret place

STATE *v* **-D, -ING, -S** to set forth in words; declare

STATS *n pl of* **STAT** statistics

STAVE *v* **-D** or **STOVE, STAVING, -S** to break or smash a hole in

STAWS *v pr t of* **STAW** SCOT. is fixed or set; stays

STAYS *v pr t of* **STAY** stops doing something; ceases

STEAD *n pl* **-S** the function or position properly or customarily occupied or served by another

STEAK *n pl* **-S** a slice of meat, typically beef

STEAL *v* **STOLE, STOLEN, -ING** to take the property of another wrongfully

STEAM *n pl* **-S** the vapor phase of water

STEED *n pl* **-S** a horse, especially a spirited one

STEEK *v* **-ED, -ING, -S** to fix, to fasten; *also* **STEIK**

STEEL *n pl* **-S** a generally hard, strong, durable, malleable alloy of iron and carbon

STEEM *v* **-ED, -ING, -S** to gleam

STEEN *n pl* **-S** a vessel of clay or stone

STEEP *v* **-ED, -ING, -S** to soak or be soaked in water or other liquid

STEER *v* **-ED, -ING, -S** to direct the course of; to guide

STEES *n pl of* **STEE** [obs] ladders; *also* **STEYS**

STEGS *n pl of* **STEG** [obs] ganders; male geese

STEIK *v* **-ED, -ING, -S** to fix, to fasten; *also* **STEEK**

STEIN	*n pl* **-S** a mug intended for serving beer	
STELA	*n pl* **-E** or **-I** an ancient upright stone slab bearing markings and used as a monument	
STELE	*n pl* **STELAE** central part of stem and roots	
STELL	*v* **-ED, -ING, -S** [obs] to place or fix firmly or permanently	
STEMS	*v pr t of* **STEM** derives, originates or is caused by something	
STENO	*n pl* **-S** informal for a stenographer	
STENT	*n pl* **-S** a slender tube inserted inside a tubular body part	
STEPS	*v pr t of* **STEP** moves the feet in walking	
STERE	*n pl* **-S** a unit of cubic measure in the metric system	
STERN	*n pl* **-S** the rear part of a ship	
STETS	*v pr t of* **STET** in printing: cancels, as of a correction	
STEWS	*v pr t of* **STEW** is upset	
STEWY	*adj* having the characteristics of a stew	
STEYS	*n pl of* **STEY** [obs] ladders; *also* **STEES**	
STIAN	*n pl* **-S** a sty on the eye; *also* **STYAN**	
STICH	*n pl* **-ES** a line of poetry	
STICK	*v* **STUCK, -ING, -S** to pierce with a pointed instrument	
STIED	*v p t of* **STY** to shut up in or live in a sty	
STIES	*n pl of* **STY** pens or enclosures for swine	
STIFF	*adj* **-ER, -EST** not easily bent; not flexible or pliant	
STILE	*n pl* **-S** a set of steps, for ascending and descending, in passing a fence or wall	
STILL	*v* **-ED, -ING, -S** to become or make calm	
STILT	*v* **-ED, -ING, -S** to raise on stilts, supporting posts	
STIME	*n pl* **-S** a glimpse	

STIMY	*v* **STYMIED, -ING, STYMIES** to hinder or obstruct; *also* **STYMIE**	
STING	*v* **STUNG, -ING, -S** to cause a stinging pain, as by insect	
STINK	*v* **STANK** or **STUNK, -ING, -S** to emit a strong, offensive smell	
STINT	*v* **-ED, -ING, -S** to put an end to; to stop; to limit	
STIPE	*n pl* **-S** the stalk of a pistil	
STIRK	*n pl* **-S** a young bullock or heifer	
STIRP	*n pl* **-S** stock; race; family	
STIRS	*v pr t of* **STIR** mixes ingredients	
STIVE	*v* **-D, STIVING, -S** to stuff; to crowd; to fill full	
STOAE	*n pl of* **STOA** ancient Greek covered walks or colonnades; *also* **STOAI, STOAS**	
STOAI	*n pl of* **STOA** ancient Greek covered walks or colonnades; *also* **STOAE, STOAS**	
STOAS	*n pl of* **STOA** ancient Greek covered walks or colonnades; *also* **STOAE, STOAI**	
STOAK	*v* **-ED, -ING, -S** to stop; to choke	
STOAT	*n pl* **-S** the ermine in its brown summer coat with black-tipped tail	
STOBS	*n pl of* **STOB** short straight pieces of wood, such as stakes	
STOCK	*v* **-ED, -ING, -S** to supply with something for future use	
STOGY	*n pl* **-IES** a long, slender cigar	
STOIC	*n pl* **-S** someone who is seemingly indifferent to emotions or pain	
STOKE	*v* **-D, STOKING, -S** to poke or stir up the fire of a furnace	
STOLA	*n pl* **-S, -E** a long garment, descending to the ankles	
STOLE	*v p t of* **STEAL** took the property of another wrongfully	
STOMA	*n pl* **-S** or **-TA** a minute epidermal pore in a leaf or stem through which gases and water vapor can pass	
STOMP	*v* **-ED, -ING, -S** to stamp with the foot	

TONE *v* **-D, STONING, -S** to hurl rocks at in order to injure or kill

TONY *adj* **STONIER, STONIEST** of or pertaining to stone

TOOD *v p t of* **STAND** rose to an upright position

TOOK *v* **-ED, -ING, -S** to set up as sheaves of grain for drying

TOOL *n pl* **-S** a single seat on legs or a pedestal and without arms or a back

TOOP *v* **-ED, -ING, -S** to bend the upper part of the body downward and forward

TOOR *v* **-ED, -ING, -S** to rise in clouds, as dust

TOPE *v* **-D, STOPING, -S** to excavate in the form of steep inclines or stopes

TOPS *v pr t of* **STOP** obstructs; renders impassable

TOPT *v p t of* **STOP** [obs] obstructed; rendered impassable

TORE *v* **-D, STORING, -S** to collect as a reserved supply

TORK *n pl* **-S** a large wading bird with white-and-black plumage

TORM *v* **-ED, -ING, -S** to move angrily or forcefully in a specified direction

TORY *n pl* **STORIES** a narration or recital of that which has occurred

TOSS *adj* facing toward the direction from which an overriding glacier impinges

TOTS *v pr t of* **STOT** runs with a springing gait; *also* **STOTTS**

TOTT *v* **-ED, -ING, -S** [obs] to bound with stiff legged gait; to bounce; *also* **STOT**

TOUP *n pl* **-S** a basin for holy water; *also* **STOWP**

TOUR *n pl* **-S** a battle or tumult; encounter; combat

TOUT *adj* **-ER, -EST** strong in structure or substance

TOVE *n pl* **-S** a device for heating or cooking

STOWP *n pl* **-S** a basin for holy water; *also* **STOUP**

STOWS *v pr t of* **STOW** puts away in some place; hides; lodges

STRAM *v* **-MED, -MING, -S** to spring or recoil with violence

STRAP *v* **-PED, -PING, -S** to fasten or secure with a flexible strip

STRAW *n pl* **-S** a thin tube used for sucking up a drink

STRAY *v* **-ED, -ING, -S** to wander, as from a direct course; to deviate

STREP *n pl* **-S** a bacterial infection of the throat

STREW *v* **-ED or STREWN, -ING, -S** to scatter, spread around

STRIA *n pl* **-E** a minute groove, or channel; a threadlike line

STRID *n pl* **-S** a narrow passage between precipitous rocks or banks

STRIP *v* **-PED or STRIPT, -PING, -S** to dismantle; to uncover

STRIX *n pl* **-ES** one of the flutings of a column

STROP *v* **-PED, -PING, -S** to sharpen razors on a leather strap

STROW *v* **-ED or STROWN, -ING, -S** to strew; to scatter

STRUM *v* **-MED, -MING, -S** to play an instrument of music by stroking or brushing the strings

STRUT *v* **-TED, -TING, -S** to walk with a lofty proud gait

STUBS *v pr t of* **STUB** bangs a toe against something accidentally

STUCK *v p t of* **STICK** pierced with an pointed instrument

STUDS *v pr t of* **STUD** sets, marks or decorates conspicuously and often at intervals

STUDY *v* **STUDIED, -ING, STUDIES** to apply the mind to learning and understanding a subject

STUFA *n pl* **-S** a jet of steam issuing from a fissure in the earth

STUFF *v* **-ED, -ING, -S** to fill by crowding something into

STULL *n pl* **-S** a framework of timber

STULM _n pl_ **-S** a shaft or gallery to drain a mine

STULP _n pl_ **-S** a short, stout post used for any purpose, as to mark a boundary

STUMP _v_ **-ED, -ING, -S** to walk clumsily; to baffle

STUMS _v pr t of_ **STUM** ferments wine by adding partly fermented grape juice to it while in the cask or vat

STUNG _v p t of_ **STING** caused a stinging pain, as by insects

STUNK _v p t of_ **STINK** emitted a strong, offensive smell

STUNS _v pr t of_ **STUN** astonishes; overpowers; bewilders

STUNT _v_ **-ED, -ING, -S** to hinder from growing to the natural size

STUPA _n pl_ **-S** a mound or monument commemorative of Buddha

STUPE _n pl_ **-S** a cloth or flax dipped in warm water or medication and applied to a hurt or sore

STURT _n pl_ **-S** disturbance; annoyance; violent quarreling

STYAN _n pl_ **-S** a sty on the eye; _also_ **STIAN**

STYED _v p t of_ **STY** shut up in or lived in a sty

STYES _v pr t of_ **STY** shuts up in or lives in a sty

STYLE _v_ **-D, STYLING, -S** to entitle; to term, name or call

STYLI _n pl of_ **STYLUS** pointed tools for writing, drawing or engraving

STYMY _v_ **STYMIED, -ING, STYMIES** to thwart; to hinder

SUAVE _adj_ **-R, -ST** sweet; pleasant; delightful

SUBAH _n pl_ **-S** a province of India

SUBER _n pl_ **-S** a cork

SUCCI _n pl of_ **SUCCUS** fluids, such as gastric juices or vegetable juices contained in or secreted by living tissue

SUCKS _v pr t of_ **SUCK** draws liquid from, by the action of the mouth

SUCKY _adj_ **SUCKIER, SUCKIEST** informal for extremely objectionable; unpleasant

SUCRE _n pl_ **-S** the basic monetary unit of Ecuador

SUDDS _n pl of_ **SUDD** floating masses of vegetation

SUDOR _n_ salty fluid secreted by sweat glands

SUDSY _adj_ **SUDSIER, SUDSIEST** foamy

SUEDE _v_ **-D, SUEDING, -S** to give leather or fabric a napped surface

SUERS _n pl of_ **SUER** people that sue

SUETS _n pl of_ **SUET** hard white fats found on the kidneys and loins of sheep and cattle

SUETY _adj_ like or full of suet; of fat

SUGAR _v_ **-ED, -ING, -S** to cover or sprinkle with sugar or some other sweetener

SUGHS _v pr t of_ **SUGH** SCOT. [obs] makes a soft moaning or sighing sound; _also_ **SOUGHS**

SUGIS _n pl of_ **SUGI** tall evergreens of Japan and China yielding valuable soft wood

SUINE _n pl_ **-S** a mixture of oleomargarine with lard or other fatty ingredients; a butter substitute

SUING _v pr part of_ **SUE** taking legal action against somebody to obtain something, usually compensation for a wrong

SUINT _n_ a peculiar, fatty substance obtained from the wool of sheep

SUIST _n pl_ **-S** a selfish person; a selfist

SUITE _n pl_ **-S** a series of things that form a unit

SUITS _v pr t of_ **SUIT** is appropriate to

SUKHS _n pl of_ **SUKH** marketplaces in North Africa and the Middle East; _also_ **SUKS, SUQS, SOOKS, SOUKS**

SULAS _n pl of_ **SULA** sea birds, including the booby

ULCI *n pl of* **SULCUS** furrows; grooves; fissures

ULFA *n pl* **-S** any antibacterial consisting of any of several synthetic organic compounds; short for sulfonamide

ULFO *adj* containing a certain univalent radical; sulfonic

ULKS *v pr t of* **SULK** to be angrily silent

ULKY *adj* **SULKIER, SULKIEST** sullenly aloof or withdrawn

ULLS *n pl of* **SULL** [obs] plows; farm implements

ULLY *v* **SULLIED, -ING, -IES** to soil; tarnish; stain

ULUS *n pl of* **SULU** sarong-like garments, worn by Melanesians, as in the Fijis

UMAC *n pl* **-S** any of a genus of trees of the cashew family

UMMA *n pl* **-S** or **-E** a comprehensive treatise in philosophy

UMOS *n pl of* **SUMO** a Japanese form of wrestling; the wrestlers of sumo

UMPS *n pl of* **SUMP** reservoirs for liquid

UNNA *n pl* **-S** the way of life prescribed as normative in Islam; *also* **SUNNAH**

UNNS *n pl of* **SUNN** East Indian leguminous plants

UNNY *adj* **SUNNIER, SUNNIEST** filled with sunlight

UNUP *n pl* **-S** the time of sunrise

UPER *adj* excellent; the highest degree

UPES *n pl of* **SUPE** actors without speaking parts; supernumeraries

UPRA *adv* above; over; on top of

URAH *n pl* **-S** a soft, twilled fabric of silk or rayon

URAL *adj* pertaining to the calf of the leg

URAS *n pl of* **SURA** some of the 114 chapters or sections of the Koran

SURDS *n pl of* **SURD** voiceless speech sounds

SURER *adj* **SURE** in a more sure manner; safely; certainly

SURFS *v pr t of* **SURF** rides the swells of the sea which break upon the shore with a board or body

SURFY *adj* **SURFIER, SURFIEST** consisting of, abounding in or resembling surf waves

SURGE *v* **-D, SURGING, -S** to rise and move in a billowing or swelling manner

SURGY *adj* surging; billowy; or swelling

SURLY *adj* **SURLIER, SURLIEST** unfriendly, rude, somewhat threatening

SURRA *n pl* **-S** an often fatal infectious disease of domestic animals, especially to horses, transmitted by biting insects

SUSHI *n pl* **-S** a Japanese dish with thin slices of fresh raw fish and cooked rice wrapped in seaweed

SUSUS *n pl of* **SUSU** dolphins; *also* **SOOSOOS**

SUTRA *n pl* **-S** a basic text of Buddhist scripture; *also* **SUTTA**

SUTTA *n pl* **-S** a basic text of Buddhist scripture; *also* **SUTRA**

SWABS *v pr t of* **SWAB** cleans with a mop or swab

SWADS *n pl of* **SWAD** [obs] clowns; country bumpkins

SWAGE *n pl* **-S** a tool used in bending or shaping cold metal

SWAGS *v pr t of* **SWAG** hangs or moves; sways; swings

SWAIN *n pl* **-S** a young man dwelling in the country

SWALE *n pl* **-S** a tract of low, marshy ground

SWAMI *n pl* **SWAMIES** a Hindu ascetic or religious teacher; *also* **SWAMY**

SWAMP *v* **-ED, -ING, -S** to overwhelm; to submerge an area in water

SWAMY *n pl* **SWAMIES** a Hindu ascetic or religious teacher; *also* **SWAMI**

SWANG *v p t of* **SWING** moved in a curve or arc

SWANK *adj* **-ER, -EST** ostentatious; pretentious

SWANS *v pr t of* **SWAN** declares or affirms solemnly and formally as true

SWAPS *v pr t of* **SWAP** exchanges; trades; *also* **SWOPS**

SWARD *n pl* **-S** land covered with grassy turf; *also* **SWARTH**

SWARE *v p t of* **SWEAR** [obs] archaic past tense of SWEAR

SWARF *n pl* **-S** fine metallic filings or shavings removed by a cutting tool

SWARM *v* **-ED,-ING,-S** to move together in large numbers

SWART *adj* producing a swarthy complexion

SWASH *n pl* **-ES** a splash of water or other liquid hitting a solid surface

SWATH *n pl* **-S** the width of a scythe stroke or a mowing-machine blade; *also* **SWATHE**

SWATS *v pr t of* **SWAT** strikes or slaps with sharp blows; *also* **SWOTS**

SWAYS *v pr t of* **SWAY** moves or wields with the hand; swings

SWEAR *v* **SWARE** or **SWORE** or **SWORN, -ING, -S** to make a solemn declaration

SWEAT *v* **-ED** or **SWEAT, -ING, -S** to perspire

SWEDE *n pl* **-S** a cruciferous plant with a thick bulbous edible yellow root

SWEEP *v* **SWEPT, -ING, -S** to clean with a broom or brush

SWEER *adj* lazy

SWEET *adj* **-ER, -EST** having the taste of sugar

SWELL *v* **-ED, SWOLLEN, -ING, -S** to increase in size or volume

SWEPT *v p t of* **SWEEP** cleaned with a broom or brush

SWIES *n pl of* **SWY** Australian two-up games

SWIFT *adj* **-ER, -EST** moving or capable of moving with great speed

SWIGS *v pr t of* **SWIG** drinks in long draughts; gulps

SWILL *v* **-ED, -ING, -S** to drink great drafts of a liquid

SWIMS *v pr t of* **SWIM** moves progressively in water by means of strokes with the hands and feet

SWINE *n pl* **SWINE** a domestic pig

SWING *v* **SWANG** or **SWUNG, -ING, -S** to move in a curve or arc

SWINK *v* **-ED, -ING, -S** [obs] to toil

SWIPE *v* **-D, -ING, -S** to hit or try to hit with a swinging blow

SWIRL *v* **-ED, -ING, -S** to move with a twisting or whirling motion

SWISH *v* **-ED, -ING, -ES** to move with a hissing or whistling sound, as a whip

SWISS *n pl* **-ES** any of various fine sheer fabrics of cotton from Switzerland

SWITH *adv* [obs] quickly

SWOBS *n pl of* **SWOB** cleaning implements consisting of absorbent materials fastened to handles; *also* **SWABS**

SWOON *v* **-ED, -ING, -S** to faint; *also* **SWOUN**

SWOOP *v* **-ED, -ING, -S** to move in a sudden sweep

SWOPS *v pr t of* **SWOP** exchanges; trades; *also* **SWAPS**

SWORD *n pl* **-S** a weapon having a long and usually sharp blade with a cutting edge

SWORE *v p t of* **SWEAR** made a solemn declaration

SWORN *v p t of* **SWEAR** made a solemn declaration

SWOTS *v pr t of* **SWOT** strikes or slaps with sharp blows; *also* **SWATS**

SWOUN v -ED, -ING, -S to faint; *also* **SWOON**

SWUNG v p t of **SWING** moved in a curve or arc

SYBOE n pl -S SCOT. a spring onion; *also* **SYBO, SYBOW**

SYBOW n pl -S SCOT. a spring onion; *also* **SYBO, SYBOE**

SYCEE n pl -S silver money made in the form of ingots and formerly used in China

SYCES n pl of **SYCE** stablemen or grooms, especially in India; *also* **SICES, SAICES**

SYKES n pl of **SYKE** small streams; gutters; *also* **SIKES**

SYLES n pl of **SYLE** [obs] young herrings; *also* **SILES**

SYLIS n pl of **SYLI** former monetary units of Guinea

SYLPH n pl -S a slim, graceful woman or girl

SYLVA n pl -S or -E the forest trees of an area; *also* **SILVA**

SYNCH v -ED, -ING, -S to cause to harmonize and operate in unison; *also* **SYNC**

SYNCS v pr t of **SYNC** causes to harmonize and operate in unison; *also* **SYNCHS**

SYNDS v pr t of **SYND** rinses something, usually with water; *also* **SYNES**

SYNED v p t of **SYNE** rinsed something, usually with water; *also* **SYNDED**

SYNES v pr t of **SYNE** rinses something, usually with water; *also* **SYNDS**

SYNOD n pl -S an ecclesiastical council

SYNTH n pl -S a synthesizer

SYPHS n pl of **SYPH** syphilis

SYREN n pl -S a warning signal that is a loud wailing sound; *also* **SIREN**

SYRTS n pl of **SYRT** [obs] areas of quicksand; bogs; *also* **SIRTS**

SYRUP n pl -S a thick sweet sticky liquid; *also* **SIRUP**

SYSOP n pl -S a system operator

TA n BRIT. an expression of gratitude

TE n the seventh subtonic note of any musical scale

TI n the seventh tone of the diatonic musical scale; *also* **SI**

TO prep in the direction of

THREE LETTERS

TAB v -BED, -BING, -S to name or designate

TAC n used in old records for a kind of customary payment by a tenant

TAD n pl -S a small amount

TAE prep SCOT. to

TAG v -GED, -GING, -S to attach a label to

TAI n any of several sparoid fishes of the Pacific Ocean

TAJ n a tall, conical cap worn by Muslims

TAM n a tight-fitting Scottish cap

TAN v -NED, -NING, -S to convert hide into leather by soaking in chemicals

TAO n the ultimate principle of the universe

TAP v -PED, -PING, -S to strike, knock gently

TAR v -RED, -RING, -S to cover with tar, a thick, black, viscous liquid

TAS n [obs] a heap; *also* **TAAS**

TAT v -TED, -TING, -S to make lacework by knotting or looping; *also* **TATT**

TAU n the 19th letter of the Greek alphabet

TAV n the 23rd letter of the Hebrew alphabet

TAW v -ED, -ING, -S to convert skins into white leather

TAX *v* **-ED, -ING, -ES** to place a charge on something like property, income or goods

TAY *n* an Irish dialect word for tea

TEA *n pl* **-S** dried leaves used to make a drink by infusing them in water

TEC *n* informal for a police officer who investigates crimes

TED *v* **-DED, -DING, -S** to spread out grass for drying

TEE *v* **-D, -ING, -S** to drive a golf ball from a small peg, a tee

TEF *n* an annual grass of North Africa, grown for its grain; *also* **TEFF**

TEG *n* a sheep in its second year; *also* **TEGG**

TEN *n* the whole number after nine

TET *n pl* **-S** the ninth letter of the Hebrew alphabet; *also* **TETH**

TEW *v* **-ED, -ING** to prepare by beating or pounding

TEX *n* a unit of weight used to measure the density of textiles

THE *adj* indicating one as distinct from another

THO *conj* despite the fact; shorten form of though

THY *adj* a possessive form of the pronoun thou

TIC *n pl* **-S** a local and habitual twitching especially in the face

TIE *v* **-D, TYING, -S** to fasten or secure

TIG *v* **-GED, -GING, -S** SCOT. to touch lightly, as in the game of tag

TIL *n* the sesame plant

TIN *v* **-NED, -NING, -S** to plate or coat with tin; an easily shaped metallic element

TIP *v* **-PED, -PING, -S** to push or knock over

TIT *n* a small insectivorous bird, the European meadow pipit; a titlark

TOD *n* BRIT. an English unit of weight used mainly for wool

TOE *v* **-D, -ING, -S** to touch, to kick, to drive

TOG *v* **-GED, -GING, -S** to clothe

TOL *v* to take away, as in a fee; *also* **TOLL**

TOM *n* the male of various animals

TON *n pl* **-S** a unit of weight used in the United States equal to 2,000 pounds

TOO *adv* in addition

TOP *v* **-PED, -PING, -S** to excel; to rise above others

TOR *n* a high-pointed hill; a rocky pinnacle

TOT *n pl* **-S** a small child

TOW *v* **-ED, -ING, -S** to draw or pull behind by a chain or rope

TOY *v* **-ED, -ING, -S** to amuse oneself idly

TRY *v* **TRIED, -ING, TRIES** to attempt

TSK *v* **-ED, -ING** a sucking noise used to express disappointment

TUB *v* **-BED, -BING, -S** to pack or store something in a tub, an open flat-bottomed vessel

TUE *n* the parson bird

TUG *v* **-GED, -GING, -S** to pull or draw with great effort

TUI *n pl* **-S** a bird of New Zealand

TUM *v* **-MED, -MING** to tease wool in a preliminary carding operation

TUN *v* **-NED, -NING** to put into or store in a tun, a large cask for beer or wine

TUP *n pl* **-S** a male sheep

TUR *n pl* **-S** a large, long-horned, wild goat native to Europe

TUT *v* **-TED, -TING** to make a disapproving sound

TUX *n pl* **-ES** an informal word for a tuxedo

TUZ *n* a lock or tuft of hair

TWA *n* SCOT. two; *also* **TWAE**

TWO *n* the next whole number after one

TYE *n* a knot; a tie

TYG *n* flat-bottomed drinking cup, generally with two or more handles

FOUR LETTERS

TAAS *n* [obs] a heap; *also* **TAS**

TABI *n pl* **-S** a sock with a separation for the big toe; worn with thong sandals by the Japanese

TABS *v pr t of* **TAB** names or designates

TABU *n pl* **-S** a rejection of some types of behavior or language because they are socially unacceptable; *also* **TABOO**

TACE *n* one of a series of armor used to protect the lower trunk and thighs; *also* **TASSE, TASSET**

TACH *n pl* **-S** an informal term for a tachometer, a measuring instrument for indicating rate of rotation

TACK *v* **-ED, -ING, -S** to attach something with a tack, a short nail with a sharp point and a flat head

TACO *n pl* **-S** a tortilla folded around a filling

TACT *n* sensitivity in dealing with others or difficult issues

TADS *n pl of* **TAD** small amounts

TAEL *n pl* **-S** any of several small-necked freshwater ducks

TAGS *v pr t of* **TAG** attaches a label to

TAHA *n pl* **-S** an African weaver bird

TAHR *n pl* **-S** an animal resembling a goat; *also* **THAR**

TAIL *n pl* **-S** the back, last, lower or inferior part of anything

TAIN *n pl* **-S** a thin tin plate

TAIT *n* a small nocturnal and arboreal Australian marsupial

TAKA *n pl* **-S** a monetary unit of Bangladesh

TAKE *v* **TOOK, -N, TAKING, -S** to get into one's possession

TALA *n pl* **-S** the basic unit of money in Western Samoa

TALC *n* a fine grained mineral having a soft soapy feel

TALE *n pl* **-S** a report, account or story

TALI *n pl of* **TALUS** anklebones

TALK *v* **-ED, -ING, -S** to utter words

TALL *adj* **-ER, -EST** high in stature; brave; bold; courageous

TAME *v* **-D, TAMING, -S** to make docile, or domestic

TAMP *v* **-ED, -ING, -S** to firmly pack something down by tapping it

TANG *n pl* **-S** a coarse blackish seaweed

TANK *n pl* **-S** a large basin or cistern; a receptacle for liquids

TANS *v pr t of* **TAN** to convert hide into leather by soaking in chemicals

TANT *n pl* **-S** a small scarlet spider

TAPA *n* inner bark of a paper mulberry tree

TAPE *v* **-D, TAPING, -S** to fasten or attach with tape, a strip of sticky material

TAPS *v pr t of* **TAP** to strike, knock gently

TARE *v* **-D, TARING, -S** to weigh as to determine the tare, the weight of the packing material or container

TARN *n pl* **-S** a steep-banked mountain lake or pool; *also* **TAIRN**

TARO *n pl* **-S** a tropical, starchy, tuberous root

TARP *n pl* **-S** a waterproofed canvas

TARS *v pr t of* **TAR** covers with tar, a thick, black, viscous liquid

TART *n pl* **-S** a small open pie with fruit filling

TASK *v* **-ED, -ING, -S** to assign a piece of work to somebody

TASS *n* SCOT. a cup or small goblet; *also* **TASSIE**

TATE *n* a small portion of anything consisting of fibers like of hair

TATS *v pr t of* **TAT** to make lacework by knotting or looping

TATT *v* **-ED, -ING** to make lacework by knotting or looping; *also* **TAT**

TATU *n* about three feet long exclusive of tail; *also* **TATOU**

TAUT *adj* **-ER, -EST** tight; stretched; not slack; close

319

TAWS *v pr t of* **TAW** to convert skins into white leather

TAXA *n pl of* **TAXON** a taxonomic categories or units, as a species or families

TAXI *v* **-ED, -ING** or **TAXYING, -S** or **-ES** to move slowly on the ground before takeoff or after landing an airplane

TEAK *n pl* **-S** a tall tree of E. Indies, with hard timber

TEAL *n pl* **-S** a small, short-necked, dabbling river duck

TEAM *n pl* **-S** a number of persons associated together in any work

TEAR *v* **TORE, TORN, -ING, -S** to pull apart or into pieces by force

TEAS *n pl of* **TEA** dried leaves used to make a drink by infusing them in water

TEAT *n pl* **-S** the small projection of a mammary gland

TECH *n pl* **-S** an informal term for a technician

TEDS *v pr t of* **TED** spreads out grass for drying

TEED *v p t of* **TEE** to have driven a golf ball from a small peg, a tee

TEEL *n* the oil of a sesame plant

TEEM *v* **-ED, -ING, -S** to be full of things, to abound

TEEN *n pl* **-S** a teenager

TEES *v pr t of* **TEE** drives a golf ball from a small peg, a tee

TEFF *n* an annual grass of North Africa, grown for its grain; *also* **TEF**

TEGG *n* a sheep in its second year; *also* **TEG**

TEJU *n* large, blackish, yellow-banded South American lizard

TELA *n pl* **-E** a delicate tissue or web-like structure

TELE *n pl* **-S** BRIT. a television set; *also* **TELLY**

TELL *v* **TOLD, -ING, -S** to utter or recite in detail; to narrate

TEMP *v* **-ED, -ING, -S** to work as a temporary employee

TEND *v* **-ED, -ING, -S** to be attentive to; to be disposed, inclined

TENT *n pl* **-S** a portable shelter

TEPA *n pl* **-S** a crystalline chemical compound

TERM *n pl* **-S** period of time that something lasts

TERN *n pl* **-S** a long-winged aquatic bird

TEST *v* **-ED, -ING, -S** to examine or try

TETE *n* a kind of wig; false hair

TETH *n pl* **-S** the ninth letter of the Hebrew alphabet; *also* **TET**

TETS *n pl of* **TET** more than one of the ninth letter of the Hebrew alphabet; *also* **TETHS**

TEXT *n pl* **-S** words written or printed

THAE *pron* SCOT. these, those

THAN *conj* expressing comparison or diversity of two elements

THAR *n pl* **-S** an animal resembling a goat; *also* **TAHR**

THAT *pron pl* **THOSE** used to refer to or indicate something

THAW *v* **-ED, -ING, -S** to melt or defrost

THEE *pron* the objective form of thou

THEM *pron* the object of a verb or preposition to refer to two or more people or things previously mentioned

THEN *adv* next in time, space or order; immediately afterward

THEW *n pl* **-S** muscle or muscular strength

THEY *pron* used to refer to people or things previously mentioned

THIN *v* **-NED, -NING, -S** to make or become thinner, smaller from one side to the other side

THIO *adj* containing sulfur

THIR *pron* BRIT. these

THIS *pron pl* **THESE** the person or thing just mentioned

THOU *pron* the one being addressed, especially in a literary, liturgical or devotional context

HRO *prep* informal spelling of through, in one side and out the other; *also* **THRU**

HRU *prep* informal spelling of through, in one side and out the other; *also* **THRO**

HUD *v* **-DED, -DING, -S** to make a heavy, dull sound

HUG *n pl* **-S** a person who acts violently, especially to commit a crime

HUS *adv* as a result

IAR *n* a tiara

ICE *n pl* **-S** an old word for a Yorker, a ball bowled to strike the ground about a bat's length in front of the wicket in the game of cricket

ICK *v* **-ED, -ING, -S** to emit recurring clicking sounds

ICS *n pl of* **TIC** local and habitual twitches especially in the face

IDE *n pl* **-S** rise and fall of the oceans water

IDY *adj* **TIDIER, TIDIEST** orderly and neat

IED *v p t of* **TIE** fastened or secured

IER *n pl* **-ED, -ING, -S** to arrange things in rows rising one above another

IES *v pr t of* **TIE** fastens or secures

IFF *n pl* **-S** a petty quarrel

IFT *n* a fit of pettishness, or slight anger

IGH *n* [obs] a close, or inclosure; a croft

IGS *v pr t of* **TIG** SCOT. to touch lightly, as in the game of tag

IKE *n pl* **-S** a small child, especially a boy; *also* **TYKE**

IKI *n pl* **-S** a wooden or stone image of a Polynesian god

ILE *v* **-D, TILING, -S** to cover with a tile, a plate or thin piece of baked clay

ILL *v* **-ED, -ING, -S** to plow and prepare land for the raising of crops

ILT *v* **-ED, -ING, -S** to cause to slope, as by raising one end

TIME *v* **-D, TIMING, -S** to measure how long something takes

TIND *v* [obs] to kindle; *also* **TEEND**

TINE *n pl* **-S** a slender pointed projecting part

TING *v* **-ED, -ING, -S** to give forth a light ringing sound

TINK *n* a sharp, quick sound

TINS *v pr t of* **TIN** plates or coats with tin; an easily shaped metallic element

TINT *v* **-ED, -ING, -S** to give a slight color

TINY *adj* **TINIER, TINIEST** very small

TIPI *n pl* **-S** a Native American tent; usually of conical shape; *also* **TEPEE**

TIPS *v pr t of* **TIP** pushes or knocks over

TIPU *n* a semi-evergreen South American tree

TIRE *v* **-D, TIRING, -S** to grow weary

TIRL *v* **-ED, -ING, -S** SCOT. to make a rattling noise

TIRO *n pl* **-S** a beginner in a field or activity; *also* **TYRO**

TITH *adj* tight; nimble

TITI *n pl* **-S** a New World shrub or small tree

TIVY *adv* with great speed; a huntsman's word or sound

TIZA *n* another word for the mineral ulexite

TOAD *n pl* **-S** a tailless, stout-bodied, leaping amphibian

TOBY *n pl* **TOBIES** a drinking mug in the shape of a stout man wearing a three-cornered hat

TOCO *n* a toucan having a very large beak

TODY *n pl* **TODIES** a tiny insectivorous bird, green and red in color

TOEA *n pl* **-S** a monetary unit in Papua New Guinea

TOED *v p t of* **TOE** touched, kicked

TOES *v pr t of* **TOE** touches, kicks

TOFF *n pl* **-S** BRIT. informal term for an upper-class or wealthy person

TOFT *n pl* **-S** BRIT. a homestead

TOFU *n* a protein-rich food made of coagulated soybean extract

TOGA *n pl* **-S** or **-E** a one-piece cloak worn by men in ancient Rome

TOGS *v pr t of* **TOG** clothes

TOIL *v* **-ED, -ING, -S** to work long and hard

TOKE *v* **-D, TOKING, -S** to take a puff on a cigarette or pipe

TOLA *n pl* **-S** a S. Asian unit of weight

TOLD *v p t of* **TELL** uttered or recited in detail; narrated

TOLE *v* **-D, TOLING, -S** to draw, or cause to follow; to allure by some bait

TOLL *v* **-ED, -ING, -S** to take away, as in a fee; *also* **TOL**

TOLT *n* a writ by which a cause pending in a court baron was removed into a country court

TOLU *n* an aromatic yellowish brown balsam

TOMB *n pl* **-S** a pit in which the dead body of a human being is deposited; a grave

TOME *n pl* **-S** an especially large heavy book

TOMS *n pl of* **TOM** the male of various animals

TONE *v* **-D, TONING, -S** to give a particular intonation or inflection to

TONG *v* **-ED, -ING, -S** to seize, hold or manipulate with tongs, a grasping device

TONS *n pl of* **TON** a unit of weight used in the United States equal to 2,000 pounds

TONY *adj* **TONIER, TONIEST** marked by an elegant or exclusive manner or style; *also* **TONEY**

TOOK *v p t of* **TAKE** to have gotten into one's possession

TOOL *v* **-ED, -ING, -S** to work something using a handheld device that aids in accomplishing a task

TOOM *adj* SCOT. [obs] empty

TOON *n pl* **-S** a reddish brown aromatic wood

TOOT *v* **-ED, -ING, -S** to blow or sound a horn

TOPE *v* **-D, TOPING, -S** to drink liquor to excess

TOPH *n pl* **-S** a kind of sandstone

TOPI *n pl* **-S** a pith helmet worn for protection against sun and heat; *also* **TOPEE**

TOPO *adj* commonly used abbreviation for a topographic map, a detailed description of a place

TOPS *v pr t of* **TOP** excels; rises above others

TORA *n* the body of wisdom and law contained in Jewish Scripture; *also* **TORAH**

TORC *n pl* **-S** a collar, necklace usually twisted and made of precious metal; *also* **TORQUE**

TORE *v p t of* **TEAR** pulled apart or into pieces by force

TORI *n pl of* **TORUS** a ring-shaped molding at the base of a column; *also* **TORES**

TORN *v p part of* **TEAR** pulled apart or into pieces by force

TORO *n pl* **-S** a bull

TORR *n* a unit of pressure

TORT *n pl* **-S** a wrongful act that injures another for which damages can be sought by the injured party

TORY *n pl* **TORIES** a political conservative

TOSE *v* **-D, TOSING, -S** [obs] to tease, or comb, as wool

TOSH *n* BRIT. informal for foolish nonsense

TOSS *v* **-ED, TOST -ING, -ES** to lightly throw something

TOST *v p part of* **TOSS** to have lightly thrown something

TOTA *n* the grivet, a small monkey

TOTE *v* **-D, TOTING, -S** to haul; to lug

TOTS *n pl of* **TOT** small children

TOTY *n* [obs] a sailor or fisherman

TOUR *v* **-ED, -ING, -S** to travel from place to place

TOUT *v* **-ED, -ING, -S** to solicit customers

TOWN *n pl* **-S** a population center that is larger than a village and smaller than a city

TOWS *v pr t of* **TOW** draws or pulls behind by a chain or rope

TOWY *adj* composed of, or like, tow

TOYS *v pr t of* **TOY** amuses oneself idly

TOZE *v* [obs] to pull violently; to touse

TOZY *adj* soft, like wool that has been teased

TRAD *n* traditional jazz as revived in the 1950s

TRAM *n pl* **-S** BRIT. a streetcar

TRAP *v* **-PED, -T, PING, -S** to catch or hold in a cage

TRAY *n pl* **-S** a flat, broad low rimmed object on which dishes, glasses, etc., are carried

TREE *v* **-D, -ING, -S** to force somebody up a tree, any perennial woody plant of considerable size

TREF *adj* not conforming to dietary laws; *also* **TEREFAH**

TREK *v* **-KED, -KING, -S** to make a slow or arduous journey

TREN *n* [obs] a fish spear

TRET *n pl* **-S** an allowance to purchasers, for waste or refuse matter

TREY *n pl* **-S** a card, dice or domino with three pips

TRIG *v* **-GED, -GING, -S** BRIT. to make clean or neat

TRIM *v* **-MED, -MING, -S** to make neat or tidy by clipping or pruning

TRIO *n pl* **-S** a composition for three parts or three instruments

TRIP *n pl* **-S** a brief journey or pleasure excursion

TROD *v p t of* **TREAD** stepped or walked on or over

TROG *v* **-GED, -GING** BRIT. informal for walk heavily or laboriously; trudge

TROP *adv* too much

TROT *v* **-TED, -TING, -S** to run; to jog; to hurry

TROW *v* **-ED, -ING, -S** [obs] to believe

TROY *adj* expressed in a system of weights used for precious metals and gemstones

TRUB *n pl* **-S** [obs] a truffle

TRUE *adj* **-R, -ST** real or correct

TRUG *n pl* **-S** BRIT. a shallow gardening basket

TSAR *n pl* **-S** a male monarch or emperor; *also* **CZAR, TZAR**

TUBA *n pl* **-E** or **-S** a trumpet; the lowest range brass wind instrument

TUBE *n pl* **-S** a hollow cylinder, of any material

TUBS *v pr t of* **TUB** packs or stores something in a tub, an open flat-bottomed vessel

TUCH *n pl* **-S** [obs] a dark-colored kind of marble; a touchstone

TUCK *v* **-ED, ING, -S** to make one or more folds in

TUET *n* the lapwing bird

TUFA *n pl* **-S** a soft or porous stone formed by depositions from ground water; *also* **TOPHE**

TUFF *n pl* **-S** a hard volcanic rock composed of compacted volcanic ash

TUFT *v* **-ED, -ING, -S** clusters of elongated strands attached at a base

TUGS *v pr t of* **TUG** pulls or draws with great effort

TUIS *n pl of* **TUI** a bird of New Zealand

TULE *n pl* **-S** a large bulrush growing abundantly

TULL *v* [obs] to allure; to tole

TUMP *v* **-ED, ING, -S** to overturn mainly used in the Southern United States

TUNA *n pl* **-S** a warm water game fish of the family Scombridae; *also* **TUNNY**

TUNE *v* **-D, TUNING, -S** to adjust to the proper pitch

TUNG *n* a Chinese tree bearing seeds that yield tung oil

TUNK *n* a sharp blow; a thump

TUNS *n pl of* **TUN** large casks for beer or wine

TUPS *n pl of* **TUP** male sheep

TURD *n pl* **-S** a piece of solid excrement

TURF *v* **-ED, -ING, -S** to spread a surface layer of earth containing a dense growth of grass and its matted roots; sod

TURK *n pl* **-S** an American plum weevil that is very destructive to plums, nectarines, cherries and many other stone fruits

TURM *n pl* **-S** [obs] a troop; a company

TURN *v* **-ED, -ING, -S** move to face a different direction

TURS *n pl of* **TUR** large, long-horned, wild goats native to Europe

TUSH *n pl* **-ES** an expression indicating contempt

TUSK *v* **-ED, -ING, -S** to stab something or someone

TUTU *n pl* **-S** a short ballet skirt

TUZA *n* a Mexican pocket gopher; *also* **TUCAN, TUGAN**

TWAE *n* SCOT. two; *also* **TWA**

TWEE *adj* BRIT. affectedly dainty or refined

TWEY *n* [obs] two

TWIG *v* **-GED, -GING, -S** BRIT. to observe or notice

TWIN *n pl* **-S** being one of two babies born to the same mother on the same occasion

TWIT *v* **-TED, -TING, -S** to taunt or ridicule

TYEE *n pl* **-S** a food fish, type of salmon

TYER *n* [obs] one who ties, or unites

TYIN *n* a monetary unit of Kazakhstan

TYKE *n pl* **-S** a small child, especially a boy; *also* **TIKE**

TYMP *n* a hollow water-cooled iron casting in the upper part of the archway in which the dam stands

TYND *v* [obs] to shut; to close

TYNE *v* BRIT. [obs] to lose; to perish

TYPE *v* **-D, TYPING, -S** to key words using a keyboard or typewriter

TYPO *n pl* **-S** a mistake in printed matter

TYPP *n pl* **-S** a unit of yarn size

TYPY *adj* **TYPIER, TYPIEST** characterized by strict conformance to breed or variety; *also* **TYPEY**

TYRE *n pl* **-S** BRIT. a ring or band of rubber placed over a rim of a wheel

TYRO *n pl* **-S** a beginner in a field or activity; *also* **TIRO**

TYTO *n* a barn owl

TYYN *n* a monetary unit of Uzbekistan

TZAR *n pl* **-S** a male monarch or emperor; *also* **CZAR, TSAR**

FIVE LETTERS

TABBY *n pl* **TABBIES** a domestic cat with a striped coat

TABER *v* **-ED, -ING, -S** to beat on a small drum; *also* **TABOR, TABOUR**

TABES *n* progressive emaciation, wasting of the body

TABID *adj* affected by tabes

TABIS *n pl of* **TABI** socks with a separation for the big toe; worn with thong sandals by the Japanese

TABLA *n pl* **-S** a pair of small drums used in Indian music

TABLE *v* **-D, TABLING, -S** to postpone discussion of something

TABOO *n pl* **-S** a rejection of some types of behavior or language because they are socially unacceptable; *also* **TABU**

TABOR *v* **-ED, -ING, -S** to beat on a small drum; *also* **TABER, TABOUR**

TABUN *n* a nerve gas used in chemical warfare

ABUS *n pl of* **TABU** a rejection of some types of behavior or language because they are socially unacceptable; *also* **TABOOS**

ACET *n pl* **-S** musical instruction to be silent

ACHE *n* [obs] something used for taking hold or holding; a buckle or clasp

ACHS *n pl of* **TACH** an informal term for tachometers, measuring instruments for indicating rate of rotation

ACIT *adj* understood or implied without being stated openly

ACKS *v pr t of* **TACK** attaches something with a tack, a short nail with a sharp point and a flat head

ACKY *adj* **TACKIER, TACKIEST** sticky to the touch

ACOS *n pl of* **TACO** a tortilla folded around a filling

AELS *n pl of* **TAEL** any of several small-necked freshwater ducks

AFFY *n pl* **TAFFIES** a chewy candy made of sugar or molasses

AFIA *n* a lower quality variety of rum; *also* **TAFFIA**

AHAS *n pl of* **TAHA** African weaver birds

AHRS *n pl of* **TAHR** animals resembling a goat; *also* **THARS**

AIGA *n* a subarctic, evergreen coniferous forest

AILS *n pl of* **TAIL** the back, last, lower or inferior parts of anything

AINS *n pl of* **TAIN** thin tin plates

AINT *v* **-ED, -ING, -S** to spoil or pollute something

AIRA *n* a South American carnivorous mammal; *also* **TAYRA**

AIRN *n pl* **-S** a steep-banked mountain lake or pool; *also* **TARN**

TAKAS *n pl of* **TAKA** monetary units of Bangladesh

TAKEN *v p part of* **TAKE** to have gotten into one's possession

TAKER *n pl* **-S** one who gets or receives

TAKES *v pr t of* **TAKE** gets into one's possession

TAKIN *n pl* **-S** a large heavily built animal related to the goats and the musk ox

TALAR *n pl* **-S** an ankle-length robe

TALAS *n pl of* **TALA** the basic units of money in Western Samoa

TALED *n pl* **-S** a kind of quadrangular piece of cloth put on by the Jews when repeating prayers in the synagogues

TALER *n pl* **-S** a formerly used German coin; *also* BRIT. a ring or band of rubber placed over a rim of a wheel

TALES *n pl of* **TALE** reports, accounts or stories

TALKS *v pr t of* **TALK** to utter words

TALKY *adj* **TALKIER, TALKIEST** containing too much dialogue

TALLY *v* **TALLIED, -ING, TALLIES** to reckon or count

TALON *n pl* **-S** the claw of a bird of prey

TALUK *n pl* **-A** a large estate in India

TALUS *n pl* **TALI** a bone in the ankle

TAMAL *n pl* **-ES** a Mexican dish

TAMED *v p t of* **TAME** to have made docile, or domestic

TAMER *adj* more docile, or domestic

TAMES *v pr t of* **TAME** makes docile, or domestic

TAMIS *n pl* **-ES** a sieve, or strainer, made of a kind of woolen cloth

TAMMY *n pl* **TAMMIES** a woolen cap of Scottish origin

TAMPS *v pr t of* **TAMP** firmly packs something down by tapping it

TANAS *n pl of* **TANA** a tree shrew

TANGA *n* a former monetary unit of Tajikistan

TANGO *v* **-ED, -ING, -S** to perform a Latin American ballroom dance

TANGS *n pl of* **TANG** a coarse blackish seaweed

TANGY *adj* **TANGIER, TANGIEST** having or suggestive of a tang

TANKA *n pl* **-S** a Japanese verse form in five lines

TANKS *n pl of* **TANK** a large basin or cistern; a receptacle for liquids

TANSY *n pl* **TANSIES** a strong aromatic perennial plant

TANTO *n pl* **-S** a Japanese short sword or dagger

TANTS *n pl of* **TANT,** a small scarlet spider

TAPAS *n/pl* a small Spanish snack often served at a bar

TAPED *v p t of* **TAPE** to have fastened or attached with tape, a strip of sticky material

TAPER *v* **-ED, -ING, -S** to become gradually narrower

TAPES *v pr t of* **TAPE** fastens or attaches with tape, a strip of sticky material

TAPIR *n* a nocturnal, herbivorous mammal having short legs, heavy body and flexible upper lip

TAPIS *n* [obs] tapestry or comparable material used for draperies, carpeting and furniture covering

TARDO *adj* slow, used as a direction in music

TARDY *adj* **TARDIER, TARDIEST** after the expected or usual time; delayed

TARED *v p t of* **TARE** to have weighed as to determine the tare, the weight of the packing material or container

TARES *v pr t of* **TARE** weighs as to determine the tare, the weight of the packing material or container

TARGE *n pl* **-S** [obs] a small, round shield or target

TARIN *n* any of small yellow singing bird; *also* **TERIN**

TARNS *n pl of* **TARN** a steep-banked mountain lake or pool; *also* **TAIRNS**

TAROC *n pl* **-S** a game of cards with allegorical images; *also* **TAROK**

TAROK *n pl* **-S** a game of cards with allegorical images; *also* **TAROC**

TAROS *n pl of* **TARO** tropical starchy tuberous roots

TAROT *n pl* **-S** a set of 78 playing cards including pictorial cards used for fortune-telling

TARPS *n pl of* **TARP** waterproofed canvases

TARRE *v* [obs] to set on, as a dog, to incite

TARRY *v* **TARRIED, -ING, TARRIES** to delay

TARSE *n* a male falcon

TARSI *n pl of* **TARSUS** a group of small bones forming the ankle

TARTS *n pl of* **TART** small open pies with a fruit filling

TARTY *adj* **TARTIER, TARTIEST** tart; somewhat sour

TASCO *n* a kind of clay for making melting pots

TASKS *v pr t of* **TASK** assigns a piece of work to somebody

TASSE *n* one of a series of armor used to protect the lower trunk and thighs; *also* **TACE, TASSET**

TASTE *v* **-D, TASTING, -S** to try food with the mouth

TASTO *n* a key or thing touched to produce a tone

TASTY *adj* **TASTIER, TASTIEST** having a good taste

TATAR *n pl* **-S** a ferocious person

TATCH *n* a spot or stain; a trick

TATER *n pl* **-S** a potato

TATOU *n* about three feet long exclusive of tail; *also* **TATU**

TATTY *adj* **TATTIER, TATTIEST** somewhat worn, shabby, or dilapidated

TAUNT *v* -ED, -ING, -S to reproach with severe or insulting words

TAUON *n pl* -S a very large subatomic particle of the lepton family

TAUPE *n* a brownish gray color

TAWED *v p t of* TAW converted skins into white leather

TAWER *n pl* -S one who taws; a dresser of white leather

TAWIE *adj* SCOT. docile

TAWNY *adj* TAWNIER, TAWNIEST of a dull yellowish brown color

TAWSE *n pl* -S a leather strap having one end cut into thongs

TAXED *v p t of* TAX to place a charge on something like property, income or goods

TAXER *n pl* -S a bureaucrat who levies taxes; *also* TAXOR

TAXES *v pr t of* TAX to place a charge on something like property, income or goods

TAXIS *v pr t of* TAXI moves slowly on the ground before takeoff or after landing an airplane

TAXOL *n* a substance obtained from a small yew tree

TAXON *n pl* TAXA a taxonomic category or unit, as a species or family

TAXOR *n pl* -S a bureaucrat who levies taxes; *also* TAXER

TAXUS *n/pl* yews, evergreen trees or shrubs

TAYRA *n pl* -S a South American carnivorous mammal; *also* TAIRA

TAZZA *n pl* -S or TAZZE a shallow cup or vase on a pedestal

TAZZE *n pl of* TAZZA shallow cups or vases on a pedestal

TEACH *v* TAUGHT, -ING, -ES to impart the knowledge of or skill

TEADE *n* a torch

TEAKS *n pl of* TEAK tall trees of E. Indies, with hard timber

TEALS *n pl of* TEAL small short-necked dabbling river ducks

TEAMS *n pl of* TEAM more than one group of people associated together in any work

TEARS *v pr t of* TEAR pulls apart or into pieces by force

TEARY *adj* TEARIER, TEARIEST wet with tears

TEASE *v* -D, TEASING, -S to mock or make fun of playfully; to annoy

TEATS *n pl of* TEAT small projections of a mammary gland

TECHY *adj* TECHIER, TECHIEST peevish; irritable

TECTA *n pl of* TECTUM a bodily structure resembling or serving as a roof especially the dorsal part of the brain

TECUM *n* a fine, strong fiber used for cordage from a Brazilian palm; *also* TUCUM

TEDDY *n pl* TEDDIES a stuffed toy bear

TEEMS *v pr t of* TEEM to be full of things, to abound

TEEND *v* [obs] to kindle; *also* TIND

TEENS *n pl of* TEEN teenagers

TEENY *adj* TEENIER, TEENIEST informal for tiny

TEETH *n pl of* TOOTH hard bonelike structures found in a mouth used for biting and chewing

TEGUA *n pl* -S an ankle-high moccasin worn in parts of Mexico and the Southwest

TEIID *n pl* -S a tropical American lizard

TEKKI *n pl* -ES an informal term for a technician who is highly proficient and enthusiastic about some technical field; *also* TECHIE

TEIND *v* -ED, -ING, -S to tithe income or produce

TELAE *n pl of* TELA a delicate tissue or web like structure

TELCO *n pl* -S a public utility that provides telephone service

TELES *n pl of* TELE BRIT. television sets; *also* TELLIES

TELEX	v **-ED, -ING, -ES** to send a message through a telegraphic communications system
TELIA	n pl of **TELIUM** a sorus on the host plant of a rust fungus
TELIC	adj directed or tending toward a goal
TELLS	v pr t of **TELL** utters or recites in detail; narrates
TELLY	n pl **TELLIES** BRIT. a television set; also **TELE**
TELOI	n pl of **TELOS** an end or goal; ultimate purpose
TELOS	n pl **TELOI** an end or goal; ultimate purpose
TEMPI	n pl of **TEMPO** the speed at which music is or ought to be played
TEMPO	n pl **-S** or **TEMPI** the speed at which music is or ought to be played
TEMPS	v pr t of **TEMP** works as a temporary employee
TEMPT	v **-ED, -ING, -S** to try to get someone to do wrong
TENCH	n pl **-ES** freshwater fish of the carp family
TENDS	v pr t of **TEND** to be attentive to; to be disposed, inclined
TENDU	n pl **-S** an Asian ebony tree
TENET	n pl **-S** an opinion, doctrine or principle held as being true
TENGE	n **-S** a basic monetary unit of Kazakhstan
TENIA	n pl **-S** or **-E** a tapeworm; also **TAENIA**
TENON	v **-ED, -ING, -S** to make a projection on the end of a piece of wood shaped for insertion into a mortise to make a joint
TENOR	n pl **-S** the highest natural adult male singing voice
TENSE	adj **-R, -ST** taut or rigid; stretched tight
TENTH	n pl **-S** a tenth part
TENTS	n pl of **TENT** portable shelters
TENTY	adj **TENTIER, TENTIEST** watchful; also **TENTIE**
TEPAL	n pl **-S** a division of a perianth of a flower
TEPAS	n pl of **TEPA** crystalline chemical compounds
TEPEE	n pl **-S** a Native American tent; usually of conical shape; also **TIPI**
TEPID	adj moderately warm; lukewarm
TEPOR	n gentle heat; moderate warmth; tepidness
TEPOY	n pl **-S** a small, three-legged stand; also **TEAPOY**
TERAI	n pl **-S** a subtropical sunhat with a wide brim
TERCE	n the third of the canonical hours; also **TIERCE**
TERES	n either of two muscles in the shoulder
TERET	adj cylindrical but usually slightly tapering at both ends, circular in cross section and smooth-surfaced; also **TERETE**
TERGA	n pl of **TERGUM** the dorsal surface of a body segment of an arthropod
TERIN	n any of small yellow singing bird; also **TARIN**
TERMA	n the terminal lamina of the brain
TERMS	n pl of **TERM** periods of time that something lasts
TERNE	n an alloy of lead and tin
TERNS	n pl of **TERN** a long-winged aquatic bird
TERRA	n pl **-E** highland areas son the surface of the moon or a planet
TERRY	n pl **TERRIES** a pile fabric with uncut loops on both sides like for bath towels
TERSE	adj **-R, -ST** abrupt, short, brief
TESLA	n pl **-S** the basic unit of magnetic flux density
TESTA	n pl **-E** the hard outer coat of the seed
TESTS	v pr t of **TEST** examines or tries
TESTY	adj **TESTIER, TESTIEST** irritated; exasperated

TETEL *n pl* **-S** a large African antelope

TETHS *n pl of* **TETH** more than one of the ninth letter of the Hebrew alphabet; *also* **TETS**

TETRA *n pl* **-S** a small colorful tropical freshwater fish

TETRI *n* a monetary unit of the Republic of Georgia

TETTY *adj* [obs] testy; irritable

TEUCH *adj* SCOT. tough; *also* **TEUGH**

TEUGH *adj* SCOT. tough; *also* **TEUCH**

TEWED *v p t of* **TEW** to prepare by beating or pounding

TEXAS *n* a structure on a river steamboat containing the pilothouse and the officers' quarters

TEXTS *n pl of* **TEXT** words written or printed

TEYNE *n pl* **-S** [obs] a thin plate of metal

THACK *n* SCOT. [obs] dialectical form of thatch, the weatherproof outer layer of a roof

THANE *n pl* **-S** SCOT. a person of rank holding land from the king; *also* **THEGN**

THANK *v* **-ED, -ING, -S** to express gratitude to

THARM *n pl* **-S** [obs] intestines in the belly

THARS *n pl of* **THAR** animals resembling a goat; *also* **TAHRS**

THAVE *n pl* **-S** a ewe lamb of the first year; *also* **THEAVE**

THAWS *v pr t of* **THAW** melts or defrosts

THAWY *adj* liquefying by heat after having been frozen

THEBE *n* a monetary unit of Botswana

THECA *n pl* **-E** a protective case or sheath especially a pollen sac or moss capsule

THEFT *n pl* **-S** the act or crime of stealing

THEGN *n pl* **-S** SCOT. a person of rank holding land from the king; *also* **THANE**

THEIN *n* caffeine; *also* **THEINE, THEINA**

THEIR *adj* belonging to them

THEME *v* **-ED, -ING, -S** to give something a certain character

THERE *adv* at or in that place

THERF *adj* [obs] not fermented; unleavened

THERM *n pl* **-S** BRIT. a unit of heat

THESE *pron pl of* **THIS** the people or things just mentioned

THETA *n pl* **-S** the eighth letter of the Greek alphabet

THEWS *n pl of* **THEW** muscle or muscular strength

THEWY *adj* having well developed muscles

THICK *adj* **-ER, -EST** heavy and compact in form or stature

THIEF *n pl* **THIEVES** one who steals

THIGH *n pl* **-S** the part of the leg between the hip and the knee

THILL *n pl* **-S** either or two long shafts of a horse cart or carriage between which the animal is fastened

THINE *pron* used to indicate the one or ones belonging to thee

THING *n pl* **-S** an inanimate object

THINK *v* **THOUGHT, -ING, -S** to use the mind to consider ideas

THINS *v pr t of* **THIN** makes or becomes thinner, smaller from one side to the other side

THIOL *n pl* **-S** a sulfur compound

THIRD *n pl* **-S** one of three equal parts

THIRL *v* **-ED, -ING, -S** to cause sharply exhilarating excitement in; *also* **THRILL**

THOLE *v* **-D, THOLING** SCOT. [obs] to endure or tolerate

THONG *n pl* **-S** a narrow strip of leather, used for binding or lashing

THORN *n pl* **-S** a modified branch in the form of a sharp, woody spine

THORP *n pl* **-S** a small village; hamlet; *also* **THORPE**

THOSE *pron pl of* **THAT** used to refer to or indicate something

THOWL *n pl* **-S** a wooden or metal pin

THRAW *v* SCOT. to twist; distort

THREE *n pl* **-S** a number; one more than two

THREW *v p t of* **THROW** propelled through the air with a motion of the hand

THRIP *n pl* **-S** a minute black insect which sucks plant sap

THROB *v* **-BED, -BING, -S** to pulsate or pound with abnormal force

THROE *n pl* **-S** a pang or spasm of pain

THROW *v* **THREW, -N, -ING, -S** to propel through the air with a motion of the hand

THRUM *v* **-MED, -MING, -S** to monotonously play a stringed instrument

THUDS *v pr t of* **THUD** to make a heavy, dull sound

THUGS *n pl of* **THUG** people who act violently, especially to commit a crime

THUMB *n pl* **-S** the short, thick first digit of the human hand

THUMP *v* **-ED, -ING, -S** to strike or beat with something thick or heavy

THUNK *v* **-ED, -ING, -S** to make an abrupt, muffled sound

THURL *n* the hip joint in cattle

THUYA *n pl* **-S** another spelling of a genus Thuja, cone-bearing evergreen tree

THYME *n* an aromatic herb for seasoning

THYMI *n pl of* **THYMUS** a glandular structure in the body

THYMY *adj* **THYMIER, THYMIEST** abounding in or fragrant with thyme

TIARA *n pl* **-S** an ornamental often jeweled headdress

TIBIA *n pl* **-S** or **-E** the inner and thicker of the two bones of the lower human leg

TICAL *n pl* **-S** a monetary unit of Siam

TICKS *v pr t of* **TICK** emits recurring clicking sounds

TIDAL *adj* relating to or affected by tides

TIDED *adj* affected by the tide

TIDES *n pl of* **TIDE** rise and fall of the oceans water

TIERS *n pl of* **TIER** to arrange things in rows rising one above another

TIFFS *n pl of* **TIFF** petty quarrels

TIGER *n pl* **-S** a large carnivorous feline mammal

TIGHT *adj* **-ER, -EST** firmly held together; compact; not loose or open

TIGON *n pl* **-S** a tiglon; the hybrid of a male tiger and a female lion

TIKES *n pl of* **TIKE** small children, especially boys; *also* **TYKES**

TIKIS *n pl of* **TIKI** a wooden or stone image of a Polynesian god

TIKKA *adj* an Indian dish of marinated meat cooked on a skewer

TIKUS *n* a bulau; an insectivorous mammal

TILAK *n pl* **-S** a distinctive spot worn on the forehead by Hindus

TILDE *n pl* **-S** the accentual mark placed over a letter to indicate its pronunciation

TILED *v p t of* **TILE** covered with tiles, plates, or thin pieces of baked clay

TILER *n pl* **-S** a worker who lays tiles

TILES *v pr t of* **TILE** covers with tile, plates or thin pieces, of baked clay

TILLS *v pr t of* **TILL** to plow and prepare land for the raising of crops

TILTH *n* **-S** cultivation of land; tillage

TILTS *v pr t of* **TILT** to cause to slope, as by raising one end

TIMAL *n* the blue titmouse, a small singing bird

TIMED *v p t of* **TIME** measures how long something takes

TIMER *n pl* **-S** a timekeeper

TIMES	*v pr t of* **TIME** measures how long something takes
TIMID	*adj* **-ER, -EST** showing fear and lack of confidence
TINCT	*v* **-ED, -ING, -S** to tinge; to color
TINEA	*n pl* **-S** a fungous infection of the skin or nails
TINED	*adj* to furnish with tines
TINES	*n pl of* **TINE** slender pointed projecting parts
TINGE	*v* **-D, -ING** or **TINGING, -S** to dye with a color
TINGS	*v pr t of* **TING** gives forth a light ringing sound
TINNY	*adj* **TINNIER, TINNIEST** of, containing, or pertaining to tin
TINTO	*n* a red Madeira wine
TINTS	*v pr t of* **TINT** to give a slight color
TIPIS	*n pl of* **TIPI** Native American tents; usually of conical shape; *also* **TEPEES**
TIPPY	*adj* **TIPPIER, TIPPIEST** likely to tip or tilt
TIPSY	*adj* **TIPSIER, TIPSIEST** fuddled or foolish from the effects of liquor
TIRED	*v p t of* **TIRE** to have grown weary
TIRES	*v pr t of* **TIRE** grows weary
TIRLS	*v pr t of* **TIRL** SCOT. makes a rattling noise
TIRMA	*n* the oyster catcher
TIROS	*n pl of* **TIRO** beginners in a field or activity; *also* **TYROS**
TISAR	*n* the fireplace at the side of an annealing oven
TITAN	*n pl* **-S** a person of exceptional importance and reputation
TITER	*n pl* **-S** the strength of a solution or the concentration of a substance; *also* **TITRE**
TITHE	*v* **-D, TITHING, -S** to pay a tenth of one's income, especially to a church; *also* **TYTHE**
TITIS	*n pl of* **TITI** New World shrubs or small trees

TITLE	*v* **-D, TITLING, -S** to furnish with an identifying name
TITRE	*n pl* **-S** the strength of a solution or the concentration of a substance; *also* **TITER**
TIVER	*n* a kind of ocher which is used in marking sheep in some parts of England
TIZZY	*n pl* **TIZZIES** a state of frenzied excitement
TOADS	*n pl of* **TOAD** tailless stout-bodied leaping amphibians
TOADY	*v* **TOADIED, -ING, TOADIES** to engage in excessive deference and attention to others for self-serving reasons
TOAST	*v* **-ED, -ING, -S** to dry and brown by the heat of a fire
TODAY	*n* the present day
TODDY	*n pl* **TODDIES** the sweet sap of several Asian palm trees, used as a beverage
TOEAS	*n pl of* **TOEA** monetary units of Papua New Guinea
TOFFS	*n pl of* **TOFF** BRIT. informal term for upper-class or wealthy people
TOFFY	*n pl* **TOFFIES** candy of brittle but tender texture made by boiling sugar and butter together; *also* **TOFFEE**
TOFTS	*n pl of* **TOFT** BRIT. a homestead
TOGAE	*n pl of* **TOGA** one-piece cloaks worn by men in ancient Rome
TOGAS	*n pl of* **TOGA** one-piece cloaks worn by men in ancient Rome
TOGUE	*n pl* **-S** lake trout
TOILE	*n pl* **-S** a sheer linen fabric
TOILS	*v pr t of* **TOIL** works long and hard
TOISE	*n pl* **-S** an old French unit of length
TOKAY	*n pl* **-S** a small Asian lizard, a gecko
TOKED	*v p t of* **TOKE** to take a puff on a cigarette or pipe
TOKEN	*n pl* **-S** something of sentimental value
TOKER	*n pl* **-S** one that tokes

331

TOKES *v pr t of* **TOKE** to take a puff on a cigarette or pipe

TOLAN *n pl* -S a chemical compound

TOLAR *n pl* -S or -JEV a monetary unit of Slovenia

TOLAS *n pl of* **TOLA** S. Asian units of weight

TOLED *v p t of* **TOLE** to have drawn, or caused to follow; allured by some bait

TOLES *v pr t of* **TOLE** draws, or causes to follow; allures by some bait

TOLLS *v pr t* **TOLL** takes away, as in a fee

TOLYL *n pl* -S a univalent chemical radical

TOMAN *n pl* -S a coin of Iran

TOMBS *n pl of* **TOMB** pits in which the dead body of a human being is deposited; graves

TOMES *n pl of* **TOME** especially large heavy books

TOMIA *n pl of* **TOMIUM** the cutting edge of the bill of a bird

TOMMY *n pl* **TOMMIES** a British soldier

TONAL *adj* pertaining to tone

TONDI *n pl of* **TONDO** a circular painting

TONDO *n pl* **TONDI, -S** a circular painting

TONED *v p t of* **TONE** to have given a particular intonation or inflection to

TONER *n pl* -S a light astringent for the face

TONES *v pr t of* **TONE** gives a particular intonation or inflection to

TONEY *adj* **TONIER, TONIEST** marked by an elegant or exclusive manner or style; *also* **TONY**

TONGA *n pl* -S a two-wheeled carriage of India

TONGS *v pr t of* **TONG** seizes, holds or manipulates with tongs, a grasping device

TONIC *n pl* -S a liquid that increases strength and restores healthy functions

TONNE *n pl* -S a unit of weight

TONUS *n pl* -ES body or muscular tone; tonicity

TOOLS *v pr t of* **TOOL** to work something using a handheld device that aids in accomplishing a task

TOONS *n pl of* **TOON** reddish brown aromatic woods

TOOTH *n pl* **TEETH** a hard bonelike structure found in the mouth, used for biting and chewing

TOOTS *v pr t of* **TOOT** blows or sounds a horn

TOPAZ *n pl* -ES a colorless, blue, yellow, brown or pink mineral

TOPED *v p t of* **TOPE** drank liquor to excess

TOPEE *n pl* -S a pith helmet worn for protection against sun and heat; *also* **TOPI**

TOPER *n pl* -S one who drinks frequently or to excess

TOPES *v pr t of* **TOPE** drinks liquor to excess

TOPHE *n pl* -S a soft or porous stone formed by depositions from ground water; *also* **TUFA**

TOPHI *n pl of* **TOPHUS** a deposit of urates in the skin

TOPHS *n pl of* **TOPH** a kind of sandstone

TOPIC *n pl* -S the main subject of a discussion

TOPIS *n pl of* **TOPI** pith helmets worn for protection against sun and heat; *also* **TOPEES**

TOPOI *n pl of* **TOPOS** a traditional or conventional literary or rhetorical theme or topic

TOPOS *n pl* **TOPOI** a traditional or conventional literary or rhetorical theme or topic

TOQUE *n pl* -S a woman's small hat without a brim

TORAH *n* the body of wisdom and law contained in Jewish Scripture; *also* **TORA**

TORCH v **-ED**, **-ING**, **-ES** to set something on fire

TORCS n pl of **TORC** collars, necklaces usually twisted and made of precious metal; also **TORQUES**

TORES n pl of **TORE** a torus; a ring-shaped molding at the base of a column; also **TORI**

TORET n a ring for fastening a hawk's leash to the jesses

TORIC adj relating to or shaped like a torus

TORII n a gateway to a Japanese Shinto temple

TOROS n pl of **TORO** bulls

TORSE n pl **-S** a wreath of twisted silk

TORSI n pl of **TORSO** the trunk of the human body

TORSK n pl **-S** a large edible marine fish

TORSO n pl **TORSI**, **-S** the trunk of the human body

TORTA n pl **-S** a delicious tart

TORTE n pl **-S** or **-N** a very rich cake

TORTS n pl of **TORT** a wrongful act that injures another for which damages can be sought by the injured party

TORUS n pl **TORI** a ring-shaped molding at the base of a column

TOSED v p t of **TOSE** [obs] to tease, or comb, as wool

TOSES v pr t of **TOSE** [obs] to tease, or comb, as wool

TOSSY adj tossing the head, as in scorn or pride

TOSTO adj a musical term meaning quick, rapid

TOTAL v **-ED**, **-ING**, **-S** to add things together

TOTED v p t of **TOTE** hauled; lugged

TOTEM n pl **-S** an object serving as the emblem of a family or clan used as a reminder of its ancestry

TOTER n pl **-S** one that carries something

TOTES v pr t of **TOTE** hauls; lugs

TOTTY adj SCOT. [obs] unsteady; dizzy; tottery

TOUCH v **-ED**, **-ING**, **-ES** to come in contact with

TOUGH adj **-ER**, **-EST** stiff, rigid, not flexible

TOURN n a spinning wheel

TOURS v pr t of **TOUR** to travel from place to place

TOUSE v **-ED**, **-ING** to pull to pieces or handle roughly

TOUTS v pr t of **TOUT** solicits customers

TOUZE n a touse, a pulling; a disturbance

TOWED v p t of **TOW** drawn or pulled behind by a chain or rope

TOWEL v **-ED** or **-LED**, **-ING** or **-LING**, **-S** to wipe dry with an absorbent cloth

TOWER v **-ED**, **-ING**, **-S** to rise and overtop other objects

TOWIE n pl **-S** a form of contract bridge for three players in a game

TOWNS n pl of **TOWN** population centers that are larger than villages and smaller than cities

TOWNY n pl **TOWNIES** resident of a college town not affiliated with the college; also **TOWNIE**

TOXIC adj of or relating to a toxin or poison

TOXIN n pl **-S** a poisonous substance

TOYED v p t of **TOY** to have amused oneself idly

TOYER n pl **-S** one that amuses oneself

TOYON n pl **-S** a chiefly Californian ornamental evergreen shrub

TRABU n an edible herring from East India; also **TRUBU**

TRACE n pl **-S** a mark left by anything passing; also **TRACK**

TRACK n pl **-S** a mark left by anything passing; also **TRACE**

TRACT n pl **-S** a region or quantity of land or water

TRADE *v* **-D, TRADING, -S** to be engaged in the exchange, purchase or sale of goods

TRAGI *n pl of* **TRAGUS** the piece of skin-covered cartilage in front of the opening of the external ear

TRAIK *v* **-ED, -ING, -S** to become ill

TRAIL *v* **-ED, -ING, -S** to drag or stream behind, as along the ground

TRAIN *v* **-ED, -ING, -S** to teach and form by practice

TRAIT *n pl* **-S** a distinguishing feature of your personal nature

TRAMP *v* **-ED, -ING, -S** to walk heavily and firmly; *also* **TROMP**

TRAMS *n pl of* **TRAM** BRIT. a streetcar

TRANK *n pl* **-S** the piece of leather from which one glove is cut

TRANS *adj* in organic chemistry, having certain atoms or radicals on opposite sides of a non-rotatable parent structure

TRANT *v* [obs] to traffic in an itinerary manner; to peddle

TRAPE *v* **-D, TRAPING, -S** to walk about in a slatternly manner

TRAPS *v pr t of* **TRAP** catches or holds in a cage

TRAPT *v p t of* **TRAP** [obs] caught or held in a cage

TRASH *v* **-ED, -ING, -ES** to throw away or destroy

TRASS *n pl* **-ES** a white to gray volcanic rock

TRAVE *n pl* **-S** an architectural term for a crossbeam

TRAWL *v* **-ED, -ING, -S** to fish using a net that drags along the sea bottom

TRAYS *n pl of* **TRAY** flat broad low rimmed objects on which dishes, glasses, etc., are carried

TREAD *v* **TROD, or -ED, TRODDEN, -ING, -S** to step or walk on or over

TREAT *v* **-ED, -ING, -S** to regard or behave towards someone in a particular way

TREED *v p t of* **TREE** forced somebody up a tree, any perennial woody plant of considerable size

TREEN *adj* utensils made of wood

TREES *v pr t of* **TREE** forces somebody up a tree, any perennial woody plant of considerable size

TREKS *v pr t of* **TREK** makes a slow or arduous journey

TREND *v* **-ED, -ING, -S** to veer or lean in a particular direction

TRESS *n pl* **-ES** a long lock or ringlet of hair

TRETS *n pl of* **TRET** allowances to purchasers, for waste or refuse matter

TREWS *n/pl* tight-fitting plaid pants

TREYS *n pl of* **TREY** a cards, dice or domino with three pips

TRIAC *n pl* **-S** a type of device that functions as an electrically controlled switch for alternating current

TRIAD *n pl* **-S** a group or union of three

TRIAL *n pl* **-S** a judicial examination of evidence and laws by a competent tribunal

TRIBE *n pl* **-S** a group of people often of related families, who live and share the same language, culture and history

TRICA *n pl* **TRICAE** an apothecium in certain lichens

TRICE *v* **-D, TRICING, -S** to haul and tie up a sail by means of a rope

TRICK *v* **-ED, -ING, -S** to deceive

TRIDE *adj* short and ready

TRIED *v p t of* **TRY** to have attempted

TRIER *n pl* **-S** one who experiments or tests; *also* **TRIOR**

TRIES *v pr t of* **TRY** attempts

TRIGO *n pl* **-S** wheat; field of wheat

TRIGS *v pr t of* **TRIG** BRIT. makes clean or neat

TRIKE *n pl* **-S** informal for a tricycle

TRILL *v* **-ED, -ING, -S** to sing or play with quickly repeated high notes

TRIMS *v pr t of* **TRIM** to make neat or tidy by clipping or pruning

TRINE *adj* threefold; triple

TRIOL *n pl* **-S** a chemical compound containing three hydroxyl groups

TRIOR *n pl* **-S** one who experiments or tests; *also* **TRIER**

TRIOS *n pl of* **TRIO** compositions for three parts or three instruments

TRIPE *n pl* **-S** the large stomach of ruminating animals used for food

TRIPS *n pl of* **TRIP** brief journeys or pleasure excursions

TRIST *v* [obs] to trust

TRITE *adj* **-R, -ST** over familiar through overuse

TROAT *v* **-ED, -ING, -S** to cry, as a buck in rutting time

TROCK *v* **-ED, -ING** SCOT. to truck; *also* **TROKE**

TROCO *n* an old English lawn game also called lawn billiards

TRODE *n* [obs] tread; footing

TROIC *adj* pertaining to Troy

TROIS *n/pl* a commonly used French word meaning the three

TROKE *v* **-ED, -ING** SCOT. to truck; *also* **TROCK**

TROLL *v* **-ED, -ING, -S** to fish with a rod whose line runs behind a slow moving boat; *also* **TROUL**

TROMP *v* **-ED, -ING, -S** to walk heavily and firmly; *also* **TRAMP**

TRONA *n* a grayish or yellowish monoclinic mineral

TRONE *n pl* **-S** SCOT. a weighing device; a spring balance

TROOP *v* **-ED, -ING, -S** to come or gather in crowds or large orderly group

TROPE *n pl* **-S** a figure of speech

TROTH *n pl* **-S** loyal or pledged faithfulness

TROTS *v pr t of* **TROT** runs; jogs; hurries

TROUL *v* **-ED, -ING, -S** to fish with a rod whose line runs behind a slow moving boat; *also* **TROLL**

TROUT *n pl* **-S** a food fish of cool fresh waters

TROVE *n pl* **-S** a valuable discovery

TROWS *v pr t of* **TROW** [obs] believes

TRUBU *n* an edible herring from East India; *also* **TRABU**

TRUCE *n pl* **-S** a state of peace agreed to between opponents for a period of time

TRUCK *n pl* **-S** any of various forms of a vehicle used for carrying goods

TRUED *v p t of* **TRUE** positioned something to make it balanced

TRUER *adj* more real or correct

TRUES *v pr t of* **TRUE** positions something to make it balanced

TRUGS *n pl of* **TRUG** BRIT. shallow gardening baskets

TRULY *adv* sincerely

TRUMP *v* **-ED, -ING, -S** to surpass; to outdo

TRUNK *n pl* **-S** the main stem of a tree

TRUSS *v* **-ED, -ING, -ES** to seize and hold firmly

TRUST *v* **-ED, -ING, -S** to place confidence in; to rely on,

TRUTH *n pl* **-S** factual, reality

TRYMA *n pl* **-TA** a type of nut having a tough outer shell

TRYST *v* **-ED, -ING, -S** to mutually agree to meet at a certain place

TSADE *n pl* **-S** the 18th letter in the Hebrew alphabet; *also* **SADHE, TSADI, SADE, SADI**

TSADI *n pl* **-S** the 18th letter in the Hebrew alphabet; *also* **SADHE, TSADE, SADE, SADI**

TSARS *n pl of* **TSAR** male monarchs or emperors; *also* **CZARS, TZARS**

TSEBE *n pl* **-S** a springbok, a South African gazelle

TSINE *n* a wild ox

TSKED *v p t of* **TSK** a sucking noise used to express disappointment

TSUBA *n* the guard on the end of a Japanese sword

TUBAE *n pl of* **TUBA** trumpets; the lowest range brass wind instruments; *also* **TUBAS**

TUBAL *adj* pertaining to a tube

TUBAS *n pl of* **TUBA** trumpets; the lowest range brass wind instruments; *also* **TUBAE**

TUBBY *adj* **TUBBIER, TUBBIEST** short and fat

TUBED *adj* of a tire, having an inner tube

TUBER *n pl* **-S** a fleshy underground stem or root of a plant

TUBES *n pl of* **TUBE** hollow cylinders, of any material

TUCAN *n* a Mexican pocket gopher; *also* **TUGAN, TUZA**

TUCKS *v pr t of* **TUCK** makes one or more folds in

TUCUM *n* a fine, strong fiber used for cordage from a Brazilian palm; *also* **TECUM**

TUDOR *adj* of or relating to a style of English architecture

TUFAS *n pl of* **TUFA** soft or porous stones formed by depositions from ground water; *also* **TOPHES**

TUFFS *n pl of* **TUFF** a hard volcanic rock composed of compacted volcanic ash

TUFTS *n pl of* **TUFT** clusters of elongated strands attached at a base

TUFTY *adj* **TUFTIER, TUFTIEST** abounding with tufts

TUGAN *n* a Mexican pocket gopher; *also* **TUCAN, TUZA**

TULES *n pl of* **TULE** large bulrushs growing abundantly

TULIP *n pl* **-S** a beautiful single showy flower

TULLE *n pl* **-S** a kind of silk lace or light netting

TUMID *adj* swollen; distended

TUMMY *n pl* **TUMMIES** the stomach

TUMOR *n pl* **-S** a swelling, prominence or growth

TUMPS *n pl of* **TUMP** overturns mainly used in the Southern United States

TUNAS *n pl of* **TUNA** game fish of the family Scombridae, warm-water fish; *also* **TUNNY**

TUNED *v p t of* **TUNE** adjusted to the proper pitch

TUNER *n pl* **-S** one who tunes musical instruments

TUNES *v pr t of* **TUNE** adjusts to the proper pitch

TUNIC *n pl* **-S** a loose-fitting garment

TUNNY *n pl* **TUNNIES** a game fish of the family Scombridae, warm-water fish; *also* **TUNA**

TUPEK *n pl* **-S** a tent that is an Eskimo summer dwelling; *also* **TUPIK**

TUPIK *n pl* **-S** a tent that is an Eskimo summer dwelling; *also* **TUPEK**

TUQUE *n pl* **-S** a knitted woolen cap

TURBO *n pl* **-S** a commonly used abbreviation for turbocharger in automobiles

TURDS *n pl of* **TURD** pieces of solid excrement

TURFS *v pr t of* **TURF** spreads a surface layer of earth containing a dense growth of grass and its matted roots; sod

TURFY *adj* **TURFIER, TURFIEST** covered with, consisting of, resembling turf

TURIO *n pl* **-NES** a shoot or sprout from the ground

TURKS *n pl of* **TURK** American plum weevils that are very destructive to plums, nectarines, cherries and many other stone fruits

TURMS *n pl of* **TURM** [obs] troops; companies

TURNS *v pr t of* **TURN** moves to face a different direction

TUSHY *n pl* **TUSHIES** the buttocks; *also* **TUSHIE**

TUSKS *v pr t of* **TUSK** stabs something or someone

TUSKY *adj* having tusks

TUTEE *n pl* **-S** one who is being tutored

TUTOR *n pl* **-S** a private instructor

TUTTI *n pl* **-S** an ensemble of musicians in a concerto

TUTTY *n pl* **TUTTIES** an impure oxide of zinc

TUTUS *n pl of* **TUTU** short ballet skirts

TUXES *n pl of* **TUX** an informal term for tuxedos

TUYER *n pl* **-S** a fixture through which air is forced to the interior of a blast furnace; *also* **TUYERE, TWYER**

TWAIN *n/pl* archaic or literary for two

TWANG *v* **-ED, -ING, -S** to strum something carelessly

TWANK *v* **-ED, -ING, -S** to twang

TWEAG *v* [obs] to tweak

TWEAK *v* **-ED, -ING, -S** to pinch and pull with a sudden jerk and twist

TWEED *n pl* **-S** a rough woolen fabric

TWEEN *n pl* **-S** a child between middle childhood and adolescence, usually between 8 and 12 years old

TWEET *v* **-ED, -ING, -S** to utter a chirping sound, as of a young bird

TWERP *n pl* **-S** an informal term for a silly, insignificant or contemptible person; *also* **TWIRP**

TWICE *adv* in two cases or on two occasions; two times

TWIGS *v pr t of* **TWIG** BRIT. observes or notices

TWILL *v* **-ED, -ING, -S** to weave diagonal lines into textiles

TWILT *n pl* **-S** SCOT. a quilt

TWINE *v* **-D, TWINING, -S** to twist together or around something

TWINS *n pl of* **TWIN** two babies born to the same mother on the same occasion

TWINY *n* a strong string of two or more strands twisted together

TWIRE *v* [obs] to peep or leer

TWIRL *v* **-ED, -ING, -S** to rotate rapidly, to spin

TWIRP *n pl* **-S** an informal term for a silly, insignificant or contemptible person; *also* **TWERP**

TWIST *v* **-ED, -ING, -S** to contort; to writhe; to distort

TWITE *n pl* **-S** a European tree sparrow

TWITS *v pr t of* **TWIT** taunts or ridicules

TWIXT *prep* between

TWYER *n pl* **-S** a fixture through which air is forced to the interior of a blast furnace; *also* **TUYERE, TUYER**

TYEES *n pl of* **TYEE** food fish, type of salmon

TYING *v pr part of* **TIE** fastening or securing

TYIYN *n pl* **-S** a monetary unit of Kyrgyzstan

TYKES *n pl of* **TYKE** small children, especially boys; *also* **TIKES**

TYPAL *adj* typical

TYPED *v p t of* **TYPE** keyed words using a keyboard or typewriter

TYPES *v pr t of* **TYPE** keys words using a keyboard or typewriter

TYPEY *adj* characterized by strict conformance to breed or variety; *also* **TYPY**

TYPIC *adj* typical

TYPOS *n pl of* **TYPO** mistakes in printed matter

TYPPS *n pl of* **TYPP** units of yarn size

TYRES *n pl of* **TYRE** BRIT. rings or bands of rubber placed over the rim of a wheels

TYROS *n pl of* **TYRO** beginners in a field or activity; *also* **TIROS**

TYTHE *v* -D, **TYTHING, -S** to pay a tenth of one's income, especially to a church; *also* **TITHE**

TZARS *n pl of* **TZAR** male monarchs or emperors; *also* **TSARS, CZARS**

UH *interj* used to express hesitation or uncertainty

UM *interj* used to express doubt or uncertainty or to fill a pause when hesitating

UP *v* -PED, -PING to raise

US *pron* the objective case of the pronoun we

UT *n pl* -S the musical note C in the French solemnization system, now "do"

THREE LETTERS

UDO *n pl* -S a Japanese herb

UEY *n pl* -S a complete reversal of direction of travel; a u-turn

UGH *interj* exclamation expressive of disgust, horror or recoil

UKE *n pl* -S a small guitar having four strings

ULE *n pl* -S a Mexican and Central American tree

ULU *n pl* -S a short-handled knife with a broad crescent-shaped blade, used by Eskimo women

UMM *interj* used to express doubt or hesitation

UMP *v* -ED, -ING, -S to serve as an umpire, an official who enforces the rules of a game

UNI *n pl* -S AUS. informal for a university

UPO *prep* [obs] upon

UPS *n pl of* **UP** those above, e.g. the higher ups

URB *n pl* -S an urban area

URD *n pl* -S an annual bean grown in India

URN *n pl* -S type of vase for preserving the ashes

URP *v* -ED, -ING, -S to vomit

USE *v* -D, **USING, -S** to put into service

UTE *n pl* -S AUS. a utility vehicle

UTS *n pl of* **UT** a musical note

UTU *n* satisfaction and reward in Maori culture

UVA *n pl* -S a small pulpy or juicy fruit containing several seeds, having a thin skin, as a grape

UZI *n pl* -S a type of submachine gun made in Israel

FOUR LETTERS

UDAD *n* a wild sheep of North Africa; *also* **ARUI, AOUDAD, AUDAD**

UDAL *n pl* -S [obs] a freehold hereditary estate; still used in Shetland and the Orkney islands

UDON *n* a Japanese noodle made with wheat flour

UDOS *n pl of* **UDO** Japanese herbs

UEYS *n pl of* **UEY** complete reversals of direction of travel; U-turns

UFOS *n pl of* **UFO** unidentified flying objects

UGLI *n pl* -ES a large sweet juicy hybrid between tangerine and grapefruit

UGLY *adj* **UGLIER, UGLIEST** offensive to the sight; contrary to beauty

UKES *n pl of* **UKE** small guitars having four strings

ULAN *n pl* -S a kind of light cavalry of Tartaric origin armed with lances; *also* **UHLAN**

ULES *n pl of* **ULE** Mexican and Central American trees

ULEX *n pl* -ES a spiny shrub

ULNA *n pl* -S or -E the inner and longer of the two bones of the human forearm

ULUS *n pl of* **ULU** short-handled Eskimo knives

UMBO *n pl* **-S** or **-NES** bump on plant or animal part

UMPS *v pr part of* **UMP** serves as an umpire, an official who enforces the rules of a game

UNAI *n pl* **-S** a sloth that has two long claws on each forefoot and three long claws on each hind foot; *also* **UNAU**

UNAU *n pl* **-S** a sloth that has two long claws on each forefoot and three long claws on each hind foot; *also* **UNAI**

UNBE *v* [obs] to cause not to be

UNCE *n pl* **-S** [obs] a claw

UNCI *n pl of* **UNCUS** hook-shaped processes or parts in biology

UNCO *adj* SCOT. unusual, strange or foreign

UNDE *adj* [obs] waving or wavy, as in a heraldic line that separates the two parts of the field

UNDO *v* **UNDID, -ING, -ES** to reverse, as what has been done

UNIS *n pl of* **UNI** AUS. informal for universities

UNIT *n pl* **-S** an amount or quantity adopted as a standard of measurement

UNTO *conj* [obs] until; till

UNTY *v* [obs] to untie

UPAS *n pl* **UPAS** or **-SES** a deciduous tropical tree that yields a latex used as an arrow poison

UPDO *n pl* **-S** an upswept hairdo

UPON *prep* on

URBS *n pl of* **URB** urban areas

URDS *n pl of* **URD** annual beans grown in India

UREA *n* chief component of urine

URGE *v* **-D, URGING, -S** to push; to drive; to impel

URIC *adj* in or relating to or obtained from urine

URNS *n pl of* **URN** type of vases used for holding ashes

URPS *v pr t of* **URP** vomits

URRY *n* a blue or black clay near a vein of coal

URUS *n pl* **-ES** a large extinct long-horned European wild ox

URVA *n pl* **-S** a crab-eating mongoose native to India

USED *v p t of* **USE** put into service

USER *n pl* **-S** one who uses, puts into service

USES *v pr t of* **USE** puts into service

UTES *n pl of* **UTE** AUS. utility vehicles

UTIA *n pl* **-S** any species of large West Indian rodent

UVAS *n pl of* **UVA** small pulpy or juicy fruits containing several seeds, having a thin skin, as grapes

UVEA *n pl* **-S** vascular middle layer of the eye made up of the iris, ciliary body and choroid

UVIC *adj* pertaining to, or obtained from, grapes specifically, designating an organic acid

UZIS *n pl of* **UZI** type of submachine guns made in Israel

FIVE LETTERS

UDALS *n pl of* **UDALS** in Shetland and Orkney, a freehold; property held by udal or allodial, right

UDDER *n pl* **-S** bag-shaped mammary gland of cows, sheep and goats

UHLAN *n pl* **-S** a kind of light cavalry of Tartaric origin armed with lances; *also* **ULAN**

UKASE *n pl* **-S** edict, order or proclamation by an absolute authority

ULAMA *n/pl* the body of mullahs, Muslim scholars trained in Islamic law and theology; *also* **ULEMA**

ULANS *n pl of* **ULAN** a kind of light cavalries of Tartaric origin armed with lances; *also* **UHLANS**

ULCER *n pl* **-S** an open sore on the skin or the surface of an organ which does not heal without treatment

ULEMA *n/pl* the body of mullahs, Muslim scholars trained in Islamic law and theology; *also* **ULAMA**

ULNAE *n pl of* **ULNA** the inner and longer of the two bones of the human forearm; *also* **ULNAS**

ULNAR *adj* of or relating to or near the ulna

ULNAS *n pl of* **ULNA** the inner and longer of the two bones of the human forearm; *also* **ULNAE**

ULTRA *adj* extreme; far beyond the norm

UMAMI *n* a strong savory taste

UMBEL *n pl* **-S** a cluster of flowers with stalks of nearly equal length originating from a common point

UMBER *v* **-ED, -ING, -S** to color with a brown pigment

UMBOS *n pl of* **UMBO** bumps on plants or animal parts

UMBRA *n pl* **-S** or **-E** shade or a shadow resulting from total obstruction of light

UMIAK *n pl* **-S** a large open boat made of skins stretched on a wooden frame

UMPED *v p t of* **UMP** served as an official who enforces the rules of a game

UNAIS *n pl of* **UNAI** sloths that have two long claws on each forefoot and three long claws on each hind foot; *also* **UNAUS**

UNAPT *adj* deficient in aptitude, not fitting or suitable

UNARM *v* **-ED, -ING, -S** to divest of weapons

UNARY *adj* consisting of or involving a single element or component

UNAUS *n pl of* **UNAU** sloths that have two long claws on each forefoot and three long claws on each hind foot; *also* **UNAIS**

UNBAR *v* **-RED, -RING, -S** to unbolt, to remove an obstruction

UNBID *adj* not ordered or invited; *also* **UNBIDDEN**

UNBOX *v* **-ED, -ING** to remove from a box

UNCAP *v* **-PED, -PING, -S** to remove a cover or restriction

UNCES *n pl of* **UNCE** [obs] claws

UNCIA *n pl* **-E** an ounce, in prescriptions

UNCLE *n pl* **-S** the brother of one's father or mother

UNCUS *n pl* **UNCI** a hook-shaped process or part in biology

UNCUT *adj* not severed

UNDER *prep* lower than; below

UNDID *v p t of* **UNDO** reversed, as what had been done

UNDUE *adj* not appropriate or suitable; improper

UNFED *adj* without food to eat

UNFIT *v* **-TED, -TING, -S** make unsuitable

UNFIX *v* **-ED, -ING, -ES** to unfasten

UNGOT *adj* [obs] not obtained; *also* **UNGOTTEN**

UNHAT *v* **-TED, -TING, -S** to remove a hat

UNHIP *adj* informal for not cool

UNIFY *v* **UNIFIED, -ING, UNIFIES** to become one, to combine

UNION *n pl* **-S** the state of being joined or united

UNITE *v* **-D, UNITING, -S** to become one, to combine

UNITS *n pl of* **UNIT** amounts or quantities adopted as a standard of measurement

UNITY *n pl* **UNITIES** the state or quality of being in accord

UNLAY *v* **UNLAID, -ING, -S** to untwist, as a rope

UNLED *adj* without guidance

UNLIT *adj* without illumination; not burning; *also* **UNLIGHTED**

UNMAN *v* **-NED, -NING, -S** to cause a loss of courage

UNMET *adj* not satisfied or fulfilled

UNMEW *v* **-ED, -ING, -S** to set free or release

UNPEG *v* **-GED, -GING, -S** to remove a peg from, to unfasten by removing a peg

UNPEN *v* **-NED, -NING, -S** to release from confinement

UNPIN *v* **-NED, -NING, -S** to remove pins from, to loosen

UNRIG *v* **-GED, -GING, -S** to strip a ship of rigging

UNRIP *v* **-PED, -PING, -S** to undue by tearing or pulling forcibly away

UNSAY *v* **UNSAID, -ING, -S** to take back or retract what has been spoken

UNSET *adj* not fixed or ready

UNSEW *v* **-ED** or **-N, -ING, -S** to undo the sewing of, to remove stitches

UNSEX *v* **-ED, -ING, -S** to castrate

UNTIE *v* **-D, UNTYING, -S** to undo or loosen a knot

UNTIL *prep* up to a time or point

UNWED *adj* not married

UNWIT *v* **-TED, -S** [obs] to render devoid of wit; derange

UNZIP *v* **-PED, -PING, -S** to open the zipper of

UPDOS *n pl of* **UPDO** upswept hairdos

UPEND *v* **-ED, -ING, -S** to set, turn or stand on end

UPPED *v p t of* **UP** raised

UPPER *adj* in a higher place or on a level above another

UPSET *v* **-TING, -S** to disturb

URAEI *n pl of* **URAEUS** the sacred serpent on the headdress of ancient Egyptian rulers

URARE *n* a dark resin obtained from several South American plants, can be used as a poison; *also* **CURARE, URARI**

URARI *n* a dark resin obtained from several South American plants, can be used as a poison; *also* **CURARE, URARE**

URASE *n pl* **-S** an enzyme that breaks down urea to form ammonium carbonate; *also* **UREASE**

URATE *n* a salt of uric acid

URBAN *adj* of, in, constituting or comprising a city

UREAL *adj* of or pertaining to urea

UREDO *n* a skin irritation; hives; *also* **URTICARIA**

URGED *v p t of* **URGE** pushed; drove; impelled

URGER *n pl* **-S** one that urges or importunes

URGES *v pr t of* **URGE** pushes; drives; impels

URIAL *n pl* **-S** reddish sheep of southern Asia

URINE *n* a waste product secreted through liquid excretion

URPED *v p t of* **URP** vomited

URVAS *n pl of* **URVA** crab-eating mongooses native to India

USAGE *n* the act, manner or amount of using or employing

USERS *n pl of* **USER** those who use, put into service

USHER *v* **-ED, -ING, -S** to conduct to a seat or place

USING *v pr part of* **USE** putting into service

USNEA *n pl* **-S** or **-E** lichen characterized by a hanging body in which the root, stem and leaf are not distinguished

USUAL *adj* common or ordinary

USURP *v* **-ED, -ING, -S** to take the place of, to seize control with no authority

USURY *n pl* **USURIES** the act or practice of lending money at an exorbitant rate of interest

UTERI *n pl of* **UTERUS** the reproductive organs of female mammals

UTIAS *n pl of* **UTIA** any species of large West Indian rodents

UTILE *adj* useful

UTTER *v* **-ED, -ING, -S** to give audible expression to

UVEAL *adj* of or relating to the uvea of the eye

UVEAS *n pl of* **UVEA** vascular middle layers of the eye constituting the iris, ciliary body, and choroid

UVULA *n pl* **-S** or **-E** the small fleshy lobe above the back of the tongue

VAC *n pl* **-S** informal term for vacuum cleaner, an appliance that cleans surfaces by sucking dirt and other material into a bag or cylinder

VAE *n* SCOT. an inlet, bay or creek; *also* **VOE**

VAG *v* **-GED, -GING, -S** to arrest as a vagrant

VAN *n pl* **-S** an enclosed boxlike motor vehicle having rear or side doors and side panels especially for transporting people

VAP *n* [obs] that which is vapid, insipid or lifeless; especially, the lifeless part of liquor or wine

VAS *n pl* **VASA** a vessel or duct in the body of a person or animal

VAT *n pl* **-S** a large container used to hold liquid

VAU *n pl* **-S** the sixth letter of the Hebrew alphabet; *also* **VAV, WAW**

VAV *n pl* **-S** the sixth letter of the Hebrew alphabet; *also* **VAU, WAW**

VEE *n pl* **-S** the letter "V"

VEG *v* **-GED, -GING, -ES** informal term meaning to engage in relaxing or passive activities

VET *v* **-TED, -TING, -S** to check up on somebody, especially when determining suitability for something

VEX *v* **-ED** or **-T, -ING, -ES** to make angry or annoyed by little provocations

VIA *n pl* **-S** road, passage, right of way

VID *n pl* **-S** commonly used abbreviation for video, a magnetic tape or digital file containing visual images

VIE *v* **-D, VYING, -S** to strive for superiority; to contend; *also* **ENVIE**

VIG *n* informal for a bribe, interest paid to a usurer, or a betting charge; *also* **VIGORISH**

VIM *n pl* **-S** exuberant vitality and energy; vigor

VIN *n pl* **-S** French word used also in English speaking countries to mean wine

VIS *n pl* **VIRES** force or power

VIZ *adv* to wit; that is; namely

VOE *n pl* **-S** SCOT. an inlet, bay or creek; *also* **VAE**

VOW *v* **-ED, -ING, -S** to make a solemn promise

VOX *n pl* **VOCES** a voice or sound

VUG *n pl* **-S** a small cavity in a rock or lode; *also* **VUGG, VUGH, VOGLE**

VUM *interj* a regional term used in New England to express surprise

FOUR LETTERS

VACS *n pl of* **VAC** an informal term for vacuum cleaners, an appliance that cleans surfaces by sucking dirt and other material into a bag or cylinder

VAGI *n pl of* **VAGUS** cranial nerves

VAGS *v pr t of* **VAG** arrests as a vagrant

VAIL *v* **-ED, -ING, -S** to take off or tip (one's hat, for example) as a sign of respect or submission

VAIN *adj* **-ER, -EST** excessively proud, especially of personal appearance

VAIR *n* fur used as a trimming on medieval robes

VALE *n pl* **-S** a tract of low ground, or of land between hills; *also* **VALLEY**

VAMP *v* **-ED, -ING, -S** to improvise a musical introduction or accompaniment for a solo line

VANE *n pl* **-S** the blade of a bird's feather; each feather has two vanes, one on each side

VANG *n pl* **-S** a rope running from the peak of a gaff to a ship's rail or mast, used to steady the gaff

VANS *n pl of* **VAN** enclosed boxlike motor vehicles having rear or side doors and side panels especially for transporting people

VANT *v* [obs] to speak boastfully of, to brag about; *also* **VAUNT**

VARA *n pl* **-S** a unit of length used in Spain, Portugal and Latin America that can be from 32 to 43 inches

VARE *n pl* **-S** a term used in provincial England for a weasel

VARI *n pl* **-S** the ring-tailed lemur of Madagascar

VARK *n* the bush hog, or boshvark; a pig

VARY *v* **VARIED, -ING, VARIES** to change to something else

VASA *n pl of* **VAS** vessels or ducts in the body of a person or animal

VASE *n pl* **-S** an open jar of glass or porcelain used as an ornament or to hold flowers

VAST *adj* **-ER, -EST** very great in number, size, amount, extent or degree

VATS *n pl of* **VAT** large containers used to hold liquid

VATU *n pl* **VATU** a monetary unit of Vanuatu

VAUS *n pl of* **VAU** more than one of the sixth letter of the Hebrew alphabet; *also* **VAVS, WAW**

VAUT *n* [obs] a vault; a leap

VAVS *n pl of* **VAV** more than one of the sixth letter of the Hebrew alphabet; *also* **VAUS, WAWS**

VEAL *n pl* **VEAL** a milk-fed calf; *also* **VEALER**

VEDA *n pl* **VEDA** one or all of the most ancient sacred writings of Hinduism

VEEP *n pl* **-S** informal for vice president, an official with a rank below a president, who can take the president's place if necessary

VEER *v* **-ED, -ING, -S** to change direction; to turn; to shift

VEES *n pl of* **VEE** more than one of the letter "V"

VEIL *n pl* **-S** a cover; disguise; a mask; *also* **VELE**

VEIN *n pl* **-S** one of the vessels which carry blood

VELA *n pl of* **VELUM** soft palates, upper back parts of mouths

VELD *n* an area of open grassland, especially in southern Africa; *also* **VELDT**

VELE *n* [obs] a cover; disguise; a mask; *also* **VEIL**

VELL *v* BRIT. a term used in provincial England meaning to cut the turf from, as for burning

VENA *n pl* **-E** a blood vessel that carries blood from the capillaries toward the heart; a vein

VEND *v* **-ED, -ING, -S** to sell

VENT *v* **-ED, -ING, -S** to provide with an opening for the escape of gas or liquid

VERA *adj* SCOT. very

VERB *n pl* **-S** a word indicating action or the existence of a state or condition

VERD *n* [obs] greenness; freshness

VERT *n* green forest vegetation especially when forming cover or providing food for deer

VERY *adj* **VERIER, VERIEST** true; exact; precise

VEST *v* **-ED, -ING, -S** to invest or endow with something

VETO *v* **-ED, -ING, -ES** to refuse to consent to or approve something

VETS *v pr t of* **VET** checks up on somebody, especially when determining suitability for something

VEXT *v p t of* **VEX** made angry or annoyed by little provocations; *also* **VEXED**

VIAL *n pl* **-S** a small container for liquids; *also* **PHIAL**

VIAS *n pl of* **VIA** roads, passages, rights of way

VIBE *n pl* **-S** a particular kind of feeling or ambience

VICE *n pl* **-S** a moral fault or failing

VIDS *n pl of* **VID** commonly used abbreviation for videos, magnetic tapes or digital files containing visual images

VIED *v p t of* **VIE** strived for superiority; contended

VIES *v pr t of* **VIE** strives for superiority; contends

VIEW *v* **-ED, -ING, -S** to see or behold something

VIGA *n pl* **-S** a rafter or roof beam, a trimmed and peeled tree trunk whose end projects from an outside adobe wall

VILD *adj* [obs] loathsome, disgusting; *also* **VILE**

VILE *adj* **-R, -ST** loathsome, disgusting; *also* **VILD**

VILL *n pl* **-S** a territorial division under the feudal system; township

VIMS *n pl of* **VIM** exuberant vitalities and energies; vigors

VINA *n pl* **-S** a seven-stringed instrument of India; *also* **VEENA**

VINE *v* **-D, VINING, -S** to grow like a vine, a climbing plant

VINO *n pl* **-S** Spanish and Italian word used also in English speaking countries to mean wine, especially wine that is cheap or of inferior quality

VINS *n pl of* **VIN** French word used also in English speaking countries to mean wines

VINT *v* **–ED, -ING, -S** to make wine

VINY *adj* **VINIER, VINIEST** of or pertaining to vines, climbing plants

VIOL *n pl* **-S** a stringed musical instrument played with a curved bow that was a precursor to the violin family

VIRE *n* an arrow with a rotary motion, formerly used with the crossbow

VIRL *n pl* **-S** SCOT. a ring or cap usually of metal put around a wooden shaft to strengthen it or prevent splitting; *also* **FERRULE**

VISA *n pl* **-S** an endorsement in a passport that allows the bearer to enter or leave, and travel in or through, the country issuing it

VISE *v* **-D, VISING, -S** to hold, press or squeeze

VITA *n pl* **-E** a short account of a person's life

VIVA *interj* a shout of acclamation used to express enthusiastic support for somebody

VIVE *adj* SCOT. lively; brisk

VOES *n pl of* **VOE** SCOT. inlets, bays or creeks

VOID *v* **-ED, -ING, -S** to make ineffective or invalid

VOLE *n pl* **-S** a small rodent similar to a mouse but with a shorter tail and legs and a stocky body

VOLT *n pl* **-S** a unit of electric potential

VOTE *v* **-D, VOTING, -S** to express or signify the mind, will or preference

VOWS *v pr t of* **VOW** makes a solemn promise

VROU *n pl* **-S** a Dutch or Afrikaner woman; *also* **VROW, VROUW**

VROW *n pl* **-S** a Dutch or Afrikaner woman; *also* **VROU, VROUW**

VUGG *n* a small cavity in a rock or vein, often lined with crystals; *also* **VOGLE, VUG, VUGH**

VUGH *n* a small cavity in a rock or vein, often lined with crystals; *also* **VOGLE, VUG, VUGG**

VUGS *n pl* **-S** small cavities in a rock or vein, often lined with crystals; *also* **VOGLES, VUGGS, VUGHS**

VYCE *n* [obs] a kind of clamp with gimlet points for holding a barrel head

FIVE LETTERS

VACUA *n pl of* **VACUUM** space from which all air or gas has been extracted; *also* **VACUUM**

VAGAL *adj* of or relating to the vagus nerve

VAGUE *adj* **-R, -EST** not clearly expressed or understood

VAGUS *n pl* **VAGI** a cranial nerve

VAILS *v pr t of* **VAIL** takes off or tips (one's hat, for example) as a sign of respect or submission

VAKIL *n pl* **-S** a lawyer or legal representative in a court of law in India; *also* **VAKEEL**

VALES *n pl of* **VALE** tracts of low ground, or of land between hills; *also* **VALLEYS**

VALET *v* **-ED, -ING, -S** to act as a personal servant to

VALID *adj* based on evidence that can be supported

VALOR *n* marked courage or bravery

VALSE *n pl* **-S** a ballroom dance in triple time, especially one of French origin; *also* **WALTZ**

VALUE *v* **-D, VALUING, -S** to set a price for or determine the worth of

VALVE *v* **-D, VALVING, -S** to regulate the flow of by means of a device that controls the flow of a gas or liquid

VAMPS *n pl of* **VAMP** improvises a musical introduction or accompaniment for a solo line

VANED *adj* equipped with feathers, as an arrow

VANES *n pl of* **VANE** the blades of a bird's feather; each feather has two vanes, one on each side

VANGS *n pl of* **VANG** ropes running from the peak of a gaff to a ship's rail or mast, used to steady the gaff

VAPID *adj* dull; lacking interest or liveliness

VAPOR *v* **-ED, -ING, -S** to evaporate

VARAS *n pl of* **VARA** more than one of a unit of length used in Spain, Portugal and Latin America that can be from 32 to 43 inches

VARES *n pl of* **VARE** a term used in provincial England for weasels

VARIA *n/pl* a miscellany, especially of diverse literary works

VARIS *n pl of* **VARI** ring-tailed lemurs of Madagascar

VARIX *n pl* **VARICES** an enlarged and convoluted vein, artery or lymphatic vessel

VARNA *n pl* **-S** a social caste in Hindu society

VARUS *adj* of, relating to, or being a deformity in which an anatomical part is turned inward toward the midline of the body

VARVE *n pl* **-S** a layer or series of layers of sediment deposited annually in a still body of water, which can be counted back to date a specific layer

VASAL *adj* of, relating to, or connected with a vessel or duct of the body

VASES *n pl of* **VASES** open jars of glass or porcelain used as ornaments or to hold flowers

VASTY *adj* **-IER, -IEST** [obs] immense; huge

VATIC *adj* of or characteristic of a prophet; *also* **VATICAL**

VAULT *v* **-ED, -ING, -S** to spring over an object, especially by pushing on it with the hands or using a pole

VAUNT *v* **-ED, -ING, -S** to speak boastfully of, to brag about; *also* **VANT**

VEALY *adj* **VEALIER, VEALIEST** not fully developed; immature

VEENA *n pl* **-S** a seven-stringed instrument of India; *also* **VINA**

VEEPS *n pl of* **VEEP** informal for vice presidents, officials with a rank below a president, who can take the presidents' place if necessary

VEERS *v pr t of* **VEER** changes direction; turns; shifts

VEERY *n pl* **VEERIES** a small, brown and cream-colored thrush native to N. America

VEGAN *n pl* **-S** somebody who does not eat meat, fish, dairy products or eggs

VEGES *v pr t of* **VEG** informal term meaning engages in relaxing or passive activities

VEGIE *n pl* **-S** informal for vegetable, a plant with edible parts, especially leafy or fleshy parts that are used mainly for soups or salads; *also* **VEGGIE**

VEILS *n pl of* **VEIL** covers; disguises; masks

VEINS *n pl of* **VEIN** vessels which carry blood

VEINY *adj* **VEINIER, VEINIEST** having or showing veins, vessels which carry blood

VELAR *adj* pronounced with the back of the tongue close to, or in contact with, the soft palate

VELDT *n* an area of open grassland, especially in South Africa; *also* **VELD**

VELUM *n pl* **VELA** the soft palate, the upper back part of the mouth

VENAE *n pl of* **VENA** blood vessels that carry blood from the capillaries toward the heart; veins

VENAL *adj* open to persuasion by corrupt means, especially bribery

VENDS *v pr t of* **VEND** sells

VENGE *v* **-D, VENGING, -S** [obs] to avenge; exact satisfaction for a wrong

VENIN *n* any of the specific toxic constituents of animal venoms; *also* **VENENE, VENINE**

VENOM *n pl* **-S** poison of any kind; spite; malice

VENTS *v pr t of* **VENT** provides with an opening for the escape of gas or liquid

VENUE *n pl* **-S** the place where an event is held

VERBS *n pl of* **VERB** words indicating action or the existence of a state or condition

VERGE *v* **-D, VERGING, -S** to move or lean in a particular direction

VERSE *v* **-D, VERSING, -S** to instruct somebody in a something

VERSO *n pl* **-S** a left-handed page of a book, usually printed with an even page number

VERST *n pl* **-S** a Russian unit of linear measure equivalent to about two thirds of a mile; *also* **WERST**

VERTU *n* a love of or taste for fine objects of art; *also* **VIRTU**

VERVE *n* vigor and energy

VESTA *n* a short wooden match

VESTS *v pr t of* **VEST** invests or endows with something

VETCH *n pl* **-ES** or **VETCH** climbing or trailing plants of the pea family

VEXED *v p t of* **VEX** made angry or annoyed by little provocations; *also* **VEXT**

VEXER *n pl* **-S** one who annoys

VEXES *v pl of* **VEX** makes angry or annoyed by little provocations

VEXIL   *n pl* **VEXILLA** the large upper petal of a papilionaceous flower; *also* **VEXILLUM**

VIALS   *n pl of* **VIAL** small containers for liquids

VIAND   *n pl* **-S** a store or collection of food, especially the food that makes up a meal or a feast

VIBES   *n pl of* **VIBE** a particular kinds of feeling or ambience

VICAR   *n pl* **-S** one who acts in the place of another, specifically an administrative deputy

VICES   *n pl of* **VICE** moral faults or failings

VIDEO   *n pl* **-S** the visual part of a television broadcast, movie, etc.

VIEWS   *v pr t of* **VIEW** sees or beholds something

VIEWY   *adj* **VIEWIER, VIEWIEST** conspicuous or striking; showy

VIGAS   *n pl of* **VIGA** rafters or roof beams, trimmed and peeled tree trunks whose ends project from an outside adobe wall

VIGIA   *n pl* **-S** something marked on a chart as a hazard to navigation, although its existence, position and nature are unconfirmed

VIGIL   *n pl* **-S** a watch kept during normal sleeping hours

VIGOR   *n pl* **-S** active physical or mental force or strength

VILER   *adj* more loathsome, more disgusting

VILLA   *n pl* **-S,** a country house or estate

VILLI   *n pl of* **VILLUS** long, soft, fine hairs on certain plants

VILLS   *n pl of* **VILL** territorial divisions under the feudal system; townships

VIMEN   *n pl* **VIMINA** a long, flexible shoot or branch

VINAL   *n* a synthetic textile fiber that is a long-chain polymer consisting largely of vinyl alcohol units

VINAS   *n pl of* **VINA** seven-stringed instruments of India; *also* **VEENAS**

VINCA   *n pl* **-S** any of several green shrubs with glossy leaves and flat flowers with five petals; *also* **PERIWINKLE**

VINED   *v p t of* **VINE** grew like a vine, a climbing plant

VINES   *v pr t of* **VINE** grows like a vine, a climbing plant

VINIC   *adj* of, found in, or derived from wine

VINOS   *n pl of* **VINO** Spanish and Italian word used also in English speaking countries to mean wines, especially wines that are cheap or of inferior quality

VINYL   *n* a type of plastic

VIOLA   *n pl* **-S** a stringed instrument of the violin family, slightly larger and lower in pitch than a violin

VIOLS   *n pl of* **VIOL** stringed musical instruments played with curved bows that were precursors to the violin family

VIPER   *n pl* **-S** a venomous snake

VIRAL   *adj* relating to, typical of, or caused by a virus

VIRES   *n pl of* **VIS** forces or powers

VIRGA   *n* wisps of precipitation from the underside of a cloud that evaporate before reaching the ground

VIRID   *adj* bright green with or as if with vegetation; verdant

VIRLS   *n pl of* **VIRL** rings or caps usually of metal put around wooden shafts to strengthen them or prevent splitting; *also* **FERRULE**

VIRTU   *n* a love of or taste for fine objects of art; *also* **VERTU**

VIRUS   *n pl* **-ES** a parasitic particle that can only replicate within a host cell

VISAS *n pl of* **VISAS** endorsements in a passport that allow the bearer to enter or leave, and travel in or through, the country(s) issuing it

VISED *v p t of* **VISE** held, pressed or squeezed

VISES *v pr t of* **VISE** holds, presses or squeezes

VISIT *v* **-ED, -ING, -S** to go or come to see someone or something

VISOR *v* **-ED, -ING, -S** to cover or protect with a shield to shade or protect the eyes; *also* **VIZOR**

VISTA *n pl* **-S** a pleasing view or outlook

VITAE *n pl of* **VITA** short accounts of a people's lives

VITAL *adj* necessary to life

VITTA *n pl* **-E** a band or streak of color on the body of an animal

VIVID *adj* full of life

VIXEN *n* **-S** a female fox

VIZIR *n* formerly a high officer in a Muslim government; *also* **VIZIER**

VIZOR *v* **-ED, -ING, -S** to cover or protect with a shield to shade or protect the eyes; *also* **VISOR**

VOCAB *n* informal for vocabulary, usually referring to an alphabetical list of words and phrases supplied with definitions or translations

VOCAL *n pl* **-S** the sung part of a piece of music

VOCES *n pl of* **VOX** voices or sounds

VODKA *n pl* **-S** a colorless liquor distilled from rye, wheat, etc.

VODOU *n* a religion of the West Indies noted for its interest in sorcery, charms and fetishes; *also* **VOODOO, VODOUN, VODUN**

VODUN *n* a religion of the West Indies noted for its interest in sorcery, charms and fetishes; *also* **VOODOO, VODOU, VODOUN**

VOGIE *adj* SCOT. proud; vain

VOGUE *v* **-D, VOGUING** or **VOGUEING, -S** to dance by imitating poses of fashion models

VOGLE *n pl* **-S** small cavities in a rock or vein, often lined with crystals; *also* **VUGS, VUGGS, VUGHS**

VOICE *v* **-D, VOICING, -S** to express or utter

VOIDS *v pr t of* **VOID** makes ineffective or invalid

VOILA *interj* behold; there it is

VOILE *n pl* **-S** a thin, sheer fabric used for garments

VOLAR *adj* relating to the palm of the hand or sole of the foot

VOLES *n pl of* **VOLE** small rodents similar to mice but with a shorter tails and legs and stocky bodies

VOLTA *n* a turning; a time in music, used to signify that the part is to be repeated

VOLTE *n pl* **-S** in dressage, a circular movement executed by a horse; *also* **VOLT**

VOLTI *v* turn over quickly; turn the page

VOLTS *n pl of* **VOLT** units of electric potential

VOLVA *n pl* **-S** a cup-shaped structure that encircles the base of the stalk of some mushrooms

VOMER *n pl* **-S** a thin, flat bone of the nasal septum

VOMIT *v* **-ED, -ING, -S** to throw up food

VOTED *v p t of* **VOTE** expressed or signified the mind, will or preference

VOTER *n pl* **-S** one who expresses or signifies the mind, will or preference

VOTES *v pl of* **VOTE** expresses or signifies the mind, will or preference

VOUCH *v* **-ED, -ING, -ES** to give one's personal assurance or guarantee

VOWED *v p t of* **VOW** made a solemn promise

VOWEL *n pl* **-S** a type of speech sound

VOWER *n* one who vows, makes a solemn promise

VOXEL *n pl* **-S** the 3D equivalent of a pixel

VROOM *v* **-ED, -ING, -S** to run an engine at high speed; *also* **VAROOM**

VROUW *n pl* **-S** a Dutch or Afrikaner woman; *also* **VROW, VROU**

VROUS *n pl of* **VROU** Dutch or Afrikaner women; *also* **VROWS, VROUWS**

VROWS *n pl of* **VROW** Dutch or Afrikaner women; *also* **VROUS, VROUWS**

VUGHS *n pl of* **VUGH** small cavities in a rock or vein, often lined with crystals; *also* **VOGLES, VUGS, VUGGS**

VUGGS *n pl of* **VUGG** small cavities in a rock or vein, often lined with crystals; *also* **VOGLES, VUGS, VUGHS**

VUGGY *adj* **VUGGIER, VUGGIEST** abounding in vuggs, small cavities in rocks or veins

VULVA *n pl* **-E** or **-S** the external genital organs of the female

VYING *v pr part of* **VIE** striving for superiority; contending

WE *pron* used by speaker to refer to himself or herself and one or more other people considered together

WO *interj* stop; stand; hold; a command mostly for animals; *also* **WHOA**

THREE LETTERS

WAD *v* **-DED, -DING, -S** to form into a mass

WAE *n* SCOT., BRIT. woe or sorrow

WAG *v* **-GED, -GING, -S** to move repeatedly from side to side

WAH *n pl* **-S** the red panda

WAN *v* **-NED, -NING, -S** to become pale

WAP *v* **-PED, -PING, -S** to strike forcibly; *also* **WHAP, WHOP**

WAR *v* **-RED, -RING, -S** to engage in an armed conflict with somebody

WAS *v p t of* **BE** existed; first and third person singular past tense of to be

WAT *n pl* **-S** a Buddhist temple in Thailand or Cambodia

WAW *n pl* **-S** the sixth letter of the Hebrew alphabet; *also* **VAV, VAU**

WAX *v* **-ED, -ING, -ES** to polish, especially with a soft solid substance that melts easily

WAY *n pl* **-S** a path or physical means of getting from one place to another

WEB *v* **-BED, -BING, -S** to ensnare or entangle in a structure of delicate, threadlike filaments characteristically spun by spiders

WED *v* **-DED, -DING, -S** to take as a spouse; join in marriage

WEE *adj* **-R, -ST** very small, little

WEM *n pl* **-S** [obs] a spot; blemish; stain

WEN *n pl* **-S** the runic alphabet equivalent to the modern "W"; *also* **WYN, WYNN**

WEP *v p t of* **WEEP** [obs] expressed sorrow, grief or anguish

WET *v* **-TED, -TING, -S** to become damp or soaked with water

WEX *v* **-ING** [obs] to grow

WEY *n pl* **-S** an old British or Scottish measure of weight for dry goods

WHA *pron* SCOT. [obs] a word for who

WHO *pron* used to refer to a person or group of people, used as the object of a verb

WHY *n pl* **-S** a reason or cause of something

WIG *n pl* **-S** a hairpiece covering the head and made of real or synthetic hair

WIN *v* **WON, -NING, -S** to be victorious in a competition or contest

WIS *v* **-SED** or **-T, -SING, -ES** [obs] to know, think or suppose

WIT *v* **WIST, -TING, -S** or **WOST** or **WOT** [obs] to know or become aware of something; *also* **WEET**

WIZ *n* informal for a person of amazing skill or accomplishment

WOE *n pl* **-S** a tremendous grief; misery

WOK *n pl* **-S** a pan with a curved base used for stir-frying, steaming and braising food

WON *v p t of* **WIN** was victorious in a competition or contest

WOO *v* **-ED, -ING, -S** to solicit in love; to court

WOT *v pr t of* **WIT** [obs] knows or becomes aware of something; *also* **WITS, WOST, WEETS**

WOW *v* **-ED, -ING, -S** to impress or delight somebody greatly

WOX *v p t of* **WAX** [obs] polished

WRY *v* **WRIED, -ING, WRIES** to contort, to writhe, to twist

WUD *adj* SCOT. insane; mad

WYD *adj* [obs] wide

WYE *n pl* **-S** the letter "Y"

WYN *n pl* **-S** the runic alphabet equivalent to the modern "W"; *also* **WEN, WYNN**

WYS *adj* [obs] wise

FOUR LETTERS

WACK *adj* in snowboarding, informal for bad or unlucky; *also* **WACKER**

WADD *n* black lead; graphite

WADE *v* **-D, WADING, -S** to walk through water

WADI *n pl* **-S** or **-ES** an oasis, especially in North Africa; *also* **WADY**

WADS *v pr t of* **WAD** forms into a mass

WADY *n pl* **WADIES** an oasis, especially in North Africa; *also* **WADI**

WAFF *v* **-ED, -ING, -S** to wave or flutter

WAFT *v* **-ED, -ING, -S** to pass easily or gently through air

WAGE *v* **-D, WAGING, -S** to engage in, as a war

WAGS *v pr t of* **WAG** moves repeatedly from side to side

WAHS *n pl of* **WAH** red pandas

WAID *adj* [obs] oppressed with weight; crushed; weighed down

WAIF *n pl* **-S** a wanderer; a castaway

WAIL *v* **-ED, -ING, -S** to express sorrow audibly; to weep

WAIN *n pl* **-S** a wagon or cart

WAIR *n* in carpentry, a plank that is six feet long and one foot wide

WAIT *v* **-ED, -ING, -S** to stay or rest in expectation

WAKE *v* **-D** or **WOKE** or **WOKEN, -ING, -S** to come back to a conscious state after sleeping

WALD *n* [obs] an elevated treeless tract of land; *also* **WOLD**

WALE *v* **-D, WALING, -S** to make a streak or ridge on the skin, especially by the stroke of a whip

WALK *v* **-ED, -ING, -S** to move along on foot; to advance by steps

WALL *v* **-ED, -ING, -S** to fortify or surround somebody or something with an upright structure that acts as a boundary

WALM *v* [obs] to roll; to spout; to boil up

WALY *interj* SCOT., BRIT. [obs] an exclamation of grief

WAME *n pl* **-S** SCOT. a belly or abdomen

WAND *n pl* **-S** a stick or baton used by a magician

WANE *v* **-D, WANING, -S** to decline; to fail; to sink

WANG *n pl* **-S** [obs] the jaw, jawbone or cheek bone

WANS *v pr t of* **WAN** becomes pale

WANT *v* **-ED, -ING, -S** to feel a need or desire for something

WANY *adj* **WANIER, WANIEST** waning; decreasing; declining; *also* **WANEY**

WAPP *n* a fair leader

WAPS *v pr t of* **WAP** strikes forcibly; *also* **WHAPS, WHOPS**

WARD *v* **-ED, -ING, -S** to watch over

WARE *v* **-D, WARING, -S** to make aware; to warn

WARK *n* [obs] a building

WARM *v* **-ED, -ING, -S** to make warm

WARN *v* **-ED, -ING, -S** to make aware

WARP *v* **-ED, -ING, -S** to turn or twist out of shape

WARS *n pl of* **WAR** engages in an armed conflict with somebody

WART *n pl* **-S** a firm abnormal elevated blemish on the skin

WARY *adj* **WARIER, WARIEST** cautious of danger; carefully watching

WASE *n* a bundle of straw, or other material, to relieve the pressure of burdens carried upon the head

WASH *v* **-ED, -ING, -ES** to cleanse with soap and water

WASP *n pl* **-S** a stinging insect

WAST *v p t of* **BE** [obs] existed; second person singular past tense of be

WATS *n pl of* **WAT** Buddhist temples in Thailand or Cambodia

WATT *n pl* **-S** a unit of power or activity

WAUK *v* SCOT. to come back to a conscious state after sleeping; wake

WAUL *v* **-ED, -ING, -S** to cry like a cat; to squall; to wail; *also* **WAWL, WOUL**

WAUR *adj* SCOT. less good than something else; worse

WAVE *v* **-D, WAVING, -S** to move one's hand to and fro in greeting or as a signal

WAVY *adj* **WAVIER, WAVIEST** rising or swelling; a series of smooth curves, as the ocean

WAWL *v* **-ED, -ING, -S** to cry like a cat; to squall; to wail; *also* **WAUL, WOUL**

WAWS *n pl of* **WAW** more than one of the sixth letter of the Hebrew alphabet; *also* **VAUS, VAVS**

WAXY *adj* **WAXIER, WAXIEST** having the paleness of wax, a resinous substance

WAYK *adj* [obs] deficient in strength of body; feeble; *also* **WEAK**

WAYS *n pl of* **WAY** paths or physical means of getting from one place to another

WEAK *adj* **-ER, -EST** deficient in strength of body; feeble; *also* **WAYK**

WEAL *n pl* **-S** reddened area on the skin from being hit with something; *also* **WHEAL**

WEAN *v* **-ED, -ING, -S** to gradually deprive somebody of something they like or that is a habit

WEAR *v* **WORE** or **WORN, -ING, -S** to have something on the body as covering, adornment or protection

WEBS *v pr t of* **WEB** ensnares or entangles in a structure of delicate, threadlike filaments characteristically spun by spiders

WEDS *v pr t of* **WED** takes as a spouse; joins in marriage

WEED *v* **-ED, -ING, -S** to pull plants that crowd out cultivated plants

WEEK *n pl* **-S** a period of seven days

WEEL *adj* [obs] well

WEEN *v* **-ED, -ING, -S** to think; to imagine; to fancy; to suppose

WEEP *v* **WEPT, -ING, -S** to express sorrow, grief or anguish

WEER *adj* smaller; littler

WEET *v* **-ED, -ING, WOT** [obs] to know or become aware of something; *also* **WIT**

WEFT *n* the crosswise threads that are passed over and under the warp threads on a loom to make cloth

WEIR *n pl* **-S** a fence or dam built across a stream to catch or retain fish; *also* **WIER**

WEKA *n pl* **-S** a flightless bird native to New Zealand

WELD *v* **-ED, -ING, -S** to join together by heating

WELE *n* [obs] prosperity; happiness

WELK *v* **-ED, -ING, -S** [obs] to cause to wither; to wilt; *also* **WHELK**

WELL *v* **-ED, -ING, -S** to come up, as in water from the earth or tears in one's eyes

WELS *n/pl* a large freshwater catfish native to central and eastern Europe

WELT *v* **-ED, -ING, -S** to reinforce or trim a seam with a tape or covered cord

WEMS *n pl of* **WEM** [obs] spots; blemishes; stains

WEND *v* **-ED, -ING, -S** to proceed

WENS *n pl of* **WEN** the runic alphabet equivalent to modern "Ws"; *also* **WYNS, WYNNS**

WENT *v p t of* **GO** left a place

WEPT *v p t of* **WEEP** expressed sorrow, grief or anguish

WERE *v p t of* **BE** existed

WERN *v* [obs] to refuse

WERT *v p t of* **BE** [obs] existed

WEST *n* the direction that lies directly ahead of one facing the setting Sun or that is located toward the left side of a compass

WETS *v p r t of* **WET** becomes damp or soaked with water

WEYS *n pl of* **WEY** an old British or Scottish measure of weight for dry goods

WHAM *v* **-MED, -MING, -S** to hit or crash into something with a forceful, resounding blow

WHAP *v* **-PED, -PING, -S** to strike forcibly; *also* **WAP, WHOP**

WHAT *pron* the thing which; that which

WHEE *interj* used to express extreme pleasure or enthusiasm

WHEN *adv* used to ask the time or moment at which something is done or occurs

WHET *v* **-TED, -TING, -S** to make a feeling, sense or desire more keen or intense

WHEW *interj* used to express relief, surprise, dismay or disgust

WHEY *n* the watery part of curdled milk

WHID *v* **-DED, -DING** to move nimbly

WHIM *n pl* **-S** a sudden turn or start of the mind; a temporary eccentricity

WHIN *n pl* **-S** a very spiny and dense evergreen shrub with fragrant golden-yellow flowers

WHIP *v* **-PED** or **WHIPT, -PING, -S** to strike with a lash, a cord, a rod

WHIR *v* **-RED, -RING, -S** to make a continuous soft buzzing or whizzing noise; *also* **WHIRR, WHUR**

WHIT *n* the smallest degree or amount imaginable; a bit

WHIZ *v* **-ZED, -ZING, -ZES** to make a humming, hissing or buzzing noise; *also* **WHIZZ**

WHOA *interj* stop; stand; hold; a command mostly for animals; *also* **WO**

WHOM *pron* used to refer to a person or group of people, used as the object of a verb or preposition

WHOP *v* **-PED, -PING, -S** to strike forcibly; *also* **WAP, WHAP**

WHUP *v* **-PED, -PING, -S** informal for beat; thrash

WHUR *v* **-RED, -RING, -S** [obs] to make a continuous soft buzzing or whizzing noise; *also* **WHIR, WHIRR**

WHYS *n pl of* **WHY** the reasons or causes for something

WICK *v* -ED, -ING, -S to take or transfer liquid by capillary action

WIDE *adj* -R, -ST having a great extent every way; extended; spacious; broad

WIER *n pl* -S a fence or dam built across a stream to catch or retain fish; *also* **WEIR**

WIFE *n pl* **WIVES** a married woman

WIGS *n pl of* **WIG** hairpieces covering the head and made of real or synthetic hair

WIKE *n* [obs] a temporary mark or boundary

WILD *adj* -ER, -EST savage; uncivilized; not refined by culture

WILE *v* -D, **WILING** to entice or lure, especially by trickery

WILL *v* -ED, -ING, -S to decree, dictate or order

WILT *v* -ED, -ING, -S to begin to wither; to lose freshness and become flaccid

WILY *adj* **WILIER, WILIEST** full of tricks; crafty

WIMP *n pl* -S a person who is regarded as weak or ineffectual

WIND *v* -ED, -ING, -S to entwist; enfold; encircle

WINE *n pl* -S an alcoholic drink made by fermenting the juice of grapes

WING *v* -ED, -ING, -S to travel swiftly or send something with great speed

WINK *v* -ED, -ING, -S to close one eye for a short time

WINS *v pr t of* **WIN** is victorious in a competition or contest

WINY *adj* **WINIER, WINIEST** having the taste or qualities of wine; *also* **WINEY**

WIPE *v* -D, **WIPING, -S** to rub with something, as for cleaning

WIRE *v* -D, **WIRING, -S** to fasten with a thread or slender rod of metal

WIRY *adj* **WIRIER, WIRIEST** slim but strong

WISE *adj* -R, -ST having knowledge; knowing; enlightened

WISH *v* -ED, -ING, -ES to have a desire or yearning; to long

WISP *v* -ED, -ING, -S to move like something delicate or faint

WIST *v* -ED, -ING, -S [obs] know; think or suppose

WITE *v* -D, **WITING** SCOT. to reproach; to blame; to censure; *also* **WYTE**

WITH *prep* expresses some situation or relation of nearness, proximity, association, connection

WITS *v pr to of* **WIT** [obs] knows or becomes aware of something; *also* **WOT, WOST, WEETS**

WIVE *v* -D, **WIVING, -S** to marry a woman

WOAD *n pl* -S a yellow-flowered plant whose leaves were formerly used to make blue dye

WOES *n pl of* **WOE** tremendous grief; miseries

WOKE *v p t of* **WAKE** came back to a conscious state after sleeping; *also* **WAKED**

WOKS *n pl of* **WOK** pans with curved bases used for stir-frying, steaming and braising food

WOLD *n pl* -S an elevated treeless tract of land; *also* **WALD**

WOLF *n pl* **WOLVES** a predatory carnivorous canine mammal

WOMB *n pl* -S the uterus

WONE *v* [obs] to dwell

WONG *n* [obs] a field

WONK *n pl* -S an expert in matters of policy, especially government, economy or diplomacy

WONT *v* -ED, -ING, -S [obs] to have the habit of doing something

WOOD *n pl* -S the hard substance under the bark of a tree

WOOF *n pl* -S the sound of a barking dog

WOOL *n* a fabric made from the hair of sheep

353

WOOS *v pr t of* **WOO** solicits in love; courts

WORD *n pl* **-S** a meaningful unit of sounds or written letters used to communicate a thought or idea

WORE *v p t of* **WEAR** had something on the body as covering, adornment or protection; *also* **WORN**

WORK *v* **-ED, -ING, -S** to function or operate

WORM *v* **-ED, -ING, -S** to move slowly or carefully

WORN *v p t of* **WEAR** had something on the body as covering, adornment or protection; *also* **WORE**

WORT *n pl* **-S** an infusion of malt that is fermented to make beer

WOST *v pr t of* **WIT** [obs] knows; *also* **WITS, WEETS, WOT**

WOUL *v* [obs] to cry like a cat; to squall; to wail; *also* **WAUL, WAWL**

WOVE *v p t of* **WEAVE** formed, as cloth, by interlacing threads; *also* **WEAVED**

WOWE *v* [obs] to woo

WOWF *adj* [obs] disordered or unsettled in intellect; deranged

WOWS *v pr t of* **WOW** impresses or delights somebody greatly

WRAP *v* **-PED** or **WRAPT, -PING, -S** to enclose in paper and fasten

WRAW *adj* [obs] angry; vexed; wrathful

WRAY *v* **-ED, -ING, -S** [obs] to reveal; to disclose

WREN *n pl* **-S** a small singing bird

WRIT *n pl* **-S** a written court order demanding that the addressee cease the action described in the order

WUSS *n pl* **-ES** or **-IES** informal for a person who is physically weak and ineffectual

WYES *n pl of* **WYE** more than one of the letter "Y"

WYND *n pl* **-S** SCOT. a narrow lane or alley

WYNN *n pl* **-S** the runic alphabet equivalent to the modern "W"; *also* **WEN, WYN**

WYNS *n pl of* **WYN** the runic alphabet equivalent to modern "Ws"; *also* **WENS, WYNNS**

WYTE *v* **-D, WYTING** SCOT. to reproach; to blame; to censure; *also* **WITE**

FIVE LETTERS

WACKE *n* a soft, earthy, dark-colored clay created by the decomposition of volcanic rock

WACKO *n pl* **-S** an eccentric person

WACKY *adj* **WACKIER, WACKIEST** entertainingly silly; *also* **WHACKY**

WADDY *n pl* **WADDIES** AUS. a stick; a wooden weapon; *also* **WADDIE**

WADED *v p t of* **WADE** walked through water

WADER *n pl* **-S** one who walks through water

WADES *v pr t of* **WADE** walks through water

WADIS *n pl of* **WADI** oases, especially in North Africa; *also* **WADIES**

WAFER *n pl* **-S** a thin crisp biscuit

WAFFS *v pr t of* **WAFF** waves or flutters

WAFTS *v pr t of* **WAFT** passes easily or gently through air

WAGED *v p t of* **WAGE** engaged in, as a war

WAGER *v* **-ED, -ING, -S** to take risk on an uncertain event

WAGES *v pr t of* **WAGE** engages in, as a war

WAGON *n pl* **-S** a child's four-wheeled cart with a long handle

WAHOO *n pl* **-S** a large tropical fish of the mackerel family that weighs up to 120 pounds

WAIFS *n pl of* **WAIF** wanderers; castaways

WAILS *v pr t of* **WAIL** expresses sorrow audibly; weeps

WAINS *n pl of* **WAIN** wagons or carts

WAIST *n pl* **-S** the typically narrowed part of the body between the ribs and hips

WAITS *v pr t of* **WAIT** stays or rests in expectation

WAIVE *v* **-D, WAIVING, -S** to give up; to decline; or reject

WAKED *v p t of* **WAKE** came back to a conscious state after sleeping; *also* **WOKE**

WAKEN *v* **-ED, -ING, -S** to become conscious, active or aware after sleeping

WAKER *n* a person who rouses another from sleep

WAKES *v pr t of* **WAKE** comes back to a conscious state after sleeping

WALED *v p t of* **WALE** made a streak or ridge on the skin, especially by the stroke of a whip

WALER *n pl* **-S** any Australian saddle horse of mixed ancestry

WALES *v pr t of* **WALE** makes a streak or ridge on the skin, especially by the stroke of a whip

WALKS *v pr t of* **WALK** moves along on foot; advances by steps

WALLA *n* a person identified by a particular occupation or activity; *also* **WALLAH**

WALLS *v pr t of* **WALL** fortifies or surrounds somebody or something with an upright structure that acts as a boundary

WALLY *adj* SCOT. fine; splendid

WALTZ *v* **-ED, -ING, -ES** to perform a ballroom dance in triple time; *also* **VALSE**

WAMES *n pl of* **WAME** SCOT. bellies or abdomens

WAMUS *n pl* **-ES** a heavy outer jacket; *also* **WAMMUS, WAMPUS**

WANDS *n pl of* **WAND** sticks or batons used by magicians

WANED *v p t of* **WANE** declined; failed; sank

WANES *v pr t of* **WANE** declines; fails; sinks

WANEY *adj* **WANIER, WANIEST** waning; decreasing; declining; *also* **WANY**

WANGO *n* a boomerang

WANGS *n pl of* **WANG** [obs] the jaws, jawbones or cheek bones

WANLY *adv* in a weak or pale manner

WANTS *v pr t of* **WANT** feels a need or desire for something

WANTY *n pl* **WANTIES** [obs] a leather tie; a short wagon rope

WARDS *v pr t of* **WARD** watches over

WARED *v p t of* **WARE** made aware; warned

WARES *v pr t of* **WARE** makes aware; warns

WARMS *v pr t of* **WARM** makes warm

WARNS *v pr t of* **WARN** makes aware

WARPS *v pr t of* **WARP** turns or twists out of shape

WARTS *n pl of* **WART** firm abnormal elevated blemishes on the skin

WARTY *adj* **WARTIER, WARTIEST** having firm abnormal blemishes on the skin

WASHY *adj* **WASHIER, WASHIEST** watery or weak, as diluted coffee or tea

WASPS *n pl of* **WASP** stinging insects

WASPY *adj* **WASPIER, WASPIEST** resembling a wasp, a stinging insect

WASTE *v* **-D, WASTING, -S** to use up or spend carelessly

WATAP *n pl* **-S** a stringy thread made from conifer roots formerly used by some Native Americans for sewing and weaving; *also* **WATAPE**

WATCH *v* **-ED, -ING, -ES** to be attentive or vigilant

WATER *v* **-ED, -ING, -S** to wet or supply with water; to moisten

WATTS *n pl of* **WATT** units of power or activity

WAULS *v pr t of* **WAUL** cries like a cat; squalls; wails; *also* **WAWLS**

WAVED *v p t of* **WAVE** moved one's hand to and fro in greeting or as a signal

WAVER *v* **-ED, -ING, -S** to vacillate irresolutely between choices

WAVES *v pr t of* **WAVE** moves one's hand to and fro in greeting or as a signal

WAVEY *n pl* **-S** a wild North American goose, as the snow goose or blue goose

WAWLS *v pr t of* **WAWL** cries like a cat; squalls; wails; *also* **WAULS**

WAXED *v p t of* **WAX** polished

WAXEN *adj* having a smooth, pale, translucent surface like that of wax, a soft solid substance that melts easily

WAXER *n pl* **-S** one who polishes with or applies wax, a soft solid substance that melts easily

WAXES *v pr t of* **WAX** polishes

WEALD *n pl* **-S** BRIT. a woodland; forest

WEALS *n pl of* **WEAL** reddened areas on the skin from being hit with something; *also* **WHEALS**

WEANS *v pr t of* **WEAN** gradually deprives somebody of something they like or that is a habit

WEARS *v pr t of* **WEAR** has something on the body as covering, adornment or protection

WEARY *adj* **WEARIER, WEARIEST** tired, exhausted

WEAVE *v* **-D** or **WOVE, WOVEN** or **-D, WEAVING, -S** to form, as cloth, by interlacing threads

WEBBY *adj* **WEBBIER, WEBBIEST** having open interstices or resembling a web

WEBER *n pl* **-S** a unit of magnetic flux

WEDEL *v* **-ED, -LING, -S** to ski on snow with short quick parallel turns

WEDGE *v* **-D, WEDGING, -S** to force into a narrow space

WEDGY *adj* **WEDGIER, WEDGIEST** resembling a wedge in shape, having a thick end that tapers to a thin edge

WEEDS *v pr t of* **WEED** pulls plants that crowd out cultivated plants

WEEDY *adj* **WEEDIER, WEEDIEST** full of or consisting of plants that crowd out cultivated plants

WEEKS *n pl of* **WEEK** two or more periods of seven days

WEELY *n a* kind of trap or snare for fish made of twigs

WEENS *v pr t of* **WEEN** thinks; imagines; fancies; supposes

WEENY *adj* **WEENIER, WEENIEST** exceptionally small; tiny

WEEPS *v pr t of* **WEEP** expresses sorrow, grief or anguish

WEEPY *adj* **WEEPIER, WEEPIEST** inclined to weep; tearful

WEEST *adj* smallest; littlest

WEETS *v pr t of* **WEET** [obs] knows; *also* **WITS, WOST, WOT**

WEIGH *v* **-ED, -ING, -S** to determine how heavy something is

WEIRD *adj* **-ER, -EST** of a strikingly odd or unusual character; strange

WEIRS *n pl of* **WEIR** fences or walls built across a stream to catch or retain fish; *also* **WIERS**

WEKAS *n pl of* **WEKA** flightless birds native to New Zealand

WELCH *v* **-ED, -ING, -ES** to avoid payment; *also* **WELSH**

WELDS *v pr t of* **WELD** joins together by heating

WELKS *v pr t of* **WELK** [obs] causes to wither; wilts; *also* **WHELKS**

WELLS *n pl of* **WELL** comes up, as in water from the earth or tears in one's eyes

WELLY *n pl* **WELLIES** BRIT. a loose waterproof rubber boot coming to or above the knee; *also* **WELLIE**

WELSH *v* **-ED, -ING, -ES** to avoid payment; *also* **WELCH**

WELTS *v pr t of* **WELT** reinforces or trims a seam with a tape or covered cord

WENCH *n pl* **-ES** [obs] a young woman; also a female servant

WENDS *v pr t of* **WEND** proceeds

WENNY *adj* **WENNIER, WENNIEST** having the nature of a wen, a common cyst of the skin

WERST *n pl* **-S** a Russian unit of linear measure equivalent to about two thirds of a mile; *also* **VERST**

WESTY *adj* dizzy; giddy

WETLY *adv* in a wet state or condition; moistly

WHACK *v* **-ED, -ING, -S** to strike sharply; to beat

WHALE *v* **-D, WHALING, -S** to hunt for whales

WHALL *n* a light color of the iris in horses; a wall-eye; *also* **WHAUL**

WHAME *n* a breeze or burrel-fly; a fly of the genus *Tabanus*

WHAMS *v pr t of* **WHAM** hits or crashes into something with a forceful, resounding blow

WHANG *v* **-ED, -ING, -S** to propel or strike with force

WHAPS *v pr t of* **WHAP** strikes forcibly; *also* **WAPS, WHOPS**

WHARF *v* **-ED, -ING, -S** to take to or store on a wharf, a platform for docking ships

WHARP *n/pl* a kind of fine sand from the banks of the Trent, used as a polishing powder

WHAUL *n* a light color of the iris in horses; a wall-eye; *also* **WHALL**

WHEAL *n pl* **-S** reddened area on the skin from being hit with something; *also* **WEAL**

WHEAT *n* a cereal grass and its grains

WHEEL *v* **-ED, -ING, -S** to change direction as if revolving on a pivot

WHEEN *n pl* **-S** BRIT. a quantity; a goodly number

WHELK *v* **-ED, -ING, -S** [obs] to cause to wither; to wilt; *also* **WELK**

WHELM *v* **-ED, -ING, -S** to cover with water; submerge

WHELP *v* **-ED, -ING, -S** to give birth to young, especially baby carnivores

WHERE *adv* at, in, or to what place

WHETS *v pr t of* **WHET** makes a feeling, sense or desire more keen or intense

WHICH *pron* specifies what particular one or ones

WHIFF *v* **-ED, -ING, -S** to perceive by inhaling through the nose

WHILE *n* a period of time especially when short and marked by the occurrence of an action or a condition

WHILK *n* an Australian marine mollusk

WHIMS *n pl of* **WHIM** sudden turns or starts of the mind; temporary eccentricities

WHINE *v* **-D, WHINING, -S** to utter a high-pitched plaintive or distressed cry

WHINS *n pl of* **WHIN** very spiny and dense evergreen shrubs with fragrant golden-yellow flowers

WHINY *adj* **WHINIER, WHINIEST** tending to complain in a feeble or petulant way; *also* **WHINEY**

WHIPS *v pr t of* **WHIP** strikes with a lash, a cord, a rod

WHIPT *v p t of* **WHIP** struck with a lash, a cord, a rod; *also* **WHIPPED**

WHIRL *v* **-ED, -ING, -S** to turn round rapidly; to cause to rotate with velocity

WHIRR *v* **-ED, -ING** to make a continuous soft buzzing or whizzing noise; *also* **WHIR, WHUR**

WHIRS *v pr t of* **WHIR** to make a continuous soft buzzing or whizzing noise; *also* **WHIRRS, WHURS**

WHISH *v* **-ED, -ING, -S** to move with a hissing sound

WHISK *v* **-ED, -ING, -S** to make a sudden agile movement

WHIST *n* a card game played between two pairs of players in which each side tries to win more tricks than the other

WHITE *adj* **-R, -ST** of the color of pure snow

WHIZZ *v* **-ED, -ING, -ES** to make a humming, hissing or buzzing noise; *also* **WHIZ**

WHOLE *n* a complete amount or sum

WHOMP *v* **-ED, -ING, -S** to strike with a sharp noise or thump

WHOOF *v* **-ED, -ING, -S** to make a deep gruff sound

WHOOP *n pl* **-S** a loud cry of exultation or excitement

WHOOT *v* [obs] to hoot

WHOPS *v pr t of* **WHOP** strikes forcibly; *also* **WAPS, WHAPS**

WHORL *n pl* **-S** something spiral shaped

WHOSE *pron* the possessive case of who or which

WHOSO *pron* whoever; whatever person

WHUMP *v* **-ED, -ING, -S** to bang, to thump; to thud

WHUPS *v pr t of* **WHUP** informal for beats; thrashes

WHURS *v pr t of* **WHUR** make a continuous soft buzzing or whizzing noise; *also* **WHIRS, WHIRRS**

WICKS *v pr t of* **WICK** takes or transfers liquid by capillary action

WIDDY *n pl* **WIDDIES** SCOT. a band or rope made of twigs; *also* **WIDDIE**

WIDEN *v* **-ED, -ING, -S** to enlarge; to spread; to extend

WIDER *adj* having a greater extent; more extended; more spacious; more broad

WIDOW *n pl* **-S** a woman who has lost her husband by death

WIDTH *n pl* **-S** the extent of something from side to side

WIELD *v* **-ED, -ING, -S** to govern; to rule; to handle effectively

WIERS *n pl of* **WEIR** fences or walls built across a stream to catch or retain fish; *also* **WEIRS**

WIERY *adj* [obs] wet; moist; marshy

WIGAN *n* a stiff plain-weave cotton fabric used for interlining

WIGGY *adj* **WIGGIER, WIGGIEST** wild, exciting, crazy

WIGHT *n pl* **-S** [obs] a supernatural being

WILCO *interj* used especially in radio communications to indicate agreement or compliance

WILED *v p t of* **WILE** enticed or lured, especially by trickery

WILES *v pr t of* **WILE** entices or lures, especially by trickery

WILLS *v pr t of* **WILL** decrees, dictates or orders

WILNE *v* [obs] to wish; to desire

WILTS *v pr t of* **WILT** begins to wither; loses freshness and becomes flaccid

WILWE *n* [obs] a willow tree

WIMPS *n pl of* **WIMP** people who are regarded as weak or ineffectual

WIMPY *adj* **WIMPIER, WIMPIEST** pertaining to a weak, cowardly person

WINCE *v* **-D, WINCING, -S** to shrink; to flinch

WINCH *v* -ED, -ING, -ES to pull or lift up with or as if with a winch, a hauling or lifting device

WINDS *v pr t of* **WIND** entwists; enfolds; encircles

WINDY *adj* WINDIER, WINDIEST abounding in or exposed to the wind

WINED *v p t of* **WINE** had wine, an alcoholic beverage

WINES *n pl of* **WINE** alcoholic drinks made by fermenting the juice of grapes

WINEY *adj* WINIER, WINIEST having the taste or qualities of wine; *also* **WINY**

WINGS *v pr t of* **WING** travels swiftly or sends something with great speed

WINGY *adj* WINGIER, WINGIEST having wings; rapid; swift

WINKS *v pr t of* **WINK** closes one eye for a very brief moment

WINZE *n pl* -S a small mine shaft sunk from one level to another

WIPED *v p t of* **WIPE** rubbed with something, as for cleaning

WIPER *n pl* -S someone or something which rubs for cleaning

WIPES *v pr t of* **WIPE** rubs with something, as for cleaning

WIRED *v p t of* **WIRE** fastened with a thread or slender rod of metal

WIRER *n pl* -S a person who installs wiring, a network of conductors that carry electricity

WIRES *v pr t of* **WIRE** fastens with a thread or slender rod of metal

WIRRA *interj* IRISH used to express lament, grief or concern

WISED *v p t of* **WISE** became informed or aware of

WISER *adj* having more knowledge; more knowing; more enlightenment

WISES *v pr t of* **WISE** becomes informed or aware of

WISLY *adv* [obs] certainly

WISPS *v pr t of* **WISP** moves like something delicate or faint

WISPY *adj* WISPIER, WISPIEST resembling something delicate or faint

WISTS *v pr t of* **WIST** [obs] knows; thinks or supposes

WITCH *v* -ED, -ING, -ES to affect something using witchcraft

WITED *v p t of* **WITE** reproached; blamed; censured; *also* **WYTED**

WITES *v pr t of* **WITE** reproaches; blames; censures; *also* **WYTES**

WITHE *v* -ED, -ING, -S bind something with strong flexible twigs

WITHY *adj* composed of withes, strong flexible twigs

WITTS *n/pl* tin ore freed from earthy matter by stamping

WITTY *adj* WITTIER, WITTIEST using words in an apt, clever and amusing way

WIVED *v p t of* **WIVE** married a woman

WIVER *n pl* -S [obs] mythical two-legged winged dragon-like creature; *also* **WIVERN; WYVERN**

WIVES *n pl of* **WIFE** married women

WIZEN *v* -ED, -ING, -S to wither; to dry; to shrivel

WOADS *n pl of* **WOAD** yellow-flowered plants whose leaves were formerly used to make blue dye

WODGE *n pl* -S BRIT. a bulky mass or chunk; a lump; a wad

WOFUL *adj* sad; mournful; *also* **WOEFUL**

WOKEN *v p part of* **WAKE** to have come back to a conscious state after sleeping

WOLDS *n pl of* **WOLD** elevated treeless tracts of land

WOLFS *v pr t of* **WOLF** devours voraciously

WOMAN *n pl* **WOMEN** or **WOMYN** an adult female person

359

WOMBS *n pl of* **WOMB** uteruses

WOMBY *adj* [obs] hollow; capacious

WOMEN *n pl of* **WOMAN** adult female persons; *also* **WOMYN**

WOMYN *n pl of* **WOMAN** adult female persons; *also* **WOMEN**

WONKS *n pl of* **WONK** experts in matters of policy, especially government, economy or diplomacy

WONKY *adj* **WONKIER, WONKIEST** knowledgeable about policy details

WONTS *v pr t of* **WONT** has the habit of doing something

WOODS *n pl of* **WOOD** the hard substance under the bark of trees

WOODY *adj* **WOODIER, WOODIEST** like or consisting of wood; ligneous

WOOED *v p t of* **WOO** solicited in love; courted

WOOER *n pl -S* one who courts another

WOOFS *n pl of* **WOOFS** the sounds of a barking dog

WOOLD *v -ED, -ING* to wind, or wrap, especially around a mast or yard made of two or more pieces

WOOLY *adj* **WOOLIER, WOOLIEST** made of wool, a fabric made from the hair of sheep; *also* **WOOLLY**

WOOPS *interj* used to express apology or mild surprise; *also* **WHOOPS**

WOOSH *v -ED, -ING, -S* to make a hissing or rushing sound; *also* **WHOOSH**

WOOSY *adj* [obs] oozy; wet

WOOTZ *n/pl* steel imported from the East Indies for making edge tools

WOOZY *adj* **WOOZIER, WOOZIEST** dazed or confused

WORDS *n pl of* **WORD** meaningful units of sounds or written letters used to communicate a thought or idea

WORDY *adj* **WORDIER, WORDIEST** containing many words; full of words

WORKS *v pr t of* **WORK** functions or operates

WORLD *n pl -S* the earth and the surrounding heavens

WORMS *v pr t of* **WORM** moves slowly or carefully

WORMY *adj* **WORMIER, WORMIEST** abounding or infected with worms, invertebrates having long, flexible bodies

WORRY *v* **WORRIED, -ING, WORRIES** to be concerned, anxious, troubled or uneasy

WORSE *adj* less good than something else

WORST *adj* the least good, most unpleasant

WORTH *adj* having monetary or material value

WORTS *n pl of* **WORT** infusions of malt that are fermented to make beer

WOULD *aux v of* **WILL** used to express a polite request

WOUND *v -ED, -ING, -S* to inflict an injury on

WOVEN *v p part of* **WEAVE** formed, as cloth, by interlacing threads; *also* **WEAVED**

WOWED *v p t of* **WOW** impressed or delighted somebody greatly

WRACK *v -ED, -ING, -S* to cause the ruin or destruction of; *also* **WRECK**

WRANG *adj* SCOT. incorrect, wrong

WRAPS *v pr t of* **WRAP** encloses in paper and fastens

WRAPT *v p t of* **WRAP** enclosed in paper and fastened; *also* **WRAPPED**

WRATH *n* violent anger; indignation; rage; fury

RAWL *v* [obs] to cry, as a cat

RAWS *v pr t of* **WRAW** [obs] reveals; discloses

REAK *v* **-ED, -ING, -S** to cause to happen

RECK *v* **-ED, -ING, -S** to cause the ruin or destruction of; *also* **WRACK**

RENS *n pl of* **WREN** small singing birds

REST *v* **-ED, -ING** to gain control or power

RICK *v* **-ED** BRIT. to twist suddenly so as to sprain

RIED *v p t of* **WRY** contorted, writhed, twisted

RIER *adj* more contorted; *also* **WRYER**

RIES *v pr t of* **WRY** contorts, writhes, twists

RING *v* **WRUNG, -ING, -S** to twist and compress

RIST *n pl* **-S** the joint between the hand and the arm

RITE *v* **WROTE, WRITTEN, WRITING, -S** to form characters, letters or figures, as representative of sounds or ideas

RITS *n pl of* **WRIT** written court orders demanding that the addressee cease the action described in the order

RONG *v* **-ED, -ING, -S** to treat unjustly

ROTE *v p t of* **WRITE** formed characters, letters or figures, as representative of sounds or ideas

ROTH *adj* full of wrath; incensed

RUNG *v p t of* **WRING** twisted and compressed

RYER *adj* more contorted; *also* **WRIER**

RYLY *adv* in a contorted manner

RURST *n pl* **-S** German or Austrian sausage

RUSHU *n/pl* Chinese martial arts considered collectively

WYNDS *n pl of* **WYND** SCOT. narrow lanes or alleys

WYNNS *n pl of* **WYNN** the runic alphabet equivalent to modern "Ws"; *also* **WENS, WYNS**

WYTED *v p t of* **WYTE** reproached; blamed; censured; *also* **WITED**

WYTES *v pr t of* **WYTE** reproaches; blames; censures; *also* **WITES**

X

XI *n pl* **-S** the 14th letter of the Greek alphabet

XU *n pl* **-S** a minor unit of currency in Vietnam

THREE LETTERS

XIS *pl of* **XI** more than one of the 14th letter of the Greek alphabet

XUS *n pl of* **XU** more than one of a minor unit of currency in Vietnam

FOUR LETTERS

XEME *n* an Arctic fork-tailed gull

XYST *n* a long and open portico for athletic exercises; *also* **XYSTUM, XYSTUS**

FIVE LETTERS

XEBEC *n pl* **-S** a small three-masted vessel; *also* **ZEBEC**

XENIA *n* the direct effect of pollen from one strain of plant upon the endosperm of another strain, resulting in hybrid characteristics

XENON *n* a colorless odorless highly unreactive gaseous element

XENYL *n* the radical characteristic of a compound

XERES *n/pl* [obs] a dry to sweet amber wine; *also* **SHERRY**

XERIC *adj* requiring only a small amount of moisture

XERIF *n* a shereef, a descendant of Muhammad

XEROX *v* **-ED, -ING, -ES** common term meaning to produce a copy of a document on a xerographic copier

XYLAN *n* a substance found in cell walls of plants

XYLEM *n* the supporting and water-conducting tissue of vascular plants

XYLIC *adj* pertaining to, derived from, or related to xylene, a volatile liquid hydrocarbon

XYLOL *n pl* **-S** a volatile liquid hydrocarbon used in solvents, aviation fuels, resins and dyes; *also* **XYLENE**

XYLYL *n* any one of several univalent radicals derived from the three xylenes

YA *pron* you

YE *pron* [obs] BRIT. used as the plural of thou

YI *n* faithful performance of one's specified duties to society in Chinese ethical philosophy

YO *interj* used as an exclamation to get someone's attention, express excitement, greet someone, etc.

YU *n* a precious jade

THREE LETTERS

YAH *interj* used as an exclamation of disgust

YAK *v* **-KED, -KING, -S** to talk persistently; *also* **YACK**

YAM *n pl* **-S** a plant having an edible tuberous root

YAP *v* **-PED, -PING, -S** to bark, to yelp

YAR *adj* **-ER, -EST** quick, agile, lively; *also* **YARE**

YAW *v* **-ED, -ING, -S** to deviate erratically from a set course

YAY *interj* an exclamation of pleasure, approval, elation or victory

YBE *v* [obs] been

YDO *v* [obs] done

YEA *n pl* **-S** an affirmation; an affirmative reply or vote

YEH *adv* informal for yes; *also* **YEAH**

YEN *v* **-NED, -NING, -S** to yearn, to desire

YEP *adv* informal for yes; *also* **YUP**

YER *prep* [obs] before

YES *v* **-SED, -SING, -SES** or **-ES,** to give an affirmative reply

YET *adv* at this time

YEW *n pl* **-S** an evergreen tree that has flat dark green needles and scarlet fruits

YEX *v* [obs] to hiccup; *also* **YOX, YUX**

YGO *v* [obs] gone

YIN *n* the passive female principle in Chinese philosophy

YIP *v* **-PED, -PING, -S** to give a high-pitched bark

YIS *adv* [obs] yes

YIT *adv* [obs] dialectal form of yet

YOB *n pl* **-S** BRIT. informal for a rowdy boy, hooligan; *also* **YOBBO, YOBBOE**

YOD *n pl* **-S** the tenth letter of the Hebrew alphabet; *also* **YODH**

YOK *v* **-KED, -KING, -S** informal for to laugh or joke boisterously; *also* **YOCK**

YOM *n* day, a Hebrew word used with various Jewish feast days

YON *adv* at a distance, but within view; *also* **YONDER**

YOT *v* [obs] to unite closely

YOU *n pl* **-S** something or someone closely identified with or resembling the person addressed

YOX *v* [obs] to hiccup; *also* **YEX, YUX**

YUK *v* **-KED, -KING, -S** informal for to laugh or joke; *also* **YUCK**

YUM *interj* excellent; delicious

YUP *adv* informal for yes; *also* **YEP**

YUX *v* [obs] to hiccup; *also* **YEX, YOX**

FOUR LETTERS

YACK *v* **-ED, -ING, -S** to talk persistently; *also* **YAK**

YAFF *v* **-ED, -ING, -S** SCOT. to bark, yelp

YAGI *n pl* **-S** a directional radio and television antenna

YAKS *v pr t of* **YAK** talks persistently; *also* **YACKS**

YALD *adj* SCOT. barren, sterile; *also* **YELD**

YAMS *n pl of* **YAM** plants having edible tuberous roots

YANG *n* the active, male cosmic principle in Chinese dualistic philosophy

YANK *v* **-ED, -ING, -S** to pull with a quick strong movement

YAPS *v pr t of* **YAP** barks, yelps

YARD *v* **-ED, -ING, -S** to enclose, collect or put into a yard, an enclosed tract of ground

YARE *adj* **-R, -ST** quick, agile, lively; *also* **YAR**

YARK *v* [obs] to make ready

YARN *v* **-ED, -ING, -S** informal for to tell a story or a long tale

YARR *v* [obs] to growl or snarl as a dog

YAUD *n* SCOT. an old mare; *also* **YAWD**

YAUP *v* **-ED, -ING, -S** to talk or complain loudly, coarsely and sometimes meaninglessly; *also* **YAWP, YAULP**

YAWD *n* SCOT. an old mare; *also* **YAUD**

YAWL *n pl* **-S** a small boat kept on a ship

YAWN *v* **-ED, -ING, -S** to open the mouth wide and take a long breath, usually involuntarily, because of tiredness or boredom

YAWP *v* **-ED, -ING, -S** to talk or complain loudly, coarsely, and sometimes meaninglessly; *also* **YAUP, YAULP**

YAWS *v pr t of* **YAW** deviates erratically from a set course

YEAH *adv* informal for yes; *also* **YEH**

YEAN *v* **-ED, -ING, -S** to bear young, used of a goat or sheep

YEAR *n pl* **-S** the time taken for the earth to make one revolution around the sun, about 365 days

YEAS *n pl of* **YEA** affirmations; affirmative replies or votes

YECH *interj* an informal expression for contempt or disgust; *also* **YUCH, YECCH, YUCCH**

YEGG *n pl* **-S** informal for a thief, especially a burglar or safecracker

YELD *adj* SCOT. barren, sterile; *also* **YALD**

YELK *n pl* **-S** the yellow part of an egg; *also* **YOLK**

YELL *v* **-ED, -ING, -S** to cry or shout out loudly

YELP *v* **-ED, -ING, -S** to utter a sharp, shrill cry, usually from pain

YENS *v pr t of* **YEN** yearns, desires

YERK *v* **-ED, -ING, -S** to strike or whip

YERN *v* **-ED, -ING, -S** [obs] to long for, to have a strong desire for; *also* **YEARN**

YETI *n pl* **-S** the abominable snowman, a big creature resembling a human covered in hair

YETT *n pl* **-S** SCOT. a gate

YEUK *v* **-ED, -ING, -S** SCOT. to itch; *also* **YUKE**

YEWS *n pl of* **YEW** evergreen trees that have flat dark green needles and scarlet fruits

YIFT *n pl* **-ES** [obs] gift

YILL *n* SCOT. ale

YIPE *interj* used to express fear, or surprise, or dismay; *also* **YIPES**

YIPS *v pr t of* **YIP** gives a high-pitched bark

YIRD *n* SCOT. earth

YIRR *v* -ED, -ING, -S SCOT. to snarl

YLEM *n pl* -S a form of matter hypothesized by proponents of the big bang theory to have existed before the formation of the chemical elements

YOBS *n pl of* **YOB** BRIT. informal for rowdy boys, hooligans; *also* **YOBBOS, YOBBOES**

YOCK *v* -ED, -ING, -S informal for to laugh or joke boisterously; *also* **YOK**

YODH *n pl* -S the tenth letter of the Hebrew alphabet; *also* **YOD**

YODS *n pl of* **YOD** more than one of the tenth letter of the Hebrew alphabet; *also* **YODHS**

YOGA *n* a system of exercises practiced as part of the Hindu discipline

YOGH *n pl* -S a letter used in the writing of Middle English representing modern day "gh" or "y"

YOGI *n pl* -S someone who has mastered yoga; *also* **YOGIN**

YOKE *v* -D, YOKING, -S to fit animals with a yoke, a wooden frame for harnessing two draft animals to whatever they have to pull

YOKS *v pr t of* **YOK** informal for laughs or jokes boisterously; *also* **YOCKS**

YOLK *n pl* -S the yellow part of an egg; *also* **YELK**

YOLL *v* [obs] to yell

YOND *adv* [obs] yonder, over there

YONI *n pl* -S the female principle in Hinduism

YORE *n* in time long past, in old time, long since

YOTE *v* [obs] to pour water on; to soak in, or mix with, water

YOUL *v* [obs] to yell, to yowl

YOUR *adj* belonging to the person spoken to

YOUS *n pl of* **YOU** something or someone closely identified with or resembling the people addressed

YOWE *n pl* -S SCOT. a female sheep; *also* **EWE**

YOWL *v* -ED, -ING, -S to utter a loud, long and mournful cry

YREN *n* [obs] iron

YUAN *n pl* **YUAN** a Mandarin Chinese monetary unit; *also* **KWAI**

YUCA *n pl* -S any plant belonging to the agave family native to warmer regions of America; *also* **YUCCA**

YUCH *interj* an informal expression for contempt or disgust; *also* **YECH, YECCH, YUCCH**

YUCK *v* -ED, -ING, -S informal for to laugh or joke; *also* **YUK**

YUGA *n pl* -S any of the four stages in Hindu theology

YUKE *v* -ED, -ING, -S SCOT. to itch; *also* **YEUK**

YUKS *v pr t of* **YUK** informal for laughs or jokes; *also* **YUCKS**

YULE *n pl* -S Christmas or Christmastime

YURT *n pl* -S a circular, domed, portable tent used by nomads in Mongolia, Siberia and Turkey

YUTZ *n pl* -ES a person variously regarded as ineffectual, foolish, disagreeable, contemptible

YVEL *adj* [obs] evil

YWAR *adj* [obs] aware

YWIS *adv* [obs] certainly, most likely, truly, probably; *also* **IWIS**

FIVE LETTERS

YABBY *n pl* -IES an Australian crayfish; *also* **YABBIE**

YACCA *n* a West Indian timber tree

YACHT *v* -ED, -ING, -S to sail in a yacht, an elegantly furnished vessel

YACKS *v pr t of* **YACK** talks persistently; *also* **YAKS**

YAFFS *v pr t of* **YAFF** SCOT. barks, yelps

YAGER *n* a hunter; *also* **JAEGER, JAGER**

YAGIS *n pl of* **YAGI** directional radio and television antennas

YAHOO *n pl* -S a boorish or crass person

YALAH *n* the oil of the mahwa tree

YAMEN *n pl* **-S** residence of an official in the Chinese Empire

YAMMA *n pl* **-S** variant of llama, a woolly-haired S. Am. ruminant

YANKS *v pr t of* **YANK** pulls with a quick strong movement

YAPOK *n pl* **-S** an aquatic opossum

YAPON *n pl* **-S** a holly shrub or small tree; *also* **YUPON, YAUPON**

YARDS *v pr t of* **YARD** encloses, collects or puts into a yard, an enclosed tract of ground

YARER *adj* more quick, agile, lively

YARNS *v pr t of* **YARN** informal for tells a story or a long tale

YAULD *adj* SCOT. active, nimble

YAULP *v* **-ED, -ING, -S** to talk or complain loudly, coarsely and sometimes meaninglessly; *also* **YAUP, YAWP**

YAUPS *v pr t of* **YAUP** talks or complains loudly, coarsely and sometimes meaninglessly; *also* **YAWPS, YAULPS**

YAWED *v p t of* **YAW** deviated erratically from a set course

YAWEY *adj* pertaining to yaws, an infectious disease

YAWLS *n pl of* **YAWL** small boats kept on a ship

YAWNS *v pr t of* **YAWN** opens the mouth wide and takes a long breath, usually involuntarily, because of tiredness or boredom

YAWPS *v pr t of* **YAWP** talks or complains loudly, coarsely and sometimes meaninglessly; *also* **YAUPS, YAULPS**

YCLAD *v* [obs] to adorn or cover with clothing

YDRAD *v* [obs] dreaded

YEANS *v pr t of* **YEAN** bears young, used of a goat or sheep

YEARN *v* **-ED, -ING, -S** to long for, to have a strong desire for; *also* **YERN**

YEARS *n pl of* **YEAR** the time taken for the earth to make more than one revolution around the sun, more than 365 days

YEAST *v* **-ED, -ING, -S** to ferment

YECCH *interj* an informal expression for contempt or disgust; *also* **YECH, YUCH, YUCCH**

YECHY *adj* **YECHIER, YECHIEST** informal for yucky

YEGGS *n pl of* **YEGG** informal for thieves, especially burglars or safecrackers

YELKS *n pl of* **YELK** the yellow parts of eggs; *also* **YOLKS**

YELLS *v pr t of* **YELL** cries or shouts out loudly

YELPS *v pr t of* **YELP** utters sharp, shrill cries, usually from pain

YENTA *n pl* **-S** one that meddles, a blabbermouth, a gossipy woman; *also* **YENTE**

YENTE *n pl* **-S** one that meddles, a blabbermouth, a gossipy woman; *also* **YENTA**

YERBA *n pl* **-S** a plant with pungent aromatic rootstock used for a beverage resembling tea

YERKS *v pr t of* **YERK** strikes or whips

YERNE *adv* [obs] eagerly, briskly, quickly

YERNS *v pr t of* **YERN** [obs] longs for, has a strong desire for; *also* **YEARNS**

YESES *v pr t of* **YES** gives an affirmative reply

YETIS *n pl of* **YETI** abominable snowmen, big creatures resembling humans covered in hair

YETTS *n pl of* **YETT** SCOT. gates

YEUKS *v pr t of* **YEUK** SCOT. itches; *also* **YUKES**

YEUKY *adj* SCOT. itchy

YEWEN *adj* made of yew, a poisonous evergreen tree

YEXED *v p t of* **YEX** hiccupped

YEXES *v pr t of* **YEX** hiccups

YIELD *v* **-ED, -ING, -S** to give up, surrender

YIKES *interj* used to express fear, shock, astonishment

YINCE *adv* SCOT. once

YIPES *interj* used to express fear, surprise or dismay; *also* **YIPE**

YIRRS *v pr t of* **YIRR** SCOT. snarls

YLEMS *n pl of* **YLEM** forms of matter hypothesized by proponents of the big bang theory to have existed before the formation of the chemical elements

YOBBO *n pl* **-S** or **-ES** BRIT. informal for a rowdy boy, hooligan; *also* **YOB, YOBBOE**

YOCKS *v pr t of* **YOCK** informal for laughs or jokes boisterously; *also* **YOKS**

YODEL *v* **-ED** or **-LED, -ING** or **-LING, -S** to sing so that the voice fluctuates rapidly between the normal chest; *also* **YODLE**

YODHS *n pl of* **YODH** more than one of the tenth letter of the Hebrew alphabet; *also* **YODS**

YODLE *v* **-D, YODLING, -S** to sing so that the voice fluctuates rapidly between the normal chest; *also* **YODEL**

YOGHS *n pl of* **YOGH** letters used in the writing of Middle English representing modern day "gh" or "y"

YOGIC *adj* pertaining to a system of exercises for attaining bodily or mental control and well-being

YOGIN *n pl* **-S** someone who has mastered yoga; *also* **YOGI**

YOGIS *n pl of* **YOGI** people who have mastered yoga; *also* **YOGINS**

YOJAN *n* a measure of distance varying from four to ten miles, but usually about five; *also* **YOJANA**

YOKED *v p t of* **YOKE** to have fitted animals with a yoke, a wooden frame for harnessing two draft animals to whatever they have to pull

YOKEL *n pl* **-S** an unsophisticated person

YOKES *v pr t of* **YOKE** fits animals with a yoke, a wooden frame for harnessing two draft animals to whatever they have to pull

YOLKS *n pl of* **YOLK** the yellow parts of eggs; *also* **YELKS**

YOLKY *adj* resembling yolk, the yellow part of an egg

YONIC *adv* the stylized representation of the female genitalia that in Hinduism is a sign of generative power

YONIS *n pl of* **YONI** female principles in Hinduism

YOUNG *adj* **-ER, -EST** being in the first part of growth or life

YOURN *pron* [obs] a form of the possessive case of you; *also* **YOURS**

YOURS *pron* a form of the possessive case of you; *also* **YOURN**

YOUSE *pron* you, usually used in addressing two or more people

YOUTH *n pl* **-S** young person

YOWES *n pl of* **YOWE** SCOT. female sheep; *also* **EWES**

YOWIE *n pl* **-S** an unidentified yeti-like animal said to exist in parts of Australia

YOWLS *v pr t of* **YOWL** utters loud, long, and mournful cries

YUCAS *n pl of* **YUCA** plants belonging to the agave family native to warmer regions of America; *also* **YUCCAS**

YUCCA *n pl* **-S** any plant belonging to the agave family native to warmer regions of America; *also* **YUCA**

YUCCH *interj* an informal expression for contempt or disgust; *also* **YECH, YUCH, YECCH**

YUCKS *v pr t of* **YUCK** informal for laughs or jokes; *also* **YUKS**

YUCKY *adj* **YUCKIER, YUCKIEST** messy or disgusting; *also* **YUKKY**

YUGAS *n pl of* **YUGA** more than one of the four stages in Hindu theology

YUKES *v pr t of* **YUKE** SCOT. itches; *also* **YEUKS**

YUKKY *adj* **YUKKIER, YUKKIEST** messy or disgusting; *also* **YUCKY**

YULAN *n pl* **-S** a deciduous Chinese tree

YULES *n pl of* **YULE** Christmases or Christmastimes

YUMMY *adj* **YUMMIER, YUMMIEST** delicious

YUPON *n pl* **-S** a holly shrub or small tree; *also* **YAPON, YAUPON**

YUPPY *n pl* **YUPPIES** informal for a young, well-educated city dweller who has a professional career and an affluent lifestyle; *also* **YUPPIE**

YURTS *n pl of* **YURT** circular, domed, portable tents used by nomads in Mongolia, Siberia and Turkey

ZA *n* informal for pizza

ZO *n* **-S** or **ZO** a cross between a cow and a yak; *also* **DZO, ZHO**

THREE LETTERS

ZAG *n pl* **-S** an angular shape characterized by sharp turns in alternating directions

ZAP *v* **-PED, -PING, -S** to strike suddenly and with force, to destroy

ZAX *n pl* **-ES** a tool for trimming and puncturing roofing slates

ZED *n pl* **-S** BRIT. the letter "Z"

ZEE *n pl* **-S** the letter "Z"

ZEK *n pl* **ZEKS** an inmate in a Soviet labor camp

ZEN *v* **-NED, -ING, -S** to meditate; to experience the feeling of calm

ZEP *n pl* **-S** regional term for a large sandwich made of a long crusty roll split lengthwise with meat and/or cheese; a submarine sandwich

ZHO *n pl* **ZHO** or **ZHOS** a cross between a cow and a yak; *also* **DZO, ZO**

ZIG *n pl* **-S** an angular shape characterized by sharp turns in alternating directions

ZIP *v* **-PED, -PING, -S** to open or close with a zipper, a fastener with interlocking teeth

ZIT *n pl* **-S** informal for a blemish on the skin; a pimple

ZOA *n pl of* **ZOON** animals which are developed from a fertilized egg; *also* **ZOONS**

ZOO *n pl* **-S** a facility where wild animals are housed for exhibition

ZOS *n pl of* **ZO** more than one of a cross between a cow and a yak; *also* **DZOS, ZHOS**

ZUZ *n pl* **ZUZIM** an ancient Hebrew silver coin

FOUR LETTERS

ZAGS *n pl of* **ZAG** angular shapes characterized by sharp turns in alternating directions

ZAIM *n pl* **-S** a Turkish chief who supports a mounted militia

ZAIN *n pl* **-S** a horse of a dark color, neither gray nor white, and having no spots

ZANY *adj* **ZANIER, ZANIEST** entertainingly strange or amusingly unusual

ZAPS *v pr t of* **ZAP** strikes suddenly and with force; destroys

ZARF *n pl* **-S** an ornamental metal holder for a hot cup of coffee, used in the Middle East

ZEAL *n* energetic enthusiasm; fervor, especially for a cause or idea

ZEBU *n pl* **-S** a domesticated ox having a humped back, long horns and a large dewlap

ZEDS *n pl of* **ZED** BRIT. more than one of the letter "Z"

ZEES *n pl of* **ZEE** more than one of the letter "Z"

ZEIN *n pl* **-S** a simple protein obtained from corn

ZEKS *n pl of* **ZEK** inmates in Soviet labor camps

ZENS *v pr t of* **ZEN** meditates; experiences the feeling of calm

ZEPS *n pl of* **ZEP** regional term for large sandwiches made of a long crusty roll split lengthwise with meat and/or cheese; submarine sandwiches

ZERK *n pl* **-S** a grease fitting

ZERO *n pl* **-S** or **-ES** the numerical symbol 0, representing the absence of any quantity or magnitude

ZEST *v* **-ED, -ING, -S** to grate the skin of a citrus fruit for use as flavoring

ZETA *n pl* **-S** the 6th letter of the Greek alphabet

ZHOS *n pl of* **ZHO** more than one of a cross between a cow and a yak; *also* **ZOS, DZOS**

ZIGS *n pl of* **ZIG** angular shapes characterized by sharp turns in alternating directions

ZILL *n pl* **-S** one of a pair of small metallic cymbals used by belly dancers

ZIMB *n* a large, venomous, two-winged fly of Ethiopia

ZINC *v* **-ED, -ING -S** to cover a metal with a corrosion-resistant coating of zinc, a metallic element; *also* **ZINK**

ZINE *n pl* **-S** informal for an inexpensively produced, self-published, underground publication

ZING *v* **-ED, -ING, -S** to make a brief high-pitched humming or buzzing sound

ZINK *v* **-ED, -ING, -S** to cover a metal with a corrosion-resistant coating of zinc, a metallic element; *also* **ZINC**

ZIPS *v pr t of* **ZIP** opens or closes with a zipper, a fastener with interlocking teeth

ZITI *n pl* **ZITI** a medium-sized tubular pasta in short pieces

ZITS *n pl of* **ZIT** informal for blemishes on the skin; pimples

ZOEA *n pl* **-S** or **-E** a larval stage of a crab

ZOIC *adj* pertaining to animals or animal life or action

ZONA *n pl* **-E** or **-S** an anatomical zone or layer

ZONE *v* **-D, ZONING, -S** to divide into locally circumscribed places characterized by some distinctive features

ZONK *v* **-ED, -ING, -S** to lose consciousness or become stupefied from exhaustion

ZOOM *v* **-ED, -ING, -S** to move speedily, especially while emitting a loud low-pitched buzzing noise

ZOON *n pl* **-S, ZOA** an animal developed from a fertilized egg

ZOOS *n pl of* **ZOO** facilities where wild animals are housed for exhibition

ZOPE *n* a European freshwater fish with a deep thin body and yellowish color

ZORI *n pl* **-S** a simple Japanese flat sandal with a thong, usually made of straw or leather

ZOUK *n* a dance music of the French West Indies

ZUBR *n pl* **-S** an auroch, a European bison

ZYME *n pl* **-S** an agent that causes fermentation

FIVE LETTERS

ZAIMS *n pl of* **ZAIM** Turkish chiefs who support mounted militia

ZAINS *n pl of* **ZAIN** horses of a dark color, neither gray nor white, and having no spots

ZAIRE *n pl* **ZAIRE** or **-S** formerly, a monetary unit of the Democratic Republic of Congo

ZAKAT *n pl* **-S** an Islamic religious tax

ZAMAN *n* a large ornamental tropical American tree, also known as the rain tree

ZANZA *n pl* **-S** an African musical instrument with strips of metal fixed to a wooden sound board

ZAPPY *adj* **ZAPPIER, ZAPPIEST** very quick or speedy; *also* **ZIPPY**

ZARFS *n pl of* **ZARF** an ornamental metal holders for hot cups of coffee, used in the Middle East

ZAXES *n pl of* **ZAX** a tool for trimming and puncturing roofing slates

ZAYAT *n* a public shed, or portico, for travelers and worshipers, found in most Burmese villages

ZAYIN *n pl* **-S** the 7th letter of the Hebrew alphabet

ZAZEN *n* a form of meditation as practiced in Zen Buddhism

ZEBEC *n pl* **-S** a small Mediterranean vessel with three masts; *also* **XEBEC**

ZEBRA *n pl* **-S** an animal native to Africa resembling a horse but with a black-and-white striped hide

ZEBUS *n pl of* **ZEBU** a domesticated ox having a humped back, long horns and a large dewlap

ZEINS *n pl of* **ZEIN** simple proteins obtained from the corn

ZERKS *n pl of* **ZERK** grease fittings

ZEROS *n pl of* **ZERO** more than one of the numerical symbol 0, representing the absence of any quantity or magnitude; *also* **ZEROES**

ZESTS *v pr t of* **ZEST** grates the skin of a citrus fruit for use as flavoring

ZESTY *adj* **ZESTIER, ZESTIEST** marked by zest or pleasant taste

ZETAS *n pl of* **ZETA** more than one of the 6th letter of the Greek alphabet

ZHLUB *n pl* **-S** a person regarded as clumsy, stupid or unattractive; *also* **SHLUB, SCHLUB**

ZIBET *n pl* **-S** a carnivorous cat-like wild animal closely allied to the civet, that is eaten in China; *also* **ZIBETH**

ZIEGA *n* curd produced from milk by adding acetic acid

ZILCH *n* informal for zero or nothing at all

ZILLS *n pl of* **ZILL** a pair of small metallic cymbals used by belly dancers

ZINCS *v pr t of* **ZINC** covers a metal with a corrosion-resistant coating of zinc, a metallic element; *also* **ZINKS**

ZINCY *adj* pertaining to zinc, a metallic element; *also* **ZINCKY, ZINKY**

ZINEB *n pl* **-S** an agricultural fungicide formerly used on fruits and vegetables

ZINES *n pl of* **ZINE** informal for inexpensively produced, self-published, underground publications

ZINGS *n pl of* **ZING** makes a brief high-pitched humming or buzzing sound

ZINGY *adj* **ZINGIER, ZINGIEST** energetic, enthusiastic, lively

ZINKS *v pr t of* **ZINK** covers a metal with a corrosion-resistant coating of zinc, a metallic element; *also* **ZINCS**

ZINKY *adj* pertaining to zinc, a metallic element; *also* **ZINCKY, ZINCY**

ZIPPY *adj* **ZIPPIER, ZIPPIEST** very quick or speedy; *also* **ZAPPY**

ZIRAM *n* an organic zinc salt used as an agricultural fungicide

ZIZEL *n pl* **-S** a large Eurasian ground squirrel; *also* **SUSLIK**

ZIZIT *n/pl* the fringes or tassels worn by orthodox Jewish men; *also* **ZIZITH**

ZLOTY *n pl* **ZLOTIES** or **ZLOTY** the basic monetary unit of Poland

ZOEAE *n pl of* **ZOEA** a larval stage of crabs

ZOEAL *adj* pertaining to a peculiar larval stage of crabs

ZOEAS *n pl of* **ZOEA** a larval stage of crabs

ZOKOR *n pl* **-S** an Asiatic burrowing rodent

ZOMBI *n pl* **-S** a person markedly strange in appearance or behavior; *also* **ZOMBIE**

ZONAE *n pl of* **ZONA** anatomical zones or layers; *also* **ZONAS**

ZONAL *adj* of or pertaining to anatomical zones or layers

ZONAS *n pl of* **ZONA** anatomical zones or layers; *also* **ZONAE**

ZONED *v p t of* **ZONE** divided into locally circumscribed places characterized by some distinctive features

ZONER *n pl* **-S** one who divides into locally circumscribed places characterized by some distinctive features

ZONES *v pr t of* **ZONE** divides into locally circumscribed places characterized by some distinctive features

ZONKS *v pr t of* **ZONK** loses consciousness or becomes stupefied from exhaustion

ZOOID *n pl* **-S** an individual invertebrate that reproduces non-sexually by budding or splitting

ZOOKS *interj* used as to express surprise, shortened form of gadzooks

ZOOMS *v pr t of* **ZOOM** moves speedily, especially while emitting a loud low-pitched buzzing noise

ZOONS *n pl of* **ZOON** animals developed from fertilized eggs; *also* **ZOA**

ZOOTY *adj* typical of a zoot-suiter; flashy in manner or style

ZORIL *n pl* **-S** a carnivorous African mammal resembling a skunk; *also* **ZORILLA, ZORILLE**

ZORIS *n pl of* **ZORI** simple Japanese flat sandals with thongs, usually made of straw or leather

ZOWIE *interj* used to express astonishment or admiration

ZUBRS *n pl of* **ZUBR** aurochs, European bison

ZUCHE *n pl* **-S** a stump of a tree

ZUZIM *n pl of* **ZUZ** ancient Hebrew silver coins

ZYMES *n pl of* **ZYME** agents that cause fermentation

ZYMIC *adj* pertaining to, or produced by, fermentation